Bernard Clayton's

COOKING

SIMON & SCHUSTER
New York • London • Toronto • Sydney • Tokyo • Singapore

ACROSS AMERICA

Cooking with More Than 100

of North America's Best Cooks

and 250 of Their Favorite Recipes

by BERNARD CLAYTON, Jr.

SIMON & SCHUSTER
Simon & Schuster Building
Rockefeller Center
1230 Avenue of the Americas
New York, New York 10020

Copyright © 1993 by Bernard Clayton, Jr.
All rights reserved
including the right of reproduction
in whole or in part in any form.
SIMON & SCHUSTER and colophon are
registered trademarks of Simon & Schuster Inc.
Designed by Edith Fowler
Manufactured in the United States of America

10 9 8 7 6 5 4 3 2 1

Library of Congress Cataloging-in-Publication Data

Clayton, Bernard.
  [Cooking Across America]
  Bernard Clayton's Cooking Across
America : with more than 100 of North
America's best cooks and 250 of their
favorite recipes.
     p.   cm.
   Includes index.
   1. Cooks—United States—
Biography. 2. Cookery,
American.   I. Title.   II. Title:
Bernard Clayton's Cooking Across
America
TX649.A1C53   1993
641.5'092'273—dc20
[B]   *92-15637   CIP*
ISBN: 0-671-67290-8

Title page photo: Jerry Mitchell

Permissions can be found on page 589.

With Thanks

This book was made possible with the help and understanding of several hundred people from coast to coast, border to border, and in Hawaii. Many are profiled in the following pages. Others came on the scene momentarily and departed. Their help was just as important.

A special thanks to:

Gail Weinhold, owner of a small variety store in Wilson, Kansas, who uncovered for me a wealth of Czech food talent in her rural community.

Barbara Fenzl, Phoenix, one of the many talented people in the International Association of Culinary Professionals. She helped me research foods in the Southwest.

Tom Jackson, an ex-Louisiana oil-field worker whose restaurant, TJ's in the Aspens, is tucked away in a wooded grove high on the eastern slope of the Sierra Nevada mountains in California and who shared with me his knowledge of Cajun cooking.

Jerry DiVecchio, a *Sunset* magazine editor, whose advice about food I have listened to with respect since we were crew members on an expedition through the Grand Canyon more than a quarter century ago. It was on that trip that she bought for the magazine my recipe for sourdough bread ($10), thereby costing me my amateur standing.

William Barkell, an Upper Peninsula native, who unfolded for me the fascinating history and lore of Michigan's Copper Country.

Bernard Bruinsma, Tacoma, who knows as much about baking and flour and yeast as any one in the country, has answered my pleas for help again and again through several books. I have learned, too, about cooking from Patsy Bruinsma, his equally talented wife.

Three editors at Simon & Schuster with whom I worked during the life of this book—Carole Lalli, Kerri Conan, and Toula Polygalaktos. They were a joy. For weeks on end I would simply vanish into America and report to them now and then with postcards from such places as Gila Bend, Arizona, and Forge Village, Massachusetts, and dozens of other post offices along the way. Not once did they question why I was at that place or ask where I was going next. Bless them for their faith!

Dick Yoshimura, Seattle, head of the Mutual Fish Company, whose knowledge of seafood boggles the mind and who is gracious in the sharing of that knowledge.

Joan Raines, my agent, while she never left her New York office, was with me the entire way flashing signs of encouragement and giving directions whenever the road seemed impossibly long.

Again and again I turned to my library for help. These books have been most helpful, and I thank their authors and their publishers:

Sylvia Thompson, *Feasts and Friends*, North Point Press.

Marjorie Standish, *Cooking Down East*, Guy Gannett Publishing Company.

Schyuler Ingle and Sharon Kramis, *Northwest Bounty*, Simon & Schuster.

Beatrice Ojakangas, *Scandinavian Cooking*, H. P. Books.

John Doerper, *Eating Well: A Guide to Foods of the Pacific Northwest*, Pacific Search Press.

Paula Wolfert, *Paula Wolfert's World of Food*, HarperCollins.

Ann Theoharous, *Cooking the Greek Way*, Holt, Rinehart and Winston.

Lydie Marshall, *Cooking with Lydie Marshall*, Alfred A. Knopf.

Lillian B. Marshall, *Cooking Across the South*, Oxmoor House.

Rocio Lamadriz, Piedad Robertson, and Olga de Zaldo, *Secrets of Cuban Entertaining*, Byron Kennedy and Company.

Marion Cunningham, whose *Fannie Farmer Cookbook* and the *Fannie Farmer Baking Book* are in a small selection of gospels within easy reach on my desk, along with *Joy of Cooking*, *Larousse Gastronomique*, and my dictionary and thesaurus.

The several volumes of *Foods of the World*, Time-Life Books, Time Inc.

Richard H. Collins, *The New Orleans Cookbook*, Alfred A. Knopf.

Jude W. Theriot, *La Cuisine Cajun*, Pelican Publishing Company.

In addition to my somewhat formalized approach to finding good cooks and good food, we have stopped the van to ask *one* question of dozens of postmen, librarians, clergy, editors, firemen, desk clerks, as well as mothers pushing baby carriages and men pitching horseshoes:

"Where in town is a good place to eat?"

The replies, while appreciated, were not always rewarding. Nevertheless, I thank them all.

To mothers and grandmothers who let the kids have fun in the kitchen, which, years later, made possible this book about men and women who love to cook and do it so very well.

A Paean to Marje

In the life of this book Marje Clayton has been van driver, navigator, riding mechanic, councilor, advisor, picnicker, dresser, dog walker, conversationalist, reader, taster, tester, mate, editor, critic, companion, nurse, confrere, photographer, wife, seamstress, and—I mean this kindly—goad.

And as my grammarian, with a basket of punctuation marks in hand, she skipped joyfully through pages of copy sprinkling commas and semicolons.

None of these roles come as a surprise for she is no stranger to me. I have known her for some time. Fifty years to be exact. It was between pages 800 and 807 that we celebrated a Golden Wedding anniversary.

Thank you, Marjorie!

CONTENTS

INTRODUCTION

THIS BOOK describes more than 100 cooks from all quarters of this country and their love of cooking expressed in 250 of their favorite recipes.

In three years on the American road I discovered no grand design for a national cuisine. No great truth was revealed that would encapsule American food in one neat paragraph. Instead, I found that this country's cuisines, a wonderful blend of ethnic and regional foods, were as many and as diverse as its peoples.

On the day we decided we would travel the whole of the United States and several Canadian provinces to write about our best home cooks and chefs, I posted this brief paragraph above the typewriter. For three years it defined my day.

This will be more than a book of recipes. I am as interested in the cook as a person as I am in the thorough step-by-step presentation of the recipe. I believe these together have been the principal reasons readers have found pleasure in reading and cooking with my books.

I also wrote—rather grandiloquently I later thought—that I would drive however many miles it required and take whatever time was necessary to write these profiles and recipes. I thought at the time we could not possibly drive more than 18,000 miles. With a calendar in front of me, I roughly calculated that the project could be done in two years' time or less, including testing recipes and writing. When we parked the van in front of the house for the last time, the odometer registered 36,932

17

miles. Three years and several months later I flew to New York and handed the 8½-pound manuscript to my editor.

We talked, cooked, and dined with a broad spectrum of good cooks, from a Louisiana counter cook, a many-starred chef in Santa Fe, a Miss Indian America in Butte, a Jackson Hole dude-ranch cook, a cooking-school teacher in San Francisco, the mistress of a bed-and-breakfast on California's high desert, a baker in upstate New York, a Pillsbury Bake-Off finalist in Illinois, to a Mormon housewife with six young sons in Salt Lake City, a Mississippi steamboat chef, and a game hunter in Iowa. Plus almost a hundred other equally high-ranked cooks along the way.

The range of food was impressive. Lobster in Maine, crabs in Maryland, and gumbo in New Orleans were expected. Surprises were a delicate lime and white chocolate torte on a Wyoming dude ranch, delicious Czech kolaches in the kitchen of a Kansas farmhouse far out on the prairie, and fresh gooseneck barnacles, a marine delicacy plucked a few hours earlier from rocks in the waters on the Canadian side of the Juan de Fuca Strait and served with tuberous begonia vinaigrette sauce.

This was a dream assignment. It meant traveling wherever we wanted to go, staying however long or short as we liked. If there was a blizzard in Montana we went southwest to New Mexico; hot and muggy in Louisiana, we drove northwest to Vancouver Island. We erred only twice—an unscheduled heat wave in Seattle and a deep blanket of snow at Lake Arrowhead in southern California.

In the all-encompassing search, our van rolled over a network of roads, highways, interstates, parkways, boulevards, pikes, streets, and lanes and aboard ferries. We shunned the Interstate system when we could, especially in the South where the highways ran down thick evergreen corridors that effectively screened out most forms of life. Out West the Interstate was a different matter. There the highways blended into and became part of the desert and plains. The long, broad ribbons of concrete were dwarfed by the vastness of the sky and the land. Cars and trucks in the distance were as ants.

We drove a GMC van. No, *cruised* would be a better word. To *drive* implies stress. This was highway *cruising*. Delightful. Every morning we looked forward to climbing up into the cab to spend the rest of the day perched above traffic, nearly at eye level with the trucks. The van was a cardinal-red color with broad silver stripes. We realized how easy it would be to pick us out should we speed. So we didn't. No tickets, not even a warning, for the entire journey. Not one flat tire. The only casualty was a scratch on the running board.

We did not sleep in the van although we were prepared to do so if there was no room at the inn. We sought out a hotel or motel or a bed-and-breakfast. However, the longer we were on the road the more we appreciated hotels and motels where the beds were certain to be long and wide and there would be room to spread our travel gear on table and dresser tops not cluttered with the host's prized objets d'art and memorabilia found in most B&Bs.

Where would we look to find these good cooks we were in search of? In the beginning I thought finding them would be difficult. It was not. Every community is as proud of its good cooks as it is of the town band or the high school basketball team, and willing to talk about them. I knew, of course, I could not land in town and demand of the sheriff: "Take me to your best cook!"

Thanks to work I had done on earlier books as well as to correspondence with readers, I began with a list of a number of fine cooks. Time and again I tapped into the extensive network in every state and Canadian provinces of fellow members of the International Association of Culinary Professionals. Fellow cookbook authors graciously gave me suggestions.

To find that special cook in the town, city, village, or farm community where I was told good food was the norm but where I knew no one, I telephoned ahead. If the town had a newspaper, I talked with the publisher or the editor or reporter who wrote the social news and often substituted as the food columnist, all of whom knew the local talent well. One editor volunteered his wife. The newspaper editor in one small city in the Upper Peninsula of Michigan would not winnow down his list of four to a single cook for fear that the word would get out to those left off the list and they would come storming into his office. The Chambers of Commerce and tourist bureaus, especially those in small cities and towns, were also eager to help.

Only one recipe was denied us. The owner of a crossroads bakery in an Amish farm community in Kansas regretted he could not let me have his whole wheat bread recipe even though I offered a dozen of mine in return. He had become locally famous for the loaf and felt quite protective about it. I understood.

It was a remarkable journey not only for the wealth of material I got but for the warmth and openness with which we were welcomed into homes and into people's lives. They took us in, gave us cherished recipes, took us shopping. They demonstrated techniques and introduced us to their friends.

Many cooks knew me through my books so I came into their kitchens as an acquaintance. Nevertheless, it took thought, time, and effort to welcome us into their lives. It was not an easy matter to invite a writer into your kitchen, especially if he is a bear of a man, six feet four and 240 pounds. I asked a thousand questions. Marje made notes. I took scores of photos. I disrupted routines. These cooks shuffled family schedules. Their neighbors picked up kids at school so they could be with us.

They planned picnics and outings and gave dinner parties. They spent hours and sometimes days in preparation for our visits.

Without exception those occasions—and they were *occasions*—were as delightful as they were rewarding.

My photographs of these cooks along with their kitchens, markets, garden produce, dishes, kids, mountains, Indian ponies, helpful spouses, dogs, seals, deserts, and desserts and Marje's notes have spurred the memory about a thousand and one things that otherwise might have escaped. While several hundred rolls of film passed through my Nikon cameras, photographs of a half-dozen people important to this book are absent, not by design, but because at the moment I was engrossed with someone's cooking skills, I should have been behind the camera. This I regret. Cooking sessions and interviews were also recorded on one of three tape recorders and then I transcribed at home. (I carried spares for fear one of them would go dead or the tape would tangle and fail to capture some precious words.)

It also became evident as we traveled across America that cooks in small towns and on farms and ranches are no longer stuck in the last century. They are no longer rural in the sense of being isolated from the rest of the world. They share with the city all of the wonderful ingredients that come from near and far places—made possible by transportation and refrigeration—to enhance and enrich the American table.

In sum, wherever it was in this country, if the food was fine tasting and the cook an uncommon person, they belonged in the book.

B.C., Jr.

I   DEEP SOUTH

Mississippi   Alabama

THE NELSON FAMILY REUNION—CAROLYN NELSON

Two Personae—Mrs. Henry (Geraldine) Gholson

Geraldine Gholson, *right*,
and Julia Ann Faulkner

"Without a doubt Mrs. Henry Fort Gholson is the finest cook in the county," Walter Webb, editor and publisher of the local newspaper, the *South Reporter*, said. "I consider her to be two women."

One is the socially active Mrs. Gholson, whose late husband ran one of the town's banks. She is on the boards of the Symphony League, the English Speaking Union, and the Brooks League Art Gallery in Memphis, fifty miles away, as well as the Holly Springs Garden Club, which

23

sponsors the annual Holly Springs Pilgrimage. The other Mrs. Gholson, the cook, takes off her shoes in the kitchen, hangs her wristwatch from her apron string, and goes to work in a no-nonsense manner with her maid/cook/friend Julia Ann Faulkner. Together the two women move around the maple table in the center of the small kitchen with a grace and ease that bespeaks years of togetherness.

"But I don't consider myself a professional," said Geraldine. "While I am in the catering business, I am selective about for whom I cook. I have never catered in a home that I've not first been a guest in the parlor."

Geraldine grew up in a small lumber town of three hundred people near Meridian where her father was the mill's electrical engineer.

"My mother was determined that her children would grow up with manners. I can remember that whenever one of us put an elbow on the table we had to finish the meal with an egg held in the armpit. Mother said there were no such things as *company* manners. We were as good as company, so good manners prevailed all of the time. No matter that the main supper dish was turnip greens and meat loaf, it was served on silver. Always linen napkins.

"I think the way we present food *en table* is as important to us in the South as the way it is prepared. We think dining in the home should be a social occasion. If we can, we like to make every day of the year festive. We don't wrap up the silver and hide it in the closet. We use our silver every day. Of course, we polish it to death but no matter. Nor would it ever enter my head to use paper napkins."

Nor does Geraldine do less for her catered affairs. She carries with her a complete sterling-silver service, crystal, and linen to serve sixty when needed. "It's elegant!" she said.

Silver has long played a role in the life of Holly Springs. Olga Reed Pruitt, local historian/author, wrote: "During the War Between the States, every family in Holly Springs had a secret hiding place for its treasures. Outwitting the Yankee was a grim game in which everyone participated. A favorite place was the potato house where the silver was hidden in the soft dirt under the vegetables."

Geraldine and I were driving past the courthouse on Van Dorn Street and discussing the brunch she would prepare the next day. "Let me tell you just how small a town we are," she said, smiling. "When I'm not wearing a hat, I can drive around the square a dozen times and not get more than a friendly wave or two. But let me put on a hat and at least two people will step from the curb to flag me down. 'Hey, I see you are going to Memphis. Will you stop and pick up a package for me?' Now that's a small town!"

By the second turn around the courthouse—no one waved at us—we had decided on brunch. It would include a Sausage-Apple Ring filled with scrambled eggs and topped with grated cheese, a Creole Sauce on the side; Baked Garlic-Cheese Grits; baked apples stuffed with mince-meat and topped with sour cream; tiny muffins dipped in sugar and hot biscuits. Fresh strawberries, orange and melon slices would surround the entrées.

SAUSAGE-APPLE RING

[SERVES 8]

A molded ring of crisp and richly browned sausage surrounding scrambled eggs topped with grated cheese has been the centerpiece of brunches created by Geraldine Gholson for a generation to celebrate weddings, graduations, and football games (Ole Miss is just down S.R. 7 at Oxford).

"When I know hungry people are to be served—hungry people who like good food—I make this sausage ring," she said. "Pork is a Southern tradition and I think this is one of the most attractive and appetizing ways to present it."

There is a choice of several kinds of bulk sausages carried by my supermarket in Indiana and for certain occasions I favor the highly seasoned Portuguese or Italian sausages for this dish. Use your favorite scrambled eggs recipe for the filling.

INGREDIENTS

2 pounds bulk sausage
1½ cups cracker crumbs
2 eggs, lightly beaten
½ cup milk
¼ cup minced onion
1 cup finely chopped apples

16 eggs
¼ cup milk or buttermilk
Salt and pepper, to taste
½ cup shredded cheese
½ cup chopped fresh parsley
Sprinkle of paprika

EQUIPMENT

One 9 x 3-inch ring mold, well greased or 1 shallow baking pan. Cut a circle of parchment paper or foil to place under the meat; the sausage ring can also be fashioned by hand directly onto the baking sheet.

continued

PREPARATION 8 mins.	In a large mixing bowl stir together the sausage, cracker crumbs, eggs, milk, onion, and chopped apple. Press the mixture evenly into the ring mold.
CHILLING overnight	Chill the ring several hours or overnight.
PREHEAT	Preheat the oven to 350° 20 minutes before baking.
BAKING 350° 1 hour	Unmold onto a shallow baking pan or baking sheet with raised edges. Place the pan on the middle shelf of the oven and bake for 1 hour. Although the meat must bake 1 hour, it can be removed from the oven after 45 minutes, covered with foil, and held to bake the final 15 minutes later, so that it may be served hot and browned.
COOK	In a large mixing bowl scramble the eggs, stir in the milk or buttermilk, and salt and pepper to taste. Cook to the desired consistency over medium heat.
FINAL STEP	Remove from the oven and slip the sausage ring onto the serving dish. Fill the ring with the scrambled eggs and top with the cheese, parsley, and paprika. Serve with Creole Sauce (see below).

CREOLE SAUCE

[MAKES 1 PINT]

While this Creole Sauce is served with the sausage dish at Geraldine's brunch, its spicy tang goes well with a number of dishes ranging from hamburger to fish.

INGREDIENTS	*2 tablespoons butter or margarine* *½ cup finely chopped celery* *1 medium onion, finely chopped* *1 small bell pepper, seeded and chopped* *4 ripe tomatoes, peeled, cored, seeded, and chopped or one* * 16-ounce can tomatoes* *½ teaspoon salt, if desired* *½ teaspoon chili powder* *2 dashes Tabasco sauce* *Pinch of sugar*
PREPARATION 10 mins.	In a large skillet heat the shortening and add the celery, onion, and bell pepper. Cover and cook for 10 minutes over

medium-low heat, until the vegetables are translucent and tender.

COOKING
30 mins.
Add the tomatoes and cook down, uncovered, over low heat until thick, about 15 minutes. Sir in the salt, chili powder, Tabasco, and sugar and cook for an additional 15 minutes.

FINAL STEP
Remove from heat and allow to cool before serving. The sauce may be kept in the refrigerator for several weeks or frozen.

BAKED GARLIC-CHEESE GRITS

[SERVES 8—CUPS OR CASSEROLE]

In the South, grits are beloved with any meal. But I have long felt that grits were bland—no message. Geraldine's grits, made with garlic and cheese, carry a big message: Good! She bakes them in custard cups or timbales and turns them out in a cluster of small brown-capped mounds on a silver platter.

Craig Claiborne, the consummate Southerner, says that he doesn't know of any dish, including buttermilk biscuits and red-eye gravy, that is more down-home Southern than grits. If you are Southern born, he believes, grits become addictive from the cradle. Claiborne says breakfast in the South without grits borders on the unthinkable.

INGREDIENTS
1 cup quick-cooking grits
½ cup (1 stick) margarine or unsalted butter
One 8-ounce roll garlic cheese (see Note)
2 eggs, lightly beaten
½ cup milk
Salt, to taste

Note: If garlic cheese, a commercially packaged product, is not available, mix 1½ cups grated Cheddar cheese with 1 teaspoon finely minced garlic.

EQUIPMENT
Eight custard cups or timbales, buttered; or one 2-quart casserole, buttered

PREHEAT
Preheat the oven to 375° while the grits are cooking.

PREPARATION
25 mins.
Cook the grits according to the package instructions. Melt the shortening and cheese in the warm grits and stir to blend. Put aside to cool somewhat before adding the eggs. Blend the eggs and milk together and stir into the grits. Salt to taste. Carefully pour the mixture into the custard cups or the casserole.

continued

BAKING   Bake for about 45 minutes or until a knife inserted comes out
375°   cleanly.
45 mins.

FINAL STEP   If in cups, turn out onto a serving dish with their browned tops
               up. Serve hot!

⟩⟩⟩⟩⟩ On the Road—HOLLY SPRINGS, MISSISSIPPI

A Small Southern Town

From our house in southern Indiana, it is literally all downhill to the Gulf of Mexico. Water running off my lawn flows down a network of tributaries in a relatively narrow north-south corridor to reach the Gulf a thousand miles distant. Great rafts of hardwood logs from here were regularly floated down the Ohio and Mississippi rivers in the 1800s to be sold to lumber mills in New Orleans. I have wondered, too, if with conditions just right, a car, given a push in my driveway, might not roll downhill the whole distance to the Gulf. I had not worked out the logistics of how to get such a performance from the family car, so we traveled in a GMC van powered by a mighty engine.

For the first leg of the trip it was difficult to tell from the terrain that we had ever left home. The low green hills down the river valleys of Indiana, through Kentucky and into Tennessee and finally across the Mississippi state line hardly changed at all.

Driving down to see Mrs. Henry Gholson of Holly Springs (pop. 7,285), I fancied I would find a sleepy small town where nothing much happens, or, for that matter, ever happened. I could not have been more wrong.

When we turned off S.R. 7 onto Memphis Street and drove around the courthouse square and past the antebellum mansions on College Avenue, I sensed that Holly Springs had more than a tradition of good food which had encouraged the visit. Paint was peeling off some of the older houses. ("Too poor to paint, too proud to whitewash," Mrs. Gholson later explained.) But the downtown was alive with traffic, both auto and afoot. It was a busy, prosperous place.

Holly Springs came into being in the early 1800s around a spring, "deep and wide enough to swim a horse," in a luxuriant grove of holly trees, according to the town's historian, Olga Reed Pruitt. It crowned the ridge along which a Chickasaw Indian trail once led from the Mississippi River, sixty miles west.

In the decade before the Civil War more cotton was raised in the surrounding bottom land than in any other place in the country. The town was booming—forty lawyers in twelve law firms, nine doctors, several private schools for "young ladies and young gentlemen," literary societies, a theater group, and a dance society.

"With two thousand inhabitants," Ms. Pruitt wrote, "the town enjoyed a graceful, leisurely way of life. The business panic was over and many handsome mansions threw wide their doors to a lavish social life such as benefited the position of cultured ladies and gentlemen of the times. People were just beginning to enjoy the fruits of their labors in hewing a town out of the wilderness."

The Civil War stopped that way of life abruptly.

It is not much talked about, but a future president of the United States made Holly Springs his home for a time. Gen. Ulysses S. Grant, with his family, lived in the big Walter Place mansion for several months while he put an iron grip around Vicksburg on the Mississippi River to the west. The town suffered sixty-one raids during the war; the most devastating was by a Southern force led by General Van Dorn which destroyed Grant's supply base here.

Cotton is no longer king; it's been replaced by soybeans, cattle, and corn. Baldwin assembles its pianos here and Sunbeam makes a line of appliances. The town has several private schools as well as Rust College, with some six hundred students. Its campus was once a campground for Grant's troops.

Holly Springs had the requisite Kentucky Fried Chicken franchise and the kids in town are hoping McDonald's will soon make up its mind where it is going to build its long-proposed outlet. Two restaurants on the courthouse square serve home-cooked meals, mostly fried, and it was clear the best food in town is to be found at home.

▰▰▰▰▰HOLLY SPRINGS, MISSISSIPPI

Bed-and-Breakfast—Mrs. T. Jackson Stubbs, Jr.

WALTER WEBB

We seldom stay at bed-and-breakfast homes because most of their beds are too short for my long frame. Nor do I care for the often forced camaraderie with the host and other guests at the breakfast table when I am just out of bed.

Hamilton Place was a surprise and a delight. We were the only guests, the beds were long and firm, and the breakfasts were delicious. The hostess, Mrs. T. Jackson Stubbs, Jr.—Linda to her friends—was not only pretty but charming.

The house stands impressively on a gentle rise at the end of Memphis Avenue. On the National Register of Historic Places, it is one of the dozen lovely antebellum houses open to the public during the town's annual springtime Pilgrimage.

Hamilton Place is furnished in large part with Louis XVI pieces. A Steinway piano in the music room is credited by historians with so having won the heart of a Union general, Benjamin Grierson, a talented pianist, that the officer ordered his troops not to ravage Holly Springs.

Linda lives in the world of food. When she is not making breakfast for guests and her family, she is the consulting dietitian to the hospitals and nursing homes in the area.

Marje and I were served breakfast at a small table in the formal dining room—set elegantly with the family's silver and crystal and linen. Fresh-cut flowers were from the garden outside the bedroom. The breakfast itself was elegant—compote of fresh fruit, orange juice, a sausage casserole, Angel Biscuits, a cream cheese pastry loaf, strawberry butter, crispy pear preserves, coffee and tea.

BREAKFAST CASSEROLE

[SERVES 12]

Light and fluffy as a soufflé, this sausage casserole is assembled the day before and refrigerated overnight before baking.

This is a great dish to do ahead and have baked for company days or weeks in advance. The baked dish is cut into a dozen servings, each wrapped separately in plastic wrap and frozen. Later, thaw the desired number before reheating in the oven or microwave.

INGREDIENTS	*1 pound bulk pork sausage* *6 slices bread* *1½ cups shredded Cheddar cheese* *8 eggs, lightly beaten* *2 cups milk* *1 teaspoon dry mustard* *¼ cup (½ stick) unsalted butter, melted*
EQUIPMENT	One 9 x 11 x 2-inch (3-quart) casserole, well greased
PREPARATION 12–15 mins.	In a skillet fry the sausage until browned, stirring well to crumble. Drain. While the sausage is draining, tear or cut the bread into 1-inch squares.
ASSEMBLING 10 mins.	Cover the bottom of the casserole with the bread pieces, then cover with the sausage and cheese. Mix together the beaten eggs, milk, and dry mustard. Pour over the casserole mixture and drizzle on the melted butter.
CHILLING overnight	Cover the casserole with plastic wrap and place in the refrigerator to chill overnight.
PREHEAT	Preheat the oven to 350° 20 minutes before baking.
BAKING 350° 45 mins.	Remove the casserole from the refrigerator and let stand for 15 minutes while the oven preheats. Bake for 45 minutes, or until set.
FINAL STEP	Serve hot; or cool to wrap later and freeze.

ANGEL BISCUITS

[MAKES 3 DOZEN BISCUITS]

Recipes for angel biscuits are about as common as the number of angels said to dance on the head of a pin. This is a new one, and the biscuits are made a special way. Light and fluffy, they will have a particular appeal to anyone on a low-sodium diet. Linda Stubbs has been on such a diet for ten years and makes these with low-sodium baking powder and potassium bicarbonate (cream of tartar).

Her angel biscuits are rolled, cut, and baked flat. Other cooks, however, fold their biscuit circles in half after placing them on the baking sheet. The 2 layers open in the oven like angel wings.

INGREDIENTS

4 cups all-purpose flour, approximately
¼ cup sugar
4 teaspoons low-sodium baking powder
1 teaspoon potassium bicarbonate (cream of tartar)
1 package dry yeast
2 tablespoons vinegar, to sour the milk
2¼ cups milk
1 cup shortening, of choice
½ cup (1 stick) unsalted butter or butter blends, melted, to brush

EQUIPMENT

One baking sheet, greased or Teflon

PREPARATION
BY HAND OR
MIXER
12 mins.

In a large mixing or mixer bowl stir together the dry ingredients, including the yeast. The mixer flat beater blade is good for this.

Stir the vinegar into the milk to sour.

Drop chunks of shortening into the dry mix; work in the shortening either with your hands, 2 knives cutting across each other, or a pastry blender. The flour will resemble grains of rice. If using the mixer, the flat beater will cut the shortening into tiny pieces.

KNEADING
3 mins.

Slowly pour the milk into the dry ingredients and shortening; mix thoroughly with a wooden spoon. If using the mixer, slowly pour in the milk to form a soft dough that clings together. Turn the dough onto a floured work surface, kneading gently for 10 to 12 strokes, adding additional flour if the dough is sticky.

Note: To bake later, the dough may be refrigerated or frozen in one piece or cut into biscuits.

SHAPING
10 mins.

Roll out the dough ½ inch thick. Cut circles with a 2-inch cookie cutter. Dip each biscuit into the melted butter and place on the cookie sheet.

RISING 20 mins.	Let the biscuits rise for 20 minutes.
PREHEAT	Preheat the oven to 425° while the biscuits are rising.
BAKING 425° 15–20 mins.	(If frozen, remove from the refrigerator the night before.) Bake for 15 to 20 minutes or until golden brown.
FINAL STEP	Take from the oven—and serve with lots of butter and other good things.

⌇⌇⌇⌇On the Road—NATCHEZ, MISSISSIPPI

Antebellum

We arrived in town after a drive down the Natchez Trace, the serene and lovely parkway coming down through the state from Tennessee. We were expected for a special picnic of venison, catfish, and chicken in Woodville, a small town below Natchez near the Louisiana state line, so our stay here would be brief.

Unfortunately, the Trace does not lead all the way into the old city nor does the mood continue. It comes to an abrupt halt ten miles short in clusters of filling stations, mini-marts, video stores, and franchise food cafés. But once through this hodgepodge, there is the Mississippi River and the beautiful old town and its thirty antebellum houses.

We parked the van and walked the old streets. A dozen of the old houses were open today to visitors. We narrowed our choice down to two —the stately and elegant Stanton Hall with a luncheon of Southern-fried-chicken-with-brown-gravy in its Carriage House Restaurant and, later in the day, Longwood, a puzzling, sad, and intriguing mansion left unfinished by artisans who marched off to battle when the Civil War started.

The docent from the Pilgrimage Garden Club, which owns Stanton Hall, described the handsome town house "as the full flowering of Southern Greek Revival planter architecture." The front and back parlors joined to form a seventy-two-foot-long room with massive mirrors at each end that reach to the sixteen-foot ceiling. Light from the bronze chandeliers was reflected back and forth between the mirrors, making the room seem limitless. Four of us on the tour were lost in its vastness.

We walked to the high bluff above the Mississippi River, a choice platform for viewing. But at the moment there wasn't much to view. No traffic. Not even a fisherman's skiff. Not only had a severe drought upstream drastically cut the river's breadth but it seemed also to have taken away its spirit. It just lay there—a brown body of water with no personality and little energy. It wasn't what I expected.

We left the river and drove into the country to Longwood, the mansion with its odd Byzantine onion-shaped dome.

Dr. Haller Nutt, a wealthy cotton planter, began the octagonal house at Longwood in 1860. Workmen had just begun work on the interior of the second level when Fort Sumter was fired on. The craftsmen, most of them from Northern states, dropped their saws and hammers and marched off to join the Union army. They never returned. The rooms on the ground floor, which were to have been work and recreational areas, became instead quarters for the Nutt family, left destitute by the war.

Dr. Nutt called the house with its great dome his "Oriental Villa." In a letter to a friend he described the house as "a remembrancer of Eastern magnificence which looms up against the mellowed azure of the Southern sky." He planned to include such unheard-of amenities as bathrooms and closets. Mirrors positioned in the sixteen-sided cupola were to reflect sunlight down to other mirrors below to light the dark interior. Elaborate furnishings, mosaic floors, marble mantels, statues and stairways were shipped from France and England only to be caught in the Federal blockade of Southern ports. None of it reached Longwood. Nevertheless, the ground floor has since been beautifully furnished with period pieces.

It was a shock then when I climbed the stairs to the second level, opened the door, and stepped into a cavernous space that looked like the inside of a barn—the construction timbers stood exposed and raw just as they were the day the carpenters walked out of the house. Twenty-two rooms were to be built on two floors in this huge space now occupied only by an occasional butterfly and a few birds. Somewhere in this emptiness was to have been a grand dining room, and I thought of all the dining pleasures not taken.

It was hard to believe. "Just a shell," Marje said. "It looked so elegant when we came up the road."

We left right after for Woodville and a picnic with three local women and their families.

◤◤◤◤◤WOODVILLE, MISSISSIPPI

Three Cooks—
Mrs. Bettye Plitt,
Mrs. Sallye Morris,
Mrs. Mary Lee Bell

Left to right, Bettye, Sallye, and Mary Lee

A few years ago the anthropology department of Harvard University chose the small town of Woodville (pop. 1,512) as best typifying the antebellum South in appearance, customs, and traditions. I chose it because of its good cooks.

The head of the Woodville Civic Club, Ernesto Calderia, suggested I talk with one or more of three Woodville ladies, all excellent cooks, who are close friends and often work together as a team on civic and church projects. Their husbands hunt and fish so the ladies know a great deal about cookery. "With luck," he continued, "you might get all three."

The next day I addressed a letter to each—Mrs. Bettye Plitt, Mrs. Sallye Morris, and Mrs. Mary Lee Bell. I had hoped to get at least one.

A week later this formal reply arrived from Mrs. Bettye Plitt:

"Mrs. Sallye Morris, Mrs. Mary Lee Bell, and myself have met to discuss your letter. After much deliberation, all three of us have decided to work with you on your book."

Woodville, founded in 1811, is one of the oldest towns in Mississippi. It is deep in the southwestern pocket of the state that juts into Louisiana, above Baton Rouge. The Mississippi River, to the west, is less than twenty miles away.

There was a relaxed hospitality in Woodville. People stopped me on the street to ask if I wasn't the author man come to town to talk with the women about cooking. One lady gave me her cookbook on game when I was unsuccessful in finding a copy of my own.

We stayed in Square Ten, an old house that had been remodeled into a bed-and-breakfast inn. We arrived to find the key in an envelope taped to the front door along with a welcoming note explaining the hosts had gone away for a few days. Would we please leave the rent money on the mantel when we left? We were to help ourselves to breakfast things in the kitchen.

Sallye, Bettye, Mary Lee, Marje, and I had our planning session on the shaded patio of the inn. The temperature stood at 101°. We talked of a whole array of Southern dishes, many of them best suited for cool weather. As hot as it was, it was clear our meal should be a picnic. And it should be in the deep shade of Sallye Morris's big pecan tree. Preparation for the picnic would be done in her air-conditioned kitchen.

Sallye would make the rolls, dewberry cobbler, Mexican corn bread, and the tartar sauce. Mary Lee would go to the country to get fresh-picked ears of corn and make the slaw. She would also bring fish her husband had caught—fillets of bass and yellow catfish from the Mississippi River. Bettye was to bring the chicken and, as a special treat for Marje and me, strips of venison tenderloin. She would also make several gallons of iced tea. The author was to bring the beer.

Five hours went into the preparation of the picnic. Husbands arrived to set up a battery of three portable propane stoves. Children arrived to eat. The bass and catfish fillets were to be deep-fried in oil in one kettle and the chicken and strips of venison in another. On the third stove, water in a big aluminum pot was coming to a boil for the corn.

Tobie Morris, Sallye's husband, lowered venison strips into the hot oil.

"Venison today doesn't taste like you will remember it," Tobie said. "Then it was probably tough and strong tasting. Twenty or so years ago there were so few deer that we had almost no experience in preparing the meat. If you bagged one you could expect to get your picture in the paper. Now the deer population has exploded.

"This year deer wandered all over town and played havoc with the gardens. For several mornings a large buck walked down Main Street as if he was going to the post office.

"We are having corn-fed venison this afternoon," he said. "The very best!" He handed me a piece. It was crispy and delicious, sweet and a bit nutty tasting. None of the strong game flavor I had always associated with venison.

"It's so good, I'm surprised it hasn't been franchised!" I said.

The women, the food, and the children moved out of the house to the big picnic tables under the pecan tree. Tobie, satisfied that the oil in a second pot was hot, dropped in pieces of fish. While it seemed early to me, Mary Lee began the corn. "My way to do corn is to bring the water to a hard boil, put in the corn, turn off the heat and leave the ears in the hot water for about twenty minutes." Bettye, a big bowl of floured chicken by her side, tended the pot on the third stove.

QUICK-FRIED RIVER CATFISH

[SERVES 6]

There was a special delight in eating catfish filleted from a big 12-pounder fished straight out of the Mississippi River, not from a fish netted in a farmer's pond and programmed for growth from the day it was hatched until the day it was fried. After one bite, the word *scrumptious* came to mind.

Frank Bell had caught the fish the night before in a wire net that had been shaped into a hollow log and dipped in tar to fool a fish into thinking it was a good place to hide.

Frank had earlier caught several bass. These were filleted, too, and prepared along with the catfish. This recipe calls for brushing the fillets with prepared mustard before rolling in cornmeal. He preferred peanut oil for frying the fish.

INGREDIENTS

1 cup prepared mustard, of choice
2 cups cornmeal
2 pounds catfish fillets, cut into 1-inch-wide strips
Salt and pepper, to taste
Peanut oil, of sufficient depth to deep-fry

EQUIPMENT

One heavy, deep pot or skillet; slotted spoon or tongs

PREPARATION
12 mins.

Put the mustard in a shallow pan or on a length of foil. Do the same with the cornmeal. Season the catfish strips with sprinklings of salt and pepper. Coat the strips liberally with mustard; then drop in the cornmeal and dredge well. Set aside while the oil heats.

DEEP-FRYING
375°
10–12 mins.
per batch

The oil should be hot enough to brown a 1-inch bread cube in 1 minute. Don't overheat. Add the fish before the oil begins to smoke.

Gently immerse the strips in the hot oil with the slotted spoon or tongs. Don't crowd the pieces. Fry for 5 or 6 minutes; turn the strips over and continue frying for an additional 5 minutes. Allow the temperature to return to 375° before frying the next batch. Expect to fry 5 or 6 batches.

FINAL STEP   Remove the fish and drain on paper towels. Serve hot.

QUICK-FRIED TENDERLOIN OF VENISON

[SERVES 4]

Marinating venison, as with other game, serves two functions—to enhance flavor and to tenderize. Many love the wild taste of venison and prefer not to marinate it, particularly if it was a tender cut from a young deer. Older animals and the less tender cuts benefit from marination.

In this Woodville recipe, the meat is cut into strips and then marinated for at least 2 to 3 hours.

INGREDIENTS
2 eggs, lightly beaten
1 tablespoon Worcestershire sauce
1 teaspoon Cajun seasoning or Tabasco sauce
2 pounds venison tenderloin, cut into ½ x 5-inch strips
2 cups flour
Vegetable oil, of sufficient depth to deep-fry

EQUIPMENT
One deep skillet, 3- to 4-quart kettle, or electric fryer. Wire basket, slotted metal spoon, and long-handled metal tongs are helpful.

PREPARATION
2 hours or
more

In a medium bowl beat the eggs and add the seasonings. Stir in the venison strips and marinate for at least 2 hours; all day, if feasible.

Place the flour in a pan and coat the venison strips. Set aside while the oil heats.

DEEP-FRYING
375°
10 mins. per
batch

Heat the oil to 375°. It should be hot enough to brown a 1-inch bread cube in 1 minute. Don't overheat.

Gently immerse the floured strips into the hot oil. Fry for 5 minutes—turn the strips and continue frying for an additional 5 minutes. Allow the oil to return to 375° between batches.

FINAL STEP
Remove the strips from the pan and drain on paper towels. Serve hot.

CORN BREAD

[MAKES 2 PANS; SERVES ABOUT 10]

Hush puppies, those small balls of fried corn bread, are traditionally served in the South with fried fish, especially catfish, but the Woodville picnic broke with tradition. The women baked an equally delicious and appropriate dish—corn bread prepared with hot peppers and cheese.

INGREDIENTS
8 ounces bacon
1 large onion, grated
3 to 4 jalapeño chili peppers, chopped
¼ cup chopped bell pepper
2 cups self-rising cornmeal; or 2 cups cornmeal, 4 teaspoons
     baking powder, and 1 teaspoon salt
1 cup buttermilk, room temperature
1 egg, beaten
6 ounces sharp Cheddar cheese, grated
One 16-ounce can yellow cream-style corn
½ cup chopped green onions

EQUIPMENT
Two 9 x 11-inch or 9 x 9-inch baking pans, ungreased. (That will be done later.)

PREHEAT
Preheat the oven to 450°. At the same time place the ungreased baking pans in the oven. Later the batter will be poured into the sizzling hot pans to form a thick, crisp crust.

PREPARATION
20 mins.
Cut the bacon into small ¼-inch pieces and fry until crisp. Set aside. Reserve the bacon grease.

Pour 1 tablespoon of bacon fat into a small skillet and sauté the onion, jalapeño and bell peppers until soft, about 10 minutes.

In a large bowl stir together the remaining ingredients. Blend in the 3 sautéed vegetables and the bacon bits.

GREASING PANS
5 mins.
With hot pads, take the pans from the oven and pour a tablespoon of bacon grease into each. Tilt the pans so the sides are greased as well.

Return the greased pans to the oven for 5 minutes before pouring in the batter. After pouring in the batter spread it evenly with a rubber scraper or wooden spoon.

BAKING
450°
30 mins.
Bake until the bread tests done, about 30 minutes, and a wooden toothpick or metal skewer inserted in the center comes out clean.

FINAL STEP
Remove the bread from the oven. Let the pans cool somewhat on metal racks before cutting the bread into serving pieces.

continued

This bread will keep for several days, thanks to the bacon fat and cheese, and may be frozen for months.

DEWBERRY COBBLER

[SERVES 8]

Dewberry. While the name has the ring of luscious fruit sculptured in the early morning mist, it is a member of the big blackberry family (*Rubus flagellaris*). Its many cousins include the boysenberry, loganberry, and youngberry—all delicious and all can be used in this recipe.

If self-rising flour isn't at hand for this recipe (Southern cooks are devoted to it), substitute 1 cup all-purpose flour plus ¼ teaspoon *each* baking powder and salt.

INGREDIENTS	*1 quart dewberries, or berries of choice* *2 cups sugar* *1 cup self-rising flour (see above)* *1 cup milk* *¼ cup (½ stick) margarine or unsalted butter* *1 teaspoon ground cinnamon, to dust top* *1 teaspoon graded nutmeg, to dust*
EQUIPMENT	One 9 x 5 x 3-inch baking pan, greased
PREHEAT	Preheat the oven to 375°.
PREPARATION 10 mins.	In a saucepan cook the berries and 1 cup of sugar over medium-low heat until the sugar is dissolved, about 10 minutes. In a small bowl mix together the flour, milk, and remaining 1 cup of sugar.
ASSEMBLING 10 mins.	Over a low heat melt the shortening in the baking dish. Spread the berries over the bottom of the dish. Add the flour mixture to the dish. Stir *gently* to blend. Sprinkle the top with cinnamon and nutmeg.
BAKING 375° 30 mins.	Place in the oven and bake to a golden brown, until solid to the touch, about 30 minutes.
FINAL STEP	Remove from the oven, cool—but only briefly—and serve. The cobbler should be served warm—with a large dollop of whipped cream or ice cream. Before ice cream came to her house, Sallye Morris remembers her mother passing a bowl of rich golden cream, so thick it had to be spooned rather than poured.

∿∿∿GULF SHORES, ALABAMA

Fisherman—Walter Tatum

Walter Tatum knows a lot about fish and crab and shrimp and other things that swim in the sea. He is a marine biologist. He is also a fine cook whose specialty is seafood.

I found him by happenstance. One morning we were driving on the highway leading to the shore when I saw the sign in a grove of pine trees —Marine Resources Division, State of Alabama. "This is where I might find a fish expert," I said to Marje and wheeled the van into a parking space in front of a small wood-framed building.

I had in mind the scene we saw the night before of dozens of people wading in the shallow water within a stone's throw of the beach, all carrying torches and spears. What were they hunting for?

"Yes, you have come to the right place," the receptionist said when I told her why I was there. "You're in luck. My boss not only knows a lot about marine life but he's a great cook. A prizewinning cook at that."

Tatum was at his desk shuffling papers and smoking a pipe with an incredibly short stem. He was deeply tanned from hours on the water. As Chief Marine Biologist for the state of Alabama, his domain is the five hundred miles of estuarine shorelines of the Mississippi Sound, Mobile Bay, and the Gulf Coast front beaches. His headquarters here are located on what became an island when the Intracoastal Canal was dug in 1933 and divorced it from the mainland.

I told him about the arresting sight we had seen along the shore fronting Biloxi. We saw dozens of patches of brightly lit water moving slowly in the shallows. For a moment they seemed not to be attached to anything worldly. Moving with the lights, I then realized, were men and women carrying propane lanterns, with gigs poised to spear fish on the bottom.

"They were intent on the outline of a flounder, a flatfish resting horizontally under a thin blanket of sand, both eyes facing upward," Tatum explained. "They're looking for the eyes which will be brightly illuminated by the lantern light. This pinpoints the faint outline of the fish in the sand. It's a deadly giveaway."

Curiously, Tatum said, the young flounder from the Gulf's east coast are programmed by their parents to drift to the bottom with the right eye up. Later the under eye moves around the head to join up with the other to become a right-eyed flounder. The west coast flounder, on the other hand, drops to the bottom with its left eye up, hence left-eyed.

It was a flounder that won him his first prize at the South Baldwin County Seafood Cookoff. "A right-eyed, as I recall. When I created the recipe I knew with the first bite I had a winner. The word *grand* leaped to mind so I called it Flounder *Grandeur*."

Tatum has a number of fish recipes that he believes are winners but unfortunately the Seafood Cookoff is no longer being held. He hopes it will come back someday, and when it does he will enter his Quick Old-fashioned Dinner-in-a-Pot and Golden Puff Flounder, which were created by the National Marine Fisheries Service.

FLOUNDER GRANDEUR

[SERVES 6]

Tatum's prizewinning dish is as simple to prepare as it is good. It may be done in advance and held in the refrigerator for a day or two. While this is a versatile recipe, he suggests using only saltwater fish since the meat is moister than that of freshwater fish.

Tatum also recommends this dish to be made with shrimp.

INGREDIENTS
2 pounds flounder fillets, or other flat fish of choice
Salt
1 cup dry white wine
¾ cup mayonnaise
½ cup finely chopped onions
1½ cups grated sharp Cheddar cheese
2 teaspoons seasoned salt, such as Adolph's

2 tablespoons chopped green onions, to garnish
2 tablespoons chopped red bell pepper, to garnish

EQUIPMENT — One deep baking dish, buttered

PREHEAT — Preheat the oven to 400°.

PREPARATION
10 mins.

Lightly salt the fillets and set aside for 5 minutes.
Place the fillets in the baking dish and add the wine. Spread the mayonnaise evenly over the fillets. Cover with the onions and cheese. Add 2 or 3 shakes of seasoned salt.
Garnish with the green onions and bell pepper bits.

BAKING
400°
16 mins.

Bake in the oven for 15 minutes. Then run the fish under the broiler to give the cheese a rich brown top.
Serve immediately.

GOLDEN PUFF FLOUNDER

[SERVES 6]

These flounder fillets are broiled for a few minutes, then topped with a creamy mixture of onion, parsley, pimento, and cayenne pepper lightened with beaten egg white and put back under the broiler to cook a golden brown.
Other flatfish may be used in this recipe—sole, turbot, or halibut.

INGREDIENTS

2 pounds flounder fillets, fresh or frozen and thawed
⅓ cup melted shortening or oil
1 teaspoon salt
Dash white pepper
½ cup mayonnaise or salad dressing of choice
2 eggs, separated
2 tablespoons each finely chopped onion, parsley, and pimento
½ teaspoon cayenne pepper
Oil, to brush

EQUIPMENT — One broiler pan, greased

PREPARATION
10 mins.

Skin the fillets and cut into 6 serving portions. Set aside.
In a bowl mix the shortening or oil, salt, and pepper. Add the mayonnaise or dressing. Beat the egg yolks and add to the mixture. Stir in the onions, parsley, pimento, and cayenne pepper.
Beat the egg whites to a stiff peak and fold into the mixture. Set aside.

continued

BROILING
8–11 mins.

Place the fish on the well-greased broiler pan and brush with oil. Broil about 3 inches from the source of the heat for 3 to 4 minutes. Turn carefully and brush with more oil. Broil 3 to 4 minutes longer or until the fish flakes easily when tested with a fork. Top the fish with the mayonnaise mixture. Broil about 5 inches from the source of the heat for 2 or 3 minutes, or until golden brown.

Serve immediately.

QUICK OLD-FASHIONED DINNER-IN-A-POT

[SERVES 6 TO 8]

When the South Baldwin County Seafood Cookoff is resumed, Walter Tatum says he wants to enter this favorite recipe created by cooks with the National Marine Fisheries Service, one that can be prepared and served in less than an hour.

INGREDIENTS

*1 pound fresh flounder or other thick fish fillets, or frozen,
    thawed*
6 cups hot water
6 chicken bouillon cubes
1 cup thinly sliced carrots
2 medium onions, cut into 8 wedges
2 tablespoons cornstarch
¼ cup cold water
2 cups broccoli pieces, flowerettes and stems
½ teaspoon each dried basil and oregano
⅛ teaspoon freshly ground black pepper
1 cup sliced fresh mushrooms
1 tomato, cored, peeled, seeded, and cut into 8 wedges
2 tablespoons sliced stuffed olives
Sour cream, to garnish (optional)

EQUIPMENT

One Dutch oven or large 6-quart sauce pot

PREPARATION
25 mins.

Cut the fillets into 2-inch squares.

Combine the hot water, bouillon cubes, carrots, and onions in the pot and bring to a boil. Cover and cook over medium heat until the carrots are tender, about 10 minutes.

Combine the cornstarch and cold water; stir until free of lumps. Add the cornstarch to the hot liquid, stirring constantly until the cornstarch is cooked and the stew has thickened, about 3 minutes.

Add the broccoli, basil, oregano, and pepper and cook uncovered for 5 minutes.

Add the fish squares, mushrooms, tomato, and olives. Stir carefully to mix.

COOKING
5–8 mins.

Cover the pot and cook until the fish flakes, about 5 to 8 minutes. Don't overcook or the meat will fall apart.

FINAL STEP

Ladle the stew into dishes or large bowls. Top each serving with a dollop of sour cream, if desired. Delicious served with toasted French bread slices.

⋙DEMOPOLIS, ALABAMA

The Nelson Family Reunion
—Carolyn Nelson

A summertime reunion of the family under the trees or in the park shelterhouse is the penultimate showcase for cooks. Once a year it is an opportunity to affirm the family's reputation for good cooks and good eaters as well as count the number of new babies, kiss pretty cousins, tell the old folks how well they look, and to pitch a few horseshoes.

This year the Nelson family of Alabama, with roots in the farming communities of Nanafalia and Sweetwater, drove to the Ralph Nelson farm, off S.R.10, between the two settlements, to celebrate their second annual reunion. And Marje and I were invited.

"Not quite as many are here this year, but that leaves more food for those of us who are," said Cousin James who has been the moving force behind the reunions. He is also the husband of Carolyn Nelson, the talented cook we had driven to Demopolis to be with in her kitchen while she got ready for the reunion.

Demopolis, a small city of some eight thousand on the banks of the Tombigbee River, was started in 1817 by a group of French exiles who were granted four townships by Congress to establish vineyards and olive groves. The women were habitués of the French court; the men were mainly officers of Napoleon's armies. They failed to cope with the wilderness and within a decade the colonists had scattered. Only the name, Demopolis, which means "city of the people," remains of those bright visions.

Carolyn, a fifth-grade teacher in a private academy in Demopolis, the author of two cookbooks, and the organist in the First Baptist Church, also caters.

She was a marvel to behold in the kitchen. Within a two-hour period she had put together Happy Chicken, breasts double-dipped in margarine and coated with seasoned flour and baked; a country corn casserole, Corn Bread Salad, strawberry fruit salad, and two cakes. One was a spectacular five-layered beauty deeply coated with caramel icing; the other she called Nun's Cake. She smiled.

"When I first discovered this cake recipe it was called Better-Than-Sex Cake. I thought the church organist should be more circumspect so I gave it a new name."

Carolyn's latest cookbook is *Down Home Cooking with Country Leftovers*, a collection that reflects a dedication to Southern cooking that doesn't rest on deep-fried food.

"There is no question that there has been a dramatic change in Southern cooking over the past twenty years," Carolyn said, "and I am delighted with it!"

There was a time, of course, and not so long ago, when cooking in most Southern kitchens consisted chiefly of fats and frying, peas and beans, an occasional vegetable in season, flour, sweet milk, buttermilk, and chicken.

Carolyn remembers as a child having meat only on Sunday, and that was usually fried chicken. Hog-butchering time gave the family fresh and smoked pork for "winter meat." Until her father bought a refrigerator—she was twelve—those were the only meats she had tasted.

"Foods were fried with the exception of a boiled fresh ham at Christmas or boiled chicken in chicken pie or dumplings. Hog fatback seasoned all vegetables. Peas, beans, turnips, and soups were drowned in grease.

Even today many older people, especially those who grew up in the country, consider vegetables tasteless unless seasoned heavily with bacon or fatback and dripping with fat."

The favorite meal when she and James were married was peas (seasoned with bacon), fried okra, fried corn, tomatoes, and corn bread made with plenty of bacon grease in it. For meat—a choice of chicken, ham, pork chops, or steak—always fried!

Today she seldom fries anything.

"Another habit I brought into marriage was fixing three big meals a day—baking biscuits for breakfast and corn bread for lunch and dinner."

How has that changed, I wanted to know.

"Now we have a light breakfast, a light lunch, with supper in the evening as the main meal. One lifelong habit that I have succeeded in breaking is that of serving dessert with each meal. Fresh fruits have found their way to our table at dessert and replaced cakes and pies most of the time. I say most of the time because sometimes I can't help myself —my happiest hours are still those spent in my kitchen baking cakes, pies, cookies, and breads."

The dishes of two dozen Nelson cooks were spread the length of the fifty-five-foot picnic table in the shade of the huge tree in Cousin Ralph's front yard. "There's some real down-home cooking from several good country kitchens here," Carolyn says, "and some that's not." She nodded toward two cakes from the supermarket with price tags still on them.

When all the dishes were on the table and uncovered, Cousin James asked Cousin Frank to say grace. Some eighty members of the Nelson family bowed their heads for the blessing, and then moved to the long table to admire the cornucopia and praise the cooks.

Carolyn's Happy Chicken came first and then came: country baked ham, chicken and dressing, fried chicken, beans and franks, plain baked beans, roast beef, sliced turkey, barbecued pork, chicken salad, potato salad, Jell-O fruit salad, sweet potato casserole, chicken potpie, colored butter beans, green beans, pink-eyed hole peas, potato chips, sliced tomatoes, corn casserole, country corn, layered salad, pear salad, deviled eggs, broccoli, corn bread and muffins, rolls and crackers, pecan pie, blueberry pie, apple pie, Caramel Cake, strawberry fruit salad, coconut lemon cake, brownies, almond squares, German chocolate cake, Nun's cake, velvet cake, pound cake, 7-Up cake with pineapple frosting, and apple and peach cobblers.

Last year the presentation of Carolyn's five-layered caramel cake was a disaster. In the hot car ride to the reunion the icing melted; it couldn't be cut without smearing and tearing the slices apart. "And it was so pretty, too." This year Carolyn chilled the cake in the refrigerator to firm it up. Before she left home she wrapped each slice in plastic wrap. I carried it on my lap to the picnic—and stood fascinated at the table to watch it disappear almost like magic.

CORN BREAD SALAD

[SERVES 8]

This salad is different and delicious. Loaded with good things, it is substantial and can be a meal by itself. The recipe is for 8 but it is easily doubled for a picnic or family reunion.

INGREDIENTS

4 cups roughly crumbled corn bread
2 cups cooked chicken, chopped pea size
1 cup chopped green onions
1 cup chopped parsley
½ bell pepper, chopped
½ cup chopped pickles (of choice)
½ cup chopped water chestnuts
1 tablespoon diced pimento
1 cup peas (1 small can)
¾ cup Shoepeg or whole-kernel corn
1½ tablespoons sugar
1 teaspoon paprika, plus extra for sprinkling
1 teaspoon salt
1 teaspoon freshly ground black pepper
1 teaspoon poultry seasoning (optional)
¼ teaspoon cayenne pepper, or to taste
1 cup mayonnaise, or enough to moisten

PREPARATION
30 mins.

In a large bowl add all the ingredients except the mayonnaise in the order they are listed above. Mix well before adding the mayonnaise. At this point I get into mixing with my hands to be certain the mayonnaise is well distributed.

Taste. I like my salad hot so I usually add more red pepper, but that's a personal choice.

CHILLING
2 hours

Cover the bowl and chill for several hours.

FINAL STEP

Sprinkle with paprika before serving.

HAPPY CHICKEN

[SERVES 6]

Describing Happy Chicken in her cookbook, Carolyn Nelson says this is the favorite recipe of the family—"including brothers, cousins, aunts, uncles, in-laws, and outlaws." Carolyn and I differ in the preparation of the recipe in two small ways. I like to flatten the meat with a whack or two of the side of a cleaver. She prefers not to flatten it; she likes it plump. I like to dip the floured chicken in melted butter; Carolyn prefers margarine.

INGREDIENTS
6 chicken breasts (from 3 chickens), skin removed
1 cup all-purpose flour
1 cup (2 sticks) unsalted butter or margarine
1 teaspoon salt
1 teaspoon freshly ground black pepper
½ cup sherry
¼ cup chopped parsley, to garnish

EQUIPMENT
One medium (12 x 8 x 2-inch) baking dish, buttered, or lined with aluminum foil and buttered

PREHEAT
Preheat the oven to 350° while preparing the breasts.

PREPARATION
25 mins.

Flatten the breast meat, if desired, and set aside. Spread the flour on a length of foil. Melt the butter or margarine in a saucepan of sufficient size to allow the meat pieces to be dipped and coated.

Season the breasts with salt and pepper. Coat each with flour and dip into the melted butter or margarine. Coat again with flour and dip into the butter for the second time. (The dish may be prepared ahead to this point, covered, and refrigerated overnight.)

After each piece has been dipped twice, place it in the baking pan. Don't overlap. Sprinkle the breasts liberally with sherry before placing them in the oven.

BAKING
350°
1 hour

Place the uncovered dish on the middle shelf of the oven and bake for 1 hour. Baste with sherry every 15 minutes.

FINAL STEP
Sprinkle the breasts with chopped parsley before serving.

CARAMEL CAKE

[SERVES 12]

There was a run on the Caramel Cake the moment it was uncovered on the picnic table at the Nelson reunion. And for good reason—it was handsome, delicious, and rich.

For cake baking Carolyn prefers all-purpose rather than cake flour. She also does not wash her cake pans in soapy water. She uses plain warm water. Most soaps have a grease-cutting agent that will cause cakes to stick even though each time the pan is greased anew. And above all, she says, keep cake pans out of the dishwasher!

To assure that her cake rises uniformly—without a hump in the center or without the cake falling—Carolyn protects her pans in the oven with a collar of heavy aluminum foil around the outside of the pan, folded to the height of the pan. Inside are folded several thicknesses of paper toweling. Before the collar is used, the foil is loosened somewhat and the paper soaked with water. The collar is reshaped and pinned around the outside of the pan. The cold collar slows the baking action along the outer edge while allowing the center, away from the heat, to bake.

INGREDIENTS	*3 cups all-purpose flour* *4 tablespoons baking powder* *1 cup shortening (Crisco), room temperature* *2 cups sugar* *5 eggs, room temperature* *1¼ cups buttermilk* *1 teaspoon vanilla extract*
EQUIPMENT	Three 8-inch round cake pans. Butter and fit the bottom of each with a circle of wax paper; butter the paper. Prepare the aluminum rings as described above.
PREHEAT	Fifteen minutes before baking, place 2 racks in the center area of the oven and preheat to 350°.
PREPARATION BY HAND OR MIXER 13 mins.	Sift together the flour and baking powder and set aside. In a mixing or mixer bowl cream together the shortening and sugar. Be certain they are well blended and that the sugar has dissolved. Add the eggs one at a time. Stir vigorously with a wooden spoon or mixer flat beater after each egg is added. Stir in the flour, a portion at a time, alternating with the buttermilk. Stir in the vanilla.

PREPARATION BY PROCESSOR 4 mins.	After sifting the flour and baking powder, attach the metal blade. Drop the shortening and sugar into the work bowl and process until blended, about 1 minute. Add the eggs, one at a time, and process for 1 minute, stopping once to scrape the work bowl. Spoon the dry ingredients into the bowl. Process for 5 seconds. Pour in the buttermilk and add the vanilla. Process just until the ingredients are combined. Run the spatula around the inside of the work bowl again—and pulse one more time. Do not overprocess.
BAKING 350° 30 mins.	Divide the batter equally among the 3 prepared cake pans. Bake until a toothpick inserted in the centers comes out clean, about 30 minutes.
FINAL STEP	Remove from the oven and let cool in the pans for 5 minutes, then invert onto a wire rack.

Icing for Caramel Cake

[SUFFICIENT TO COVER A 3-LAYER CAKE]

This is not an icing to be rushed, but it is an icing to be praised. Outstanding.

Carolyn gave its history: "When Ken Broughten was in my first-grade class, he brought me some of the best caramel candy I had ever put in my mouth. I asked him to bring me the recipe, but the next day he told me there was no recipe. His aunt and mother had it in their heads. They were gracious enough to come to my house and let me take it down on paper while they made the candy. They said it was an old family recipe that came with a wood stove when it was bought many years ago. Then I used the recipe for icing, and the cake became a sensation with my family and at church socials and school affairs."

Allow between 1½ to 2 hours to make this icing. It's worth every minute.

INGREDIENTS	*1¼ cups each sugar and water* *3⅛ cups (3 cups plus 2 tablespoons) sugar* *17 ounces (1 large can plus 1 small can) Carnation evaporated milk* *½ cup (1 stick) margarine (regular—not soft or whipped)* *2 teaspoons vanilla extract* *1½ cups chopped almonds or walnuts*
EQUIPMENT	One large, deep stainless skillet or stainless Dutch oven

continued

PREPARATION
20 mins.

Spread the sugar evenly in a skillet over high heat. Watch for the first bubble to appear. When it does, start stirring, and slowly stir until all of the sugar is dissolved and transparent.

Add the water. The mixture will harden, but let it boil until dissolved.

Meanwhile mix the 3⅛ cups sugar and the evaporated milk in a 2-quart container. Heat in a microwave on "reheat" or in saucepan over medium heat until the sugar is dissolved.

COOKING
15 mins.

Cook the sugar-water mixture over medium heat for about 15 minutes, or until it reaches a very fast bubbly stage. Don't rush it at this stage. Let some of the water cook out.

Combine the sugar-water and milk-sugar in the large pot and cook over medium-high heat until it boils. Add the margarine.

STIRRING
234°
1–1½ hours

Turn the heat to medium and stir every 3 or 4 minutes, until the mixture reaches the soft-ball stage—234° with a candy thermometer. This can take 1½ hours, depending on the humidity in the kitchen. Remove from the heat and add the vanilla extract and nuts.

BEATING
30–60 mins.

Use a spoon or a hand-held mixer. Beat until the icing reaches spreading consistency. By hand it will require about an hour of beating, with the electric mixer, less time and effort.

FINAL STEP

Spread the icing on the cake layers and sides. If the icing becomes too stiff, add a few drops of hot water and stir.

II MIDWEST and PLAINS

Illinois Kansas Missouri

Mississippi River

Backcountry

The crisp feel of fall was in the air. One or two leaves on my new gum tree, anticipating their first autumn on my lawn, had already turned from green to gold. I joined my neighbor, Foster Curry, in setting out trash cans, and picking newspapers off the drive.

"Have a good one," he said about our trip. Elsie Thomas, a neighbor one house beyond, was walking her dog. She called to say that she would phone the boarding kennel every other day to be certain Timothy was happy. She was concerned that he was not going with us.

It was time to go. Marje was driving the first couple hundred miles. I was in the navigator's seat, surrounded by maps, reading the newspaper and making notes on the day's journey.

This would be a backcountry loop—away from Interstate highways —down through the lovely wooded rolling hills of southern Indiana, Illinois, and Missouri and onto the undulating prairie of Kansas. However, our return to Indiana would be on I-70, rewarding only because speed and time would be a priority.

We wheel slowly through small towns and villages and past grammar schools and playgrounds, a journey replete with hundreds of images of America: an old cemetery starkly alone on the brow of a hill, trees branching out and over to shade the wayfarer; mailboxes in all sizes and colors giving few hints of the personalities of the people in the houses beyond; a dog soaking up the warmth of the sun on the concrete strip past his house, which he considers to be his own. There are places where chickens still wander across the road as they did when I was a kid in farm country.

A pleasurable way to go.

The Westerfield House—
Jim and Marilyn Westerfield

We turned the van off Illinois 15 and drove down a corridor of tall pines leading to a large log cabin set in a wide clearing. There was a cornfield out back and, beyond, a dense woods. The garden in front was landscaped with a covering of herbs growing in beds between paths of pebbles, carefully raked each morning into delicate furrows as a Japanese gardener would do.

Abraham Lincoln, whose law office was in Springfield, knew well this part of Illinois—the high plateau region east of the Mississippi River —but he would not have recognized this unusual three-story log building —the Westerfield House—the home of Jim and Marilyn Westerfield.

It is more than a home, of course. It is a first-rate restaurant, celebrated in the area around St. Louis (twenty-five miles away) for its festive seven-course dinners by candlelight during the Christmas season and its summertime "herbal" luncheons. Three bedrooms, elegantly furnished with Colonial antiques and collectibles, are for bed-and-breakfast lodgers. (I was startled to find a dressmaker's form all in black lace standing by my side in the bathroom.)

I had talked with Jim and Marilyn at a meeting of food people in St. Louis some months earlier and had been fascinated with the story of the Westerfield House. Instead of leading quiet lives in retirement—he had been a wholesale-food executive and she, an accountant-bookkeeper— the two chose the demanding lives of restaurateurs and innkeepers. And to do it in a log house set in a clearing in remote woods!

"When we built the log house in 1978," Jim explained, "we only had vague thoughts about an inn, but it wasn't until we were encouraged by friends who came here for overnight visits that we decided in 1983 to go for it."

"With no experience other than that we were both excellent home cooks, overnight we began serving six-course meals for guests. We had a lot of desire. It all came together beautifully and has remained so. We have never had an unpleasantness."

Marilyn is chef. Her domain is the kitchen below where, with two helpers, she prepares and sends up one flight of steep stairs seven-course meals for as many as seventy diners. Jim, a tall, lank man with a silver-speckled beard, is factotum in charge of all other things including his beloved herb gardens.

He and I were walking through the gardens, which cover an area larger than a tennis court. "There are more than a hundred and forty different herbs growing here, of which there are forty different varieties of mint. I have grouped them in three areas." I was furiously jotting down herb names as we walked.

"Here is the 'back-door herb garden' that every lady of the house would have planted by the kitchen door 260 years ago. It includes, among others, dill, oregano, lovage, parsley, thyme, and scented geraniums. She baked with the latter and used it as a cologne."

The middle garden was for the family's medicinal needs, Jim explained.

"Here is artemisia for sore muscles, knees, and back. Leaves of wormwood were placed in stored clothing and linens to repel insects, especially moths. Southernwood, too, was death to moths. This is teucrium for gout and indigestion. Old woman is bottled in alcohol for a week and then mixed with goose fat to make an ointment good for all pains and hurts. Feverfew repels bugs. It also makes a comforting brew."

Beyond was the garden Jim called the "herbs of legend."

"The most revered, of course, are the herbs on which the Christ child lay in the manger—lady's bedstraw, rosemary, pennyroyal, and thyme."

The Westerfield's summertime herbal-luncheon guests are first taken by Jim on a tour of the gardens. A typical lunch prepared by Marilyn would be rosemary wine; herbed crisps; summer greens and herb salad; lemon chicken pie; sage-glazed carrots; and, for dessert, ice cream flavored with lavender.

"When we introduced herbal luncheons two summers ago I was blissfully unaware of what I was creating. Now it's standing room only, with a limit of seventy guests."

The Christmas season for the Westerfields begins in November when Jim lays in a supply of 3,000-foot-tall red tapers to be burned in 101 candle holders in the dining rooms. No electric lights. He also fashions large fans of bright red apples (three bushels) and pineapples for display over the fireplace and along the walls. And he polishes the silver buckles on his slippers, part of the Colonial garb he and Marilyn wear during the holiday season.

The Christmas season ends the day after New Year's when they collapse after hosting and serving dinners every night for almost two months. They escape to Florida.

They offer a bed-and-breakfast and gourmet-dinner package most of the year but beg off during the frantic Christmas season.

Jim's other love is his huge collection of Windsor chairs, popular in the eighteenth century in England and America, with spreading legs, a back of spindles, and a saddle seat. All the chairs in the dining rooms are Windsors. In our bedroom alone we had a choice of several Windsors plus one tiny Windsor in a dollhouse.

ABSOLUTELY MIDWESTERN SALAD

[SERVES 6]

A dozen herbs and spices in oil, vinegar, and mayonnaise are mixed and tossed separately with the salad greens, then tossed with the cream cheese and blue cheese dressing.

INGREDIENTS

3 ounces cream cheese, room temperature
3 ounces blue cheese, room temperature, crumbled
5 to 6 tablespoons water
1 egg
2 tablespoons fresh lemon juice
1 cup vegetable oil, of choice

¼ cup red wine vinegar
2 tablespoons mayonnaise
2 tablespoons chopped fresh chives
1 tablespoon sugar
1½ teaspoons Worcestershire sauce
¾ teaspoon each paprika and salt
1 garlic clove, crushed and finely minced
¼ teaspoon prepared hot mustard
¼ teaspoon white pepper
8 cups torn salad greens
1 egg, hard-cooked, chopped
Seasoned salt, to sprinkle
Black pepper, ground over the salad

PREPARATION
10 mins.

Beat the 2 cheeses in a small bowl until smooth. Beat in 1 table-spoon of water at a time until the mixture can be poured. Set aside.

For the dressing, in a food processor bowl or blender combine the egg, lemon juice, and ¼ cup oil and process for 15 seconds. Add the remaining oil in a slow, steady stream. Add the vinegar, mayonnaise, chives, sugar, Worcestershire, paprika, salt, garlic, mustard, and white pepper. Process until smooth.

ASSEMBLING
4 mins.

Combine the salad greens in a large bowl, with enough dressing to coat. Sprinkle with the chopped egg and seasoned salt and toss gently. Add 2 to 3 tablespoons of the cheese mixture and pepper to taste, and toss again.

FINAL STEP

The oil and cheese mixtures not used can be covered and kept separately in the refrigerator for up to 2 weeks.

BAKED HAM–SWISS–CHEDDAR IN PHYLLO

[MAKES 2 ROLLS]

This Westerfield favorite is ham and two different cheeses sandwiched together, then wrapped in phyllo dough and baked.

INGREDIENTS

6 sheets phyllo dough, 14 x 18 inches, thawed if frozen
½ cup (1 stick) unsalted butter, melted, to brush
4 thin slices ham, about 7 x 4 inches
2 thin slices Cheddar cheese, about 7 x 4 inches
2 thin slices Swiss cheese, about 7 x 4 inches

continued

EQUIPMENT   One cookie sheet, lightly buttered

PREHEAT   Preheat the oven to 375°.

PREPARATION   Keep the phyllo wrapped until the ham and cheeses have been
10 mins.   cut to size.
        Place 1 phyllo sheet on a damp towel with the short edge of
the dough nearest you. Brush sparingly with butter; continue
layering 2 more sheets in this manner. Set aside and proceed
with the next 3 sheets in the same way.

ASSEMBLING   Fold the phyllo in half. Place a slice of ham on the phyllo,
20 mins.   leaving at least a 1½-inch margin of dough uncovered at each
side. Place a slice of Cheddar cheese over the ham. Repeat with
another piece of ham, and top with Swiss cheese. Fold the mar-
gins in and brush with butter. Lift one end of the phyllo and
carefully roll it jelly-roll fashion, starting with the short end.
        Place the roll, seam side down, on the prepared cookie sheet
and brush with butter. Repeat with the remaining phyllo, ham,
and cheeses.

BAKING   Bake for 20 to 25 minutes, until golden brown.
375°   Serve immediately.
20–25 mins.

WILD RICE–STUFFED VEAL BIRDS

[SERVES 2]

Jim Westerfield's recipe is for 4 veal birds to be served to 2 persons.
Rather much, I think. At our house we usually serve one each if the
balance of the meal is substantial. When the birds are served, they look
like breasts of small game birds, hence the whimsical name.

INGREDIENTS   *½ cup chicken stock, homemade (see page 562) or store-bought*
2 tablespoons thoroughly rinsed wild rice
3 tablespoons unsalted butter
2 ounces mushrooms, finely chopped
2 tablespoons freshly grated Parmesan cheese
2 tablespoons minced fresh parsley
½ pound veal, cut evenly into 4 thin slices
¾ cup beef stock, homemade (see page 560) or store-bought
½ cup dry white wine
1 tablespoon minced shallot

1 teaspoon minced fresh thyme, or ½ teaspoon dried
Salt and freshly ground black pepper, to taste

PREPARATION
1 hour

Bring the chicken stock to a boil in a small saucepan over medium-high heat. Stir in the wild rice. Reduce the heat to low, cover tightly, and simmer until the rice is tender, about 45 minutes, adding more stock if necessary.

Melt 1 tablespoon of the butter in a small skillet over medium heat. Add the mushrooms and cook until tender and liquid has evaporated, about 3 to 4 minutes. Reserve the skillet; do not clean. Drain any excess stock from the cooked rice and the mushrooms, add the cheese and 1 tablespoon of the parsley to the mushrooms.

Pound the veal slices very thin. They will be about 3 x 8 inches.

ASSEMBLING
8 mins.

Spoon one quarter of the wild rice mixture onto each veal scallop. Roll up and secure with thread. Toothpicks can be used but they make the birds awkward to turn.

COOKING
25 mins.

Heat 1 tablespoon of the butter in the reserved skillet over medium-high heat. Add the veal birds and brown on all sides, about 5 minutes total. To the skillet add ¼ cup of the beef stock, the white wine, shallot, thyme, and remaining tablespoon of parsley and bring to a boil. Simmer gently until the veal is cooked, about 15 minutes.

Transfer the veal to a platter and keep warm.

Add the remaining ½ cup of beef stock to the skillet, increase the heat to high, and boil to reduce by half, scraping up any browned bits. Whisk in the remaining tablespoon of butter and season with salt and pepper.

FINAL STEP

Remove the strings or toothpicks from the veal. Pour the sauce over the birds and serve.

GOUGÈRE

[SERVES 8 TO 10]

This puffed Burgundian pastry is made with tablespoons of dough, in 2 layers, arranged in close order in a circle, and baked. The French serve it cold, cut in wedges as an appetizer, or hot in smaller pieces as hors d'oeuvres.

INGREDIENTS

1 cup water
½ cup (1 stick) unsalted butter, room temperature
1 cup all-purpose flour
4 eggs
1½ cups grated Gruyère cheese
1 teaspoon salt
½ teaspoon dry mustard

EQUIPMENT

One baking sheet, lightly buttered, with a 9-inch circle marked

PREHEAT

Preheat the oven to 450°.

PREPARATION
10 mins.

Combine the water and butter in a medium pan and bring to a rolling boil over medium heat (be certain the butter is completely melted). Add the flour all at once and beat with a wooden spoon until the mixture forms a ball and comes away from the sides of the pan. Remove from the heat.

Add the eggs, one at a time, beating vigorously after each addition, until the dough is smooth and shiny. Blend in the remaining ingredients.

ASSEMBLING
5 mins.

On the baking sheet form the marked circle by arranging table-spoons of dough with the sides touching. Repeat, making a second layer of dough directly on top of the first.

BAKING
450°
10 mins.
325°
15 mins.

Bake for 10 minutes at 450°. Reduce the oven heat to 325° until the gougère is puffed and lightly browned, about 15 minutes more.

FINAL STEP

Immediately poke several holes around the gougère to release the steam. Slide onto a serving plate, slice, and serve.

LINDSBORG, KANSAS

A Kansas Sweden—
Alice Brax, Reverend J. Q. Woodard

A sign on the outskirts of town read: *Välkommen till Lindsborg.*

A small town of about three thousand in the middle of Kansas, Lindsborg was founded in 1869 by a band of Swedish immigrant farmers most of whom were named "Lind." It calls itself "Little Sweden, USA," and is pridefully Swedish to its very roots.

Marje and I walked to the town park to look over the Swedish pavilion given by the Swedish government from its exhibit at the 1904 St. Louis World's Fair. The grandest moment in the life of the town was King Carl Gustaf's visit to dedicate the building in 1976.

The only excitement when we walked through the empty building was caused by three small girls who rattled doors and windows to scare us and then, giggling and laughing, raced back across the street to their doll carriages.

We walked up the red-brick Main Street, wide and tree-lined, past the *apotek* (pharmacy), *bibliotek* (library), *stadhus* (city hall), the *conditori* (bakery), and the *stuga* (tavern). Despite this display of things Swedish, I counted more Fords and Chryslers on the street then Volvos, and by the train tracks a huge elevator for Kansas wheat. "That elevator by itself could probably hold all the wheat grown in Sweden," Marje re-marked.

The power structure in town is impressively Swedish—Mayor Olson, President of the School Board Anderson, Chamber of Commerce President Anderson, Librarian Lofgren, and Circuit Court Judge Anderson.

The food in town is impressively Swedish but not lavishly so, at least it was not during our stay. The nearest thing to a smorgasbord was the steam-table buffet at the Swedish Crown Restaurant. It obviously was put together with its noontime business clientele in mind and featured as many wheat-belt favorites (peas, carrots, beans, wieners) as it did Swedish (meatballs, boiled potatoes, marinated herring).

Swedish cooking—plain and delicious—came with bed and break-fast at the Swedish Country Inn, just off Main Street. In its time it had been a feed store, a buggy company's sales room, a hotel, and finally a dormitory for men students from nearby Bethany College.

When the Applequist family bought the old building ten years ago there were birds nests in the upstairs closets and holes in the walls thanks to high-spirited college boys. Now it is a spiffy, twenty-room inn with all the comforts of a neat and tidy Swedish home plus a sauna on the lower level. While the inn serves breakfast only to overnight guests, others may come to the noon buffet. There is no dinner *and* no smorgasbord.

Nevertheless the food is all-Swedish, so much so that Alice Brax, the chef, feels she must tell first-time visitors to the dining room: "Break-fast is not American—no bacon, no pancakes, no doughnuts. It is all Swedish." It's *husmanskost*. City people would call it country cooking.

Breakfast was a choice of three breads (limpa rye, potato, and whole wheat), three cheeses (caraway, Swiss, and farmer), summer sausage, head cheese, bologna, sliced boiled eggs, herring, meatballs, cereal, bran muffins, and slices of a Swedish cardamom braided loaf.

I was in the kitchen with Alice when she was making a classic *hus-manskost* dish—*Ostkaka*, a dessert that is a baked dish of curdled cream and milk and eggs.

Alice was born in Lindsborg at a time when almost everyone in town spoke Swedish. "I grew up thinking everyone spoke two languages, so when I moved away as a young woman and let it be known I spoke Swedish I was shocked to find I was considered, well, odd. I was called 'that dumb Swede from Kansas.' Even though most often it was spoken in jest, I hated it. I had to come back home to appreciate my heritage."

She visited Sweden for the first time ten years ago as a retirement present after two decades as director of food services at Bethany College, the small Lutheran school in town noted for its annual week-long Mes-siah Festival.

"I came back from Sweden full of enthusiasm for its food and almost immediately learned that the newly opened Swedish Inn wanted a Swedish cook. After cooking for college kids for so many years this was a wonderful release."

While Lindsborg cooks can find ingredients for almost all Swedish dishes on the shelves at Lee's Market, it is a retired Southern Baptist minister who makes Swedish meatballs for almost everyone in the community. "Nobody in Lindsborg does their own meatballs anymore, not even here at the inn," explained Alice. "The Reverend Woodard has the town's business. He does them so perfectly."

The Reverend J. Q. Woodard, a spirited eighty-two-year-old retired Baptist minister with a handsome set of mutton-chop whiskers, moved here from Texas a few years ago to be near his wife's family. While he has made himself available for interim pulpit duty, his celebrity has come from the thousands of meatballs he has made while standing at a butcher's block in the back of the market. The butcher grinds the meats, the reverend fashions the tight little balls—two at a time between his palms. His production is about fifteen pounds of meatballs at a time, several times a week, depending on demand. One year for *Hyllingsfest*, a weekend festival celebrating Lindsborg's pioneer and cultural past, he shaped about twelve thousand.

KÖTTBULLAR
(Swedish Meatballs)

[MAKES ABOUT 40; SERVES 6 OR 8]

The Reverend Woodard shapes meatballs 2 at a time between his palms, but they can also be done between 2 teaspoons dipped in cold water. Chill the mixture overnight in the refrigerator so the meat isn't sticky when a small portion is pinched off to roll.

While many Swedish cooks fry meatballs in butter or oil, these are baked, hence nearly free of fat. I vary the Woodard recipe slightly by cooking the onions before mixing rather than adding them raw.

INGREDIENTS

½ tablespoon butter
½ cup finely chopped onion
1 pound lean ground beef
½ pound lean ground pork
1 egg, lightly beaten
¾ cup bread crumbs
½ cup milk
1 teaspoon salt
½ teaspoon sugar
½ teaspoon freshly ground black pepper
½ teaspoon ground allspice   continued

EQUIPMENT	One baking sheet
PREPARATION 15 mins.	In a small frying pan, melt the butter over moderate heat. When the foam subsides, add the onion, cover, and cook for about 5 minutes, until they are soft and translucent.
	In a large bowl, combine all the ingredients including the onion. Knead vigorously with both hands or beat with a large spoon until the mixture is well blended, smooth, and fluffy. (An electric mixer at medium speed will do the job nicely.)
PREHEAT	Preheat the oven to 350°.
SHAPING 15 mins.	Shape the meat into balls about the size of a walnut or golf ball. (My creation usually weighs about ½ ounce.) Arrange the meatballs in one layer on the baking sheet.
	(If you wish to save some of the uncooked meatballs for later, place them on a flat tray in the freezer. When frozen, drop them in a plastic bag for storage.)
BAKING 350° 18–20 mins.	Place the baking sheet in the oven and bake for 18 to 20 minutes, or until the meatballs are browned and show no pink when one is broken open.
FINAL STEP	Serve either hot or at room temperature. Leftovers can be kept frozen.

OSTKAKA
(Dessert Pudding)

[SERVES 8]

Ostkaka has been described as a pudding and a cheesecakelike dessert. It is topped with lingonberries and a touch of whipped cream. A light sprinkling of thinly sliced almonds is another touch.

After the rennet has been added to the warm milk to form the curds, most of the resulting whey is spooned off. The rule: Spoon off just half as much whey as the volume of milk with which you began. One whey to two milk. Discarding too much whey will result in a dry *Ostkaka*. Some cooks drain off the whey through a cheesecloth placed in a large sieve or colander. This is fine, but if you use this technique, don't allow the whey to drain completely. Take off only half the total volume. The discarded whey need not be thrown away. Use as the liquid in a bread recipe.

Ostkaka may be baked in a baking dish from which it will be spooned into dessert dishes, or it can be baked in individual cups.

The traditional topping is lingonberries—whole or as a canned sauce —but other sweetened berries do as well. Some Swedish cooks serve it with *kräm*, a pudding made with any fruit juice, cooked with sugar and cornstarch until thick.

INGREDIENTS	*8½ cups whole milk*
	1 rennet tablet
	1 tablespoon warm water
	½ cup all-purpose flour
	2 eggs
	½ cup sugar
	½ cup light cream (half-and-half)
	½ teaspoon almond extract
	½ teaspoon salt
	Lingonberries, fresh or sauce, or other berries
	½ cup sliced almonds (optional)
	Whipped cream (optional)

EQUIPMENT

One 10 x 6 x 2-inch baking dish, or 1 dozen individual cups, buttered

PREPARATION
25 mins.

In a 3-quart saucepan heat 8 cups of milk to lukewarm (98° to 100°).

Meanwhile, dissolve the rennet tablet in the warm water. In a small bowl, mix the flour into the ½ cup of milk; stir until smooth and add to the lukewarm milk. Stir the rennet into the milk-flour mixture, and put aside until the mixture sets, about 10 minutes.

PREHEAT

Preheat the oven to 325°.

SEPARATING
8 mins.

When the curd has formed, with a knife cut in a pattern of 1-inch squares, roughly made. Precision not required. The curd will shortly separate from the whey, in about 5 minutes.

With a ladle or cup lift out 1 quart of the liquid whey. Discard it or reserve for another use. (See above.)

ASSEMBLING
8 mins.

In a medium bowl combine the eggs, sugar, cream, almond extract, and salt. Stir into the curd. Turn the mixture into the prepared baking dish or individual containers.

BAKING
325°
55–60 mins.

Bake for 55 to 60 minutes, or until the center is firm when tested with a knife blade. The surface may look slightly wet.

FINAL STEP

Serve hot or cold with lingonberries or other berries. Sprinkle with almonds, if desired, and top with whipped cream.

KARDEMUMM A FLÄPA
(Swedish Cardamom Braid)

[MAKES 1 PLUMP FOOT-LONG LOAF]

One of the Swedish Country Inn's favorites is this handsome plump loaf woven with 3 strands of dough rich with butter, eggs, raisins, and spice. Braided bread has a crafted look that delights the eye, and this loaf in particular has the taste to delight the palate.

INGREDIENTS

3 cups bread or all-purpose flour, approximately
1 package dry yeast
¼ cup sugar
½ teaspoon salt
¼ cup nonfat dry milk
½ cup hot water (120°–130°)
12 tablespoons (1½ sticks) unsalted butter, softened at room
*   temperature*
1 egg, room temperature
1 teaspoon ground cardamom
⅓ cup golden or dark raisins
1 egg white, slightly beaten with 2 tablespoons sugar, to glaze

EQUIPMENT

One large baking sheet, greased or Teflon. If for a small oven, however, the baking sheet must be small, which may mean dividing the dough and baking 2 smaller loaves rather than 1 large one. The braided dough will be about 12 inches long and expand somewhat during baking.

PREPARATION
BY HAND OR
MIXER
15 mins.

In a mixing bowl measure 1 cup of flour and add the yeast, sugar, salt, and dry milk. Blend with a wooden spoon. Pour in the hot water and stir with 25 strong strokes, or 2 minutes with the mixer's flat beater.

Cut the soft butter into several pieces and drop into the batterlike dough. Add the egg, cardamom, and raisins.

Stir in the remaining 2 cups of flour, ¼ cup at a time, first with the spoon and then by hand, or with the mixer's flat beater and then the dough hook. The dough will form a rough mass and clean the sides of the bowl. Because of the large amount of shortening, the dough will not be sticky. It will be firm but not stiff.

KNEADING
8 mins.

Turn the dough out onto a lightly floured work surface. With a strong push-turn-fold action, knead until the dough is smooth and elastic, or knead under the dough hook, for about 8 minutes.

**PREPARATION
BY PROCESSOR
5 mins.**

Attach the metal blade. Measure 1 cup of flour into the work bowl and add the yeast, sugar, salt, and dry milk. Pulse to blend. Pour in the hot water. Pulse several times until the batter is smooth. Drop in the butter, egg, and cardamom, and with the machine running add the remaining flour—¼ cup at a time— until the batter becomes a shaggy rough ball of dough carried around the bowl by the force of the blade.

**KNEADING
50 secs.**

Knead for 50 seconds with the machine running. If the dough clings to the sides of the bowl, add a few sprinkles of flour.

(The raisins may be added to the dough the last few seconds of the kneading process but they will be cut into small bits by the blade. Or the raisins can be worked into the dough after the first rising.)

**FIRST RISING
1 hour**

Return the dough to the bowl (it need not be greased again because of the high butter content of the dough). Cover the bowl with plastic wrap and put aside at room temperature until the dough has doubled in volume, about 1 hour.

**SHAPING
20 mins.**

Punch down the dough and turn it onto a floured work surface. Knead the dough briefly to work out the bubbles.

Divide the dough into 3 equal parts—and roll under the palms into a roll about 14 inches long. Beginning in the middle of the strands, braid loosely to one end, reverse the loaf and again braid from the middle to the end. Pinch the ends closed.

**SECOND RISING
1 hour**

Cover with wax paper and leave until doubled in bulk and puffy to the touch, about 1 hour.

PREHEAT

Preheat the oven to 350° 20 minutes before baking.

**BAKING
350°
45 mins.**

Before baking, brush the braid with the beaten egg white and sugar. Bake until the loaf tests done, about 45 minutes. The crust will be a rich brown, and a wooden toothpick or metal skewer inserted in the center of the loaf will come out clean and dry.

FINAL STEP

Remove the braid from the oven. Use a metal spatula to lift the braid off the baking sheet because the hot loaf is somewhat fragile and might break unless it has cooled.

◆◆◆◆On the Road—DEPARTING LINDSBORG, KANSAS

Mummy's Arm

Marje was in the navigator's seat in the van when suddenly she chortled. She had been reading some of my Lindsborg notes.

"The mummy's arm! I can't believe it. You made it up."

I protested that I had not.

Yesterday when we had gone to the McPherson County Old Mill Museum, down on the Smoky Hill River, she had gone in one direction and I the other, our usual mode for museum visiting. I had seen it. She had not.

I thought it was a piece of charred wood or a length of beef jerky when I first saw it in the glass case along with a number of other Lindsborg treasures. But it wasn't until I stooped down to read the legend that I realized I was looking at an *arm*.

The card read:

"This forearm of an Egyptian mummy, purported to be that of a 3,000-year-old Egyptian princess, was obtained by Bishop Mackay Smith, the father of the donor, while on a trip up the Nile in 1875. Lack of room in his trunk prevented his getting the entire mummy."

◆◆◆◆R.F.D., WILSON, KANSAS

Two Lady Bakers—
Amelia Branda and Ida Mae Goodman

Down a red dirt road that leads through wheat fields and pasture lands south of Wilson, a small town of 876 which calls itself the Czech capital of the state, live two women, mother and daughter, who have a remarkable bakery operation going in their country kitchens.

Ida Mae Goodman, *left*,
and Amelia Branda

The two women bake kolaches, the delicious fruit, nut, and cream cheese–filled buns that is to a Czech what a croissant is to a Parisian. (Kolaches come in several shapes—rounds with the filling in the center, small squares with the corners brought together on the top, or little filled turnovers.)

Ida Mae Goodman, the daughter, begins her day at 4:00 A.M. when she starts the first of many batches of dough to be used that day. Two hours later she loads everything into the family car and drives up the road one mile to join her mother, Amelia Branda, in her kitchen. Amelia, too, had begun her day making dough. For ten hours, five days a week, the two women make and bake several hundred kolaches which are then placed on a long picnic table in the living room to cool before being packed in cartons for delivery.

To keep the operation in flour, every three weeks the truck from Shaw's Grocery in Wilson delivers a quarter of a ton of all-purpose flour.

Mrs. Branda, who is eighty-two but looks and moves twenty years younger, for many years did special-order cake baking for the community but stopped to join her daughter in the kolaches enterprise.

The remarkable thing is that the mixing and kneading of all the dough for thousands of these delicious buns is done by hand: no mechanized help beyond what could be found in any small farmhouse kitchen. No mixer. No blender. The only concession to high tech is a small microwave oven in which frozen fillings are thawed. The cooking of the fillings and the baking—one batch after another all during the day —is done on and in an ordinary-size kitchen range.

"It isn't that we like to do everything by hand," Ida Mae explained, "but so far we can't afford the equipment."

Because their kolaches have become so popular locally and in such faraway places as Salina and Great Bend and Hays that they are considering renovating an old mobile home into a commercially equipped bake shop and, perhaps, allow themselves the luxury of outside help.

For now, the women work in the kitchen bakery regardless of weather. Neither heat nor blizzard and deep snow has yet kept Ida Mae from driving the road each day to her mother's. Only once did a storm knock down the power line leading to the house, but they lit candles and continued to work until the power came back on.

Each week 750 kolaches go in three deliveries to Shaw's Grocery where they sell for $2.65 a dozen. Originally Shaw had planned to freeze and put aside a supply of the buns, but the fresh-made ones sell out so fast that none are left to freeze. (If you should plan to stop at Shaw's to sample the kolaches, phone ahead—[913] 658-2120.) The rest are special ordered for receptions and parties and by folks who love them on any occasion.

KOLACHES

[MAKES 32 BUNS]

The two women use a variety of fillings for their kolaches—apricot, cherry, prune, poppy seed, raisin, cottage cheese, apple, and pineapple —and all of them made in the small kitchen. Recipes for making the fillings follow. You may wish to make these beforehand. Store-bought canned jams, jellies, and pie fillings can also be used.

As to choice of shortening: I like butter alone or in combination with vegetable shortening. But, of course, many Czech cooks prefer lard.

INGREDIENTS

¾ cup (6 ounces) shortening, room temperature
½ cup granulated sugar
1 teaspoon salt
3 egg yolks
1 cup milk
5 cups all-purpose flour, approximately
2 packages dry yeast
Fillings (see recipes below)
Confectioners' sugar, to sprinkle (optional)

EQUIPMENT

Two baking sheets, greased

PREPARATION BY HAND OR MIXER
10 mins.

In a mixing or mixer bowl cream by hand or with the mixer flat beater the shortening, sugar, salt, and egg yolks. Mix in the milk. Measure in 2 cups of flour. Add the yeast. Stir to blend well.

When the batter is smooth, add the remaining four, ½ cup at a time, and each time stir vigorously. When the dough has formed a mass that can be lifted out of the bowl and placed on the floured work surface, the dough is ready to knead. Or, if using a mixer, attach the dough hook.

KNEADING
8–10 mins.

Knead the dough with an aggressive push-turn-fold motion or under the dough hook for 8 minutes, or until the dough is smooth and elastic. At this point it should not stick to the work surface or the sides of the mixer bowl. Add sprinkles of flour if the dough continues to be sticky during the kneading period.

FIRST RISING
1 hour

Place the dough in a greased bowl, cover tightly with a length of plastic wrap, and put aside at room temperature to double in bulk, about 1 hour.

FIRST SHAPING
20 mins.

Punch down the dough and place it on the work surface. Divide the dough into 4 equal pieces. Roll each piece into a long cylinder about 1½ inches in diameter. With a knife cut each cylinder into 8 equal pieces.

Roll each small piece into a tight ball and place on the greased baking sheet. Space 2 inches apart. Cover with a length of wax paper and set aside to rise again.

SECOND RISING
20 mins.

Allow the balls of dough to rest and rise for about 20 minutes.

SECOND
SHAPING
15 mins.

Press each ball into a circle about 2½ inches across, and form a small rim around the edges. This is more than just a depression made with the thumb—this calls for pressure and pulling by opposing index fingers to flatten the dough but leaving the rim intact. If the dough is not pressed down sufficiently it will rise and push out the filling.

Place a tablespoon of filling in the center of each circle.

To make a square packet: Pat out a square 3 inches on a side, and place a full teaspoon of filling in the center. Bring the four corners together on the top, pressing them together to adhere. Brush with melted butter.

THIRD RISING
30 mins.

Cover the kolaches loosely with wax paper and let rise again until the dough is "light," that is, puffy, about 30 minutes.

PREHEAT

Preheat the oven to 375° while the buns rise.

BAKING
375°
25–30 mins.

Place the kolaches in the oven and bake for 25 to 30 minutes, or until the dough is a golden brown.

Don't overbake.

continued

FINAL STEP   Remove from the oven and, if you wish, sprinkle with confectioners' sugar. Place on racks to cool. These freeze well.

Prune or Apricot Filling

[WILL FILL 36 KOLACHES]

INGREDIENTS   *1 pound pitted dry prunes or apricots*
½ cup sugar
1 cup cooking liquid, from above
1 tablespoon lemon juice
1 teaspoon grated lemon rind
½ teaspoon ground cinnamon

PREPARATION   Cover the prunes with cold water; stir in the sugar, and bring to
6–7 mins.   a boil. Reduce the heat and cook slowly, stirring constantly, until
smooth and thick. Remove from the heat and strain, keeping 1
cup of the cooking liquid. To the cooked prunes and the saved
liquid add the lemon juice, grated rind, and cinnamon.

Poppy Seed Filling

[WILL FILL 36 KOLACHES]

INGREDIENTS   *½ pound ground poppy seeds*
1 cup water
1 cup milk
1 tablespoon butter
1 teaspoon vanilla extract
½ teaspoon ground cinnamon
1 cup sugar
½ cup crushed graham crackers
½ cup softened raisins

PREPARATION   Boil the poppy seeds in the water until thickened. Add the milk
18 mins.   and boil slowly for about 10 minutes. Add the butter, vanilla,
and cinnamon, then the sugar; continue cooking for about
5 minutes. Take from the heat, add the graham crackers and
raisins.

Note: Both of these fillings will keep indefinitely refrigerated.

∿∿∿WILSON, KANSAS

The Sauerkraut Lady—Laverne Libal

A jolly woman whose beautiful smile is bracketed by deep dimples, Laverne Libal is fiercely proud of her Czech ancestry and Wilson. She is constantly pushing town fathers to promote the town's potential.

"There's the annual Czech After-Harvest Festival each July, but that's not enough. The very least we could do would be to put up a big billboard over on the Interstate."

Laverne had a new perm for our meeting in her kitchen. She had taken time off from her job in the meat department of the I.G.A. so she could show me how to make sauerkraut and to give me recipes. Her husband, Jack, an insurance adjuster, stayed home to shred the cabbage, which is his job.

"We get our cabbage from Colorado," he explained. "It's too hot in Kansas to grow good kraut cabbage." He pushed the head of cabbage back and forth over the blade of an old wooden box cutter or shredder, the shredded pieces dropping into a bowl below.

The Libals make about fifty gallons of sauerkraut a year, most of it served during the annual festival and the balance given to friends and eaten at home. Today they made only enough to fill a one-gallon crock.

"It is not a heavy brine solution," she said. "Only about one cup of salt to each gallon of shredded kraut."

The Libal kraut is so mild and delicious that it can be eaten right from the crock, unlike store-bought kraut that must be rinsed in running water to remove the heavy brine solution.

SAUERKRAUT, HOW TO MAKE

[MAKES 1 GALLON]

The secret to making sauerkraut is to force the cabbage shreds to give up their juices which, with the salt, will become the preserving brine. Some use a hand-held wood stamper to press the shreds into the bottom of the crock, but Laverne much prefers her fist so as not to mash or bruise the sauerkraut.

The least amount Laverne makes is 5 gallons. I have cut the recipe to 1 gallon.

INGREDIENTS
10 pounds fresh cabbage
1 cup salt

EQUIPMENT
One 1-gallon stone crock; kraut or vegetable shredder. (It can be done in a food processor but it would be long and arduous.)

PREPARATION
1 hour
Remove and discard the tough outer leaves of the cabbage head. Shred the cabbage and put down enough shreds to make 1 layer in the crock—about 1 inch of cabbage—and sprinkle the layer heavily with salt.

Using your fist, punch down hard against the shreds but take care not to mash or bruise them.

When the water from the cabbage begins to rise to the top of the first layer as you punch it down, sprinkle it with salt, about 1 tablespoon. Lay down the second layer, about 2 inches deep, and mash it with your fist to produce water. Continue layering the cabbage and salt to within 2 inches of the top of the crock.

SITTING
2 weeks
The crock is left *uncovered* at room temperature for 2 weeks, not touched except to add water if the brine evaporates down to the level of the kraut.

FINAL STEP
Can the kraut in sterile glass jars, or freeze.

SAUERKRAUT KRISPS

[SERVES 6]

This unusual sauerkraut dish is a mixture of kraut, flour, and shortening rolled thin, shaped into strips or 3-inch squares, and sautéed. I have also made them quite small to be served as a surprise hors d'oeuvre. Please note that I call for shortening in this recipe, but lard is preferred by most Czech cooks I know.

INGREDIENTS
2 cups all-purpose flour
½ teaspoon salt
½ cup shortening, chilled
1½ cups sauerkraut, drained (reserve juice)
6 to 8 teaspoons water, if needed

OPTIONAL COATINGS
1 egg, beaten, to brush
Milk, to brush
Caraway seeds, to sprinkle
Poppy seeds, to sprinkle
Coarse salt, to sprinkle

EQUIPMENT
One baking sheet

PREHEAT
Preheat the oven to 425°.

PREPARATION
15 mins.
In a bowl combine the flour and salt. Cut the shortening into chunks and work it into the flour with a fork until it resembles coarse cornmeal, as with a piecrust. Add the sauerkraut to the bowl plus teaspoons of the reserved juice or water to make a moist, soft ball.

ASSEMBLING
15 mins.
Divide the dough into 2 parts for easier handling. Roll each on a floured work surface. Roll very thin: ¼ inch for crisp, or ⅜ inch for chewy. Cut into strips or squares, as desired.
The tops may be brushed with egg or milk and sprinkled with a choice of seeds or coarse salt or whatever.

BAKING
425°
10–15 mins.
Place on the ungreased baking sheet and bake for 10 to 15 minutes, or until lightly browned.
Serve immediately. Watch the surprised looks.

CZECH SAUERKRAUT

[SERVES 6]

This is Laverne's favorite sauerkraut recipe. Sometimes she will add sausage or ham pieces or ham hocks.

INGREDIENTS
2 pounds fresh sauerkraut
1 teaspoon caraway seeds
1 large onion, finely chopped
1 tablespoon shortening
1 tablespoon flour
1 teaspoon sugar (optional)

PREPARATION
15 MINS.

Drain the sauerkraut. Taste for sharpness. Wash and drain again if it tastes too briny. Place in a medium saucepan. Add the caraway seeds and enough water to cover. With forks pull apart and loosen the sauerkraut.

COOKING
35 mins.

Cook, covered, over medium heat for 25 minutes.

In the meantime, in a small skillet, sauté the onion in the shortening until soft and lightly browned, about 10 minutes. Stir in the flour and sugar, if desired, and cook for an additional 5 minutes, until slightly thickened.

Stir the flour mixture into the sauerkraut and cook for an additional 5 minutes.

Serve hot.

KANSAS CITY, MISSOURI

Barbecue Encampment—Alan Uhl

I got up before dawn, dressed and drove a half dozen miles across Kansas City to be there when the sun came up. At a distance it was a scene reminiscent of a soldier's bivouac or a hunters' camp in the wilderness. Smoke curled up from a dozen fires tended by bearded men in big, floppy campaign hats. Friends shouted early morning greetings to friends across the way. Almost every hand held a mug of steaming black coffee.

A man with a hatchet cursed a dull blade as he split chunks of wood into slender splinters which he carefully placed just so on a bed of coals. Others, still asleep on cots, had drawn blankets over their heads to fend off the day as the warming sun reached into the camp. It had been cold, almost freezing during the long, watchful night. The piquant smoke carried with it the delicious smell of meat cooking over low fires.

It was not in a wilderness but a clearing in the heart of Kansas City —Parking Lot A on the grounds of a vast complex of livestock show barns, and a football stadium—where one of the most prestigious barbecue contests in the United States was under way.

I went to the campgrounds to find out just what is *barbecue* to this gathering of some of its fervent practitioners. To these gathered stalwarts *barbecue* meant cooking meat by smoke in a covered unit in which the controlled temperature is low—225° is considered nearly ideal—and moisture is abundant. Some people soaked chips or chunks of wood and dropped them onto the charcoal embers, while others built their fires out of wood alone. The choice of woods is strictly personal. Some flavor the meat with a dry rub of spices, while most marinate the meat for long periods before cooking and mopping on marinade during the process.

I also found that to many in this group the word is *barbeque*, spelled with a *q*. One man explained: "Take the abbreviation B.B.Q., who ever heard of a B.B.C.?" To the contest sponsors, however, it was barbecue.

With this in mind, I toured the grounds.

Briskets of beef, one for each of the sixteen contestants, were cooking in a collection of barbecue "cookers" that ranged from a small covered home-style grill to cavernous barrel-like cookers. The meats had been carefully tended and mopped with secret sauces, referred to as "the mop," at intervals during the long night. Now they were being wrapped with aluminum foil and set aside in warming ovens to be judged later in the day. Five other meats which take less time to prepare—baby back ribs, pork shoulders, legs of lamb, sausages, and chicken breasts—were cut and trimmed by sleepy cooks and made ready for grilling and smoking.

The barbecue contestants had arrived at the grounds the day before in cars, trucks, motor homes, and vans pulling trailers loaded with paraphernalia to compete in the annual American Royal National Invitational Barbecue Cookoff. They were champions from across the country. David Veljacic, a fireman in Burnaby, British Columbia, flew into town with twenty-five pounds of his favorite apple and oak woods for smoking packed in two suitcases. The Society loaned him a cooker.

While it was a pro-am affair, most entrants were caterers and chefs who specialize in barbecue. They were there to try for $10,000 in prizes as well as the publicity a blue ribbon would give their businesses. One or two teams were just good buddies who came together for several beers and the fun of it. Some came with spouses who helped keep fires going, passed instruments, brought beers, and took turns at mopping marinades.

Roy Green, who drove up from Euless, Texas, called himself a "barbecue gypsy," one of a fraternity who travel nationwide on an informal barbecue circuit. He had just won the World Invitational Rib Championship in Virginia.

Green, a caterer, travels across the country towing Bubba, a one-ton steel barbecue cooker shaped like an armadillo. "Oh, there's some money in the contests but mostly we do it for braggin' rights back home." He grinned. He said he usually cooks only beef and ribs, today for the first time he would try lamb.

"I told my daddy I don't know much about lamb. He said just keep cookin' it till the wool falls off!" He gave Bubba an affectionate kick in its tires.

I talked with the man who was chopping wood when I arrived at sunup. "I found that if you go straight hickory, it is going to be bitter." said Paul Kirk. "Hickory is a very predominant smoke. I like cooking with oak, always have, and I have used straight oak and won contests with it. I use a lot of applewood that gives what I say is a little sweeter smoke. Whether it does or not—in my mind it does. I'm not a fan of green wood, smoky as it is. I'd just as soon have at least six months age on it. It burns a little better and still you get good effect."

Carolyn Wells, one of the Society's founders, was charging from one end of the campground to the other in a golf cart delivering pieces of meat to cooks ready to go to work. "The pieces of meat must be uniform. We also keep it refrigerated until the last minute or catch heck from the health department," she explained as she parked the cart.

What's the secret of delicious barbecue?

"Buy the best pieces of meat you can afford, use a wood accent, cook it slow, try to maintain a two hundred twenty-five–degree heat, put in a source of moisture, baste every twenty minutes. My husband and I think marinating and basting are more important than dry rubs or sauces on the meat after it is cooked. The marinade flavors the meat; during basting the vinegar evaporates to leave spices clinging to the meat. We are very heavy on marinades."

I followed the trail of an especially fine-smelling plume of smoke to a brisket being turned over by the gloved hands of Alan Uhl, an insurance executive and one of the founders of the Kansas City Barbecue Society, sponsors of the event. In 1988 he was the Kansas state champion. At the moment he was mopping the last of a bucket of marinade over a blackened brisket that after twelve hours in smoke and heat looked like it had been pulled through a sooty flue.

"Just you wait till I peel off the cheesecloth that's holding the sauce on and you will see something beautiful. It will taste even better, I promise."

Uhl poked his brisket with a fork. "It's done," he announced, and asked Sally, his wife, to hand him the scissors to cut away the cheesecloth.

The brisket, stripped of its cloth wrapping, lay exposed. It was an inviting dark brown. "I need only a pound of this for the judging so, here, have a smidgen." It was delicious. Tender. A light smoky flavor, touched with spice.

Uhl looked pleased at my pleased look.

It is fashionable among barbecue aficionados to carry a sobriquet or *nom de grille*. Alan's is The Great Barbecue Battler. (Others in the encampment included the Baron of Barbecue, The K. C. Rib Doctor, The Sultan of Slab, and The Honorable Sir Loin.)

The Great Barbecue Battler had several suggestions for would-be champions.

• A covered cooker is essential. It doesn't have to be elegant. Uhl's is an old upright freezer, with the smoke and heat piped into it from an outside firebox. (I have a Brinkmann and a Weber on my patio.)

• Moisture is essential to the smoking process. The necessary moisture can be produced by basting the meat, using either a pan of water alongside the meat or scattering wood chips or chunks that have been soaked in water over the glowing coals.

• You must have a way of knowing at what temperature the meat is cooking. Buy a reliable thermometer; a Taylor is a good one for under $10 at the hardware store. Rest it horizontally through a hole in the cover or lid, above the meat. Barbecue when the heat reaches 250° but maintain it at 225°.

• Buy thick leather gloves to handle the metal parts of the cooker and feed the fire. Buy white cotton gloves to hold the brisket when wrapping, mopping, unwrapping, and slicing.

• Always wrap the brisket or other large pieces of meat, such as a leg of lamb, in three layers of cheesecloth to blanket the marinade against the meat during the long hours it is in the cooker. The rule generally applies that when the meat doesn't have skin over it or a layer of fat on it, wrap it in cheesecloth. Fine for rabbit and also turkey breasts.

• As far as fuel is concerned, it matters little to Uhl whether the wood he tosses on the charcoal has been soaked in water or is dry. Use whatever combination maintains the 225° temperature. Hickory, oak, mesquite, and fruit woods are the best. Never, never use any kind of pine or evergreen.

Why be a competitor?

"Why indeed? Cooking at home on the patio is one thing but loading everything into my pickup, driving who knows for how far (next summer Coeur d'Alene, Idaho), setting up, sweating, shivering, getting rained on, grossly undersleeping, sometimes drinking too much, packing it all again, driving home, unloading, cleaning up, putting it away, collapsing. . . .

"I guess we all like to do things we are good at. Certainly a love of good food is important. Taking a lump of meat, sometimes tougher than an old shoe, and turning it into a tender delight that almost melts in your mouth . . . well. . . .

"I just love the taste of meat cooked in some fashion involving heat and smoke from natural sources. Nothing has given me more pleasure over the decades than going outside to cook. I know my neighbors think I am cuckoo when I clear away the snow so I can pull the grill out of the garage. Crazy, isn't it?"

Uhl is a contributor to the Society's authoritative book, the *Passion of Barbeque*, in which recipes are rated according to the time it takes to prepare them. There are three categories—One Bone, Two Bone, and Three Bone.

One Bone: meat, poultry, and seafood that can be done in fifteen minutes to an hour. The chapter promises: "Home by five, barbeque by seven."

Two Bone: creations that require more time, normally two to four hours. The chapter is subtitled: "A well-spent afternoon."

Three Bone: twelve to fifteen hours. "A smoke marathon."

Alan Uhl's recipe for brisket is a Three Bone.

UHL'S BRISKET OF BEEF

[SERVES 10 TO 12 HUNGRY EATERS WITH AMPLE LEFTOVERS]

Dedicate a day and a night to the Uhl brisket: 12 hours to season the meat in a plastic bag before wrapping it in cheesecloth, saturating it with marinade, and slow-cooking it in smoky moist heat for 12 to 15 hours. Total time is about 24 hours, and worth every aromatic moment.

It begins with the selection of a whole brisket, weighing in the neighborhood of 10 pounds. Ask the butcher to trim away the fat, including the fat bubble between the two sections. It will be tied into a neat bundle of solid meat that will weigh about 6 to 7 pounds.

In the final hour or 2, unwrap the cheesecloth and discard. Place the meat on heavy aluminum foil, spread barbecue sauce over it, and seal the foil tightly. Put it back in the cooker and it will become so tender that only an electric knife can slice it without tearing.

INGREDIENTS

One 10-pound brisket of beef, trimmed of fat to about 6 or 7 pounds

SEASONING
Equal parts salt, coarsely ground black pepper, garlic granules, and paprika
Cayenne pepper, small amount (optional)

MARINADE
4 cups beef stock, homemade (see page 560) or store-bought
½ cup olive or vegetable oil
½ cup red wine vinegar
1 cup Worcestershire sauce
2 teaspoons dry mustard
1 teaspoon crumbled bay leaf
2 teaspoons paprika
1½ teaspoons chili powder
1½ teaspoons garlic granules
2 teaspoons salt
1½ teaspoons Tabasco sauce

EQUIPMENT

Covered grill, charcoal, soaked wood chips or water pan (see above)

PREPARATION
overnight

To make the seasoning, stir the ingredients together in a small bowl. Seasoning not used in this recipe can be stored for use at some other time. Rub the seasoning into the meat, place it in a plastic bag, tie, and refrigerate overnight. It can be seasoned in less time but an Uhl-brisket calls for seasoning of at least 10 to 12 hours.

At the same time make the marinade by mixing all of the

ingredients together; refrigerate overnight or longer. It will make about 1½ quarts. The marinade not used can be refrigerated.

PREHEAT
30 mins.

Start the charcoal fire a half hour before putting on the meat.

COOKING
12–15 hours

After the fire has been started, remove the meat from the plastic bag and wrap it in 2 or 3 thicknesses of cheesecloth. Thickly brush with marinade and place it in the covered grill or smoker. The wet marinade will hold the cloth in place.

Maintain the fire and smoke at the temperature outlined above. Brush with marinade every 1 to 2 hours.

Try not to open the cooker to mop the marinade more than hourly. The less you open the cooker, particularly in cold weather, the faster the meat will cook. The brisket can go 2 and 3 hours without basting, but curiosity often dictates otherwise.

TESTING
2 hours before
serving

Two hours before serving, pierce the meat with a fork to determine its tenderness. Forking the raw meat before cooking will help to judge its progress later.

Rewrap the meat in aluminum foil and return it to the cooker for 1 hour before serving. See above.

Slice and serve!

BARBECUE RUB

[MAKES ABOUT 1 CUP]

Rubs are just what the name implies—dry spice combinations meant to be rubbed on the meat to be grilled or smoked. Some cooks use both a marinade and a rub, depending on the recipe.

This is a dry rub created by Uhl. It's especially good on lamb.

INGREDIENTS
2 teaspoons ground cloves
4 teaspoons dry mustard
4 teaspoons ground ginger
2 tablespoons dried mint
1 teaspoon garlic granules (not garlic salt!)
2 teaspoons paprika
1½ teaspoons dried rosemary
1 teaspoon black pepper
1 teaspoon salt

PREPARATION
Mix together all the ingredients in a small bowl and store in a covered container until needed.

⌁⌁⌁⌁*THE STEAMBOAT* MISSISSIPPI QUEEN

On the Upper Mississippi River—
Chef Paul Wayland-Smith

JUDI BOTTONI

It seemed a good time to leave the road for a week and take to the river.

Marje and I are steamship people to the marrow. We have been aboard passenger liners and freighters in both the Atlantic and Pacific, plus the Tasman Sea, in fair weather and foul. I have suffered *mal de mer* to the extreme in the Mediterranean, and exulted in the mirror-smooth sea off Baja California.

A cruise trip on the Mississippi River aboard a steamboat would be different.

We boarded the *Mississippi Queen* with four hundred other passengers alongside a wharf in St. Paul. A pretty Southern belle hostess, the wind rustling her petticoats and bonnet, welcomed us aboard the steamboat—seven decks tall, imposing in girth and decor. Unlike an ocean-going ship, the *Mississippi Queen* rode low in the water, the lowest of her decks barely six feet above the river. Her huge paddle wheel, turning slowly in the water, was at the ready waiting for a command from the wheelhouse.

A steamboat is not a ship, no matter how big it is. I had to watch terminology when I talked with Capt. Lawrence Keeton, who has spent more than half a century on the river. He kindly but firmly pointed out that a ship is for the sea and a boat is for inland waters. It is a *boat*.

The *Mississippi Queen* is the largest river steamboat ever built. About four hundred feet long, she moves across the surface of the water grandly with scarcely a quiver, rock, roll, or pitch. Her wake at top speed —eight miles an hour (knots are not known here)—is less than that kicked up by a small fishing boat speeding past. The first night aboard I placed a glass of water on the railing outside our cabin. One hundred miles later, through several river locks, not a drop was spilled. No ocean liner ever offered such tranquillity.

Ocean liners always have a "hum," a sense of many machines working below, and the vibration from the propeller shaft, especially if the vessel is running fast in a pounding sea. There is none of this aboard the *Mississippi Queen*. She is quiet. If I wanted noise I had to walk all the way aft to the deck immediately above the giant paddle wheel to hear the loud splash-splash-splash as it churned through the water. Occasionally the steamboat's great whistle would sound but that was it.

When I was not grabbing a camera to photograph the *Queen* going through a lock or a small but mighty towboat shepherding fifteen to twenty huge coal barges upriver or training binoculars on bald eagles resting on the limbs of dead trees at the river's edge, I was faced with a formidable social program much like one found aboard a Caribbean cruise ship.

Daily I faced the daunting choice of activities: first-run movies, bingo games, Hollywood Squares (river version), happy-hour specials in the Paddlewheel Lounge, a renewal of wedding vows (four couples obliged with a certificate to frame), square-dancing demonstrations by a touring California group, and a cocktail party for war veterans. There were lessons on the steam calliope, tours of the pilothouse, kite flying from the Sun Deck, afternoon teas, and elaborate stage shows in the Grand Saloon by the boat's talented troupe of a dozen entertainers and musicians. Busy, busy.

Today, however, I hunkered down on the railing to watch the world go by—the forests, the steep cliffs, the high bluffs, the barges, the duck blinds. Tonight the lights of small towns twinkled in the distance; the boat's powerful searchlight fastened on one channel marker and then leaped to another. There was no rush of waves against the vessel as there is at sea, so the night was undisturbed. I could hear the honking of Canadian geese in flight, winging south in the light of a hunter's moon.

It was the twenty-seven locks and dams on the Upper Mississippi, however, that afforded the most excitement. There was the long glide into the lock, the majestically slow closing of the huge gates behind us, followed by the odd sensation of sinking as the water disappeared and the boat settled between massive concrete walls to the level of the river below. The forward lock opened and the boat slowly eased out and into the main river channel.

Regardless of where she was on the Mississippi River—upper or lower—the *Mississippi Queen* was a crowd-gathering spectacle—all white with a sexy yellow and red trim, her name in tall metal letters along her side, a dozen American flags along the Sun Deck waved and snapped a constant salute. People in cars, buses, and trucks stopped along the highways to wave, honk, ring bells, fire a shotgun, shout a greeting. I saw a slow-moving Soo Line freight train on tracks hugging the river come to a complete stop. The engineer hung out his window, blew the whistle, and waved both arms.

Tom Murphy is a seventy-year-old Irishman who wears the shoulder boards of a purser but carries the title of P.S.R.

"That's for Passenger Service Representative or, in fewer words, concierge. I do whatever has to be done to make passengers happy. Well, almost. It is a new position on cruise ships to share the pursuer's workload, especially the social end."

Murphy has an irrepressible and sometimes irreverent sense of humor yet carries the dour expression of a purser who has been asked the same question a thousand times. His favorite passenger non sequitur: "When does the 10 o'clock shore tour leave?"

What is there about riverboat travel that makes it so appealing that some people come back to cruise eight, ten, and twenty times? So many people come back, in fact, that the boat has a party each cruise just for the returnees. This time 116 were there. One gentleman was on his seventeenth cruise. One returnee was ninety-one years old.

"At sea, aboard a passenger liner, after you have passed the Statue of Liberty or gone under the Golden Gate Bridge, all you will see for the next week or two weeks is water and more water. There's nothing happening when you are out on deck that you can share with a fellow passenger. Nothing on which to peg a conversation.

"But here on the river strangers will exclaim together about the sunset or point out a deer standing at water's edge or call to a fisherman proudly waving his catch for them or offer to photograph one another against a pretty landscape. They love to sit at lunch or dinner and watch the panorama of shore life pass by. They love to share these experiences."

The subject at our table turned to food, which has had a curious history aboard the boat.

For a number of years the food was tugboat fare, more to the liking of hard-working river men than of vacationing landsmen. Because New Orleans is the boat's home port, the food had come under the spicy and hot influence of Cajun cooks. Fine for the occasional dish, said passengers, but a bit much as a steady diet.

But that has changed. The *Queen* brought aboard Chef Paul Wayland-Smith, who had been a chef on other steamboats plying the Mississippi, to create a different cuisine. This has meant almost all new dishes for the *Mississippi Queen* and the training of a staff of twenty-eight to follow through.

Departing the *Mississippi Queen* at the St. Louis wharf, I read some of the comments about the cruise in the steamboat's guest book. Some were to be expected: "Impressive," "Swell," "I shall return," and "Real neat." Others were more pragmatic: "Relaxing but fattening," "Closet too small for all my shoes," and "The jury is still out!"

I wrote: "It is grand at times and fun all the time!"

BRAIDED SALMON AND FLOUNDER

[SERVES 6]

This is a handsome presentation of strips of pink salmon woven with strips of white flounder into a checkerboard, poached and served with a lemon-dill white sauce. If flounder is not to be found in the market, any of the flatfish can be used. Most of the time in my market it is sole.

When buying the fish, have in mind that 18 strips of salmon 4 inches long and ½ inch wide will be cut from the salmon fillets. An equal amount is cut from the flounder.

INGREDIENTS

1 pound each salmon and flounder fillets
3 cups water
2 cups white wine
½ cup lemon juice (if more liquid is needed to cover the fish, add in this ratio)

WHITE SAUCE
½ cup white wine
2 tablespoons lemon juice
3 black peppercorns
2 bay leaves
½ cup heavy cream
2 tablespoons butter
Fresh dill, chopped, or dry, to garnish

EQUIPMENT

One fish poacher or shallow saucepan

PREPARATION
20 mins.

Wash the fillets carefully. Cut the salmon fillets into 18 strips 4 inches long and ½ inch wide. Repeat with the flounder. Weave the strips in and out into a checkerboard pattern, alternating pink and white.

POACHING 12 mins.	Heat the water/wine/lemon liquid in the poacher or saucepan and bring to a simmer. Leave this mixture over low heat for 5 minutes. Then place the fillets carefully in the water and poach for 5 to 6 minutes, with the water barely simmering. Lift the fish carefully from the pan, set them in a warmed serving dish and keep hot.
SAUCE 10–12 mins.	While the fish pieces are poaching, prepare the sauce. In a small saucepan pour the white wine, lemon juice, peppercorns, and bay leaves and bring to a boil. Simmer over low heat until the liquid is reduced to ¼ cup. Strain. Add the cream and bring back to a simmer. Whisk in the butter.
FINAL STEP	Dress the fish with the sauce and garnish with the dill.

MISSISSIPPI MUD PIE

[SERVES 8]

Eating Mississippi Mud Pie on the *Mississippi Queen* traveling downstream on the Mississippi River is an irresistible combination. Besides, it is irresistibly good.

The creation begins with a pan of brownies. Spread this with a layer of mocha ice cream. Follow this with a layer of whipped cream. Freeze. When it comes from the freezer, cover each serving with chocolate sauce, sprinkle with pecans, and shower with dark chocolate shavings.

INGREDIENTS	*BROWNIES* *4 ounces (4 squares) unsweetened chocolate* *1 cup (2 sticks) unsalted butter* *2 teaspoons vanilla extract* *4 eggs, well beaten* *1½ cups sugar* *½ teaspoon salt* *⅔ cup cake flour* *½ teaspoon baking powder* *1 quart mocha ice cream, or of choice (softened somewhat to spread)* *2 cups cream whipped* *Chocolate sauce, to pour* *Chopped pecans, to sprinkle* *Dark chocolate shavings, to sprinkle*

continued

EQUIPMENT

One 8 x 11-inch baking pan, buttered and lined with buttered wax paper or parchment paper; 1 baking sheet

PREHEAT

Preheat the oven to 350°.

PREPARATION
15 mins.

Place the chocolate and butter in the top of a double boiler and set over medium-low heat. Stir frequently until the mixture is melted and smooth, then remove from the heat and set aside to cool for a few minutes.

Add the vanilla, eggs, sugar, and salt to the mixture and beat until thoroughly combined. Add the flour and the baking powder and mix well.

Spread the batter evenly in the prepared pan.

BAKING
350°
45 mins.

Bake for about 45 minutes, until the top is dry and a toothpick inserted in the center comes out barely clean.

COOLING AND
FREEZING
overnight

Remove from the oven and let the brownies rest in the pan for about 5 minutes, then turn out onto a rack, and peel off the paper.

Place the whole brownie on a baking sheet. Spread with ice cream and ¼-inch topping of whipped cream.

Cover and freeze overnight.

FINAL STEP

To serve, cut the whole brownie into portions and place on individual dessert plates. Top with the chocolate sauce, pecans, and dark chocolate shavings.

III   SOUTHWEST, CALIFORNIA, and HAWAII

Missouri en route to New Mexico

Arizona   Nevada   California   Hawaii

Enter Timothy

A new dimension was added to our travels in the van. It was Timothy, our Cairn terrier. I had fought the idea all the way, but suddenly it became a package deal—either Timothy and my wife or no Timothy, no wife.

In the past he had been left behind for long periods. When we were gone two months to Australia he was left with friends, but he has not been invited back even though I have dropped broad hints that he would like to be. I learned later he scratched a door panel—and that scratched any future invitation.

I had long chats with Dr. Koeppen, our veterinarian, about the psychological effect of a long kennel stay on a dog. Usually the dog is withdrawn for the first few days, he said, but then falls into the kennel's pattern of life and enters into the fun of it. His appetite returns. He barks joyfully with the other dogs at the slightest sound or movement in or out of the building. He goes to bed early. He seems to genuinely like it. But that was never successfully demonstrated to my wife, who has a strong anthropomorphic bias. She knew that Timothy would suffer all the things she would suffer were she confined in a cage for weeks at a time.

On earlier trips across the country, in preparation for Timothy, I asked the staff in motels and hotels about pets. My AAA and Mobil Travel Guides are good indicators. Mobil has the silhouette of a dog among the symbols if the motel permits pets. A line struck through the dog if it doesn't. Some AAA motels welcome small animals only.

In my inquiries I discovered that dogs (and their masters) usually are kept on the ground floor of consenting motels so as not to disturb guests below with sounds of padding paws or scratching. I discovered, too, that in some motels special rooms are set aside for guests with pets. Some motels ask for a deposit of a few dollars to cover damage if there is any.

On the eve of the trip, I took Timothy to be examined for travel by Dr. Koeppen. Timothy had been sneezing a lot when he got up in the mornings, but otherwise I thought he was in good shape. So did Dr. Koeppen. He gave Timothy a shot for his sneezing and some purple pills for a slight cough.

I bought an extra box of prescription diet from the doctor and stowed it in the back of the van. We left early in the morning . . . with dog.

~~~~~*HERMANN, MISSOURI*

Vintage 1847—Chef Gary Buckler, Ethel Scheer

We had been in Hermann three years earlier for recipes for my bread book, and were so intrigued by the town, its people, and its food that we shifted our planned route to the Southwest to visit it again.

We found our way here the first time because of the Vintage 1847

Restaurant, the inspiration of its chef, Gary Buckler, and Debby, his wife. Gary had come to Hermann a dozen years ago with a degree in viticulture and enology from California State University to manage the Stone Hill vineyards. Almost from his first day on the job he was captivated with the thought of turning the old barn near the wine cellars into a restaurant. The barn had been built in 1900 to stable the winery's dozen horses, which were used to cart wine shipments down the long hill to the railroad and to the riverboats as well as to work in the vineyards.

The old feed chutes and troughs along with the horse stalls were cleaned and painted. Kick marks on the walls from hooves of angry horses were left untouched. Pieces of a 12,000-gallon wine cask was used to make doors, tables, and benches. One portion of the stable became the wine-tasting room.

Throughout the year, Vintage 1847 draws a steady stream of visitors from St. Louis (60 miles) and Kansas City (120 miles). For eleven months of the year the menu is Missouri regional, but in October it is *German*.

"We have guests who wouldn't dream of ordering schnitzel or sauerbraten any time of year but during Octoberfest—that's what they want," said Gary. "It has to be traditional German. We do all of the favorites—smoked sausages, smoked fowl, roasted chicken with spaetzle dumplings and red cabbage—and hardly ever a steak or a lobster."

Buckler's network of suppliers in the region embraces hunters, trappers, and fishermen. In December he calls on them for game for the Beast Feast, an annual cancer benefit dinner. The menu is wholly game from the country thereabouts—snapping turtle soup, roast young possum, muskrat stew, duck, pheasant, venison, roast beaver tail, and wild turkey.

"I seldom know in advance what I will be serving. I have to hear from the hunters as to what they are bringing me before I put together the menu. One year we had a coyote. Made a delicious pâté. I kept that a secret until after it had been served."

STUFFED RAINBOW TROUT MISSOURIANA

[SERVES 6]

I have never cared for trout, even one that I have pulled kicking and flipping from an icy snow-fed mountain stream and rushed to a skillet less than 10 feet away. For me trout never quite lives up to its billing.

Never, that is, until I had Trout Missouriana one night at the Vintage. I couldn't believe how good it was, and when I did the recipe at home I immediately wrote along the recipe margin: "Best trout I ever had."

The fish is baked *en papillotes*, heart-shaped pieces of parchment, which are brought to the table for presentation.

INGREDIENTS	*6 whole boneless rainbow trout*
	6 ounces bacon, cut into ¼-inch pieces
	1 medium onion, finely chopped
	1 garlic clove, finely chopped
	6 ounces ham, cut into ¼-inch pieces
	1 teaspoon dried basil
	1 teaspoon dried tarragon
	1 tablespoon chopped fresh parsley
	½ teaspoon white pepper
	2 teaspoons salt
	½ cup white wine
	¼ cup bread crumbs
	Butter, to dot
EQUIPMENT	Six 16 x 24-inch pieces of parchment paper. Fold each lengthwise, cut a large heart as for a valentine, and lightly oil on the inside. One large baking sheet, oiled.
PREHEAT	Preheat the oven to 400°. At the same time preheat the baking sheet.
PREPARATION 27 mins.	Fitting: Lay a trout on the parchment heart to be certain that the margins are ample to fold and seal later.
	Fry bacon over medium heat until crisp, about 8 minutes. Lift bacon from the pan with a slotted spoon and set aside. Sauté

onion and garlic in the same pan until soft and translucent, about 8 minutes. Add ham and cook until it is heated, about 4 minutes. Stir in the basil, tarragon, parsley, white pepper, and salt. Add the white wine and bacon pieces. Simmer the mixture for 7 minutes, then stir in the bread crumbs. Set aside.

ASSEMBLING
10 mins.

Open each heart and place the trout on it. Stuff each with the crumb mixture and dot with butter.

Starting at the V of the heart, fold and roll the parchment edges tightly together to completely seal.

BAKING
400°
12 mins.

Place the trout on the preheated baking sheet and place in the oven for 12 minutes.

FINAL STEP

Serve, still sealed, to each person. The aromas from the opened package will prepare the taste buds for the enjoyment to come.

PÂTÉ MOUSSE DE FOIE ST. LOUIS

[SERVES 12 PARTY GUESTS]

INGREDIENTS

1 pound chicken livers
3 tablespoons Marsala wine
3 tablespoons brandy
1 teaspoon salt
1 teaspoon dried basil
½ teaspoon freshly ground black pepper
½ teaspoon dried thyme
½ teaspoon ground allspice
1 small onion, finely chopped
1 garlic clove, chopped
6 ounces (1½ sticks) unsalted butter
½ cup heavy cream, to whip

MARINATING
1–2 hours

In a bowl combine the livers, Marsala, brandy, salt, basil, pepper, thyme, and allspice. Marinate for at least 1 hour.

COOKING
12 mins.

In a medium pan sauté the onion and garlic in 2 ounces of butter until translucent. Add the chicken livers with all of the liquid and spices. Sauté until the pink blush is gone. Set aside and allow to cool.

PUREEING
15 mins.

Puree the cooled liver mixture in 2 batches in a food processor or blender. To each batch add 2 ounces of butter a small portion at a time. Process until the liver is a smooth paste.

REFRIGERATING
30–45 mins.

Scrape the paste into a mixing bowl, stir well, cover, and refrigerate for another 30 to 45 minutes to cool.

overnight

Whip the cream until stiff, fold into the cooled liver paste, scrape into a serving dish, cover, and refrigerate overnight.

FINAL STEP

Serve the pâté when chilled. Or you may wish to decorate the top of the pâté with design pieces cut from vegetables placed in a beef gelatin glaze:

Dissolve 1 scant teaspoon gelatin in 1 cup beef stock. Decorate the top of the mousse with blanched decorations cut from scallions and turnip. Gently ladle the beef stock over the entire top of the mousse, cover, and refrigerate until served. It will keep for at least 5 days refrigerated.

KAFFEE KUCHEN
(German Coffee Cake)

[MAKES TWO ROUND 9-INCH LOAVES]

One thing Vintage 1847 diners anticipate is the baking of Ethel Scheer, whose great-great-grandfather Schawmberg emigrated to Hermann from Germany. Ethel, who speaks German so well that on her first visit to Germany she was taken for a local, is a gentle, quiet-spoken woman whose skills are impressively professional though self-taught.

One of her best creations, adapted from a family recipe, is *Kaffee Kuchen*, a coffee bread. The rich risen dough is dimpled by the fingertips, spread lightly with sour cream, and sprinkled with cinnamon and sugar just before it goes into the oven. The *kuchen* comes from the oven plump with streaks of brown and pools of sour cream across the top. Another simple yet delicious topping for the coffee cake is melted butter sprinkled with sugar and cinnamon. Ethel Scheer uses this same dough to fashion delicious dinner rolls.

INGREDIENTS

Dough
1 package dry yeast
2 tablespoons sugar
½ teaspoon salt
2½ to 3 cups all-purpose or bread flour, approximately
⅔ cup milk, warmed
5 tablespoons unsalted butter, room temperature
1 egg

⅔ cup sour cream

Topping
½ cup sugar
1 teaspoon ground cinnamon
⅛ teaspoon salt

EQUIPMENT

Two 9-inch baking pans, buttered, or Teflon

PREPARATION BY HAND OR MIXER
8 mins.

Place the yeast, sugar, salt, and 1½ cups of flour in a mixing bowl. Pour in the warm milk; stir vigorously by hand or with a mixer and add the butter and egg. This stage is an easy one for the electric mixer.

When the ingredients are thoroughly blended, add the balance of the flour, ½ cup at a time, and stir to make a soft mass that can be lifted from the bowl and placed on the work surface, or left in the mixer bowl to knead under the dough hook. If the dough is sticky, add liberal sprinkles of flour. It helps to work with dough using a metal spatula or dough blade.

KNEADING
10 mins.

If by hand, knead the dough with a strong push-turn-fold motion to develop a dough that is soft and elastic. Add small sprinkles of flour if the moisture breaks through and the dough seems sticky.

If with a mixer dough hook, knead at medium/low speed (No. 2 on my KitchenAid), dropping in sprinkles of flour if the dough continues to stick to the edge of the bowl. When sufficient flour has been added, the dough will remain a mass around the hook as it revolves.

By hand or in the mixer, knead for a total of 10 minutes, or until the dough is smooth and elastic and feels alive and warm to the touch.

FIRST RISING
1 hour

Place the dough in a greased bowl, cover tightly with plastic wrap, and leave at room temperature to double in volume, about 1 hour.

SHAPING
10 mins.

Divide the dough into 2 pieces. Shape each into a ball. Press flat and roll to shape the dough to fit the baking pan. The dough should be about ½ to ¾ inch thick.

SECOND RISING
1 hour

Cover the pans with plastic wrap or cloth, and leave the dough to rise to double in volume—not quite to the top of pan—about 1 hour.

PREHEAT

Preheat the oven to 375° about 20 minutes before the bake period. Mix together the topping ingredients and put aside.

BAKING
375°
30 mins.

Uncover the pans. Dimple the dough lightly with your fingertips in a pattern of choice, and spread thinly with sour cream. Liberally sprinkle the topping mixture over the sour cream.

Place the pans in the middle shelf of the oven and bake until the breads are deep brown, and with a solid bottom crust, about 25 minutes.

FINAL STEP

Allow the breads to cool for 10 minutes before turning them from the pans onto a rack.

My mother always cut her coffee bread in wedges; I cut mine across the loaf into thin slices—easier to toast later.

WINTER'S FAVORITE GINGERSNAPS

[MAKES ABOUT 4 DOZEN COOKIES]

Ethel's first and lasting love is Winter's Favorite Gingersnaps. Her mother baked them for her when she was a child, and then, for years when the family lived on a farm, she did batches of these gingersnap treats for the children's school bus classmates.

These gingersnaps, which some would call molasses cookies, are made with a mild molasses. I like mine with a little more personality so I use the dark variety.

INGREDIENTS

¾ cup (1½ sticks) unsalted butter, room temperature
¾ cup vegetable shortening
2 cups sugar
2 eggs, beaten
½ cup molasses
4 cups all-purpose flour
2 teaspoons baking soda
2 teaspoons ground cinnamon
2 teaspoons ground cloves
2 teaspoons ground ginger
½ teaspoon salt
Vegetable oil to moisten
Sugar, to dip

EQUIPMENT

Two cookie sheets, greased; flour sifter

PREPARATION
10 mins.

Cream together the butter, shortening, and sugar until light and fluffy. Add the beaten eggs and molasses and beat together.

Sift together the dry ingredients.

In a large bowl, add the dry ingredients, a portion at a time, to the butter-egg mixture. With a wooden spoon stir together to form a soft dough.

CHILLING
3 hours–
overnight

Cover and chill the dough for 3 hours, at least, or overnight.

PREHEAT

Preheat the oven to 375° 20 minutes before baking.

ASSEMBLING
8 mins.

Shape the dough into small balls about the size of a walnut and place on the cookie sheet. Choose a flat-bottom glass. Moisten the bottom with vegetable oil. Dip into sugar and flatten each ball. Repeat until all are flattened.

BAKING
375°
10–12 mins.
per batch

Bake for 10 to 12 minutes per batch. Repeat baking for the balance of the dough.

Remove from the oven and cool on a wire rack.

XXXXXX *On the Road—HERMANN, MISSOURI*

A German Town

We drove into Hermann over a narrow two-lane bridge high above the Missouri River. It was so tight a fit that I was fearful that the mirrors sticking out like ears on the van would scrape the beams of the bridge or the sides of an approaching car. Thankfully they did neither of these. It is an impressively long bridge over an impressively wide river. The bridge is old, built in an era when engineers took pride in exposing all of the iron trussing. It sets the appropriate mood for returning to the past.

Hermann was settled in 1837 by the German Settlement Society of Philadelphia. The town has aged gracefully through the years with little change in spirit or appearance. It is a neat, tidy place with swept streets and sidewalks and freshly painted buildings. Nothing is ramshackle.

Chosen by the Deutsche Ansiedlung Gesellschaft zu Philadelphia because its location on the Missouri River reminded the settlers of the Rhine Valley, the town's charter stipulated that it must be "characteristically German in every particular." The town of twenty-five hundred is solidly and determinedly German. Its forty-page telephone book is a good measure of its German-ness. Names range from Aufederheide, Mundwiller, through Rohlfing, Oelschlaeger, to Zwilling and Zimmerman. We stayed at the German Haus and lunched at the Burger Haus. Street-corner trash cans are labeled SCHUND.

Each year with German drive and German pride, Hermann celebrates a number of festivals. In March it is the Wurstfest when the town pays tribute to its sausage makers. In May it is the Maifest when the lovely old homes of the town are opened to visitors. In August it is the Great Grape Stomp and in September the Volksmarch, a walk of 6.2 miles through the historic districts of the town. Each year more than a hundred thousand "outlanders" visit Hermann, some coming on special Amtrak trains from Kansas City and St. Louis. Problems have cropped up in this paradise, however, and townspeople are concerned about the popularity of its wine tastings, especially among college students in the region pouring into town in chartered buses during the festivals.

Despite the incursions of thousands each year, Hermann natives stoutly maintain their town is a Shangri-La. Jim Held, who owns the Stone Hill Winery, said: "This is what my German forebears wanted—a lovely valley apart from the rest of the world with their language and culture intact. The language has mostly disappeared but we are holding on to the rest as best we can."

〽〽〽〽〽*On the Road—ELLSWORTH, KANSAS*

Fire!

It was Halloween. We were in a comfortable motel in Ellsworth. Rural setting. Quiet. Clean.

In the middle of the night, in the middle of a deep sleep, a thousand sirens started to whoop, whoop, whoop in my ear! I leaped out of bed in terror. Where was I? Home? No, Kansas. Tornado? Kansas has tornadoes. I stepped outside. No tornado. A clear, still, starlit night. Fire? No smell of smoke.

A giant siren on a tall pole behind the motel finally quit wailing. Ellsworth has volunteer firemen and this had been a call for them to come running. In the distance I could hear a fire truck, with its siren full blast, racing away in the night. The next morning the motel manager said he hoped I hadn't been bothered. He had forgotten to warn me about the Civil Defense (and fire) siren just outside. The fire itself was a Halloween prank. To create some excitement, some town kids had torched a half dozen bales of hay in a field south of town. The rancher wanted help in putting out the fires.

I thought to myself that the ranch fires couldn't have been very big compared to the ones we used to have around my hometown when the big kids thought nothing of setting fire to a haystack the size of a barn. And that was after barricading the road with logs and stones so the fire truck couldn't get through.

There was smoke and flame around us the next day as we drove west of Ellsworth, but it was controlled burning. Ranchers were harvesting grain (milo) and when a field is finished the stubble is set afire. There was no wind. Great black columns of smoke rose straight up thousands of feet into the sky, blotting out the sun and throwing deep shadows on the ground.

"This must have been what it was like when the Indians set fire to prairie grasses to stampede the buffalo," Marje said. "Look, in other fields the big rolls of hay look like buffalo hunched over grazing." The rolls were like those set afire by the kids on Halloween.

For most of the day we were never out of sight of grain elevators rising like solitary skyscrapers on the horizon or oil-well pumps looking like huge grasshoppers nodding serenely in the fields.

"If we are still spotting look-alikes, I think the anhydrous ammonia tanks, for fertilizing the fields, look like covered wagons at a distance," Marje said.

Suddenly, while Marje was driving, we heard geese honking. She pulled to the side of the road. Overhead were dozens of flights of hundreds of migrating Canadian geese flying in V formations, not in a random pattern but precisely diagonally across the road. Waves of geese. It was impossible to count even the number of flights stretching from horizon to horizon. Some flights had only six and eight birds while others had forty and fifty. They were coming from the wetlands in Cheyenne Bottoms, near Great Bend, flying south.

Late in the afternoon we sighted the Rocky Mountains at Point of Rocks. It is also the place where Kit Carson saved a rancher's daughter during an Indian attack. Signs in the rest area warned to be on the lookout for rattlesnakes. Timothy visited his first cactus. I had warned him. He was attentive and cautious. No needles!

Despite smoke and flame it was a particularly pleasant day on the road. We shared the vast earth and enormous sky with few others. Little traffic.

The only honking came from geese.

⋙⋙SANTA FE, NEW MEXICO

Coyote Cafe—Chef Mark Miller

Mark Miller did not look at all like the celebrated chef/restaurateur I knew him to be. Almost hidden behind a mountain of restaurant linens, he was reconciling an $8,000 computer error.

"This is *not* the exciting side of the business, believe me. But, what the hell, I leave tomorrow on a three-week camel safari in Africa!"

Miller, considered an outstanding chef by his peers across the country, says of himself: "I'm a pretty good cook." Chef or cook, Miller, a witty, bearded man with graying red hair, probably knows more about traditional as well as the new Southwest cuisine than anyone around. With advanced degrees in anthropology and studies in ethnology, Miller has had no problem blending it all together.

We were talking in Miller's small office on the top floor of what had been Santa Fe's Greyhound bus terminal on Water Street until artisans and artists turned the cavernous space into a warm and playful place to

dine, the Coyote Cafe. Coming into the café, I looked above the staircase to see a grim-comic Mexican papier-mâché All Souls' Day mariachi band playing a silent serenade. A menagerie of carved folk-art animals (howling coyotes among them) stalked among the cactus and sand on a broad ledge above the long counter separating the cooks from the customers. The open kitchen was in a constant state of sizzle with meats grilling over pecan-wood coals. It is the Coyote's food—bite for bite and taste for taste—that delights.

Some dishes are simple, some elaborate—a corn and chicken soup; fat golden brown corn cakes topped with shrimp sautéed in chipotle butter; a black pepper pizza; a tortelike confection of corn and cilantro crepes with shreds of barbecued duck, corn-flour ravioli stuffed with spicy chorizo sausage in a goat cheese sauce; a salad of smoked quail with Gruyère cheese and potatoes; chilies rellenos filled with smoked corn and wild mushrooms; caramelized goat's milk custard layered with chocolate and covered with whipped cream and toasted *piñones*.

For Mark it has been an exciting adventure to rediscover and adapt a cuisine that has been known to the natives of the old Southwest for centuries but largely ignored by others in recent times.

As an anthropologist with academic credentials in several fields, Miller is no stranger to trekking in faraway places—river rafting in the Andes; horseback riding across Spain. But closest to his heart have been his journeys by foot and horseback into remote regions of the Southwest and Mexico to explore the native culture. "These people were remarkably sophisticated in their knowledge and preparation of foods, yet little of this is to be found in official reports or personal papers. "No one wrote cookbooks then," he said. There was a rueful note in his voice.

"The native culture throughout the old Southwest was raised to a high state in the arts as well as other aspects of their lives. Look at the exquisite basketry and beadwork, the vast network of irrigation canals, and the hundreds of pages of Navajo poetry. Sun-dried tomatoes are new on the American table but two hundred years ago they were being dried on mission roofs.

The Pueblo Indians had at least thirty varieties of corn and thirty varieties of squash which, geometrically, gave the Indians at least 600 possible dishes. The Pima tribe had 100 recipes for pine nuts. One tribe along the Gulf Coast in Mexico created more than 250 separate dishes using salmon. Miller reasons that if they could create that many recipes for one fish, imagine what they must have done with the rest of the bounty at hand—other kinds of fish, shellfish, game, berries, fruit, and wild and domesticated plants.

"A culture in which a woman would work a thousand hours on a pair of beaded moccasins would not be content with a diet of gruel."

"It never occurred to the early Spanish explorers and later, the Anglos, to take more than a passing interest in the native cuisine. Explorers, hunters, and settlers noted in their diaries that the natives were 'cooking something in a pot.' What was in the pot was of little interest."

It is not always easy for Miller to find a supplier of native foodstuffs. The old sources have dried up. Farmers have moved to town. It is easier to buy a can of tomatoes in the supermarket than it is to grow them yourself.

"Lamb is an example. Churro sheep were introduced five hundred years ago by the Spanish; the fine fleece prized for spinning by Navajo women. The churro is a small animal that feeds on wild snowberries and sage. It has all dark meat, no fat, and is somewhat chewy and gamy but has no cholesterol. It has not been served in restaurants for more than a century yet it is a delicious meat that I like even better than venison.

"After a long search I have found a small rancher who would raise churro for me. When he gets into full production the lamb will cost a third of what I pay for venison raised commercially in Texas."

Miller wants to change the perception of what is really good Mexican and Southwest food. He has written a cookbook, *Coyote Cafe* (Ten Speed Press), a handsomely illustrated book, centered on what he calls the "four magic plants" of the Southwest—beans, corn, squash, and chilies—the foundation foods of the Southwest cuisine for hundreds of years.

"Food does not have to be European to be good. We are learning to eat and like food that has real taste.

"Well, most of us are." He sighed. "I recently rode into the back-country with cowboys searching for lost stock. I caught and grilled several beautiful trout stuffed with wild mushrooms gathered along the way. The cowboys refused to eat either the trout or the mushrooms! 'We don't want to die,' they yelled."

Why the name Coyote? "The coyote is one of the ancestor spirits of the Pueblo Indians. He is a fun-loving prankster. He makes things *not* happen and he brings things to life. He is just right for the cafe."

YUCATÁN LIME SOUP

[SERVES 4]

This is the Coyote Cafe's version of chicken soup. It is Mark Miller's favorite soup, brothy and country feeling—with the smoky flavor of grilled chicken, the sparkling sour taste of lime, the crunch of tortilla strips, and the simple richness of chicken stock.

At the Coyote, the soup is served in colorful soup plates, not bowls, so the ingredients don't sink beneath the surface and disappear. The lime juice goes in at the very end so as not to lose its sharpness.

Note: If chilies, fresh, dried, or powdered, and other ingredients used in these recipes are not available in your supermarket, try a small specialty market, an Oriental market, or check the Latin community in your area. Mail order is also available, of course.

INGREDIENTS

½ pound skinless, boneless chicken breast
1 pound tomatoes, Roma preferred
6 cups rich chicken stock, homemade (see page 562) or store-bought
10 garlic cloves, roasted, peeled, and finely chopped
4 serrano chilies, chopped in rings
1 bunch cilantro (coriander), tied (remove 12 sprigs for garnish)
4 rings white onion, ¼-inch-thick slices
1 poblano chili, roasted, peeled, and julienned
8 teaspoons fresh lime juice
1 tablespoon roasted ground Mexican oregano
Thin strips of tortilla (¼ x 3 inches), deep-fried, to garnish
4 lime wedges, to garnish

PREPARATION
10 mins.

Grill or broil the chicken until brown but still moist, and shred by hand into ¼ x 2-inch strips. Set aside.

With a black iron skillet over medium-high heat, cook the tomatoes until blackened all over, and roughly chop.

COOKING
24–34 mins.

Place the tomatoes in a saucepan with the stock, garlic, serranos, and cilantro. Simmer, covered, over low heat for 20 to 30 minutes. Remove the cilantro.

Divide the chicken equally between the soup plates.

Broil the onion rings until cooked but not blackened, about 4 minutes, and add to the plates together with the poblano chili.

ASSEMBLING
5 mins.

Ladle the soup over, and stir in 2 teaspoons of lime juice per plate. Garnish each plate with cilantro sprigs, a pinch of oregano rubbed between the fingers, tortilla strips, and a lime wedge.

FINAL STEP

The soup could also be served in a large tureen surrounded by the garnishes, and ladled at the table.

This dish with homemade tortillas, or bread and salad, makes an excellent lunch or *aprés*-ski meal.

HORNO-STYLE LEG OF GOAT

[SERVES 6 TO 8]

In Madrid many years ago I had my first taste of goat at a café while the heels of a pretty flamenco dancer on the stage just above me beat a savage tattoo within inches of my plate. Both experiences were memorable. I found the same delicious goat at Coyote Cafe but not the dancer.

A *horno* is the beehive-shaped adobe oven used by Mexican women principally in rural areas. The Coyote Cafe doesn't have one, nor do I. Instead the Coyote Cafe wraps the leg in potter's clay and bakes it in a slow oven for about 4 hours. So do I.

The best time of year to prepare this dish is around Easter, when Greek communities traditionally cook young goat; Mexican and Spanish food markets also usually carry fresh goat.

Alternatively, this can be made with leg of lamb.

INGREDIENTS

10 pounds baking clay
One 4- to 5-pound goat leg, bone in
5 tablespoons olive oil
3 white onions, julienned
24 garlic cloves, thinly sliced
Salt and pepper, to taste
10 bunches mint, washed, trimmed of lower stems

EQUIPMENT

One baking sheet; parchment paper; mallet

BEFOREHAND

On parchment paper, roll out the clay into a 12 x 15-inch rectangle approximately ½ inch thick, and cover with a piece of foil the same size. Let the clay sit while preparing the goat. Line the baking sheet with parchment paper.

PREHEAT

Preheat the oven to 225°,

continued

PREPARATION
16 mins.

Heat 3 tablespoons of oil in a large skillet over high heat until almost smoking, reduce to medium and sear the leg of goat for about 4 minutes per side. Allow to cool.

Sauté the onions in the remaining 2 tablespoons of oil until the onions are tender.

Make 6 cuts of approximately 2 inches in length across the leg and against the grain down to the bone on both sides. Stuff the cuts with the garlic and onions, and salt and pepper the leg.

ASSEMBLING
5–10 mins.

Place half of the mint on the foil as a bed for the leg of goat. Place the leg on top of the mint, and cover with the remaining mint. Fold the foil around the leg, leaving the bone exposed, and crimp the foil to seal. Trim any sinews off the bone. Fold the clay over the foil in the same manner as the foil and pinch to secure. Decorate the clay or etch patterns if the fancy takes you.

BAKING
225°
4¼ hours

Place on the parchment-covered cookie sheet and roast for about 4 hours.

Remove and allow to rest for 10 to 15 minutes.

FINAL STEP

Crack the clay open with a mallet over newspapers. Carve and serve the meat. Ask your guests to come to the kitchen or back-yard to see it done.

CHIPOTLE SHRIMP WITH CORN CAKES

[SERVES 6]

I gave this dish of shrimp, chipotles, and corn cakes an A+ on the margin of my journal. I have made it since at home and have given it the same high score. Make the Ranchero Sauce ahead of time and re-frigerate.

INGREDIENTS

18 corn cakes (recipe follows)
8 cups water
Juice of 1 lemon
1 tablespoon crushed peppercorns
1 tablespoon sea salt
2½ pounds uncooked medium shrimp (about 54)
1 cup (2 sticks) unsalted butter, softened
4½ tablespoons pureed canned chipotle chilies
2 green onions, chopped
1 cup Ranchero Sauce (recipe follows)

PREPARATION
30 mins.

Prepare the corn cakes and keep them warm. In a large pan, bring the water to a boil, add the lemon juice, peppercorns, and salt. Add the shrimp and cook for 45 seconds to 1 minute. Drain, cool, peel, and devein.

To prepare the chipotle butter, roughly puree together the butter, ½ pound of the peeled shrimp, and 1½ tablespoons of the chipotle puree. Set aside at room temperature.

Just before serving, toss together the remaining pound of cooked shrimp with the remaining 3 tablespoons of chipotle puree and heat through on a griddle, about 2 minutes.

ASSEMBLING

Place 3 corn cakes on each plate. Place 3 shrimp on top of each cake and spread the chipotle butter liberally over the shrimp. Sprinkle the chopped green onions over the shrimp.

FINAL STEP

Serve the Ranchero Sauce at the side of the corn cakes.

Corn Cakes

[MAKES 18 TO 20 CAKES]

These corn cakes can also be served alone for breakfast or as an appetizer, or with fowl such as duck and quail. The buttermilk gives the batter an appealing tanginess.

INGREDIENTS

¾ cup all-purpose flour
½ cup coarse cornmeal (polenta)
½ teaspoon each baking powder and baking soda
1 teaspoon each salt and sugar
1¼ cups buttermilk
2 tablespoons butter, melted
1 egg, beaten
1 cup fresh-cut corn kernels
2 green onions, chopped

PREPARATION
11 mins.

Place the dry ingredients in a bowl and mix together. In a large bowl, whisk the buttermilk and butter together and then whisk in the egg. Gradually add the dry ingredients to the liquid and whisk until thoroughly incorporated.

Puree ½ cup of corn, and fold it into the batter along with the remaining whole kernels and the green onions. Add a little buttermilk if necessary to thin the batter.

continued

COOKING
30 secs.
each side

Using an ungreased pan over medium heat, ladle 1 tablespoon corn cake batter and form 3-inch cakes. Cook until golden brown, about 30 seconds each side.

FINAL STEP

Stack and keep warm until served.

Ranchero Sauce

[MAKES 4 CUPS]

Mark Miller considers this the original tomato sauce, the granddaddy of the most widely used sauce in the world today. It goes not only with shrimp and corn cakes but eggs, chicken, pork, tamales, and seafood.

INGREDIENTS

1½ pounds tomatoes, Roma preferred
3 serrano chilies
1 cup finely chopped white onions
1 tablespoon finely chopped garlic
1 tablespoon peanut oil (or lard)
3 poblano chilies, roasted, peeled, seeded, and cut into julienne strips (about ¾ cup), a few strips reserved for garnish
1 small bunch cilantro (coriander), tied
1 teaspoon salt

PREPARATION
16 mins.

Lightly blacken the tomatoes and serranos in a skillet or under the broiler, about 4 to 5 minutes. Chop together and set aside.

Sauté the onion and garlic in the oil in a saucepan over low heat until the onions are soft but not brown, about 10 minutes.

COOKING
20–30 mins.

Combine all the ingredients in the saucepan. Cook, partially covered, over low heat for 20 to 30 minutes, adding water if necessary. Remove the cilantro.

FINAL STEP

Garnish with a few strips of julienned poblanos. The sauce keeps well refrigerated.

⧓⧓⧓⧓ *CHIMAYÓ, NEW MEXICO*

Restaurante Rancho de Chimayó— Laura Ann Jaramillo

There was a time, not too many years ago, when people in search of exceptional Southwestern cooking drove for hours on a narrow winding road over high mountains and through deep valleys to reach this restaurant in the picturesque four-hundred-year-old village of Chimayó, about thirty miles north of Santa Fe.

For a long time the place was a well-kept secret, until Craig Claiborne, then food editor of *The New York Times*, revealed to the outside world the existence of Restaurante Rancho de Chimayó in a story he called "Getting There Is Half the Fun."

Located in the little valley of Chimayó, seven thousand feet above sea level and kept green by two small tributaries of the Rio Grande, the restaurant was the inspiration of Arturo Jaramillo, who realized that vacationers hungry for Mexican food would travel miles into the Sangre de Cristo Mountains for dishes cooked as he remembered them in his grandmother's house. Jaramillo, a descendant from a family of original Spanish settlers in the region, turned part of the family's old adobe ranch house into a restaurant. While it was no easy task for a diner to reach the restaurant, it became famous locally for the authenticity of its Mexican-American dishes.

Then one day a new highway through the mountains was opened

that reduced driving time from Santa Fe to a half hour. Now it was just a pleasant afternoon drive to reach the restaurant, with time to visit one or two of the artist studios in the vicinity. During the summer months, the restaurant was serving more than a thousand people a day. Patrons who loved the Rancho were saddened by the huge crowds and the shift away from authentic dishes. Arturo left the valley to open a restaurant in the city.

Enter the Jaramillo daughter, Laura Ann, a 1984 graduate in marketing from Trinity University in San Antonio. She was two years old when the restaurant opened; at five she was busing dishes, and at eight she was waiting tables and carrying drinks from the bar. At twelve she was promoted to an assistant cook. Now, after college, she was back in business determined to restore its old glory.

We dined by the soft light of a kerosene lamp. The ambiance was pleasing. The sopaipillas served with the meal were delicious. I said to Marje we would come back someday when Laura Ann had all of her plans in place.

An after-dinner drink, the Chimayó cocktail, was sufficient to light my path back across the road to the Hacienda Rancho de Chimayó, the old family home where we were spending the night. A renovation program was under way on the seven guest rooms in an old adobe house snuggled against a red stone cliff.

For our room it was not the best of times. Furnished with veneered furniture from the 1920s, my mattress and springs crashed to the floor twice before I decided it was easier to let them rest on the floor. The hammered brass shade on my bedside lamp fell to the floor with a loud clatter each time I tried to adjust the light.

Masons, erecting a fireplace, had left disconnected an electric baseboard heater. With no heat, it was a long, cold night. Workmen had also left a deep depression in the floor to make way for the stonework. I stumbled into it twice walking across the room in the dark.

Next morning when I told Laura Ann about the room's shortcomings, I could tell by the cold glint in her eyes that the bed would never again fall and the lamp would ever after have a secure shade. And the depression in the floor would be filled with fireplace stones yet today.

SOPAIPILLAS

[MAKES 18 TO 24 PUFFS]

Sopaipillas, golden puffs to be filled with honey, are a favorite at the *restaurante* and served with its highly seasoned dishes. Serve hot from the kettle. Break off a corner of the puff, fill with honey, and it becomes a fine accompaniment for Mexican foods.

INGREDIENTS	*Vegetable oil or fat, to deep-fry* *1¾ cups all-purpose flour* *2 teaspoons baking powder* *1 teaspoon salt* *2 tablespoons shortening* *⅔ cup cold water, approximately* *Honey, to accompany*
EQUIPMENT	One deep kettle or skillet; 1 slotted spoon
PREHEAT	Preheat the oil or fat to 385° while preparing the dough.
PREPARATION BY HAND OR MIXER 8 mins.	Sift the flour, baking powder, and salt into a mixing bowl. Cut the shortening into the flour with a pastry blender, crossed knives, or the fingers. The flat beater of the electric mixer is also excellent for this chore. The mixture will resemble coarse meal. Add water by the tablespoon but only enough to make a stiff dough.
KNEADING 4 mins.	Turn the dough onto a lightly floured work surface and knead until smooth and somewhat elastic. It will be responsive under the hands but not as much as a fully developed bread dough.
PREPARATION BY PROCESSOR 5 mins.	Attach the steel blade. Measure the dry ingredients into the work bowl and drop pieces of the shortening over the mixture. Cover and pulse 3 or 4 times to cut the shortening into tiny pieces in the flour. With the processor running, pour in enough water through the feed tube to form a ball of dough that will ride on the blade and clean the sides of the bowl.
KNEADING 40 secs.	When the ball has formed, process to knead for 40 seconds.
RESTING 10 mins.	Place the dough on the work surface, cover with a cloth or a length of wax or parchment paper and allow to rest for 10 minutes.
SHAPING 5 mins.	Roll the dough into a rectangle about 12 x 15 inches, and very thin—no more than ⅛ inch thick. With a pastry wheel or knife, cut into 2- or 3-inch squares.

continued

FRYING
1–2 mins. per
batch

Drop 2 or 3 squares of the dough into the hot fat. Turn several times with a slotted spoon so each sopaipilla puffs and browns evenly. Remove and drain on paper towels.

Serve immediately with honey.

CHIMAYÓ COCKTAIL

[MAKES 1 COCKTAIL]

INGREDIENTS

1½ ounces tequila
1 ounce apple cider
¼ ounce each lemon juice and crème de cassis

EQUIPMENT

One cocktail shaker

PREPARATION
1 min.

Pour all of the ingredients over ice and shake well.

〰〰〰On the Road—TAOS, NEW MEXICO

Welcome?

The sign in big letters alongside the highway read: BE-PU-WA-VE. Below, in smaller letters: WELCOME TO THE INDIAN PUEBLOS.

The trip had been planned around the hope that I might find a recipe for Indian fry bread. There are eight Indian communities spread in a fifty-mile arc along the Rio Grande from Tesque Pueblo, near Santa Fe in the south, to the largest and most fabled of them all, Taos Pueblo in the north.

It was a typically magnificent New Mexico morning when we left Sante Fe, the kind that you come to expect here almost every day— brilliant azure sky with layers of white clouds placed on the horizon just so, for the benefit of photographers and painters. The road was wide and occasionally it swept within sight of the Rio Grande to let you see the small green irrigated farms along its banks. There was the occasional billboard urging you to come to play bingo on the reservation next Thursday night and, just off the reservation, a wine-tasting drive-in.

Our first pueblo was a surprise. I had thought, mistakenly as it turned out, that all pueblos were colorful buildings of stone or adobe with apartments terraced one above the other. Not so. This pueblo was, in fact, several blocks of small, unpainted frame houses fronting on dusty dirt streets. Backyards held a collection of stripped automobiles, goats, chickens, and sheep. It was lonely. There was not a child or stray dog anywhere in sight. It was early Sunday afternoon and I decided it must be professional football that was keeping everyone indoors. It did not look like a place for a recipe. We drove on.

Lesson for the day: A pueblo is both a building and a tribe, the latter can be housed in anything of choice.

Taos is the most famous of the pueblos. The two smooth-walled, multistoried apartmentlike buildings, one on either side of the narrow Taos River that flows through the pueblo, are five hundred years old and they have had a powerful effect on visitors, especially artists.

This was not a dance or feast day in the pueblo, so the only Indians I saw were the unsmiling Indian in the ticket office, five men roofing one of the adobe buildings, and a man digging a small post hole in the parking lot.

It was not the fees that put me off as much as a typewritten sheet titled "Visitor Etiquette" which the man at the gate handed me when he gave me my tickets and tags. "You must obey Indian law" the page began, and the rules ranged from don't enter buildings except shops and don't feed or pat stray dogs to don't put feet in or wade in the river, don't climb buildings, and don't throw rocks.

It was a curious, unfriendly place that I don't care to visit again. Even for a recipe. I was warned in Santa Fe that once inside the pueblo, rules for photographers were strict. Many times, I was told, irate Indians had snatched cameras away from visitors and dashed them to the ground or had ripped the film out of the camera. With the latest model Nikon in hand I was apprehensive.

Later I was to learn that some of the pueblos are considered "dead" villages in the sense that only a few religious and ceremonial leaders live there; most of the people live elsewhere. The families bring bedding and other gear and move back into the buildings just for the ceremonial dances. Not so Taos. It was alive but distant.

It was late afternoon on the drive back to Santa Fe that something beautiful and very exciting happened. There had been brief but heavy showers moving intermittently across the valley between intervals of brilliant sunshine. Rain, sun, rain, sun. The rain had just put down a sheet of water on the pavement.

Looking ahead into the sun, the highway stretched as a shimmering silver ribbon and each car and truck was enveloped in a radiant silver cocoon as the sun shone through the mist thrown up by tires. The drive on the silver highway lasted for about fifteen minutes and then it was wiped out as rain clouds gathered again.

A lovely phenomenon.

SANTA FE, NEW MEXICO

The Pink Adobe— Rosalea Murphy

When Rosalea Murphy arrived in Santa Fe as a bride from New Orleans she brought with her a cookbook and a young lady's slight experience in a Creole kitchen. Santa Fe was a small, lazy, sleepy town, and the towns-people bought wood off the backs of burros that were driven in from the country each morning.

"I was young but knew a lot more about food than I did anything else, so in 1944, the last year of the war, I leased an adobe building that the owner had painted pink and opened the Pink Adobe." She began with a two-burner gas plate, an ancient secondhand oven, and a large marble slab resting on a butler's stand. "I rolled out thousands of piecrusts on that marble slab. When it was accidentally broken years later I sat down and bawled."

The present Pink Adobe is on the old Santa Fe Trail not far from the Plaza, the heart of the city. It is in what was the Barrio de Analco, a three-hundred-year-old former barracks built with thirty-six-inch-thick walls and with small narrow windows, not much more than slits, placed high to protect against arrows.

Murphy began the Pink Adobe with two items on the menu. One was Dobeburgers, hamburgers smothered with a spicy sauce. The other was her apple pie, the recipe for which she had brought from New Orleans. Both were immediate hits. While the Pink Adobe now serves native specialties featuring the region's characteristic blue corn tortillas, the burgers and pie remain the restaurant's favorites.

"I wouldn't dare change the menu or the dishes," she explained. "They've become such a tradition. The other evening a couple who had been here on their honeymoon came back to celebrate their twenty-fifth anniversary with Dobeburgers just like before. They cried with joy at first bite!"

Murphy admits somewhat ruefully that if she had to do it over again she would have added jalapeño peppers to the sauce to make it even more spicy. It is too late now to change the recipe, she said. (The recipe below offers the option of jalapeño peppers.) Murphy is an accomplished painter. When we went to her home studio we found her at her easel finishing a series of oil paintings of vegetables. She has illustrated her cookbook of restaurant favorites, *Cooking with a Silver Spoon*.

Murphy is writing a new book titled *The View from Table Ten*, her favorite corner table in the Dragon Bar across the alleyway from the Pink Adobe. In the subdued light of the old building she holds court each evening to a steady stream of writers and painters and sculptors who come by her table to exchange news and gossip about what's happening in the city's art colony.

"I must confess that my first love was painting. I got into food to support my art. Food became the monster. I couldn't escape. I have no regrets, however. It has all come together in a pretty wonderful life in Santa Fe."

SANTA FE LAYERED BEAN DIP

[SERVES 6]

Rosalea said a good meal should start with a taste teaser. It should be spicy and salty enough to create a small thirst and be a forerunner of dishes to follow. Her layered bean dip served with tostados is a good way to begin.

INGREDIENTS

FIRST LAYER
2 cups cooked pinto beans (1 cup dry) (see page 248 to prepare)
1 tablespoon minced onion
1 cup grated sharp Cheddar cheese
6 drops Tabasco sauce
Salt, to taste
2 tablespoons bacon or ham fat

SECOND LAYER
2 medium ripe avocados
2 tablespoons fresh lemon juice
½ teaspoon each salt and freshly ground black pepper

THIRD LAYER
1 cup sour cream
½ cup mayonnaise
½ teaspoon cayenne pepper or taco seasoning

FOURTH LAYER
One 7-ounce can pitted ripe olives, drained and chopped
3 medium tomatoes, peeled and coarsely chopped
1 cup chopped green onions

Tostados, to serve

FIRST LAYER
10 mins.

Drain and mash the beans in a bowl. Add the onion, cheese, and Tabasco and blend well. Add salt to taste. Heat the fat in a large iron skillet and add the bean mixture. Over medium heat, stir until the cheese is melted and the whole mixture is bubbling. Set aside.

SECOND LAYER
10 mins.

Peel, pit, and mash the avocados in a bowl with the lemon juice, salt, and black pepper.

THIRD LAYER
1 min.

In a separate bowl mix together the sour cream, mayonnaise, and cayenne or taco seasoning.

FOURTH LAYER
1 min.

Mix together the olives, tomatoes, and chopped green onions.

ASSEMBLING
5 mins.

Spread half of the bean mixture on a large shallow serving platter. Top with half of the avocado mixture. Spread with half the third layer and half the fourth layer.

Repeat with the balance of each of the four mixtures. Olives, tomatoes, and green onions on top.

FINAL STEP

Serve with the tostados. For delicious tostados, cut a dozen flour tortillas in quarters and deep-fry. Salt lightly.

DOBEBURGER

[SERVES 6]

The Dobeburger was one of the first Pink Adobe offerings, and it has been a Santa Fe favorite for more than forty years. The secret is the sauce. Until the sauce is spread over the grilled hamburger, the sandwich is not out of the ordinary. But add the Dobe sauce and it becomes a creation.

INGREDIENTS

1½ pounds fresh ground round steak

Sauce
1 cup mayonnaise
1 teaspoon Tabasco sauce
Generous sprinkle dried savory
½ cup catsup
Sprinkle each of garlic salt and celery salt

6 hamburger buns
Butter, for buns

EQUIPMENT

Grill, charcoal

PREPARATION
5 mins.

Shape the ground round into 6 patties and set aside.
To make the sauce, mix all of the ingredients together until the mixture is smooth.

BROILING
8–10 mins.

Broil the meat to desired doneness over a charcoal fire.

FINAL STEP

Toast and butter the hamburger buns. Add the hamburgers and cover with a generous serving of the sauce.

ADOBE APPLE PIE

[SERVES 6]

This is the favorite dessert in the Pink Adobe. Rosalea has no idea how many pies she has made—"thousands, hundreds of thousands, maybe millions." At any rate she is pleased that all have been eaten with "gusto."

INGREDIENTS

CRUST
2 cups flour
1 teaspoon salt
¾ cup shortening or lard
6 to 7 tablespoons ice water

FILLING
1½ pounds apples of choice, peeled, cut into ¼-inch-thick slices
2 tablespoons fresh lemon juice
½ teaspoon each grated nutmeg and ground cinnamon
½ teaspoon granulated white sugar, plus extra for sprinkling
¼ cup raisins
1 cup brown sugar
2 tablespoons each flour and butter, room temperature
½ cup broken pecans
¼ cup milk

SAUCE
½ cup (1 stick) unsalted butter, room temperature
1½ cups confectioners' sugar
1 tablespoon boiling water
1 teaspoon brandy or rum

EQUIPMENT

One 9-inch pie pan

PREPARATION
10 mins.

Crust: measure the flour and salt into a medium bowl. With a knife cut the fat into several small pieces and drop into the flour. Toss and work the fat and flour together with a pastry blender, 2 knives, or fingers working quickly, until the mixture resembles coarse meal.

Sprinkle in the water, a tablespoon at a time, stirring with a fork. Gently toss the loose particles around the bowl to absorb the moisture. Add water as needed to bring together the particles in a moist mass that holds together with no dry or crumbly places apparent.

CHILLING
1 hour

Wrap the ball of dough in plastic wrap or foil and place in the refrigerator to chill, 1 hour or more.

SHAPING
10 mins.

Remove the dough from the refrigerator and divide into 2 pieces. Thinly roll 1 piece and line the pie pan. Roll the second piece for the top crust and place in the refrigerator for a few minutes while the crust is being filled.

PREHEAT

Preheat the oven to 425°.

FILLING
10 mins.

To fill the pie, spread the apple slices over the bottom crust and sprinkle with the lemon juice, nutmeg, and cinnamon. Spread white sugar and raisins evenly over the apples.

Mix together the brown sugar, flour, and butter in a small bowl; when well blended spread over the contents of the pie tin and sprinkle with the pecans. Add the milk, saving 1 tablespoon to brush.

Cover the pie with the top crust and crimp the edges. Prick the top with a fork or cut vents in an artistic pattern with a sharp knife.

BAKING
425°
15 mins.
375°
35 mins.

Place the pie on the lower shelf of the hot oven. After 15 minutes reduce the heat to 375° and continue baking for an additional 35 minutes, or until juice bubbles from the center vents.

Five minutes before the pie is finished baking, brush the top with milk (or cream) and sprinkle with some granulated sugar.

SAUCE
6 mins.

While the pie is baking prepare the brandy hard sauce. Cream the butter until it is light. Beat in the sugar and add the water. Beat in the liquor.

FINAL STEP

Remove the pie from the oven and place on a wire rack to cool. Serve warm or at room temperature with the brandy hard sauce.

〰〰〰ALBUQUERQUE, NEW MEXICO

The Hirsts— Marie Hirst

MELINDA HIR[

It was the Hirsts, our hosts in Albuquerque, who directed us to Charlie's Front Door (see below), but it was at home with Marie in the kitchen and Lee helping that we had some of the best food in New Mexico. Especially the cheese quiche.

Normally I shy away from quiche. Over the last decade it has been done to a soggy death, so I felt constrained to exclaim even halfheartedly about the entrée when Marie presented it at the table. Nevertheless, I had to admit that it was a handsome dish—golden brown and puffy. Two bites into the quiche it was clear that I was eating a superior dish with crisp crust all the way to the bottom—not a soggy particle to be had.

I should have known to expect as much at the Hirst table. They are a remarkable couple in their sixties. Not only has she flown seaplanes into remote regions of the world to scuba dive, but she was one of the first women in the country to fly a jet (in the company of test pilot Chuck Yeager). She also races road cars. We were in the guesthouse across the patio from the big house; at 4:30 each morning I was dimly aware that lights had been turned on in the garden greenhouse; Marie had begun her day by potting plants, to be followed by piano practice. For Lee, each work day is capped late in the afternoon with a six-mile run. Last year he flew to Australia to win the four hundred–meter race in the sixty-five to seventy age group in the Melbourn Masters' World Games. On the weekend he is a member of the local rugby team.

Marie and Lee are also business partners, owners of a successful New Mexico public relations firm. But it is the kitchen where I like to think of Marie.

THREE-CHEESE QUICHE

[SERVES 6]

Easy to prepare and bake in 45 minutes, Marie's quiche makes its own golden crisp crust.

INGREDIENTS	*2 teaspoons butter, room temperature, to coat* *2 tablespoons finely grated Parmesan cheese* *2 cups roughly grated Cheddar cheese* *1 cup roughly grated Swiss cheese* *2 eggs* *¾ cup milk* *¾ cup flour, approximately* *½ teaspoon salt* *Pinch of freshly ground black pepper*
EQUIPMENT	One quiche pan or pie plate
PREHEAT	Preheat the oven to 425°.
PREPARATION 5 mins.	Butter the pan or pie plate. Sprinkle with 1 tablespoon of grated Parmesan cheese. Mix the Cheddar and Swiss cheeses together and then spread them in the pan, mounding the cheeses toward the center as with filling a pie pan with apple slices. In a bowl stir together the eggs and milk. Add the flour, ¼ cup at a time, to give the mixture the consistency of heavy cream. Stir in the salt and pepper. Pour the milk mixture over the cheeses. Sprinkle with the remaining tablespoon of grated Parmesan.
BAKING 425° 40 mins.	Bake the quiche until brown and bubbly, about 40 minutes. Serve hot.

POSOLE

[SERVES 4]

My mother knew that one of my very favorite dishes in the whole wide world was hominy. She cooked it with bacon bits in a light white sauce. Before she cooked it, I would beg a cold spoonful out of the can.

Today I have equal affection for posole, hominy's cousin from Mexico and the Southwest. Like hominy, it is dried whole corn kernels treated with slaked lime (calcium hydroxide), with the husks discarded. It is a traditional Mexican Christmas dish, and is believed to bring good news in the new year.

Most posole dishes can be made with hominy. In the Southwest frozen posole can be purchased in most supermarkets.

INGREDIENTS	*2 cups dried posole or hominy*
	2 smoked ham hocks, or ½ pound smoked bacon, cut into 1-inch chunks
	3 large garlic cloves, chopped
	1 tablespoon red chili powder
	1 small onion, finely chopped
	4 tablespoons roughly chopped Mexican oregano leaves, or 2 tablespoons dried
	1 teaspoon freshly ground black pepper
	4 quarts water
	2 cups white wine
	1 teaspoon salt
EQUIPMENT	One 6-quart saucepan, with cover
SOAKING	Rinse the posole under cold running water. Put in a bowl, cover with cold water, and leave to soak overnight.
PREPARATION 5 mins.	Drain the posole and rinse again. Put it in a medium saucepan with the whole ham hocks or bacon chunks, the garlic, chili powder, onion, oregano, and black pepper. Salt will toughen the kernels so it is added after the kernels are tender.
COOKING 4 hours	Cover the posole with the water. Bring to a boil over moderate heat, skimming occasionally. Simmer the posole gently, covered, until the kernels are puffed and tender, about 4 hours. Add wine as necessary to keep the posole covered. Add salt.
FINAL STEP	Allow to cool. Cut the meat from the ham hocks into small pieces and return to the posole. Discard the bones and the oregano leaves.

ALBUQUERQUE, NEW MEXICO

Front Door–Back Door—Charlie Elias

You are given the choice of two doors to enter when you visit Charlie's to dine on some of the best food in Albuquerque.

While the food served behind each door comes from the same kitchen, Charlie's Back Door is the neighborhood's favorite bar, with food secondary. Charlie's Front Door, where food is paramount and liquor subordinate, is just twenty-three feet away—under the same roof —but to get to the Back Door you must go outside, follow footprints painted on the walk down the alley, and go around a corner. Waiters scurry through the kitchen on their way to serve clientele in both places, but it must be an emergency, with special permission from the chef, to take the shortcut. It's just not done.

Charlie Elias was born in Santa Fe, up the road about sixty miles, into a Lebanese-Irish-Spanish family that loved food in the tradition of the Southwest: hot, with lots of chilies. After Korea he thought about studying dentistry on the G.I. bill but, instead, opened the Back Door behind a friend's package liquor store in 1966. His mother, Mary Martinez, helped put together the Door's first menu, which Charlie proudly says has changed little in the intervening years.

The Back Door was so successful that in 1972 Charlie opened the Front Door.

"You want the best place to eat in Albuquerque, right?" my friend Lee Hirst wanted to know when we arrived in the city.

On and off over the years I had eaten with Lee at some of the best restaurants in New York City, so I knew that he knew good food and undoubtedly had spotted several good places since moving to Albuquerque from the East a few years before. "Marie agrees with me that Charlie's is about the best place around here," he added. I prize his wife's judgment highly.

We went into the Back Door first. The light was subdued and the ambiance pleasurable. But we needed more light to read the menu, see the food, and take notes, so we went out the door, up the alley, turned the corner, and went in the Front Door. Same pleasurable ambiance but there was enough light to read the menu.

I liked Charlie immediately. He put before me a small dish of white corn kernels which looked enough like hominy to be hominy. It was posole, a close cousin; both have an earthy subtle flavor with robust texture. I loved Charlie's posole.

Good things kept coming to the table. Green Chili Stew. Green Chili Enchiladas. Puffy sopaipillas stuffed with chili meat. Blue corn tortillas layered with cheese. I saw a Hungry Indian—a sandwich—being served at the next table, but I was too full to go for it. I did admire it— half-pound hamburger held between flat sopaipillas with lettuce, tomato, onion, cheese, green chili strips, and French fries. Next time.

The food was so good that we went back the next noontime and I had Charlie's Eggs, a dish of scrambled eggs layered with Green Chili Stew and topped with melted cheese. It has become a classic at the double Doors.

GREEN CHILI ENCHILADAS

[SERVES 6]

Enchiladas are corn tortillas either rolled around fillings or stacked between fillings, coated with a sauce and garnished. Probably no other Mexican dish has so many variations of fillings, sauces, and garnishes.

Charlie's enchilada is a green chili–and–onion filling layered between 2 tortillas and topped with cheese. Tortillas may be softened initially by steaming them in a colander. Wrap them in a towel and place over a pan of simmering water for 10 minutes.

The enchiladas may be prepared separately on ovenproof serving plates or together in a large baking pan.

INGREDIENTS

1½ pounds lean pork, cut into ½-inch cubes
⅓ cup flour
1 tablespoon vegetable oil
½ cup diced fresh or frozen green chilies
2 garlic cloves, finely chopped
1 teaspoon salt
2 cups water
3 tablespoons vegetable oil
12 yellow corn tortillas
1 large white onion, finely chopped
6 ounces Longhorn Cheddar cheese, coarsely grated

EQUIPMENT

One stockpot; 6 ovenproof serving plates or 1 large baking pan

PREPARATION
1 hour

Dust the pork cubes in flour. Heat the oil in a large skillet and cook the meat over medium-high heat until well browned, about 10 minutes.

Add the chilies, garlic, salt, and water. Bring to a gentle boil over medium heat, covered, and boil for 30 minutes.

Reduce the heat to maintain a simmer for 20 minutes. Add water if necessary to keep the sauce the consistency of catsup, wet but not runny.

Keep hot while putting together the enchiladas.

FRYING
36 mins.

Heat the oil in the skillet. Drop the tortilla in the hot oil and cook for 2 minutes, flip, and cook for 1 minute. Repeat with the other tortillas. Place on a paper towel.

PREHEAT

Preheat the oven to 450° 20 minutes before baking.

ASSEMBLING
18 mins.

Place 1 tortilla flat on a ovenproof serving plate. Sprinkle with the onion and grated cheese, as desired. Cover with the green chili sauce and top with a second tortilla. Sprinkle the top generously with grated cheese.

Repeat with the other enchiladas on each plate (or use a large baking pan).

BAKING
450°
4 mins.

Place in the hot oven until the cheese is melted and bubbly, about 4 minutes.

Serve hot.

GREEN CHILI STEW

[SERVES 8 OR MORE]

Green Chili Stew is delicious and filling, a meal in itself, great for robust appetites such as to be found at tail-gate parties, *après*-toboggan on the big hill out in back, or when the kids are home from college.

INGREDIENTS
½ cup lard or shortening of choice
2 pounds lean pork, cut into 1½-inch cubes
¼ cup all-purpose flour, to dredge
2 pounds potatoes, peeled, cut into cubes
6 cups crushed or finely chopped tomatoes
*1½ cups chopped fresh or frozen green chilies (This is for
    medium "hot"—add more for hot hot.)*
3 garlic cloves, finely chopped
½ ounce pequín chilies or Tabasco sauce
1 tablespoon salt
4 quarts water
Tortillas, to accompany

EQUIPMENT
One 6-quart heavy sauce pot or kettle

PREPARATION
15 mins.
Heat the lard or other shortening over medium heat in the sauce pot. Dredge the pork cubes in flour and drop into the sauce pot to brown, about 15 minutes. Watch carefully that the flour does not burn.
When the pork is well browned add the remaining ingredients.

COOKING
1½ hours
Simmer, covered, over low heat for 35 minutes. Bring to a boil for 20 minutes, and return to a simmer for 30 minutes to finish. Taste and adjust seasoning. Perhaps more Tabasco?

FINAL STEP
Serve hot with tortillas. And perhaps a cold Mexican beer.

CHARLIE'S EGGS

[SERVES 6]

Charlie did these one morning for a friend who wanted eggs cooked in a different way. They were such a success that the dish has been part of the Front Door's regular menu ever since. There was only one other egg recipe on our entire journey across America that measured up. It was the Lobster Scramble (page 505) at Port Clyde, Maine. Both outstanding.

INGREDIENTS

12 large eggs
Salt and freshly ground black pepper, to taste
4 cups Green Chili Stew, heated (see recipe above)
2 cups grated Longhorn Cheddar cheese

EQUIPMENT

Six ramekins or ovenproof plates

PREHEAT

Preheat the oven to 450°.

PREPARATION
5 mins.

Scramble the eggs until they are just beyond creamy but not stiff. Add salt and pepper. Divide and place on individual ovenproof plates. Cover generously with the chili stew. Liberally cover the stew with cheese.

BAKING
6 mins.

Place in the oven to melt and bubble the cheese, about 6 minutes.

FINAL STEP

Serve bubbling hot. Watch for looks of surprised delight on guests' faces.

~~~~ALBUQUERQUE, NEW MEXICO

Native Cuisine—Zora Hesse

The slimmest of the dozens of cookbooks we collected on our journey across America, the *Southwestern Indian Recipe Book* with just fifty-two pages, was one of the best. There were only thirty-eight recipes, all from women of the Apache, Papago, Pima, Pueblo, and Navajo tribes. Some recipes were those used by the aborigines before the first contact with Europeans.

The recipes written by the author were spare, no words wasted. On each page was a drawing of life among the various cultures—gathering wood, weaving, decorating pottery, cooking, and baking in an outdoor oven. Drawings of pots and baskets marked those recipes that were wholly aboriginal.

Tracing the author was no easy matter. The name on the cover was

one word: Hesse. He or She? Inside it became Zora Hesse. The introduction was signed with initials: Z.G.H., Albuquerque, New Mexico. Not much to go on. No Zora Hesse in the Albuquerque phone book. I called the publisher at Filter Press in Palmer Lake, Colorado.

"Oh, yes," said Mr. G. L. Campbell, "it is *Mrs.* Hesse. You will find her a delightful person. I had a deuce of a time talking her into doing the book. Would you like her phone number? You will like her."

I called Mrs. Hesse who, I was to learn, was known to about everyone in the state—a former Democratic national committee woman from New Mexico, also an anthropologist, an authority on Indian cultures, and the wife of a distinguished Albuquerque surgeon.

Marje and I were invited for a meal of native Indian dishes in the Hesse home, a showplace of native art that would delight the heart of a museum curator. The art had been collected by the couple in travels over the world, but principally it was of Southwestern Indian rugs, baskets, dolls, and pottery.

"Some of it was given to Frank in trade when he was practicing on the reservation," Zora explained. "Most of the pieces were given in friendship."

Zora was a bride for only a few months when Frank was sent from Boston to the small Arizona town of Sacaton on the sprawling Gila River Indian Reservation where he was the Public Health doctor. He had been drafted in 1955 and assigned to the Public Health Service. "It was classic bureaucratic rationale. Frank was asked which he would prefer—Hawaii or San Francisco? The next day he was sent to the Arizona desert.

"*That* came as a shock, but from the very beginning we were absolutely engrossed with the Indian culture. We were so close to native life.

There was no air-conditioning, and it was miserably hot in the summertime. Yet those were the best years of our lives. We had time to be a family as well as to start one. There was no diaper service and I had to be on constant guard to keep the wild horses from eating the diapers hung on the line to dry."

For both of them it began an admiration for the Indians of the Southwest—Apache, Pima, Papago, Pueblo, and Navajo—that remains undiminished four decades later. On the reservation, Zora, trained as an anthropologist, became friends with the Indian women. They were intrigued with this quiet young woman from the outside who was openly so respectful of their culture. "I was never pushy." Yet she had an unbounded curiosity about the way they lived.

"Above all there was a great reverence for any and all things from the earth among these peoples. You need only to watch and experience the joyful Corn Dance to know the intimacy, harmony, and intangible bond between Mother Earth and her children."

Zora stopped. "The mention of corn reminds me of the first time Frank and I were invited by an Indian friend to celebrate her fourteen-year-old grandson's first deer kill. Nothing was promised but we thought, of course, venison would be the pièce de résistance of the meal."

When they came into the house there was the deer, crowned with a handsome set of antlers, laid out on the floor of the living room. Friends of the family stood around in a circle admiring the beast. On a small table near the door was a bowl of corn pollen. Each guest took a pinch, sprinkled it over the deer, and then stood back for a moment in silence before nodding and lauding the skill of the young hunter.

"With the ceremony complete, we were escorted into the next room to be seated for the meal which I had thought might be the venison. No. Beef stew. Dessert was canned peaches."

It was Zora's fervor for the culture that got her into writing her cookbook.

At a dinner party one night a book publisher was speaking highly of an Indian cookbook he had read, and was particularly taken by a tuna casserole recipe.

"Tuna! Tuna in the desert?" Zora exclaimed. "I laughed so hard in disbelief that he challenged me to write a better one. 'Of course I can,' I said, and promptly forgot about it. A month later he phoned to ask how the book was doing. 'What book?' I cried. 'Your book,' he said. 'You had better get it written because a number of bookstores are already taking orders for it.' So I did."

Authentic native dishes, be forewarned, are not haute cuisine but all are nutritious. Most of the ingredients used by Zora are available in supermarkets and stores throughout the Southwest and in specialty shops elsewhere in the country. Canned roasted green chilies may be substituted for the fresh one; for those who prefer a milder pepper, green bell peppers can be used.

Some, however, are difficult to obtain unless a desert is handy. The needles on tender new leaves of the prickly pear cactus must be carefully picked off before slicing and frying. The buds of the cholla cactus are picked off with tongs, then the cactus is dropped into boiling water until the thorns fall off. Drain, spread with butter, salt, and serve.

RED CHILI STEW

[SERVES 4]

This is a stew cooked by Pueblo women that may be made with pork, lamb, or beef stew meat. The oregano and garlic powder are not aboriginal, of course, and may be left out for the sake of authenticity. I like it either way.

INGREDIENTS

5 dried red chilies, stems and seeds removed
1 piece pork fat, to oil
1 pound lean pork, cut into small cubes
Salt, to taste
1 teaspoon dried oregano
½ teaspoon garlic powder

PREPARATION
35 mins.

Place the red chilies in a medium saucepan, cover with water, and bring to a boil over medium-high heat. Turn low to simmer, covered, for 25 minutes.

Heat a large skillet or saucepan, sauté the piece of fat until the bottom of the pan is coated with oil, then discard.

Drop the pieces of pork in the skillet and sauté over high heat until all the sides are well browned, about 5 minutes.

PUREEING
8 mins.

Into a processor work bowl or a blender drop half the peppers and sufficient water from the chili pot to make a puree the consistency of catsup. Scrape into the skillet with the meat. Repeat for the balance of the chilies and add the salt, oregano, and garlic.

COOKING
30 mins.

Stir the mixture together and add the chili water to cover. Cover and cook over medium heat for 30 minutes.

Serve hot.

MEAT JERKY

Dried meat was a staple of all Indian tribes. This method of preservation is how it is done by the Apache and Navajo. Lean venison, lamb, mutton, or beef can be used. Be certain it is lean meat—fatty meat can become rancid.

PREPARATION
several days

Slice meat into thin ¼-inch slices. Salt moderately on both sides.
Hang meat on a line in full sun to dry. Turn from side to side frequently.
As the sun starts to set, bring the meat indoors to hang in a dry place. Return outdoors the next day in full sun.
Depending on climate and humidity, the meat will dry in a few days.

FINAL STEP

Store the jerky in a covered container. Jerky can be eaten as is or used in stews.

KNEEL-DOWN BREAD

[SERVES 6]

The name of this custardlike bread came from watching Indian women kneeling to grind corn kernels into pulp on a metate, a grinding stone. The pulp can be made this old-fashioned way, or in a food processor. It's then wrapped in corn husks and baked under a bed of coals (the old-fashioned way), or baked in the oven. For variety, add chopped green chilies or chopped tomatoes to the corn pulp before baking.

INGREDIENTS

5 ears of corn with husks
1 teaspoon salt
2 eggs, well beaten (for modern version only)

PREPARATION:
Navajo style
1 hour

Beforehand, build a wood fire and burn down to hot coals.
Carefully remove the husks from the corn and dampen liberally with water; set aside. Cut and scrape the corn from the cobs. Grind the corn kernels to a pulp in the metate. Add the salt.
Make a layer of half the corn husks and spoon the pulp over the top. Cover with the remaining husks and form into a package.

BAKING
1 hour

Place the packet in a bed of hot ashes with a few hot coals on the top. Bake for 1 hour.

continued

PREPARATION:
modern style
15 mins.

Preheat oven to 350° 15 minutes before baking.

Husk the ears and scrape the kernels from the cobs and zap once or twice in a food processor or blender. Keep it coarse. Don't make it into a puree. The kernels can also be mashed in a bowl with a wooden pounder. Add the eggs to the puree.

Shape the pulp into a loaf and place on aluminum foil; wrap into a package. Or pour the pulp into a buttered casserole.

BAKING

Bake at 250° for 1 hour.

FINAL STEP

Open the package and enjoy. Or take to the table in the casserole.

PUEBLO CHILI FRITTERS

[MAKES 8]

Of all the Indian dishes prepared in the Hesse kitchen, this is Frank's favorite. It is one of mine, too. The fritters are about the size of a golf ball. Instead of baking powder, the ancients used powdered deer horn.

INGREDIENTS

Cooking oil, to deep-fry
2 tablespoons minced onion
1 tablespoon unsalted butter
½ cup all-purpose flour
⅓ cup water
1 egg, slightly beaten
½ teaspoon baking powder
1 tablespoon roasted green chili, peeled, seeded, and chopped

EQUIPMENT

One large pot or deep skillet

PREHEAT

Preheat the oil in a pot or deep skillet to 360°.

PREPARATION
15 mins.

Sauté the onion in the butter in a small skillet until the onion is soft and translucent, about 10 minutes.

In a mixing bowl place the flour and slowly pour in the water, stirring constantly, to make a medium-thick batter. Stir in the egg and baking powder. Add the chili and onion and mix well.

DEEP-FRYING
6 mins.

Drop the batter by the tablespoonful into the hot oil. Fry until lightly brown, about 3 minutes on each side.

FINAL STEP

Drain on paper towels and serve hot.

TUCSON, ARIZONA

Mexican-Sonoran— Madge Griswold

"Come to dinner," Madge Griswold had written.

It was no quickly scrawled handwritten note. The invitation was a ten-page background paper on food as well as an itinerary precisely tailored for what I had told her I wanted to do in Arizona. In addition to dining at the Griswold house, she promised we would see and visit with the butcher, the baker (no candlestick maker), the greengrocer, the chili shopkeeper, the tortilla lady, and a dozen others.

"You must also see the kind of country we live in and where a lot of our food is produced," she wrote. She had scheduled detailed visits to the Santa Cruz chili factory, a vineyard, a quick visit (five minutes, as it turned out) to Nogales on the Mexican border, a quiet moment at the Tumacacori mission; back to Tucson and a visit to the Grande Tortilla Factory, Kretschmer's Broadway Market, G & L Oriental Imports, and, finally, Tony's Italian Deli ("for the good smells of an Eastern Italian take-out shop").

And it was all to be. I walked out the hotel door precisely at 9:00 A.M. and introduced myself to Madge, who was seated in her Saab, as she had written she would be, with maps spread across the dash. It was a beautiful day under a cloudless and brilliant blue sky that stayed with us for the seven-hour journey.

Madge drove and talked about Southwestern culture and food while I basked in the beauty and grandeur of the hills and mountains and valleys.

"You know," she said, "food writers who live elsewhere categorize all the cuisines in this part of the country as one 'Southwestern' style of cooking. Nothing could be further from the truth!

"The Southwest is an enormous area, stretching from Texas in the east to California in the west. The food of Texas is markedly different from the food of Arizona. Both are different from the foods of New Mexico, where Santa Fe food is even different from that of Las Cruces. Both are in the same state."

We stopped so I could photograph a string of fat beef cattle winding their way downhill to a water hole.

"Arizona's traditional food is milder and more gentle than that of its sisters to the east. New Mexico's chili dishes are seasoned with pure chilies, chili paste, or chili powder, unadulterated by other spices. Here, in Arizona, foods are more frequently served with or wrapped in giant paper-thin tortillas, unlike the smaller corn and flour tortillas made elsewhere. New Mexican foods are frequently laced with subtle hints of cloves or cinnamon. Not in Arizona."

A hawk leaped into flight from the top of a telephone pole which slowed the conversation.

"If you want," she continued, "you can say that everything below the Gila River in this state is traditional Mexican/Sonoran. The Pima County Board of Supervisors once jokingly suggested that this region secede from the rest of Arizona and form a new state called Baja Arizona.

"Above the Gila River," she continued, "is a large metropolitan area —Phoenix and the suburban cities of Tempe, Mesa, Sun City, and others—that does not have a strong Hispanic influence or cultural tie. The climate and the terrain are Southwestern but the food is contemporary American."

We had driven through Nogales, looked through the high wire fence into Mexico, and turned back north.

Is there such a thing as an authentic Southwestern cuisine?

"No, I don't think so. Each community has a slight twist or variation to a dish, as does each family. And each will tell you that his or her version is the authentic one. In reality, the diversity of foods is as immense as the territory. Ultimately, your interpretation of authentic may be whichever version you were first introduced to."

The blue sky had darkened. A storm from California out of the Pacific was kicking up ugly brown clouds of dust from a mountain of mine tailings, in contrast to our sun-drenched departure from the city a few hours earlier.

"I would characterize Tucson's contribution to Southwestern food as rich flavors laced with pure seasoning and a surprising lack of heat— except in some local salsas. Food in Tucson has been influenced by not only the Mexican state of Sonora, to the south, but the Tohono O'Odham (Papago) Indians who are native to this area. We love the giant paper-thin tortillas that come flat, crisp, and cheese-laden or wrapped around chili, bean, or other fillings to make enormous *burros* that are far larger than *burritos* (little *burros*) found elsewhere.

"This is the region of the green-corn tamale made from field corn ground with cheese and fluffed with lard, then laced with fresh green chilies and more cheese. Delicious. Beans are refried with good lard and a hint of onion. There are no cinnamon or clove flavors as there are in some *adobados* of New Mexico."

There were a few drops of rain on the Saab's windshield as we pulled under the porte cochere of the hotel. In seven hours we had toured southern Arizona, visited the Tucson markets, the shops, the small tortilla factory, and had talked constantly about food.

"That's the final word until dinner at our house when we can talk more about food."

So many dishes had been planned that Madge had divided the meal into two sessions—aperitif and hors d'oeuvres tonight with the main course tomorrow night.

Tonight: chicken liver mousse (Arizona range chicken), with Seville oranges (from the Griswold tree) and Dijon mustard; Cornmeal Brioche; cauliflower flowerettes with a dipping sauce of homemade mayonnaise laced with home-cured black olives (from the Griswold tree) and hot-pepper sauce; pecan puffs (profiteroles) laced with bits of chopped, toasted Arizona pecans.

The next evening was even more ambitious. During the day we had visited a half-dozen markets collecting a score of items for the meal, including a leg of Arizona lamb. It was a working dinner party with four people in the kitchen for two hours chopping, sautéing, cutting, blanching, and talking about food!

Shrimp from the Gulf of California that had been tossed in a salsa and spread delicately over a small *topopo* (tostada) was the first course. The second course was one I highly favored: Roasted Red Pepper and Red Chili Soup garnished with tortilla strips fried crisp in oil.

The entrée was brought to the table by Ralph Griswold, who had grilled the butterflied leg of lamb over a bed of mesquite flavored with an occasional piece of hickory bark that had been brought from their old home place in New Jersey. The lamb slices were garnished with slices of wild *Boletus* mushrooms harvested in the forested mountains of northern Arizona. The meat was accompanied by puree of potato and celery root and a salad of radicchio and endive.

ROASTED RED PEPPER AND RED CHILI SOUP

[SERVES 6]

Everything in this soup gets roasted: the peppers, the shallots, the garlic, the tomato, and the chili powder. Roasting deepens the flavor immeasurably and the gentle treatment of the garlic and shallots renders them mellow and mild.

Chili powder is used rather than chilies because it is widely available in many places where fresh red chilies are not. The powder is heated briefly in oil to intensify the flavor. The soup is garnished with tortilla strips crisply fried in safflower or corn oil.

INGREDIENTS

4 corn tortillas, to garnish
¼ cup oil, to fry tortilla strips
4 large red bell peppers
2 large shallots, split lengthwise, skins left on
4 large garlic cloves, skins left on
2 medium fresh tomatoes, stems removed, skins and
    seeds left intact
4 cups beef or chicken stock, preferably homemade
    (see pages 560 or 562) or store-bought
1 tablespoon extra-virgin olive oil
2 tablespoons mild chili powder
Salt, to taste
1 teaspoon lemon juice

EQUIPMENT

One baking sheet

PREPARATION
Overnight

Cut the tortillas into strips ⅜ inch wide the day before so they may dry uncovered overnight. Fry the strips in a neutral oil until crisp. Drain immediately on paper towels. (This is a delicious garnish not only for soups but for salads, too.)

ROASTING
8–10 mins.

Cut the peppers into eighths lengthwise and remove the stems, ribs, and seeds. Place the wedges on a baking sheet, skin side up, and roast them under a broiler until the skin blisters and blackens, about 8 to 10 minutes. Remove them from the broiler and place in a brown paper sack. Close the bag tightly and let stand for 15 minutes. Peel the skin from the peppers and set aside.

6–8 mins.

Place the cut shallots, skin side up, on a baking sheet, along with the garlic cloves and tomatoes. Roast until the skins brown but do not burn, turning the tomatoes once, about 6 to 8 minutes.

SIMMERING
20 mins.

Cut the tomatoes into rough pieces. Combine the roasted peppers, shallots, garlic, and tomatoes in a heavy (nonreactive) saucepan with 2 cups of stock. Simmer until the vegetables are very tender, about 20 minutes.

PUREEING

Retrieve the garlic cloves and shallots. Trim off the skins. Pour the peppers and tomatoes into a blender and add the trimmed shallots and garlic cloves. Process until the mixture is pureed. This should be done in 2 batches. Reserve in a bowl.

Rinse the saucepan with warm water and remove any bits of vegetables that remain and return the pureed mixture to the saucepan. Add the other 2 cups of stock to the blender and whirl briefly to pick up any pieces of vegetables that remain.

COOKING
10 mins.

Add the stock to the saucepan with the puree and slowly reheat the soup.

In another saucepan, heat the olive oil and add the chili powder, just as if making a roux with flour and butter. Stir until the chili has a nicely roasted scent. Be careful not to burn it. Stir the mixture into the soup. Add the salt and lemon juice.

FINAL STEP

Serve the hot soup in warmed plates or glass bowls, garnished with the crisp tortilla strips.

CORNMEAL BRIOCHE

[MAKES 1 LOAF]

Madge Griswold adapted a recipe for the traditional French brioche and, by adding cornmeal, endowed it with a Southwestern personality. It may be made in a mixer or food processor, but it also offers the opportunity to make it the old-fashioned way, by hand, crashing the dough down into the bowl.

INGREDIENTS

2½ cups all-purpose flour, approximately
2½ cups stone-ground cornmeal
1 package dry yeast
¼ cup nonfat dry milk
1 tablespoon sugar
2 teaspoons salt
1 cup warm water (105°–115°)
1 cup (2 sticks) unsalted butter, room temperature
5 eggs, room temperature, plus 1 beaten egg mixed with
*   1 tablespoon milk*

EQUIPMENT

Two medium (8 x 4-inch) loaf pans, greased or Teflon

continued

PREPARATION
BY HAND
OR MIXER
15 mins.

Into a large bowl pour 1 cup each white flour and cornmeal, the yeast, dry milk, sugar, salt, and water. Beat in an electric mixer for 2 minutes at medium speed, or for an equal length of time with a large wooden spoon or spatula. Add the butter and continue beating for 1 minute.

Stop the mixer. Add the eggs, one at a time, and the remaining 1½ cups of flour, ½ cup at a time, beating thoroughly with each addition.

The dough will be soft and sticky, and it must be beaten until it is shiny, elastic, and pulls from the hands or sides of the bowl.

KNEADING
10–15 mins.

Grab the dough in one hand, steadying the bowl with the other, and pull a large handful of it out of the bowl, about 14 inches aloft, and throw it back—with considerable force. Continue pulling and slapping back the dough for about 15 minutes. Don't despair. It is sticky. It is a mess. But it will slowly begin to stretch and pull away as you work it.

If using a heavy-duty mixer, at medium speed, the flat beater blade is better than a dough hook for this mixing. It should take about 10 minutes.

FIRST RISING
2–3 hours

Cover the bowl with plastic wrap and put in a warm place (80° to 85°) until the dough has doubled in volume.

REFRIGERATING
4 hours or
overnight

Stir down the dough. Place the covered bowl in the refrigerator. The rich dough must be thoroughly chilled—at least 4 hours—before it can be shaped.

SHAPING
5 mins.

Place the chilled dough on the floured work surface and divide into 2 pieces. Place in the prepared loaf pans.

SECOND RISING
2½ hours

Cover the pans with wax paper and leave at room temperature until the pieces have doubled in volume, about 2½ hours.

PREHEAT

Preheat the oven to 375° 20 minutes before baking.

BAKING
35 mins.

Brush the top with the egg-milk glaze.

Place the pans on the middle shelf of the oven and bake until the loaves are light brown, 35 minutes. Turn the pans around midway during the baking period.

FINAL STEP

Place the pans on the metal rack and turn on the side to loosen the loaves. Gently turn out the loaves. The hot loaves must be handled with care until cooled.

TINY SHRIMP TOPOPOS
WITH SALSA CRUDA AND AVOCADO

[SERVES 6]

Shrimp poached in tequila with avocado and a salsa of fresh chilies and tomatoes are served cool, not icy cold, for a first course.

Note: The shrimps and the salsa may be prepared ahead of time. You cannot peel and slice the avocado beforehand because it will turn brown.

INGREDIENTS

1 small onion, diced
½ stalk celery, sliced
½ carrot, diced
1½ cups tequila
18 uncooked medium shrimp, peeled and deveined

SALSA
1 yellow Hungarian pepper
1 jalapeño pepper
1 Anaheim pepper
¼ cup finely chopped green onions, including green part
2 medium tomatoes, or 1 large tomato, peeled, seeded, and
*   chopped*
Pinch of salt
Pinch of sugar

1 ripe avocado
1 tablespoon finely chopped cilantro (coriander)

PREPARATION
30 mins.

Combine the onion, celery, and carrot in a small saucepan. Add the tequila and simmer for 15 minutes. Add the shrimp and turn the heat off. Shrimp cook very quickly. They are poached completely once they turn pink. Remove the shrimp from the liquid and cool to room temperature, covered lightly. (Refrigerate if the dish is not to be assembled immediately.)

For the salsa: Use rubber gloves to handle the peppers and do not let the seeds or ribs touch the skin. Cut the chilies into tiny (⅛-inch) dice. Toss the scallions with the chopped tomato and diced chilies. Season with the salt and sugar. (Chill, covered, if you are not serving immediately.)

ASSEMBLING
20 mins.

Arrange a cone of salsa on each plate. Halve the shrimp lengthwise and place 6 shrimp halves against the side of each salsa cone. Peel and thinly slice the ripe avocado and cut each slice in half crosswise. Arrange the slices between the shrimp slices. (Avocado can be kept from browning by adding lemon juice.)

Serve garnished with chopped cilantro.

XXXXX*MESA, ARIZONA*

Big John—John Boehm

The view from the cottage was across the tenth tee, down the length of the fairway, to the Superstition Mountains, jagged and misty in the late afternoon sun. Golfers came, hit balls, and rode off in their carts. Timothy, at his ease on the patio, loved it. Some spoke to him. There was excitement when a ball hit from some distant tee rolled immediately in front of him. He had not seen anything quite like it before.

The Arizona Golf Resort in Mesa, east of Phoenix, was Timothy's rightful place for it was because of him we discovered this oasis in the desert. We had been driving through parched, barren land all day, and I knew we were onto something the moment we drove through the elegant white archways flanked by palms. The grass was green and there was a lot of it. Trees all over the place. It bespoke gentility, old money. I saw a bumper sticker: SNOW BIRDS HAVE GREEN BILLS.

When I phoned for a reservation earlier, a pleasant voice assured me: "Yes, we love dogs." The Mobil travel guide, with its little canine icon, indicated the resort did love dogs, but I thought I had better check since the accommodations sounded almost too good to be true.

It was because of Timothy that we met Chef John Boehm.

John Boehm weighs close to three hundred pounds and stands an impressive six feet two inches. Top this off with a tall chef's hat and you can understand why it is not difficult to notice him when he comes into the dining room to chat with guests.

John has problems, as do all chefs, but his are somewhat different.

During the Arizona "high season" when it is cold in the northern United States but delightful here, his clientele is largely retired folk who, according to the chef, bring with them their "preferences and prejudices." They don't want to be challenged with new dishes. No Mexican food, no chilies, no spices, just keep it cool. They don't want to wait forty-five minutes for a special dish to be prepared.

"I let them have whatever they want and offer it to them six ways—poached, pan-fried, broiled, baked, sautéed, or blackened. The last is as close as I can get to being innovative."

The food was good; one soup particularly: Mesa Vegetable. It was rich with Cheddar cheese, cream, and garden vegetables—broccoli, cauliflower, onions, and celery. It was made with chicken stock and a hint of garlic. Not for a diet but a special treat.

MESA VEGETABLE SOUP

[SERVES 6]

This delicious soup is first thickened with a butter-flour roux and then with cheese and heavy cream.

INGREDIENTS
½ cup each *broccoli, cauliflower, onions, and celery, all cut into small (⅜-inch) dice*
1 garlic clove
6 cups chicken stock, homemade (see page 562) or store-bought
2 cups dry white wine
2 bay leaves
½ teaspoon white pepper
½ teaspoon salt, if needed
¾ cup (1½ sticks) unsalted butter
⅓ cup flour
3 cups roughly shredded medium Cheddar cheese
1 cup heavy cream
¼ cup chopped fresh parsley, to garnish

PREPARATION
25 mins.

Combine all of the vegetables in a large saucepan and add the garlic, stock, wine, and bay leaves. Bring to a boil. Reduce to a simmer over medium-low heat, cover, and cook until the vegetables are tender, about 20 minutes. Season with the white pepper and salt.

ROUX
10 mins.

Meanwhile, in a small skillet melt the butter over medium heat and add the flour, a tablespoon at a time, stirring until the flour is absorbed. Cook the roux over low heat for 10 minutes. Do not burn. Stir the roux into the soup.

ASSEMBLING
8 mins.

Remove from heat and add the grated cheese. Stir in the cream. Reheat soup.

Serve hot with a sprinkling of chopped parsley.

⋙ On the Road—NEVADA'S HIGH DESERT

Cottontail Ranch

The Cottontail Ranch is a bordello of renown in Nevada's high desert country. It is in a cookbook because the big sign out front bidding the traveler welcome lists "food and drink" along with a variety of other services. There is no mistaking it for something it isn't because the sign says bluntly, in tall letters—BORDELLO. Nevada law allows such things.

The Cottontail Ranch is a forlorn cluster of a half-dozen mobile homes joined together and standing alone on acres and acres of nothing but sagebrush and a few cows. It is on the southwest corner of the intersection of S.R. 266 and U.S. 95, the latter a remote but fast highway for trucks running between Reno and Las Vegas. From here the less-used S.R. 266 goes west over the White Mountains and drops down into Bishop, a small California city snuggled against the Sierra Mountains.

We had driven this way a number of times in the past to visit our daughter and family in Bishop. Each time as I approached the intersection with its strung-together clutch of small buildings, my curiosity was piqued.

It was late November. My daughter had warned me several times that an early winter snow could make the mountain highway impassable and, if so, we should continue north to Tonopah before turning west.

"Snow on Westgard Pass, which is above seven thousand feet, is what you have to worry about," she had written. "So be sure you make inquiry before you take the road."

"Why don't I stop at the Cottontail Ranch," I said to Marje, and make inquiry? She and Timothy would wait in the van. (I learned later that visiting dogs were tolerated but wives never!)

With some trepidation, I walked across the dusty parking lot where but one car was parked, put my hand on the doorknob, and pulled the door open. Inside, across a small alcove, was a second door, perhaps a dozen feet away. I turned the second doorknob but it was locked. On the wall beside the door was a bell button and a small sign: FOR PLEASURE PUSH THIS BUTTON! I was struck with how polished and worn the knob and the button were.

I pushed the button. Nothing happened. I pushed a second time. For a moment nothing happened and it was in that moment I realized how silly this all was—and turned to leave.

The door opened. There stood a smiling woman in a brief black bra and scanty black panties posing with one arm resting against the doorsill and the other outstretched, friendlylike toward me. A filmy pink boa was caught in the motion of her arm. My mind flashed to Marlene Dietrich leaning against a doorsill in a western movie. But only for a moment. The woman in front of me was not very attractive. A bit too old. A bit too plump. The hair too black. Nevertheless, she exuded hospitality.

"Won't you come in?" She smiled, and waved her arm toward the dark interior behind. The boa fluttered.

For a moment I was speechless.

"Please come in," she implored, and with a flourish of her boa, stepped back to allow me to come across the threshold on which I was firmly planted and intended to remain so.

"No, no . . . my wife . . . my wife is outside and . . . so is the dog," I blurted. This was not going well. "Is there snow on Westgard Pass?"

She stared at me as if I had spoken in tongues.

"Is there snow on Westgard Pass?" I repeated bravely—brave now that my intentions had been made clear.

The arm and the pink boa stopped waving. She looked absolutely bewildered. Stunned. The boa slipped off her shoulders. It occurred to me she might think I was giving her a coded message.

"I don't know what you are talking about," she said in a small voice. She seemed about to cry. I had to get out of there. "Thanks anyway," I said and backed away from the button that one pushed for pleasure.

Suddenly an older woman, in jogging gear, whom I assumed was the madame, appeared and put a motherly arm around the girl. "What is it you want?" she demanded. I had no choice. "Is there snow on Westgard Pass?"

"Snow on what?" Her voice was rising.

"Good-bye, and thank you." I fled through the door.

I scrambled into the van. Marje was laughing. "No recipe?" she asked. Just as I started to close the door the driver of the other vehicle came down the steps and shouted across at me.

"Fella, there's *no* snow on Westgard Pass."

And indeed there wasn't.

⌇⌇⌇⌇BISHOP, CALIFORNIA

The Matlick House—Nanette Robidart

Bed-and-breakfast homes are like snowflakes—no two are alike. And, like snowflakes, some last in memory, others do not.

One Marje and I remember is the Matlick House, in Bishop, a small California high-desert town (part Paiute Indian reservation) where our daughter and family have lived for two decades. Standing on the lawn of the Matlick House, looking west, the view is of the magnificent Sierra Nevada mountains less than ten miles distant. In winter, when the mountains are blanketed with deep snow almost down to the town, the view is awesome.

The locals take it for granted—it happens every winter, they point out—but I can't be so casual, because the Sierra occupies a very special place in my being. Over a period of several years I backpacked the length of the John Muir Trail that follows the spine of the mountains from Yosemite south to Mount Whitney. Once having done that you embrace the memory forever.

Mistress of the Matlick House is Nanette Robidart, a handsome, slender woman, an accountant, who came from Los Angeles a few years ago to purchase the ranch house built in 1906 in the center of what was then an apple orchard. Now the house shares the acreage with a mobile-home park, a shopping center, and a few horses in a small pasture. With five guest bedrooms, the inn is large enough not to have the intimate closeness of some small B&B establishments where, like it or not, you become a member of the family.

Nanette sets a fine breakfast table. Many of her guests come to Bishop to hike the mountain trails or ski, so to assuage big appetites, slices of home-smoked bacon and ham are stacked high, and platter-sized apple-walnut pancakes move steadily from the kitchen to the dining room. Everyone knows that you eat more at high altitudes—Bishop is nearly a mile high—so I sometimes have scrambled eggs and pumpkin bread as well.

Nanette commands a pleasant but tight ship. She expects her guests to be comfortable yet well mannered: "Treat my home as your own home —and lock the front door when you leave." This pleasant greeting was part of a lace-framed announcement in our room which suggested other points of etiquette: "Sorry, no smoking inside—how about the front porch?" and "I want you to be comfortable but I don't feel good about waste—please turn off the heater when you are warm." Also: "Please honor my checkout time. It is very difficult and embarrassing for me to have to ask you to hurry up and leave."

Timothy was not supposed to be a guest. House rules. However, when Nanette met him she succumbed to his charms and said he could stay *this* time. Frankie, her Persian cat, almost as big as Timothy, immediately took up guard duty at our door. She sat for hours for the opportunity to see him as he came into the hall. He, on the other hand, intimidated by her brashness, brushed past her as fast as running down stairs would allow. Frankie followed him until Timothy was in the van. "I think she likes him," Nanette said. Timothy was not certain.

Matlick House breakfasts were bountiful. On the third morning I pleaded for smaller portions of everything except the pancakes.

APPLE-WALNUT PANCAKES

[MAKES 1 DOZEN]

INGREDIENTS

1⅓ cups all-purpose flour
2 teaspoons baking powder
½ teaspoon salt
1 tablespoon sugar
2 eggs
1¼ cups milk
3 tablespoons oil, of choice
1 apple (she prefers Granny Smith)
1 teaspoon ground cinnamon
¾ cup chopped walnuts or pecans   *continued*

EQUIPMENT   One griddle or waffle iron

PREPARATION   In a medium bowl mix the flour, baking powder, salt, and sugar.
5–10 mins.   Beat the eggs in a separate bowl, add milk and oil, and blend well
with a fork. Pour the liquid into the dry ingredients, and beat
until smooth.

Grate the apple. To complete the batter, stir in the apple,
cinnamon, and nuts.

COOKING   Heat a griddle or waffle iron. Pour the batter to form cakes of
20 mins.   desired size.

Serve hot—with butter and maple syrup.

OWENS VALLEY PUMPKIN BREAD

[MAKES 1 LARGE OR 2 SMALL LOAVES]

Crushed pineapple is mixed with pumpkin, walnuts, and raisins, spiced
with cloves, cinnamon, and nutmeg to make this fine-tasting quick bread
that is a specialty of the Matlick House

INGREDIENTS   *1⅔ cups all-purpose flour*
1½ cups sugar
¼ teaspoon baking powder
1 teaspoon baking soda
1 teaspoon each grated nutmeg, ground cloves and cinnamon
½ cup vegetable oil
½ cup crushed pineapple, drained
1 cup fresh or canned pumpkin
2 eggs, well beaten
1 cup each chopped dates and chopped walnuts
1 cup raisins

EQUIPMENT   One large (9 x 5-inch) or two small (7 x 3-inch) loaf pans, greased
or Teflon, lined with wax paper, buttered

PREHEAT   Preheat the oven to 375°.

PREPARATION   In a large mixing or mixer bowl stir together the flour, sugar,
20 mins.   baking powder, and baking soda. Add the spices.

In a separate bowl blend together the oil, pineapple, pumpkin, and eggs. By hand or with the mixer flat beater stir the liquid
into the dry ingredients, blending well.

Fold the dates, nuts, and raisins into the batter.

BAKING
375°
50–60 mins.

Spoon the batter into the prepared pan(s) and place in the oven. Bake until the bread is a light brown, 50 to 60 minutes, and tests done when a wooden toothpick inserted in a loaf comes out clean and dry.

FINAL STEP

Remove the bread from the oven. Turn the pan on its side; carefully pull the loaf out by gently tugging on the wax paper lining. Cool the bread on a metal rack.

MATLICK HOUSE BUTTERMILK SCONES

[MAKES 16 WEDGE-SHAPED OR 3 DOZEN ROUND SCONES]

A Scot at the breakfast table at Matlick House would immediately be transported home by a taste of Nanette's scones. While traditional scones are thought of as wedge-shaped pieces cut from a round "bannock" either before or after it is baked, these are cut with a biscuit cutter. It depends on the occasion. To serve at a tea calling for a delicate presentation, use a 1½-inch biscuit cutter, as would an English host. For a hungry gathering at breakfast, I like a large, fat bannock or scone cut into wedges. Leftover scones are excellent when split and toasted.

INGREDIENTS

3 cups all-purpose flour
½ cup sugar
1 tablespoon baking powder
1 teaspoon salt
½ cup (1 stick) cold unsalted butter
1 cup currants or raisins
2 eggs
⅔ cup buttermilk
1 egg mixed with 1 tablespoon milk or cream, to brush

EQUIPMENT

One baking sheet; biscuit or cookie cutter of choice; pastry brush

PREHEAT

Preheat the oven to 375°.

PREPARATION
15 mins.

Into a mixing bowl or mixer bowl measure the dry ingredients. Stir with a wooden spoon or with the mixer flat beater. With your fingers, pastry cutter, or flat beater cut the butter into the dry ingredients. Stir in the currants.

Shape a depression in the flour and break in the eggs and pour in the buttermilk. Stir together to blend. Gradually pull the flour into the buttermilk mixture with a mixing spoon or spatula.

continued

If it is too moist and sticks to your hands or beater blade, add sprinkles of flour.

Work with the dough as little as possible to achieve a soft, pliable ball. Don't aggressively knead, which will toughen it. If under the dough hook, work at low speed for less than a minute.

SHAPING
15 mins.

For large scones: Divide the dough into 2 pieces. Press each piece into a circle about ¾ inch thick. Place on the baking sheet and with a knife lightly score the bannock into the desired number of pie-shaped pieces. For the small scones: Pat and press the dough with the knuckles into a rough 8-inch circle about ¾ inch thick. Cut the pieces with a biscuit cutter and place on the baking sheet. Don't twist the cutter when stamping out the scones or they may bake lopsided. Small scones may also be made by pressing or rolling the dough into an oblong ¾ inch thick. Shape into 1½-inch squares with deep cuts, but do not separate them entirely. They will break apart easily when baked.

Brush the egg glaze mixture over the top of the scones.

BAKING
375°
18–20 mins.
per batch

Bake in the oven until the scones are a lovely golden brown, 18 to 20 minutes. Midway in the baking period turn the baking sheet.

FINAL STEP

Gently break the large bannocks into scones. Serve while hot or warm at breakfast, tea, or brunch. (Kids love them anytime.)

〰〰〰SEBASTOPOL, CALIFORNIA

Dinner at Sebastopol—Russell and Scotty Specter

A meal by the Specters of Sebastopol is a performance—a cut above entertainment—with great flourishes of pots and pans, fire and smoke, spice and wine, chopping and grating, knives and whisks, all accompanied by conversation about the latest best meal one has had and where one is dining next week.

Russell Specter is a passionate cook. Flame and motion attend. His wife, Scotty, equally passionate but conservative, runs a quieter kitchen

when she is there alone. Things bake more slowly and for longer periods of time. The stirring of the pot is done quietly. Aromas are delicate. She moves unhurried from table to stove.

Scotty has been cooking since she was a child on a Texas ranch. Russell's tenure in the kitchen is shorter but one held with great enthusiasm. Together they prepare memorable meals. They love to cook and they do it extremely well. It is a marriage made in the kitchen. "My food appealed to Russell right off. The first thing we did when we met was to discuss where we would have our first meal. We decided on a Cuban restaurant."

Russell: "We consider restaurants the prime form of entertainment. We really do. We don't belong to clubs or anything of the kind. We don't gamble. We like music and food and wine."

"Our wine bill is something to behold!" Scotty added.

A decade ago, after earlier marriages, they met and shortly thereafter bought a two-family house in San Francisco. He lived with his daughters in one of the two flats. She lived with her children in the other. Two sets of children under one roof—separate but equal. "Good friends all of us," said Scotty. When the children left, Russell and Scotty married and moved into a ranch house on the edge of an apple orchard in Sebastopol with the coastal mountain range to the west. "It's been a good marriage," said Scotty. "Never an argument or quarrel. Now and then an 'energy' exchange, but that's the extent of it."

The Specters' four acres burst with growing things. Two goats, six chickens, one cat, one dog, three Japanese koi (carp) in a large wooden tub, and a host of birds, rabbits, and the occasional raccoon and skunk. Large sections are given over to herb and vegetable gardens.

To reach the Specter place on Watertrough Road we drove north over the Golden Gate Bridge for about forty miles. It is the heart of what the people who live here unashamedly claim to be the best place in the world to live. Sonoma County. The great horticulturist Luther Burbank thought so; so did Jack London and now Charlie Brown's creator, Charles Schultz.

The county is bound on one side by the Pacific Ocean, to the north by redwood country. It is a transition zone where two climates meet, creating micro-climates among the zone's hills and valleys. Melons will grow on one side of a hill but may not on the other. To the south is Marin County, where one end of the Golden Gate Bridge is anchored and which has absorbed a lot of people fleeing San Francisco. They haven't yet reached Sonoma. It remains essentially rural.

Russell, short, pleasantly portly with a full beard touched with silver, looks perfect for the part of a London barrister in an English mystery. In fact, he is a lawyer, specializing in labor relations. He had been in one of my baking courses several years before at Tante Marie's Cooking School in San Francisco. I sensed immediately his enthusiasm for and an appreciation of good food and good cooking.

We were at the Specters for two memorable meals, both prepared with all Sonoma foodstuffs. First there were slices of foie gras, plump and rich, which Russell sautéed lightly in duck fat and a touch of olive oil, with shallots. The slices were served with big chunks of sourdough bread. We ate the whole one-pound liver and looked to Russell for more. But now it was slices of a beautiful wild mushroom, a cepe, the size of a grapefruit, which he sliced and sautéed in the same pan, but this time he flambéed it with cognac.

Through all of this we were having first a Piper-Sonoma Vintage 1984 Blanc de Noir and then a van der Kamp Bruts Sonoma 1983 Valley Champagne. The salad—seven greens from a neighbor's garden plus baked baby beets—was tossed with walnut oil, balsamic and champagne vinegars. For three days the beef chunks for the main course had been marinating in a California Zinfandel, oregano, thyme, aniseed and bay leaves. With the beef Russell served two reds—Ravenswood Merlot (Sonoma County, 1984) and Heitz Wine Cellars Napa County Cabernet Sauvignon 1982.

Dessert: locally grown Bartlett pears, poached in a Sonoma burgundy, bay leaf, peppercorns, and honey.

The next day, because Russell had built an adobe oven from plans in my bread book, we had a leg of Sonoma lamb baked in it. What a wonderful place Sonoma is!

ADOBE OVEN ROAST LAMB

[SERVES 6]

This leg of Sonoma lamb was roasted in a wood-fired adobe oven that Russell had constructed last summer out by his garden. It can be prepared equally well in a regular oven, gas or electric. Missing, however, will be the fun and satisfaction of stoking a fire of your own making. Missing, too, will be the fragrance of fruit wood burning to fire the interior of the oven to a white heat. In 2 hours or so the ashes will be raked out, the roast put inside, and the door closed to be opened only to brush the meat with marinade.

Slits are cut in the meat and stuffed with a mixture of rosemary, anchovies, and garlic. The leg is marinated overnight in a marinade of wine, pomegranate juice, and olive oil.

INGREDIENTS   *One 5- to 6-pound leg of lamb*

STUFFING
½ cup chopped fresh rosemary
2 tablespoons anchovy paste
4 garlic cloves, mashed

MARINADE
1 cup red wine
1 cup pomegranate juice
2 onions, chopped
6 garlic cloves, minced
1 teaspoon salt
1 tablespoon freshly ground black pepper
½ cup olive oil

EQUIPMENT   One large roasting pan; thermometer, if adobe oven is used

PREPARATION   Cut a dozen ½-inch-deep slits across the grain of the meat with the point of a paring knife.

In a small bowl mash together the stuffing ingredients to make a thick paste.

Stuff the paste into the slits.

MARINATING
overnight   Mix together the marinade ingredients. Place the leg of lamb in a bowl or the roasting pan, pour over the marinade. Cover and refrigerate overnight.

Two hours before placing the meat in the oven remove from the refrigerator and let stand at room temperature.

Before baking, pour off all but 1 cup of the marinade, which will be brushed on the meat as it bakes.

continued

PREHEAT   Preheat the oven to 375° 15 minutes before roasting, or test
                     adobe oven for temperature.

ROASTING   Place the lamb, fat side up, in an open roasting pan and place in
375°   the oven. Brush with the marinade 2 or 3 times during roasting.
1½ hours   Roast for about 1½ hours, or until a meat thermometer registers
                     145° for medium-rare, 165° for well done.

FINAL STEP   Allow the roast to rest for 5 to 10 minutes before carving.

SONOMA STEW

[SERVES 6]

Overnight marination and long hours in a slow stew pot can turn the
least expensive pieces of beef into a tender, fine-tasting dish. This is an
elegant stew for which the beef pieces and the vegetables are roasted
separately and joined just before serving, which allows each to retain its
special flavor.

Scotty favors a gelatinous cut of beef (shin or foreshank). It has a
great deal of connective tissue but it also has a great beef flavor. You
won't find a better piece of beef for this stew. A mix of short ribs and
rump or chuck can be substituted. Scotty's recipe is her version of Ca-
talan Estofat of Beef from an admired cookbook, *Paula Wolfert's World
of Food* (HarperCollins).

Note: Allow at least 24 hours to prepare the beef. The vegetables are put
in the oven to roast 2 hours before serving.

INGREDIENTS   *MEAT*
                     4 to 5 pounds boneless beef foreshank, cut into 1-inch cubes
                     2 bottles strong dry red wine
                     *¼ pound blanched salt pork, cut into lardons, ¼ inch across
                         and 1 inch long*
                     4 tablespoons extra-virgin olive oil
                     *½ teaspoon each coarse salt and freshly ground white pepper,
                         or to taste*
                     2 large yellow onions, cut into eighths
                     2 large carrots, cut into 1-inch chunks
                     1 celery rib, cut into 1-inch chunks
                     8 garlic cloves, unpeeled
                     ½ teaspoon each dried oregano, fennel seed, thyme
                     2 bay leaves, crumbled
                     3 cloves

1 stick cinnamon, crushed
¼ teaspoon whole white peppercorns, lightly crushed
¼ teaspoon flour
3 tablespoons red wine vinegar
4 tablespoons anisette, if desired

VEGETABLES
3 tablespoons olive oil
18 small white onions, peeled
18 small new potatoes, or 1½ pounds larger red potatoes, peeled
*   and chunked*
¼ teaspoon fennel seeds
Sprigs of thyme and 2 bay leaves
Coarse salt and freshly ground white pepper, to taste
Parsley, chopped, to garnish

EQUIPMENT

One large flameproof casserole; 1 roasting pan

MARINATING
24 hours

Place the beef cubes in a bowl and cover with the red wine. Cover with plastic wrap and keep in a cool place or refrigerate for 24 hours.

Stir them once or twice during marination.

The following day, drain the beef, reserving the wine. Dry the meat on paper towels. Lightly pound each piece with a mallet or a hammer on a small board.

PREPARATION
30 mins.

Cook the lardons in the olive oil in the casserole over low heat, stirring occasionally, until the fat is rendered and the lardons are lightly browned, about 15 minutes. With a slotted spoon transfer them to a bowl.

Increase the heat to high and sauté the beef in several batches, turning the pieces until browned all over, about 10 minutes for each batch. Transfer the meat to the bowl with the lardons. Season with the salt and pepper.

8–10 mins.

Add the vegetables, garlic, herbs, and spices to the casserole and brown them lightly, stirring. Pour off all but 3 tablespoons of fat, sprinkle it with the flour, stir, and allow it to brown evenly. Deglaze with the vinegar, then gradually stir in the reserved red wine.

PREHEAT

Preheat the oven to 250° 15 minutes before cooking.

COOKING
250°
2½–4 hours

Return the meat to the casserole. If the meat is not covered by wine, add water. Bring the mixture to a boil and cover the vessel with parchment or foil to make a tight fit with the lid.

Set the casserole in the oven. Cook until the meat is tender, about 4 hours for the shank but less time for pieces from better cuts, about 2½ hours. Test with a fork.

Remove the beef to a plate and cover it loosely with foil to keep moist.

SAUCE
20–25 mins.

Strain the cooking liquid, pressing down the vegetables to extract the juices. Skim the fat off the top of the liquid. Pour into a large saucepan and boil it over high heat until the liquid is reduced to 2 cups, about 15 minutes. Add the anisette, if desired, to the sauce and return to a boil.

REFRIGERATING
overnight

Remove the sauce from the heat and let cool. Pour it over the meat, cover and refrigerate overnight.

PREHEAT

Preheat the oven to 350° 15 minutes before roasting.

ROASTING
350°
1½ hours

About 2 hours before serving, remove the meat and sauce from the refrigerator to bring them to room temperature.

Meanwhile, cover the bottom of a roasting pan with the olive oil and add the vegetables and herbs. Roll the vegetables to coat evenly. Roast until the vegetables are glazed, crusted, and tender, about 1½ hours. Blot off the excess oil. Season with salt and pepper.

ASSEMBLING
25 mins.

About 20 minutes before serving, reheat the meat and sauce in the casserole over moderately high heat. Add the vegetables and simmer for 5 minutes to blend the flavors. Season with a good pinch of mixed coarse and fine salt and freshly ground pepper to taste.

Serve garnished with the chopped parsley.

SAN FRANCISCO, CALIFORNIA

Tante Marie—Mary Risley

Mary Risley teaches cooking in San Francisco, one of the most food-aware cities in the country. Its diners are noted for their sophisticated palates and its markets for an abundance of superb foodstuffs from land and sea. Mary's school is in the center of it all.

It is called Tante Marie's Cooking School and it ranks high among the best culinary schools in this country and abroad. It has been compared to La Varenne and Cordon Bleu. A host of famous chefs teach for Mary. To drop a few names: Jacques Pepin, Jim Dodge, Giuliano Bugialli, Marion Cunningham, Carol Field.

Several times I have gone to the school to teach bread and pastry. Each time I have been impressed by the enthusiasm with which Mary and the students approach food. It's fun. It's exciting. It's never dull. Yet Mary is demanding. I once saw a crestfallen student burst into tears when Mary reprimanded her sharply for cutting a carrot julienne when it should have been diced. When she had set the student right, Mary put her arm around the girl. I heard her tell the girl: "Listen, don't take it personally. What you have just heard from me is nothing compared to what will come down around your head when the *sous-chef* in a big restaurant catches you doing a dumb thing like that in *his* kitchen."

There are only fourteen students enrolled at any one time in the school's modest quarters at the base of Telegraph Hill within walking distance of Fisherman's Wharf, the Italian section of North Beach, and Chinatown. The school is in the very heart of good eating in San Francisco!

Mary started the school with a single student who was overwhelmed by the faculty of visiting chefs, cooks, teachers, and food specialists. "She really had it made," Mary said. "Never has one student had so much put before her by so many." The school's program has not changed in the intervening years; Mary teaches the morning participation classes and the outside faculty teaches in the afternoon and evening. The school year is nine months, broken into trimesters.

When I joined the class as part of the research for this book, most of the students were from California. Three were from far away—Texas, Tennessee, and Connecticut. Most were in their late twenties and early thirties. One young woman with a law degree was making a career change to food writing. A young man who had fallen and severely injured his back on a construction job was being retrained to someday become a chef in a small restaurant. One student aspired to be a waiter. One wanted to combine food styling with teaching. The rest of them looked to becoming cooks/chefs and caterers.

Mary: "I know, however, that when twelve or fourteen students say they want to spend a lifetime in the food business, the average is that one or two, usually young women, will peel off and return to Texas or Michigan or northern California to get married. They will raise a family —and with their enviable San Francisco credentials become the best cooks in town. That's fine with me. Their kids will think twice before going to McDonald's."

I wanted to know if cooking is more and more moving away from the home? Is there less good cooking? The answer to both, Mary said, is absolutely yes. What concerns her is with both heads of the household working there will be less and less cooking. Families will come to rely more and more on other people to cook their food. The mediocrity of food concerns Mary. Children are growing up to accept fast food as the norm. They are growing up not knowing the difference between good and bad food.

"Airline food is an example of future cuisine," she said grimly.

It was the week of Christmas break and we cooked and baked for a gala at Mary's house to mark the end of the first trimester.

The "guys," as Mary called all of them, had passed oral and written exams with good marks. The two rooms were filled with festive banter. Work was moving ahead on an impressive array of foods—salmon in parchment, leg of lamb *en croûte*, wild mushrooms *en papillote*, terrines and canapés and beggar's purses (caviar and crème fraîche wrapped in small crêpes and tied with scallions), spiced beef with homemade horseradish sauce, roasted pecans, and the traditional bûche de Noël as well as chocolate truffles. A delicious Red Pepper Tart crept into the action, as did an Omelette Soufflé au Grand Marnier.

"Guys, take a break." Mary said. "I'm going to make you one of the best omelettes ever." And she started beating egg yolks in a large copper bowl.

As we stood around the big work table eating omelette (and it *was* the best ever), Mary gave her annual graduation address. It took all of four minutes at the most.

"Now that you all have passed the first course with flying colors, I know that you are thinking even more about your future in food. If you want to start a catering business or open a restaurant, don't rush into it. Set that as a distant goal, say five or ten years. In the beginning go to work for someone already in the business. If you make mistakes, you do it on their money. Not yours. Next, get some accounting experience. An MBA degree is not a bad place to start."

Late one afternoon Mary and I were talking in her home kitchen. A telephone hooked to an answering machine rang constantly.

"That's Food Runners." She paused. "That gives balance to my life," she said, nodding in the direction of a small room off her kitchen. "When restaurants, bakeries, markets, and caterers are left with surplus or extra food at the end of the day or a week, and produce that is slightly blemished or a bit overripe, they call here. My house is the dispatch center for a corps of volunteer drivers—some two hundred at present—who pick up the food and deliver it to the city's shelters to feed the hungry.

"It all began two years ago. I had seven boned ducks and a large veal pâté that would have been a sin to throw away. I called the homeless shelter at Glide Memorial Church. They were delighted. I delivered the ducks and that started Food Runners.

"The last phone call," Mary said, checking the machine, "was from Zuni Cafe. They have two gallons of pears for us. Yesterday, for example, an accounting firm canceled a reception for one hundred guests but forgot to cancel the catering order. The firm was left with four trays of cheeses, salami, and hors d'oeuvres. We delivered it to the Larkin Street center for wayward kids."

Food Runners has no budget. It is all-volunteer.

"I spoke of the balance that Food Runners gives to my life. At Tante Marie's I work a lot with big names and big egos. Several of my visiting teachers believe the food world revolves around them and only they hold the secret of good cooking. Recently one devoted a full forty-five minutes to drying a handful of cashews in the oven. Imagine, almost an hour of class time to dry a few nuts. I offered her a glass of grapefruit juice. 'Oh no, it would ruin my palate for the day.' Really!"

But balance came back into her life later that day when she took a leg of lamb over to the Haight-Ashbury family shelter. The cook is a Sioux Indian, a handsome giant of a man, with long hair tied in a ponytail, a tattoo on one arm, and a gold earring.

"He moves with such ease and grace among his pots and pans; extemporizing all the time—a dash of this, a big pinch of that—and never knowing from one meal to the next what he will have to work with. His kitchen is always filled with such glorious aromas. You know even before tasting the food that it is delicious. He is a genius—doing so much with so little. He can cook for me anytime!"

POULET AU VINAIGRE
(Chicken in Vinegar)

[SERVES 4]

This is a departure from the many bland presentations of chicken. Mary's *Poulet au Vinaigre* is piquant, bordering on a slightly acidic, vinegary taste. Tantalizingly so. My kitchen notes give it a consistent A+.

INGREDIENTS

1 chicken, cut into 8 pieces, breastbone intact
Salt and freshly ground pepper, to sprinkle
2 tablespoons unsalted butter
¼ cup red wine vinegar
¼ cup water

SAUCE
2 garlic cloves, minced
¼ cup red wine vinegar
1 tablespoon tomato paste
Pinch each of salt and freshly ground black pepper, or to taste
2 tablespoons butter (optional)

1 tablespoon chopped parsley, to garnish
2 tablespoons fresh tarragon (optional), to garnish

PREPARATION
8–10 mins.

Sprinkle the chicken pieces with salt and pepper to taste. Brown in the butter (or use none in a Teflon pan) on all sides over medium heat for 8 to 10 minutes.

COOKING
20 mins.

Add the red wine vinegar and water, cover, and cook gently for about 20 minutes. Remove the chicken to a serving plate, and keep warm, uncovered. The breastbone can be removed now, if desired.

SAUCE
10 mins.

In the skillet add the garlic and sauté for 1 minute. Add red wine vinegar and bring to a boil, scraping up all the sediment in the pan. Add the tomato paste, salt, and pepper.

The sauce should be peppery and slightly vinegary. The butter may be swished into the sauce, bit by bit, if a richer dish is desired.

FINAL STEP

Spoon the sauce over the chicken, and sprinkle with the parsley and tarragon, if desired.

RABBIT STUFFED WITH SPINACH AND BACON

[SERVES 6]

In Indiana we have an abundance of live rabbits in the woods and frozen rabbits in the supermarkets, but rarely can I find a boned rabbit. Mary Risley, in a city that has everything, seems to have no problem getting one from her butcher. Here, my butcher just shakes his head. (Actually he said: "You want a boned *what?*") Nevertheless, it is a delicious dish and well worth going hunting for a boned rabbit.

INGREDIENTS

One 5-pound rabbit, boned, reserving liver
3 tablespoons brandy
Pinch of thyme
¼ pound smoked bacon
1 pound fresh spinach, or frozen, thawed
1 teaspoon plus a pinch of salt
3 tablespoons unsalted butter
2 tablespoons minced shallots
⅓ cup bread crumbs
½ teaspoon freshly ground black pepper
1 tablespoon Pernod
4 strips thin bacon
1 pound caul fat or fatback
1 each carrot, celery stalk, and small onion, all coarsely
*   chopped*
½ cup chicken stock, homemade (see page 562) or store-bought

EQUIPMENT

One baking pan; string

continued

PREPARATION
1–2 hours

Either bone the rabbit yourself or have the butcher bone it and reserve the bones.

Marinate the liver in brandy, with a pinch of thyme and set aside for 1 to 2 hours.

STUFFING
40 mins.

Cut the bacon into small dice and brown lightly in a skillet over low heat. Cook the spinach with the pinch of salt in a heavy-bottomed pan until wilted. Drain, squeeze out excess water, and chop coarsely.

Melt the butter in a skillet and cook the shallots; add the spinach, and cook until dry. Place the shallot-and-spinach mixture in a bowl with the bacon. Add the bread crumbs, teaspoon of salt, pepper, and Pernod. Mix well.

PREHEAT

Preheat the oven to 350°.

ASSEMBLING

Spread the rabbit out in a rectangle on a work surface and spoon the stuffing over it. Cut the liver in quarters. Wrap a thin piece of bacon around each quarter and lay the quarters across one short end of the rabbit. Roll up the rabbit meat around the liver pieces and continue to roll until all the stuffing is encased.

Wrap the rabbit in caul fat or thin layers of fatback. Tie with a string.

Place the rabbit in a baking pan with the carrot, celery, and onion. Place the rabbit bones around the rabbit roll. Add the marinade from the liver and the chicken stock.

ROASTING
350°
1 hour

Roast for 1 hour or until firm to the touch, basting occasionally.

CARVING
20–30 mins.

Remove the rabbit from the pan and let cool for 20 minutes before carving into ½-inch slices.

FINAL STEP

Serve with a spoonful of the pan juice poured over each slice shaped as a pinwheel of meat and stuffing.

RED PEPPER TART

[SERVES 6]

A puff-pastry shell is filled with a mixture of sweet red peppers, garlic, red pepper flakes, and tomatoes, crisscrossed with thin strips of Gruyère cheese, and baked briefly. The shell and the red pepper mixture are prepared in advance and brought together at serving time.

INGREDIENTS

SHELL
½ pound puff pastry
2 egg yolks
1 tablespoon cream

FILLING
4 red bell peppers
¼ cup olive oil
1 small onion, thinly sliced
2 garlic cloves, minced
⅛ teaspoon red pepper flakes
1 cup peeled, seeded, and chopped tomatoes
1 tablespoon tomato paste
Salt and freshly ground black pepper, to taste
¼ cup finely chopped fresh parsley or basil
½ pound Gruyère cheese, thinly sliced

EQUIPMENT

One ungreased baking sheet; 1 roasting pan

PREPARATION
15 mins.

For the shell: Roll the puff pastry to ⅛ inch thickness. Cut a 6 x 14-inch strip, carefully trimming the edges before making the cuts. Turn the piece over onto the ungreased baking sheet.

 Lightly beat together the yolks and cream and brush some of it over the pastry. Cut ½-inch strips from the remaining pastry. Turn over and place them on the edges of the larger piece to form a border.

PREHEAT

Preheat the oven to 400° while the pastry chills.

CHILLING
20 mins.

Chill the pastry for 20 minutes. Prick all over with a fork. Brush the rim with the remaining egg-cream mixture.

BAKING
400°
30–40 mins.

Bake until the shell is a golden brown, 30 to 40 minutes. Prick the bottom of the tart several times during the baking to prevent it from puffing too much.

FILLING
15 mins.

While the tart cools, keep the oven on. Cut the peppers into quarters. Remove the seeds and ribs. Place skin side up on a roasting pan and broil until the skins are black, about 8 minutes. Drop the peppers into a brown paper bag for 5 minutes to soften the skins. Remove the skins and cut the peppers into thin strips. Lower oven heat to 350°.

COOKING
16 mins.

In a skillet heat the oil and add the sliced onion. Cook for 5 minutes over medium heat and add the garlic. Cook for 1 minute longer. Add the roasted peppers, red pepper flakes, tomatoes, tomato paste, and salt and pepper.

 Cook over moderately high heat, stirring constantly, until

most of the moisture has evaporated, about 10 minutes. Stir in the parsley and/or basil.

ASSEMBLING
5 mins.

When ready to serve, carefully spoon the red pepper mixture into the cooled tart shell. Decorate with a crisscross of thin slices of the Gruyère cheese.

Warm briefly in a 350° oven. Cut the tart into strips and serve.

OMELETTE SOUFFLÉ AU GRAND MARNIER

[SERVES 2]

This is the omelette masterpiece Mary prepared for the students on the final day of classes. It takes only minutes to make.

INGREDIENTS

3 eggs, separated
¼ cup Grand Marnier
Zest of 1 orange, grated
3 tablespoons plus 1 teaspoon sugar
1 tablespoon butter

EQUIPMENT

One omelette pan

PREPARATION
5 mins.

In a bowl beat the egg yolks until thick. Add the Grand Marnier and orange zest and beat again.

In a separate bowl whisk the egg whites until stiff, gradually adding the 3 tablespoons of sugar, and beat well. Fold the meringue mixture into the yolk mixture.

COOKING
2 mins.

Heat the butter in the omelette pan, until almost brown. Pour in the egg mixture and cook for 1 minute, or until set. Turn out onto a flameproof dish, sprinkle with the 1 teaspoon of sugar, and put under the broiler to brown slightly.

Serve at once. It is *delicious*.

ᗡᗡᗡᗡᗡ*On the Road—NAPA VALLEY, CALIFORNIA*

A Ride to Saint Helena

It was raining cats and dogs, with an occasional cruising sea gull gliding alongside, when we drove across the Golden Gate Bridge. Above, the bridge towers were hidden in fog. Looking down I could see an outbound freighter feeling its way through the mist. It was not a pretty day.

The driver, however, found it exhilarating, and even more so when she turned the car off U.S. 101 onto the curves, dips, and hills of the lesser road leading to the Napa Valley wine country.

"Isn't this just great?" Carol Field wanted to know. There was a ceiling of low fog pressing down from above. The wet blacktop glistened. The small Toyota was moving fast; I sat reassured by a tightly buckled seat belt and long legs jammed against the dash. We scooted past a slow-moving truck throwing a heavy spray our way. Windshield wipers were going full out.

"Oh, this is just like Tuscany," she said in a voice soft with nostalgia. "Isn't this beautiful—even in the rain. Look at those green fields, and those lovely live oak trees. Look at those sheep, and over there, two horses."

She is an authority on the Italian look, certainly, for she has spent many months in Italy researching three highly authoritative books, *The Hill Towns of Italy; The Italian Baker;* and her latest, *Celebrating Italy.*

The scene, though still a wet one, suddenly changed from ranch land to vineyard. We were in wine country, zipping past rows and rows of grapevines.

"It's a pity," she said. "The valley has become too popular, too appealing. Too many people, both locals and visitors, trying to travel on too few roads. The vineyards are considering moving their tasting rooms to the entrance to the valley in hopes of cutting down traffic into the interior."

Carol and I had come to Saint Helena, deep in the valley, to visit Karen Mitchell and the Model Bakery, where Carol said she believed some of the best sourdough breads in the Bay Area are being baked. And, like Steve Sullivan at the Acme Bakery in Berkeley (page 179), Karen bakes it with a homemade but highly successful leavening of fermented grapes and flour.

Karen's husband was a helicopter pilot in Vietnam, and when the war was over the two of them spent two years in France. "I loved it. I especially loved the *boulangeries.* When we came back here I was deter-

mined to start a bakery and make the same kinds of breads that we had in France."

In Saint Helena they found an old bakery with two large 12-foot-deep brick ovens, fired by gas jets swung into position in the throats of the ovens and pulled aside when the oven temperature reached 700°. During the day, as the ovens cool, different products are baked beginning with breads and, finally, in soft heat, the cakes.

Not all of her breads are leavened with natural grape yeast, but they are the ones that are the most sought after. A loaf costs $3. "It is an expensive production, up to two days counting all the steps, so we bake-off just twice a week."

Whenever she needs a new sourdough starter, Karen goes to an old vineyard nearby that has not been "nuked"—sprayed with sulfur—and there she picks a five-gallon bucket of the valley's Gamay grapes.

"I crush the grapes in the pail, cover it with a cloth to keep out the fruit flies, and put it aside for a week near the ovens where it is about a hundred degrees. By then it will be a bubbly sort of wine, with a sugar content of between one and two percent. I strain off the juice, and discard the skins and stems. Each day I lightly 'feed' the juice by mixing in a small portion of whole-wheat flour. By the end of two weeks I have a starter the consistency of a thick batter."

Making the sponge with the starter is the second step. She measures 4 pounds of the starter to which she adds 6 quarts water, 10 pounds whole-wheat flour, and 2 tablespoons salt. This thick mixture is left to ferment 6 to 12 hours in a warm place. To the sponge she adds 5 cups water, 8 tablespoons salt, and 8 to 10 pounds flour (3 of whole-wheat and the balance of white), approximately. When the dough has been kneaded, she scales it into 2-pound pieces. These are left at room temperature for 5 to 6 hours to rise.

When light and puffy, the pieces are shaped into loaves, covered, and left to rise a second time before they are baked in a 425° oven.

It was still pouring when Carol and I came out of the bakery under umbrellas. We sped back to San Francisco through hills touched with the soft green of early winter in California.

"Just like Italy." Carol sighed.

WALNUT CREEK, CALIFORNIA

Today's Farmer—Marion Cunningham

When the late James Beard was asked to suggest a cook who could write or a writer who could cook to rework and rewrite completely the venerated eighty-year-old *Fannie Farmer Cookbook*, he replied without hesitation, "Marion Cunningham!" And, as if his nomination needed support: "She is enthusiastic. One of the best."

Marion and I were seated on the patio of her home among the orchards and fields on the northwest slope of Mount Diablo, some fifty miles from San Francisco.

She laughed: "When I took the assignment from Knopf I had no idea what I was getting into. No idea. None! Until that moment, my credentials were only for helping James in the cooking-school kitchen, and cooking for the family and the P.T.A. When I said yes I thought it was something I could do in a few months. But when I got into it—with all the enthusiasm for which James gave me credit—I discovered I had taken on a monumental task. I was five years in the kitchen!"

The old book had gone through eleven editions, beginning in 1896 when it was published under the title of *The Boston Cooking-School Cook Book by Fannie Merritt Farmer.* Over the years it had become cluttered with shortcuts and elaborate recipes. Also it had gotten away from simple home cooking. Many instructions had become meaningless. Unfortunately, the old book was pushing prefab food rather than natural ingredients.

The new *Fannie Farmer Cookbook* published in 1979 was an immediate success, and, with this and subsequent books, Marion joined the ranks of best-selling cookbook authors and food authorities in this country.

Marion—tall, attractive, with a great smile and white hair pulled back into a tight bun—has a charm and a warmth about her that makes it fun to be her friend. We moved into the house to join Marje and Joyce McGillis, her associate and a computer consultant, for a lunch of sausage, polenta, fresh chopped tomato and basil salad, sourdough bread, and steamed persimmon pudding with whipped cream.

The view from the dining room was spectacular in all directions—rolling hills, live oak trees with bunches of mistletoe growing in their branches, horses and cattle in the fields in the valleys below the house, the crown of Mount Diablo in the distance against a cloudless deep blue sky. Fruit and nut trees embraced the house. Almost a half century before, Marje and I had driven across the cattle guard beyond Marion's house and up the mountain to a picnic ground near the peak. We had driven from San Francisco on rationed gas (the war had just started) for our young daughter's first picnic.

Marion picked up the conversation:

"The thing that delights me about food today is that all kinds of Americans—young people, men, career women, as well as housewives—are rediscovering the joys of real cooking, making their favorite dishes from scratch, and working with fresh ingredients. They are filling the kitchen with tempting cooking aromas and setting tables of which they can be proud.

"Yes, I think we are experiencing a true return to what we have always considered home cooking."

Here are two of my favorite recipes from her collection.

CIOPPINO

[SERVES 6]

Cioppino, a marvelous seafood stew, was created by the wives of fishermen in San Francisco's Italian fishing colony. It is to the Italians what bouillabaisse is to the French fisherman in Marseilles. It is a combined treasure of fish and shellfish. Seldom are the ingredients the same because much depends on what is available from the sea that day. If clams are not to be had, substitute mussels. If crab is scarce, substitute lobster tails. I substituted bottled clam juice for water to further accent the seafood flavor.

INGREDIENTS
2 large onions, chopped
3 carrots, chopped
3 garlic cloves, mashed
½ cup olive oil
1 cup chopped fresh parsley (reserve ¼ cup, to garnish)
4 cups tomato sauce
2 cups water or bottled clam juice
1½ teaspoons crumbled dried thyme
1 tablespoon crumbled dried basil
3 pounds clams in shell, scrubbed
2 pounds white fish fillets
2 crabs, cooked and cracked
¼ cup dry white wine
Pinch of cayenne pepper
Salt, to taste
½ cup minced parsley, to garnish

EQUIPMENT
One large kettle, with cover

PREPARATION
8 mins.
In a large kettle, sauté the onions, carrots, and garlic in olive oil until the onions are translucent and soft, about 8 minutes.

COOKING
70 mins.
Add the parsley, tomato sauce, water or clam juice, thyme, and basil. Partially cover and simmer for 45 minutes. If the soup gets too thick, add a little water.

Add the clams and simmer for 10 minutes. Add the fish and crabs, and simmer 5 minutes more.

Stir in the wine, cayenne pepper, and salt, simmer for an additional 10 minutes.

FINAL STEP
The fish and shellfish may be arranged on a large platter and served, with the broth ladled separately. Sprinkle liberally with the minced parsley.

continued

Furnish each guest with a bib as well as large napkins because fingers are expected to augment forks.

Pass nutcrackers and picks to get the meat out of stubborn crab shells.

Serve with hot, crusty peasant bread in big chunks, plenty of butter, and a hearty red wine.

SWEETBREADS À LA NAPOLI

[SERVES 4]

It was not until I had traveled extensively that I realized to my great surprise that not everyone shared my taste for sweetbreads. My mother did them beautifully. My father had an understanding with Perry Jones, the butcher, that we would have first call on a pound of this most delicate of variety meats whenever it came into his shop.

When shopping for sweetbreads, which is the animal's thymus, look for moisture and freshness. They should be rosy-colored if they come from a steer and whitish if they come from a calf or lamb. Those from a calf are considered the choicest sweetbread available.

Below is Marion's basic recipe for preparing sweetbreads. The sweetbreads may be blanched a day or so beforehand, covered loosely, and stored in the refrigerator. I have added my own touch by serving them with a creamy cheese sauce over toast rounds.

INGREDIENTS
1 pound sweetbreads, as prepared below
2 tablespoons lemon juice or vinegar
½ teaspoon salt
1½ cups heavy cream
6 tablespoons unsalted butter
2 tablespoons beef stock, homemade (see page 560) or store-bought
Salt, to taste
1 cup grated Parmesan cheese
8 pieces of toast, cut into 3½-inch rounds
8 mushroom caps

EQUIPMENT
Four individual baking dishes

BEFOREHAND
2 hours
Prepare the sweetbreads by soaking them in 1 quart of cold water in a medium saucepan for 1 hour. Remove the sweetbreads; add to the soaking water the lemon juice or vinegar and salt and bring to a boil. Add the sweetbreads and simmer gently for 15 minutes. Drain, then plunge immediately into cold water. Allow

the cold water to run over the sweetbreads to cool them rapidly. Working gently with a sharp knife, trim away the membranes and connecting tubes. Pat dry.

PREHEAT

Preheat the oven to 350°.

PREPARATION

Spoon 2 tablespoons of heavy cream into each of the baking dishes.

COOKING
10–15 mins.

Cut the sweetbreads into 8 pieces. Melt 2 tablespoons of butter in a skillet and sauté the sweetbreads quickly. When they are lightly brown, add the beef broth, stirring to blend until glazed. Salt lightly, remove the sweetbreads and set aside.

Mix the remaining 1 cup of cream with the cheese. Spread it on the toast rounds.

Melt the remaining 4 tablespoons of butter in the skillet. Sauté the mushroom caps until they darken slightly but are still firm; set aside.

ASSEMBLING
5 mins.

Put 2 toast rounds in each dish. On each piece of toast, place a slice of sweetbread and then a mushroom cap.

BAKING
8 mins.

Bake, covered with foil, for 8 minutes. Serve hot.

⋙SAN FRANCISCO, CALIFORNIA

Master Baker—Jim Dodge

Jim Dodge bakes some of the finest pastries to be found anywhere—in this or any other country. For a decade he was the pastry chef at the Stanford Court, the many-starred hotel on Nob Hill in San Francisco at the intersection of the two remaining cable-car lines. He wrote the award-winning pastry book *The American Baker*, and more recently *Baking with Jim Dodge*. In 1992 he opened an American version of a European bistro in Hong Kong called The American Pie.

Jim Dodge is the kind of friendly, bright, and witty person you look forward to seeing the next time you are in town. In recent years our paths have crossed a number of times. We have had the same editor at Simon & Schuster and, through her, we have been kept informed of

what the other was doing. We both taught classes at the highly regarded Tante Marie's Cooking School in San Francisco, and we have been on the same panel of judges for WinterBake, a national baking competition.

When he was a child, Jim spent hours in the kitchen and dining rooms of his family's hotels in New Hampshire and upstate New York. "Early we children were taught to appreciate and enjoy wholesome, carefully prepared food. Later my classical training with a Swiss chef taught me to create the full range of traditional desserts. Then I moved on to follow my own instincts and tastes."

Bit by bit he formed a philosophy about making desserts that seems right for the lives we live today. American cooks, he believes, have never felt themselves bound by European tradition that dictates the "correct" way to flavor a certain sauce or decorate a particular cake.

"Our desserts developed from the ground up—determined by the fruits, nuts, and dairy products offered by the land itself. Our country is so vast that desserts developed regional styles. Now, no matter where you live, every imaginable kind of fruit is in the market."

Jim paused. "Modern technology is both wonderful and terrible. In supplying us with all kinds of ingredients the year round, we have begun to forget the basic truth on which our rich baking heritage is based: that the time to enjoy any fruit is when it is at the peak of its season, ripe and luscious and so abundant it begs to be picked and eaten. We have been so charmed by the exotic that we sometimes pass over local produce, which has always been the best for baking."

Advice?

• Be a fussy shopper. "Let it be known you want only the best, and when your grocer goes out of his way to steer you toward it, show your appreciation. Next week he'll be waiting to tell you about his terrific new shipments of plums or nectarines. Consider the recipes you can make according to what's fresh and delicious in the market today."

• If pears are prime at the moment but pears are not what you want, do not hesitate to go to a frozen fruit of choice. "With the new techniques in flash freezing, frozen fruits—cranberries, blueberries, peaches, raspberries, and strawberries—do remarkably well.

• Desserts should start with one predominant flavor. "The magnificent strawberries or peaches or pears that are irresistibly ripe and sweet should dictate the direction the baker should go with a dessert choice. A dessert with four or five main ingredients is confusing and inevitably disappointing."

• Keep sugar to a minimum. "Too much sugar will mask the rich, lively flavors of fresh fruit with the result that you taste sweetness instead of that wonderful fresh fruit you started with. I refuse to put anything artificial or second-rate in my desserts."

• The most impressive desserts are the simplest. "Clean lines and understated decorations are always more striking than elaborate embellishments. A dessert is not a work of art to be admired from a distance; it is an invitation to pleasure, the promise of a delightful eating experience."

• A dessert's first appeal is visual. "What appears on the outside is a promise of what waits within. Once you have created anticipation, you either fulfill that anticipation or you disappoint. A cake decorated with berries promises berries inside. A cake topped with clouds of whipped cream promises lightness. If you decorate a chocolate cake with fresh cherries but there are no cherries inside, people will be disappointed, even if it's a fine chocolate cake."

• Finally, the presentation of any dessert is part of the pleasure it gives. Even if a dessert needs to be refrigerated until shortly before serving, bring it to the table whole, set on a simple, elegant plate, and let your guests enjoy the way it looks. "Part of the pleasure of a great dessert, after all, is the admiration and appreciation that comes to the cook."

BLUEBERRY-LEMON CAKE

[SERVES 12]

The lively flavor of this striking cake by Jim Dodge—a study in blue and white—comes from the simple combination of lemony whipped cream and fresh blueberries.

INGREDIENTS	*1 Génoise (recipe follows)* *5 large eggs* *¾ cup sugar* *¾ cup fresh lemon juice (about 6 lemons)* *½ cup (1 stick) unsalted butter* *2 cups whipping cream* *2 pints blueberries (the spicier the better), washed and drained*
EQUIPMENT	Pastry bag with #7 plain tip
BEFOREHAND 3–24 hours	Make the *Génoise* recipe 3 hours to 1 day ahead.
PREPARATION 20 mins.	In a bowl whisk together the eggs and sugar until light. Add the lemon juice and continue mixing until well blended. Pour into the top of a double boiler and stir constantly over simmering water until very thick, about 10 minutes. Remove from the heat and stir in the butter.
REFRIGERATING 2 hours	Transfer to a bowl and refrigerate the lemon cream until cold, about 2 hours. This step can be done a day ahead and kept refrigerated until needed.
ASSEMBLING 15 mins.	Whip the cream to soft peaks. Fold in the lemon cream until smooth and evenly colored. Place one sponge layer on a cake plate and spread about ¼ inch of lemon cream evenly over the top of the layer. Cover the cream with a layer of blueberries, gently pressing the berries into the cream. Cover the berries with another layer of cream. Place the second sponge layer on top. Set aside about 1 cup of cream for decorating and spread the rest evenly over the top and sides of the cake.
DECORATING 5 mins.	Spoon the reserved cream into the pastry bag with plain tip and pipe 12 dome-shaped mounds evenly spaced around the perimeter of the cake. Heap the remaining berries in the center inside the domes.
CHILLING 2 hours	Refrigerate for at least 2 hours.
FINAL STEP	Remove the cake from the refrigerator 30 minutes before serving.

GÉNOISE
(White Sponge Cake)

[MAKES ONE 2-LAYER 9-INCH CAKE]

INGREDIENTS	*4 tablespoons (½ stick) unsalted butter* *⅔ cup cake flour* *½ cup plus 2 tablespoons sugar* *4 large whole eggs, plus 4 large egg yolks*
EQUIPMENT	One 9-inch cake pan, with circle of parchment cut to fit the bottom. Butter the bottom and sides of the pan. Line the bottom with parchment, then flour the sides.
PREHEAT	Preheat the oven to 300°.
PREPARATION 20 mins.	Melt the butter and keep it warm (body temperature is ideal). Sift together the flour and 2 tablespoons of sugar. Toss them a little between your fingers to be certain they are thoroughly mixed. Set aside. Bring some water to boil in a large saucepan or the bottom of a double boiler. In a large stainless-steel bowl, stir together the egg yolks, whole eggs, and the ½ cup of sugar. Whisk continuously over the boiling water just until hot (don't cook the eggs), about 4 minutes. Transfer to the bowl of an electric mixer and whip at high speed until doubled in volume. The batter will be pale and thick. Beat at medium-high speed for a few more minutes, until the batter forms a ribbon and holds a deep crease, about 5 to 6 minutes. Sprinkle the flour-sugar mixture over the batter and gently but briskly fold it in. Transfer one-quarter of the batter to a small bowl; stir the melted butter and fold it in. Fold this mixture back into the rest of the batter, working quickly so that the butter does not thicken. Pour immediately into the prepared pan.
BAKING 300° 1 hour 10 mins.	Bake for about 1 hour and 10 minutes, until the center springs back when lightly touched. The top will be lightly browned, and when you press down gently on the cake, you should hear the whisper of breaking air bubbles. This is a delicate cake. It can fall 1 inch or more if you slam the oven door or open it too many times or too wide during baking.
RESTING 10 mins.	Let the cake rest a full 10 minutes in the pan before turning it out onto a wire rack. If you are not going to use the sponge

immediately, let it cool completely, about 25 minutes, then wrap it in plastic wrap and refrigerate (leave the parchment attached). You may also freeze the sponge for several days. Remove from the freezer and unwrap just before assembling the cake.

TRIMMING
5 mins.

The hard outer skin that develops on the top and bottom of a sponge cake should always be trimmed off before assembling the final cake. First cut off any raised area on the top of the sponge to make the surface completely level, and then trim off the remaining skin. Turn the cake over and trim the bottom.

FINAL STEP

It is important to keep the knife level as you cut. Use a long-blade slicer or serrated knife. Lay one hand flat on top of the cake to steady it. Make sure it is being held flat. Draw the knife through the cake horizontally in one long cut to provide 2 layers.

COCONUT CREAM PIE

[SERVES 10]

The grated white chocolate that crowns this pie brings out the flavor of the coconut. Jim is highly partial to unsweetened coconut flakes that are available in natural food stores and in most markets that sell ingredients in bulk. The flakes are more flavorful and not as dry as grated coconut. Smell the coconut before you buy it; old coconut smells stale.

   To add the aroma and tropical flavor of toasted coconut to the piecrust, add ½ cup unsweetened coconut flakes when you make it. Mix them with the flour.

INGREDIENTS

One 9-inch piecrust, made with coconut flakes if desired
2 cups milk
2 cups unsweetened coconut flakes
2 vanilla beans, split
½ cup sugar
2 tablespoons all-purpose flour
2 large eggs
4 tablespoons (½ stick) unsalted butter
1 cup whipping cream
2 ounces white chocolate

EQUIPMENT

One pie pan; pastry bag with #7 star tip

BEFOREHAND
30 mins.

Bake the desired piecrust.

PREPARATION
10 mins.

Bring the milk to a boil in a heavy-bottomed saucepan. Add the coconut. Scrape the pulp from the vanilla beans and add both the pulp and the scraped beans to the milk. Simmer together for 5 minutes.

Meanwhile, sift the sugar and flour together in a mixing bowl. Add the eggs and beat until light. Stir ¼ cup of the hot milk into the egg mixture, then pour the egg mixture into the saucepan of milk and cook at high heat, stirring vigorously with a wire whisk, until the center bubbles and the mixture is very thick, about 3 minutes.

Remove from the heat and stir in the butter. Set aside to cool.

ASSEMBLING
10 mins.

When both the pie shell and filling are cool, remove the vanilla beans and pour the filling into the shell. Smooth the top with a spatula or the back of a spoon.

Whip the cream to soft peaks and spoon it into the pastry bag. Make a circle of whipped cream rosettes around the edge of the pie.

Rake the chocolate or grate it with a vegetable peeler into long, thin curls.

Arrange the chocolate in the center of the pie, with all the pieces pointing toward the edge—creating a sunburst pattern. (If your chocolate is not in graceful pieces, just heap it in the center of the pie.)

FINAL STEP

Serve immediately, or refrigerate until ready to serve.

〰〰〰〰BERKELEY, CALIFORNIA

The Acme Bread Company— Steve and Suzie Sullivan

In the San Francisco Bay Area—a region fiercely devoted to its sourdough breads—Steve Sullivan and his Acme Bread Company bake some of the finest sourdough breads to be found.

Critics say his breads are better than the loaves that had been baked by venerable San Francisco bakeries in the century-old Bay Area sourdough tradition. Sadly, the quality of the loaves from these old bakeries' was diminished a few years back when the once fiercely independent family-owned bakeries were merged into one giant baking conglomerate. Then Steve Sullivan came along. Tall, slender, tanned, his long hair tied into a ponytail, Steve *is* the Acme Bread Company.

I had driven across the Bay Bridge to introduce myself only to discover that he had been baking with my bread books even before he started Acme. Steve baked his first bread, an Armenian loaf, when he was ten years old. Now, a decade later, Steve, his wife, Suzie, and a crew of twenty bake around the clock to keep up with the demand from Bay Area restaurants as well as customers who walk in off the street to buy at retail counters set close to the ovens in the older bakery at 1610 San Pablo Avenue. The new and larger bakery is two miles away on Ninth Avenue.

With a degree in rhetoric from the University of California, Steve's venture into baking as a livelihood began with washing dishes and scrubbing vegetables at Alice Waters's Chez Panisse restaurant in Berkeley. He moved from dishwasher to waiter and then back to the kitchen as baker. He got the job when the breads he had been baking in his apartment oven won the overwhelming approval of an informal test panel—Alice and the kitchen staff.

Steve handed me a book. I didn't recognize it. Its once blue cover was almost totally white, encrusted with flour. Its dog-eared pages were marked by notes and memos.

"That's your *Breads of France*." He laughed. "My first loaf was your

Monsieur Monfort's French Bread, which calls for a total of six hours of fermentation of the dough as it rises. Wonderful flavor. My second loaf was *Pain de Campagne Madame Doz*, its starter made with buttermilk and vinegar. I always had a real affinity for it because it is a genuinely rustic loaf."

Steve and Suzie opened the Acme in 1982. Friends chipped in to raise the necessary $40,000 to make it possible. At the same time Suzie discovered she was pregnant. ("A happy coincidence," she said.)

"When we opened," Steve explained, "some people said Berkeley didn't need another bakery. 'How about a hot dog stand? We need a really good hot dog stand.' Well, we didn't intend it to be just another Bay bakery. We were going to do something special. And I think we did."

While Steve liked the breads made with the long fermentation of yeast-raised dough to enhance the flavor as in the *pain ordinaire,* he was at the same time looking for a natural starter to give his bread a distinctive flavor and texture all its own. He found it in a small village in southern France. An understanding *boulanger* suggested he try making his own leavening with the hulls, stems, and juice of crushed grapes. The grapes should not have been sprayed, the *boulanger* added, or the bacteria necessary for fermentation will have been killed.

It was October when Steve got home. The grapes in his father's backyard were ripe and swollen on the vines. He picked several dozen bunches, wrapped them in cheesecloth, and crushed them into a large bucket. He left the crushed grapes and juice just as they were in the bottom of the bucket and added water and flour to make a thin slurry. The pail was covered with a cloth to keep out the bugs. Six hours later he returned to find the mixture foaming and frothing. Success!

"I took off about a half gallon of the liquid, and stirred in more flour to make a thick batterlike mass. It almost immediately began to work and bubble. It smelled slightly sour, but pleasantly so. I knew something good was going on." It was the genesis of all the thousands of sourdough loaves that have since come from the Acme ovens.

Not all of Acme's breads are sourdough. "Surprisingly, our French customers from the university don't care for the sourdough. It is a taste strange to them. For them and others we bake about a thousand baguettes leavened with a commercial yeast. They want the flavor that comes with a long fermentation of the dough, not from the sourness of a starter."

Unlike the old San Francisco bakers who considered their starters treasured secrets not to be revealed, Steve does not agree. "Any customer who brings in a glass jar is welcome to have some. No charge. I ask only that they treat it with affection."

The problem that most home bakers have with a sourdough starter, Steve believes, is that they don't care for it properly. They leave it unattended for months in the refrigerator and then expect immediate results when it is brought out from the cold. Give it at least forty-eight hours to regain its vitality, he says.

"If a starter has a cheesy, funky smell, throw it out. Start over. When you have a good starter going replenish it often, at least every two weeks. Give it your attention. Let it know you love it. The sourdough tradition goes back to the days when women at home baked on a regular schedule, at least once a week; this kept the starter alive and active and happy."

Advice for beginners?

"Concentrate on doing one bread until you get a feel for it. Bake it a dozen times. Don't do as I did. I was seduced and fascinated by all the different recipes. I would do a molasses bread and then a cheese bread and then jump to a rye. I didn't feel confident with the feel of dough until I zeroed in on one basic white bread. I baked it over and over again. And, finally, after about ten loaves I knew what the dough should feel like."

MONSIEUR MONFORT'S FRENCH BREAD

[MAKES 2 MEDIUM ROUND OR 4 LONG LOAVES]

This is one of the first breads to be baked by the Acme Bakery and still one of the favorites with customers. It does not get its good taste from a long-standing sour or from a "chef" left over from yesterday's dough, but from a freshly made (with yeast) dough left to rise and mature in flavor through three stages for a total of 6 hours.

INGREDIENTS
3½ cups all-purpose flour, approximately
3½ cups bread flour, approximately
2 packages dry yeast
4 teaspoons salt
3 cups hot water (120°–130°)

EQUIPMENT
One baking sheet for hearth loaves, greased or Teflon; or if available, four 18-inch-long French bread pans, greased; 1 dough blade or putty knife

PREPARATION BY
HAND OR MIXER
15 mins.
Place a dough blade or putty knife to one side before you begin.
Stir the two flours together. In a large bowl or mixer bowl measure 5 cups of the blended flour and stir in the yeast and salt. Form a well in the bottom of the bowl and pour in the hot water. If by hand, slowly pull the flour into the liquid with a wooden spoon—until it is fully absorbed. If in the mixer, attach the flat beater and mix at medium speed. Add flour, ½ cup at a time, to

make a shaggy mass that can be lifted from the bowl and placed on the work surface—or left in the mixer under the dough hook. The dough should be tacky but not hopelessly sticky.

KNEADING
10 mins.

If by hand, begin turning and folding the dough with the dough blade or putty knife. Sprinkle flour on the work surface and your hands if the dough is sticky. Continue to lift, fold, and turn for 10 minutes. Throw the dough down against the work surface to break the lift-fold-turn rhythm. The dough will become elastic but will continue to stick to moist fingers unless powdered with flour.

If in the mixer, attach the dough hook. Stop the mixer occasionally to determine the development of the dough. Add flour if sticky. The soft dough will clean the sides of the mixer but will not form the compact ball as with other doughs. Knead for 10 minutes.

PREPARATION BY
PROCESSOR
4 mins.

Attach the short plastic blade. Measure 6 cups of the blended flour and the yeast and salt into the work bowl. With the processor running, pour the hot water through the feed tube. The dough will be a heavy batter. Add the balance of the flour—½ cup at a time—to make a rough mass that spins with the blade and cleans the sides of the bowl. Stop the machine, remove the cover, and test the dough between your fingers. It should be slightly sticky but not wet. Add flour if necessary.

KNEADING
1 min.

With the processor on, knead for 1 minute.

FIRST RISING
2–3 hours

Turn the dough into a greased bowl. Cover tightly with plastic wrap, and leave at room temperature until the dough has expanded fully to more than double its volume, 2 to 3 hours.

SECOND RISING
1–2 hours

Turn back the plastic, punch down the dough, and recover the bowl. Allow the dough to double in volume, 1 to 2 hours.

SHAPING
15 mins.

Turn the dough onto the floured work surface, punch down, and knead briefly to press out the bubbles. Divide the dough, which will weigh about 3¾ pounds, into as many loaves as you want. Form into balls and let them rest for 5 minutes.

For a long loaf, flatten a ball into an oval. Fold over, flatten with blows with the sides of the open hand, fold again, and roll under the palms of the hands. If the dough resists, let it rest while preparing the other pieces. Return to the partially formed loaf and continue to roll under the palms until it is shaped. The seam will disappear.

continued

The long pieces of dough can be placed directly on a baking sheet to rise, although they will slump somewhat because the dough lacks stiffness. They can be placed in a *banneton* (a long basket lined with a cloth and liberally sprinkled with flour. The baskets will direct the dough upwards during the rise period.

By placing the shaped dough in a *couche*, a length of canvas (18 x 36 inches) or pastry cloth, and pulling the cloth up between the loaves to separate them, the home baker can do as M. Monfort does with large loaves. Sprinkle the cloth liberally with flour beforehand. The dough expands upwards and puts pressure on the loaf or loaves adjoining to do the same.

A third way is to place the long loaves in half-cylindrical, French-type pans.

Round loaves can be placed on the corners of the baking sheet to rise, but because of the softness of this particular dough it is often better to use cloth-lined baskets.

THIRD RISING
1–2 hours

Cover the loaves with a wool cloth or rest a sheet of wax or parchment paper on glasses over the dough so it doesn't touch. If it does, it may stick. The wool will not. Let the dough rise for 1 to 2 hours.

PREHEAT

Twenty minutes before the bake period preheat the oven to 425°. Place a broiler pan or similar vessel on the lowest shelf. Five minutes before baking, pour 1 cup of hot tap water into the pan.

BAKING
425°
25–30 mins.

If the loaf was raised in a basket, tip it onto your hand and lower gently onto the baking sheet. The dough raised on canvas is gently rolled onto a flat cardboard or cookie sheet held in one hand and transferred to the baking sheet.

With a razor blade, slash the top of the round loaves in a tic-tac-toe design. For the long loaves, cut a series of diagonal slashes.

Spray lightly with water as you place them in the hot oven. Five minutes later spray the loaves again. Do it from the oven door. Don't pull out the loaves or the moist, hot air will escape.

The loaves will be fully oven sprung (expanded) in about 18 minutes, at which time color will begin to tinge the crusts. The pan should now be empty of water.

Bake in the oven until the loaves are a golden brown, a total time of 25 to 30 minutes. Turn over 1 loaf and tap the bottom crust with a forefinger. A hard hollow sound means the bread is baked. If not, return to the oven for an additional 5 minutes. If the loaves appear to be browning too quickly, cover with a piece of foil or brown sack paper.

Midway in the bake period and again near the end of it, shift the loaves to expose them equally to the temperature variations in the oven.

FINAL STEP   Remove the bread from the oven. Place the loaves on a wire rack to cool. The *boulanger* stands his loaves on end so that cool air circulates around them. For a bright, shiny crust, brush lightly with water, slightly salted.
Bon appétit!

PAIN DE CAMPAGNE MADAME DOZ
(Madame Doz' Peasant Loaf)

[MAKES TWO 2-POUND HEARTH LOAVES]

The peasant bread baked by Madame Doz and Acme is made with *levain*, a portion of dough left from a previous bake. In her country kitchen in France, Madame Doz kept her *levain* for 1 and 2 weeks in a tray under the tabletop. At Acme, the turnover is faster and *levain* moves ahead from one batch of dough to the beginning of the next in a matter of hours.

A *levain* can be kept by the home baker in the refrigerator for several days, but it must be from a dough without sugar or shortening or it may spoil. Keep *levain* in a container that will allow the dough to expand during its first few hours in the refrigerator.

INGREDIENTS   *STARTER*
1½ cups bread or all-purpose flour
1 package dry yeast
⅔ cup warm water (105°–115°)
⅓ cup buttermilk, room temperature
1 teaspoon vinegar

LEVAIN
All of the starter
1 cup water, room temperature
2 cups stone-ground or plain whole-wheat flour
½ cup wheat germ
1 cup bread or all-purpose flour

DOUGH
All of the levain
2 cups water, room temperature
4½ cups all-purpose or bread flour, approximately
4 teaspoons salt
4 teaspoons water

continued

EQUIPMENT

One baking sheet, greased or Teflon, for round *boules*; long pans for *baguettes* or *ficelles*, greased

STARTER
12–36 hours

Measure the flour into a medium bowl, and stir in the dry yeast. Pour in the water, buttermilk, and vinegar. Stir to make a heavy batter. Cover tightly with plastic wrap and let stand at room temperature for a minimum of 12 hours, or until it rises and falls. The starter can be held for 24 to 36 hours if more convenient.

LEVAIN
6–12 hours

A true *levain* is taken from the dough of a previous bake, but for a beginning batch the process starts here.

Uncover the bowl containing the starter. Stir in the water, whole-wheat flour, and wheat germ.

The *levain* is to be a soft ball of dough, not a batter, so add sufficient white flour, about 1 cup, to make a solid mass. Work in the flour by hand or with the dough hook.

Replace the plastic wrap and leave at room temperature for a minimum of 6 hours. It can be left longer if convenient. The ball of dough will rise and spread under the plastic sheet and then take on the appearance of a heavy batter.

DOUGH BY HAND
2¼ hours

Two things are different in this bread recipe. The white flour is made into a soft dough and then blended with the ball of *levain*. The salt is not added until later in the kneading. But don't forget it—set it aside now as a reminder.

Uncover the *levain*, stir it down with a rubber scraper or by hand and lift onto the work surface. Round it into a ball and set aside.

Pour the water into the bowl, and add 1½ cups of flour. Stir to blend into a thick batter. Add the rest of the flour, about ¼ cup at a time, to make a soft dough that can be lifted from the bowl. Place it on the work surface and knead the dough until it is smooth, adding sprinkles of flour if it is sticky.

Press the *levain* into a flat oval and cover with the ball of white dough. Fold the two together and continue folding and kneading by hand or with the dough hook until the two are completely blended.

The combined doughs should be elastic yet firm, so add additional flour as the kneading begins. A test is to shape the dough into a ball and see how well it retains its shape when you remove your hands. If the dough slouches badly, it needs more flour. If it holds its shape yet is elastic and responds to the finger pushing back—there may be enough flour. On the other hand, it should not be a stiff ball.

KNEADING
16 mins.

The combined doughs will blend into a light brown ball, sprinkled with tiny darker brown flakes. Use a forceful push-turn-fold motion, aggressively throwing the ball of dough down against the work surface from time to time. If the dough remains sticky, cover it with sprinkles of flour. Knead under the mixer dough hook for the same length of time, 8 minutes.

Stop the kneading for a moment to dissolve the salt in the 4 teaspoons of water. Press the dough flat with a depression in the center to hold the salt solution. Fold the dough over the liquid and return to kneading.

The dough may be slick and squishy until the liquid is absorbed; if so, sprinkle with a bit of flour. Knead for an additional 8 minutes, or a total of 16.

DOUGH BY
PROCESSOR
8 mins.

Both the *levain* and the ball of white dough can be made by hand in a bowl, as above, saving the processor for later.

Attach the short plastic dough blade.

Drop the *levain* in the processor's work bowl. Pulse for a moment and then drop in the ball of white dough. Pulse until the 2 doughs are well blended.

Pour the salt mixture into the bowl, and pulse to blend. Add ¼ cup of flour to absorb the liquid. If the dough is sticky and does not clean the bowl, add sprinkles of flour.

KNEADING
45 secs.

When the dough forms a shaggy mass and rides on the dough blade as it whirls around the bowl, knead for 45 seconds.

FIRST RISING
2 hours

Place the dough in the washed and greased bowl, cover tightly with plastic wrap, and leave at room temperature until it has more than doubled in volume, about 2 hours.

SHAPING
10 mins.

The dough can be shaped in any of the French loaves described on pages 183–84.

Remove the plastic wrap and punch down the dough with your extended fingers. Turn the dough onto a work surface and divide into as many pieces as you wish loaves. The dough will weigh about 4 pounds.

SECOND RISING
1½ hours

Cover with a cloth or wax paper and leave at room temperature to rise to *triple* its original bulk, about 1½ hours.

PREHEAT

Place broiler or other shallow pan in the oven; preheat to 450° about 20 minutes before baking. Five minutes before baking, pour 1 cup water in the pan to create steam. Use a long-handled container to pour the water.

continued

BAKING
450°
35–40 mins.

Uncover the loaves. Those in *bannetons* are turned over on the baking sheet. Those in the cloth folds (*couches*) are rolled onto a length of cardboard. Lift and roll off onto the baking sheet. Those already in pans or on a baking sheet, leave as is.

Cut the tops with a razor blade.

Place the loaves on the middle rack of the oven, or, if the top shelf is also used, be aware that bread bakes faster there and must be switched with breads on the lower shelf midway through the bake period.

Loaves are done when golden brown and crusty, about 35 to 40 minutes. Turn over one loaf and tap the bottom crust with a forefinger. If the bread sounds hard and hollow, it is baked.

FINAL STEP

Place the loaves on a metal rack to cool, or stack on end so the air can move around them freely. The loaves will crackle loudly as the crusts cool and crack.

Try to wait until the bread is almost cool before breaking it into chunks or slicing.

On the Road—LAKE ARROWHEAD, CALIFORNIA

Snow

At the time—midsummer in Indiana—it seemed like such a dandy idea.

The plan was that in December we would establish a southern California base high in the mountains at Lake Arrowhead, above San Bernardino. We had been there many times in both summer and winter to see our son, Jeff, and his wife, Linda. It seemed like an ideal place from where to move in all directions throughout the Los Angeles area and yet live most of the time above the smog and away from the daily grind of freeway congestion.

Other Christmases at Lake Arrowhead had been picture-perfect. At the most, a light sprinkle of snow, just enough for Santa's sleigh to make a landing.

This time it was different. It began to snow in the early afternoon of Christmas Eve. It was the most unusual snow I had ever seen. The flakes fell straight down. Big fat flakes. And they FELL. It was a true snow*fall*. They didn't swirl and blow. I watched fascinated. It snowed right through the night and into Christmas Day. It slowed for a few hours and then began again.

The first inkling I had that we were in for trouble was the ride at night in our son-in-law Dick's four-wheel-drive pickup across the mountain from our apartment to Jeff's place on Alpine Drive. There had been just enough traffic on the roads to pack the snow and make them ideal for sledding, which the neighborhood kids were doing with gusto.

But the roads were not ideal for us. Coming up the hill we spun into a snowbank, ricocheted, and slid backward down the hill. I remembered a back road that might get us there. It led *down* the hill. This time we slid right past Jeff's drive, spun around and into a snowbank.

There were three of us in the front seat of the truck. Susan, our daughter, was in back with the Christmas presents and the two dogs—Timothy and his mother, Katie. The car was now slipping backward continuing down the hill, with Susan looking out of the rear window telling Dick which way to steer. If the truck went into a free fall we would go over the steep embankment at the bottom of the hill. The only way to slow the backward descent was to miss the telephone poles and mailboxes yet keep the side of the truck brushing into the snowbanks until we could get to a somewhat level place at the bottom of the hill.

Susan's left, looking out the rear window, was Dick's right. It got confusing. So Susan called out instructions according to "your ring finger." Like: "More toward your ring finger." It was deathly quiet in the cab except for the ring-finger directions from Susan and the fast, shallow breaths of Marje, who was hyperventilating, which she later swore did not happen. Again we were at the bottom of the hill. We would try it one more time. If not successful it would be up to Santa to deliver the gifts and attend the family party.

Slow didn't do it, so Dick would have to approach the drive with speed. It worked. We took the back road again that led down the hill, and as we sped and slipped down toward the house, Dick abruptly whipped the truck into the drive.

For a moment there was quiet in the cab. Silent night. Then joyous yells and congratulations to the driver. The dogs barked. It was over.

For one week it snowed and thawed and snowed and rained and snowed and froze until it was impossible to drive anyplace without chains. Names of streets should have given me a clue as to what to expect —Matterhorn, Teton, Zermatt, Yukon, Everest, Alpine Way, Rim of the World, Rim Forest, Skyforest, etc. The worst winter in a decade, everybody said, and even Jeff who had been driving up and down the mountain for a dozen years thought it was unusual. Yet his tone implied that flatlanders just didn't know how to cope.

Isolated in our mountain retreat in Arrowhead Village should not be construed as a deprivation. We were less than a hundred feet away from the Lake Arrowhead Hilton Hotel with its cafés and sports club. Across from our apartment was Stater Bros. supermarket, provisioned throughout the snowstorm by determined drivers in big trucks.

But isolation meant that I could not get on with the book, the purpose of the trip. We would leave the mountain after New Year's and establish a new base on the ocean where there would be freedom of movement.

STUDIO CITY, CALIFORNIA

Cook and Friend— John Florea

John Florea has been my friend for almost a half century, yet I never cease to be amazed at his ability to be where great things happen and great food is served.

I was chief of the Time-Life bureau in San Francisco during the first months of World War II at a time when the city, blacked out from dusk to dawn, was fearful that at any moment the Japanese might bomb what remained of the badly crippled Pacific fleet tied up for repairs below our apartment on Telegraph Hill. John was a new photographer for *Life* in

Los Angeles covering Hollywood and photographing Marine Raiders in training at Camp Pendleton.

Shortly thereafter we were war correspondents for the magazines, based in Honolulu and attached to the Nimitz command. From then on John would pop in and out of my life at unexpected times and in unexpected places.

Food would always be a part of the scenario, because John loves to cook. John loves to eat. He travels with an array of spices and herbs in an attaché case. A sharp chef's knife means as much to him as a sharp photo negative.

Tonight we were in his Studio City kitchen watching him put together Rumanian dishes that he loves to prepare, *Sarmales* (stuffed cabbage rolls), and *Mamaliga Cu Brinza* (a delicious cornmeal mush with cheese). John, whose given name is Ionel Tiber Nicholai Povare, is a proud and, at times, defiant second-generation Rumanian. In 1982 the Rumanian Society of America named him its Man of the Year.

While he trimmed cabbage leaves, I sat on a stool and stirred cornmeal; we talked about the unforgettable times we shared. There was the afternoon on the beach below Diamond Head when we shot a home-movie sequence of the two of us laboring to husk a coconut to get out the meat for a fresh coconut pie. We never did get it out.

The most memorable event for us was the day Japan signed the surrender papers aboard the U.S.S. *Missouri*. It was Sunday, September 2, 1945. The place was choked with battleships, carriers, cruisers, destroyers—almost everything in the Pacific fleet was there. It was an august gathering. The *Missouri* was the centerpiece. She was the focus of all attention. There was a traffic jam of small boats getting admirals and generals and captains and colonels and war correspondents out to the ship before the deadline—11 o'clock—when the Japanese delegation was to come aboard.

I was in a launch, one of dozens jockeying for position at the ladders onto the *Missouri*. We were waved off twice and each time as we approached I was in awe of the vastness of her broadside. From my tiny cockleshell she was enormous, a giant steel wall. The Stars and Stripes above the mainmast was the same that had flown over the Capitol in Washington on the day Japan attacked Pearl Harbor. I could hear a military band rehearsing "Anchors Aweigh" somewhere on the ship. It was the third time around when a voice rang out from someplace high on the battleship.

"Hey, Bernie Clayton," a familiar voice boomed down across the water. "Dinner tonight, my ship!" Good lord, it was Florea!

I thought he was in Europe. After a year in the Pacific, he was sent by *Life* to the European theater where he had gone into Germany with Patton's troops, photographed the meeting of American and Russian soldiers, and had taken the first pictures in Buchenwald. But here he was. I should have known.

Once aboard, I was directed to the navigation bridge looking down on the table where MacArthur and the official party stood as the Japanese delegation came aboard. I saw Florea on a platform specially erected for photographers near the table. I gave him the high sign. Yes, dinner tonight! He had no idea how hungry I was for food, real food.

When the Japanese walked to stand before the table, the entire ship became silent. I could hear the scratching of the pen in the hand of Mamoru Shigemitsu, the Japanese foreign minister. Suddenly it was over. World War II had come to an end.

At that instant a remarkable thing happened. More than two thousand warplanes that had been circling out of sight during the ceremony now came low in formation over the *Missouri*. Everyone aboard the battleship—admirals and generals and sailors and soldiers and correspondents—stood transfixed by a sight that would never be repeated. Clouds of planes—fighters and bombers—filled the sky. The thunder and din of thousands of engines was as fearsome as it was thrilling.

Later in the day I made my way to John on the U.S.S. *Annacon*, a Navy command ship. In his camera case he was carrying several bottles of wine he had scrounged for this celebratory end-of-the-war dinner he had helped arrange in the officers' mess.

For the first time in months I dined on *real* food—roast turkey, glorious mashed potatoes and giblet-rich gravy, peas in a buttery sauce, tart cranberries, stacks of fresh-baked bread, and slabs of real butter and *huge* platters of ice cream.

To me it was unbelievable. I had been on Army rations for months in the Philippines, and for the past ten days in Japan, eating food prepared in the dingy, greasy kitchen of the shabby Grand Hotel on the Yokohama waterfront that smelled and tasted powerfully of fish. Old fish. The Army had commandeered the hotel for the press corps. No complaints. It was the best the Army could find. But those Navy guys. . . .

John learned to cook before he took his first photograph. He was eleven years old when he was introduced to the kitchen. In the mornings, while he was still in bed and before she left for work in a San Francisco knitting mill, his mother fried breakfast eggs and left them in the skillet covered with a pan lid.

"I hated those cold eggs. I buried them in the backyard. One day when she was planting vegetables my mother discovered them. She didn't say a word but marched me into the kitchen for my first lesson in fixing my own food. I haven't buried an egg since."

John left *Life* after the war to direct TV episodes and full-length motion pictures including "Bonanza," "Mission Impossible," "Flipper," "Sea Hunt," *Seven Brides for Seven Brothers*, and "MacGyver"—a total of more than six hundred over three decades. His photographs hang in New York City's Museum of Modern Art. He also picked up an Emmy in 1974 for his production of "The Runaways."

SARMALES
(Stuffed Cabbage Rolls)

[MAKES 18 SMALL ROLLS]

This is a winter kind of dish. Think of blustery winds, of snow drifting across the lane, of ice skating, of Santa Claus, and of kids in from sledding. But not always so.

The first time I had *sarmales* was in Hawaii. Palm trees. Warm trade winds. Sand castles. Scuba. Surf. It was Christmas week. For several hours one afternoon, John was in the kitchen of the comfortable old beach house our families were sharing, busy putting together, among many dishes, *sarmales*. They were a hit, and have remained so in this family for many Christmas dinners since.

INGREDIENTS

One 3-pound head of cabbage
4 tablespoons vegetable oil
2 medium onions, finely chopped (about 2 cups)
½ cup finely chopped celery
¾ cup raw rice
½ pound each ground pork, veal, and lean beef
2 teaspoons salt, or to taste
1 teaspoon freshly ground black pepper
¼ pound bacon, cut into ½-inch pieces
1½ pounds sauerkraut with liquid
2 smoked ham hocks
3 cups chopped tomatoes
2 cups water
1 pint sour cream

EQUIPMENT

One stockpot or casserole

PREPARATION
30 mins.

Core the cabbage and drop it into a large pot of boiling water, cooking briskly for about 10 minutes. Remove the cabbage (letting the water continue to boil), carefully detach as many of the outer leaves as you can and reserve them.

Return the rest of the cabbage to the boiling water and cook for a few minutes longer. Remove and again detach as many more leaves as possible. Repeat this process until you have separated 18 individual leaves. Put aside for the moment. Reserve the unused leaves.

In a large skillet heat the oil and add *half* of the chopped onions and all of the celery. Cover and sauté for 10 minutes, or until the onions are soft and translucent. Add the rice. Cook for an additional 5 minutes.

In a large bowl combine the pork, veal, beef, salt, and pepper and stir in the onion-rice mixture. Mix together until the ingredients are well combined.

WRAPPING
20 mins.

Lay the cabbage leaves side by side and, with a small knife, trim the tough rib end from the base of each leaf. Place 1 heaping tablespoon of the meat filling in the center of each leaf and roll up all of the leaves tightly, tucking in the ends as if you were wrapping a package. Set the rolls aside.

PREHEAT

Preheat the oven to 350°.

FRYING
10 mins.

In a large skillet fry the bacon; add the balance of the onions, cover, and cook until golden brown. Combine the bacon-onion mixture with the sauerkraut and juice in a large bowl.

ASSEMBLING
10 mins.

Chop the remaining cabbage leaves coarsely and line the bottom of a stockpot or casserole. Spread half of the sauerkraut mixture over the top of the chopped leaves.

Place the ham hocks on the bed of sauerkraut. Surround with the stuffed cabbage rolls. Cover this with the remaining sauerkraut.

Spread the tomatoes over the top and add 2 cups of water. Bring the mixture to a boil over a medium flame on the stove top.

BAKING
350°
2 hours

Place the stuffed cabbage in the oven *uncovered* and bake for 2 hours.

FINAL STEP

When the cabbage rolls are served, top each with a dollop of sour cream. Serve with a slice of *Mamaliga Cu Brinza* (recipe follows), a great companion.

A delicious wine to accompany this dish is a Rumanian Premiat.

MAMALIGA CU BRINZA
(Cornmeal Mush with Cheese)

[SERVES 8]

No matter how cornmeal is prepared—corn pone or spoon bread—it delights me. I thought I had tried every possible cornmeal recipe, but along came John Florea with a new delicious dish, a Rumanian one, put together in layers.

INGREDIENTS
5 cups water
1½ cups cornmeal, preferably yellow
2 teaspoons salt
½ pound bacon slices, cut into ½-inch pieces
2 tablespoons bacon drippings (from above)
¾ pound Cheddar cheese, roughly grated, divided into thirds
1 cup sour cream

EQUIPMENT
One casserole or deep pie dish, buttered

PREPARATION
1 hour
In a small bowl mix 1½ cups of the water, the cornmeal, and salt. Stir to mix well and set aside for an hour.

While the cornmeal is soaking, fry the bacon pieces over medium heat, about 6 minutes. Divide the bacon bits into thirds and set aside. Reserve the drippings.

COOKING
25 mins.
Bring the remaining 3½ cups of water to a boil in a medium saucepan, and stir in the cornmeal mixture—stirring constantly so there are no clumps. When the mush begins to thicken, cover and cook for 20 minutes. Stir 2 or 3 times while it cooks.

Add the bacon drippings as you stir.

PREHEAT
Preheat the oven to 350°.

SHAPING
15 mins.
Spoon the cooked mush onto a buttered platter. Dip your hands in cold water and shape the mush into a round cake about 9 inches in diameter and 1½ inches high.

Let the cake stand for 15 minutes to cool and stiffen.

ASSEMBLING
10 mins.
Hold a long thread taut, draw it horizontally through the cool mush to cut the first of three ½-inch layers. With a spatula lift off the first layer and place in the casserole.

Spread one third each of the bacon and cheese over the layer.

Repeat the cut for the second layer. Place on top of the first layer and spread another third of bacon and cheese.

Repeat for the third and final layer. Spread the remaining

bacon and cheese on top of the cake and top with the sour cream.

BAKING
350°
15–20 mins.

Bake until the cheese melts, 15 to 20 minutes.

FINAL STEP

Allow the *mamaliga* to cool for 15 minutes before slicing to serve.

XXXXX*IDYLLWILD, CALIFORNIA*

Chimney House—Sylvia Thompson

The first time I met Sylvia Thompson was aboard the French passenger barge *Palinurus*. The vessel, a converted coal barge, was tied to a pier on the Bourgogne Canal in southeastern France. She and Gene, her husband, had driven down from Paris to have dinner with her mother, one of our fellow passengers. The owner of a neighboring vineyard was also invited and, thoughtfully, brought a number of bottles of his best wines. It was a gala candlelight affair. Laughter and song rang through a night that otherwise would have known only the croak of bullfrogs.

To my delight, I discovered Sylvia was a cook and cookbook author. She and I talked for hours about food and writing and vowed to develop a correspondance to continue the discourse.

Today we climbed a California mountain to see Sylvia and Gene, our first meeting since the canal fête a decade earlier. We had come to dinner at Chimney House, their home high in the San Jacinto Mountains in southern California. We came from our resort cabin on Lake Arrowhead in the San Bernardino Mountains—for a crow it would have been a short direct flight, but for us, by auto, down one mountain, across a wide plain, and up the other, it was a three-hour drive.

It had snowed heavily in the mountains the night before; the turnoff road was nowhere in sight. Only a rope stretched between trees leading up a small rise gave indication that life existed beyond. Suddenly Gene, in heavy boots, appeared at the top. "This is it," he shouted. "Pull yourselves up on the rope because it's icy."

Chimney House, a three-story redwood and cedar chalet designed by Sylvia, was built around a river rock chimney that was the only thing left standing when an earlier dwelling burned to the ground. The house —a spectacular aerie at a six-thousand-foot elevation—rests on a giant granite boulder thrusting its way through trees into space. Beyond, the ring of mountains rise to eleven thousand feet above the desert floor; from their summit, you can see the Pacific ocean forty miles to the west.

In her fourth and most recent book, *Feasts and Friends*, Sylvia wrote about her life as a child of celebrated Hollywood parents. Her mother was a film star and a talented cook whose elegant Hollywood dinner parties were legendary.

It was her mother who was our fellow passenger on the French canal barge. It was not until the third day aboard that it came to me that the handsome older woman, Mrs. Sheeman, the artist, who was always at her easel recording life along the canal in watercolors, was the lovely actress Gloria Stuart.

Sylvia was also the daughter of a writer, and from childhood she had wanted to be a writer, too. "Then I married a writer. Finally the day came when I was free to do the writing I had always talked about. Gene said write what you know about. I realized then that what I knew best was food—the cooking, eating, and sharing of it with friends.

"For a number of years I was my mother's apprentice in the kitchen," Sylvia said. "Yet our styles could not be more dissimilar. My style has evolved over the years from an interest in the complex to a passion for simplicity.

"My mother has never made a roast beef in her life. It wouldn't interest her. Her style is based on the intricacies of composition. It borders on the baroque. Everyone adores it."

Sylvia was standing at the big kitchen stove set in place so that the cook need only glance up from pots and pans to see sky, mountains, trees, birds, storm, snow.

"More and more I find myself cooking country fare, dishes that are elegant in their simplicity," she said.

When we came she had been testing tomato recipes and was especially pleased with a rosemary tomato and mushroom sauce. She was also in the midst of what she called a "polenta frenzy." Sautéed chicken breasts, she had decided, would be splendid with both. "Cornmeal mush is beloved from Mississippi to Rumania, but to me there's something about the Italian polenta that's, well, magic."

POLENTA, VENETIAN STYLE

[SERVES 6]

This recipe from a friend of Sylvia's in Venice makes one of the most satisfying dishes imaginable. Cornmeal that has been freshly ground and is slightly coarse makes the best polenta. Try grinding it yourself with dried corn kernels from a health food store.

Although polenta is traditionally cooked in a slope-sided copper kettle and stirred with a wooden paddle, any deep heavy saucepan and sturdy wooden spoon will do.

Sylvia does not agree with authoritarian Italians who insist one must stir from start to finish—an ordeal. "That's because their grandmothers made them do it to keep them out of mischief! It is not necessary, believe me."

INGREDIENTS

7 cups water
1 tablespoon salt
2 cups medium-coarse yellow cornmeal (preferably not degerminated)

EQUIPMENT

One 4-quart saucepan; 1 wooden paddle (see above); a length of string to cut polenta

COOKING
50 mins.

In a saucepan bring the water and salt to a boil. Turn the heat to medium high and, whisking constantly and watchfully, add the cornmeal in a slow, steady stream—you want no lumps.

Turn the heat to medium. Every 4 or 5 minutes, stir from the bottom to the top. As a crust forms around the pot, be careful not to stir it into the mush. Cook for at least 45 minutes—the longer the better.

SLICING
5 mins.

Turn the polenta onto a work surface, preferably a wooden board. The mush will spread. Immediately slice with a string into 1-inch-wide pieces.
    Serve hot.

SAUTÉED BREAST OF CHICKEN

[SERVES 4]

INGREDIENTS

1½ pounds skinless, boneless chicken breasts
Flour, to dust lightly
3 tablespoons light-flavored olive oil, or half oil and half
    unsalted butter
½ teaspoon white pepper, or 8 turns of pepper mill
Sprigs of parsley, to garnish

PREPARATION
8 mins.

Trim the chicken breasts, removing all fat, gristle, and ragtag bits. Pat dry. Cover with a length of plastic wrap, and with a meat pounder or the bottom of a sturdy plate flatten the breasts so they're all of uniform thickness. Dust both sides with flour and shake off the excess. Warm a serving platter.

COOKING
5–6 mins.

In a large skillet over medium-high heat, heat the oil (or oil/butter) until hot. Sauté the chicken for 3 minutes on the first side, turn, and sauté the second side until the flesh on top is springy, 2 to 3 minutes.

FINAL STEP

Place the breasts on the platter and garnish them with parsley.

LIGHT PLUM TOMATO AND MUSHROOM SAUCE

[SERVES 6]

This tomato sauce is delicious over chicken, polenta, and pasta, or slices of grilled eggplant and zucchini—or any combination thereof. Although olive oil adds silkiness and sheen, for those on a diet, this sauce is lovely without it.

    While all the ingredients may be prepared in advance, the sauce tastes freshest when ladled as soon as possible from the skillet. While ripe tomatoes are best, out of season use prime quality, canned plum tomatoes, drained and broken up with your fingers into smallish lumps.

INGREDIENTS

2 pounds firm, ripe, flavorful plum tomatoes
3 to 4 tablespoons light-flavored olive oil (optional)
8 ounces mushrooms, thinly sliced
3 large garlic cloves, finely chopped
1 teaspoon chopped fresh rosemary, or ½ teaspoon dried
1 teaspoon freshly ground black pepper, about 12 turns of
    pepper mill
½ teaspoon salt, or to taste
Parmesan cheese, freshly grated, to sprinkle (optional)

PREPARATION
10–15 mins.

Drop the fresh tomatoes into boiling water—count to 10—then lift out. Core and peel, then cut in half crosswise. Press out the seeds and juice. Coarsely chop.

COOKING
15 mins.

In a large heavy skillet, warm 2 tablespoons of olive oil or heat the skillet dry. Add the mushrooms and toss over high heat, stirring constantly, until all sides glisten, about 2 minutes. Add the garlic and sauté, stirring for another minute. Turn into a bowl.

In the unrinsed skillet, blend the tomatoes, rosemary, pepper, and a splash of olive oil, if desired. Cook over high heat, stirring frequently, until the sauce is thick, about 10 minutes. Add the mushrooms and garlic and stir for another 2 minutes to heat them. Add salt.

FINAL STEP

After ladling, a sprinkle of Parmesan cheese over each serving is a flavor plus.

◆◆◆◆◆On the Road—BY AIR TO HAWAII

Aloha

Only once in the three years devoted to this book did we forsake the open road for the sky. We flew to Hawaii (without Timothy).

Truth be told, we went, not as tourists, but as one-time residents. Our several years living on the slope of Diamond Head and in the upper Manoa Valley, were some of the best years of our lives. Jeff, our son, was born there, hence a bona fide *kamaaina*—a native. Those years were not necessarily the happiest, however; much of that period was wartime, a time of turmoil during which Hawaii was trying to sort out whether it wanted to be a territory or a state.

This visit to Hawaii came exactly a half century from the day I arrived aboard the S.S. *Lurline* as a brand-new war correspondent fitted in a brand-new Abercrombie and Fitch gabardine officer's uniform (thanks to a Time-Life expense account).

Surprisingly, I discovered fine dining on that first voyage. The *Lurline*, a Matson luxury liner which had sailed the Pacific only a short while before, was now a troopship but still carried her peace-time chefs, a battalion of cooks and helpers, and, most importantly, foodstuffs from the company's rapidly diminishing store of all good things to eat. The *Lurline* was jam-packed with several thousand troops, but it was heaven at the table.

Now, fifty years later, we were back in the Islands, not aboard the *Lurline* but enjoying instead the cooking of Kusuma Cooray who, a number of years before, had come from Sri Lanka to make an impressive contribution to Hawaii's cuisine.

∿∿∿∿*HONOLULU, HAWAII*

A Golden Palate—Kusuma Cooray

Within moments of her birth, Kusuma Cooray's father had placed a tiny pinch of gold dust scraped from a gold sovereign and drops of her mother's milk on the baby's tongue—the Sri Lankan ceremony of *ran-kiri*, which literally means "golden milk," to bless the child with a lifetime of good fortune.

Much later, Kusuma, now one of Hawaii's most respected chefs and teachers, was preparing luncheon in the kitchen of her high-rise apartment (forty stories) in downtown Honolulu within a block of where, a half century before, I had worked in an office at Time-Life in what was then one of the tallest buildings in town (five stories). Ranjit, her husband, stood by to wheel the dishes on a small trolley down to the lovely tropical garden surrounding a swimming pool set in a small forest of palms and ferns. We were a party of six for a luncheon that ranged across several cultures—herb soup, saffron rice with raisins, red shrimp curry,

kale with coconut and lemon juice, chicken curry, braised salmon with a creamy mustard sauce, wi-apple chutney, tomato apricot chutney, and finally, bananas flambé.

On the trip back to Hawaii some years ago I had sought out Kusuma for recipes for my books on soups and stews and we have been friends ever since.

A handsome woman with a richly smooth voice, Kusuma came to Honolulu on vacation in 1974 after studies at the National Bakery School and Cordon Bleu Cookery School in London and La Varenne Ecole de Cuisine in Paris. Two things happened almost immediately to keep her in the Islands. First, she met Ranjit Cooray, a fellow Sri Lankan and a graduate student in botanical studies at the University of Hawaii, and second, she was introduced to Doris Duke, the tobacco heiress who lived on Black Point in a spectacular house at the very edge of a cliff overlooking the breaking waves of the Pacific. Ranjit, she married; Duke hired her and for nine years she was chef-in-residence in the Hawaii house and, at other times, in the Duke homes in New Jersey and Rhode Island.

We were standing in her small kitchen deep-frying pappadams, the fresh, crackly thin Indian breads, before joining the garden party.

"Doris was a wonderful teacher," Kusuma said. "She had all of the credentials, certainly. She had traveled the globe and knew the cuisines of most peoples of the world. She was an understanding yet demanding critic. Demanding, but not harshly so. She liked healthy cooking because she is very careful about her diet. She specially liked and appreciated foods from my part of the world, Sri Lanka.

"She had a great influence on my cooking. She taught me no matter how simple the dish is, treat it with respect and use only the finest ingredients. Use nothing less than the best."

Kusuma left the Duke house to become executive chef of one of Honolulu's most cherished restaurants, The Willows, noted for its coconut cake (my favorite), its Hawaiian dishes, and its open dining areas built around large lily ponds teeming with koi, the colorful Japanese carp. With Kusuma in the kitchen, The Willows won several national awards for an outstanding cuisine.

Two years ago she decided she would do full time what she had loved doing part time—teaching. While at The Willows she had conducted workshops in cake decorating, chocolate work, and East Asian cooking.

At the same time, the state of Hawaii was completing a $10 million state-of-the-art culinary teaching complex at the Kapi'olani Community College on a beautiful campus near Diamond Head Crater. The complex was being built to keep ahead of the ever-increasing demand among restaurants and hotels in the Islands for trained young men and women desperately needed in all phases of food service for the booming tourist trade. The college was delighted to learn that Kusuma was receptive to joining the faculty. She was named chef-instructor of International cuisine.

"I left The Willows because I finally tired of the rigorous seven-day-a-week, around-the-clock demands put on a restaurant's executive chef. But, equally important, I wanted to be in touch with the younger generation and to share my knowledge of food and the art of cooking."

Later Kusuma and I were walking through the spectacular kitchens and classrooms at Kapi'olani. She laughed. "I took one look at these several beautifully designed and spacious kitchens and all of this gleaming stainless steel and the large classrooms equipped with the latest high-tech teaching aids and I knew this is where I wanted to teach. I seriously doubt that there is a finer kitchen anywhere on earth. It's a dream kitchen."

Equally spectacular is the student-run Ohelo dining room with a sweeping view of Honolulu and of ocean and beaches stretching from Diamond Head Crater to Koko Head.

"It has become one of Honolulu's finest restaurants. It has been such a success that people must make reservations weeks in advance."

HERB SOUP

[SERVES 6]

Kusuma Cooray loves to cook with herbs. This soup created by her for
The Willows restaurant is a delight for the gardener or for friends who
have access to all of these herbs. Most of them can be purchased fresh
in supermarkets, herb shops, and farmer's markets. It may, however, be
difficult at times to find them all. Doing without 1 or 2 herbs will not
greatly affect the good flavor of the soup, but try to get them all if you
can.

INGREDIENTS

2 tablespoons clarified butter (see page 241)
½ teaspoon each fennel, cuminseed, and dill seeds
2 tablespoons chopped onion
½ cup each coarsely chopped leafy tops of fresh parsley,
*   coriander, and fennel*
¼ cup each coarsely chopped fresh sweet basil and mint
2 medium tomatoes, finely diced
6 cups chicken stock, homemade (see page 562) or store-bought
¼ teaspoon freshly ground black pepper
Salt, to taste, if desired
2 tablespoons lemon juice, or to taste
1 cup plain yogurt, to garnish

COOKING
15–17 mins.

In a medium (3-quart) saucepan heat the clarified butter over a
low flame. Add the fennel, cumin, and dill seeds; cook and stir
for 2 minutes.

    Add the chopped onion and cook, stirring occasionally, until
the onion is soft and light gold in color, about 8 minutes. Add
the fresh herbs, then the diced tomatoes. Cook over high heat
for another 2 minutes.

    Add the chicken stock. Season with the pepper, salt, and
lemon juice, and simmer for 5 minutes.

    There is a choice of texture. Serve the soup as is, or put
through a food processor or blender for a creamier soup.

FINAL STEP

Serve hot, with a dollop of yogurt in each bowl.

ISSO CURRY
(Red Shrimp Curry)

[SERVES 6 TO 8]

While Hawaiian curried dishes had long been favorites of those who frequented The Willows, it was not until Kusuma introduced Sri Lankan curries that the restaurant earned its three national awards for excellence.

The lemongrass used in Sri Lankan and Indian cooking can be found in many supermarkets and shops catering to the Asian community. It is one of 30 perennial grasses exuding an aromatic oil used as a seasoning or for the manufacture of oil in pharmaceutical and perfume industries.

INGREDIENTS

1½ pounds medium to large raw shrimp
2 tablespoons butter or oil
1 medium onion, thinly chopped
3 garlic cloves, thinly sliced
1 teaspoon grated ginger
1 stem lemongrass, cut into 2-inch lengths
1 ripe tomato, peeled, seeded, and chopped
1 tablespoon curry powder
½ teaspoon ground turmeric
2 teaspoons paprika
1½ cups fresh or canned coconut milk (cow's milk may be substituted)
Salt and lemon juice, to taste
Rice, to accompany, if desired

PREPARATION
15 mins.

Peel, devein, and rinse the shrimp. Set aside.

COOKING
23–27 mins.

Heat the butter or oil in medium sauté pan, add the chopped onion, garlic, ginger, and lemongrass pieces. Sauté over medium heat until the onion bits are soft and translucent, 10 to 12 minutes.

Add chopped tomato and cook for 5 minutes. Stir in the curry powder, turmeric, and paprika. Combine well.

Add the coconut milk and bring to a simmer, uncovered. Stir the shrimp into the mixture and cook for 8 to 10 minutes over low heat. Don't overcook or the shrimp will toughen.

FINAL STEP

Season with salt and lemon juice and remove from the heat. Remove the lemongrass before serving. Serve hot with rice.

MALLUN
(Kale with Coconut and Lemon Juice)

[SERVES 4 TO 6]

This is a handsome side dish—deep green speckled with white coconut bits. Delicious, too. Serve hot with fish, chicken, or meat.

INGREDIENTS

1 pound fresh kale, young leaves preferred
1 teaspoon butter
1 tablespoon chopped onion
½ cup water
Pinch of ground turmeric
¼ cup grated fresh or frozen coconut (unsweetened)
Salt and freshly ground black pepper, to taste
Lemon juice, to taste

PREPARATION
10 mins.

Trim the kale leaves, discarding the tough stalks. Wash well to remove any sand. In a medium saucepan bring 2 inches of water to a boil, add the kale and cook for 2 minutes. Drain and refresh with cold water. Drain and shred or finely slice the leaves and set aside.

COOKING
11 mins.

Place the butter and onion in the saucepan and sauté over medium heat until the onion is soft and translucent, about 6 minutes.

Return the shredded kale to the saucepan with the onion, add the ½ cup water, turmeric, and coconut. Stir together well and cook over moderate heat for 5 minutes.

FINAL STEP

Remove from the heat and season with salt, pepper, and lemon juice.

Serve hot and admire its greenness—and good taste.

WATALAPPAM
(Spicy Coconut Custard)

[SERVES 6 TO 8]

If there is a Sri Lankan national dessert dish, the much favored *watalappam* is it. I can always find canned coconut milk in the specialty foods department of my local supermarket and, occasionally, frozen fresh.

Palm sugar is obtained by "tapping" the young palm tree and collecting the sugary sap that flows from the cut. It can be found in markets catering to an East Indian clientele. Brown sugar may be substituted in this recipe.

INGREDIENTS	*1 cup palm or dark-brown sugar* *¼ cup water* *5 eggs, room temperature* *2½ cups thick coconut milk* *½ teaspoon ground cardamom* *¼ teaspoon grated nutmeg* *Pinch of ground cloves* *1 tablespoon rose water* *¼ cup roasted and slivered cashews or almonds, to garnish*
EQUIPMENT	One 1-quart baking dish or 8 ramekins or custard cups, buttered; length of parchment paper
PREHEAT	Preheat the oven to 275°. Set a shallow pan large enough to hold the baking dish or ramekins in the oven and fill with 1 inch of hot water.
PREPARATION 10–15 mins.	Over low heat dissolve the sugar in the water until it's the consistency of a thin syrup (320°). Set aside to cool. Beat the eggs in a bowl. When the sugar syrup is cool, add it to the eggs. Add the coconut milk. Stir in the spices and rose water. Strain the custard into the baking dish or ramekins.
BAKING 275° 1¼ hours	Carefully place the dish or ramekins in the pan of hot water, and rest the parchment paper over them. Bake for 1¼ hours; the custard is set when a knife inserted in the center comes out clean.
FINAL STEP 2 hours– overnight	Remove from the oven and garnish with cashews or almonds. After the custard has cooled, place in the refrigerator to chill completely before serving.

IV   SOUTHEAST

Georgia   Florida

Spring

We drove 380 miles the first day on our way to the Georgia cooks. Through Kentucky horse country, the mares stood unconcerned for a photograph as curious foals inched toward my camera. Black barns and black fences. Green buds pushing open on branches. Red cardinals and black crows. Tobacco fields planted and covered with long strips of white cloth.

In eastern Kentucky and Tennessee the Interstate flows through sweeps of undulating hills and deep valleys, unlike the smaller, shorter hills in southern Indiana. The vistas are grand and exciting. Thirty miles north of Knoxville we saw the first redbuds that would soon become a blanket of pink on the hills as we drove farther south.

Despite great natural beauty, the states of Tennessee and Kentucky have allowed their beautiful hills to be littered with signs demanding to be read. The signs are placed close, side by side, and stacked one above the other until the entire hillside is screaming for attention—signs for gas and oil and budget motels and Coke and Pepsi and local natural wonders ranging from caves to waterfalls. Against one beleaguered hill with only a fringe of beautiful trees left in place, I counted twenty-two huge signs.

Gatlinburg is on the edge of the Great Smoky Mountains National Park. Marje and I had been there years before on our honeymoon. It was then a small town in the mountains and as late as 1940 visitors from the outside world were a curiosity. No longer. Gatlinburg has changed. While the population of the town is about four thousand, the citizens are outnumbered ten to one judging from the march of tourists up and down the street and in and out of the shops. Once it was the outlanders who were few and far between, now it is the locals.

The national park forms the southern boundary of the town. One moment we were surrounded by souvenir shops, franchise ice cream parlors, hot dog stands, and shlock in general and were beat upon by heavy truck traffic and then, within a few feet, were the quiet forest and a sparkling river.

Within the park boundaries it is wilderness, formerly home of the Cherokee Indians, who were chased out in 1830. They now live on a reservation on the south edge of the park. In the early 1900s loggers cut down much of the virgin timber but did not destroy the beauty of the place. (A measure of the park's wildness is the more than six hundred black bears that roam through the forest.) Thirty-three miles later the wilderness road ended, as it began, in a rush of schlock and souvenir tomahawks, bows and arrows, and pottery bears.

Our first night in Georgia was at a Holiday Inn two miles south of Madison, a lovely town whose antebellum homes were virtually untouched during the War Between the States. Dogwood burgeoned into tunnels of white flowers over the streets. Swatches of brilliant pinks and reds of azaleas vied with the dogwood for attention. Magnolia trees, some three stories tall, with their shiny, waxy leaves, not yet in bloom, were waiting no doubt for the other beauties to depart before taking center stage.

It was spring in the South.

EATONTON, GEORGIA

A Country Kitchen—Joseph B. DeLoach III

We scattered chickens and roused a sleeping dog in the middle of the gravel lane as we drove up to the big DeLoach house. We also interrupted a wedding ritual. Walking solemnly through a bed of irises alongside the house were a half-dozen kids performing the ceremony. The bride wore a kitchen curtain. The groom: shorts only. They stopped to wave.

Nearby, Joe, in bib overalls, a pink T-shirt, and baseball cap, was painting a window sash. Later he took off his cap, slipped on an apron, and became the cook we had come to see.

Livestock were everywhere. Two small pigs, Eunice and Kay, named after Joe's secretaries at the local school, were squealing for attention. They would become bacon and ham by the time Joe finished rebuilding an antebellum smokehouse out back. The meat would be for the family and Joe's catering business.

While waiting for the pigs to reach maturity, Joe and Melody, his wife, are kept busy with 3 milk cows, 27 beef cattle, 100 or more chickens, 1 turkey cock, 2 dogs, 1 cat with kittens, and 3 children on three hundred acres of Georgia land that has been in the family since 1850. The impressive two-story structure is known locally as the Jenkins Hill House, named after a great-grandfather.

Until recently the DeLoach ménage included a flock of guinea hens that was decimated one by one, because the birds persisted in flying low across the road in the evening to roost in an oak tree at the very time auto traffic going past from the nearby town of Eatonton was the heaviest.

Joe and Melody, both forty, are teachers in the Putnam County School in the nearby town of Eatonton (population: 4,833) where he also counsels kids between the ages of eight and thirteen. On Sundays he teaches Bible class to the youth of the Eatonton Methodist Church, *after* which he serves them brunch.

To do all of these things—milk the cows, slop the pigs, spade the big garden, prune fruit and nut trees, collect the eggs—Joe's day begins at 4:00 in the morning and ends about 9:30 in the evening. But not always.

The night before, the cows broke down a fence and twenty animals tramped around the front yard until they were rounded up about midnight.

When he has done the chores at the barn and henhouse, he comes back to the kitchen to prepare breakfast for the whole family while Melody is wakening and supervising the scrubbing and dressing for school of Joseph, who is six; Rebecca, ten; and Jessica, 13. They would be together again in the late afternoon—ranged along the kitchen counter with their homework—where Joe, available for consultation, would be fixing dinner.

Joe treasures food. He loves to grow it in the garden, on the hoof, and in the orchard. He loves to cook it and he loves to eat it. Slender and wiry, it doesn't show. And it pleases him to have others enjoy it too.

"I don't consider myself a gourmet cook by any stretch of the imagination. I don't do European dishes and I don't fancy *nouvelle cuisine*. I just cook basic, simple food. People have called it country cooking. I call if just food."

Joe admits his cooking is not exactly slimming, because he favors real butter and milk from the family's cows and eggs from their own hens. "But you don't have to eat everything in sight," Joe said. "I don't use bacon fat. I like to take a slice of ham from the back part of the ham, cut it into little pieces, and fry it down to give my beans and collards that good Southern flavor. So what I prepare is done by taste. Mine. If you don't like what I like I guess you are out of luck. Sorry."

Joe and Melody grow just about everything on the place except corn and sorghum cane. "We tried both out in front of the house for a couple of years. We cut the stalks by hand with a cane knife. Let me tell you that's the hardest work in the world. And the raccoons were harvesting more corn than we were so we finally gave up. Now we get corn to grind for our grits and meal from my daddy down the road. We do it in a little old hand grinder that's been hooked to a washing-machine motor. It turns out meal by the sackfuls in just no time."

Joe's great-great-grandfather owned slaves and raised cotton on the land and, for a reason that family history can't explain, sold the slaves and some of the land at the very *beginning* of the War Between the States and put it all into Confederate currency.

"We still have every dollar of it." Joe grinned. "It's in a cigar box over at the bank. After all, you never know. . . ."

Joe has a special reverence for a favorite great-aunt, Annie Laurie Jenkins, who surfaces again and again when he talks about food, the family, and the farm.

"Aunt Lollie, whose home this was until she died, loved good food and loved to serve it. Perhaps that's what got me into the catering business. If you came to her house you never left without being offered something if nothing more than a biscuit or a piece of cake or a cookie. In the kitchen she used to say, 'Momma made it this way' or 'Momma used this ingredient instead of that one.' She would go on telling me not only how she cooked but how it had been handed down through the family. Her way is the way I cook today. Simple things but good!"

We were in the big kitchen talking while he put the finishing touches to Aunt Lollie's chicken salad. The ingredients for the salad were put through an old 1897 hand grinder. At the same time he began the family's evening meal. The main course would be Ham and Red-Eye Gravy done in a special way. The ham slices were fried only lightly, the gravy made and poured over the ham, then the ham was put in the oven to bake. Later he fried a chicken so I could see it done the Southern way. Or, more appropriately, Joe's way.

SOUTHERN FRIED CHICKEN

[SERVES 4]

We were in the chicken yard to select a bird for the frying pan. Mixed in with the plump laying hens were a dozen bantam chickens. Dinner was *not* a bantam.

INGREDIENTS

One 2½-pound fryer chicken, cut into pieces
1 teaspoon salt
⅛ teaspoon freshly ground black pepper
2 cups vegetable shortening, approximately
Flour, to roll

Note: Occasionally Joe will vary his seasoning by adding a little lemon pepper, garlic salt, onion powder, or Old Bay seasoning.

EQUIPMENT

One 12-inch cast-iron skillet; 1 baking sheet, if desired.

PREPARATION
2 hours

Two hours prior to frying the chicken, wash the pieces and drain in a colander. Salt and pepper them, and place in the refrigerator.

Put the shortening in the skillet to melt. There should be enough to come halfway up the sides of the pan, and two thirds of the way up the sides of the chicken when it is in the pan.

While the fat is heating, put the flour on wax paper or spread on a baking sheet. Roll the still damp chicken in the flour. Knock off any excess. For a thicker crust, dip twice and don't knock off the excess.

COOKING
20 mins.

To test the oil, dip the tip of a leg into it. If it sizzles, the oil is hot enough. It should be around 375°, just below the smoking point. Place the pieces skin side down in the pan. The pieces should touch but not overlap.

Cover loosely. Reduce the heat to medium-high, and cook for 9 to 10 minutes, or until dark golden. Remove the cover, turn the chicken with tongs, and cook for 8 to 10 minutes more.

FINAL STEP

Drain on paper towels. The chicken should be dry and crisp, not greasy.

CHICKEN SALAD

[SERVES 4]

Joe's beloved Aunt Lollie sold her salad curbside at the Eatonton farm market in the town square each Saturday during the Depression. The salad is made a day ahead and left overnight to "season." Joe uses homemade pickles, but any good-quality sweet pickle will do fine. The salad can also be made with ham or beef.

INGREDIENTS

One 2½-pound chicken, cut into pieces
2 celery stalks, chopped
1 medium onion, chopped
2 carrots, chopped
1 teaspoon salt

2 eggs, hard-cooked
2 celery stalks
½ cup sweet pickles
1 tablespoon prepared mustard
¼ cup mayonnaise
1 tablespoon vinegar, of choice
Garlic power, onion powder, and freshly ground black pepper,
    to taste after the ingredients have been mixed together

EQUIPMENT

Meat grinder with coarse cutting disc or food processor

PREPARATION
50 mins.

Wash the chicken pieces under cold running water. Place in a pot or saucepan and cover with water. Add the celery, onion, carrots, and salt.

Bring the water to a gentle boil, reduce the heat to a simmer and cook for 45 minutes. Do not cover.

continued

Remove the chicken from the pot and allow the pieces to cool. At the same time cool the stock before refrigerating or freezing. Remove the chicken from the bone and cut into pieces that will feed handily into a meat grinder or food processor.

GRINDING
AND MIXING

Feed the chicken pieces, eggs, celery, and pickles through the grinder. In a bowl mix the salad lightly but thoroughly with the mustard, mayonnaise, vinegar, and seasonings.

In the processor, place the chicken pieces and the rest of the ingredients in the processor bowl and process briefly (3 to 4 pulses). Don't make it a pulp. Process only into small particles to give the salad texture.

REFRIGERATE
Overnight

Refrigerate the salad overnight.

FINAL STEP

Serve the salad on a bed of lettuce or in tomato shells.

HAM WITH RED-EYE GRAVY

[SERVES 6]

While Joe uses water to make his gravy, many Southerners like it made with leftover black coffee, red wine, or Coca-Cola.

INGREDIENTS

½ slice ham per person (6)
Rind and fat from ham
⅓ cup hot water (120°–130°)

EQUIPMENT

One ovenproof skillet

PREHEAT

Preheat the oven to 250°.

PREPARATION
8 mins.

Place the ham slices in an ovenproof skillet and cook until lightly browned. Remove the ham. Cut off the rind and fat and return these to the skillet with the hot water. Bring to a boil and cook for 2 to 3 minutes. Remove the rind.

BAKING
250°
1 hour

Return the ham to the skillet. Spoon the liquid over the slices, cover, and bake for 1 hour.

FINAL STEP

Place the ham on a platter or plate and pour the gravy over.

~~~~~SAVANNAH, GEORGIA

Elizabeth on 37th—Elizabeth Terry

Considering the orchids and accolades that have been heaped on Elizabeth Terry since she and her husband, Michael, opened their restaurant —Elizabeth on 37th—ten years ago, it would be understandable if they were two people caught up in the glitz and glamour of becoming famous. She has been called "a southern sensation" by *Time*, while Craig Claiborne says she makes "irresistible versions of old Southern standbys like succotash."

Elizabeth, mid-forties, bespectacled—and attractively so on both counts—came to our table last night in a white chef's toque, jacket, and slacks. She moved easily from table to table talking with guests in the several dining areas on the main floor. "This is my moment to be in touch. I want to know how they like the food." We made a date for later.

Elizabeth was picking the day's harvest of herbs for the kitchen when we arrived. The herb garden was landscaped into a wide ornamental border fronting 37th Street. "We have enough here for everyone—the kitchen, the neighbors, and our guests, if they want to pick them," she said, waving a bunch of marsh marigolds in one hand and sprigs of sorrel in the other. "I think it sets off the house beautifully, don't you?"

We moved to chairs in the deep shade on the verandah. Overhead a ceiling fan whirled slowly though it wasn't needed in the coolness of the morning.

When they came to Savannah from Atlanta ten years ago, "eating out" usually meant a choice of country ham with red-eye gravy, fried shrimp, fried oysters, fried fish or fried chicken, with grits and an assortment of beans and greens. Not very exciting. But that has changed dramatically and she is pleased they have been a part of that change.

When the Terrys opened their restaurant they chose to build the cuisine around the dishes that Savannah people prepared and served on special occasions in their own homes. "I researched generations-old Georgia recipes and as a result I have been able to bring back some dishes with a new flair."

Among these old Southern recipes is rack of lamb coated in pistachios; a flounder stuffed with fish mousse and served with a basil-lime hollandaise; an oyster and sausage turnover; a ragout with wild mushrooms and rosemary; country butter bean and wild rice soup with ham; and roasted eggplant and shrimp with okra, onion, and thyme.

"It's fun to be innovative and yet not get so far out in front that we lose our customers," she said. Yet Elizabeth does things differently. "For instance, many think the only way to prepare a Southern favorite, collard greens, is to boil them for an hour or so with a ham hock and plenty of bacon fat. We like collard greens but we use them differently. We steam them and make a bed for salmon.

"We don't use fatback in our cooking, not even in our lentil soup, which is a traditional way of making it. To flavor vegetables we fry bacon but pour off all the fat and discard it. When we make chicken stock we chill it, lift off and discard the fat.

"We think we have to be responsible about such things. We do little salting in the kitchen. Sometimes our guests complain. 'The food is too bland,' they say. Most of the time the complaints come from those who smoke." She smiled.

Neither Elizabeth nor Michael had thought of food as a career until it was agreed that they would move from Atlanta to Savannah to enjoy a less hectic life. Michael, a Harvard Law graduate, was director of legal services for Atlanta. She had studied physiology at Lake Erie College in Painesville, Ohio, and in Atlanta was a probation officer for a time before she began to cook in a small deli which specialized in soup and cheese.

The Terrys' intentions were modest when they moved—perhaps a small luncheon place, a small law practice, and a small house. That went out the window when they saw the two-story mansion with its imposing façade, Palladian windows, and elegant entrance at 105 East 37th Street that had been built in 1900 by a Georgia sugar baron.

"That changed our thinking—and our lives," said Michael. The local banker, somewhat reluctant to finance something as uncertain as a restaurant, finally agreed to do so if the loan would be made to Elizabeth alone, since the bank at that moment was trying to enhance its equal-rights loan record.

"I wasn't black but I was a woman," said Elizabeth.

"So, to please the loan officer, we named it [the restaurant] Elizabeth," Michael continued. "There is a tearoom connotation in the name that we didn't want, so we decided in the very beginning we would always serve large portions. Nothing tearoomy."

Elizabeth said she never thought she could become a brassy, demanding female, but she was forced to become one to get good produce for the restaurant. "The produce merchants thought I was crazy, especially when I told them the stuff they were sending me wasn't fit to eat. They had been getting by with it for years—pushing out old produce before they sold the new. I kept sending it back. I would tell them 'I can't use this old stuff. It's tired.' We went round and round. Now they are bringing in good things, fresh, and different—four kinds of mushrooms and the lovely pencil-thin asparagus stalks instead of the old fat ones, and much more."

On the other hand, Elizabeth, from the very beginning, exulted in the quality and variety of seafood at her disposal—fish, including red snapper, grouper, shad, sea trout, sea bass, and what she calls "those incredible crabs and shrimp and oysters."

In a variation of life in many English farmhouse inns, the Terrys and their two daughters live on the second floor of the house. "Literally, we live on top of our work. We like it that way. When we leave for work in the morning we simply go down a flight of stairs. The only traffic to worry about may be a daughter frantically rushing back up to get a school book she forgot."

GEORGIA RAGOUT
WITH WILD MUSHROOMS AND ROSEMARY

[SERVES 6 OR 8]

While any species of mushrooms can be used, domestic as well as wild, Elizabeth prefers the shiitake. I use whatever I can find that day at my supermarket, and all seem to do equally well. This is a rich satisfying dish that Elizabeth serves with roasted potatoes that can be prepared in the oven after the ragout has cooked and kept warm. On occasion I have served the ragout with rice.

INGREDIENTS

2 pounds stew beef, cut into ¾-inch cubes
Oil, to brush
1½ cups red wine
½ pound bacon, cut into ¼-inch pieces
1 carrot, thinly sliced
½ medium onion, sliced
2 celery stalks, thinly sliced
2 garlic cloves, minced
2 leeks, thinly sliced
2 cups rich chicken stock, homemade (see page 562) or store-
    bought
¾ cup chopped tomatoes in juice
¼ cup minced fresh sage and rosemary
1 cup diced ham
2 cups mushrooms (wild if available)
Salt and freshly ground pepper, to taste

2 large baking potatoes, peeled and cut into ½-inch cubes
½ cup water
2 tablespoons cornstarch, or 2 teaspoons arrowroot
1 tablespoon cooking oil
Salt and freshly ground pepper, to taste

EQUIPMENT

One roasting pan; 1 cookie sheet

PREHEAT

Preheat the oven to 500°.

BROWNING
6 mins.

Place the beef cubes in the roasting pan and brush lightly with the oil. Brown for 6 minutes. Remove the pan from the oven and add the red wine.
    Reduce the oven temperature to 325°.

COOKING
10 mins.

In a large skillet fry the bacon until crisp. Add the carrot, onion, celery, garlic, and leeks. Cover the skillet and sweat the vegetables over low heat until soft and translucent, about 10 minutes.

BAKING
325°
1½ hours

Place the vegetables in the roasting pan with the beef, adding the stock, tomatoes (and their juice), minced herbs, ham, and mushrooms. Add salt and pepper to taste. Cover the pan with a tight-fitting lid or aluminum foil and put in the oven. Bake for 1½ hours.
    While the beef is baking, peel and cube the potatoes. Cover with cold water and set aside.
    Remove the pan from the oven. Thicken the juices by stirring in the ½ cup water and cornstarch or arrowroot. This will also give the dish an attractive gloss. Set aside and keep warm.
    Turn the oven up to 500°.

ROASTING
7 mins.
: Drain the potatoes and pat dry. Toss potatoes with the oil, salt and pepper, and spread on a cookie sheet. Roast in the oven for about 7 minutes until crisp and golden.
Serve both dishes hot.

ELIZABETH'S PECAN-ALMOND TART

[MAKES TWO 8-INCH TARTS]

This delicious tart is made even more so with a dollop of Butterscotch-Bourbon Sauce. Begin with a favorite pie dough, homemade or store-bought.

INGREDIENTS
1 cup sugar
1½ cups light Karo syrup
6 tablespoons cold unsalted butter, cut into chunks
5 eggs, lightly beaten
2 teaspoons vanilla extract
2 cups chopped pecans
½ cup sliced, toasted almonds
*Two 8-inch unbaked pie shells, homemade (see page 565) or
    store-bought*

EQUIPMENT
Two 8-inch pie pans

PREHEAT
Preheat the oven to 350°.

PREPARATION
7–8 mins.
In a medium pot bring the sugar and syrup to a boil and hold for 2 minutes. Remove from the heat and stir in the butter. Add the eggs and vanilla—stirring all the while. When the butter has completely melted, pour the mixture into the pie shells. Spread the pecans *first* over the top and then the almonds. This may seem a heavy portion of nuts, but it isn't.

BAKING
350°
30 mins.
Bake for 30 minutes, or until a cake-testing pin or toothpick inserted in the flan comes out dry.

FINAL STEP
Serve with the Butterscotch-Bourbon Sauce (recipe follows) or vanilla ice cream.

Butterscotch-Bourbon Sauce

[MAKES 2 CUPS]

INGREDIENTS

⅔ cup light Karo syrup
1½ cups brown sugar
4 tablespoons (½ stick) unsalted butter
⅔ cup heavy cream
¼ cup bourbon whiskey

PREPARATION
25 mins.

In a small pan bring the syrup, brown sugar, and butter to a boil while stirring with a wooden spoon, about 6 minutes. Remove from the heat and stir in the cream.

Cool about 20 minutes and stir in the bourbon.

Serve at room temperature.

XXXXX*TYBEE ISLAND, GEORGIA*

The Breakfast Club—Cheryl and Joseph Sadowsky

On a sandbar fronting the Atlantic, eighteen miles east of Savannah, is Tybee Island (pop. 2,240), a beach community of modest homes, vacation cottages, a boardwalk, a fishing pier, and a few motels. It has changed little over the past half century but it may soon. It has been discovered by developers and there may go the neighborhood. But not quite yet.

The Breakfast Club is a small restaurant of a few booths and a long counter owned and run by Cheryl and Joseph Sadowsky, who came from Chicago a dozen years ago. Everything in the small frame restaurant revolves around eggs. Anything you want for breakfast you can have so long as it comes from a hen. By midmorning, empty egg shells are flowing over the rim of a tall refuse can onto the floor.

GRILLE CLEANER'S SPECIAL

[SERVES ONE HUNGRY DINER OR TWO LESS SO]

My notes for the Grille Cleaner's Special reflect that I found it "staggering in size" but "delicious."

INGREDIENTS	*1 cup thinly sliced Polish sausage*
	2 teaspoons bacon fat or cooking oil
	1½ cups finely diced cooked potatoes
	1 small onion, diced
	2 eggs
	1 tablespoon each finely chopped onion and green pepper
	Salt and freshly ground black pepper, to taste
	One 3 x 6-inch slice Monterey Jack cheese
	One 3 x 6-inch slice Cheddar cheese
EQUIPMENT	One 8-inch skillet
PREPARATION 30 mins.	Fry the sausage slices in a lightly oiled skillet over medium-low heat until partially cooked, about 4 minutes. Remove from the skillet.
	Add the bacon fat or oil and spread the potatoes evenly over the bottom of the same skillet with the onions scattered over the top and cook over medium-low heat. As the potatoes cook, press them down with a spatula several times. Cook until the bottom is golden brown, about 10 minutes. Turn the potatoes over, brown the other side, then remove to a plate.
PREHEAT	Preheat the oven to 400° while the potatoes are cooking.
ASSEMBLING 5 mins.	Spread the fried sausage pieces close together over the bottom of the skillet. Spoon a ½-inch layer of cooked potatoes over the sausages.
	In a bowl stir together the eggs and the chopped onion and green pepper. Pour the mixture over the potatoes. Salt and pepper to taste.
	Lay the slice of Monterey Jack cheese diagonally across the upper half of the creation. Place the slice of Cheddar across the bottom half.
BAKING 400° 5 mins.	Place the skillet in the oven for 5 minutes or until the cheese bubbles.
FINAL STEP	Serve in the skillet or slip onto a plate. It is meant for one person but it can be shared.

Red Barn on Frederica Road—Bennie Gentile

As we crossed over the waterways and marshes from the Georgia mainland to St. Simons Island, I was looking forward to meeting Bennie Gentile and eat the dish that had made him famous.

Bennie was a street-smart kid from Albany with little ambition when, in the depths of the Great Depression in the early thirties, he joined the Civilian Conservation Corps. "Best thing that ever happened to me—got me off the streets and into the woods and, eventually, into food, and I have loved it."

Today Bennie is famous all along the Georgia coast for the food he serves at his Red Barn on Frederica Road. Don't expect a sign on the barn to tell you, yes, this is the place. But even without it you can't miss the big red structure since it is the largest *red* building on St. Simons. Nor does Bennie advertise. People just seem to know where it is and find it time and again.

Bennie, a handsome seventy-year-old man, calls himself a professional. His credentials are impressive. He holds a card in the bartender's union. He is a professional cook and chef; in his fifty years in the kitchen he has done it all. He is a professional restaurateur; the highly successful Red Barn is a testament to that.

"Good bartenders make good cooks and good cooks make good bartenders," Bennie believes. "A bartender has to know the inventory behind the bar as well as the taste of his whiskeys and liqueurs—and how they go together. A cook must know his ingredients and how they go together to produce a certain taste and texture. Both must have a sense of timing and coordination and movement."

Bennie's most favored dish is Shrimp Mull—a thick mixture rich with shrimp, tomato, garlic, and onion and cooked with one of two meats—smoked sausage or fresh salt pork—ladled over a snowy hillock of rice. The dish with sausage, the "inside mull," is for restaurant guests, while the mull made with fried-out fatback, the "outside mull," is reserved for affairs catered out-of-doors.

SHRIMP MULL (Inside)

[SERVES 10 TO 12]

Delicious as it is even in small servings, Shrimp Mull is hardly worth making unless you plan to make a lot. It is easy to refrigerate or freeze the basic sauce along with the sausage, for use another day, but don't freeze the shrimp. Whether you make the "inside" or the "outside" mull, be certain all of the fat is cooked out of the meat and discarded except for one tablespoon in which to sauté the onion.

As the mull cooks down, it may be necessary to add more tomatoes and their liquid. The mull, however, should be thick enough to spoon, not ladle, and hold its shape on a mound of rice.

INGREDIENTS	*4 pounds uncooked fresh shrimp*
	2 pounds country sausage, bulk or in links
	2 medium onions, chopped
	2 garlic cloves, diced
	Two 8-ounce cans tomato sauce
	One 16-ounce can tomatoes, chopped (include liquid)
	One 6-ounce can tomato paste
	1½ cups catsup
	1 teaspoon sugar
	2 teaspoons freshly ground black pepper
	1 teaspoon salt, or to taste
	6–8 cups long grain rice

EQUIPMENT   One deep skillet or pot

PREPARATION
25 mins.

Peel and devein the shrimp. Set aside. If the sausage is in links, cut and remove the casings and break apart the sausage meat with a fork.

COOKING
1 hour
25 mins.

Fry the sausage until it is crispy brown and the fat has been cooked out of it, about 15 minutes. Lift the sausage from the skillet with a slotted spoon and place on a length of paper towel to absorb the fat. Set aside. Discard all of the fat in the skillet except 1 tablespoon in which to sauté the onion and garlic.

Sauté the onion and garlic in the skillet over a low fire until translucent, about 10 minutes. Return the sausage to the skillet and add the balance of the ingredients, except the shrimp and rice.

Stir the mixture, cover, and place over medium-high heat to bring to a boil. Lower the heat and simmer the sauce for an hour. Stir frequently.

Prepare the rice according to package directions 30 minutes before the shrimp are to be dropped into the sauce.

continued

ASSEMBLING
3–5 mins.

During the *final* minutes of cooking the sauce, add the shrimp and stir well. When the shrimp are pink, remove the completed mull from the heat. The exact time will depend on the size of the shrimp, but certainly no longer than 5 minutes for the largest shrimp.

FINAL STEP

Place a serving of rice on each plate. Crown it with mull!

▰▰▰CROSS CREEK, FLORIDA

A Fine Cook Remembered—
Marjorie Kinnan Rawlings/Sally Morrison

Sally Morrison

Cross Creek Cookery was one of the first cookbooks to come into my kitchen. It was written by author Marjorie Kinnan Rawlings, who won the Pulitzer prize for *The Yearling*. Her mother's baking powder biscuits hold an honored place in my first cookbook, because it is my mother's recipe, too. As a loving tribute to both mothers, the recipe is included here.

When I learned that Rawlings's old "cracker" farmhouse at Cross Creek, where she lived and wrote for a quarter of a century, had been restored by the state of Florida, we made plans to go there. What a joy it was to find the house restored to the way it was when she was alive, not as a stuffy museum without spirit, complete with a woodburning kitchen stove in daily use and a larder filled with home-grown things, canned and fresh.

Rawlings was an unknown writer when in 1928 she bought the old house with its breezeways, its many windows, and deep porches set down in a seventy-two-acre citrus farm. But by the time she died in 1953, after a string of other successful books including *Cross Creek*, *Jacob's Ladder*, and *The Sojourner*, her fame was such that she lost the privacy she so loved. When she bought the farm, the road in front was little more than a dirt lane she and the neighbors used to go to town. She led but lost a fight against a wide paved highway favored by the truckers.

Rawlings was a remarkable woman but so is Sally Morrison, the resident park ranger, curator, and caretaker, who chops kindling for the old stove and cooks on it, picks wild oranges in the grove for marmalade, feeds the chickens and collects the eggs, hoes in the garden and picks beans and collard greens. She has also written a fine cookbook, *Cross Creek Kitchens*.

A dozen years ago, while a park ranger in Montana, Sally leaped at the invitation to come to Cross Creek to breathe life into the place, which had been declared a state historic site.

Sally moved into the long-neglected house, cleared away the rubble and brush, nailed down loose boards, repaired the plumbing. She cleaned the wood stove, bought a new stovepipe, and had the chimney repaired. She began filling the empty jars in the pantry with the seasonal bounty of fruits and vegetables. Absent for some thirty years, the smells of gingerbread and corn bread spread through the homestead once again.

Smoke curled up from the chimney as we drove up to the house and parked the van in the deep shade of a pecan tree. When we walked around to the back porch the smell of wood smoke mingled with the odors of good things cooking in the kitchen.

"The formality of a museum didn't belong here where a woman's life and love and laughter were so rich," Sally said, smiling. "I took down the DO NOT USE signs that were posted everywhere, removed the pink ribbons pulled across the red 'fainting' couch to keep people from sitting on it, and each morning placed a bouquet of fresh roses on the breakfast table. It was a home again.

"That's the way it should be," said Sally. "Marjorie Rawlings loved to cook. Rich food. Lots of butter and lots of cream—from Dora, her Jersey cow. She called herself an introverted writer and an extroverted cook, one who cooked with emotion, not measurement.

"Writing to her was agony but cooking was a joy. Cooking took her mind off the difficulties of writing."

Sally was stirring marmalade made with the wild or sour oranges from the few remaining trees in the grove at the side of the house. Now and then she took a stick of kindling from the wood basket and punched it into the firebox.

Food that was natural and native intrigued Rawlings, said Sally. "She was a fine hunter and fisherman. In her cookbook she has recipes that range from pot roast of bear, alligator-tail steak, and jugged rabbit, to fried coot, blackbird pie (with the real birds before they became illegal to shoot), and, one of her favorites, turtle. The only wild thing she couldn't bring herself to prepare was rattlesnake.

"The wilderness around Cross Creek that she loved has been cleared away and the bears are gone," Sally said, "but only last week a fourteen-foot 'gator was found struggling to get across a country lane near here. It had been badly shot up by someone. Fish and Game officers released him on an island out in the middle of Orange Lake to recuperate."

When Marje and I left the house to return to Gainesville we stopped on the bridge over the Creek—a lovely clear, quiet stream, lined with cypress trees and fishing camps. A boat was slowly moving over the water in the deep shadows of the trees. The Creek, which is how Rawlings fondly addressed it, is less than a mile long and links Orange Lake with Lochloosa Lake and it was these waters that so impressed the author in her many books about life in rural Florida.

Sally's cookbook (Triad Publishing Company, Gainesville, Florida) is exceptional, but she has refused to allow it to be widely distributed for fear in some way it might overshadow or detract from the Rawlings legend.

SWEET 'TATER PIE

[SERVES 8]

The first time I had sweet potato pie—it was Sally's—I was dumbfounded. It was just about the best piece of pie *of any kind* I had ever eaten. It was difficult to believe that such an ungainly looking tuber could produce something so light and beautiful. "I realize most people don't share my passion for a sweet potato in all of the ways it can be prepared," Sally said, "but I have yet to meet anyone who doesn't like my sweet potato pie!"

True, Sally, true.

INGREDIENTS
1½ cups mashed cooked sweet potato
⅓ cup honey or cane syrup
2 eggs, lightly beaten
¾ cup milk
½ teaspoon grated nutmeg
¼ teaspoon salt
1 tablespoon orange juice or rum (optional)
⅓ cup chopped pecans
One 9-inch unbaked pie shell, homemade (see page 565) or
store-bought

EQUIPMENT
One 9-inch pie pan

PREHEAT
Preheat the oven to 450°.

PREPARATION
5 mins.

Have a pie shell at hand—homemade or store-bought.
Combine the potatoes with the honey or syrup. Mix thoroughly. Add the eggs, milk, nutmeg, and salt. Add the orange juice or rum, if desired. Pecans may be added to the filling or sprinkled on top. I like the latter. Pour into the shell.

BAKING
450°
15 mins.
325°
30 mins.

Bake for 15 minutes, then lower the temperature to 325° and bake for 30 minutes, or until firmly set.
Place the pie on a wire rack to cool.

SPRING GREENS AND SPRING CHICKEN

[SERVES 4–6]

With the first burst of spring growth, when turnip greens, mustard greens, or collards in her garden are especially tender, Sally simmers them slowly with a whole chicken to make a light, uncomplicated dish to be served with a few splashes of hot pepper vinegar (or Tabasco) and a pan of corn bread.

Old-timers in the Cross Creek community considered early spring greens to be a blood purifier, and the broth with chicken or ham to be an invigorating tonic.

Welcome spring!

INGREDIENTS

½ cup chopped green onion, with tops
2 garlic cloves, minced
1 tablespoon butter
One 2- to 3-pound frying chicken, cut in pieces
2 to 3 hot peppers (optional)
A mess of tender greens—a mixture of turnip, mustard, and collard greens—enough chopped to fill loosely a 3-quart pan. They will cook down. Spinach may be substituted for one.
½ teaspoon salt
½ teaspoon freshly ground black pepper
Hot pepper vinegar or Tabasco sauce, to splash on finished dish

COOKING
1 hour

In a 3-quart soup pot, sauté the onion and garlic in butter until they are translucent and soft, about 10 minutes. Place the chicken pieces in the pot, add the hot peppers, if desired, and water to cover. Cover the pot and simmer over low heat until the chicken is tender, about 45 minutes. The meat should pull easily from the bones.

Set the chicken aside and allow to cool for a few minutes, then remove the chicken from the bones and cut into bite-sized pieces.

Bring the chicken broth to a boil and add half the greens. Turn the heat to low and cook, covered, until the greens cook down, about 5 minutes. Add the salt and pepper and the rest of the greens and simmer, uncovered, just until the greens are tender. Don't overcook.

FINAL STEP

Serve in individual bowls—a serving of chicken in each bowl topped with broth and tender greens.

Serve with hot pepper vinegar or Tabasco on the side. If there is cooked rice in the house we often add a spoonful or two to the bowl.

MOTHER'S BISCUITS

[MAKES 2 DOZEN]

My mother baked such beautiful baking powder biscuits that for a long time I felt intimidated by the thought of doing them myself. Finally, I dared.

The recipe that started me along this delicious byway was from *Cross Creek Cookery*. My mother's recipe was never committed to paper. But after a consultation with my sister, I am satisfied this biscuit is as good as my mother's.

INGREDIENTS	*2 cups all-purpose flour* *4 teaspoons baking powder* *½ teaspoon salt* *2 tablespoons butter* *1 (scant) cup milk, room temperature*
EQUIPMENT	One baking sheet, greased and cornmeal-dusted, Teflon or covered with parchment paper
PREHEAT	Preheat the oven to 450°.
PREPARATION BY HAND OR MIXER 10 mins.	Mix the flour, baking powder, and salt together in a mixing or mixer bowl, and sift twice. Work in the butter with your fingertips or with a wire pastry blender, or in the mixer (flat beater) until the mixture resembles coarse grain. Add only enough milk to hold the dough together. The exact amount varies with the flour.
SHAPING 6 mins.	While it is considered heresy to handle biscuit dough needlessly, Mrs. Rawlings's mother believed that to make a flaky, layered biscuit one had to roll out the dough, fold it over itself in 4 layers, roll out again to a thickness of ½ inch, and cut with a 2-inch cookie cutter. Place the biscuits on the baking sheet.
BAKING 450° 12–14 mins.	Bake until the biscuits are a golden brown and raised to about 1½ to 2 inches, 12 to 14 minutes. Serve hot.

▰▰▰ TARPON SPRINGS, FLORIDA

The Sponge Divers—Maria Koursiotis

In 1961, with three small children tagging along, Maria Koursiotis left the lovely but impoverished Greek island of Kalymnos in the Aegean Sea to join her husband, a sponge fisherman, in Tarpon Springs. The first

time she visited the town's markets, she was astounded by the variety and abundance of foods. To this day she remembers the thrill of it.

Maria had come from a village where meat was eaten only twice a year—lamb at Easter and on the feast day of the village's patron saint. Fish, too, was relatively scarce, for after thousands of years fishing, much of the Aegean had been almost emptied of fish. Her husband, John Koursiotis, a sponge fisherman in the rich beds off the Florida coast, had prospered with two 40-foot boats. Sponge prices were high. But it didn't last.

In 1971 disaster hit Tarpon Springs when a "red tide" wiped out the sponge beds and closed down the town's chief industry. Crippled by the "bends" that came with years of deep diving for sponges, John came ashore. Maria took command and did what she wanted to do from the moment she arrived in Tarpon Springs. She opened a family-style restaurant, Mama Maria's, on Athens Street, across from the town theater.

It is a small restaurant, about fourteen tables, but its reputation is big in Tarpon Springs where she competes with the famous Louis Pappas, and the lesser-known Acropolis Taverna, the Crazy Greek Eatery, Demetrios, Dodecanese, Old Athens, Pia's Athenian Corner, ZeeZee's, and Zorba's Lounge and Restaurant.

Maria cooks the dishes she cooked in Greece but with Florida overtones. Collard, chard, turnip, mustard and beet greens appeal to Maria, who serves them boiled, dressed with oil and lemon. The fish, fresh from offshore and served whole, is a choice of red snapper or porgy broiled over charcoal with olive oil, lemon juice, and oregano. The grouper sandwich is the fish fillets wrapped in pita bread. Chicken is blanketed with thin slices of feta cheese and braised. Maria roasts her own lamb at the restaurant for special feast days. But down the street is the National Bakery, which bakes the crusty, chewy bread that Maria serves, and at Easter the bakery roasts upward of fifty lambs for its regular customers, an Aegean tradition that has its roots in Greece where fuel was so scarce and costly that a family's baking and roasting were done in the baker's ovens.

Maria is the cook. Daughter Georgia is the waitress/cashier. She was also my interpreter; her mother spoke no English and I spoke no Greek.

While sponge fishing has come alive again and prices have risen astronomically, Maria wishes for the old days when there were fewer tourists in town and things were cheaper.

"It was quieter then, too. All of our families were very close. We were divers. Our men came from Greece and were born into Greek families here. It was something that was passed on from father to son. They all looked after each other. Now all of that has changed. The price for sponges is so high everyone with a boat is diving, and they don't understand how dangerous it can be. Years went by without a death among our men, but there's been three deaths recently. There are now about two hundred men and women diving for sponges from about fifty boats of every description and with all kinds of equipment."

I told the two women about our sponge-diving excursion at the Sponge Docks the day before, a thirty-minute outing for tourists. Tickets were $4 each. There were nine of us aboard plus a crew of several elderly men whom I took to be divers long retired. The captain stood at the wheel and explained the finer points of sponge diving, with particular emphasis on its dangers. A second man sat tinkering with the engine. A third man stood by to fasten down the diver's helmet to his suit and to handle the air hose and safety rope that followed the diver in the water. As for the diver, he clanked aboard with thick lead weights on his boots, eating a can of cold pork and beans.

I had thought the boat with this experienced crew would take us offshore into deep, clear waters where the sponges flourished. Instead, the boat dropped anchor in the black, oily waters of the inner harbor, ten minutes from the dock. The diver, an old man with a gallant mustache and wearing a beret inside his helmet, clamped shut his faceplate and dropped over the side.

"This is a dangerous business," said the captain gravely, looking commanding. "You see he has a rope tied to his waist so that we can quickly pull him aboard if he gets into trouble."

The old man had disappeared beneath the surface, with a trail of bubbles following his route across the channel. He had gone perhaps twenty feet when there was a heave on the safety line. One of the passengers gasped. "No, no, there's not to worry, he's not in trouble," the captain said. "He's found the sponge bed!" Urged by the captain, we clapped and shouted, which I doubted the diver could hear. Suddenly, the old man, his diving suit inflated and buoyant, shot half out of the water triumphantly waving a soggy black mass that I took to be a sponge.

When I asked the captain how a sponge could possibly grow in such black polluted water, he said that this was a special kind of sponge grown here just for this diving exhibition. He ignored my comment that the diver must have walked on his knees in this shallow water to keep his helmet under water.

The passengers poked and fingered the one specimen. One couple had their pictures taken holding it, and some kids sat on the diver's lap for a photo when he unbolted his helmet. The captain passed around a selection of postcards for sale, and then the boat turned back for the short trip to the dock where a tour bus waited to embark fifty passengers for the sponge dive.

How could he possibly find a sponge in that water, I wanted to know?

Georgia laughed. "He had it up his sleeve. After all, you did see how it would have been done over a real sponge bed. It was worth $4, wasn't it?"

Yes it was, I said, if only to have seen the old man shoot to the surface waving the sponge he had palmed.

STEFADO
(Greek Beef Stew)

[SERVES 4]

Stefado (also *stifátho*) is often the pièce de résistance of the large noon-day meal in Greece. Bits of feta cheese and walnuts sprinkled over the top distinguish this stew from all others. This is the beef version. In Greece it is also made with veal or hare.

INGREDIENTS
2 pounds lean beef, cut into 1-inch cubes
1 tablespoon olive or cooking oil
24 small white pearl onions, peeled
2 tablespoons butter
1 teaspoon granulated sugar
½ cup red wine
1½ cups water
1 tablespoon red wine vinegar
¾ cup tomato paste

Sachet d'épice
2 bay leaves, crumbled
8 peppercorns
One 2-inch stick cinnamon
1 garlic clove, mashed

1 tablespoon brown sugar
Salt, to taste
2 tablespoons cornstarch (optional)
3 tablespoons cold water (optional)
½ cup coarsely broken walnuts
½ pound feta, coarsely crumbled

PREPARATION
10 mins.

Trim off any fat and connective tissue from the beef.

SAUTÉING
15 mins.

In a medium saucepan or heavy pot with lid, heat the oil over medium-high heat until it begins to smoke. Add the beef cubes and spread over the bottom. Don't crowd. Stir with a wooden spoon until all sides are brown, about 4 minutes. Remove with a slotted spoon and set aside. Repeat with the balance of the meat.

While the meat is sautéing, place the onions in a small saucepan of cold water. Bring to a boil and drain immediately.

When the meat is sautéed, drop the butter into the saucepan and add the onions. Sprinkle with sugar (to caramelize) and sauté to a light golden color over medium heat, about 10 minutes. Stir the onions to color uniformly. Lift out the onions with a slotted spoon and set aside. They will be added to the stew after it has cooked for an hour or so.

COOKING
1½–2 hours

Return the meat to the saucepan and add the wine, water, vinegar, tomato paste, *sachet*, and brown sugar. The liquid should barely cover the meat. Add water if necessary. It may also be necessary to add small amounts of water from time to time during cooking to maintain that level. Bring the liquid to a boil, reduce the heat, and simmer with the lid on for 1 to 1½ hours, or until the meat is tender when pierced with the point of a sharp knife or fork.

Remove the *sachet*. Taste for seasoning, especially salt. Carefully spoon the onions into the stew and mix thoroughly. Replace the cover and simmer for an additional 30 minutes.

Note: If you wish the stew to be thicker, stir together the cornstarch and cold water until smooth. Add to the stew, bring to a boil, and boil for 1 minute, stirring.

FINAL STEP

The nuts and feta cheese may be sprinkled generously over the stew in a tureen or passed at the table.

BAKED LAMB SHANKS
WITH TOMATO SAUCE

[SERVES 4]

I have often thought that there must be a Greek branch or two on the Clayton/Condon family tree, for I love lamb in all its forms, especially the shank. When Marje prepares it for dinner I am at the table early and leave late. She knows it is a sure way to get my attention.

This recipe from Mama Maria's is one of the best. Serve with rice.

INGREDIENTS
4 lamb shanks, about ¾ pound each
Salt and freshly ground black pepper, to taste

SAUCE
2 teaspoons olive oil
1 large onion, thinly sliced
1 garlic clove, finely chopped
1 cup dry white wine
9 medium tomatoes, peeled, seeded, and finely chopped, or
    3 cups chopped canned tomatoes, drained
1 teaspoon dillweed
½ teaspoon dried oregano
2 tablespoons brown sugar

Cooked rice to accompany, if desired

EQUIPMENT
One covered roaster or a baking dish with tight-fitting lid, bottom brushed with olive oil

PREPARATION
30–35 mins.
Season the lamb shanks with salt and pepper. Place them in the roaster over medium-high heat for 10 minutes, turning them to sear and brown. Remove the lamb and set aside.

For the sauce: Pour the olive oil into the roaster over medium heat. Add the onion and garlic, cover, and sweat until they are soft and translucent but not browned, about 10 to 12 minutes.

Add the remaining sauce ingredients. Stir together and bring to a simmer for 10 minutes.

PREHEAT
While the sauce is simmering, preheat the oven to 300°.

BAKING
300°
2 hours
Place the lamb in the roaster with the sauce. Cover and bake for 1½ hours.

Remove the cover, turn the shanks, spoon some sauce over them. Continue to bake for an additional 30 minutes.

While the lamb is in the oven prepare the rice, if desired.

SAUCE 8 mins.	Place the shanks on a platter or individual plates. Reduce the sauce by half, about 8 minutes.
FINAL STEP	Serve directly from baking dish or arrange the shanks on a heated platter, surround with rice, and pour the sauce over the meat. Pass the sauce as well.

⋙FORT MYERS, FLORIDA

A Tropical Island—Mona Moffat

Mona Moffat is a Floridian, a writer, columnist, teacher, and cook. She loves Florida. It is warm, sunny, pleasant, and not too expensive. But what she likes most about it is the feeling it gives of being cut off, but not quite, from the rest of the country.

"Florida is really a tropical island." She had spread out a map of the state to illustrate her point. "It is only happenstance, a geological quirk, that a narrow land bridge (one hundred miles across) ties the state to the U.S. mainland.

"This island mentality of ours stems in part from the thousands of true islands that make up our shoreline—Sanibel, Captiva, Estero, Pine,

Cabbage Key, Marco, to name the famous ones, plus the string of island keys down to Key West. To complete the island analogy: We are bound by water on nearly every side—the Atlantic Ocean and the Gulf of Mexico. So, you see, except for our slim land connection with the South, we are very nearly an island—in fact as well as in feeling."

The two of us had talked about cooks and cooking at an earlier meeting of food people in St. Louis, and had made plans to meet in her kitchen in Fort Myers. Mona, a strikingly handsome woman with much grace and style, has written, cooked, and counseled on two continents. With her children in college, in 1969 she sailed to Greece on a cruise ship and was so impressed with the country that she stayed for twelve years as columnist/editor for the *Athens Daily Post* and a consultant to a number of European restaurants. She is now a food columnist for the *Fort Myers News Post* and is developing a program for cooks who collect recipes in their personal computers.

Floridian cooking, Mona feels, reflects the insular state of mind, this feeling of making do with what is at hand and not looking to the rest of the country but standing alone.

"The early Florida cuisine was based on products indigenous to it, and this prevails in one way or another to this day. It was no great hardship, of course, because Florida was and is magnificently endowed with riches both on the land and in the sea."

Importantly, she pointed out, the same tropical island atmosphere that attracted people to Florida has also drawn talented chefs and enterprising restaurateurs. The result is a blend of many divergent styles of cuisine that is truly cosmopolitan, without losing its Floridian roots. The local food markets feature not only ethnic ingredients of all sorts, but foods imported from other states, foods that are staples to so many of us from the North, West, and East.

Mona, nevertheless, is of two worlds—Florida and Greece—and it was to be Greek night when we met in her kitchen to cook and talk about food.

When I phoned earlier in the day to confirm our date, Mona said that she thought we might like a change from what we had been eating on our drive down the west coast of Florida.

"It is going to be my other favorite food—Greek!" she said, and with such enthusiasm that I didn't dare mention that we had just come from Mama Maria's at Tarpon Springs. It really didn't matter because both Marje and I have a passion for Greek food.

KEFTÉTHES
(Meatballs)

[MAKES 50 SMALL EGG-SIZED MEATBALLS]

These featherweight meatballs lightly fried in oil and butter appear on all festive occasions in Greece, and every Greek seems to have his or her own treasured recipe. This is Mona's.

For family meals, shape the balls the size of a small egg; for cocktail parties, the size of a large marble. Ask the butcher to mix the meat two or three times to give the meatballs the light, fluffy quality so sought after.

If desired, they may be baked instead of fried. Do so without flour, in a 350° oven, until well browned on all sides.

INGREDIENTS

1 cup unseasoned bread crumbs
½ cup milk
1 cup finely minced onion
8 tablespoons (1 stick) butter
1 pound lean ground beef
1 pound lean ground pork
2 eggs, beaten
1½ tablespoons each finely chopped fresh mint and parsley
2 teaspoons salt
¼ teaspoon freshly ground black pepper
½ teaspoon ground cinnamon
½ cup all-purpose flour
3 tablespoons olive oil

PREPARATION
20 mins.

In a small bowl soak the bread crumbs in the milk and set aside.

In a small skillet sauté the onion in 1 tablespoon of butter over low heat until lightly browned, about 8 minutes. Remove and scrape the onions into a large mixing bowl.

Add the soaked crumbs, 2 tablespoons of butter, the meats, the eggs, and the seasonings. Knead the mixture by hand for at least 5 minutes to blend all of the ingredients thoroughly.

Shape the small balls between your palms, and roll each lightly in the flour.

FRYING
10 mins.
per batch

Melt 5 tablespoons of butter in a large skillet, and add the olive oil. Heat until it has a fragrance. Fry the meatballs in the hot oil until brown, carefully rolling them with a spatula or wooden spoon to brown on all sides, about 10 minutes for each batch.

As they brown, remove with a spoon and place on paper towels to drain. Replenish butter and oil if needed.

continued

FINAL STEP   Put the drained *keftéthes* in a covered bowl or casserole and place in a warm oven until serving time. The cover not only keeps them hot but moist as well.

These can be refrigerated. Reheat in a 325° oven.

BAKLAVA TROPICAL

[MAKES ABOUT 2 DOZEN DIAMOND-SHAPED PIECES]

In a tropical variation of the Greek national pastry, baklava, Mona spooned pineapple, coconut, and almond bits between the layers of phyllo dough and, when it came from the oven, poured on a syrup flavored with dark rum, Key lime juice, and honey. Typically, baklava is layered only with nuts.

Phyllo, the Greek word for "leaf," is sometimes spelled *filo* or *fillo*. In the United States it is possible to buy both phyllo leaves and phyllo/strudel leaves, which can be used interchangeably. They can be purchased frozen in supermarkets or ordered fresh from Greek specialty stores. Phyllo is so tedious to make that even in Greece the bake shops buy the leaves ready-made from specialty bakers.

INGREDIENTS   *PASTRY*
1 pound (approximately 25) phyllo/strudel leaves

FILLING
¾ pound (3 sticks) unsalted butter, to brush
1 cup grated coconut
1 cup finely diced preserved pineapple (8 slices)
½ cup finely chopped almonds
⅓ cup sugar
¼ teaspoon ground cardamom
2 teaspoons ground cinnamon
1 teaspoon ground cloves

SYRUP
1 cup sugar
2 cups water
Juice and rind of 2 Key limes, or ¼ cup bottled Key lime juice
*   and zest of 1 lime*
3 whole cloves
1 stick cinnamon
1 cup honey (bland)
½ cup dark rum

EQUIPMENT

Most commercial phyllo leaves are about 17 x 11 inches, hence a 13 x 9-inch pan or dish is ideal and will produce about two dozen 2-inch diamonds. Butter the dish liberally.

BEFOREHAND
Overnight or
2 hours

For the pastry: Remove the package of phyllo leaves from the freezer to allow thawing overnight in the refrigerator or 2 hours at room temperature. When the package is opened and the leaves unfolded, cover with a moistened cloth to prevent the leaves from drying and breaking.

PREPARATION
10 mins.

Clarify the butter in a saucepan by melting it very slowly over low heat, about 10 minutes. Skim off the foam, spoon the butter into a small bowl or cup, and discard the milky solution that remains.

Mix together in a bowl the remaining filling ingredients.

PREHEAT

Preheat the oven to 350°.

ASSEMBLING
15–20 mins.

Count out 8 phyllo sheets, cover, and refrigerate while assembling the others. These are for the top.

Lay a sheet of phyllo on the bottom of the buttered pan, brush it with some clarified butter, and lay another sheet on top. Butter that sheet and repeat for 8 layers of buttered phyllo. Sprinkle a quarter of the filling mixture evenly over the phyllo.

Lay on 3 more sheets, brushing each with clarified butter. Sprinkle with a quarter of the filling.

Continue layering with 3 sheets of buttered phyllo and mixture until all the leaves and filling are used.

The final layer is the reserved 8 sheets. Tuck the edges down smoothly and secure with melted butter.

PATTERNING
10 mins.

Lay out a pattern on the top leaf with a ruler or yardstick. The traditional shape is a diamond, but pastries may also be cut into squares and triangles. Use a sharp knife to cut through the pastry, including the bottom layer. This in-depth cut will allow the syrup to permeate all of the baklava when it is poured on after baking.

BAKING
350°
1½ hours

Sprinkle the top leaves with water or spray with an atomizer to prevent the top leaves from curling during baking.

Place the baking dish in the middle of the oven. Bake for 1½ hours, or until the phyllo has risen and has a rich golden color.

SYRUP
20 mins.

Although the syrup can be made several days before it is needed and held in the refrigerator, it may be more convenient to make the syrup while the baklava is in the oven.

continued

In a saucepan combine the sugar, water, lime juice and zest, cloves, and cinnamon. Stir to dissolve. Bring to a boil. Lower the heat and simmer for 15–20 minutes. Remove from the heat and discard the spices. Add the honey and rum. The syrup must be warm but not hot to pour over the pastry when it comes from the oven.

SOAKING
overnight

Pour the syrup over the baklava, and let it sit overnight so that the syrup can permeate all of the leaves and attain peak flavor.

FINAL STEP

Separate the diamond-shaped pieces and serve.

The baklava may be stored in a covered container at room temperature for 4 to 5 weeks.

Wrapped securely in foil or plastic, baked or unbaked, baklava can also be frozen. If frozen, place the unbaked baklava directly into a 350° oven for 1½ hours, then reduce the heat to 325° and bake for an additional hour, or until the pastry is puffed and golden. It may be kept frozen for 3 months.

NAPLES, FLORIDA

The Chef's Garden—Chef Tony Ridgway

In the upscale resort city of Naples (pop. 17,581) where dining out is de rigueur and home cooking is not, the Chef's Garden is the place to go for some of the best food to be found anyplace in the southern sector of Florida's Gulf Coast. I was told so in Indiana and then at least three more times as we traveled south down Florida's west coast. I came to believe it even before I got there one warm spring day for lunch—and I found it to be true. Good food. The Michelin guide would certainly agree that it is worth a detour.

Tony Ridgway baked his first loaf of bread when he was nine and first cherry pie when he was eleven. He knew what he wanted to be when he left the Air Force to return to civilian life: chef/restaurateur. And he wanted to do it in Naples where as a kid he had wintered with his parents. One restaurant was available—the Wurst Place, a German café specializing in bratwurst and knockwurst.

Chefs Tony Ridgway, *left*,
and Michael Etienne

"The owners were quite attached to the café and when I changed the name *and* the menu they were certain I had ruined everything," he said.

Today there is an occasional bratwurst on the menu for old times' sake, but more often it is a baked Brie with walnut vinaigrette dressing, escargots and wild mushroom Bourguignon, spicy shrimp and prosciutto eggroll, or spinach and fresh mango salad. For an entrée, you have a choice of sautéed Gulf shrimp and sun-dried tomatoes and curried butter sauce; sweetbreads sautéed with cream, tarragon, and Dijon mustard; or sautéed veal with prosciutto in a sauce of baby artichokes and tomato.

Or it may be what Ridgway calls a "memory dish." When he and the chefs, cooks, and staff people get together several times a month there is a nostalgic and somewhat sentimental moment given over to dishes each fondly calls up from memory, such as a meat loaf a favorite aunt prepared or a grandmother's chicken and dumplings. It will be tasted and tested in the kitchen, and if all hands agree, it will go on the menu from time to time. One such recipe was a chocolate bread pudding I had. It was made with pieces of day-old croissant rather than stale bread.

SEAFOOD CAESAR SALAD

[SERVES 4]

While Caesar salad is believed to have originated in southern California in the 1920s, it has long since found its way to Florida and elsewhere. Ridgway has given it a new taste and texture with seafood rather than cheese and oil alone.

INGREDIENTS

DRESSING
1 tablespoon capers
2 teaspoons Dijon mustard
2 eggs
1 garlic clove, mashed and finely chopped
1½ tablespoons Worcestershire sauce
1 tablespoon prepared horseradish
2 teaspoons tomato puree
3 tablespoons each lemon juice and red wine vinegar
6 tablespoons olive oil
Salt and freshly ground black pepper, to taste

SALAD
2 medium heads of romaine lettuce
1 pound medium shrimp, cooked, peeled, and deveined
½ pound crab meat
½ cup grated Parmesan
½ cup croutons, brushed with garlic

PREPARATION
5–10 mins.

For the dressing: In a food processor add all of the dressing ingredients except the last two. With the machine running, slowly add the oil in a steady stream. Season to taste with salt and pepper. This can be done ahead.

For the salad: Separate the leaves of romaine, wash, and dry. Break the romaine into bite-sized pieces and place in a salad bowl.

ASSEMBLING
5 mins.

Pour the dressing over the lettuce, then toss lightly with wooden spoons until it's well distributed. Add the seafood and cheese. Toss.

FINAL STEP

Scatter the croutons over the top and serve at once on chilled salad plates.

CHOCOLATE BREAD PUDDING

[SERVES 6]

Ideally there should be several day-old croissants on hand for this pudding. If not, day-old bread slices or even a leftover brioche or two will do. Begun a long time ago by thrifty cooks anxious not to waste a smidgen, bread pudding has overcome its humble origins and is now accepted, even begged, to come to the table.

Ridgway has given it a delicious turn with chocolate.

INGREDIENTS
1 to 2 large croissants, cut into ½-inch pieces
2 cups heavy cream
½ cup sugar
1 vanilla bean, split in half
Pinch of salt
6 egg yolks
¾ pound semisweet chocolate, chopped

EQUIPMENT
Six 6-ounce custard cups, or one 5- or 6-cup baking dish, buttered and dusted with sugar; water bath for cups or baking dish.

PREHEAT
Preheat the oven to 325°.

PREPARATION
20 mins.
Divide the croissant pieces among the cups or the baking dish. Set aside.

In a heavy saucepan combine the cream, sugar, vanilla bean, and salt. Scald the mixture but do not boil. Remove the vanilla bean.

In a mixing bowl lightly whip the egg yolks and add half of the scalded cream mixture; pour the mixture back into the saucepan. Add the chocolate and stir over medium heat until it is melted, about 15 minutes. Do not allow to boil!

BAKING
325°
45–50 mins.
Divide the chocolate mixture among the custard cups or pour into the baking dish. Make certain all the croissant pieces are covered with the chocolate mixture.

Place the cups or baking dish in a pan of water and bake until the custard is set, 45 to 50 minutes. Test with a knife. If the blade comes out clean, it is done.

~~~~~MIAMI, FLORIDA

Latino Foods—Maria Elena Cardenas

Home to a million Hispanics, Dade County is a treasury of Latino foods. But unless you know the language, it is best to keep to the dining room and stay out of the kitchen. I feel underfoot in a busy kitchen where the magic is cast in a foreign tongue. I know only enough Spanish to ask for a glass of *agua* and then, to the waiter, *gracias*. Hardly enough to quiz a busy cook. So, it was obvious that Marje and I needed help when we arrived in Miami to explore its Latino cuisine.

Help came from a remarkable woman who is a cook, a writer, and an internationally known translator. She is Maria Elena Cardenas, who was born in Cuba. As a young girl she moved to New York City to be with her family in exile. A graduate of Vassar College, she came to Miami to become a certified federal court interpreter in several languages. For a number of years she has been a widely read columnist for the Spanish edition of the *Miami Herald*.

For two days we toured Miami and environs with Maria, visiting Cuban and Spanish restaurants and markets. I drove. Maria talked. Marje took notes.

"The Cuban cuisine is fascinating. There has been a complex layering of culinary traditions, and in fact, the cuisine, even after five centuries of direct Spanish influence, still relies very heavily on indigenous tubers and vegetables and also on the many African food crops carried to Cuba by the slaves brought to work in the cane fields."

I turned a corner. Marie continued.

"The Spaniards successfully grew Old World plants such as oranges, cabbages, carrots, radishes, and sugarcane, but fared less well with olive trees, grapevines, wheat, oats, and barley. Those cereals were essential elements to the Spanish diet and their failure would have been disastrous had it not been for the starch-laden native crops.

"We are going to stop at this X-Tra Market," she said, directing the van off the highway into the big Dadeland Mall.

In the huge warehouse we walked past eight-foot-tall mountains of green and yellow plantains, white and yellow yams, sweet potatoes, malanga (a member of the taro family), cassava (an edible root), soursop (a fruit often made into ice cream or a drink), and calabaza (squash) on long display counters.

"We Cubans cling with a passion to our traditional cuisine. By growing and preparing native tubers, vegetables, and fruits—and this sounds a bit overblown but it's true—we reinforce our sense of cultural identity and establish a link with our past."

The visit was the only time I have ever been forbidden to take a photograph of a banana. I had just taken a flash picture of the plantains and was focusing on the bananas when a tight-lipped assistant manager rushed up to demand that I stop. "You can't do that!" he cried. "You must put the camera down or leave the store. It's the rule."

As I uncoupled the flashgun, he said permission would have to come from the head office, which was in another city. I thanked him and we left.

We drove to Islas Canarias, a small Cuban restaurant at the corner of Twenty-seventh Avenue and Northwest Third, where President Reagan lunched during his 1983 Miami visit. Maria had been his interpreter that time. The pace in the café was frenetic and the food abundant! First, black bean soup followed with a variety of *saladitos*—small chunks of potatoes in garlic mayonnaise; shrimp salad; chicken and cod croquettes; and a mélange of mussels, shrimp, tiny clams, roast pork, chorizo, blood sausage, and squid in a broth. Entrées: fresh sugar-cured pork shanks; a whole red snapper in green sauce; and *tortilla*, an ambitious dish that consisted of an omelette on a bed of potatoes, sauced with shrimp, squid, and mussels.

"This is only lunch." Marie laughed. "You should be here for dinner!"

Someplace in this outpouring of food was a giant platter of beans and rice. But most delicious was *Pastel de Pollo*, a chicken potpie.

During the meal the cook sent out samples of fried plantains she wanted us to taste, both green and ripe. A member of the banana family, plantains are less sweet and more versatile. They can be cooked and eaten at various stages of ripeness, and each stage has its own treatment and taste. Green or unripe plantains, which are almost as hard as potatoes, are often simply boiled in salted water and served with meat, in place of boiled potatoes. They are good cut into slivers, deep-fried, and served as chips.

"When a plantain is fully ripe it is glorious," Maria said. "Sliced into rounds, sautéed in butter, it is crisp outside and soft inside. It is mild, but its definite sweetness blends beautifully with pork or chicken and makes beef more interesting, too."

We were back in the van.

"Cuban food is trendy," Maria said, "and it could be the next cuisine to be discovered. While it is hardly haute cuisine, wait until the country discovers the Cuban sub."

To make the sub, she explained, first split lengthwise a ten-inch roll. Layer on a slice of boiled ham, a slice of Swiss cheese, mustard, pickles, and, to top it off, a slice of roast beef. Butter the *outside* of the roll, top and bottom. Place it in a sandwich toaster/grill, the kind used to make grilled cheese sandwiches. Force the grill as far down as it can go—squashing the roll as flat as possible. Grill until the cheese melts.

"It is the rage in south Florida," said Maria.

MOROS Y CRISTIANOS
(Black Beans with Rice)

[SERVES 6]

This version of the traditional Cuban dish is quick and easy to make. It's another fine leftover dish, since it calls for beans that are already cooked.

INGREDIENTS

2 cups cooked black beans
¼ cup olive oil
1 large onion, finely chopped
2 pimentos, sliced
4 garlic cloves, mashed and finely chopped
½ teaspoon dried oregano
2 cups water
1½ cups raw rice
2 teaspoons salt

BEFOREHAND
2 hours or
overnight

There are two ways to soak beans before cooking, either one will greatly reduce occasional gas discomfort. Both involve discarding the water in which the beans have been soaked.

The least complicated way is to soak the beans overnight in water (2 to 3 inches above the beans to cover) to allow for absorption. Drain the beans, discard the water, cover with fresh water, and cook. If time is a factor, the beans may be quick-soaked by covering them with water and bringing them to a boil for 2 minutes. Set aside and allow them to soak for 1 hour. Drain and discard the water. (Lentils do not have to be soaked before cooking, nor do those beans with package instructions that say soaking is not required.)

COOKING
45 mins.

In a medium saucepan or skillet heat the oil and add the onion, pimentos, and garlic. Cover and cook over medium heat until the onion is soft and transparent, about 12 minutes. Stir in the black beans and oregano. Add the water.

When the water boils, add the rice and salt. Reduce the heat to a simmer. Cover with a sheet of wax paper and place one sheet of paper toweling over the wax paper—and cover with a lid. Cook at low heat for 30 minutes.

FINAL STEP   Taste for seasoning. Can be kept refrigerated for several days or frozen.

PASTEL DE POLLO
(Chicken Potpie)

[SERVES 4]

If she had to choose, *Pastel de Pollo* would be the one dish Maria would pick that would be typical of Cuban cooking. It is baked in an ordinary pie pan and served with rice. It is also an ideal leftover chicken dish, since it calls for cooked chicken. Maria adapted this recipe from the excellent *Secrets of Cuban Entertaining*.

INGREDIENTS   *PIECRUST*
2 cups flour
2 tablespoons baking powder
½ teaspoon salt
1 tablespoon sugar
¼ cup (½ stick) unsalted butter, chilled
½ cup shortening, vegetable or lard, chilled
1 egg
1 tablespoon white wine, if desired

STUFFING
1 large onion, finely chopped
1 green bell pepper, chopped
1 garlic clove, minced
2 tablespoons olive oil
2 cups cooked chicken, cut into ½-inch dice
1 teaspoon salt
½ teaspoon cayenne pepper
Dash Tabasco sauce
Pinch of ground cumin
1 cup chopped tomatoes
1 cup tomato sauce
1 tablespoon capers
¼ cup chopped olives
2 tablespoons raisins
¼ cup red wine

1 egg yolk stirred with 1 tablespoon milk, to glaze

continued

EQUIPMENT	One 10-inch pie pan
PREPARATION 15 mins.	For the crust: Mix the dry ingredients. Cut in the butter and shortening until the mixture resembles coarse cornmeal. Make a hole in the center of the mixture. Place the egg and wine in the hole. Toss the mixture to blend the ingredients. Shape into a ball.
CHILLING 1 hour	Place the dough in wax paper and put in the refrigerator for at least 1 hour to chill while preparing the filling.
COOKING 40 mins.	For the stuffing: Sauté the onion, green pepper, and garlic in the olive oil over medium heat until the onion is soft and transparent, about 12 minutes. Add the diced chicken and stir together. Add the remaining stuffing ingredients. Reduce the heat to a simmer and cook for 25 minutes, or until the sauce thickens.
PREHEAT	Preheat the oven to 350°.
ASSEMBLING 15 mins.	Set the chicken aside while shaping the dough in the pie pan. Divide the ball of dough into 2 pieces. Roll the first piece into a round about ⅛ inch thick and fit it into the pie pan. Pour in the chicken mixture. Roll out the top crust and place gently over the chicken mixture. Pinch the edges together as with a covered pie, or allow the crust to float free over the mixture. Brush the top with the egg yolk mixture.
BAKING 350° 1 hour	Bake for 1 hour, or until golden brown. Take hot to the table.

SOPA DE FRIJOLES NEGROS (Black Bean Soup)

[SERVES 6 TO 8]

This black bean soup is memorable. Thick and dark and not highly spiced, it is as satisfying as any meat dish, and generally served with side dishes of rice and cut-up onion.

The annatto oil used here gives a reddish-orange color and adds a mild flavor to meat and poultry dishes as well as seafood sauces. It can be made at home by cooking in a skillet over high heat ⅓ cup annatto (achiote) seeds in ½ cup vegetable oil for 1 minute. When cooled, strain and store the oil in a glass jar in the refrigerator. Discard the seeds.

This version is adapted from Time-Life's excellent Foods of the World series, *The Cooking of the Caribbean Islands*. However, I have prepared the beans in a different and easier way.

INGREDIENTS

2 cups (1 pound) dried black beans
4 cups chicken stock, homemade (see page 562) or store-bought
2 tablespoons annatto oil (see above)
1 cup finely chopped onions
2 teaspoons finely chopped garlic
8 ounces lean cooked ham, finely chopped (about 2 cups)
1 large firm tomato, peeled, seeded, and finely chopped,
*   or ½ cup canned tomatoes*
2 tablespoons malt vinegar
½ teaspoon ground cumin
Freshly ground black pepper, to taste

EQUIPMENT

One heavy 4- to 5-quart casserole

BEFOREHAND
2 hours or
overnight

To prepare dried beans for cooking, see page 248.

PUREEING
15 mins.

Combine 1 cup of cooked beans and 1 cup of chicken stock at a time in a blender or food processor. Do not puree too much because the beans should have a roughness to them. As you proceed, scrape the mixture into a large bowl or pan with a spatula.

COOKING
40 mins.

In a heavy casserole, heat the annatto oil over moderate heat until a light haze forms above it. Add the onions and garlic, cover, and, stirring frequently, cook until the onions are soft and transparent, about 10 minutes.

Stir in the ham, tomatoes, vinegar, cumin, and a few grindings of pepper. Bring to a boil and, stirring frequently, cook briskly until the mixture thickens enough to coat a spoon heavily, about 12 minutes.

Add the bean puree and simmer over low heat until the soup is heated through, about 15 minutes.

FINAL STEP

Taste for seasoning. Ladle the soup into a large tureen or individual soup plates and serve at once.

▚▚▚▚▚▚*On the Road—MIAMI TO KEY WEST*

Paradise Lost

The 108-mile drive across the forty-two bridges of the Overseas Highway (U.S. 1) to the town of Key West left me exhilarated, yet dispirited.

The beauty of sky and sparkling turquoise water, the excitement of just being there, was extraordinary—like a first balloon ride or seeing the Eiffel Tower for the first time. On the long and high bridges the sensation was one of flying. Where the key was narrow and the white sands on both sides reached nearly to the van, I was excited by the nearness of the Atlantic Ocean on one side and the Gulf of Mexico on the other.

Many years ago, in the pre-Castro days, when Havana was wicked and I worked for a San Francisco steamship/hotel company, I flew to Cuba with the company's president to see if some features of Havana's resort hotels might be incorporated into our new hotel in Hawaii, the Princess Kaiulani, then in the design stage. (There were none.)

We flew in a DC-3, low and slow the full length of the Keys en route from Miami to Havana. Although I had flown many times over the islands in Hawaii and knew them well, I was unprepared for the unique beauty of the Keys. Islands of vivid green—palms and mangroves—tied together across great stretches of water by a narrow strand of highway that had been the Florida East Coast Railway until the killer hurricane of 1935. From a DC-3 flying at eight hundred feet, the Keys looked idyllic. I wanted to go back someday to see it at ground level.

Today I did. On the bridges, over the sun-dappled blue and green waters, and driving across the narrow keys through sand so white and bright I had to shade my eyes, it was as spectacular as I thought it would be. Perhaps even more so.

But when a key was wide enough to afford a turnoff from the highway, it was ugly strip-city. Dozens of miles of schlock. It was auto parts/mini-malls/fast food. Key Largo and Marathon took the prizes for tastelessness.

In an informal survey from the van, Marje jotted down these signs for roadside businesses: snorkel trips, scuba diving, pizza, ocean-front lots for sale, Arby's, bait, sugarcane juice, Kampgrounds, Jehovah's Witnesses Kingdom Hall, Paradise Pub, Red Feather Natural Foods, The Shell Man, Frijole Mexican Foods, shrimp sale from a truck tailgate. The Cracked Conch Foods, Winn-Dixie Supermarket, karate, Barefoot Key R. V. Park, and a state highway warning of a crocodile crossing. Not to mention Humphrey Bogart's boat, the *African Queen*, parked in the side yard of a motel.

When we got to Key West we found it forlorn. They were filling large areas around the north side of the city with coral pumped from the bay floor to make more room for more franchise-food places and more motels and more hotels. It was no longer the laid-back land of Hemingway. The charming streets of this southernmost outpost of the continental United States were a tangle of T-shirt shops and overrun with visitors.

My friend Sarah Benson, who lives seventeen miles down the highway from Key West, like other conchs, is unhappy with the ugliness that has crept into paradise. Her husband, an electrical contractor who makes frequent business trips to Miami, is more than unhappy with all of this. He is enraged.

"On the drive my husband simply freaks out. 'We need one goddamn good hurricane to wipe out all this trash,' he will storm. He rants and raves for the two hours it takes to get us to Miami. Yes, it is hideous, but I just don't look at it.

"When we drive through places like Marathon and Key Largo I put my nose in a book. Or I drive and hand him a book and say 'Read to me.' Or I get him working on a big set of electrical plans so he won't look up until I yell 'Look at that' and we are someplace over water. I say, 'Now isn't that beautiful,' and he looks up and agrees.

"That's how I maintain the peace!"

KEY WEST, FLORIDA

Farthest South—Sarah Benson

Sarah Benson lives on Summerland Key, close to the seventeen-mile marker on U.S. 1 on your way to Key West.

Miles away from New York City, about as far south as one can get, she tests recipes in her kitchen for *Gourmet* magazine and also writes its two most popular columns—"You Asked for It" and "Sugar & Spice." After years of a four-hour-a-day commute between a New Jersey home and the magazine's offices in Manhattan, she and her husband were

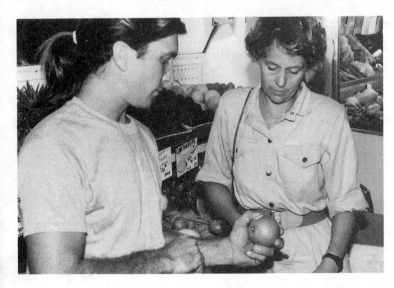

Russell Pantelis (Bucko)
and Sarah Benson

determined to live a less hectic life—either a ranch in Wyoming or the Keys in Florida. Warm Florida winters won over those of cold Wyoming.

"There are a lot of really good cooks in the Keys and they are doing imaginative things," she said. I made notes of several recipes I would test at home in Indiana. She mentioned one with guava paste. It's not one of my favorite foods.

"Oh, it would be if you lived in the Keys. When you go out in the Gulf or ocean fishing you take with you three items for survival—just in case—cream cheese, Ritz crackers, and guava paste. You could ride out a hurricane for days with those three, and water or a few soft drinks."

At one time not so long ago, food shopping in the Keys was a problem. But no longer, thanks to Bucko and his Waterfront Market. All know him as Bucko. I dug deep to find that his name is Russell Pantelis. A bundle of frenetic energy, he has made the lives of Key West cooks almost sublime. Each day his big semi-trailer shuttles between Key West and Florida City and, at times, Miami, to bring premium produce back to the town.

"When test-cooking for the magazine as well as for my classes, I can get almost anything that you can get in mid-America. Oh, I can't get the real hoity-toity cheeses that people in Memphis and Chicago can get. But, oh, the fish!"

FISH BAKED IN SALT

[SERVES 6]

One of Sara Benson's favorite ways to prepare those fish she so admires is to bake them in a blanket of salt. The fish is moist, tender, tasty, and not a bit salty. Patting and shaping a salt blanket around the fish seems to work better with a large 4- to 5-pound fish than with smaller ones.

Until you get the consistency of the salt mixture just right after doing it once or twice, place the salt and the fish on a length of aluminum foil fitted in the baking pan that can be drawn up to cradle the fish—but not cover it—to hold the wet salt in place. Sarah said the slushy mixture should resemble "wet snow."

Sarah's fish for this recipe is red snapper, but other large fish such as sea bass, mullet, or porgy will do as well. I save up a supply of frozen egg whites left from baking to make my salt blanket.

INGREDIENTS	*4½ to 5 pounds kosher salt*
	12 egg whites
	One 4½- to 5-pound whole fish, cleaned and fins removed
	Lemon wedges, to garnish
EQUIPMENT	A baking pan slightly larger than the fish. For a tighter fit, place the aluminum sheet inside the pan.
PREHEAT	Preheat the oven to 450°.
PREPARATION 10 mins.	Place the salt in a large bowl. Lightly beat the egg whites and stir into the salt until the mixture has the consistency of wet snow.
	Spread about one third of the salt mixture on the baking pan. Place the fish on the salt and cover the fish completely and thickly—1 to 1½ inches—with the salt mixture.
BAKING 450° 1 hour	Bake for 1 hour. When the fish is ready it should look like a well-baked loaf of bread.
FINAL STEP	To serve, break the crust along both sides with a sharp knife and lift off the top. Lift the fish onto a serving platter and divide into portions. Serve with lemon wedges.

FRESH TOMATO SOUP WITH BASIL

[MAKES ABOUT 8 CUPS]

This delicious tomato soup with leeks is made with both chicken and beef stock and is a favorite of Sarah's cooking classes. It is easy to make and it can be done in just about 30 minutes.

INGREDIENTS

2 tablespoons unsalted butter
2 cups finely chopped leeks
4 ripe tomatoes, peeled, seeded, and chopped
4 cups chicken stock, homemade (see page 562) or store-bought
2 cups beef stock, homemade (see page 560) or store-bought
Salt and pepper, to taste
⅓ cup finely chopped fresh basil leaves

COOKING
17–22 mins.

In a medium saucepan melt the butter and cook the leeks over medium-low heat only to soften, about 5 minutes.

Add the tomatoes and cook for 2 minutes. Add the stocks and simmer the soup for 10 to 15 minutes. Add salt and pepper to taste.

FINAL STEP

Stir in the basil just before serving. This soup is equally delicious cold.

STRAWBERRY ICE

[MAKES 2 QUARTS]

There is no better time than a hot, humid evening in Key West to be introduced to Strawberry Ice—a refreshing concoction of Sarah Benson's made of fresh-picked fruit from the mainland, orange and lime juices, and a modest splash of Grand Marnier.

INGREDIENTS

3 pints strawberries, fresh picked and hulled (frozen berries, partially thawed, may be substituted)
1¾ cups sugar
1½ cups orange juice
½ cup lemon juice, or 3 tablespoons Key lime juice, if available
¼ cup orange-flavored liqueur

EQUIPMENT

One freezeproof container

PREPARATION
15 mins.

In a blender puree the ingredients in batches and mix all together. Pour into the container.

FREEZING overnight	Freeze the mixture overnight, stirring several times during the process.
FINAL STEP	Allow the ice to soften slightly before serving. It can be kept in the freezer for months, that is if any is left should the family discover it. It's that good.

▰▰▰▰KEY WEST, FLORIDA

Baker Bob—Bob Baker

On a hot, humid evening at sundown in Key West, when there's not a whisper of a breeze to move the smallest leaf, dining out in an open-to-the-sky second-story café has overwhelming appeal. Up there, a zephyr might by chance find its way through the tops of the coconut palms. The Rooftop Cafe is such a place.

    The waiter seated us out of doors. While the stars would be out soon, he thoughtfully brought a candle. The menu was comprehensible. The type was large, easy to read. The prices were reasonable. The list of entrées were sensible, not a myriad of items that confuse. There were just three soups, four seafood and five meat and fowl entrées, one house salad, three pasta dishes, and a choice of four desserts. It was clear the chef was directing attention to the things he does best.

It got better. A light breeze from the water moved gently across the deck and touched the bougainvillea and hibiscus blossoms. The candle flame flickered. A half moon slipped into view.

"This is the way to go." I sighed softly so as not to disturb the flame.

The food was excellent. Marje had yellowtail flounder, one of the Keys' best fish, sautéed in olive oil with a squeeze of lime. I had one of the best dishes I had in Florida: butterflied shrimp sautéed with curry, banana, and raisins—and thickened slightly with heavy cream. Rice to accompany.

I introduced myself to the chef. He said he uses my cookbooks. I liked him immediately.

Bob Baker, a bearded thirty-two-year-old, is not a conch; he was born in New York City, quit law school to sell croissant sandwiches from the Runaway Cafe, a lunchmobile parked each morning on Water Street at Hanover Square. At night it was driven back to a friend's garage across town. "We did well, and for two years we were the only mobile *boulangerie* in the city and I became 'Baker Bob.' "

Bob, who speaks fluent French, came to the Rooftop five years ago to interpret for and learn from a chef from Brittany. When the chef returned to France, Bob became Chef Bob.

"I love Key West. Some people don't. A lot of them, certainly cooks and chefs, get antsy and want to get back to the mainland after they have been here a while. But this is my kind of place. I wear shorts. I walk a few blocks to work. I don't have to take the subway. I do as I please. If tonight I feel like making Grouper Carmen Miranda with apples and grapes and bananas, I do it.

"Fish is our glory here, but almost everything else—fresh produce, the lot—has to be schlepped down from the mainland one hundred miles away. Local conch has been almost fished out; it is protected, so we import frozen conch from Costa Rica and Honduras for conch steaks and chowders. Oysters are from Georgia and clams from Long Island. I like clams on the menu but at thirty-seven dollars for one hundred it kills the food costs. We do get some shrimp and stone crabs locally, and they are superb."

Here is a superb dish made with superb shrimp.

BUTTERFLIED CURRIED SHRIMP

[SERVES 4]

The first time I prepared this Key West dish I forgot to add the cream. The guests, unaware of my lapse, thought it was wonderful. "Don't change a thing!" they cried. But I did. The next time I remembered the cream. The result: double wonderful. If ever a bite can truly be said to melt in your mouth, this is it.

Don't overload with curry. Use a light touch. Serve on a nest of fluffy rice. With large shrimp, you should have about 5 to 6 to a serving. Ample for such a rich dish.

INGREDIENTS	*1½ pounds uncooked large shrimp*
	1 banana, not too ripe, on the green side
	⅓ cup raisins
	1 tablespoon curry powder
	Salt and pepper, to taste
	½ to ¾ cup heavy cream
	1 tablespoon clarified butter (see page 241)
	2 tablespoons finely chopped tomato or red bell pepper, to garnish
EQUIPMENT	One large skillet
PREPARATION 15–20 mins.	Peel, devein, and butterfly the shrimp. Cut the banana into thin ¼-inch slices. Have the raisins, curry powder, salt, pepper, and thick cream at your side for a quick assembly during the brief time the shrimp are sautéing.
COOKING 3–4½ mins.	Melt the butter in a large skillet over low heat to prevent shrimp from curling. Place the shrimp cut side down.
	Quickly add the raisins, curry powder, salt and pepper, cream, and banana slices. Gently stir together. Allow the mixture to simmer, uncovered, over very low heat for 2 or 3 minutes to cook and coat the shrimp. The shrimp should be a light pink. Don't overcook.
FINAL STEP	Serve the shrimp on rice, or with rice at the side. Garnish with a sprinkle of chopped tomato or red pepper.

⋙KEY WEST, FLORIDA

The Best Key Lime Pie—Joan Bernreuter

Joan Bernreuter, *right*, and
pastry chef Barbara Brigham

After savoring the tart goodness of a piece of Key Lime Pie, it is difficult
to believe that it is a child of adversity. Had there been a cow grazing on
remote Key West in the 1800s, today's pie would taste entirely different.
There was no fresh milk within a hundred nautical miles so housewives
turned to sweetened condensed milk, which, when combined with the
juice of the island's plentiful limes, produced the Keys' culinary icon.

We had driven the length of the Keys to have a piece of Key Lime
Pie in Key West where it all began.

I hoped to find the real thing; I had been warned there were impos-
tors. Some are artificially colored green when the pie's true color is a
light yellow, made so by the egg yolks. Some are stiffened with Jell-O or
cornstarch; others are made with graham cracker crusts. Some are
topped with whipped cream instead of a lovely meringue, whose peaks
and valleys have been toasted brown in the oven. Some are even made
with kiwi into mousse and cheesecake variations.

Today the journey was rewarded. We found *the* Key Lime Pie at the
Deli Restaurant, a rather ordinary-looking café on a corner of a residen-
tial block about a quarter of a mile from the town's old business district.
The pie has brought fame to the Deli. I first learned about the Deli and
its owners, Joan and John Bernreuter, from a small paragraph in *The
New York Times*.

Joan's recipe is true "conch"—born in the Keys. If you are a native of the Keys you can rightly call yourself a conch, after the large mollusk with the spiral shell found in surrounding waters. While Joan is only a "near conch," having been born in Mississippi some seventy years ago, the recipe came down through three generations of island-born Bernreuters.

She and John are unhappy with what they consider a sacrilege, and they have gone public with the family's closely held pie recipe. "We've kept it a secret a long time. I thought: Why should I tell them how to do it? I'll just let them sweat it out. But I've changed my mind. I am getting older. What good does it do me to take it to the grave? No, I would just as soon let people know how the original is to be made."

In the beginning, Key West housewives wanted to put to good use the bushels of fruit falling from the lime trees. The lime is about the size of a golf ball, somewhat scraggly looking, with brown spots which discolor and scar the skin. While some people use the larger and more available Persian or Tahitian limes grown abundantly elsewhere in Florida, these limes are never used in an authentic Key lime pie. The Key limes are tarter and sharper.

In the early days, chickens scratched in every yard. Eggs were cheap and plentiful. The yolks went into the pie filling, the whites were whipped into the meringue topping.

Now, unfortunately, Key limes are scarce even here where a disease and a hurricane wiped out commercial growers a half century ago. Nevertheless, most homeowners in the Keys have at least one Key lime tree in their yards. And a bushel of limes carried to the neighboring supermarket will bring a handsome price. While the Deli relies on friends for its fruit, most juice used by restaurants and bakeries comes in bottles from Key Largo, Mexico, and the Bahamas.

Bottled Key lime juice can be purchased in many specialty food stores. My neighbor who winters in Florida brings me a few bottles when he returns north in the late spring.

KEY LIME PIE

[MAKES ONE 8- OR 9-INCH SINGLE-CRUST PIE]

Joan's secrets? First, beat the egg yolks and sweetened condensed milk together. Pour in the lime juice but stir *briefly*—no more than a half-dozen "turns." She emphasizes a very *brief* stir. "If you take too many turns, the acidic lime juice will break down the egg mixture—the filling will be runny. That's why so many cooks use Jell-O or cornstarch."

Eagle Brand milk is the milk of choice in the Deli kitchen. I was delighted to hear that, for I was an Eagle Brand baby, and my mother was certain that was why I grew taller than my father.

The second secret is with the meringue. She does not use cream of tartar to stabilize the egg whites. She thinks that is important to the pie's good taste. She makes the meringue in the mixer; only after the egg whites are fluffed does she pour in sugar, a little at a time.

Graham cracker crusts?

The very thought chokes Joan. "Oh, God, no!" For years she made her own flour piecrusts with Crisco. Now the pressure of making 10 to 12 Key Lime Pies a day ($12 each) has forced her to go commercial. "We tested every piecrust on the market and we finally settled on frozen Pet. We couldn't make them any better."

INGREDIENTS	*One 14-ounce can sweetened condensed milk*
	4 whole eggs, separated
	½ cup Key lime juice
	One 8- or 9-inch baked pie shell, homemade (see page 565) or
	frozen store-bought
	½ cup sugar
EQUIPMENT	One 8- or 9-inch pie pan
PREHEAT	Preheat the oven to 450°—to brown the meringue only.
BEFOREHAND	Make or buy the pie shell.
PREPARATION 12 mins.	Pour the condensed milk into a mixer bowl, add the egg yolks, and beat at moderate speed for 2 minutes.

Stop the mixer. Slowly pour the lime juice into the milk-egg mixture. With a spoon or spatula gently fold the juice into the mixture. *Do not beat.* Pour into the pie shell.

Note: Be certain the beaters and bowl have been washed clean of milk and egg yolk.

Beat the egg whites to hold a peak—and then gradually add the sugar.

With a rubber spatula, pile the meringue around the outer edge of the pie, touching it to the shell; then fill toward the center. Use all of the meringue. Build it high and deep. Finally, give the meringue an artistic swirl.

BAKING 450° 5 mins.	Brown overall until golden, about 5 minutes.
CHILLING 2 hours	Cool on a wire rack before placing the pie in the refrigerator to chill for at least 2 hours.

∿∿∿ *On the Road—CEDAR KEY, FLORIDA*

A Tranquil Place

After driving the length and breadth of Florida in the company of too many cars and trucks going too many directions at the same time, Cedar Key promised to be a welcome retreat.

I had found Cedar Key sticking out on the map like a tiny finger, about a dozen miles south of where the Suwannee River flows into the Gulf of Mexico. The small fishing village is on Way Key, the largest of about forty small barrier islands in the Cedar Key group. It had been a booming settlement a century ago. Fish teemed in the offshore waters and begged to be caught. The big cedar trees for miles around were cut and shipped north to make pencils. Then the boom collapsed, leaving it a backwater town of fewer than a thousand souls. The railroad quit running. Cattle grazed where the cedar forests had been, and not many fish were left.

"Sure looks quiet and peaceful. Picturesque as promised," Marje said as we crossed one of the several small bridges leading into the town. A fishing boat, its owner beating on its engine with a hammer, was tied to a rickety pier in the bayou. Gulls swooped across the water while a dozen or so pelicans sat solemnly on pilings waiting for the small fishing fleet to return at dusk.

We drove to the Island Hotel, which is as old as the town, 150 years, and has a place in the National Register of Historic Places. The ten-room

building was built of hand-hewn cypress boards and faced in tabby, a mixture of lime rock and crushed oyster shells.

The hotel was quaint but dowdy. The welcome mat at the foot of the stairs was badly soiled. We were put in the Richard Boone suite. It was comfortable enough, though there were only three twisted wire clothes hangers on a nail in the wall and our bags were opened on the floor for lack of any other place for them. A mosquito net hanging from the ceiling enclosed the bed. The restaurant, happily, had a deserved reputation for good food.

It was a quiet town. A peaceful town. Not much traffic. In the afternoon I strolled down the *middle* of Main Street for a couple of blocks just to prove it could be done. I wish I had been more observant. I did not see the sign or, if I did, I paid it little attention. It was a big banner, red letters on white canvas, stretched loosely across the front of a tavern less than a hundred yards from our corner room at the hotel. I went back later to check it out. It read: COME PARTY TONIGHT WITH NANCY LUCIA AT THE L&M BAR.

After dinner, I was rocking in one of the chairs on the covered balcony outside our room when I grew curious as to why traffic on the otherwise quiet street below was picking up, and motorcycles and trucks and Jeeps and big old cars were parking under our windows. They didn't disturb me. Not at that moment.

It was ten o'clock and we were asleep when it happened—the crash of brass cymbals at my ear could not be more terrifying. It was heavy metal mayhem! The town was rocking! The buildings were shaking! Full volume! The decibels were leaping!

The sound from the L&M Bar was ricocheting off a motel across the street and directly into our room. At first I was simply annoyed. I thought this too would pass. I couldn't believe it was happening in this sleepy little town. In my PJs I walked out on the balcony and looked down at Main Street. As far as I could see it was jammed with pickup trucks, motorcycles, automobiles, everything but a farm tractor and I wouldn't have been surprised to see that.

From miles around they had come to Cedar Key to celebrate Friday night. By midnight I was so caught up with the action that I stayed on the porch, rocking in my chair and listening and looking. It must have been hot inside the L&M Bar, because couples kept drifting out to cool off in passionate embraces against the building wall across the street.

It got louder as the night wore on. I wondered how the souls in the motel directly across the street could sleep, or had they joined the party?

It now became funny—the race of cars and trucks and motorcycles down Main Street, the jockeying for parking space in front of the hotel, and the cowboys and girls in embraces across the street. "Sure gives you a great feel of the country," I called to Marje who was in bed reading. She did not share my anthropological interest in the scene below.

At two o'clock the band quit, but the partying on the street carried on for another hour. I received a number of friendly greetings shouted up to the balcony. Finally it was quiet. For an hour or so.

Suddenly trucks were barreling up and down Main Street. It was still pitch black. I looked out. Fishermen were coming in trucks, cars, and motorcycles to their fishing boats moored in the marine basin.

At that predawn moment we decided that we would limit our stay at Cedar Key to one night.

∿∿∿GAINESVILLE, FLORIDA

The Sovereign—Chef Elmo Moser

Gainesville—a beautiful small city of 85,000 in north Florida—is just a name on a map and a gas stop on I-75 for most travelers who rush down from the Northern states to winter in exotic places like Naples and Coral Gables and Captiva and then rush back home in the spring. No dawdling along the way.

The Mobil travel guide does little to divert this North-South flow. The guide devotes six lines to the city, describing it as a university town that once was called Hogtown and says one of Gainesville's manufacturing plants makes bows and arrows.

In this sense we were ignorant, too.

Going south, we pulled off the Interstate because (1) it was mid-afternoon of a long day on the road, and (2) we found a motel that would accept Timothy as a guest.

We also discovered The Sovereign, a restaurant several miles across town, beyond the University of Florida campus (35,000 students), in an old brick and beam carriage house that had been rehabbed into a smart, upscale café with a delightful cuisine. Our desk clerk, who had worked there as a waiter, thought we might enjoy it. We did!

A month later, going home by a different route, and after having had only one dinner at The Sovereign, we detoured 150 miles to reach Gainesville and the restaurant—to dine, to spend time in the kitchen, and to talk food with the owners, a remarkable couple.

Chef Elmo Moser, short, bearded, brimming with good humor and wit, Swiss-born, and schooled in the classic cuisine, is married to a raven-haired, dark-eyed beauty born in Mexico who one day a week dedicates the menu to Mexican foods.

"I do it because Elmo likes hot food," Lupe explained. She was the cashier in a Los Angeles restaurant where Elmo was chef. She greeted him one day with a foil-wrapped package of burritos when he stopped at her house to drive her to work.

"My car was always breaking down. I took the wheel and told him to scoot over. I would drive—he would eat. He liked it. We got married!"

When they bought the old carriage house in 1976—it had been a restaurant through three bankruptcies—the accepted cuisine there and elsewhere in town had been black-eyed peas, grits, and barbecue.

Today the menu was saltimbocca sautéed with prosciutto, veal Oscar with crab meat, baked moussaka, scallops ceviche, beluga caviar with iced Absolut vodka, rack of baby lamb, fresh flounder stuffed with crab meat, and drunken fish and seafood doused in bourbon broth with rice! These dishes have won for them a rack full of Golden Spoons from *Florida Trend* magazine.

In the beginning Lupe didn't believe the restaurant's clientele would accept Mexican food, so she prepared it only for Elmo and the waiters. "For about a year I did this. They cleaned their plates and asked for more. That was enough for me to go public." As a consequence, Thursday night is Latino cuisine.

On our second visit to The Sovereign, Lupe took us to our table and, as she did the first time we came, checked the basket of breads on the table. "After all, you *are* the bread man," she said. She beckoned the waiter, who had waited on us the time before, and told him to bring a fresh basket of bread and rolls.

"What's with it with you guys?" he asked when she walked away. "Every time you come into the restaurant she orders the bread changed!"

SHRIMP ELMO

[SERVES 4]

Sautéed shrimp on a bed of spinach sprinkled with black and green olives and Swiss and blue cheese is an easy, quick dish to make. Serve with rice or boiled potatoes. Good!

INGREDIENTS	*20 ounces fresh leaf spinach, or frozen, thawed* *2 tablespoons butter* *Garlic salt, to taste* *Salt and freshly ground black pepper, to taste* *24 (about 1½ pounds) uncooked large shrimp, peeled and deveined* *4 shallots, chopped* *2 tablespoons fresh lemon juice* *Splash of white wine* *8 each black olives and green olives, pitted and sliced* *4 ounces each Swiss cheese, grated, and blue cheese, crumbled*
EQUIPMENT	One au gratin platter
PREHEAT	Preheat the oven to 375°.
PREPARATION 14 mins.	In a medium skillet sauté the spinach with 1 tablespoon of butter, the garlic salt, salt and pepper, about 5 minutes. Place in an au gratin platter and keep warm. In a second skillet sauté the shrimp and the shallots with 1 tablespoon of butter until the shrimp are pink and lightly done, about 4 minutes. Add the lemon juice and white wine.
ASSEMBLING	Place the sautéed shrimp and shallots on top of the spinach, sprinkle with the olives and mixed cheeses.
BAKING 375° 5 mins.	Bake for 5 minutes. Serve hot.

ROAST PORK YUCATÁN

[SERVES 6]

Here is one of Lupe's Thursday-night Mexican contributions. It has an A+ in my kitchen notebook, especially when made with the bone left in the loin to enhance the flavor that comes with an overnight marination. Use achiote paste, made from the seeds of a small tree that grows in the Yucatán which is prized for the yellow color and earthy flavor it imparts to food, and the juice of bitter orange.

Achiote paste, also called annatto paste, can be found in markets that cater to Mexicans and Latinos. If the true bitter orange is not to be had, substitute a mock juice made with the juice of 3 oranges, 2 lemons, and 1 lime.

Serve with white rice.

INGREDIENTS

2 garlic cloves, mashed and finely chopped
1 tablespoon salt
1 tablespoon freshly ground black pepper
One 3- to 4-pound pork loin
1½ teaspoons achiote paste, if available (see above)
1 cup bitter orange juice (see above)
2 tablespoons white vinegar
1 banana leaf (optional)
1 teaspoon cornstarch dissolved in 1 tablespoon water (optional)

EQUIPMENT

One medium roasting pan or Dutch oven with lid

PREPARATION
10 mins.

Make a mixture of garlic, salt, and pepper and rub into the meat. Set the meat aside in a large bowl for the moment.

In a small bowl dissolve the achiote paste in the bitter orange juice and vinegar. Pour this over the pork and, if you have a banana leaf growing outside your door as Lupe does, cover the meat with it.

MARINATING
6 hours
or overnight

Marinate 6 hours or overnight. Cover the bowl loosely with plastic wrap. Turn 2 or 3 times during the marinating period.

PREHEAT

Preheat the oven to 325° 20 minutes before roasting.

BAKING
325°
2½ hours

Place the meat in the roasting pan and pour the marinade over it. Cover and bake for about 2½ hours.

Remove the meat from the pan and set aside. Strain the juice and, if needed, thicken with the dissolved cornstarch. Simmer for a few minutes.

FINAL STEP

Carve the meat and pour the juice over each serving.

CHICKEN JERUSALEM

[SERVES 4]

Made with chicken, mushrooms, and artichoke hearts, this dish takes no more than 5 minutes to prepare and 15 minutes to cook. A pleased diner wrote in the guest book: "An enticing offering. All ingredients go splendidly with the chicken."

INGREDIENTS

4 skinned and boned chicken breasts
Salt and pepper, to taste
Flour, to coat
½ cup vegetable oil
One 11-ounce can artichoke hearts, sliced
1 tablespoon butter
½ cup finely chopped fresh chives or green onions
1 cup thinly sliced mushrooms
8 ounces sour cream, room temperature
White wine (optional)

PREPARATION
5 mins.

With a wide knife blade or rolling pin, flatten down the high part of the breast pieces to make a uniform surface. Salt and pepper the chicken. Roll lightly in flour, shaking off the excess.

COOKING
15 mins.

Heat the oil in a medium skillet and sauté the chicken over medium heat until just done, about 5 minutes. Remove from the pan and keep warm.

Heat the artichoke hearts in a small skillet and set aside.

Drain the oil from the pan. Add the butter, heat, and sauté the chives or green onions and the mushrooms until the mushrooms are tender, about 8 minutes. Remove the skillet from the heat and stir in the sour cream. Heat again until hot but not bubbling. If the sauce seems too thick, add a little white wine.

FINAL STEP

On a serving platter, place the heated artichoke hearts on the warm chicken, and dress with the sauce.

V GREAT LAKES STATES

Indiana Illinois Wisconsin Michigan

Farm Country

Many of the great highways and railroads in the United States cross Indiana and they do so in the northern half of the state, which, while fertile, is monotonously flat. Aside from small cities like Lafayette and Muncie and towns like Delphi and Wabash and the town where I grew up, Zionsville, the rest of it is given over to a vast green carpet of corn and soybeans. Few livestock remain.

I have driven the 150 miles between Indianapolis and Chicago and not seen a cow or a hog. Fences have been pulled down to allow huge tractors and combines to move freely through the fields and harvest to the very edge of the road.

The north and south halves of the state are divided geographically so precisely that one might think The Creator had drawn a straight line from the Ohio state line to Illinois on the west and commanded: "Flat farmland up here—hills and forests down there!"

I live in the "down there" part of the state, on a great watershed that falls away to the Ohio River. Each time I go upstate, from south to north, I am struck with how organized the north is with its orderly division of farm land along straight lines compared to our meanderings along streams and rivers and around hills and up valleys.

We drove north to see a Hungarian friend who lives in the rural part of the state within a few miles of the great steel mills of Gary and East Chicago fringing Lake Michigan. It was midsummer. The weather, hot but with ample rain, had been ideal for the crops. It was August and the corn was elephant-eye high.

272

Driving on a country road with the tall walls of corn coming right down to the berm within a few feet of the car, you get the odd, disoriented sensation of moving through a green corridor which meets other green corridors at intersections. Millions of stalks of corn are uniformly alike. Look up and you see only a narrow slice of sky framed by green. There is no distant horizon. Nothing to give perspective. I have had the same uncomfortable feeling driving through French vineyards in the midst of thousands of grapevines where every turn in the road looks exactly like the turn just passed.

CROWN POINT, INDIANA

The Teacher—Judith Goldinger

Judith Goldinger burst into my kitchen/studio one spring morning with a large glistening white food processor cradled in her arms. Behind her an associate struggled with bags of vegetables and fruits and sacks of flour.

"We've come to show you how it works," she said as she introduced herself—and took over. It would be the first time—and the last—that I was to be a spectator in my own kitchen. I was edgy, but concern changed to admiration as the morning progressed.

Within minutes the food processor was merrily slicing and shredding a mountain of vegetables. "Now, watch this disc," she said, and a stream of perfectly cut carrots shot into the work bowl. "Now, this blade," and a ball of dough spun around the plastic bowl. Suddenly there was a multicourse luncheon, including a hot bread, spread across my big maple worktable. I hadn't turned a hand. I was impressed.

Now, a month later, Marje and I were driving to Judith's home in the country outside Chicago to have a Hungarian meal. A red, white, and green Hungarian flag, tied to a tall staff in the Goldinger front yard, flew in a brisk breeze.

Born in Budapest between World Wars I and II, Judith came of age during the take-over of her country by the Soviets. "I was twenty years old, a wide-eyed, idealistic young woman working as a secretary in the Department of Interior. I was terribly wrapped up in demonstrations in support of Premier Imre Nagy when he stood up against the Russians. I was warned it would happen, and it did—I spent the next three years in prison." When she got out she was allowed to emigrate to America. They considered it good riddance, she said.

Judith was twelve years old when her mother enrolled her in a Budapest school which taught housekeeping skills to young ladies. " 'You will marry a rich man,' my mother said, 'so you must be able to direct the household staff. You must know how to cook, how to prepare a menu, how to shop for food. You must know how to sort the laundry and count the pieces. You must know the proper place settings. All these things and more you must learn. You must be ready!' "

Judith laughed. "Oh, poor Mama. I married for love."

Her husband, Frank Goldinger, a landscape architect for a large Chicago cemetery, is a tall, broad-shouldered man with a commanding mustache and Vandyke beard. He was born in Hungary but did not meet Judith until after he emigrated to the United States. Frank is the traditionalist of the family, insisting that Hungarian food cannot be considered Hungarian food unless it is prepared as it is in the motherland. "No lard tonight," he teased. "And you call this a Hungarian meal!"

He turned to me. "I love the flavor lard gives to all dishes and there is nothing in the world I find more delicious than a piece of rough peasant bread spread with goose fat or lard. Now it is low-cholesterol this and low-cholesterol that. I do miss it."

The Holy Trinity of the Hungarian kitchen is lard, paprika, and onions. A traditional meat dish such as Chicken Paprika would be unimaginable without the three to give it flavor and body. Paprika is produced by grinding the dried pods of the *capsicum annum* pepper. In Hungarian cooking, paprika adds a spark as well as flavor, but it need not be especially hot. While it is on the spice rack in almost every American kitchen, Judith says American cooks use paprika timidly, as though it would bite, or they merely sprinkle some on pale food for a touch of color.

Paprika is what sets Hungarian cooking apart from Polish or German or French, she said. "It is the base for a variety of soups and stews and sauces in which the paprika is sprinkled on onions and then sautéed in lard. The green pepper, too, is much used: as garnish or cooked.

"Hungarian food is food cooked with love. Hungarians want texture changes and visible evidence—namely chopped ingredients, smoothly blended sauces, soups, and stews slowly simmered—of the effort that has gone into preparing their food. Not many shortcuts or hurry-up steps. It could be called conspicuous preparation.

KÖRÖZÖTT
(Liptauer Cheese Spread)

[MAKES 2 CUPS]

Körözött is a delicious cheese mix to be spread over thin slices of a coarse peasant bread. While this mix originated in coffee houses in Budapest, it has since become a national hors d'oeuvre to be served at home. While the several ingredients in Judith's Körözött were swirled together in a food processor, the traditional way is to place the ingredients separately on a serving tray and invite each guest to mix his or her own as taste dictates. Judith uses either feta or chèvre.

INGREDIENTS
¼ pound (1 stick) unsalted butter
½ pound cream cheese
¼ pound feta cheese
1 tablespoon grated onion
1 tablespoon Hungarian paprika
½ teaspoon anchovy paste
½ teaspoon dry mustard
½ teaspoon caraway seeds

PREPARATION
5 mins.
Cream the butter and cheeses in a food processor. Add the onion and the other seasonings and blend well.

FINAL STEP
Serve with a hearty peasant bread on a platter surrounded with radishes and green onions.

PAPRIKÁS CSIRKE
(Chicken Paprika)

[SERVES 5 TO 6]

Chicken Paprika is a delicious example of Hungarian cooking. The meat is coated with thick gravy that clings to the pieces. Sour cream and sweet cream or yogurt are mixed with a little flour and stirred in at the end just before serving.

Judith serves this chicken with the delicious tiny egg dumplings in the following recipe.

INGREDIENTS

1 large chicken, a 4- to 5-pound stewing hen if possible, cut up
1 teaspoon salt, plus extra for chicken
2 tablespoons lard or home-rendered chicken fat
1 cup finely chopped onions
1 garlic clove, finely chopped
1½ tablespoons Hungarian paprika
1 large ripe tomato, peeled and chopped, or 1 cup canned
1 cup chicken stock, homemade (see page 562) or store-bought
1 cup sour cream
2 tablespoons all-purpose flour
2 tablespoons heavy cream or plain yogurt
1 green bell pepper, sliced into thin strips

PREPARATION
5 mins.

Pat the chicken pieces dry with paper towels and salt them generously.

BROWNING
10–12 mins.

In a large skillet, heat the lard over high heat until a light haze forms over it. Add as many chicken pieces, skin side down, as will fit in one layer. After 2 or 3 minutes or when the pieces are a golden brown, turn them with tongs and brown the other side. Remove the pieces as they brown and continue with uncooked ones. This will take about 12 minutes in all.

COOKING
35–45 mins.

Pour off the fat, leaving only a thin film. Add the onions and garlic, cover and smother over medium-low heat until lightly colored, about 8 minutes.

Off the heat, stir in the paprika and 1 teaspoon of salt and stir until the onions are well coated. Add the tomato. Return the skillet to the heat and add the chicken stock. Bring to a boil, stirring in the brown bits from the bottom and sides of the pan.

Return the chicken pieces to the skillet. Bring the liquid to a boil again, turn the heat to its lowest point, and cover the skillet tightly. Simmer the chicken for 25 to 35 minutes, or until the juice from a thigh runs yellow when it is pierced. (*Note:* If the bird is a real stewing chicken it may need more cooking time and probably more liquid than the young, small supermarket chicken.)

When the chicken is done remove to a platter. Skim the surface fat from the skillet.

SAUCE
9–12 mins.

In a mixing bowl, stir the sour cream, flour, and heavy cream or yogurt, then stir the mixture into the simmering juices. Simmer for 6 to 8 minutes, or until the sauce is think and smooth.

Return the chicken to the skillet. Add the green pepper slices. Baste with the sauce, and simmer for 3 or 4 minutes to heat the pieces through.

FINAL STEP

Remove from the heat and let stand for a few minutes before serving.

NOKKEDLI
(Tiny Egg Dumplings)

[SERVES 6]

These dumplings are easy to make but require a certain degree of skill in cutting them uniformly from a piece of dough and pushing them into a pot of simmering water. But the trick will come quickly.

The dumplings can be made with vegetable shortening instead of lard, but they won't have quite the taste that is cherished by Hungarians.

INGREDIENTS

1 egg
1 tablespoon lard or vegetable shortening, melted, plus
    2 teaspoons
8⅓ cups water
1 teaspoon plus 1 tablespoon salt
1½ cups all-purpose flour

EQUIPMENT

A small cutting board that can be held in one hand at the edge of the pan of simmering water while the second hand cuts the dough with a knife and pushes the dumplings into the water

PREPARATION
10 mins.

In a small bowl mix the egg, melted lard, ⅓ cup of water, and 1 teaspoon of salt.

In a larger bowl pour the flour and make a crater in the center. Stir in the egg-lard mixture to form a soft dough—just beyond stickiness when handled.

continued

Stir the tablespoon of salt into the 2 quarts of water and bring to a boil in a 3-quart saucepan.

SHAPING
10 mins.

Place 3 or 4 tablespoons of the dough on the wooden board held at the edge of the pan of water. With the dull side of a knife, cut and push tiny portions of the dough into the simmering water. Dip the blade in the water occasionally so the dumplings do not stick to the blade. When all the dumplings have surfaced, remove with a slotted spoon into a colander. Rinse with cold running water.

REHEATING
3 mins.

Heat the 2 teaspoons of lard in a skillet over medium-high heat. Toss the dumplings in the skillet for about 3 minutes to reheat.

FINAL STEP

Served with the Chicken Paprika the two make an attractive and delicious couple. The recipe can be doubled to have dumplings to spare to be reheated for a later meal.

◤◥◤◥◤◥On the Road—CHICAGO

A City to Like

Chicago is a favorite city of mine. I was assigned to the Time-Life Chicago bureau in 1940, the first full-time *Life* editorial representative to be sent out of New York. The magazine was new and I was twenty-three. Our daughter was born there. When World War II started, I reluctantly left to open a bureau in San Francisco.

I find reason to like Chicago more each time I visit. This time it was three outstanding restaurants—Prairie (see below), Avanzare, and Scoozi, the later two owned by Lettuce Entertain You Enterprises, Inc., a sharp, innovative outfit which has created a sensation in the city with these and a dozen other restaurants.

It was a night off. No anxiety about an interview with a cook or chef or working in a kitchen. Nothing but the pleasure of dining with friends in a good restaurant.

Scoozi is in a barnlike building on West Huron Street with exposed wooden timbers supporting a roof the length of a basketball court. Informal. The chef calls the menu "country Italian." Outstanding was the shared smoked pheasant and wild mushrooms on polenta. For the three of us it was charred jumbo sea scallops; risotto with spinach; ricotta cheese and wild mushrooms; grilled tuna with an avocado, basil, and caper relish; chicken breast stuffed with goat cheese; and a special order of fusilli, roasted eggplant, peppers, olives, and pine nuts in extra-virgin olive oil.

The Avanzare, a sister restaurant, is a more upscale place on East Huron with a menu inspired by the kitchens of northern Italy. A sampling there included grilled asparagus and sun-dried tomatoes with feta; baked polenta covered with Italian sausage, goat cheese, and tomato sauce; veal scallopini with wild mushrooms, radicchio, and orzo, topped with a creamy sauce; red chili pasta with shrimp, eggplant, ricotta, and sun-dried tomatoes; and spinach pasta with a filling of three cheeses.

The word "sweetbreads" on a menu will blind me to any other item no matter how exquisite. This has been so since I was a child. Tonight my entrée was sweetbreads garnished with crayfish and pine nuts. Superb.

ＣＨＩＣＡＧＯ, ILLINOIS

Prairie—Chef Stephen Langlois

If it grazes, swims, or grows within a few hundred miles of Chicago, you may expect to find it on the menu at Prairie. If it does not come from the Midwest, it doesn't come through the kitchen door. "We don't do shrimp and oysters from coastal waters nor do we have sweet corn from Mexico in the middle of the winter," Chef Stephen Langlois explained.

The inspiration for the Prairie cuisine is credited to Frank Lloyd Wright, the renowned Midwest-born architect. When it was decided to build a restaurant as part of a hotel complex in historic Printer's Row on south Dearborn Street, Wright came immediately to mind, although the building, a historic landmark, had not been his design.

"We found a Wright directive to his students that encompassed everything we wanted but hadn't been able to put into words. 'Make it regional in character, traditional in values and uniquely modern.' And that's the way we went," said Langlois.

Named for Wright's Prairie school of architecture, the interior combined honey-colored oak and earth tones for which the architect was noted. Tables, chairs, and tableware recall the angular designs found in his many buildings in the Chicago area. Overall, attractive and spare.

But it was in the Prairie's cuisine that the Wright dictum had had the greatest influence. "It set the course. We went completely heartland but not just with corn, beef, chicken, and pork. Not just mashed potatoes and gravy. It was to be, as Wright said, uniquely modern. And I think we have done it," said Langlois.

"Our Schaum torte is an example. It is a German-American classic and a typical Wisconsin dessert—traditionally a meringue shell filled with ice cream and canned strawberry syrup," Langlois explained. "I thought it was too sweet, goopy, and gooey. We updated it with a walnut-laced meringue shell, split and filled it with homemade apple-cinnamon ice cream, topped with fresh berries."

How has it been accepted by Schaum-lovers? "Interestingly, a few hard-liners say we ruined it, while most say, 'God, this is great. Even better than Mama's.' "

Chicken in all of its forms has long been a favorite of Midwest families. Langlois seasoned his roast chicken just with salt, pepper, and paprika. It is served over bacon–corn bread dressing. In place of gravy, there is a rich cream sauce flavored with fresh sage and chives. Grilled chicken is marinated in walnut and vegetable oils, catsup, mustard, and honey, which becomes the sauce served with the meat as well.

For many weeks prior to the opening in 1987, Chef Langlois was on the road visiting festivals and county and state fairs in a half-dozen states, searching for best-ever apple pie recipes and tramping through a Michigan woods with a farmer looking for morel mushrooms. He gleaned traditional recipes from old cookbooks that belonged to historical societies, and churches, and in settlements records. He talked to home cooks and cooks in small-town diners and cafés.

He searched for local products and suppliers of indigenous ingredients. Ranging over ten Midwestern states, Langlois found sources for Sheboygan sausages; Wisconsin pheasant, duck, and cheese; Minnesota wild rice; Indiana persimmons; Kentucky quail; and Michigan crayfish, mushrooms, and dried fruits. He found a source for buffalo on a farm in northern Michigan which is now sending him via Greyhound a thousand pounds of buffalo loin each month. Some of it is made into summer sausages as well as used in Prairie's Kentucky burgoo.

The chef's considerable talents have taken him in a few short years from a kid sorting lobsters in a Maine seafood café to executive chef of a four-star restaurant by age twenty-seven. Head of his 1984 class at the Culinary Institute of America and picked as most likely to succeed, a year later he was selected by the *Chicago Tribune* as one of five of the city's up-and-coming young chefs.

Langlois is an articulate, confident young man, pleased with his celebrity. I found it odd to address him formally as Chef Langlois. I am forty-five years his senior and felt even older each time he referred to "the old times" and "the old days," back before electric refrigerators and freezers in the home. I could not bring myself to tell him that one of my summertime chores as a kid was to empty the pan of water collecting from the melting ice in the kitchen icebox.

BAKED STUFFED WALLEYE PIKE

[SERVES 4]

Sandwiched between pike fillets is a stuffing made with wild rice, barley, and spinach and garnished with four herbs—chervil, curly parsley, cilantro, and broadleaf parsley. The baked fish is then cut into thin slices and served surrounded by a lemon butter sauce. Each time I have this fish it gets a high mark in my kitchen notebook. Bass or bluefish fillets may be substituted.

Run your finger over the center of the fillet to feel if there are any small pin bones at the head end. If a fillet is thin, pluck out the bones with pin-nose pliers or tweezers. When the pin bones are big and strong, cut down the fillet on both sides of the bones and remove the thin strip of flesh with the pin bones embedded in it. No big chore.

INGREDIENTS

Five 8- to 10-ounce pike fillets, about 2 pounds

STUFFING
1 fillet from above
¼ pound spinach leaves, washed and stemmed
1 small carrot, diced
1 small red onion, finely chopped
1 tablespoon butter
1 egg
¾ cup heavy cream
¾ cup cooked wild rice
2 tablespoons cooked barley (optional)
Salt and white pepper, to taste

Salt and white pepper, to taste
Paprika, to sprinkle
½ cup fish stock (see page 563) or dry white wine
Lemon Butter Sauce (recipe follows)
2 tablespoons each finely chopped chervil, curly parsley,
*   cilantro, and broadleaf parsley, to garnish*

EQUIPMENT

One baking dish or casserole, buttered

CHILLING
2 hours

Chill the fish in the refrigerator for 2 hours, or for 20 minutes in the freezer. Skin one of the fillets and pull out the pin bones. Cut it into pieces to be fed into the food processor and return to the refrigerator.

PREPARATION
12 mins.

While the fish is chilling blanch the spinach. Sauté the carrot and onion in the butter until they are tender, about 10 minutes. Drain and chop the spinach.

Puree the chilled fish pieces in the food processor into a very fine paste. Add the egg and continue to puree for an additional 45 seconds.

Add the cream gradually until blended but do not overwhip. Stop the machine immediately as soon as all of the cream has been added.

Fold in the wild rice, barley (if using), spinach, carrot, and onion. Season to taste with salt and pepper.

PREHEAT

Preheat the oven to 400°.

ASSEMBLING
10–15 mins.

Trim and skin the 4 fillets and remove all pin bones (see above).

Place 1 fillet in the baking dish and season lightly with salt and pepper. Spread a portion of the stuffing mixture over the fillet. Top with the second fillet and sprinkle lightly with paprika, salt and pepper. Be certain the 2 fillets are the same size and placed tail matching tail. Repeat with the 2 remaining fillets.

Pour the fish stock or white wine around the fillets.

BAKING
400°
25–30 mins.

Bake for 25 to 30 minutes or until a small piece of the flesh can be flaked off with a fork. Don't overcook. While baking, make the Lemon Butter Sauce.

FINAL STEP

Remove from the oven and cut eight or ten ¼-inch slices. Each stuffed fish makes 2 portions.

Arrange 4 to 5 slices on each plate and surround with Lemon Butter Sauce. Sprinkle generously with the chopped herb mixture and serve.

Lemon Butter Sauce

[MAKES 1 PINT]

INGREDIENTS

½ cup fresh lemon juice
¼ cup dry white wine
¼ teaspoon black peppercorns
1 bay leaf
1 shallot, finely diced
1 bunch parsley, stems only
Splash of white wine vinegar
¾ cup heavy cream
1 cup (2 sticks) unsalted butter
Salt and white pepper, to taste

PREPARATION
20 mins.

Combine all of the ingredients except the cream, butter, and salt and pepper in a sauce pot and reduce over medium-low heat. Add the heavy cream and reduce over heat by two thirds.

COOKING
8–10 mins.

Cut the butter into 1-inch pieces. While the sauce simmers, slowly incorporate the butter, piece by piece, into the sauce with a wire whisk. After all of the butter has been added, be sure the sauce does not boil. Season to taste with salt and white pepper.

GRILLED HONEY-MUSTARD CHICKEN

[SERVES 4]

The chicken pieces are marinated in a honey-mustard mixture for 24 hours before grilling. The marinade is then transformed into a rich sauce with cream, butter, and fresh tarragon. The Prairie favors grilling/smoking the chicken over coals of either mesquite, hickory, or applewood.

INGREDIENTS

4 boneless chicken breasts, skin on
4 boneless chicken legs or thighs, skin on

MARINADE
¼ cup each vegetable oil and walnut oil
½ cup honey
½ cup tomato catsup
5 shallots, peeled and chopped
5 garlic cloves, peeled and chopped
¼ cup Dijon mustard
1 tablespoon dried tarragon
1 cup water

SAUCE
Reserved marinade
¼ cup whipping cream
½ cup (1 stick) unsalted butter cut into 1-inch pieces
Salt and pepper, to taste

½ cup chopped fresh chives

MARINATING
24 hours

Place the chicken pieces in a pan large enough to hold them in one layer.

Combine all of the marinade ingredients and pour over the chicken pieces. Cover with plastic wrap and refrigerate for 24 hours. Turn the pieces several times during the marination. Remove just before grilling. Reserve the marinade.

PREPARATION
30–40 mins.

The charcoal fire should be started in sufficient time to allow the coals to burn down to a moderate heat—not a blast furnace—in about 30 to 40 minutes.

SAUCE
15 mins.

Combine the reserved marinade and the cream in a nonaluminum sauce pot, and reduce slowly by half or until thick enough to cover the back of a spoon, about 15 minutes. Slowly incorporate the butter with a wire whisk to form a blend.

Simmer only. Do not let it boil.

Pour the sauce into a blender and at high speed blend for 2 to 3 minutes until smooth and silky.

Strain the sauce through a fine mesh strainer or cheesecloth and season with salt and pepper. Put aside.

GRILLING
15–20 mins.

Grill the chicken, skin side down, until crispy. Turn and continue to grill until done, a total of 15 to 20 minutes over a moderately hot fire.

FINAL STEP

Serve sliced or whole atop the sauce, and sprinkle liberally with the chives. Pass the sauce to guests who may wish more.

PRAIRIE PLUM KETCHUP

[MAKES 1 QUART]

If honey mustard is not your choice with chicken, try Prairie Plum Ketchup made with plums, zest of orange and lemon, spices, a touch of hot pepper and mustard, plus a dollop of port wine. It is delicious with almost any meat, especially pork.

Be forewarned, however, that it is so addictive you will be using it with just about everything. Don't think a quart is too much.

INGREDIENTS

2 teaspoons minced shallots
1 tablespoon orange zest
2 teaspoons lemon zest
6 cups canned whole plums with syrup
½ cup plum preserves
⅓ cup each orange juice and lemon juice
1 teaspoon each Dijon mustard, grated nutmeg, ground ginger,
    cayenne pepper, and salt
¼ cup port wine

PREPARATION
10 mins.

Place the shallots in a small saucepan, cover with boiling water, and simmer for 2 minutes. Drain and reserve.

Place the orange and lemon zests in the pan, add boiling water to cover, simmer the zest, covered, for 5 minutes. Drain and reserve.

Remove the pits from the canned plums and coarsely chop them.

COOKING
1½ hours

In a medium-size saucepan combine all of the ingredients except the port wine. Bring to a boil, reduce to a simmer over medium-low heat, stirring often until the ketchup thickens, about 1½ hours.

REFRIGERATING
overnight

Pour the ketchup into a clean container and refrigerate overnight.

FINAL STEP

The next day stir in the port wine.

SOUR CREAM–RAISIN PIE

[MAKES ONE 9-INCH PIE]

Sour Cream–Raisin Pie is the upscale version of a pie baked in Amish kitchens. The Prairie serves it because it is a delicious pastry.

INGREDIENTS

Two 9-inch pie shells, one for filling, the other for the lattice top (see page 565)
1½ cups dark raisins
½ cup water
½ cup each granulated sugar and brown sugar
1 tablespoon flour
¼ teaspoon each salt, grated nutmeg, and ground cinnamon
2 teaspoons lemon zest
⅓ cup lemon juice
3 eggs
1 cup sour cream
1 egg yolk stirred with 1 tablespoon water, to glaze

EQUIPMENT

One 9-inch pie pan

PREHEAT

Preheat the oven to 450°.

PREPARATION
20 mins.

Prepare the pastry dough and line the pie pan, but do not bake. Set it aside along with the dough for the lattice top.

In a saucepan place the raisins and water and bring to a boil. Lower the heat and simmer for 5 minutes.

In a bowl mix the two sugars, flour, salt, spices, lemon zest, and lemon juice. Pour into the raisin-water mixture, stirring constantly until slightly thickened. Remove from the heat and cool.

In a bowl beat the eggs with the sour cream until blended. Stir in the cooled raisin mixture. Spoon the mixture into the prepared pie shell. Roll out the dough for the lattice work; cut into strips and top to form a lattice crust. Brush the top dough strips with the yolk-water glaze.

BAKING
450°
15 mins.
350°
30 mins.

Bake for 15 minutes. Reduce the heat to 350° and continue to bake for 30 additional minutes, or until the strips are a golden brown and the filling in the center of the pie is hot and bubbling. If the edges should brown too rapidly, cover with a narrow strip of foil.

Serve warm.

〰〰〰 *CHICAGO, ILLINOIS*

A Special Barbecue—Wayne Robinson

Wayne Robinson, *right*

A measure of Wayne Robinson's talent as a cook is his made-from-scratch barbecue sauce with fourteen ingredients that any sparerib should be proud to be slathered with. While it may not win sauce contests in such barbecue hotbeds as Kansas City and Amarillo, for those who like to taste the meat beneath the sauce and not have one's pallet withered by heat, his special mixture is a blessing.

The sauce is piquant. Very. Defined by Webster: "pleasantly sharp." Precisely. Its character rests in large part on the liberal use of vinegar and lemon juice, and only a modest amount of hot stuff such as Tabasco. The vinegar is not one of those exotic ones but plain white vinegar. Jug vinegar, I would call it. The lemons are squeezed and both the juice and the lemon peel are added to the simmering sauce.

I met Wayne through a mutual friend, a writer for the food section of the *Chicago Tribune*. "He does wonderful things with his cooking—and his life," the writer said. Wayne, who is thirty-six, lives on Chicago's South Side near the University of Chicago campus. His house is just a few steps away from a Frank Lloyd Wright house which sets the tone for the quiet neighborhood of lovely old homes, many of which, including his, are being restored. His next big project is to tear out a couple of walls to enlarge the kitchen and give the cook more work space. (The ruggedly built Chambers gas stove from the 1950s, in mint condition, will stay.)

Wayne was to make a barbecue with all the trimmings—spareribs; lemon chicken; green beans; black-eyed pea and corn salad; sliced tomatoes; and for dessert, lemon cake with fresh blueberries. And a summertime beverage: fresh-squeezed lemonade.

Together we went shopping for ribs at Moo & Oink, Inc., a meat company on Stony Island Avenue. An amazing place. While it was cold in the big refrigerated building, the talk and the laughter among the customers and clerks was warm and happy. Behind butcher blocks, a dozen white-coated men and women cut, trimmed, weighed, and packaged an astounding variety and volume of meat—mountains of chicken wings, necks, legs, breasts, thighs, and feet heaped on stainless-steel tables. The pork ribs were wheeled into the room in huge steel tubs holding several hundred pounds of meat, and as each customer pointed to his or her selection it was swiftly packaged by a clerk.

Our barbecue began with the purchase of lean ribs. Wayne allows six to eight ribs to a person, more if it is the kind of an eating affair that may go on for hours with guests coming back for seconds, thirds, and fourths.

Here are my notes as Wayne moved between the kitchen and the grill outside.

• Begin by sprinkling the meat liberally with freshly ground black pepper and garlic powder. Rub in by hand.

• The ribs will be over the coals for about 2 hours so build the fire accordingly, with additional pieces of charcoal dropped on from time to time to keep a good base going. Not an inferno.

• When the meat is placed on the grill, sprinkle with vinegar, beer, and lemon juice. Repeat this each time the ribs are turned.

• Cook the ribs slowly so the heat can penetrate into the thickest meat. There should be no crust that will prevent the heat from getting into the ribs.

• While the meat is grilling, cook the sauce.

FOURTEEN-INGREDIENT SAUCE

[MAKES 6 CUPS]

Sauce is not slathered on while the meat is on the grill except for the final 30 minutes. He begins the last half hour by taking the ribs off the grill and coating them liberally with sauce. Back over the fire, he turns the meat 4 times during the final period. Each time he *drips* on additional sauce. He does not brush it on.

INGREDIENTS
2 cups white vinegar, plus some to sprinkle
¾ cup brown sugar
1 large onion, quartered
Juice of 3 large lemons, plus some to sprinkle, reserve peels
1 large garlic clove, peeled but not sliced
1 cup water
½ teaspoon freshly ground black pepper
¼ teaspoon cayenne pepper
One 6-ounce can tomato paste
½ cup Worcestershire sauce
¼ cup soy sauce
8 to 10 dashes Tabasco sauce
½ cup (1 stick) unsalted butter

PREPARATION
5–10 mins.

In a medium saucepan pour the vinegar and sugar and bring to a boil. Add the onion, plus the lemon juice and the squeezed lemon peel, and the garlic clove. Return to a boil.

Add the water and simmer for 5 minutes. Add the remaining ingredients including the butter.

SIMMERING
1 hour

Simmer for an hour or more. The sauce should have the consistency of cream; it should not be goopy or thick.

FINAL STEP

Coat the ribs, following Wayne's procedure (see above), sprinkling on additional lemon juice and vinegar.

MARINADE FOR FOUR-MUSTARD CHICKEN

[MAKES ENOUGH FOR 8 CHICKEN BREASTS]

To use, pour the marinade into a plastic bag. Add the chicken pieces. Toss until all of the pieces are covered. Refrigerate for at least an hour, longer preferably, to allow the chicken and sauce to marry well. Bring the chicken to room temperature before grilling.

INGREDIENTS
½ cup each of 4 mustards of choice (e.g.: a spicy Creole, a traditional French poupon, a very hot Diablo, and white wine)
½ cup apple juice
¼ cup red vinegar
⅛ cup white vinegar
Juice of ½ lemon
1 shallot, thinly sliced
½ teaspoon freshly ground black pepper
¼ cup olive oil

PREPARATION

Combine all the ingredients and refrigerate until needed.

PEPPER STEAK

[SERVES 4]

I think a properly peppered steak is a great way to cook a delicious piece of meat. By "properly," I mean pounding the cracked peppercorns into the surface of the steak before it is grilled—*not* using an enfeebled sauce that is poured on after the fact.

Wayne does it properly with a 1-inch-thick rib eye. The black peppercorns are cracked with a hammer or coarsely ground in a mill. Pound the pepper into the meat by hand, through a piece of plastic wrap, if desired.

INGREDIENTS

4 steaks, of choice
½ cup black peppercorns, cracked or crushed
4 tablespoons (½ stick) unsalted butter
1 shallot, thinly sliced
½ cup finely chopped onions
½ cup lemon juice
½ cup brandy

PREPARATION
15 mins.

Prepare the grill. When it is ready, pepper the steaks (see above) and drop them on the hot grill.

Immediately spread ½ tablespoon butter over each steak.

COOKING
3–10 mins.

Meanwhile, in a small skillet, sauté the shallot and onions in 2 tablespoons butter; add the lemon juice and brandy.

When the butter has melted, liberally daub onto the steaks. Turn the steaks and repeat. Grill the steaks to personal taste from 3 to 10 minutes. (Refrigerate any remaining sauce for later use.)

FINAL STEP

Serve the steaks with oven-roasted potatoes.

BLACK-EYED PEA SALAD

[SERVES 6 TO 8]

This salad begins with small cubes of ham simmered in a mixture of sugar, cloves, and mustard. The meat is mixed with the vegetables, and the salad refrigerated overnight before serving.

INGREDIENTS

4 cups frozen black-eyed peas, cooked to package instructions,
*   or 2 cups dry peas (see page 248)*
1 red bell pepper, roasted, peeled, seeded, and diced
1½ cups cooked fresh or frozen corn kernels

¾-pound slice baked ham cut into ¼-inch cubes
¼ cup brown sugar
6 whole cloves
⅛ teaspoon ground mustard
1 jalapeño pepper, seeded and minced
¼ cup water
¼ cup olive oil
¼ cup fresh lime juice
1 teaspoon freshly ground black pepper
½ teaspoon salt, or to taste
⅓ cup chopped parsley
⅓ cup thinly sliced green onions

PREPARATION

Prepare the black-eyed peas, roast the bell pepper, cook the corn kernels, and cut ham cubes and reserve.

COOKING
15 mins.

Simmer the ham cubes in a mixture of the brown sugar, cloves, mustard, jalapeño pepper, and water over medium heat for about 10 minutes.

Discard the cloves. Mix the ham cubes and juice from the skillet with the peas and the remainder of the ingredients.

REFRIGERATION
overnight

Place the salad in a covered bowl and refrigerate overnight. Stir occasionally. Serve cold.

⋙LIBERTYVILLE, ILLINOIS

Champion—Debbie Vanni

Debbie Vanni is a home cook. A particularly good one. Her dishes have won prizes and praises. One accolade came from the *Chicago Tribune* food staff. I asked a couple of the food editors and writers, whom I had known, who they considered one of the best home cooks in the paper's circulation area—a large piece of the Midwest—and their response was overwhelming: Debbie Vanni.

"When a news release comes to the newspaper carrying a list of

Debbie Vanni, *left*,
and daughters

winners of a major contest we are surprised only when her name is *not* on it. If there were world-class winners she would be among them."

We were at the Vannis in suburban Chicago for dinner. It had been a busy week for her. It began with a backyard barbecue party for the linemen of the Chicago Bears professional football team, coaches, wives, and kids. Now she was in stride for us—the *Chicago Tribune* food editor, a food stylist, two cookbook authors, and Debbie's husband, Bill. The two young Vanni girls, Kristina and Kara, ate hot dogs in the kitchen. The centerpiece of the affair was a fresh Norwegian salmon grilled by Bill, a structural engineer in earthquake damage control.

Earlier we had talked about food and bake- and cook-offs and how to win. She sandwiched me in between laundry and midmorning snacks for a hundred children at her church's summer Bible school. Later in the week she would do a Hawaiian birthday luau in the backyard for Kristina.

Through all of this, she confided, she was thinking about regional and national cooking contests—which to enter, now that the fall and winter contest season was fast approaching.

At the moment she was thinking *Pillsbury Bake-Off!* Contesters call it "the elite, the royal, the queen of contests, the *big* one!" It means fame for the one hundred chosen contestants just for being selected to go to Phoenix, plus $40,000 for the first-place winner. With a lead time of six months before recipes are to be submitted, she had decided this year to submit ten recipes in the hope of having one a winner.

This would be Debbie's second Bake-Off. The first was in 1986—the thirty-second Bake-Off contest—when she and Bill and their two daughters were flown to Orlando. She baked her Caramel Almond Apple Tart in the "Rewards and Treats" category. "I didn't win the $40,000, but the recipe was published in the Pillsbury Bake-Off book that year. We were treated grandly. It was wonderful." (Had she been the big winner, a Chicago grocery chain would have matched the $40,000.)

[Note: Culinary talent runs deep in the family. In the subsequent thirty-fifth Bake-Off at Disney World, her twelve-year-old daughter Kristina won $2,000 and a TV set for a raspberry-filled apricot cake, and Debbie's mother, Pat Bradley, won $10,000 for a creamy broccoli and wild rice soup.]

Debbie's celebrity as a cook began early. When she returned for the eighteenth reunion of high school girlfriends, the first question, after hugs and kisses: "Did you bring us your chocolate chip cookies?" Baking cookies to take to grade school started with her mother's example and then a couple of years later she took over when she had learned to bake. "I think I was about eight years old. By the time I was a senior I had established quite a reputation among my classmates."

Debbie, who holds a degree in nutrition and food science from Northern Illinois University, was the Lake County health department nutritionist at the time she was urged by a neighbor to enter the county fair contest. She came away with Grand Champion ribbons for her Almond Brioche Coffee Cake, Caramel Apple Pie, and Painted Christmas Cookies. She won so consistently in the next four years, blanking out all competition, that the fair executives asked if she wouldn't mind being a judge and give others a chance.

For her venture into the big-time competition, she won an Oster kitchen center (a combination of a number of kitchen appliances in one unit) in a Kellogg cereal contest with her bran bread. That summer she won two other contests. Prizes: Oster kitchen centers. That Christmas relatives were gifted with kitchen centers.

In 1987 she and Bill and the girls were flown by the Beef Industry Council to Sun Valley, Idaho, where she won $2,500 and a kiss from actor James Garner for her outdoor barbecue recipe. A year later she flew to Hershey, Pennsylvania, where she prepared a prizewinning Chicken with Black-Eyed Pea Salsa in the National Chicken Cooking Contest. She now is part of a circuit of amateur recipe contests and cookoffs throughout the country year-around. Sponsored by food manufacturers, trade associations, and local festivals, more than three thousand contests honor everything from apples and cheese to catfish and garlic.

"The money is not the big thing. It's nice, but winning is better. Over the years I have won a microwave oven, a number of wonderful vacations for the family, the kitchen centers, toasters, bags of groceries, as well as a bundle of blue ribbons, a box of medals and plaques that cover my kitchen wall. The twenty-five-hundred-dollar win has been the biggest, with one hundred dollars here and two hundred dollars there.

"It's the thrill of winning and the fun of going to the finals in such wonderful places as San Francisco and Sun Valley and New York City. It's a reunion—a get-together of old friends. There is a whole network of us throughout the United States. We write and keep in touch. We send news of new contests in round-robin letters. Most of us would rather win something less than "the big one," because you can't go back again if you win it."

A contest begins at Debbie's refrigerator door where she hangs dozens of announcements of likely contests. These have been winnowed from the hundreds she quickly scans in newspaper food sections, women's magazines, and mailings. These she will ponder each time she opens the refrigerator door. What prizes are offered? Where will the finals be held? Can Bill go with her? Will it be a fun place for the young girls? Are the chief ingredients readily available and at what cost? She enters about ten major contests a year.

New recipes just don't happen. There is no sudden flash of lightning, no roll of thunder, no voice in the night to reveal a winning recipe. Usually they begin with a trip to her basement where she has a library of some six hundred cookbooks including all of the Pillsbury Bake-Off books, starting with the first in 1949. Metal file drawers fairly burst with hundreds of folders filled with recipes she has clipped from newspapers and magazines over the years.

Much of this wealth of information, especially about contests, is now on her computer. She can call up statistics to show that judges in the Pillsbury contest in 1986, for example, were partial to entries whose ingredients included apples, nuts, and cream cheese. She has similar profiles of dozens of other national contests that guide her in developing new recipes.

"I ask myself what new ingredients and what new techniques can I discover in a computer search that will give a recipe that special fillip that will catch the attention of a panel of judges." When she has designed a new recipe, she will make the dish once or twice but never a third time. "It is such a waste, and it costs." (She budgets herself to $150 a week for contest costs and family food.)

Here are two of her winners.

CORN AND SAUSAGE CHOWDER

[SERVES 6]

Midwest Living magazine liked this chowder so much that it gave a microwave oven to Debbie in one of her early competitions. She prepared the chowder for lunch after we had shopped for corn at the Libertyville Farmers Market. Corn fresh from the field is best, certainly, but when it is out of season canned peg corn may be substituted to go along with the canned cream-style corn.

INGREDIENTS	*3 ears of fresh corn (2 cups kernels)* *1 pound bulk pork sausage* *1 cup chopped onions* *4 cups potatoes, cut into ½-inch dice* *2 teaspoons salt* *½ teaspoon dried marjoram* *⅛ teaspoon freshly ground black pepper* *2 cups water* *One 16-ounce can cream-style corn* *12 ounces evaporated milk* *Parsley, chopped, to garnish*
EQUIPMENT	One 4-quart soup pot
PREPARATION 4 mins.	Cook the corn in boiling water. If picked in the garden and raced to the kitchen, 4 minutes will be enough. If store-bought, about 5 minutes. Set aside to cool before cutting.
COOKING 30–35 mins.	Brown the sausage in the soup pot over medium heat for about 8 minutes. After 5 minutes of cooking, add the onions to the pot. Add the potatoes, salt, marjoram, pepper, and 2 cups water. Bring to a boil and then turn down to a simmer and cook until the potatoes test done, about 20 to 25 minutes.
ASSEMBLING 4 mins.	Add both corns and the evaporated milk and bring to a steaming heat. Don't boil.
FINAL STEP	Ladle the chowder into warm bowls, garnish with chopped parsley, and serve.

SHRIMP AND FETA GREEK-STYLE PIZZA

[SERVES 6 WITH HEARTY APPETITES]

A few months after I left Debbie I turned to a TV network show of the Pillsbury Bake-Off in Phoenix hoping to see Debbie in action. The camera panned instead to two young girls carrying a big poster: "Go for it, Mom!" It was daughters Kristina and Kara.

Debbie had gone for it with this pizza, reprinted here with permission of Pillsbury BAKE-OFF® Cooking and Baking Contest. A 12-ounce package of frozen medium shrimp, thawed and drained, can be substituted for fresh shrimp.

INGREDIENTS	*1 tablespoon cornmeal* *One 10-ounce package Pillsbury Refrigerated All Ready Pizza Crust* *1 cup shredded mozzarella cheese* *1 tablespoon olive oil* *1 pound uncooked fresh medium shrimp, shelled and deveined* *2 garlic cloves, minced* *½ cup crumbled feta cheese* *¼ cup sliced green onion, some green tops included* *1 to 2 teaspoons crushed dried rosemary, or 1 tablespoon fresh* *One 2½-ounce can sliced ripe olives, drained*
EQUIPMENT	One 12-inch pizza pan or 13 x 9-inch pan, greased
PREHEAT	Preheat the oven to 425°.
PREPARATION 5 mins.	Sprinkle the greased pizza pan with the cornmeal. Unroll the dough and place in the greased pan; starting at the center, press out with your hands. Sprinkle with mozzarella.
COOKING 1 min.	Heat the olive oil in a large skillet over medium-high heat; add the shrimp and garlic. Cook only until the shrimp are pink, about 1 minute, stirring frequently. Don't overcook.
ASSEMBLING 5 mins.	Spoon the shrimp and garlic over the mozzarella cheese. Sprinkle evenly with the feta, green onion, rosemary, and olives.
BAKING 425° 18–22 mins.	Bake until golden and bubbly, 18 to 22 minutes, or until the crust is golden brown. Cut and serve hot!

~~~~~~~~*SHEBOYGAN, WISCONSIN*

The Brat (Rhymes with Cot)—
Roland Schomberg and Harold Lindemann

The van was en route to Sheboygan, a small city of 50,000 on the western shore of Lake Michigan, north of Milwaukee. My hope was to meet up with a true bratwurst, a savory link of pork sausage of German lineage that has been the joy of the outdoor-grill set for decades.

Though Milwaukee has equally good sausage credentials, it struck me as too big and too cold for the personal relationship with a bratwurst I had in mind. We continued north on I-43 until we reached this town which pridefully calls itself "The Bratwurst Capital of the World." The brat is its icon.

To an outlander that may sound boastful, but any town that sells eleven tons, or 135,000, of these small sausages over a Fourth of July weekend, deserves the accolade. Bratwurst signs in grocery stores, supermarkets, and butcher shops demand attention, and bakeries push the special Semmel Rolls designed just for the brat. Stop anyone on the street and they are delighted to talk about brats—where to find them, how to grill them, whether beer should be mixed into the filling, etcetera.

Weeks earlier I had written Roland Schomberg, a third-generation resident of the nearby community of Sheboygan Falls and past president of the Sheyboygan County Historical Society, to ask if he would point me in the direction of some old-timers to talk to about the sausages and the best way to grill them.

As a farm kid, Schomberg helped to scald hog carcasses and turn the sausage stuffer for his mother. "When I was a kid, every farm family made its own sausages—bratwurst, which is all pork; rinderwurst, a beef sausage if they had a cow to get rid of that year; liver sausage, and head cheese—and hung its own bacons and hams." Nowadays, several large factories make, package, and ship bratwurst around the country. One of these, Johnsonville, does heavy merchandising with traditional sausages, now and then introducing new sausage creations.

We stopped for a tour of the company's big plant, set in the midst of cornfields near Sheboygan Falls, to watch a galaxy of stainless-steel machines, twist, turn, and tie thousands of sausage links at an incredible rate. In the chill room the guide pointed to the new generation of sausages—an "Irish" sausage with garlic, a brat mixed with beer and one with Chianti, a "Texas" brat with jalapeño and red pepper, and another with cheese plus beer.

Schomberg later confided that he and a number of others buy their bratwursts from neighborhood butchers who make the sausages daily according to long-held-secret recipes.

"To my taste there is nothing like the old-fashioned brat made with nothing but pork—three-quarters lean meat and one-quarter fat—and seasoned only with salt, pepper, a dash of nutmeg, and a little sugar." But even the old formulas are changing, he said. "Now it is less fat and more lean pork because of the concern over cholesterol."

German immigrants settled in the Sheboygan area in the early 1800s, bringing with them an abiding love of hearty German fare, especially sausage. Schomberg, who has traveled extensively in Germany, has yet to find a Sheboygan-style bratwurst there. "Ask for a bratwurst and you get what we call a weisswurst, a white sausage made with veal." Schomberg believes that initially veal was not available to the settlers in this country, who turned to pork for sausage, thus beginning a long love affair with bratwurst.

Harold Lindemann is one of Sheboygan's most accomplished "brat fryers." While he grills literally tons of brats at local company outings, church picnics, festivals, and fairs, his proudest achievement was on the Mall in Washington, D.C., where he and a crew grilled and served two tons of brats at the Smithsonian Festival of Folk Life in 1976.

"It was wonderful," said Lindemann, a tall, heavy-set man who loves cigars as much as he loves brats. "Those people had never tasted them before and they loved them. We charged a dollar fifty a brat, and we could hardly keep up with the demand on a sixteen-foot-long grill that was loaded all the time."

What advice does he have for grilling brats, wieners, and other sausages, as well as hamburgers, at home?

• Cardinal rule: Be spare with the charcoal. You are going to cook a small link of sausage, not a whole pig. Use only enough charcoal to cover the bottom in a single layer! The urge is to cook fast; don't.
• When the charcoal pieces are gray and ashen—no black or unburned spots—dash ¼ cup water over the hot charcoals. The resulting small steam explosion will blow away the ash to uncover the bed of coals.
• Place the sausages on a rack 7 to 9 inches above the coals. Gently grill the sausages, turning them once or twice, until firm to the touch and golden brown, about 25 to 30 minutes.
• If fire erupts from fat drippings, immediately put it out with "8 or 10 drops" of water to keep it a contained flame. Don't let it become a massive blaze. Not only will it burn the brats but it can become an "emotional mess."
• If the charcoal fire is a modest one, the brats can rest the entire

time on the grill, taking on a moist golden brown color, without split or punctured skin and without once causing panic.

    • The final step is what Lindemann calls "Beer, butter, and brats." To keep brats warm between servings, drop them into a pan of beer with a tablespoon of butter which has been brought to a simmer.

    A delicious alternative of Lindemann's is to keep the brats warm in a nest of sauerkraut. Both kraut and brat are then forked onto a Semmel roll. He suggests layers of kraut between layers of sausages until the pan or kettle is filled. Keep it hot on the stove or corner of the grill. The pan can be covered, wrapped in a blanket, and carried hot to a tailgate party.

    For pan frying, place brats in a cold skillet. Add 2 to 4 tablespoons water and cover the skillet. Gently simmer for 10 to 12 minutes. Remove the cover and increase the temperature to medium heat. Gently brown the brats for about 20 minutes. Turn them frequently with tongs. Don't prick them by turning with a fork.

    For indoor broiling, cover the bottom of the broiler pan with ½ inch of water. Place the sausages on the broiler rack. Place the rack in the oven at least 6 inches from the broiler element and broil for 10 to 12 minutes per side, or until golden brown and firm to the touch.

SEMMEL ROLLS

[MAKES 1 DOZEN ROLLS]

    In Sheboygan it is difficult to mention the brat without getting into a discussion about the Semmel, a hard, chewy roll, close cousin to a Kaiser, but with a distinctive cleavage across the top. One without the other would be unthinkable in Sheboygan.

    The baked Semmel is large—about 4 inches in diameter and rises to about 2 inches in height.

INGREDIENTS
4½ cups bread or unbleached flour, approximately
1 package dry yeast
1 tablespoon sugar
1 teaspoon salt
1½ cups hot water (120°–130°)
1 teaspoon malt extract, if available
1 egg
1 egg white
1 tablespoon shortening
Rye flour, for dusting

continued

EQUIPMENT

One baking sheet, greased or covered with parchment paper

PREPARATION BY HAND OR MIXER
8 mins.

Measure 3½ cups of flour into a mixing or mixer bowl and add the yeast, sugar, and salt. Stir to blend well. Pour in the hot water and malt extract. Mix for 1 minute with a wooden spoon or mixer flat beater until a smooth but heavy batter forms.

Add the egg, egg white, and shortening. Beat together until the mixture is smooth. If with the electric mixer, remove the flat beater and continue with a dough hook. Add flour—¼ cup at a time—until the dough is a solid but soft mass that can be lifted from the bowl, or left under the dough hook.

KNEADING
10 mins.

Knead the dough with a strong push-turn-fold motion for 10 minutes, adding liberal sprinkles of flour if the dough is wet. If in the mixer, the dough will clean the sides of the bowl and form a ball around the dough hook. If, however, it continues to cling to the sides, add sprinkles of flour.

PREPARATION BY PROCESSOR
4 mins.

Measure 3½ cups of flour into the work bowl and add the yeast, sugar, and salt. Pulse to blend. With the machine running, pour the hot water through the feed tube.

The dough will be a thick batter. Drop in the egg, egg white, and shortening. Pulse 7 or 8 times to blend completely. Add flour, ¼ cup at a time, until the dough forms a ball and rides the blade. If dough is wet and sticks to the sides of the bowl, add flour by the tablespoon, with the machine running.

KNEADING
1 min.

When the dough cleans the sides of the bowl, continue to process to knead for 1 minute. Uncover the bowl; pinch the dough to determine if it is soft, smooth, elastic, and slightly sticky when kneading is completed.

FIRST RISING
1 hour

Place the dough in a greased bowl, cover tightly with plastic wrap, and set aside to double in bulk, about 1 hour.

SECOND RISING
45 mins.

Uncover the bowl and punch down the dough with your fingers. Re-cover the bowl and allow the dough to double in volume again, about 45 minutes.

SHAPING
15 mins.

Place the dough on a floured work surface, roll it into a 12-inch-long cylinder. With a sharp knife cut 12 pieces from the length (at every inch on the ruler).

Shape the pieces under a cupped palm into smooth rounds. Cover and allow to relax for 5 minutes.

Flatten each roll with your hand to about ½ inch thick. Dust lightly with rye flour.

With a length of wooden dowel, a round wooden spoon

handle, or a pencil press a deep vertical indentation into the top of each roll. Press firmly and deeply, almost to the bottom.

As each roll is shaped, place it face down on the baking sheet.

THIRD RISING
40 mins.

Cover the rolls with a length of wax or parchment paper, and leave them at room temperature to rise—slightly less than double in size, about 40 minutes.

PREHEAT

In the meantime, prepare the oven by placing a pan under the middle shelf. Twenty minutes before the bake period preheat the oven to 450°, quite hot. Five minutes before the rolls are to go into the oven, pour 1 cup of hot water in the pan to form steam and provide a moist environment for the rolls.

BAKING
450°
25 mins.

Be certain hot water is in the pan.

Uncover the rolls, carefully turn them right side up, brush them with water or spray lightly with an atomizer of water.

Place the pan on the middle shelf of the hot oven. Three minutes later lightly spray the interior of the oven—not directly on the rolls.

Midway through the bake period turn the sheet around so that the rolls are exposed equally to temperature variations in the oven. They are done when crispy brown all over, in about 25 minutes.

FINAL STEP

Remove the rolls from the oven. If, after the rolls have cooled, they are not as crisp and crusty as you like, put them back into a hot oven for 10 minutes.

〜〜〜〜〜*On the road—EN ROUTE BRILLION*

Off the Interstate

Turn off any Interstate highway and you become part of the life of the community; no longer just a speeding, disinterested traveler intent only on reaching a Ramada Inn by nightfall. It demands a shift of gears. It demands you be alert and alive to what's going on around you. The speed and pace are slower, sometimes annoyingly so. Patience is a virtue. Cows ambling across the highway from one field to the next may hold up traffic for five minutes, but it may be the only time you and the kids will ever see a cow stop a car.

Wisconsin is a wonderful turn-off state. Up north are forests, marshes, and lakes. The southwest part of the state has rounded hills and narrow valleys. In the southeast, cows outnumber people one hundred to one, and milk and cheese are its treasure. From the freeway the only hint of this are the big purple silos rising in the distance like tall sentry towers watching over the green acres carpeted with corn and soybeans, alfalfa and oats.

We left I-43 on the outskirts of Manitowoc, on Lake Michigan, and turned west on S.R. 10. Immediately the scene changed. It was a two-lane highway shared by farm trucks, petroleum haulers, a spray rig behind a lumbering green tractor, a clutch of motorcycles with bright headlights, and a woman pedaling a bicycle along the berm. None of us seemed to be in a great hurry. Patience.

We drove thirty miles through some of the richest dairy land in the nation to visit Brillion, home of the world's best wiener.

At the first intersection, a small sign pointed to the Branch Cheese Factory, one of hundreds of family-owned cheese factories that for a century prospered making cheese for its neighbors. Today there are fewer than three hundred in the entire state, producing 40 percent of the cheese made in this country. Most of the small plants have been bought and merged by big food companies and cooperatives. I was glad to find one small plant still in existence. I said so to the lady behind the counter as she wrapped several packages of Cheddar cheese for us.

"Despite all I've heard," I said, "this family business seems to be doing all right." I could tell by the sounds out back that a number of people were hard at work. She shrugged her shoulders. "Truth to tell, we were bought last month by a Texas pizza chain looking to protect its cheese source."

We drove on down the road.

Farmhouses were relatively close together. "It would certainly promote neighborliness," Marje remarked. I said it indicated to me that a man didn't need much of this fertile land to be a successful farmer. Now in midsummer the silos were being filled with tons of chopped green silage to be fed year-round to the black-and-white milk cows. Most had never seen a pasture but lived their lives near the barn, close held for morning and evening milkings. Not for them a long slow amble, udders swinging side to side, to a distant pasture.

The number of big silos in the feed lot seemed to indicate the degree of a farmer's industry and prosperity. If the farm had only one silo rising up in the barn lot, it followed that the paint on the house was peeling, the lawn needed mowing, and the kids' bicycles were scattered on the drive. Four or five silos meant clipped shrubs, a red BMW in the driveway, and a swimming pool in the side yard.

All of this we would have missed on the Interstate.

BRILLION, WISCONSIN

The American Wiener—Clayton Arndt

The wiener is a basic American food. Nurturing and delicious, a wiener can make an event of a ball game or a picnic or a wedding reception.

I asked Marje if she thought anyone makes wieners like they did when we were kids? There was one man in the country, I told her, that has the reputation of making them even better than remembered and we would meet him shortly.

When we met Clayton Arndt later that day, I said I had heard that he made the world's best wiener. I underscored *world's best* not once but twice.

"Yes," he said, "I suppose I do."

He does it in a small packing house in the town of Brillion, Wisconsin. We had been directed there by an esteemed cook who said that before coming on to her house we must drive eighty-five miles to Brillion, even though it was in the opposite direction, to taste the best hot dog in the world. And bring her a few, please.

The Arndt wiener is simply made. The meat is fresh. Absolutely. All of it, pork and beef, comes in on the hoof in the back of the building and within hours emerges up front as a wiener. The mix is 80 percent beef and 20 percent pork. There are no fillers that puff up other wieners. The spices are mixed according to a three-generations-old family formula. The casings that form and shape the Arndt wiener are natural, sheep intestines (shipped in brine from Australia). No synthetics for Clayton Arndt.

"One of the most important steps," Clayton explained, "is to mix the meats and spices together and let the batch rest and 'cure' for forty-eight hours. This blends all the good flavors together."

The last step in making a fine wiener is to smoke it with real smoke —not a liquid smoke brushed on—twenty-four hours or more. It is now wholly cooked.

Brillion is a town of 2,907, less than twenty-five miles inland from Lake Michigan. The Arndt retail meat shop on the edge of town has become one of its biggest attractions. Hanging on the wall near the meat counter is a large map of the United States. It looked like a pin cushion: White pins representing customers were stuck in all states, including Hawaii and Alaska. Wisconsin's small meat producers cannot ship their products interstate, thanks to the large meat companies' Washington lobby. Each pin means that someone from that location came through Arndt's front door.

"Last week a man brought in a large suitcase and asked me to pack it full with nothing but wieners and sausages. He was flying that night to Hawaii to visit his son stationed in Pearl Harbor. The son had written that that was all he wanted his father to bring from home. The son got a pin on the map."

Arndt was literally born into the business—in the family's residence over the Arndt grocery, butcher shop, and slaughterhouse downtown. "I learned to count by placing twelve rings of summer sausages on a wooden pole and calling my dad so he could hang them in the smoke-house. I was only a little kid when I was given a knife to trim fat off the meat. It kept me out of Dad's way."

How best to savor the world's best wiener? To capture its full flavor and succulence, the first choice, said Clayton, is to cook it in a saucepan of water on top of the stove. Bring the water to a brisk boil. Turn off the fire! Repeat. *Turn off the fire!* Don't boil the wiener or the casing will burst and all the good juices will be lost. Only when the fire has been turned off, do you drop in the wiener. Leave it in the water for 10 to 15 minutes, remove, and eat!

Second best, Arndt said, is to grill the wiener over a modest bed of charcoal until it is heated through. Not too hot or it may burst. Turn it occasionally. Grilling is not Clayton's favorite way, for it adds a different taste to the meat that obscures the true flavor of his wiener.

When introduced to the Arndt wiener for the first time, you might be taken aback by its appearance. It is slender and slightly wrinkled. The wrinkles come in the smokehouse but disappear when the wiener is cooked and the juicy meat swells.

While Arndt by state law cannot ship his wieners across state lines, a family member or friend certainly can. You must know someone in Wisconsin. It is worth the effort. Or the law may be changed. Ask Clayton. His address is Clayton Arndt, Arndt's, 540 West Ryan Street, Brillion, WI 54110.

Happy savoring!

FISH CREEK, WISCONSIN

Door County—Russell Ostrand

If you want to surprise friends with an authentic fish boil exactly like Russell Ostrand does at the White Gull Inn, you will need a big thirty-gallon iron kettle resting on stones and a hot wood fire underneath. Small red potatoes go into the boiling water, followed by pieces of Lake Michigan whitefish. Stir in a lot of salt to make the fish oils rise to the surface.

At the appropriate moment, when the potatoes and fish are deemed done, stand back from the fire—so as not to singe your eyebrows—and, with élan, casually toss half a cup of kerosene on the glowing bed of coals.

With a great whoosh all hell breaks loose. Flames explode into a fireball that engulfs the pot; the water erupts into a boilover that cascades in a great torrent over the sides and into the fire. It also cools down the fire so you can scoop out the fish and potatoes.

Guests applaud the performance. Dinner is served.

Before I went to Fish Creek I had been cautioned several times that fish boils are overrated. I disagree. The fish, dipped into melted butter and sprinkled with lemon juice, was delicious. So were the potatoes, the

creamy coleslaw, the homemade breads, and a piece of Door County's traditional post-boil dessert, cherry pie. I suggest one change: Take off the unattractive shriveled fish skin before it is served; give the fish color with a sprinkle of paprika or a pinch of chopped parsley.

It is possible, of course, to do a less theatrical fish boil at home. The water need not boil over onto the kitchen floor and the fish oils can be skimmed off with a spoon.

Your do-it-yourself fish boil, unfortunately, will not have Master Boiler Russell Ostrand, a veteran of twenty-five years of fish boiling, who, after wiping the sweat off his brow, goes into the dining room, sits in a chair at the side of the room, a cold bottle of beer within reach, and entertains with polkas on his accordion. Ostrand is a tall, husky, genial man who retired recently as a pipe fitter at a Sturgeon Bay shipyard. His career as Master Boiler began when the pipe-fitters union invited him to do the boil at their big annual picnic. "The real reason they invited me," he said, "is because they got two for the price of one—I could play the accordion as well as boil the fish."

The fish boil was begun a century ago by Scandinavian settlers and has changed little since.

FISH BOIL

[SERVES 6]

The large amount of salt in the fish boil does not make the fish taste salty. It does make the undesirable fish oils rise to the surface, therefore the salt is necessary to the success of the recipe. Ostrand does not include onions with the potatoes as other fish boilers in Door County do, because he feels they take away from the flavor of the fish.

Lake whitefish, a relative of the salmon, is caught in cold freshwater lakes and rivers. The flesh is white, firm, and sweet-tasting. It is imported from Canada in considerable numbers.

INGREDIENTS	*12 small red potatoes* *8 quarts water* *1 pound (2 cups) salt* *2½ pounds whitefish, cut into 12 pieces* *Butter, melted, and lemon slices, to serve*
EQUIPMENT	One large pot, preferably one with a removable basket or rack; several lengths of cheesecloth
PREPARATION 10 mins.	Wash the potatoes and cut a slice from one end. Tie the potatoes in a cheesecloth bag.
COOKING 30 mins.	Bring the water to a boil in the pot. Add the potatoes and half the salt. Cook for 20 minutes. Check the doneness of the potatoes by pricking with the point of a sharp knife. Wrap the fish pieces in a length of cheesecloth and lower into the boiling water. Add the remainder of the salt. Cook for 10 minutes. With a large spoon, skim the oils from the surface of the water.
FINAL STEP	Lift the cooked potatoes and fish from the water; drain. Serve with the melted butter and lemon.

~~~~EGG HARBOR, WISCONSIN

The Very Best Cherry Pie—Kathryn Zeller

At summer's end, Kathryn Zeller would be leaving Egg Harbor and already in June she was being mourned by townspeople (all 238 of them) and visitors alike who considered a visit to her bakery one of the chief reasons to come to Door County in the first place.

Leaving Egg Harbor with Kathryn would be her cherry pies, loaves of Amish white breads, and Danish pastries, special favorites among many delicious things she had been baking for a decade of summers. She was closing her business, Butter and Eggs, to join her husband at his new faculty post at the University of Kansas, too far for a seasonal commute like the one the family has been making each spring and fall to and from Ohio.

My meeting with Kathryn a number of years ago came about when I parked in front of her shop to ask how Egg Harbor got its name. I got two versions: Before the town had a name, two small freight vessels were racing to be the first ashore with provisions for the winter. In its excitement, the crew of one vessel began pelting the other with eggs carried as cargo. The vessel under attack replied in kind. The battle raged until all the eggs were gone. A more likely story, I thought, was that early explorers found the beach covered with egg-filled duck nests.

Regardless of how named, it was in Egg Harbor that I found Kathryn's bakery. I was researching a new book on bread baking in 1987, and when I tasted her loaf of Amish white bread I asked if I could use it in the book. No problem, she said, and gave it to me. (It is in *Bernard Clayton's New Complete Book of Breads* as Egg Harbor Bread.) When she wrote that she was leaving Egg Harbor, I knew I had to rescue her wonderful pie before she and it disappeared from the Door County scene.

Door County's tart and juicy Montmorency cherries are among the finest grown in a region noted for premium fruit. Experts believe that the limestone structure in which the trees are rooted provides ideal nutrients and moisture. The water surrounding the peninsula protects the trees from spring frosts. The county each year produces 15 million pounds of cherries.

Kathryn barely dents that figure when she drives to a nearby freezer plant to scoop just-picked cherries off a conveyor belt. With these she will bake between thirty and forty cherry pies for weekend trade. Price: $6 a pie.

Kathryn, who grew up on a farm with a big orchard, is no stranger to picking and seeding cherries.

"I was one of ten kids in the family and each summer my mother took all of us to the orchard to pick enough cherries to fill three 25-gallon milk cans. Then we went to the back porch where she armed each of us with one of her hairpins to dig out the seeds. It was a picnic! We could eat as many cherries as we wanted. After the seeds were out, the cherries were put back in the milk cans, which were filled with water so air couldn't get to them and spoil them. The cherries were there for several days while Mother, upstairs in the kitchen, was busy canning them as fast as she could. We would slip down into the basement and sneak a handful. Almost as good as when they were picked right off the tree!"

She uses tapioca for thickening. The cherries are *not* cooked beforehand. When the tapioca is mixed with the cherries, the mixture is allowed to rest for fifteen to twenty minutes. "The first time I made cherry pie I didn't allow the tapioca time to absorb the juice; when we bit into the pie it was like biting into buckshot."

The pie dough should be made at least two to four hours ahead and placed in the refrigerator to mature and chill.

EGG HARBOR CHERRY PIE

[MAKES ONE 9-INCH PIE]

These are Kathryn's mother's recipes for both crust and filling. The only substitution in the recipe is the use of margarine instead of lard.

"Cholesterol, of course. Early on I had customers turn on their heels and walk out of the bakery, even after they had driven a long distance, when I said, yes, it is an old-fashioned crust with lard. No more. Ah, I do miss the flakiness of a lard crust," she said wistfully.

Note: Because cherry pies are notorious for bubbling over the sides of the pan, it is wise to spread a length of foil on the shelf below to catch any spills.

INGREDIENTS	*PIECRUST* *3 cups all-purpose flour* *1 teaspoon salt* *1¼ cups margarine, chilled* *1 teaspoon baking powder* *1 egg* *1 tablespoon vinegar* *6 tablespoons ice water* *FILLING* *3 to 4 cups fresh or frozen cherries, pitted, thawed, and* * drained; reserve ½ cup juice from either* *2½ tablespoons tapioca* *1 cup sugar for fresh cherries, ¾ cup for frozen* *6 drops red food coloring (optional)* *¼ teaspoon almond extract* *⅛ teaspoon salt* *Butter, to dot* *Sugar, to sprinkle*
EQUIPMENT	One pie pan of choice, large (9- or 10-inch)
PREPARATION	For the piecrust: Into a medium bowl measure the flour and salt. With a knife, cut the margarine into several small pieces and drop into the flour. Toss and work the fat and flour together with a pastry blender, 2 knives, or your fingers working quickly, until the mixture resembles coarse meal, with irregular particles ranging from tiny grains of rice to small peas. Add the baking powder, egg, and vinegar. Pour each ingredient into the flour mixture and stir to blend before adding the next.

Sprinkle in the ice water, a tablespoon at a time, and stir with a fork held lightly. Gently toss the loose particles around the bowl to absorb the moisture. Add water to bring the particles together in a moist (not wet) mass that holds together with no dry or crumbly places apparent.

CHILLING
2 hours

Wrap the ball of dough in plastic wrap or foil and place in the refrigerator for 2 hours or more.

About 30 minutes before rolling, remove the dough from the refrigerator, otherwise it will be difficult to work.

This dough can be frozen before or after shaping. An excellent crust for all fruit pies.

ROLLING AND
SHAPING

Instructions for rolling and shaping a pie crust can be found on page 566.

PREHEAT

Preheat the oven to 400°.

FILLING
15–20 mins.

In a large bowl, combine *all* of the filling ingredients. Let stand for 15 to 20 minutes.

ASSEMBLING
5 mins.

Pour the filling into the unbaked pie shell. Dot with butter. Add the top crust to cover, or cut lattice strips to arrange on top. Sprinkle sugar over the top. If a covered pie, cut decorative slits in the center.

BAKING
400°
50–60 mins.

Bake for 50 to 60 minutes. The crust should turn deep brown, and the filling should be bubbling gently in the center.

FINAL STEP

Place the pie on a wire rack to cool. Enjoy.

▰▰▰ON THE ROAD—MICHIGAN'S UPPER PENINSULA

Copper Country

We drove to Michigan's Upper Peninsula to find a recipe for Cornish Pasty, a delicious kind of turnover, that had been brought there more than a century earlier by miners from Cornwall who came to work the vast copper deposits.

We headquartered in Houghton (pop. 7,512), facing its sister city, Hancock (pop. 5,122), across the narrowest part of Portage Lake. Together the towns mark the beginning of the Keweenaw Peninsula that juts into Lake Superior.

This was Copper Country.

Facing each other across the waterway, the cities are like the hill towns of Europe, especially along the Rhine and Mosel rivers. No castles but equally dramatic against the sky above Hancock is a major landmark, Quincy Mining Company's old Number 2 shaft house. In Houghton, the spires of St. Ignatius Loyola Catholic Church rise like an old-world cathedral.

We drove to Laurium (pop. 2,875), the focus of our pasty search. It had been a boom town like all the others a hundred years ago, but one day the companies picked up and moved their operations to the open pit mines in the Western states where the ore was cheaper to mine. Now it is a quiet place, surrounded by abandoned mine shafts, remains of stamp mills and smelters, mountains of black tailings and memories. In its glory, the virgin forest was stripped from the hills for miles around to be cut into timber to shore up hundreds of miles of underground drifts and slopes; to fuel steam-driven machines; and to build thousands of homes, stores, churches, and meeting halls.

On a wall of the Houghton County Museum is a lithograph of Hancock as a balloonist with sketch pad would have seen it in 1890. The town is orderly and neat in the foreground; stretching for miles beyond are naked hills punctuated only by shaft houses and a few chimneys sending out wisps of smoke. The lithograph was done by a town proud of its industry, naked hills and all.

When the mining slowed and finally stopped, the trees returned. Forests again blanket the hills, partially hiding huge reinforced concrete blocks that once anchored mill machinery.

The giant foundation for one of the many technologically advanced machines still stands on the shores of Torch Lake—a massive pump that rose four-stories high and was capable of pumping 60 million gallons of water a day out of the fabled Calumet Mine. The pump was built by the Krupp Works in Essen, Germany; assembled there, tested, taken apart, and shipped across the Atlantic to New Jersey; where it was again assembled, tested, and there accepted by the mine company. But it had to be taken down once again, shipped by boat to Torch Lake, and, for the final time, reassembled. Sadly, in 1949, the great pump, no longer needed, was broken into scrap.

My historian friend in Hancock, Bill Barkell, said that in the late 1800s engineers from all over this country and Europe were called to the

Upper Peninsula to design fantastic machines to mine ore, iron as well as copper, and to do so against tremendous odds, including Lake Superior, which at any time could come crashing through the tunnel walls— and sometimes did. They built machines no one had ever thought of before.

"Yet, do you know what the engineer did at the end of the day? He hitched up a horse and drove home in a buggy. A horse and buggy, mind you!"

⋙⋙ UPPER PENINSULA, MICHIGAN

The Delectable Turnover—Eric Frimodig

The Cornish pasty is a delicious meat-and-vegetable turnover of hearty goodness, and I have traveled widely to find it. I had my first pasty in Drake's Tavern in San Francisco and from there I followed it to the old copper mining country along the rugged coast of Cornwall in England. On to Michigan's Upper Peninsula, where Cornishmen came in the mid-1800s to work the newly discovered copper deposits. Mine has been a rewarding search.

The pasty was a creation of miners' wives. No lunch bucket was

needed because it was its own edible container. A complete meal in itself
—small cubes of beef, potato, turnip, and onion—it was sturdy enough
to be carried into the mine or dropped down a mine shaft to a hungry
husband. The miner's initials were scribed into the dough so that a miner
could pick out his own pasty from a number of others resting on a mine
timber. Because it was protected by its crust, the pasty would keep warm
for hours.

What the bagel is to New York City, the pasty is to the Upper
Peninsula: ubiquitous. People stand in line for them. People tote them
frozen to distant places like Cleveland and New Orleans and Indianapolis. One man regularly asks for pasties to be sent via UPS to Los Angeles
(cost prepaid: $50 a dozen). In the Upper Peninsula, butcher shops grind
meat specially for pasties.

Roadside signs read: THE QUEEN'S PASTIES; RED ONION PASTIES, TURN
RIGHT AT LIGHT; HOT AND TIRED? PASTIES DELIVERED; LEHTO'S PASTIES,
THE ORIGINAL; PASTIES, UNBAKED $1.35, FROZEN $1.35; HOMEMADE PAS-
TIES, A TASTE OF THE UPPER PENINSULA; BESSIE'S ORIGINAL HOMEMADE
PASTIES AND SMOKED FISH.

The pasty is an Upper Peninsula phenomenon. Once you cross the
Mackinac Bridge going south into the bigger piece of Michigan (Detroit,
Grand Rapids, Lansing, and so on) no more pasties!

The best pasty in Copper County, I was told by a number of people,
was made at the Country Kitchen in Laurium. The cook/owner is Eric
Frimodig, who was born in Copper Harbor at the tip of the peninsula,
got a degree in forestry at Michigan Tech here in Houghton, spent a
couple of years with the Army in Germany, and then came back home,
not to be a forester but to make pasties.

Eric is Scandinavian, not Cornish, but his pasties are as good as any
I have had. He makes his with traditional ingredients—meat, onion,
potato, turnip or rutabaga, and seasoned with salt and pepper. Never
carrot, for it is not favored by traditionalists.

In the summertime, with vacationers pouring onto the cool peninsula to escape the heat in the lower states, the Country Kitchen's crew
of four make about five to six hundred pasties a day. On the Fourth of
July weekend it jumps to a thousand. "This year we could have sold
another five hundred but we were too exhausted."

Eric's pasties, like most others, weigh about a pound and are meant
to be eaten out of hand, or, if desired, with knife and fork. Dough is
important to a good pasty. It must hold the package together in the oven
and when bitten into; yet it must taste good. Until recently Eric favored
lard but has substituted vegetable shortening for its lower cholesterol.

Eric doesn't mind breaking with tradition. Want a garlic pasty? He'll
make it. Or a chicken pasty, a vegetarian pasty, or one with venison (if
you supply the venison), or fish? Whatever. Just call ahead. He will even

make a "cocktail" size—a three-inch pasty with a teaspoon of filling. This spring he did 750 for a high school reunion. "Not my favorite. Too tedious."

In this part of Michigan, one night a week is set aside as the family's pasty night. Office and factory workers say the pasty beats a brown-bag lunch. All day long there is constant bagging of pasties for family and company picnics, school reunions, church socials, fishermen and hunters, and for those who like to have a pasty in hand while driving across the peninsula. Or a woodsman may take an unbaked pasty with him on a backpack trip, wrap the pasty in foil, toss it in the campfire ashes, and have a completely satisfying dinner.

"There is an elderly widow lady here in town who comes through the front door at exactly 10:05 every Thursday morning for her hot pasty. I can set my watch by her."

With dozens of pasty shops in the Upper Peninsula, each trying to develop a pasty with a different and more appealing personality, there are, as a consequence, pasties to be found in all shapes and tastes. Instead of the Cornish half-moon, some cooks square the package, tucking the sides under rather than crimping them along the curved edge. Others pull the dough up on all sides and seal the pasty with a large rosette on top.

CORNISH PASTY

[FOUR 8-INCH PIECES OR 2 DOZEN SMALL]

I have suggested in this recipe that the meat be cubed, as the Cornish cooks do it, rather than have it coarse-ground as Eric does. He achieves the same texture, however, by working with partially frozen meat, which results in small clumps in the pasty. The choice is yours.

I like to do something to my pasty that I learned in San Francisco, which Cornish cooks do not. I pour a tablespoon of rich beef stock into one of the steam vents in the crust before it is served hot out of the oven. I did find one café in the U. P. that poured a heavy gravy over the pasty, which I thought a desecration.

INGREDIENTS   *DOUGH*
3½ cups (1 pound) all-purpose flour, approximately
1 teaspoon salt
½ pound (2 sticks) margarine or unsalted butter, room
*   temperature (Cornish cooks use all lard)*
¾ cup ice water

continued

FILLING
12 ounces turnips (about 3), diced small (¼ inch)
12 ounces potatoes (about 4 medium), diced small or thinly sliced
1½ pounds round or flank steak, cut into ¼-inch cubes or, if preferred, coarsely ground
1 large onion, chopped

FOR EACH PASTY
Pinch of salt
Pinch of freshly ground black pepper
1 teaspoon butter
1 tablespoon rich beef stock (see page 560) (optional)

EQUIPMENT

One large baking sheet, lined with parchment or brown sack paper, or greased lightly

PREPARATION
8 mins.

In a large bowl place 3 cups of flour and stir in the salt. Cut the margarine or butter into small pieces and drop into the flour. With a pastry blender or 2 knives work the fat into the flour until it has the consistency of coarse meal.

Slowly dribble the ice water. Work with your fingers or a fork to shape the mass of dough that is firm. If too much water has been added, the dough may be tacky. If so, add sprinkles of flour.

CHILLING
1 hour or more

Press the dough into a ball, wrap in plastic wrap or foil, and place in the refrigerator to chill and relax. Ideally, the dough should be given a day's rest before using.

(*Note:* The vegetables and meat, when diced, traditionally are placed in prescribed layers in the pasty in this order: turnips, potatoes, meat, and onions and topped with a teaspoon of butter. However, most U. P. bakers mix all the ingredients together in a bowl before filling the pasties.)

FILLING
10 mins.

Peel, dice, and slice the vegetables and the meat separately, in the order in which they will be layered. To give the meat a richer appearance in the pasty, briefly sear the steak pieces in a small skillet before continuing.

PREHEAT

Preheat the oven to 450°.

ASSEMBLING
15 mins.

Remove the dough from the refrigerator and roll it into a piece ⅛ inch thick. With an 8-inch lid as a pattern, cut circles with a pizza cutter or knife. Place these in the refrigerator to be taken out, one at a time, to fill.

The dough will be folded over the filling, so position the

vegetables and the meat on one half of the circle of dough, with a ½-inch margin around the edge left free to be pressed together. Add salt, pepper, and 1 teaspoon butter. Moisten the margin with water.

Fold the top half of the circle over the filling. Gently lift the bottom edge to meet the top, and press together. Lifting the bottom in this manner helps shape a narrow turned-up strip to make the package more secure, with less chance of its leaking.

With a spatula, lift the pasty and place it on the baking sheet. Repeat filling and folding the others.

With a knife tip or skewer, fashion a steam vent in the center of each pasty. Scribe guest's initials in one corner. Initials may also be used to indicate the kind of filling or its variation, such as no onion.

BAKING
400°
20 mins.
250°
40 mins.

Place the pasties in the middle shelf of the hot oven and immediately reduce the heat to 400°. Leave at this temperature until pasties begin to brown, or about 20 minutes. Reduce the heat to 250° and continue to bake for an additional 40 minutes, or about 1 hour total.

FINAL STEP

Serve hot with hot beef stock to accompany, if desired. Stock can also be poured into the crust.

Baked pasties are delicious frozen and reheated, but the Cornish cooks recommend freezing the unbaked pasties. Place frozen pasties directly in the hot oven but allow an additional 30 minutes to bake at 400° before reducing heat to 250° as above.

〰〰〰*On the Road—FRANKENMUTH, MICHIGAN*

Discovery

Frankenmuth: Settled 1845. Pop.: 3,753. Elev.: 645 ft. (197 m). This city was settled by a small band of Bavarian immigrants from Franconia, Germany, who came here as Lutheran missionaries to spread the faith to the Chippewas. Today, Frankenmuth boasts authentic Bavarian architecture, flower beds and that warm German hospitality.

This modest two-sentence paragraph in the Mobil Travel Guide, one of our travel bibles on the road, sent a signal that Frankenmuth was waiting to be discovered by us. Two lines of copy were hardly a mention compared to six sentences for Iron Mountain and Kalamazoo, and thirteen for Muskegon. Even Frankenmuth's position on the map was downgraded to a small black dot. I was certain I had stumbled onto something big.

Weeks before, I had made arrangements through its Chamber of Commerce to spend some time in the kitchen with one of the town's good cooks to talk about German-Bavarian food, perhaps someone who had a small garden, and we would talk about beans and carrots and corn. We were booked to stay in the Frankenmuth Bavarian Motor Lodge, described in the literature as "quaintly Old World."

We turned off I-75, below Saginaw, to drive six miles across table-flat farmland. Hardly the Bavarian Alps.

There, with corn and soybeans and alfalfa growing right to the corporation limits, was Frankenmuth waiting to be discovered. Ah, we were too late! A half century too late! Today Frankenmuth is being "discovered" each year by some 3 *million tourists!*

Everyone except me knew that it is one of Michigan's premier tourist draws.

This cornfield miracle was wrought by an amazing Frankenmuth family, the Zehnders. Starting in 1929 with an all-you-can-eat chicken dinner restaurant of modest reputation, the Zehnders almost single-handedly transformed a small Midwestern town with no distinguishing features—it's not even the county seat—into a major tourist attraction, a "theme" town that would please Disney. The town had always been proud of its old-world ties, but it wasn't until some of the Zehnders visited relatives in Germany and came back with the idea to give their chicken restaurant a Bavarian theme that the town went Alpine.

Today almost every business in Frankenmuth has been touched by the Bavarian magic. There are Bavarian leather shops, woodworking shops, clock shops, as well as butcher shops specializing in German sausages. Two breweries in town make Old German pilsener and Old German Dark. It was 90° in the shade when we drove out to Bonner's at the edge of town. At this huge year-round Christmas trim and gift shop, I was greeted by an enormous Santa Claus waving at me from across the cornfield while inside snow (artificial) was drifting across an acre of display space.

On both sides of Main Street are Zehnder restaurants. One branch of the family runs Zehnder's of Frankenmuth, a restaurant with nine dining rooms and a bakery as well as the Bavarian Haus Motel. The other Zehnders have the Frankenmuth Bavarian Inn, where seven dining rooms can seat more than a thousand customers at a time. Overlooking Main Street and connected to the inn is a Glockenspeil Tower with a thirty-five-bell carillon, town clock, and hand-carved Pied Piper of Hamelin figures jauntily moving through the doors of the tower.

On the other bank of the Cass River—you must drive or walk over a Zehnder-built but authentic wooden covered bridge to get across—is the new two-hundred-room Bavarian Inn Motor Lodge, its tower suites crowned by a large onion-shaped dome.

"Quaintly old world, did you say?" Marje asked.

I could see on the lawn an illuminated sign, the kind that welcomes Kiwanians, Lions, and Bell Telephone seminars. This one read: TODAY WE WELCOME MR. AND MRS. BERNARD CLAYTON. In my surprise I almost ran the van over the curb. Was this the fifteen minutes of celebrity that Andy Warhol said comes once to every person? I should have left it there. I should not have asked at the desk how they knew about the Claytons. The young lady explained, quite simply, that a new name is chosen at random each day from the list of arriving guests.

Nevertheless, it didn't stop me from taking a photograph of the sign. At that moment one of the assistant managers walked past. He called over. "I'll bet you're the Claytons." Caught red-handed with the camera, I admitted we were. He laughed. "Put up their names and they'll do it every time!"

The Chamber of Commerce had asked Dorothy Zehnder, a member of the family, to talk to me about home cooking. Co-owner of the Bavarian Inn Restaurant and Motor Lodge, she is the mother of several sons and daughters, all in the business. She is a member of its board of directors, and for forty years manager of its kitchen and some six hundred employees.

We sat in her window-lined office high above and overlooking the huge kitchen resplendent with stainless steel. She talked about sausages and Wiener schnitzel, sauerbraten and Kasseler Rippschen (smoked loin chop), but on the scale of 325 tons of chicken a year; 27,000 heads of cabbage; 227,673 pounds of potatoes; 15,166 gallons of milk; 117,461 pounds of beef; and 42,000 shakers of chicken seasoning.

It was awesome. Especially to one who had anticipated spending an afternoon in a small home kitchen and perhaps digging a few carrots in a garden back of the house. Completely out of my orbit.

We drove on the next day. It had been fun. We wouldn't have missed our names in lights for anything.

VI   NORTHERN PLAINS and NORTHWEST

Iowa   Minnesota   North Dakota   Saskatchewan

Montana   Washington   British Columbia

Oregon   Idaho   Wyoming   Utah

Northwest Departure

When we left the house to begin our Northwest journey, I watched Marje take a farewell walk through the house and, as has been her wont, bid good-bye to things. "Good-bye painting . . . good-bye chair . . . good-bye house." A nice way to depart.

This followed a storm in the night that brought Timothy trembling to my bedside for comfort. We sat for an hour or more while I talked to him about the wonders of nature, including lightning and thunder. While he didn't seem impressed, he quit shaking and asked to go outside for a moment.

At an Illinois rest stop on the Interstate I read a notice stuck to the mirror written on yellow tablet paper in a strong, neat hand:

"We are a couple in the gray car out in front and we would appreciate anything you could spare to allow us to buy gas to get to Cheyenne."

I walked over to the car. The man said he was embarrassed to have to ask. I gave him some money and wished them well. The man, in his forties, said he thought by nightfall he would have enough money to buy gas to move on.

North by northwest from our departure point in Indiana, beyond Illinois and into Iowa and Minnesota, is a region where almost as many Norwegians, Swedish, and Finnish are to be found as in Scandinavia. Or so it seems. It spreads over a large part of the Midwest and the upper Plains states. It is a place of _kransekage, knäckebröd, kjottboller,_ and _lefse_ —all edible, all delicious.

The first stop on the journey will be Decorah, Iowa, a lovely small town on the Iowa River, near the Minnesota state line, surrounded by thousands of acres of corn-carpeted hills and valleys with green stalks and brown tassels. It is the home of the Fjeistuls, the Amundsons, the Grimstads, the Flaskeruds, and the Wangsnesses, to name but a few of its 7,991 inhabitants. More about the Wangsnesses follows.

Decorah, the home of Luther College, considers itself the focus of Norwegian-American life and culture in the United States, and with good reason. Its Nordic Fest, a three-day summertime Norwegian festival, attracts visitors, especially those with Norwegian roots, from all over the states and some from Norway.

A few years ago if a salesman expected to do business in Decorah or out on the farms, he had to speak Norwegian or not speak at all. There was a lapse of a few years when the language was not taught in Decorah High School, but it is back, more in demand than ever now that the town has a sister city in Norway. Decorah and Fagerness each summer exchange their young people.

Ours was to be an exchange with the Wangsnesses.

～～～DECORAH, IOWA

Norwegian Town—Norma Wangsness

When I wrote to the staff of the Vesterheim, the outstanding Norwegian immigrant museum in Decorah, I asked for the name of the town's best cook. The reply was immediate, unequivocal: Norma Wangsness.

The Wangsnesses live in a big house diagonally across Water Street from the museum. Norwegian trolls peek mischievously from the upper windows. The kitchen is large, light, and airy—and equipped specially for Norma. "I'm a small woman, so I always have problems with tables too high and counter space too far off the floor. When I was young I sat on a chair with the mixing bowl in my lap and I still do that today."

Behind her is a twenty-five-year-old electric stove in mint condition. "It has a terrace top which is not produced anymore. Pity. It has two tiers of burners. Those in front are lower than the back ones. We bought it for me and our daughters who were then learning to cook and couldn't reach pans on a normal stove top."

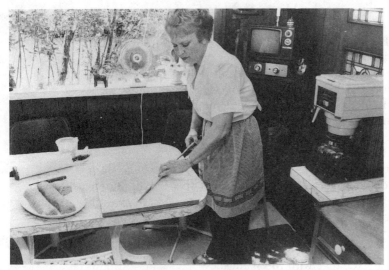

Both Willis and Norma were born in Iowa, and both trace their Norwegian ancestry back many generations. Their grandfathers were fishermen-farmers in Norway. With the help of research done when a distant cousin, Walter Mondale, was a candidate for the presidency of the United States, Norma has been able to go back several centuries to shared ancestors in the Norwegian village of Vangsnes.

A handsome, vivacious woman, Norma has been cooking almost all of her sixty years. When she was ten years old she waited tables in her mother's boardinghouse and baked cookies and cakes for pin money. When she was seventeen years old, she and Willis Wangsness (an "older man" at twenty-four) were married. They opened a restaurant in nearby Ossian. Later they ran a highly successful photo studio in Decorah—he was behind the camera and she did the retouching and tinting.

For lunch that day: *Norge kjottboller* (meatballs), *sod suppe* (sweet fruit soup), *Lefse* (a flatbread made with potato), *Havremel Flatbrød* (oatmeal flatbread), *spritsar* (a butter cookie), and *Rømmegrøt* (cream pudding), the latter considered by many to be the national dish of Norway.

The meal underscored all that I had heard about Norwegian cooking. Elemental. Vigorous tasting. Hearty. Pure. Simple.

LEFSE
(Potato Flatbread)

[MAKES ABOUT 16 PIECES]

Lefse, a flatbread made with potato, is prepared with almost reverential care in the Wangsness kitchen, where it becomes a two-person operation. Norma makes the *lefse* dough and shapes and rolls each piece. Willis moves the *lefse* to the griddle and tends it. For many years Norma's grandmother made the *lefse* for family dinners and celebrations, but when she could no longer do it, she taught Norma and Willis to be *lefse* bakers so her recipe would continue on for at least one more generation. "It is no big deal really," said Norma, "just a series of small things done well."

Traditionally, *lefse* dough is rolled out with a *lefse* rolling pin, which has long grooves along either the length of the roller or around the roller. However, Norma uses an ordinary rolling pin covered with a cloth sleeve in the early stages of rolling and then does a final roll with a *lefse* rolling pin to give the dough its traditional pattern.

To be included in the equipment is the *lefse* stick, which is about the length and heft of a yardstick tapered into a swordlike blade that can be slipped under the edge of the paper-thin *lefse* to carry it to the hot griddle. But the long handle of a wooden spoon will do as well with a bit of help getting the end under the *lefse*.

Finally, the *lefse* griddle has an electric element made just for this job. Any griddle with a flat surface will work equally well. A pancake griddle, for instance, is fine.

Willis feels strongly that only Idaho russet potatoes should be used to make the best *lefse* dough. *Lefse* is served as a bread on special occasions.

INGREDIENTS	*3 pounds potatoes, approximately, peeled, diced (5 cups riced potatoes needed)* *½ cup (1 stick) margarine* *3 tablespoons confectioners' sugar* *1 teaspoon salt* *2 cups all-purpose flour* *Butter, to spread* or *brown or white sugar, to sprinkle*
EQUIPMENT	See above.
COOKING 30 mins.	In a medium saucepan cook the potatoes in water until tender but not mushy, about 20 minutes. Drain. Press the potatoes through a potato ricer or grater.

continued

In a large bowl combine the potatoes and margarine. Cool to room temperature. Add the sugar and salt.

KNEADING
4 mins.

Mix thoroughly with your hands or a wooden spoon. Stir in 1 cup of flour, then add the remaining flour to make a stiff dough. Knead for 4 minutes. Pat the dough into a ball.

PREHEAT

Preheat the griddle to 400°.

SHAPING
10 mins.

Divide the ball of dough into 4 portions, then divide each portion into 4 equal pieces—a total of 16 pieces. On a lightly floured board, roll one piece of dough at a time to a paper-thin 10- or 11-inch circle. Make a final roll with a *lefse* rolling pin, if available, to imprint the authentic gridlike pattern.

BAKING
400°
16–32 mins.
total

Fold the dough onto a *lefse* stick or spoon handle, carry to the griddle, and unroll. Bake each piece on the griddle for 1 or 2 minutes on one side, or until the *lefse* bubbles and brown spots appear. Turn over and repeat.

Lefse will look dry but it will be flexible, not crisp. Fold in half, then in half again. Cool between cloths and store in plastic bags.

FINAL STEP

To serve, unfold and spread with butter, or sprinkle with brown or white sugar. Roll up to eat.

To freeze, wrap airtight; store in the freezer. Thaw in its wrapper.

In Norway a supply of *lefse* is kept in a table drawer and served on a wooden platter supported by a pedestal.

HAVREMEL FLATBRØD
(Oatmeal Flatbread)

[MAKES ½ POUND]

These oven-baked crackers, delightfully crisp and tasty, are served with cheese, spreads, and soups. To add fiber, replace 1 cup of the white flour with whole-wheat.

Norma's grandchildren love these and call them "granny crackers."

INGREDIENTS

2 tablespoons sugar
¾ cup (1½ sticks) unsalted butter, melted
½ teaspoon salt
1 teaspoon baking soda
1½ cups buttermilk

3 cups white flour, or 2 cups white and 1 cup whole-wheat
2 cups quick-cooking oats

EQUIPMENT

One cookie sheet; pastry cloth and pastry sleeve for rolling pin

PREPARATION
10 mins.

In a bowl stir together the sugar, melted butter, and salt. In a separate vessel add the baking soda to the buttermilk.

Alternately add the flour and the buttermilk to the sugar-butter mixture. Stir in the oatmeal.

PREHEAT

Preheat the oven to 350°.

SHAPING
20 mins.

To facilitate measuring the amount of dough needed for each piece of *flatbrøt*, divide the dough into 2 pieces and roll each into a log. Cut from the log ⅓ cup of dough—and mark the remaining length of dough accordingly.

Shape the small piece of dough into a round ball. Flatten it down on the pastry cloth with your palm. Roll paper-thin with a rolling pin covered with the pastry sleeve. Roll onto the pin or *lefse* stick and place the dough on the cookie sheet.

Either cut with a pastry cutter into squares before baking, or bake the dough and then break into pieces.

BAKING
350°
8 mins.

Place in the oven and bake for about 8 minutes, or until the flatbread is lightly browned. (The baking time depends on the thickness of the rolled dough.)

FINAL STEP

Slip the flatbread off the cookie sheet onto a metal rack to cool. (Break the dough into pieces now, if desired.) These may be stored in a covered container for weeks.

RØMMEGRØT
(Cream Pudding)

[SERVES 6 TO 8]

To make this delicious, smooth pudding, purchase the richest cream possible.

INGREDIENTS

2 cups rich whipping cream (not ultra-pasteurized)
⅓ cup all-purpose flour
1½ cups milk
½ teaspoon salt
4 tablespoons sugar
1 tablespoon ground cinnamon, to garnish

continued

COOKING
30–40 mins.

Pour the cream into the saucepan; bring to a boil over medium heat. Stir until the foam is gone.

Add the flour gradually while stirring with a whisk, keeping the mixture smooth. Beat the mixture with a wooden spoon as it cooks over a low heat. Cook and stir for about 15 minutes, until it thickens and comes away from the side of the pan.

At this point the butterfat will separate from the flour mixture. Spoon the butter into a small serving dish to serve later.

In a separate pan bring the milk to a boil and then gradually add it to the mushlike mixture. Beat with a whisk until it is smooth. Simmer for 10 to 20 minutes, stirring frequently, until the mixture thickens. Add the salt and 2 tablespoons of sugar. Beat with a whisk until smooth. If lumps will not smooth out, force the mixture through a sieve, or process in a blender or food processor.

FINAL STEP

Serve the hot pudding in dessert bowls. Top with reserved butter. Garnish with cinnamon and remaining 2 tablespoons of sugar. Syrup or honey is sometimes passed at the table.

▰▰▰▰*On the Road—MINNEAPOLIS, MINNESOTA*

A New People

In a journey across this country you see people in the places you expect to see them. No surprises: an Indian girl on a pinto pony in the New Mexican desert; an Amish man and his buggy in northern Indiana; a black youth, a boom-box jouncing at his side, walking down State Street in Chicago. It is unexpected to find a new people in Minneapolis.

They are the Hmongs, a small, dark Asiatic people in a land of blond, Nordic giants.

A preliterate mountain people without a written language, they were recruited as our allies to rescue American pilots and sabotage Communist supply lines during the secret war in Laos in the early 1970s. Hmongs later sought refuge in this country. Some ten thousand came to the

Minneapolis–St. Paul region, sponsored by local church groups; others settled in southern California. Life for them has not been easy.

Unable to read or write, the Hmongs grew up in remote mountain country practicing slash-and-burn farming on remote hilltops, relying on stories of their elders for their education and attributing sickness to evil spirits. When they came to Minnesota, they continued many of their old ways—doctoring sick children with an elixir of powdered lead. Opium, too, has been a favorite palliative and the Hmongs cannot understand why a package of it sent from home should cause such a furor with the authorities. In Laos they could hunt and fish where and when they pleased; this practice, continued in Minnesota, which has strict game laws, has vexed wardens who have found them trapping birds of all kinds and sizes in public parks and fishing for everything that swam in restricted ponds and pools.

Sara Monick, my guide to good food in Minneapolis, had driven us to the Minneapolis Public Market to see the wealth of produce available to local cooks. I was surprised to see that almost all of the stalls were presided over by Hmong women. Hmong children were everywhere. Few Hmong men were about. It is not difficult to tell a Hmong from a Minnesotan. The Hmongs are a small, squat people—in the five-foot range, round brown faces, and black hair.

Over the past decade, Sara said, many of the Hmongs have become excellent truck gardeners, thanks in large part to the University of Minnesota's program run with the belief that these refugees could better earn a living on the land raising cucumbers, bell peppers, tomatoes, and a dozen other vegetables, than by working in a factory or business where language and mores would be a greater obstacle.

Walking among the stalls stacked high with washed, polished, and trimmed vegetables, I searched for one that was not occupied by a Hmong woman, since my ability to speak Hmong is limited. I wanted to know what had happened to all the local truck gardeners that once occupied each of the several hundred sheltered stalls in the big open-air market. Above each stall was a large weathered sign with the original lessee's name, and a few words extolling the kind and quality of produce. But now these people were gone, retired from truck gardening or dead, and the Hmongs, with the city's blessing, had moved into the vacant stalls.

"B. Johnson and Son," the sign read. Underneath sat an elderly man, a Johnson, I presumed; during the course of our conversation I could not determine whether he was *fils* or *père*. He said he had been coming to this stall from his small farm in the country for more years than he cared to remember and added that most of the years had been good ones. Now, he said, he had reservations.

"I used to look forward each market day to seeing not only my customers but people in the stalls all around me. We were friends for many years, and then they got old and wore out and gave up, and then the Hmongs came.

"I have nothing against the Hmongs, mind you, but last Saturday of the twenty-seven displays here in the market twenty-five were Hmongs. Only two of us old-timers showed up.

"I have given up trying to understand them. I just can't carry on a conversation. I've tried. But they don't seem to want to learn English. A lot of them are on relief; last week one of the men was selling surplus cheese he'd been given by the government. I guess the men work in the fields but not all of the time. In the mornings they drive up, drop off the women and kids, and come back again at noon when we close. And they all drive better cars than I can afford.

"Strange people," he mused. He was more puzzled than bitter.

Several of the Hmong women had set up card tables to display small hand-stitched "story" panels depicting life in the remote hill country of Laos. Known as *pa ndau*, an ancient art of storytelling on blankets and articles of clothing, the women sew intricate designs, working from memory.

From a pile of a dozen or so, Marje chose a sixteen-inch square panel of blue cotton on which the seamstress had told the story of jungle life—a stalking tiger; monkeys in a tree; parrots on a branch; a wild boar with tusks lowered to attack; a rhino, fox, and deer; and two elephants, one drinking from a pool while its mate waved a large bouquet of pink and white flowers in its trunk. Primitive art, certainly, but done with a fine sense of color, pattern, and motion.

Scandinavian Cuisine—Karen Torp

Once in a great while Karen Torp will prepare corned beef and cabbage with soda bread to celebrate her Irish paternal roots, but more often in her kitchen it will be Swedish *skinkabullar* (meatballs), *rødkaol* (braised red cabbage), or, at Christmas time, *lutfiske* (cod). It is clear that the maternal side of the family prevails in the Torp kitchen. It is tilted even

more to the North countries if you factor in her late husband, Bill Torp, a Minneapolis physician and a first-generation Norwegian.

Marje and I fell in love with Scandinavian cuisine several decades ago when we bicycled across France and Holland, then into Denmark and Sweden. We were roughing it. All of our gear was in saddlebags strapped onto our rear fenders. And we did it all on a budget of $5 a day. It was a joy to cycle into a small village to find not one but two, sometimes three konditories anxious for us to buy their pastries. All within our tight budget. Often we spread our purchases among all of them (it seemed the right thing to do), with no concern about waistlines for we were cycling it off as fast as we put it on.

This I recalled with pleasure when Karen invited us to spend a couple of days in the Torp kitchen in Edina, a suburb of Minneapolis, a city considered by many to be the center of Scandinavian life in the United States. Actually, I had asked to be invited. Karen, I knew, was one of the outstanding cooks in a region well provided with outstanding cooks. No one passes up an invitation to dinner at the Torp house.

"What delights me most about Scandinavian cooking is that it is pure; it is simple. It is fresh; it is natural. And it can be duplicated in this country. In Minnesota we don't have the ocean but we do have thousands of lakes and Lake Superior, one of the great freshwater lakes of the world. By air we are short hours away from the sea. Fish from Norway is flown in all the time.

"Most Scandinavian dishes are relatively unknown in this country," Karen said. "Compared to the French and the Italians, we Scandinavians have been shy when it comes to spreading the word about our cuisine.

"There never has been a wave of Scandinavian cooking to sweep across the country like Chinese or Italian. Mexican and even Cajun are far out in front. True, every café and restaurant in America at one time or another has had a smorgasbord, but unfortunately many are simply buffets, a collection of hot and cold dishes the cook has put together. Maybe the time is now."

Much of the best cooking of those Northern countries commends itself to the American kitchen; almost all of it can be duplicated with American products, or for that matter, with Scandinavian products, now abundantly available in specialty stores throughout the country.

"There is a favorite story in the family that on the day my dad tasted my mother's cooking he stopped being an Irishman and became a Swede," Karen said, smiling. "There had been no tradition of Irish cooking in his home so he was a pushover for my mother, a wonderful cook. But Dad had a sophisticated palate that went beyond the ordinary, so thanks to him, when I went off to college I assumed everyone had eaten smoked oysters and eel and broccoli and Brussels sprouts."

Karen calls herself a Scandinavian cook because her curiosity and creativity are wide ranging and she doesn't want to feel confined to any one country's cuisine. "In class I'm often challenged by a student who will say: 'My grandmother—she is Danish—doesn't do it that way,' or 'That's not Swedish!' My life as a teacher is made simpler just to call everything Scandinavian!

"Recently I was shopping at the supermarket for the meats and cheeses that I would need for my smorgasbord. I overheard two ladies talking about a Danish cook I know. One said: 'I have been invited to Marjorie Johanson's party.' The other lady said: 'Oh, that's nice but all she serves is sandwiches.'"

SMÖRREBRÖD
(Open-Face Sandwich)

[MAKES 24 SANDWICHES TO SERVE 6]

Smörrebröd is a buttered open-face sandwich that may be served for all courses. When served at the table they are to be eaten with knife and fork. No fingers. If to be hand-held at a cocktail party, be certain they are tailored to be picked up.

Plan ahead, Karen urges, so you can mass produce the sandwiches on an assembly line by having all of the ingredients organized and ready. Remember, she cautions, this takes time. Visit the deli early to make your selection of meats and cheeses. Prepare all ingredients the day before but assemble smörrebröd as close to the serving time as possible. (Karen can do 1 a minute.)

She also urges a beginner to perfect his or her technique for preparing smörrebröd before tackling a party for 20.

Use firm day-old bread, chiefly rye. No squeezing-soft white bread! Most crusts are cut off but if the bread is soft it may need crust to firm it up. Cut each slice of bread in half before buttering. Spread the softened butter to the *edge* to seal the bread against unwanted moisture. Cover the bread *completely* with ingredients. Leave no space uncovered.

Put dill and lemon only on seafood, never on meat.

Karen strives for a three-dimensional effect. Get as much height as possible when putting on the ingredients. Don't pat them flat. Allow them to rise up.

Ask the butcher or deli clerk to slice the roast beef and ham as thinly as possible. When ready to assemble, pick up the slice in the center—as if lifting a delicate piece of silk—and place it on the lettuce leaf in an attractive mound.

Times of preparation are not given because each cook will go at his or her own pace.

SHARED
INGREDIENTS

8 tablespoons unsalted butter, at room temperature
12 slices rye or whole-wheat bread, cut in half (triangles or
*   rectangles). Firm white bread is a third choice.*
2 heads Boston lettuce, washed, dried, and leaves separated

continued

Roast Beef and Pickle

INGREDIENTS   *Butter, bread, and lettuce (see above)*
½ pound thinly sliced roast beef
6 small pickles, sliced and spread into fans
3 tablespoons Remoulade Sauce (see page 533)
6 sprigs parsley

PREPARATION   Butter the bread and cover with the lettuce. Place a mound of beef on the lettuce and garnish with a dab of the Remoulade. Slice each pickle several times down three-quarters of its length and spread into a fan. Place pickle on the beef and garnish with the parsley. Repeat for the remaining 5 pieces of bread.

Roast Beef, Beets, and Mushrooms

INGREDIENTS   *Butter, bread, and lettuce (see above)*
2 medium onions, thinly sliced
1 tablespoon butter
½ pound thinly sliced roast beef
6 thinly sliced beets
2 mushrooms, sliced into 6 thin slices
2 tablespoons chopped parsley

PREPARATION   Butter the bread slices and cover with a lettuce leaf. Sauté the onions in butter until browned, about 8 minutes. Place the beef on the lettuce in a mound. Place some of the sautéed onions on the meat slice. Garnish with the beet and mushroom slices, then the chopped parsley.

Ham and Orange

INGREDIENTS   *Butter, bread, and lettuce (see above)*
½ pound thinly sliced ham
6 tablespoons mayonnaise
18 segments canned mandarin oranges, well drained
6 parsley sprigs

PREPARATION   Butter the bread and cover with the lettuce. Place a mound of ham on top of the lettuce, spread on some mayonnaise, add 3 orange sections each, and a parsley sprig.

Shrimp, Lemon, and Dill

INGREDIENTS   *Butter, bread, and lettuce (see above)*
¾ pound cooked tiny shrimp or large shrimp thinly sliced
6 tablespoons mayonnaise

1½ slices lemon, cut into quarters
6 sprigs fresh dill

PREPARATION   Butter the bread and cover with the lettuce. Place two or three rows of shrimp on top of the lettuce. Pipe mayonnaise between the rows. Garnish with a lemon slice and a sprig of dill.

Shrimp, Lemon, and Cucumber

INGREDIENTS   *Butter, bread, and lettuce (see above)*
¾ pound cooked tiny shrimp or large shrimp thinly sliced
6 tablespoons mayonnaise
6 thinly cut lemon slices
6 thinly cut English cucumber slices
6 sprigs fresh dill or watercress

PREPARATION   Butter the bread and cover with the lettuce. Mound the shrimp on top of the lettuce. Place a tablespoon of mayonnaise toward one end (off center). On a work surface, place a slice of cucumber on top of the lemon slice. With a sharp knife cut from the edge to center. Twist both together and place on top of the mayonnaise. Garnish with the dill or watercress.

Radish and Jarlsberg Cheese

INGREDIENTS   *Butter and bread only (see above)*
¾ cup finely chopped radishes
2 to 3 slices Jarlsberg cheese
Parsley sprigs or chives

PREPARATION   Butter the bread only; do not use the lettuce. Spread on the chopped radishes, covering fully from edge to edge. On a work surface, cut the cheese slices into triangles and place 2 or 3 in a design of your choice on the radish spread. Garnish with the parsley sprigs or chives.

Gjetist Cheese and Green Pepper Rings

INGREDIENTS   *Butter and bread only (see above)*
6 slices Gjetist goat cheese
1 green bell pepper
Radish slices, thinly cut

PREPARATION   Butter the bread only; do not use the lettuce. On a work surface, cut the cheese slices to fit the bread. Cut 12 thin bell pepper rings, and lay over the cheese. Garnish with the radish slices.

Tilost Cheese, Red Pepper, and Green Onion

INGREDIENTS
Butter and bread only (see above)
6 slices Tilost cheese
1 red pepper (small in diameter)
2 tablespoons chopped green onions

PREPARATION
Butter the bread only; do not use the lettuce. Cut the cheese slices to fit. Slice 6 thin rings from the red pepper and lay across the cheese. Garnish each with 1 teaspoon of the chopped onions.

Herring, Onion, and Tomato

INGREDIENTS
Butter and bread only (see above)
One 8-ounce jar herring fillets in wine sauce
1 small red onion
1 or 2 cherry tomatoes
6 parsley sprigs

PREPARATION
Butter the bread only; do not use the lettuce. Drain the fillets and spread equally over the bread slices. Cut 12 thin rings from the red onion and lay 2 each over the fillets. Cut the cherry tomatoes into wedges and place on the onions. Garnish with the parsley sprigs.

Egg, Anchovy, and Cucumber

INGREDIENTS
Butter and bread only (see above)
3 hard-cooked eggs
1 can anchovies
1 English cucumber

PREPARATION
Butter the bread only; do not use the lettuce. Slice the hard-cooked eggs. Discard the egg ends. Place the egg slices on the bread. Place 1 or 2 anchovies at a diagonal and in a wiggle position as if swimming in the ocean. Cut 12 thin cucumber slices. With a sharp knife, cut each from the edge to the center, twist and place to garnish.

Meat Loaf and Onion

INGREDIENTS
Butter, bread, and lettuce (see above)
½ pound meat loaf, thinly sliced
1 medium onion, thinly sliced in rings
⅓ cup catsup
6 parsley sprigs

PREPARATION   Butter the bread and cover with the lettuce. Arrange the slices of meat on the lettuce. Place thin slices of the onion on the meat. Dab a bit of the catsup on one end of the meat (don't spread). Garnish with the parsley.

Tomato, Egg, and Chives

INGREDIENTS   *Butter, bread, and lettuce (see above)*
2 or 3 small ripe tomatoes
2 hard-cooked eggs
2 tablespoons chives or *alfalfa sprouts*

PREPARATION   Butter the bread and cover with the lettuce. Cut the tomatoes in thin slices and place over the lettuce. Cut the hard-cooked eggs into thin slices, discarding the end pieces, and place on the tomatoes. Garnish with the chives.

FINAL STEP   When all the sandwiches have been arranged on serving trays, cover with plastic wrap and store in a cool room until ready to serve.
        Karen places the filled sandwich trays in the middle of the table as a handsome centerpiece. The guests are invited to help themselves.

JANSSON'S FRESTELSE
(Jansson's Temptation)

[SERVES 6]

Legend holds that the nineteenth-century religious zealot Erik Jansson, who was adamantly opposed to the pleasures of the flesh, was sorely tempted by this crusty dish of anchovies and potatoes and threw over his principles to eat some—in secret, of course. He was discovered.

Its popularity in Sweden is roughly comparable to that of pizza in America, and its briny taste gives people a feeling of being in instant communication with the sea.

Karen's comment to me: "This dish sounds terrible, but it is truly delicious." Karen was right, and I now understand how Jansson was tempted.

Serve as a side dish or a midnight snack.

INGREDIENTS
⅓ cup unsalted butter
1 cup sliced onions
6 medium potatoes, peeled, cut in julienne strips, 2 inches long
    and ¼ inch thick as for French fries
One 3-ounce can anchovy fillets
White pepper, to taste
¾ cup cream
¼ cup dry bread crumbs

EQUIPMENT
One shallow 2-quart baking dish, buttered

PREHEAT
Preheat the oven to 350°.

PREPARATION
10 mins.
Melt 2 tablespoons of butter in a large skillet. Add the onions, stirring occasionally, and sauté 4 minutes, or until soft but not browned.

In the prepared baking dish, alternately layer potatoes, sautéed onions, and anchovies, beginning and ending with potatoes. Sprinkle each layer with a pinch of pepper. Drizzle anchovy oil remaining in the can between the layers. Dot with butter.

Pour the cream over the top. Sprinkle lightly with dry bread crumbs.

BAKING
350°
1 hour
Cover the dish and bake for 50 minutes, or until the potatoes test tender when pierced with the tip of a sharp knife and the liquid is nearly absorbed. Remove the cover and bake for an additional 10 minutes.

Serve hot or at room temperature.

SANDBAKKELS
(Butter Cookie Shells)

[MAKES 6 DOZEN COOKIES]

A dough of butter and eggs, flavored with lemon and almond, is pressed into tiny tins and baked. There are regular fluted *Sandbakkel* tins, about 2 inches in diameter and ¾ inch deep, but small tart or tartlet tins do equally well.

Karen's *Sandbakkels* are eaten as they come from the tins, while in Scandinavia they are often filled with almond paste.

INGREDIENTS
½ cup (1 stick) unsalted butter, room temperature
½ cup shortening, room temperature
1 cup sugar
1 egg

⅛ teaspoon salt
¼ teaspoon lemon extract
¾ teaspoon almond extract
5 cups all-purpose flour, approximately

EQUIPMENT

Sandbakkel or tartlet tins. The bake period is short so it will be convenient to use the same tins over again. One baking sheet.

PREHEAT

Preheat the oven to 350°.

PREPARATION
10 mins.

In a medium bowl cream the butter and shortening together. Gradually add the sugar and mix well. Stir in the egg and add the salt, lemon and almond extracts, and 4 cups of flour. If the dough is sticky add additional flour.

CHILLING
2 hours

Chill the dough in the refrigerator for 2 hours.

SHAPING
10 mins.

Pinch off a small marble-sized ball of dough and press into the tin. Working with your fingers, press well into the sides. The dough should be uniformly pressed into the tins.

Place the filled tin on the baking sheet and continue with the balance of the tins.

BAKING
350°
12–15 mins.

When the baking sheet is filled, place in the oven and bake until the cookies are a light brown, about 12 to 15 minutes.

FINAL STEP

Allow the cookies to cool slightly. Invert the tins and tap gently. If a cookie sticks, loosen it carefully with the sharp point of a knife.

These will keep for several weeks when stored in an airtight container.

⧓⧓⧓⧓⧓*On the Road—LEAVING MINNEAPOLIS*

Wild Rice: True or False

A traveler in Minnesota will almost certainly buy a souvenir packet of wild rice for the cook back home. We did. Several.

Caveat emptor! We found an impostor loose in the rice paddies.

From the locals I learned quickly there are two wild rices on the market. One is the true wild rice grown naturally in the waterways of Minnesota and harvested chiefly by Ojibwa Indians in canoes gliding through the wild plants. With a wooden flail, they knock the ripe heads into the canoe bottoms. Promotion is low key. A simple label will give the name of the family or small co-op which harvested and packaged it. Nothing fancy. The package may carry a small red sticker: "Minnesota Hand Harvested Wild Rice." It is expensive: $5 to $6 a pound.

The other rice—grown in man-made paddies—is a California product, planted mechanically in fields, drained at harvesttime to allow giant machines to thresh the rice; later the rice is put into packages with colorful but often misleading drawings of Indians paddling canoes in sylvan settings.

Not all but some of the rice is shipped to Minnesota and passed off as *the* wild rice. Price—about $2.50 a pound, half that of the real thing.

Frank Bibeau, a wild ricer and a member of the White Earth Indian Reservation, is up in arms, as are his fellow Minnesotans, over this intrusion of the cheaper and less toothsome California rice. Not only has this invasion put thousands of rice harvesters out of business (ten thousand at last count with only two thousand remaining), but the paddy-grown rice has only a portion of the flavor and little of the texture of the natural rice.

"Minnesota wild rice is a true gourmet food," he said. "The cheaper California paddy rice, often billed as 'Minnesota's state grain' in slick advertising, is not the food it pretends to be."

We learned all this after we had purchased rice at several different stores, and stowed them deep in the van for the journey cross country. When we unpacked in Indiana—and before we gave a packet to the neighbor who watered our plants and to the one who picked up our mail —I thought I had better check whether they were Minnesota or California.

To my relief, I found that I was in the clear. My purchases were well certified. One was "premium grade 100% Minnesota long grain wild rice," and the other, "authentic natural grown Minnesota wild rice."

My Indian friends will be glad to know that none of the rice we bought was from California.

FARGO, SOUTH DAKOTA

North Dakota Woman—Andrea Halgrimson

Andrea Halgrimson loves the Red River Valley of North Dakota. She loves its people and she wishes more of them would stay rather than leave for the big cities in the East and West. She loves its table-flat terrain.

Flat it is. Approaching Fargo, as we did, from the south on a clear night—as most nights are in the valley—you begin to see the lights of the city's few tall buildings peeking over the horizon more than thirty miles away. You sense the earth *is* round.

Andrea loves its food. She takes angry umbrage when out-of-state columnists write that the place is peopled only by those Swedes with frozen taste buds! She knows about writers, for she is with the city's only newspaper, *The Forum* (circulation: 60,000). She is its food editor and columnist and her readership spreads throughout the region.

"I love it here, I really do. So much of my feeling for the state is in my gut and heart that I get carried away when I talk about our way of life. This is not a backwater. People who live here tend to have a defeatist attitude because they are so accustomed to everybody else putting us down. We have a rich cultural life—museums, a symphony orchestra, two dance companies, and much more. That's part of my mission as a writer, to write and talk about the good things we have."

Halgrimson is a statuesque, sophisticated woman in her fifties with a brilliant smile and rich, deep voice. She is a commanding presence whether she is in the kitchen, at a typewriter, in a crowd, or among the books and files in the paper's library, which she heads (she lists her occupation as "cook-librarian"). On one finger are two sharply notched sterling silver rings shaped from devices used by her father, a longtime Fargo obstetrician. She does all things with flair.

Halgrimson is witty and articulate—and outspoken. She is outspoken about things she likes and outspoken about things she doesn't.

I had written Andrea months earlier through a cooking-school group to which we both belonged. Marje and I would be driving through the Dakotas, heading west, and it would be an opportunity to see a part of the country that I had not seen before and talk with some of its people. When we had mentioned to friends that our trip would take us to Fargo in search of material for the book, the reaction was one of astonishment. "Good food and good cooking in Dakota? You gotta be kidding!"

It was on that note that my correspondence with Andrea began. "A food snob in the East," I wrote, "said that there is no good food in Dakota. Is that so?" I should have ducked. The reply was immediate—and outspoken:

"In the first place there is no Dakota in the singular. There is South Dakota and there is North Dakota. As for those food snobs in the East, I have found Easterners to be some of the most provincial people I've ever met, having no sense of the beauties and culture lying beyond their overpopulated megalopolis. However, I am grateful for their attitude. If people were aware of the wonders of our state, we'd soon be inundated."

One lovely autumn day, almost a year later, we drove into Fargo. Named for the Fargo of the Wells-Fargo Express Company of frontier days, it is a comfortably small metropolis—the largest in the state—with pleasant, tree-lined streets.

Alas, said Andrea, rarely does one find good food in the restaurants of the area. "They are sadly unimaginative. Instead of sending the chef to a cooking school, they paint the dining room."

The dinner Andrea cooked for us in her small apartment kitchen was simple, delicious, and unexpectedly *spectacular*. The chickens, fat and farm-raised, were stuffed loosely with a handful of carrots, celery, and orange peel and rubbed with olive oil and thyme. Andrea carried them from the kitchen through the living room, around the sofa, through a forest of large plants and out onto the narrow balcony. Festoons of ivy draped from the ceiling and along the balcony rail. In the midst of this mini-jungle was a Weber kettle, its deep bed of red coals glowing fiercely.

Too hot, I said to Andrea. "Oh, I don't know—we'll try it anyway," she said, "and keep a close watch." The chickens, glistening with oil, were laid on the grill. The lid was closed and the cook returned to the kitchen to continue a discussion about potatoes.

A fire siren wailed, and I turned my head toward the street—and the balcony. The jungle was deep in black smoke roiling from under the kettle! Smoke hid the ivy. I yelled. Hurling an epithet and grabbing a jug of water, Andrea raced for the chickens. I looked for the fire engine. As I reached the railing, the fire truck, its siren screaming, hurried on past to its assignment elsewhere, oblivious to our impressive billow of smoke.

Confronted with Andrea's determined attack with splashes of water, the fire drew back, the coals cooled down, and the chickens continued on to a delicious conclusion. A bit sooty under the wing but of little matter.

Andrea had prepared a "fall" vegetable medley—eggplant, zucchini, peppers, onion, and garlic. The soup was mushroom, and the bread, toasted sunflower seed. There was a green garden salad. Dessert, naturally, was a lovely chocolate cake made without flour, with semisweet chocolate and ground almonds.

When we returned to Indiana weeks later I found on my desk a column Andrea had written about our visit to Fargo. She quoted my letter in which I told her I had heard there was no good food in "Dakota."

She wrote: "I invited him to *North* Dakota because I thought a guy like Clayton ought to know better. I'd change what I perceived to be his bad attitude." Well, as it turned out, she continued, she liked my wife and my dog, Timothy, and guessed I was okay. "I fell in love with them," she told her readers, "and I believe Bernard's attitude about North Dakota was altered."

Yes, considerably.

CHICKEN SOUP WITH MUSHROOMS AND CHIVES

[SERVES 6 TO 8]

This recipe calls for a fat 4- to 5-pound chicken to make a clear, rich stock in which cubes of chicken meat, sliced mushrooms, and chives are added.

INGREDIENTS

One 4- to 5-pound chicken
2 medium onions, quartered
2 carrots, coarsely chopped
1 cup chopped celery

Sachet d'Épice
1 bay leaf
¼ teaspoon dried thyme
3 sprigs of parsley

continued

Salt, if desired, to taste
Freshly ground black pepper, to taste
1 tablespoon butter
¼ pound mushrooms, thinly sliced
2 tablespoons finely chopped fresh chives
2 teaspoons fresh lemon juice
½ cup fresh parsley, snipped, to garnish

EQUIPMENT

One sieve, colander, or chinois; cheesecloth, to strain

COOKING
3–3½ hours

For the stock: In a medium (3-quart) saucepan combine the chicken, onions, carrots, celery, and *sachet*. Add water to cover. Bring to a boil, skim the surface frequently, and simmer, covered, until the chicken is tender, about 1 hour.

Remove the chicken, cool, remove the meat from the bones, and cut the white meat only into small dice, making 1½ cups. (Save the rest of the chicken for another use.)

Return the bones to the saucepan and continue to simmer for an additional 2 hours, adding water if needed to maintain the level of liquid throughout the simmering period.

STRAINING
5 mins.

Strain the stock through a sieve lined with a dampened, double thickness of cheesecloth.

Season the stock with salt and pepper. Keep hot.

SAUTÉING
3 mins.

In a small skillet melt the butter; sauté the mushrooms and chives over medium heat for about 3 minutes.

FINAL STEP

Combine the diced chicken, sautéed mushrooms and chives, and lemon juice in the stock, reheating if necessary, and ladle into a heated tureen or casserole. Snip parsley over individual servings.

TOASTED SUNFLOWER SEED BREAD

[MAKES TWO 8½-INCH LOAVES]

Butter, honey, and sunflower seeds are the heart and soul of this all-whole-wheat bread. It is a large loaf, with sunflower seeds peeking through the crusts—top, bottom, and sides. Inside, it is moist, open textured.

The bread is fine for any meal or occasion but especially good for breakfast or brunch—thinly sliced and served with sweet butter.

It keeps well in a plastic bag for at least a fortnight.

Toast the sunflower seeds in a 300° oven for 20 minutes.

INGREDIENTS

5 to 6 cups whole-wheat flour, approximately
2 packages dry yeast
2 teaspoons salt
½ cup nonfat dry milk
2¼ cups hot tap water (120°–130°)
¼ cup honey
2 tablespoons butter, room temperature
1 cup toasted sunflower seeds (see above)

EQUIPMENT

Two medium (8½ x 4½-inch) loaf pans, greased or Teflon

PREPARATION BY
HAND OR MIXER
15–20 mins.

In a large mixing bowl measure 3 cups of the whole-wheat flour, the yeast, salt, and dry milk. Stir to blend. Pour in the hot water and add the honey and butter. Stir the thick batterlike dough vigorously for 75 strokes with a wooden spoon or 3 minutes under a mixer flat beater. Add the sunflower seeds.

Add another cup of whole-wheat flour, working it into the batter with a spoon or the mixer. Add more of the flour—¼ cup at a time—until the dough forms a mass, moist and sticky. (Additional flour will be added momentarily.)

(*Note:* Let the dough rest for 4 or 5 minutes to allow the wheat particles to absorb their full quota of moisture.)

Continue adding flour, a small portion at a time, until the dough is a shaggy mass that can be lifted out of the bowl onto the work surface—or left in the electric mixer bowl to work with the dough hook.

KNEADING
8 mins.

Knead with a strong push-turn-fold motion for about 8 minutes, or until the dough is soft, elastic, and feels alive under the hands. Or knead for 8 minutes with the dough hook.

FIRST RISING
1 hour

Place the dough in a bowl, cover tightly with plastic wrap, and leave at room temperature until the dough has doubled in bulk, about 1 hour. It will be puffy.

SHAPING
15 mins.

Turn back the plastic wrap, punch down the dough, and transfer it to the work surface.

Divide the dough into 2 pieces. Press each piece into an oval, fold in half lengthwise, pinch the seam closed, and drop into a pan, seam under.

SECOND RISING
45 mins.

Cover the pans with wax paper and let the dough rise until approximately doubled in volume, about 45 minutes.

PREHEAT

Preheat the oven to 375°, about 20 minutes before the bake period.

continued

BAKING
375°
45 mins.

Bake the loaves in the moderately hot oven for 45 minutes. The loaves will be a deep brown and will pull away from the sides of the pans when done. They can be tested with a wooden toothpick inserted in the center of the loaf. If the toothpick comes out dry, the bread is done.

FINAL STEP

Remove the bread from the oven and turn the loaves onto a wire rack to cool before serving.

CHOCOLATE, CHOCOLATE CAKE WITH CHOCOLATE GLAZE

[SERVES 6 TO 8]

Andrea speaking: "For celebrations, I want chocolate. Particularly on holidays. All day. And since every day is someone's birthday, one likes to have a few hundred chocolate recipes on hand to prevent duplication. This is one of them."

Note: To toast the almonds for topping, place in a pan in a 350° oven for 5 to 8 minutes. Shake the pan to turn the nuts. Watch carefully. The nuts should be a light brown.

INGREDIENTS

One cup (5½ ounces) unblanched almonds
4 ounces semisweet chocolate, or ¾ cup semisweet chocolate chips
½ cup (1 stick) unsalted butter, room temperature, cut into pieces
½ cup sugar
3 large or extra-large eggs
Grated zest from 1 large orange
¼ cup very fine dry bread crumbs
Chocolate Glaze (recipe follows)
Toasted chopped almonds (see above), to garnish, if desired

EQUIPMENT

One 7- or 8-inch round springform pan, buttered; bottom lined with parchment paper, buttered

PREHEAT

Preheat the oven to 375°.

PREPARATION
30–35 mins.

Grind the almonds as fine as possible in a food processor or blender. Set aside.

Melt the chocolate in a heavy pan over very low heat or in the top of a double boiler over hot, not boiling, water, about 10 to 12 minutes.

Cream the butter in an electric mixer until very soft and light in color. Gradually work in the sugar, beating constantly. Add the eggs, one at a time, beating hard after each addition. At this point the batter may appear curdled.

Stir in the melted chocolate, ground nuts, orange zest, and bread crumbs. Mix thoroughly.

Pour the batter into the prepared pan.

BAKING
375°
25 mins.

Place the cake in the oven and bake for 25 minutes or until a cake tester pin or a silver knife inserted in the center of the cake comes out clean.

COOLING
35 mins.

Remove the cake from the oven; cool in the pan for 30 minutes. Turn onto a rack; lift off and discard the parchment.

Meanwhile, make the glaze.

ASSEMBLING

Place the cake on a rack over wax paper and pour the glaze all over. Tip the cake so the glaze runs evenly over the top and down the sides. Smooth the sides with a metal spatula if necessary.

FINAL STEP

Garnish the rim of the cake with toasted almonds, if desired. Serve as is, or chill.

Chocolate Glaze

INGREDIENTS

2 ounces unsweetened chocolate
2 ounces semisweet chocolate, or ¼ cup semisweet chocolate chips
¼ cup (½ stick) unsalted butter, softened and cut into pieces

PREPARATION
8–10 mins.

Combine the ingredients in a heavy saucepan or in the top of a double boiler. Melt over low heat, 8–10 minutes. Remove from the heat and beat until it is cool but can still be poured.

Curious Canadian Customs

On TV weather maps, Canada—our neighbor to the north—drops off into an abyss at the very boundary of the two countries. A blank field of gray or white (this morning on NBC the void was lavender) is all there is of Canada or, for that matter, of Mexico.

I have news for weathermen. There is more to it than meets the television eye.

Saskatchewan by itself is as big as Texas. If North Dakota has endless fields of grain, Saskatchewan—where we entered Canada—has more. If North Dakota is flat, Saskatchewan around Regina is flatter. If North Dakota is cold, Saskatchewan is colder. If North Dakota has good food —not universally, of course, but at selected locations—so does Saskatchewan. If U.S. Customs officers are curious, Saskatchewan Customs officers are curiouser.

We crossed into Canada at a remote customs/immigration station, Port Oungre, where the nice young officer had nothing much to do that afternoon. For an hour or more we were his only customer. I think he was just pleased to have someone with whom to visit. It seemed hardly possible that he thought this elderly, kindly couple was packing drugs into the province. Yet he poked through the jammed-packed van with a flashlight and a fine-tooth comb, feeling up under the seats and punching the cushions.

During the search, Marje read while Timothy and I walked into Canada. With his forepaws in the United States and his rear in Canada, we wet down the stone boundary marker. In the meantime, the agent came up with the result of his lengthy search—two bottles of wine on which I had to pay a tariff of a couple of dollars even though I promised him I would bring them unopened back to the United States. Sorry, he said. I felt I should compliment him on the thorough search, but I was afraid he might think me cheeky.

Timothy visited the stone once more, then we got into the van and drove into Canada.

≈≈≈≈REGINA, SASKATCHEWAN

Forty-eight Hours—Margo Embury, Eunice Shiplack, Kay Pasieka, Nota Solomos, Sis Eberts, Shirley Hansen, Lola Hoff

Margo Embury is a fine home cook whose knowledge of food goes far beyond her kitchen. As publishing director of a printing-distribution firm, she has been responsible for the publication of more than fifty best-selling Canadian cookbooks. She has a network of food people that has grown out of her work with several hundred cooks and authors across the country.

A kindred soul in food, Margo and I had been talking for almost a year, making plans for Marje and me to spend a few days in Saskatchewan. While it is a fair distance from Indiana—more than a thousand miles and above the forty-ninth parallel—I felt certain Canada's heralded "bread basket" would have something in its basket besides bread.

Here are my notes of a forty-eight-hour whirlwind visit with Embury and cooks, or, if you wish, two days in the life of a cookbook author.

Lola Hoff serves Margo Embury

Day One: *MORNING*

Off early to Embury's house to meet two grandmotherly women from the Ukrainian Women's Association of Canada whose cookbook has sold forty thousand copies to become a regional best-seller. Eunice Shiplack and Kay Pasieka were born in the Ukraine and came as children to Canada in 1928. Both cook Ukrainian, but there are some changes.

On Christmas Eve they no longer toss a spoonful of *kutia*, a mixture of wheat berries, poppy seeds, walnuts, and honey, to the ceiling to foretell good fortune for the coming year by how many kernels stick. Nor when baking a wedding bread, *korovai*. Traditionally it must be prepared by seven young, happily married women who must draw water from seven different wells and use flour from wheat grown in seven different fields, eggs from seven different hens, and butter churned from milk from seven different cows.

"I won't have time to search for seven young happily married women to make one loaf of bread," I told the ladies, so they suggested Paska, the traditional bread baked for the Easter celebration.

Left to right, Eunice Shiplack, the author, and Kay Pasieka

Day One: *LUNCH*

It was only midmorning, but the Ukrainian ladies insisted we lunch at a local Ukrainian restaurant, The Bukovina, for a taste of traditional dishes. The women knew the owner. Perhaps, said Mrs. Shiplack, he will let us into his restaurant early. The restaurant was open but *only* to tradesmen.

Mrs. Shiplack, a strong-willed woman, was not to be denied. We went in. Mrs. Shiplack peeked and poked into various pots and pans and invited me to do the same. It occurred to me she might be one of the owners, but then I heard a loud Ukrainian oath explode behind me. It was the chef/owner, Mr. Mariutsan. He was furious.

Unperturbed, Mrs. Shiplack translated—"Food is to be eaten, not poked—get to hell out of the kitchen!" We retired to the dining room to await the formal opening.

The food was interesting but, with one exception, nothing to write home about. Perhaps it was an off day for the cook, further aggravated by our task force under the command of Mrs. Shiplack. The exception was *Kapusnyak*, a sauerkraut-sparerib soup with just the right touch of sour.

Day One: AFTERNOON

Back to Embury's house for a Canadian Broadcast Corporation interview in the dining room with Bruce Steele, a friendly man of rotund voice and figure. He left me with the feeling that his knowledge of food as well as his willingness to talk about it was far greater than mine. I should have been the interviewer and he the interviewee.

Day One: DINNER

Dinner with Nota Solomos, a handsome woman of Greek heritage and a home economist/teacher known throughout the province, and George Kolitsas, in his restaurant, Golf's Steak House.

There is a large Greek community in Regina and while most of the restaurants in town are owned by Greeks, few of them are identified as such. It is not a matter of prejudice; it is just that Regina diners are conservative. "They don't pretend to be sophisticated. They're not comfortable in a restaurant with a name they can't pronounce or with dishes with strange-sounding words," said George. "Our beef *stefado* is on the menu simply as 'beef stew.'"

George and his three brothers also own a chain of five pizza restaurants. No Greek name for them: Houston Pizza, with no Texas connection. They just liked the name.

Solomos, the home economist, on the other hand, teaches Greek cooking to overflowing classes. "It's a three-thousand-year-old cuisine that adjusts beautifully to Saskatchewan's rich bounty of produce, meats, and seafoods. The very essence of Greek cooking is informality, and this fits perfectly into our way of life in the province."

She had brought to the dinner *Galaktoboúreko*, a delicious custard pudding-pie.

Day One: NIGHT

Ah, bed.

Day Two: MORNING

It was a long, early-morning drive through newly harvested wheat fields, a vast carpet of short golden stubble stretching to the horizon. No winding roads. This flat part of Saskatchewan was a surveyor's dream. Straight lines, no curves around hills. We drove ahead for thirty miles, turned a clean 90° right, three miles on, a 45° left, and into a barnyard alongside a modest one-story ranch house.

John and Sis Eberts live here. John is famous for his deep-pit barbecued beef served at festivals, fairs, reunions, church bazaars, and company picnics or anything else where several hundred people need to be fed. This was late summer and already he had barbecued more than one and a half tons of beef and had another month to go. He and Sis began barbecuing fifteen years ago when their daughter was candidate for the local Wheat Queen and the sponsoring group was strapped for funds.

He is also known for his practical jokes. I bear witness. I also bear a bruised ego. He looked me up and down and allowed that I was a big, strong guy. My ego was touched.

"Yes, I suppose I am," I admitted modestly.

"You might like to know just how strong," he said, and pointed to a boxlike contraption replete with dials and pulleys resting on the floor across the room. It looked like part of a homemade Nautilus machine.

John called the women to be my audience. (That should have tipped me off.) He moved me into a crouched position over the machine looking down at the dials.

"Put your feet here. Take a deep breath and then pull on this bar with all your strength!" He stepped back.

I gave the bar a mighty tug—and all Hell broke loose! Bells clanged, whistles blew, the sides of the machine fell to the floor, and a heavy board, powered by a coiled spring, cracked me across the butt! I was

John Ebert

absolutely stunned—and my beet-red face showed it! The women and John roared. I had been had. Completely.

When my poise returned, John and I talked about his famous deep-pit barbecue. It is not for the home cook but a cook for hundreds.

Beef hips are cut into two pieces, about 25 pounds each. Rubbed with a dry mix of salt, pepper, paprika, and tenderizer, the meat is left for twenty-four hours. Each piece is then wrapped tightly in cheesecloth, which is sewn in place.

He mixes flour and water into a thick paste and spreads it ¼ inch thick over the cheesecloth. The bundle is tied tightly with bailing wire. He leaves a length of wire protruding out of the pit so the bundle can be lifted out later. Finally, he wraps the package with burlap and sews it on tightly.

The pieces are soaked with water using a garden hose and tossed into a six-foot-deep pit in which a big load of wood has burned down to a three-inch-deep bed of coals. The pit is immediately closed over with a sheet of galvanized roofing, and sealed with shovelfuls of dirt. Eight hours later the packages are taken from the pit, the hard shell cut away, and the juice saved. John cuts ½-inch-thick slices. He figures that each slice weighs about ¾ pound—a thick, generous portion. The meat is forked onto fat buns of bread, moistened with a dollop of beef juice. With the big sandwich in hand, the guest moves down the line to baked beans, corn on the cob, and a big serving of Sis Eberts's special Picnic Potato Salad.

Day Two: LUNCH

Shirley Hansen was making her grandmother's Hungarian sweet mixed pickles when we arrived at the big brick farmhouse on the crest of a slope overlooking the lovely Qu'Appelle Valley that cuts two thirds of the way across the flat prairie lands of Saskatchewan.

Shirley is a rancher's wife who for the past week had been doing what she laughingly calls "meals-in-the-fields" for a half-dozen hungry threshers, including her husband. They are harvesting wheat in fields about ten miles away. The work begins in the morning when the dew has burned off the wheat and continues under headlights late into the night.

This calls for noon and evening deliveries over a period of two weeks. She delivers an enviable cuisine—roast beef and potatoes, roast turkey, baked ham, chili, sausage and sauerkraut, hamburgers and beans, soups, stews, casseroles, and "lots of puddings and pies."

We sat at a table in the sunlit kitchen overlooking her garden. She was annoyed yet pleased at the nearness of wildlife. Deer reach over the garden fence to pluck good things to eat. She brought to the table a light lunch of venison sausage (not from the garden deer, she hastened to explain), which was made with pork to add fat to bind together the lean deer meat. She served it with a crusty homemade bread, a selection of Canadian cheeses, her chutney and "chili sauce" (pears, peaches, apples, and tomatoes), rhubarb relish, plus the sweet mixed pickles that filled a dozen jars on the counter. Served with the lunch were her good-tasting Ice Cream Muffins.

The recipe is so simple: 3 cups self-rising flour plus 3 cups *melted* ice cream (any flavor—nuts and fruit are especially good); mix, pour into tins. Bake for 20 to 25 minutes at 375°.

Day Two: AFTERNOON
We drove back to Regina, retreated to the motel room to catch up on writing, and gave Timothy a long and well-deserved run in the park. When we visit ranches and farms there are always big dogs running around that outweigh him by fifty pounds, so he spends a great deal of time asleep on the backseat of the van. I sense he feels his life inside the van is better than a dog's life outside.

Day Two: DINNER
The four of us—Margo Embury, Marje, Timothy, and I—piled back into the van and drove to a small town in the Qu'Appelle Valley for a multinational dinner with a remarkable couple, Lola and Sig Hoff.

Both in their seventies, they had just returned from their third three-month volunteer mission to Jamaica where she taught cooking to would-be restaurant cooks and chefs, and he, a landscape architect, trained young men in beach restoration practices. The program, like this country's Peace Corps, is CESO, Canadian Executive Service Overseas. Married fifty years, they renewed their vows in a ceremony in Kingston attended by their Jamaican students. The three-tiered wedding cake was baked by her students.

Dinner was Scandinavian/Canadian. She is Danish, he, Swedish, so the meal is a blend. But it began Caribbean, with a Jamaican Rum Manhattan! Smooth! Powerful! Lola, who has been catering and teaching cooking for half a century, started with hors d'oeuvres of smoked salmon canapés, meatballs, and Brie and then on to the dinner table for spinach soup, home-cured ham, boiled potatoes, peas, carrots, and cauliflower. The delicious dessert was Swedish: *Äppelkaka*, an apple cake of layers of applesauce and rye bread crumbs—topped with whipped cream.

Day Two: MIDNIGHT
It was midnight when the van turned back to Regina. Early the next morning we left Saskatchewan for Glacier National Park. My regret was that the fast-paced two-day schedule did not allow us to work in the kitchen with these good cooks. All we did was eat their food.

EASTER PASKA

[MAKES ONE 9-INCH LOAF]

The Paska loaf is baked by the Ukrainian ladies as part of the blessing of the basket of foods brought to the church at Eastertime. Several layers of dough are laid down to form a lovely ornamental design of entwined cords and crosses.

INGREDIENTS
3 eggs
2 tablespoons sugar
½ cup (1 stick) unsalted butter, room temperature
1 teaspoon salt
1 cup milk, or 1 cup water plus ⅓ cup powdered milk
4½ cups all-purpose flour, approximately
2 packages dry yeast

EQUIPMENT One round 9-inch baking pan, 2 inches deep, greased or Teflon

PREPARATION BY HAND OR MIXER 10 mins.
In a mixer or mixing bowl cream by hand or with a mixer flat beater 2 eggs, the sugar, butter, and salt. Mix the milk with the butter-egg mixture. Measure in 1 cup of flour and the yeast. Stir well to blend.

When the batter is smooth, add the balance of the flour, ½ cup at a time, and each time stir vigorously. When the dough has formed a mass that can be lifted from the bowl and placed on the floured work surface, the dough is ready to knead. Or, if with a mixer, attach the dough hook. Add sprinkles of flour if the dough continues to be sticky during the kneading period.

KNEADING 10 mins.
Knead the dough with an aggressive push-turn-fold motion or under the dough hook for 10 minutes, or until the dough is smooth and elastic. At this point it should not stick to the work surface or to the sides of the mixer bowl.

FIRST RISING 1 hour
Place the dough in a greased bowl, cover tightly with a length of plastic wrap, and put aside at room temperature to double in bulk, about 1 hour.

SHAPING 10–15 mins.
This is accomplished in three steps.

First: Roll out a 1-inch-thick layer of dough to cover the bottom of the pan.

Second: Take 2 pieces of dough, and roll each under your palms to 36-inches in length. Loosely entwine the strands and place on the top of the base, around the edge of the pan.

Third: Roll 4 pieces of dough, each 10-inches long. Loosely twist 2 lengths together into a rope. Repeat with the other 2 pieces. Cross the 2 ropes at the center of the loaf. Slightly separate each end of the 2 ropes and curve all 4 ends toward the center to form a clover-leaf design. As they rise, the ends will push into the strands and secure the design.

SECOND RISING
50 mins.

Cover the dough with parchment paper or a cloth and put aside at room temperature until the dough doubles in bulk, about 50 minutes.

PREHEAT

Preheat the oven to 350° about 20 minutes before baking.

BAKING
350°
15 mins.
375°
40 mins.

Brush the loaf with 1 beaten egg.
    Place the baking pan in the oven and bake for 15 minutes at 350°. Turn the oven up to 375° and bake for 40 minutes more, or until a golden brown.

FINAL STEP

Allow the loaf to cool for 10 minutes before turning it out of the bake pan—it is somewhat fragile while hot.

KAPUSNYAK
(Sauerkraut Soup)

[SERVES 6]

This is a soup for when winter weather calls for something robust, hearty, filling, and delicious. It is thick and could well be called a stew.

INGREDIENTS

2 pounds fresh spareribs
8 cups water (with more to be added)
2 cups chopped onions
2 bay leaves
2 medium potatoes, peeled and diced a scant ½ inch
1 cup shredded carrots
1 cup chopped celery
3 cups sauerkraut
1 cup rice
½ teaspoon salt
½ teaspoon freshly ground black pepper
Chopped parsley, to garnish

PREPARATION
5 mins.

Rinse the meat. Place in a large sauce pot, cover with the 8 cups water and add the onion and bay leaves.

COOKING
About 1 hour

Bring the pot to a boil over medium-high heat, turn to a simmer, and cook, covered, until the meat is tender, about 45 minutes.

Add the potato, carrots, and celery.

Taste the sauerkraut. If it is too briny for your taste, pour it into a colander and rinse briefly. Add the kraut, rice, salt, and pepper to the pot. Stir to mix the ingredients together.

Simmer until the potatces test done when stuck with a fork, about 20 minutes.

FINAL STEP

The meat may be served as a separate course or cut into small pieces and served with the soup.

Garnish each serving with a sprinkle of parsley.

Rye bread is the traditional accompaniment.

GALAKTOBOÚREKO
(Custard Pie)

[MAKES SIXTEEN 2-INCH SQUARES]

Golden leaves of phyllo moistened with a lemon syrup surrounds this delicious custard dessert made with Cream of Wheat. It can also be made with wheat hearts, farina, or semolina.

An alternative to the syrup is to sift ½ cup of confectioners' sugar over the pastry when it comes from the oven, then sprinkle heavily with cinnamon. Allow it to cool, uncovered, for 4 hours before serving.

INGREDIENTS

20 sheets (about ¾ package) of prepared phyllo/strudel leaves
2½ cups whole milk
3 eggs
¾ cup sugar
6 tablespoons Cream of Wheat
¼ teaspoon salt
2 teaspoons unsalted butter plus ½ cup (1 stick) butter or
  margarine, melted, to brush
½ teaspoon vanilla extract
1 teaspoon grated orange zest
⅓ cup finely chopped almonds

SYRUP
1 cup sugar
1 cup water
2 teaspoons lemon or lime juice

EQUIPMENT

One 8 x 8 x 2-inch baking dish, buttered; 1 pastry brush

continued

BEFOREHAND

Follow the package instructions for thawing and keeping phyllo leaves moist while preparing the dish.

COOKING
25 mins.

Scald the milk, remove from the stove, and keep warm.

In a small bowl beat the eggs until light and fluffy. Add the sugar and beat until creamy. Slowly pour the egg mixture into the milk, stirring constantly. Stir in the Cream of Wheat, and cook over low heat until slightly thickened, 15 minutes.

Remove from the heat and allow to cool slightly. Add the salt, 2 teaspoons of butter, vanilla, orange zest, and almonds. Mix well. Set aside.

PREHEAT

Preheat the oven to 350°.

ASSEMBLING
10 mins.

Unfold the phyllo leaves into a neat stack on the work surface. Lay a slightly dampened paper towel or cloth over the leaves to prevent them from drying out and tearing during preparation.

With a pastry brush coat the pan bottom and sides with melted butter. There will be 12 sheets to form the bottom and 8 sheets for the top. The number of leaves is not critical. The first 12 leaves will cover the bottom of the pan, and up the sides. The extra lengths will be folded over the custard after it is poured.

Brush *each* sheet with butter after it is laid down.

Pour the slightly cooled filling over the sheets. Turn in the overhanging sheets across the custard top. Cover with 8 more buttered sheets, tucking under the edges to make a neat package.

Score the top sheets with a sharp knife into 2-inch squares or, if you wish, in the traditional Greek diamond shapes.

BAKING
350°
45 mins.

Sprinkle cold tap water over the top. Place in the oven for 45 minutes, or until the dessert is puffed and golden.

SYRUP
10 mins.

While the pastry is baking bring the sugar, water, and lemon or lime juice to a boil. Lower the heat to simmer for 10 minutes. The syrup must be warm, not hot, when the pastry comes from the oven.

FINAL STEP

As soon as the pan comes from the oven, pour syrup over it a tablespoon at a time. Give pastry ample time to absorb the syrup.

Let the *Galaktoboúreko* cool before following the scored marks to cut it into serving pieces.

PICNIC POTATO SALAD

[SERVES 6 TO 8]

Sis Eberts's potato salad to go with John's barbecue is equally good whether made for 6, 60, or 600.

INGREDIENTS
3 pounds potatoes (new potatoes preferred)
1 cup diced cucumber
3 tablespoons minced green onions, tops and bottoms
1½ teaspoons salt
½ teaspoon freshly ground black pepper
2 diced hard-cooked eggs

DRESSING
1½ cups sour cream
½ cup mayonnaise
¼ cup vinegar, of choice
¾ teaspoon celery seed
1 teaspoon chopped fresh or ½ teaspoon dried dillweed
1 tablespoon prepared mustard, of choice

PREPARATION
20 mins.

Scrub the potatoes with a brush, boil in salted water to cover until tender but still firm, about 15 minutes. Don't overcook.

Cool the potatoes and cut into small cubes. Place the potato cubes in a bowl and add the diced cucumber, onion, salt, pepper, and diced eggs.

ASSEMBLING
5 mins.

Mix together all of the dressing ingredients and pour over the potato mixture. Mix thoroughly.

FINAL STEP

Chill, and carry in a cooler to a picnic, a tailgate party, a class reunion, or church social.

ÄPPELKAKA
(Apple Cake)

[SERVES 4 TO 6]

While most *äppelkakas* are made with white bread crumbs, rye crumbs in Lola Hoff's cake gives it a flavor that pleased guests will find hard to divine. Rye crumbs are seldom on the market, so make your own by crumbling slices of rye bread and drying at low heat in the oven. A food processor will quickly reduce the chunks into crumbs.

INGREDIENTS	*½ cup (1 stick) unsalted butter* *2 cups dry rye bread crumbs* *2 tablespoons sugar* *1 teaspoon ground cinnamon* *3 cups homemade or store-bought applesauce*
EQUIPMENT	One 2-quart mold or soufflé dish coated with 2 teaspoons soft butter
PREPARATION 5 mins.	Melt the butter in a heavy skillet over moderate heat. Add the bread crumbs, sugar, and cinnamon. Stir with a wooden spoon and sauté for about 5 minutes.
PREHEAT	Preheat the oven to 375°.
ASSEMBLING 12 mins.	Cover the bottom of the mold or dish with a ½ inch layer of the rye crumbs. Pour on a thick layer of applesauce, then a thinner layer of bread crumbs, alternating until all of the crumbs and applesauce are used. Top with a thin layer of crumbs.
BAKING 375° 25 mins.	Bake for 25 minutes. It will be firm to the touch. Place on a wire rack to cool before serving.
FINAL STEP	Serve alone or with whipped cream.

On the Road—EN ROUTE TO MISSOULA, MONTANA

*&^%$#$#@

Leaving Glacier, we crossed the Continental Divide and coasted downhill on U.S. 2, traveling parallel to the Middle Fork of the Flathead River (running low because of a hot, dry summer), through spectacular mountain scenery, past the beautiful Flathead Lake, a stop for a bowl of chili in Polson at the foot of the lake, through the Flathead Indian Reservation and into Missoula at the mouth of Hell Gate Canyon where Lewis and Clark camped. I looked forward to coming back to the city where I had been a number of years ago. I remembered it as a nice, comfortable, attractive city.

I had two phone calls to make before we drove into town.

Weeks earlier I had talked with a lady who raised organic chickens on a farm in the nearby mountains. But when I called her she said she had just gone out of business for lack of sales.

Next, I called the woman I was to talk with about her made-at-home pies that were selling like hot cakes in Missoula stores. The story about her highly successful enterprise had appeared in *Readers' Digest* earlier in the year.

When she answered the phone I quickly realized I was talking with an angry woman. Mad as hell about *all* reporters and writers. The *Digest* story had brought down the wrath of the local health department, which made her close down her home-kitchen operation.

If I wanted to know anything about her and her pies, read the %ˆ&$#@ *Readers' Digest!*

And she hung up. BANG!

MISSOULA, MONTANA

Big Sky—Greg Patent

Greg Patent genuinely enjoys cooking, and has for most of his fifty years. He began at age eleven with baking-powder biscuits. Four years later he was doing the evening meals for his parents, both of whom worked, and at age nineteen his apricot bar won second prize ($1,000) and a trip from San Francisco to New York in the Tenth National Pillsbury Bake-Off.

Tall, darkly handsome, a marathon runner in his free time, Patent is the chef of The Mansion, a restaurant in a three-story Victorian house of high ceilings, oak paneling, and stained-glass windows. A few years back this house was pulled from the valley floor up the mountainside to rest at its present location—a spectacular overlook of the city below.

Greg and I were sitting in deep wicker chairs on the verandah of the old house and looking across the valley cupped in the distant mountains.

"While food was my passion I didn't then consider it a career. Instead, I became a zoologist—a Ph.D. from Berkeley. My first interview was here at the University of Montana. I immediately fell in love with the place—the valley, the mountains, the people, the pace of life—everything. I accepted a position on the faculty; phoned Dorothy, my wife, and told her this is where we would raise our family. There's never been a regret."

One day the manager of a local TV station who knew of Greg's interest in food asked him if he might be interested in doing a cooking show. It would have to be shot in Patent's kitchen and with only one camera.

"Not a big-budget production," he said, laughing.

Yet "Big Sky Cooking" was so successful that he produced, directed, and starred in a total of fifty-two regional shows, and wrote a cookbook about it.

In 1981, Greg was invited to do a series of TV shows for Cuisinart, the food processor company, who admired the way he used its machine on camera. First the people at Cuisinart signed him to produce a series of five-minute spots for them (in his kitchen), and then followed up by asking him to become the national spokesperson for their company, doing interviews and demonstrations on television, as well as speaking with radio, newspaper, and magazine food writers and editors. He authored a best-selling cookbook, *Patently Easy—Food Processor Cooking*, and found himself a celebrity in the field he loved. He left the university after ten years on the faculty, and took to the road.

"Then one day I had had my fill of travel—of planes, trains, buses, and cars—and came back to settle down in Missoula."

When he returned, he wrote *Shanghai Passage* (Clarion Books), a book about his exciting growing-up years in the Orient, where he was born and lived until he emigrated with his parents to San Francisco at age eleven.

"When I became chef here [Missoula] I had the advantage of knowing the food mores of this town. After all, I taught many Missoula people how to cook. Jicama, for example, had been unknown here until I introduced it on my TV show. Now all the stores have it. The same with a dozen other things. Boned turkey is big here at Thanksgiving—thanks to the 'Big Sky' TV show!

"I know the things people here in Missoula like and the things they don't like. The don't-likes would be liver, kidneys, brains, and sweetbreads. In the beginning they didn't favor veal, but I have persistently pointed out that veal at The Mansion is something special. It's expensive, true. Naturally raised in Virginia, it has no hormones, no antibiotics. Not frozen; it is vacuum-packed and flown here overnight. Great flavor. Some nights a quarter of my orders will be for veal."

Tonight he will be serving Veal Medallions with mushrooms and Cognac-Cream Sauce. "It will be sold out within half an hour," he said.

VEAL MEDALLIONS WITH COGNAC-CREAM SAUCE

[SERVES 4]

This dish is done in a series of minutes. Hot buttered noodles are a fine accompaniment.

INGREDIENTS

1½ pounds boneless veal loin, cut into ½-inch medallions (about 10)
Flour, to coat
4 tablespoons (½ stick) unsalted butter
1 tablespoon olive oil
½ pound fresh mushrooms, thinly sliced, or whole small fresh morel mushrooms
2 tablespoons minced shallots
¾ cup cognac
⅓ cup chicken stock, homemade (see page 562) or store-bought
1 cup heavy cream
Salt and pepper, to taste
2 tablespoons chopped fresh parsley, to garnish

PREPARATION

Coat the medallions lightly with flour, shaking off any excess.

COOKING
15–20 mins.

In a 12-inch skillet heat 2 tablespoons of butter and the olive oil over medium-high heat.

Cook the veal for 1 to 2 minutes on *each* side in two batches, and transfer them to a plate as they are done. Keep warm.

Pour off the fat from the skillet, keeping the browned bits in the pan. Add the remaining 2 tablespoons of butter and place over medium-high heat. When melted, add the mushrooms and shallots. Toss and cook for 1 minute.

continued

Add the cognac and ignite carefully with a match, shaking the pan all the while. When the flame subsides, add the stock and continue cooking until the liquid thickens and becomes syrupy, 3 to 4 minutes.

Add the cream and boil a minute or two to reduce slightly.

Remove the pan from the heat and season with salt and pepper. Add the veal and any juices to the skillet and cook for a minute or two, basting the medallions with the sauce.

FINAL STEP   Turn onto a heated serving platter and sprinkle with parsley.

HUCKLEBERRY PIE

[MAKES ONE 2-CRUST PIE; SERVES 8]

It was berrying time in Montana and huckleberry pie and ice cream were on The Mansion's menu. Huckleberries and blueberries have almost identical flavor. If the seeds are small, it's blueberries you have just picked; if many and large seeds—huckleberries. There is a hint of wildness in huckleberries that I like.

Greg gives the bottom crusts of his pies a special thrust of heat by preheating the heavy baking sheet on which he places the pies. (*Note:* Prepare the crust at least 1 hour ahead of time.)

INGREDIENTS   *CRUST*
1½ cups unbleached all-purpose flour, plus extra for dusting
¾ cup cake flour
½ teaspoon salt
1 cup (2 sticks) cold unsalted butter, cut into ½-inch bits
2 eggs yolks
½ cup ice water

FILLING
1 cup granulated sugar
¼ cup firmly packed light brown sugar
⅓ cup quick-cooking tapioca
1 teaspoon ground cinnamon
½ teaspoon grated nutmeg
5 cups fresh or frozen huckleberries (see Note below)
2 tablespoons lime juice
1 to 2 teaspoons granulated sugar, to sprinkle

EQUIPMENT   One 9-inch ovenproof glass pie plate; heavy baking sheet, heated (see above)

PREPARATION
15 mins.

For the crust: In a large mixing bowl, combine both the flours and salt. Cut in the butter with a pastry blender until the mixture resembles coarse crumbs. Mix together the egg yolks and ice water. Add the liquid to the flour mixture gradually while tossing with a fork. The dough will begin to gather in a ball. Shape the dough gently into a 6-inch flat disc, and dust lightly with flour.

REFRIGERATING
1 hour

Wrap the dough in plastic wrap and refrigerate for at least 1 hour.

PREHEAT

Preheat the oven and heavy baking sheet to 450°.

FILLING
5 mins.

Combine both the sugars, tapioca, and spices in a large bowl. Add the berries and lime juice and fold together gently but thoroughly with a rubber spatula.

ASSEMBLING
15 mins.

Roll out half of the chilled dough to a 13-inch circle on a lightly floured surface. Fit carefully into a 9-inch pie plate; avoid stretching the dough.

Turn the filling into the bottom crust.

Roll out the remaining dough to a 12-inch circle.

Brush the exposed edge of the lower crust lightly with water. Cover the filling with the top crust and press the edges gently to seal. Trim away excess pastry with scissors, leaving a ½-inch border. Fold the ledge of pastry under itself to make a standing rim. Flute. Cut 3 or 4 slits in the top crust for steam to escape.

Brush lightly with water and sprinkle evenly with granulated sugar.

BAKING
450°
15 mins.
350°
45–60 mins.

Place the pie on the preheated baking sheet and bake for 15 minutes at 450°. Lower the heat to 350° and continue baking until the crust is a rich golden brown and bubbling juices look slightly thickened. This will take an additional 45 minutes if fresh fruit, or about 1 hour with frozen berries.

COOLING
2–3 hours

Thoroughly cool the pie on a rack for several hours before serving. Cutting into the pie too soon may make it ooze.

FINAL STEP

Serve with a scoop of Montana Huckleberry (see below) or vanilla ice cream. (*Note:* Pick over fresh berries to remove twigs and leaves. It is not necessary to rinse them. Use frozen berries straight from the freezer. Do not thaw them first.

The best way to freeze huckleberries is to place them in a single layer on baking sheets. When frozen, transfer them to freezer storage bags. The berries will remain separate and can be stored for at least 1 year.)

MONTANA HUCKLEBERRY ICE CREAM

[MAKES ABOUT 2½ QUARTS]

This delicious ice cream can be made with blueberries if huckleberries are not available.

INGREDIENTS

1 quart fresh or frozen huckleberries
1½ cups granulated sugar
8 egg yolks
1 quart heavy cream
3 tablespoons lime juice

EQUIPMENT

One 4-quart ice cream freezer

PREPARATION
10–12 mins.

Combine the berries and 1 cup of sugar in a 3-quart saucepan. Bring to a boil, stirring, over medium heat. Cover the pan, reduce heat, and simmer for 10 minutes. Set aside.

In a mixer beat the egg yolks with the remaining ½ cup of sugar until the mixture is very thick and pale.

COOKING
20 mins.

Meanwhile, scald the cream in a 2-quart saucepan. Very slowly, add the cream to the yolks while beating at low speed. Transfer the mixture to the saucepan used to scald the cream. Cook, stirring constantly with a rubber spatula over very low heat, until the mixture thickens to a custard, about 20 minutes. The temperature will be 175°. Do not boil.

CHILLING
several hours or
overnight

Add the custard mixture to the huckleberry mixture and stir well. Set the saucepan into an ice-water bath and stir occasionally until the mixture is very cold, about 1 hour. Add the lime juice.

If desired, refrigerate the cool mixture overnight.

Freeze in the ice cream maker according to the manufacturer's instructions.

FINAL STEP

Transfer the ice cream to a storage container and store in the freezer. This ice cream does not freeze too hard to serve straight from the freezer.

MISSOULA, MONTANA

Cash and Alley Cat—Pearl Cash

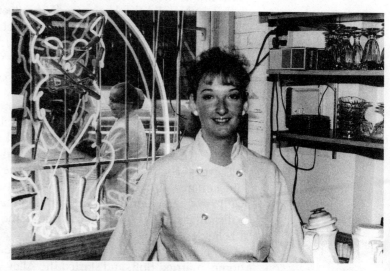

Pearl Cash is a vivacious redheaded woman who arguably is one of the best young chefs in the country. She is little known except around Missoula and that's because national food writers/critics seldom, if ever, focus attention on what's happening in faraway Montana.

I had not heard of Pearl and the Alley Cat Grill before I got to Missoula, but I'll not forget her now that we've been there. The food was exceptionally good. The Grill, which had been Daddy's, a gay bar, before Pearl took it over two years ago, is in an old building in a no-name alley. The address is 125½ West Main, but don't look for it on Main Street, because it is not there. It is half a block way. Ask for directions.

The Grill, with its high ceilings and exposed red-brick walls, is warm and comfortable and smells of good things. There's a big whiskered neon cat in the front window and a collection of feline art on the walls. (I usually don't care for cats, but these seemed right for the place.) There are a half-dozen seats at the bar, ten comfortably wide booths, and one small table for four in the back. Not large, and you may have to wait.

Lunch is chiefly sandwiches and salads. For my first lunch there I had grilled large gulf shrimp on mixed greens with mushrooms, cucumbers, peppers, carrots, and green onions tossed with a ginger nut dressing and sprinkled with toasted coconut. Dessert (and I went overboard): Viennese triple chocolate hazelnut rum torte! That held me until evening when I had grilled fresh Oregon salmon brushed with lemon pepper and butter.

Dessert: Oh, no, I couldn't.

Pearl started her career as a waitress—a young girl serving tables in a restaurant owned by a family whose son she married shortly thereafter. The two of them opened their own café, but after a while the marriage failed and so did the business. "No reflection on the food," Pearl said, "but the restaurant was too big a project. That's why the Alley Cat is small. I grew up a lot in a short time. I had read and studied and cooked enough to know that I knew good cuisine when I saw and tasted it. But I was scared. I stood in awe of big city chefs and big name cooks with their big French credentials and connections.

"So I thought I had better go to France and see what it is all about. I signed up for cooking classes and off I flew. I hadn't been there more than a month when I *knew* I knew food. I never felt so confident.

"Yet I realized that everything I had heard about French cooking was true—the food was really good, the seasoning superb, the wines outstanding—but the doing of it was not an insurmountable task! Start with good ingredients, do interesting things with them, you can prepare a dish that is as good as you can find in the best French restaurants. This I believe!

"That to me was a revelation," she continued. "Wow! I hurried home, married Bob, and started the Alley Cat. Never a regret."

GRILLED SHRIMP SALAD WITH GINGER DRESSING

[SERVES 1]

While the shrimp and salad ingredients are for 1 person in this recipe, the dressing is for 1 quart. It is so delicious that it deserves to be made in a larger quantity.

To increase the number of salad servings, simply multiply ingredients times the number of guests. Easy.

INGREDIENTS

DRESSING
1 cup vegetable oil
3 tablespoons diced peeled gingerroot
1 cup cubed onion
½ teaspoon chopped celery
⅓ cup peanut butter
2 teaspoons sugar
1 teaspoon freshly ground black pepper

¼ teaspoon cayenne pepper
1 teaspoon salt
½ cup soy sauce
½ cup lemon juice
¼ cup white wine vinegar

MARINADE
½ cup dry sherry
½ cup soy sauce
¼ cup vegetable oil
¼ cup brown sugar
2 teaspoons minced garlic
3 slices gingerroot, smashed, to release juices
¼ teaspoon freshly ground black pepper

5 uncooked large shrimp, peeled

SALAD GREENS AND VEGETABLES
1 cup mixed salad greens
4 slices red bell pepper
4 thin slices cucumber
4 thin slices tomato
4 carrot sticks
2 medium mushrooms, thinly sliced
2 thin slices red onion
Toasted coconut flakes and lemon slices, to garnish

EQUIPMENT	Skewers
PREPARATION 10 mins.	For the dressing: In a blender container or food processor bowl place the first 9 ingredients and blend at high speed until smooth. Add the remaining ingredients. Combine thoroughly. Set aside for the moment. For the marinade: Whisk together the marinade ingredients. It will make about 1½ cups.
MARINATING 30 mins.	Marinate the shrimp in the marinade for 30 minutes, then string the shrimp on a skewer.
GRILLING 8 mins.	Over medium-hot coals grill the shrimp for about 8 minutes, turning and basting with the marinade.
ASSEMBLING 5 mins.	Arrange the salad ingredients on a large plate. Top with the grilled shrimp and ginger dressing.
FINAL STEP	Garnish with the coconut and lemon slices.

⟩⟩⟩⟩⟩⟩*On the road—BUTTE, MONTANA*

Richest Hill

Butte is a peculiarly attractive city. Not at first glance, nor in the first hour, but it does come to you that there's a certain charm about the place whose most dominant feature is a huge hole in the ground, not put there by a meteor but by men digging for copper. It is the world's largest open pit mine. The hole is about all that is left of what was proudly called "the richest hill on earth."

My reaction to Butte when I looked down on the town from I-80 was —"God, it's bleak!" One of the cooks I had come to town to visit, Michele Robinson, seeing the town for the first time, put a note by her husband's coffee cup (he arrived earlier to take a job)—"Whither thou goest, there I wither!" When Guy Graham arrived in town to become a chef: "They flew me in at night so I couldn't see that big hole in the ground and immediately took me to a reception where I was surrounded by friendly natives."

Butte grows on you. It is almost but not quite a mining "theme" town. Unlike a Disney creation, Butte is for real. The big open pit mine is for real. The massive headframes silhouetted against the sky, standing on the hills like silent sentries over underground mines, are for real.

Parts of it remind me of San Francisco without the Bay—the way the houses are built close together on hillsides. Here the houses, most of them built in the late 1800s, are confined to small lots (no grass to mow nor garden to tend) so miners would waste no time getting to work or coming home. The houses, streets, and sidewalks are clean and neat; no longer do dangerous sulfurous fumes from the big smelters lay a blanket over the town to kill the trees and vegetation. On a drive up and down hilly streets with names like Quartz, Copper, Granite, and Mercury, it was obvious that there is considerable civic pride in this town of 35,000 people. The turn-of-the-century stores and office buildings were saved when the vein of rich ore petered out just before it reached the Uptown District. The area has been rehabed into an attractive business district, thanks to the city's "façade fund" that pays a share of the costs.

In the late 1800s and early 1900s, when the mines were operating full blast, Butte had a population of more than 70,000. Miners came from fifty countries. Most were single men, and to house them hundreds of boardinghouses were opened. There were scores of restaurants, small and large. One advertised in the Butte paper:

Try Mrs. Williams' cooking. When possible aid a very deserving young widow woman by taking your meals at the Klondike Restaurant, at 428 S. Arizona Street. Fresh oysters in every style. Don't forget the place nor the reason why you should go there.

In 1895, at the Old Atlantic Bar, miners getting off a shift could walk up to a buffet offering sixteen kinds of sausages, roast beef, ham, turkey, rolls, bread, five cheeses, tomatoes, pickles, beets, celery, hard-boiled eggs, molded potato salads, macaroni salads, coleslaw, lettuce, stacks of sardines, and fried chicken, all watched over by a white-coated attendant who asked only that the patron have in hand a 10¢ schooner of beer.

Mineowners and their friends ate considerably higher up on the cuisine scale. The menu for the 1899 New Year's dinner at the Montana Hotel in nearby Anaconda has an aura of elegance.

The menu, in part—bluepoint oysters; littleneck clams; planked whitefish; wild bitterroot turkey with chestnut dressing; steamed fresh lobster; broiled golden plover on toast; breast of prairie chicken with hominy fritters; haunch of bear with raspberry sauce; snow pudding; apple and lemon custard pies; assorted cakes; fruit; nuts; cheeses; and, finally, coffee.

Today most of the mines are closed and prosperity is no longer measured in tons of ore. Now it is high tech, power, timber, and energy research.

The taste for good food remains.

⋙⋘ *BUTTE, MONTANA*

Three Women, One Kitchen—Johanna Hanson, Michele Robinson, and Esther Dumont

Johanna Hanson, *left*, and Michele Robinson

Austrian Povitiza and Indian Fry Bread came from the same kitchen on a beautiful late summer's day in Butte.

Johanna Hanson, whose grandparents were born in Austria, and Michele Robinson, who was born on the Wind River Indian Reservation in Wyoming, have been close friends almost from the day they and their husbands signed up for dance classes. This led to talk about food and, recruiting four others, they started The Magnificent Ate, a gourmet club.

I had written to each about coming to Butte, not knowing they were friends. One day I had a conference call with both women on the line.

"Yes, come see us in Butte, but we will be together in one kitchen, Johanna's."

"Fair enough," I said and Marje and I left for Butte.

Johanna, who was born in the mining town of Anaconda, a few miles west of Butte, began cooking when she was in the fifth grade because her parents worked and she had the kitchen to herself.

"My grandmother had nine children so I had a half-dozen aunts who guided me around their kitchens." Johanna worked in a grocery store while in high school, and after college, taught school for several years. But with a husband and three boys at home she left teaching to cater gourmet picnic baskets for float trips on the wild rivers in the area.

We were in her kitchen to make the povitiza and the fry bread.

The first fry bread was made about 150 years ago when the Plains Indians were introduced by white settlers to wheat flour which made possible a raised dough. Unlike the Indians in the Southwest, the Plains Indians had no ovens, so they fried the bread.

Visiting county fairs and rodeos in the Western states, I had had a nodding acquaintanceship with Indian fry bread. I was never impressed. Yet I knew that somewhere, someday, I would find Indian fry bread that was more than an unfulfilled promise of a good-tasting native American dish.

I found it in the hands of Michele Robinson, with some help from tribal elders. Michele is a member of the Arapahoe tribe, a consultant in Indian history, a former aide in Washington, D.C., to a U.S. senator, a Butte Woman of the Year, and the 1964 Miss Indian America. She also has her own daily TV show. Besides those and other impressive credentials she is a top-notch cook.

But fry bread had not been her long suit until I called her long distance one day and asked if it were possible to make really good Indian fry bread. I think I even used the word "delicious." There was a hesitant moment.

"Yes, but I will need a little time," she said. Later I found out Michele did not trust her own fry bread, so she had called a number of Indian women in the community for suggestions. All agreed that the best of all fry bread cooks was Esther Dumont, a member of the Assiniboine tribe. She lived in town and had spent a lifetime raising kids and grand-kids and cooking fry bread for festivals and fairs.

"She's a friend and a dear—but she's a fierce lady when she is aroused," Michele said. "Ask any school principal in Butte when she goes to speak for her kids."

For a full day the two Indian women made fry bread and talked technique and ingredients. Mrs. Dumont even divulged the secret ingre-dient, given to her by a Cree woman, that she believed made her bread so special. Later I called her at home to thank her for sharing her exper-tise. She was at her sewing machine quilting gifts for a number of rela-tives and friends in observance of the first anniversary of the death of her eldest son.

I discovered, too, why many of the fry breads I had eaten at fairs and rodeos had tasted like nothing special. "When I called my Indian friends about making the dough," Michele said, "they just laughed. 'You don't intend to make your own dough from scratch? A lot of times we just use store-bought bread dough.' "

INDIAN FRY BREAD

[MAKES 5 TO 6 PIECES]

Fry bread is a yeast-raised dough pinched off in pieces about the size of oranges and flattened. A slit is cut in the center of the dough to better distribute the heat and the dough is put into hot fat. The result, the size of a dinner plate, will be a golden brown bread—light, puffy, and chewy. Not greasy.

Mrs. Dumont's secret ingredient was baking powder to be used in addition to yeast. Among Mrs. Dumont's other revelations:

- Let the dough rise twice.
- Keep the grease hot (365°) but not smoking.
- Use just enough oil to float the dough.
- Twist off hunks of dough to fry. Don't cut, or the seam will seal and the dough won't puff.

While Mrs. Dumont believes the best flour is a mixture of all-purpose and "commodity," a government surplus flour and only available on the reservation, Michele and I have had excellent results using only all-purpose.

INGREDIENTS	5 cups all-purpose flour, approximately 1 package dry yeast ½ teaspoon sugar 1 teaspoon salt ½ teaspoon baking powder 2 cups hot tap water (120°–130°) Vegetable oil, 2 inches deep in kettle or skillet
EQUIPMENT	One deep kettle or heavy skillet
PREPARATION BY HAND OR MIXER 10 mins.	In a large mixer or mixing bowl, pour 3 cups of flour, the yeast, sugar, salt, baking powder, and hot tap water. Stir briskly with a wooden spoon about 150 strokes, or for 2 minutes with a mixer flat beater. Add the balance of the flour and work into a moist batterlike dough with a wooden spoon and then by hand. When the dough is soft but not sticky, turn it out onto a lightly floured work surface.
KNEADING 8 mins.	Dust the dough with a sprinkle of flour and begin to knead with a push-turn-fold movement. If the moisture breaks through the skin and the dough begins to stick, sprinkle with flour. Knead for a total of 8 minutes by hand or under the dough hook.
FIRST RISING 1 hour	Put the dough in a greased bowl, cover tightly with plastic wrap, and set aside at room temperature until the dough has doubled in bulk and become puffy, about 1 hour.

PREHEAT	Preheat the oil to 365°.
SHAPING 10 mins.	Punch down the dough. Lightly oil your fingers and tear off pieces of dough about the size of an orange or baseball. Flatten each piece to about ¼ inch thickness. With a sharp knife make a slit through the center of the dough, about 2 inches long.
RESTING 20 mins.	Cover the pieces and allow the dough to rest for 20 minutes, or until the oil heats.
FRYING 25–30 mins.	Each piece is fried separately in the hot fat. When the under side is golden brown, carefully turn the bread over with tongs and cook until brown, a total of about 5 to 6 minutes. Remove and drain on paper towels.
FINAL STEP	Serve warm. The bread also does well reheated in a microwave oven, and it may be frozen. Folded over chopped tomato, shredded lettuce, grated cheese, salsa, and anything else you like, it becomes an "Indian taco." Or the foundation for an "Indian pizza."

AUSTRIAN POVITIZA

[SERVES 18 TO 24]

Povitiza is closely akin to strudel. Johanna's dough is different from strudel dough in that it is made with yeast and given a 20-minute rest period to rise before going into the oven.

Johanna's worktable was the long dining-room table over which she had spread an often-laundered damask tablecloth. The damask cloth served two purposes: The dough, when stretched over it, didn't stick because of the varied textures. When the dough was fully stretched, one long edge of the cloth was lifted to gently roll the dough (and the filling) into the long cylindrical shape. The chairs had been pulled away from the table to give her an unimpeded path as she moved around the dough, stretching and pulling it thinner and thinner, longer and longer, and wider and wider.

If there is a secret to making povitiza, she said, it is to use the backs of the hands, not the fingertips, to pull and stretch the dough. Initially, for the first few times around the table, the dough may be pulled gingerly between the thumbs and forefingers, but only for a short while. Invariably, fingertips will press into the dough and weaken it. Also remove all rings from your fingers that might tear the dough.

When she had finished, the small ball of dough had been stretched into a paper-thin sheet almost 6 feet long and 4 feet wide.

INGREDIENTS

FILLING
*2 pounds walnuts, coarsely ground in meat grinder, not food
    processor*
1 cup brown sugar
1 cup granulated sugar
1 cup honey
1 teaspoon salt
½ teaspoon ground cinnamon
3 eggs
½ cup (1 stick) unsalted butter, melted
One 12-ounce can evaporated milk

DOUGH
6 cups bread flour, approximately
1 teaspoon salt
3 eggs
1 tablespoon butter, room temperature
1 cup 2% milk
1 cup hot water (120°–130°)
2 packages dry yeast

½ cup (1 stick) each unsalted butter and margarine, to brush
2 tablespoons granulated sugar, to sprinkle
3 tablespoons confectioners' sugar, to dust

EQUIPMENT

One 12 x 18-inch baking pan. Povitiza may be cut into sections
to fit, or the entire length may be fitted U-shape into the pan to
be cut into small pieces after baking. Grease and flour the pan,
or cover the bottom with parchment paper. One table or 2 card
tables covered with damask cloth dusted with a sprinkling of
flour.

PREPARATION
30 mins.

(Note: Prepare the work surface and filling before making
dough.)
    For the filling: In a bowl combine the nuts, 2 sugars, honey,
salt, and cinnamon. In a second bowl stir together the eggs,
melted butter, and evaporated milk. Stir the two mixtures together and set aside.
    For the dough: In a medium bowl or mixer bowl measure
4 cups of flour and sprinkle with the salt. Form a well in the flour
and break the eggs into it. Add the butter. Add the milk, hot
water, and yeast. Stir by hand with a wooden spoon or mixer flat
beater. Add additional flour, ¼ cup at a time, to make a soft, but
not wet, dough.
    The mass will be sticky but sprinkles of flour will control it.

KNEADING
18 mins.

With a dough scraper in one hand, knead and toss the dough for 10 minutes on a lightly floured work surface.

Add additional flour as needed. The dough in the mixer bowl should be soft but not wet and should clean the sides of the bowl. Knead at low speed for 8 minutes. Stop the machine and feel the dough to be certain it is soft, elastic, but not sticky.

RESTING
20 mins.

Cover the dough with a cloth and allow to rest for 20 minutes.

STRETCHING
15–20 mins.

Place the dough on the floured cloth. With a rolling pin roll the dough out to a thickness of about ⅛ inch, then begin pulling and stretching it over the backs of your hands. As you finish in one position, give the dough a gentle wave so that the air lifts it off your hands, and drop it to the table. Continue around the table. Pay particular attention to the thicker areas. Work away from the thinner spots until the dough is the same uniform thickness.

If a large hole appears, patch with a piece taken from an end. Ignore smaller tears, which will not be noticed when the pastry is rolled.

DRYING
15 mins.

Stop when you feel further effort will tear the dough. With scissors or a sharp knife trim off the heavy edge.

During the drying interval, melt the butter and margarine and keep warm.

PREHEAT

Preheat the oven to 400°.

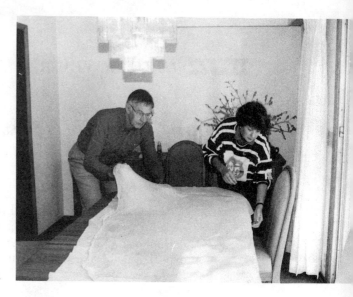

The author and Johanna

ASSEMBLING
10 mins.

Sprinkle the melted shortening over the dough. You may do this with a brush, but do so carefully.

Place the filling along the edge nearest you, in a 3-inch strip, to within 2 inches of the ends. Lift the tablecloth on the side nearest you and use it to roll the dough around the filling, jelly-roll fashion. The povitiza will become a cylinder approximately 3 to 4 inches thick.

Brush the length with more melted shortening and sprinkle with granulated sugar.

Either cut the povitiza in appropriate lengths to go into the baking pan or the uncut length can be bent and fitted.

RESTING
20 mins.

Allow the Povitiza to rest for 20 minutes.

BAKING
400°
20 mins.
350°
30 mins.

Place the pan on the middle shelf of the oven. After 20 minutes reduce the oven's heat to 350°, turn the pan end for end to expose the pastry to uniform heat.

Bake to a golden brown, another 30 minutes.

FINAL STEP

Remove from the oven and allow to cool before cutting diagonally into 3-inch serving pieces. Dust liberally with confectioners' sugar before serving.

Povitiza may be frozen. When reheating, place frozen pastry in a 350° oven for 15 minutes.

〰〰〰〰BUTTE, MONTANA

Uptown Cafe—Chefs Susan Phillips and Guy Graham

A Montana food critic looked over all the restaurants in the state and picked the Uptown Cafe as "a sleeper!" He wrote: "It is becoming the darling of the fine cuisine lovers." Darling? Hardly the words one would expect for an eatery, no matter how upscale, in the mining town of Butte.

While I was researching Montana food the message kept coming back—you must try The Uptown. When I learned The Uptown was only five years old and had been started by three young Easterners, I was intrigued. Even more so when I learned that they were impoverished—broke—when they arrived in Butte. One was an out-of-work systems analyst; one a psychologist (who next day did find work at a local clinic); and the chef, who, until the restaurant opened, taught cooking to convicts at the prerelease center.

"We were poor," said Barbara Kornet, who had been working in the city for a high-tech firm until she was laid off. She urged her two friends to quit their jobs and come west to join her in a restaurant venture. The psychologist, Susan Phillips, was a cook and a successful caterer. Guy Graham, with a background in food science, was chef of a four-star Pittsburgh restaurant.

"Fortunately for us the Yugoslavian family who owned this place was anxious to sell," Barbara continued. "Terms were so good we could hardly believe it. It was then a working-man's diner serving hefty old-world fare. They made their own kielbasa and sauerkraut and rendered their own lard."

To make the transition from lunch counter to a full-course evening dining establishment, the trio spent six weeks with the Yugoslavian owners, learning about the Butte working crowd's eating habits and preferences, and elaborating on the old menu while tossing in a dash of "nouveau."

"It was a wonderful way to get started. It was a going business, with a good clientele. Everybody got to know the three of us in association with the retiring owners. It was a smooth transition. Not a stitch was dropped when we opened as The Uptown that Monday."

Has it been a success?

"Well, you heard about us!" Barbara smiled. "When we took it over we could afford only to buy enough paint for the rear wall of the dining room. It was six months before we could buy more paint to do the rest of the room. That's the way it went for the first year or so. Now, can you believe it, we own the building—and seven of our nine apartments upstairs are rented.

"And"—she beamed—"we're no longer poor!"

The combination of personalities has worked well. "With my business background," explained Barbara, "I do all the books, paperwork, advertising.

"The other two? Well, scientists are good cooks because they are fussy to a fault about the finer points of combining ingredients, and so forth. Susan and Guy are very particular about temperature, about things like what happens molecularly when an egg heats to a certain point. This is great, but it took us two and a half years to perfect a chocolate cheesecake.

"And then they had to learn what the impact of several thousand feet gain in elevation would have on their recipes from Pittsburgh. The altitude was a shock to their approach to baking in particular."

The Uptown Cafe sends a monthly menu calendar to patrons. Meals and recipes change to reflect seasons, ethnic celebrations unique to Butte, availability of special items—such as live lobsters which Guy's cousin sends from his lobster house in Maine.

CHICKEN SALTIMBOCCA

[SERVES 4]

Over the years the Uptown Cafe has offered many varieties of sautéed chicken. Simple and quickly prepared, this entrée remains a favorite.

INGREDIENTS
4 skinless, boneless chicken breast halves
2 tablespoons clarified butter (see page 241)
Flour, to dust
1 tablespoon unsalted butter
⅓ cup dry white wine
4 slices prosciutto ham
4 thin slices provolone or Swiss cheese
1½ cups chicken stock, homemade (see page 562) or
    store-bought

¼ teaspoon rubbed sage leaves
1 teaspoon arrowroot plus 1 tablespoon water
Black pepper, freshly ground over finished dish

EQUIPMENT

One oven-proof platter

PREPARATION
10 mins.

Using a mallet or broad side of a kitchen cleaver, pound the thick end of each breast piece to a uniform thickness. This will ensure even cooking of the meat.

PREHEAT

Preheat the oven to 350°.

COOKING
15 mins.

Heat a heavy skillet over medium heat and add half of the clarified butter. While the butter is heating, dust 2 of the chicken pieces in flour and shake off any excess.

Brown the chicken quickly on both sides over medium-high heat, about 2 minutes each side. Repeat with the remaining breasts, using more clarified butter if needed.

When the chicken pieces are browned, add the butter. When the butter is a nut-brown color, add white wine and turn off the heat.

ASSEMBLING

Place the breasts on the ovenproof platter and top each with a slice of prosciutto and a slice of cheese. Place the platter in the oven.

BAKING
350°
15 mins.

Bake for about 15 minutes, or until the cheese begins to melt and brown.

SAUCE
4 mins.

Add the stock and sage to the butter and wine in the skillet. Reheat on high. Scrape up the brown bits that have stuck to the skillet during cooking. Reduce the liquid to ½ cup, about 4 minutes. Add the arrowroot. The mixture will take on a saucelike consistency.

FINAL STEP

Remove the platter from the oven. Top the meat with the sauce and freshly grated black pepper, the latter of which Chef Guy feels is truly essential to the overall flavor of this dish.

Serve immediately.

APRIL FOOL'S SALAD

[SERVES 6]

It was April 1 when Chef Guy put these ingredients together for the first time in this delicious salad, hence the name. He suggests making the dressing a day ahead so the flavors have a chance to marry. This is not a mixed salad—each ingredient is placed in order on the bed of lettuce leaves.

INGREDIENTS

Salad
1 large head red leaf lettuce
1 medium cucumber, peeled, halved lengthwise, each half cut into ⅛-inch-wide slices
18 medium very ripe strawberries, hulled and quartered
½ small red onion, very thinly sliced
½ cup lightly toasted blanched almond slivers
Freshly ground black pepper, to taste

Dressing
¼ cup raspberry vinegar
½ of 1 egg white
¼ teaspoon salt
½ teaspoon dried tarragon leaves
8 to 10 fresh basil leaves, sliced into ⅛-inch slivers
½ cup corn oil
2 tablespoons heavy cream

PREPARATION
15 mins.

For the salad: Core and wash the lettuce leaves in lukewarm water. Shake off excess water and place the lettuce in a bowl and refrigerate until ready to assemble the salad.

For the dressing: In a food processor or blender place the vinegar, egg white, salt, tarragon, and basil. Turn on the machine and add the oil in a steady stream. When the oil is incorporated, add the heavy cream.

RESTING
1 hour or
overnight

Mix the salad dressing beforehand and refrigerate for at least an hour or more. Overnight is best.

ASSEMBLING
5–10 mins.

Arrange the lettuce leaves on plates. In the order listed, divide each ingredient among the salads and arrange nicely. Dress each salad with 1 ounce of dressing. Add freshly ground black pepper.

Serve immediately.

◆◆◆◆◆◆ *On the Road—EN ROUTE TO SEATTLE*

A Favorite City

When the van rolled down the western slope of the Cascade Range into Seattle we broke the news to our companion, Timothy, that he would be staying at a kennel for the duration of our stay in the city, not the Arlington Suites ("no pets, please"). At first he didn't seem impressed, but on arriving, as always at a new boarding place, he was delighted with the smells of strange dogs and of new pillars and posts to mark.

Seattle has long been on my list of favorite cities. The list changes as the years pass: some are dropped, others added. Honolulu, now congested and un-aloha, has been dropped. So has New York City. Los Angeles and Miami were never on it. Missoula and Santa Fe, among a number of others, have been added.

But Seattle, despite some misgivings on this trip, was near the top of the list.

The downtown traffic has become a nightmare, the freeways bulge, and bumper stickers urge cash-heavy Californians who are there on real estate buying binges to go home. The unique and wonderful Pike Place Market is overrun with tourists, who photograph and pinch the fish, fruit, and giant heads of lettuce but don't buy. Understandably this annoys seafood and produce vendors who wish these people would buy more than one apple at a time.

I would have moved here forty years ago but I would have come alone. Marjorie, who wants always to keep dry and snug, had been told repeatedly about the rain, fog, mist, drizzle, and a general wetness of Seattle, so I was forever to remain a visitor, never a resident.

World War II had just begun when I came to Seattle for the first time with several San Francisco writers at the invitation of the Army to visit coastal fortifications guarding the Pacific Northwest against the Japanese. The enemy was expected to invade at any time; the wildness of the Olympic Peninsula seemed an inviting target for a landing, or so the Army and locals imagined.

I can now report to the Japanese without fear of revealing a military secret that we were *not* ready for them. They could have come ashore without expending a single shot or shell. For two days we were rushed up and down the shoreline along the Strait of Juan de Fuca, across from Victoria, B.C., with always a promise that the "big guns" were just over the brow of the next hill. I recall seeing a total of one machine gun and two rolls of barbed wire. I am puzzled to this day why the Army chose to embarrass itself, except it knew the press could not or would not report on how completely defenseless the Northwest was.

Seattle had not yet grown into a bustling cosmopolitan city renowned for its cuisine. It was a small town tucked in near-isolation in the far corner of the United States. Few planes flew there. By train and car it was two days to the big city to the south, San Francisco. Food was excellent but no one seemed excited about it. Wartime rationing had not yet affected the salmon, crab, and oyster harvest, so I was in heaven savoring seafood and hard-crusted breads instead of looking for gun emplacements.

It would be a half century before the rest of the United States and the world would know what treasures from the sea, river, forest, and farm the locals had been enjoying all along.

John Doerper, a respected food columnist, says he moved from California where everything is grown hot, dry, and tasteless to Bellingham, on cool, moist, and temperate Puget Sound above Seattle because of "the superb quality and variety of the food of the Pacific Northwest.

"The cuisine of the Pacific Northwest, which everyone now is discovering, can be as simple as a barbecued salmon, dotted with butter and a touch of garlic, and sprinkled with salt and pepper, or as complex as the exquisitely light sauces prepared by some of our outstanding chefs."

Not unlike France, where to be in a Parisian restaurant contributes greatly to the joy of French cuisine, so to be in Seattle adds immeasurably to the pleasure and delight of Northwest cooking.

On this journey we cooked and we ate out. We came away with a pocketful of recipes and notes that will make it possible, given fresh ingredients, to come close to the Northwest cuisine in your own kitchen.

For this particular visit we needed an anchor and a compass, someone who knew food and knew where to find it, whether in a restaurant, a market, a fishing trawler, or a home kitchen. Someone who would be at the other end of the phone line when a question arose.

She was Beverly Gruber and for months we had been planning the Seattle-and-environs visit. I had met her several years before when she and other Seattle members of an association of culinary professionals put together a food conference that had Julia Child, Bert Greene, and others of us walking gingerly on floating pens of farm-raised salmon in the middle of Puget Sound. As visiting members of the International Association of Culinary Professionals we also snacked on a score of different kinds of oysters and sampled Northwest wines amid tanks of fish, octopi, eels, and seals at a soiree in the city's fine waterfront aquarium.

A free-lance food consultant; owner/director of the cooking school, Everyday Gourmet; and a restaurant reviewer, Beverly knows the Puget Sound area—from Olympia in the south to Victoria and Vancouver in the north—as well as she knows the layout of her own kitchen.

She plotted our course, and did it well.

⋙ *SEATTLE, WASHINGTON*

Chef Tom Douglas

Kasu Cod—marinated and lightly grilled—is Tom Douglas's signature dish. It has become to Seattle what blackened redfish is to New Orleans. While it is not his creation, Tom brought it out of obscurity ten years ago when he discovered it in Yoshimura's Mutual Fish Company's market and placed it on the menu of his then newly opened restaurant, Cafe Sport.

The full name of the dish is sake *kasu* black cod. *Kasu* is the lees, the matter left in the distillation of the rice wine; it has been used as a food preservative by the Japanese since sake was first made, which dates back to at least A.D. 731. While cooks in Japan use *kasu* in the preparation of a wide variety of seafoods, in Seattle it is used chiefly with black cod and salmon because of their ready availability. The former actually isn't a cod but a member of the skilfish family, with white large-flaked meat, sweet and rich. Any member of the cod family can be substituted.

The fillet pieces are placed overnight in a salt-sugar brine. Rinsed, they are marinated in a mixture of *kasu*, brown sugar, *mirin* (a sweet rice wine), and sake for at least another twenty-four hours. The mixture, which smells sharply and sweetly of sake, imparts a sharp flavor to the grilled fish.

Tom Douglas is a tall, broad-shouldered bear of a man, scraggly beard and long curly hair, he is also one of Seattle's finest chefs. He put his imprint on Northwest cuisine at the Cafe Sport, which is across the street from Pike Place Market. Recently, when he realized he had become more manager than chef, he left to open his own restaurant, the Dahlia Lounge, named for his favorite flower.

"Seattle has always had one foot in the Orient, especially Japan, so when I opened Cafe Sport the first thing I put on the menu was *Kasu* Cod. However, it was not an immediate success. At first I had to force it on people. I considered two orders of *Kasu* Cod a good day. Sometimes there were none, so I had to toss out the fish. Then all of a sudden it took off.

"Now the café has at least fifty orders every day—and I'm called a genius. It underscores my belief that the best products make the best cooks except, of course, when you have idiots in the kitchen."

He brought *Kasu* Cod to the fore and at the same time introduced the city to Black Bean Soup and Dungeness Crab Cakes. Those two he brought from Delaware where he had been in the kitchen of the venerable DuPont Hotel in Newark. "Crab cakes are served by every diner on the East Coast, but when I put them on the menu here I had every food columnist in the region raving about this 'new' Seattle dish.

"I had always thought of black bean soup as a seasonal item to be served in wintertime. I took it off the menu last summer and, believe it or not, people got up and walked out of the restaurant. It's crazy."

Why bean soup in a seafood town?

"It is more a matter of climate. Any day in Seattle can be cold enough to make you think of a bowl of warming soup. Besides, I love food and I eat whatever makes my heart and soul happy. Bean soup does that.

"Here in the Northwest we tend to have things fresher, the food is healthier. Food here is more alive. In my case it is simpler. I tend to use fruits and vegetables for sauces rather than meat sauces."

He paused. "In these waters we have the finest fish in the world. They have been our claim to fame. But would you believe that some restaurants have fish flown in from Honolulu and Boston. Talk about coals to Newcastle, to mix a metaphor."

KASU *COD*

[SERVES 4]

The *kasu, mirin*, and sake can be purchased in markets catering to the Asian community in most large U.S. cities. *Kasu* is a light gray solid with the consistency of cold butter.

Tom Douglas suggests the grilled fish be served with wedges of bell pepper and small yellow or green pattypan squash strung on slender wooden skewers and grilled. The vegetables are marinated for about an hour in a bowl mixed with a cup of the *kasu* marinade.

INGREDIENTS	*BRINE* *3 tablespoons salt* *½ cup granulated sugar* *3 cups warm water* *2½ pounds cod fillets* *MARINADE* *1 cup* kasu *¾ cup each brown sugar, mirin, and sake*
EQUIPMENT	One 9 x 13-inch baking dish.
PREPARATION 2 hours or overnight	In a baking dish combine the brine ingredients; stir until the sugar and salt dissolve. Place the fish in the brine. Cover and chill at least 2 hours or overnight.
MARINATING overnight or up to 3 days	Meanwhile, in a blender or food processor, whirl together the marinade ingredients until smooth. Cover and chill until ready to use, up to 1 week; or freeze up to 3 months. Drain the fish, discarding the brine. Rinse and pat the fish dry. Place the fish in the baking dish, spread about 2 cups of the marinade over the fish, coating all sides. Cover and chill at least overnight, or up to 3 days, turning occasionally.
GRILLING 12 mins.	(*Note:* If the vegetables are to be grilled, do them first over a medium fire. Cover and cook for 5 minutes on each side. Set aside on a platter; cover to keep warm.) Lift the fillets from the marinade, brushing off the excess, and place on the grill; cover the grill and cook the fish until browned, about 6 minutes. Turn the fish over, cover the grill, and cook until the fish is opaque and moist-looking in the thickest part, about 6 minutes longer.
FINAL STEP	Place on a platter with the vegetables, if desired. The marinade is excellent for shrimp and scallops, too.

BLACK BEAN SOUP

[SERVES 6 TO 8]

The soup is pureed, with a few beans put aside to garnish. Don't process or sieve the soup too fine. It is a robust soup and it should have a degree of roughness. Two or 3 short bursts of the processor will give it the right texture.

INGREDIENTS

2½ cups (1¼ pounds) black turtle beans (see page 248)
10 cups water or to cover, to soak beans
1 tablespoon shortening
1 cup chopped onions
½ cup chopped celery
7 cups beef or chicken stock, homemade (see pages 560 or 562)
    or store-bought
2 cups water
1 teaspoon chopped fresh garlic
¼ cup sherry or Madeira
1 teaspoon salt
½ teaspoon freshly ground black pepper
2 eggs, hard-cooked, finely chopped
Lemon slices, to garnish
Parsley sprigs, to garnish

BEFOREHAND
12 hours

Cover the beans with the 10 cups of water and soak for at least 12 hours. Drain.

PREPARATION
8 mins.

Heat the shortening in a large sauce pot over medium-high heat. Add the onions and celery and sauté until tender, about 8 minutes.

COOKING
2½ hours

Add the beans, stock, 2 cups of water, and garlic. Simmer uncovered, stirring occasionally, until tender, about 2½ hours, adding water to keep the beans covered.

BY PROCESSOR
10 mins.

Set aside 1 cup of cooked beans for garnish later. Ladle the soup into the food processor in batches. Process only until roughly pureed.

HEATING
5 mins.

Turn the puree into a large saucepan and stir in the sherry or Madeira, salt, pepper, and cup of whole beans. Place over medium heat and bring to serving temperature, stirring occasionally.

FINAL STEP

Gently blend in the chopped egg and ladle into serving bowls. Garnish each portion with a slice of lemon tipped with a small sprig of parsley.

NORTHWEST DUNGENESS CRAB CAKES WITH WILD WEST REMOULADE

[SERVES 4 TO 6]

A Pacific Rim version of a long-time favorite New England dish, this recipe by Douglas is served with a mustardy lemon-herb sauce.

INGREDIENTS	*Wild West Remoulade (recipe follows)* *1 pound fresh Dungeness (or other) crab meat* *1 egg* *8 drops Tabasco sauce* *2 teaspoons each red wine vinegar and fresh lemon juice* *Zest from 1 lemon, minced* *¼ cup Dijon mustard* *⅓ cup vegetable oil* *⅓ cup each finely chopped green bell pepper, red bell pepper, and onion* *3 tablespoons finely chopped fresh parsley* *¾ cup fresh bread crumbs* *2 tablespoons butter* *Sprigs of parsley, to garnish*
EQUIPMENT	One baking pan
BEFOREHAND 10 mins.	Make the remoulade and set aside. Pick over the crab meat, drain well, and set aside.
PREPARATION 10 mins.	To make a mayonnaise, place the egg, Tabasco, red wine vinegar, lemon juice, zest, and mustard in a blender or food processor and mix thoroughly. While the machine is running add the oil in a slow, steady stream until the mixture is emulsified. Scrape into a small bowl and set aside. In a large bowl combine the peppers, onion, 1 tablespoon of parsley, crab meat, and reserved mayonnaise from above. Mix together the bread crumbs and 2 tablespoons of parsley. Add enough of the crumb-parsley mixture (¾ to 1 cup) to allow the mixture to hold its shape when formed into patties.
PREHEAT	Preheat the oven to 400°.
SAUTÉEING 6–12 mins.	On a length of wax paper, divide the crab mixture into 12 equal portions and form into small rounds. Sauté the rounds in the butter in a nonstick pan over low-medium heat until golden brown, 1 to 2 minutes each side. Press down lightly on the rounds with a spatula after they are lightly browned.

continued

BAKING 400° 12–14 mins.	Place the cakes on the pan and bake until they are cooked through, about 12 to 14 minutes.
FINAL STEP	Serve the cakes with the remoulade spooned on top or at the side as a dipping sauce. Garnish with sprigs of parsley.

Wild West Remoulade

[MAKES ¾ CUP]

INGREDIENTS	*1 egg* *2 tablespoons lemon juice* *1 tablespoon coarse-grain mustard* *Salt, to taste* *½ cup olive oil* *½ teaspoon freshly ground black pepper*, or *drops Tabasco, to taste* *1 teaspoon tomato paste* *1 tablespoon chopped fresh parsley* *½ tablespoon chopped fresh chives* *1 tablespoon chopped capers, drained* *1½ tablespoons dill pickles or cornichons*
EQUIPMENT	Food processor or blender
PREPARATION	In a processor or blender add the egg, lemon juice, mustard, and salt. With the processor running, slowly drizzle in the oil until the mixture binds. Add the remaining ingredients and continue to process until well mixed.

◣◣◣◣ *SOOKE, VANCOUVER ISLAND, BRITISH COLUMBIA*

Sooke Harbour House—
Sinclair and Fredrica Philip and Ron Cherry

I ate gooseneck barnacles dressed with a tuberous begonia vinaigrette at dinner tonight. Picked earlier from a piling in the harbor nearby, I found the small sea creatures interesting but not before I had a problem.

Sinclair Philip

Though of no major consequence, it was embarrassing. The discussion at the table had been about edible flowers, so when a plate of what I rashly assumed to be flowers in some form was served, I popped one into my mouth.

To my astonishment, and to that of my host, who saw it disappear, I bit into a rock-hard shell. It was a barnacle. I recovered, somewhat flustered, and thereafter I daintily pulled the meat out of its shell by its neck. Chewy, with the texture of escargot. Good.

It was the first course of an extraordinary meal served at the extraordinary Sooke Harbour House, an inn on the low headlands of Victoria Island overlooking the turbulent waters of the Strait of Juan de Fuca. Washington's Olympic Mountains, in another country, stretched across the southern horizon. By the address alone—1528 Whiffen Spit Road, Sooke, Vancouver Island, British Columbia—you sense that it will be an uncommon establishment. *Sui generis.* One of a kind.

It is a simple place, a white clapboard farmhouse of another era, and a new two-story addition alongside, tucked into a protected glen where Whiffen Spit, a mile-long finger of sand and rock, reaches to a lighthouse. Offshore, seals and otters and whales cavort.

The keepers of this most unusual inn are Sinclair and Fredrica Philip. He is a native British Columbian, with a doctorate in political economics and an almost awesome knowledge of Northwest food and wine. He spent ten years in France and there married Fredrica, who is from a restaurateur family and has a sure sense of design and an instinct for hospitality.

Sinclair is the creator, the innovator. Fredrica is the doer. "She tethers the balloon," explained a friend. Together Fredrica and Sinclair have created a superb restaurant, but also in this remote place on the edge of the forest and the ocean, they have established one of the most comfortable and satisfying hideaways in the Northwest. Its accommodations are luxurious. When you are here the rest of the world with its stresses and strains simply doesn't exist.

The house is surrounded by gardens of flowers that are a riot of colors—red, yellow, orange, lavender, pink, white, deep purple, and pale salmon—divided by green rectangles of herbs and vegetables into neat geometric patterns. *Everything* is organically grown.

This is important to know, because at Sooke Harbour House *everything* is edible. The onshore gardens reach down to the water's edge where Sinclair's marine garden begins. With a snorkel for the shallow water or scuba gear for the deep, he brings home not only dozens of kinds of seaweed and kelp but free-swimming scallops, rock scallops, sea urchins, and crab, all served to guests a short time later.

The dining room facing the sound is the glass-enclosed porch that wraps around the front of the Old House. There are several guest rooms, all with fireplaces and Jacuzzi tubs. Nearby is the New House, built recently and separated from the Old by flower beds and a large glass holding tank for marine life destined for the kitchen.

Each of the ten stunning guest rooms is a small gallery of art pieces and paintings as well as furnishings carefully chosen by the Philips to carry out a theme—Seagull, Edible Blossoms, Mermaid, Herb Garden, Blue Heron, Ichthyologist Study, Underwater Orchard, Forager's. We were in Kingfisher. Not fussy. Not overdrawn. A delight.

We toured the gardens, bed by bed, with Sinclair in the lead and Byron Cook, the gardener, at his side. Marje again and again uttered soft clucks of surprise tinged with amazement when it was pointed out that: no, chickweed is not a weed in *their* garden but an herb to be used in salads and, as a bonus, a palliative for rheumatism; gladiola blossoms are delicious stuffed with salmon roe; pinks (*Dianthus*) taste like cloves; and a delicate sorbet can be made with pine needles.

Sinclair stopped by the holding tank. The current inhabitants were four trout and a small octopus.

"The octopus will probably be gone in the morning," he said. "Not that we will have eaten it, but someone in the kitchen will have turned it loose with the lame excuse that it was sick or that it didn't look good enough to eat.

"The kitchen makes pets of the octopi and names them. I think this one is Harry. They are quite friendly. Really they are. They recognize the kids after a while and will return the affection. They swim to the glass, change colors, and follow when the kids walk the length of the glass. So, as I say, I doubt if Harry will be here in the morning."

Normally octopi are delivered to the kitchen by local fishermen already cleaned and ready to be prepared.

"Recently I had a phone call asking if I could use a nice octopus. I said yes, bring it over. A half hour later a big box was delivered to the kitchen. I had assumed it was cleaned. I opened the box to look down on an angry fifty-pound octopus, his tentacles going in eight directions, trying to get out!

"It took several of us to wrestle him into the holding tank. I left on a business trip the next day and when I came back he was gone. I didn't ask, 'Did we serve him or did he beguile his way to freedom?' "

When the Philips came to Sooke in 1980 they brought with them a respect, sharpened in France, for fresh locally produced foods. They have put together an amazing supply system for their kitchen. Each fisherman has Sooke House foremost in mind for the best catch as well as the most unusual. Nothing is spurned at Sooke House—no other kitchen prepares a greater variety (and quality) of seafood.

Yet the exceptional quality of the cooking extends beyond the sea and into the woods, meadows, and pastures. Oyster mushrooms, chanterelles, morels, and a score of other wild mushrooms are served in season. There is fresh local rabbit, duckling, beef, and lamb. The lamb comes from nearby oceanside pastures where they and their mothers are fed flavorful bromegrass, salt grass, wild rye, and herbs exposed to salt-laden shore breezes.

Because Sinclair had invited us to experience a wide range of wild and natural flavors, the kitchen had prepared a menu that began with the gooseneck barnacles. Next came thin slices of fresh pink abalone (farm-raised nearby) and sea cucumber (picked off the ocean floor just a few hours before) and touched with a crab apple glaze, served on a small plate decorated with edible nasturtiums. I had pulled many fat, sandy sea cucumbers from the ocean in my own snorkel explorations, but I had never eaten one. I was curious. It was indeed different—but after two bites I decided it called for an acquired taste.

Not so for a slice of delicious fresh baked halibut with a dab of sea urchin butter melting on the top, and served on a plate garnished with freshly brined Coho salmon roe and toasted seaweed.

A piece of steamed salmon atop a light chanterelle mushroom sauce followed along with the house special salad—blossoms of fuchsias, nasturtiums, Dianthus, violas, calendulas, oxeye daisies, gladiolus, Johnny-jump-ups—all edible—with arugula and lettuce dressed with an herb vinaigrette. Dessert included fresh strawberries, blueberries, and wild blackberries around a scoop of crab apple ice and decorated with a border of pearly pink rose petals.

Two days later we left the island by ferry to return to Seattle.

With Canada receding in the twilight, I wrote in my journal: "If I had one attainable wish for all readers of this book it would be to grant at least one night in Sooke Harbour House, with meals, urging them to stay the course through barnacles to crab bisque, scallops, roasted Metchosin rabbit, oysters grilled with pickled blackberries, and trout with corn and nut butter sauce."

SALMON IN CRANBERRY VINEGAR SAUCE

[SERVES 4]

The cranberry vinegar for the sauce must be made at least a week before you plan to make the dish. If you can find wild cranberries use them as they are particularly good for this vinegar. The method of quickly whisking butter into the sauce to enrich it is often used by chefs. Make sure the heat is very low and whisk vigorously as the butter is incorporated.

INGREDIENTS

VINEGAR
2 cups coarsely chopped cranberries
2 cups red wine or rice vinegar

SALMON
2 cups fish stock (see page 563)
⅓ cup cranberry vinegar
¼ cup clarified butter (see page 241)
2 small garlic cloves, minced
2 small shallots, minced
Four ½-pound salmon fillets
1 cup (2 sticks) unsalted butter, room temperature

EQUIPMENT

One ovenproof skillet

BEFOREHAND
1 week

For the vinegar (will make 2 cups): In a glass or ceramic bowl, crush the cranberries thoroughly with a potato masher. Add vinegar. Cover with plastic wrap; cut small holes in the wrap to let the vinegar breathe. Store in a cool dark place for 1 week. Strain and pour into a clean bottle.

PREHEAT

Preheat the oven to 425°.

PREPARATION
5 mins.

For the salmon: In a small saucepan, combine the stock and vinegar; bring to a boil. Remove from the heat and keep warm.

<table>
<tr><td>COOKING
2½–3 mins.</td><td>In an ovenproof skillet, heat the clarified butter over medium-high heat, and cook the garlic and shallots, stirring, for 1 minute.

Add the salmon, cook for 1 minute, and turn. Add the warm stock mixture; cook for 30 seconds longer. Remove from the heat. Tightly cover the skillet with foil. (If the skillet has a wooden handle, cover the handle with foil.)</td></tr>
<tr><td>BAKING
425°
10 mins. per
1-inch
thickness</td><td>Bake until the fish flakes with a fork, about 10 minutes per inch thickness of fish. Remove the salmon from the pan. Keep warm while preparing the sauce.</td></tr>
<tr><td>SAUCE
10–12 mins.</td><td>Return the skillet to the heat; cook the juices over high heat for 10 to 12 minutes, or until reduced to ¾ cup. Reduce heat to low; whisk in the butter, a little at a time, whisking thoroughly after each addition, to make a smooth creamy sauce.</td></tr>
<tr><td>FINAL STEP</td><td>Arrange the salmon on a heated platter. Pour the sauce around the fillets.</td></tr>
</table>

GRILLED OYSTERS WITH NASTURTIUM BUTTER SAUCE

[SERVES 1]

Nasturtium vinegar is easy to make: Fill a stainless-steel container with nasturtium flowers, leaves, and seed pods. Pour several cups of apple cider vinegar over the top. Cover with plastic wrap, leaving a small hole for breathing. Store in a cool, dry place for a few weeks before using.

Apple cider vinegar can be used in making the butter sauce but nasturtium vinegar is preferable.

INGREDIENTS   *4 large shelled oysters*

SAUCE
⅓ cup fish stock (see page 563) or store-bought clam juice
2 tablespoons dry white wine
1 teaspoon nasturtium vinegar (see above) or apple cider vinegar
Nasturtium leaves and flowers—2 large leaves and 4 flowers, coarsely chopped
½ cup (1 stick) unsalted butter, room temperature

1 or 2 nasturtium flowers, to garnish

continued

PREPARATION 3 mins.	Grill the shelled oysters until both sides are brown, about 3 minutes each side. Keep warm.
SAUCE 5 mins.	Reduce the fish stock, white wine, and vinegar in a sauté pan over high heat, to obtain about 2 tablespoons of liquid, 5 minutes. Add the chopped nasturtium leaves and flowers. Remove from the heat and whisk in the butter.
FINAL STEP	Pour the sauce on the plate, arrange the oysters on the sauce, and garnish with a small leaf and flower.

SCENTED GERANIUM AND LOGANBERRY SORBET

[SERVES 6]

There is a wide assortment of scented geranium leaves that can be used in making this delicious sorbet. Co-chef Ron Cherry suggests Rober's Lemon-Rose, M. Ninon (apricot scented), Prince Rupert (lemon scented), Shotesham Pet (filbert scented), Staghorn Oak (sandalwood scented), and Frensham Lemon.

This recipe assumes, of course, that you have an ice cream maker.

INGREDIENTS	*10 to 15 scented geranium leaves, depending upon intensity (small, young leaves are stronger)* *3 cups fresh loganberries* *1½ cups Johannisberg Riesling wine* *½ cup maple syrup*
EQUIPMENT	Ice cream maker
PREPARATION 5 mins.	Bruise and chop the geranium leaves.
COOKING 5 mins.	Over medium heat, bring the loganberries and a ½ cup of wine slowly to a boil in a heavy-bottomed pan. Stir occasionally.
STEEPING 30 mins.	Remove from the heat. Add the geranium leaves, cover with a lid, and let steep for 30 minutes.
PUREEING 2 mins.	In a blender or food processor puree the mixture. Strain out the loganberry seeds and geranium leaves.
FREEZING	Add the remaining cup of wine and the maple syrup to the puree. Pour into the ice cream machine and follow the manufacturer's instructions for freezing.

〰〰〰〰EDMONDS, WASHINGTON

A Peace Table for the Russians—Jerilyn Brusseau

Grandmother Spurgeon's cinnamon roll has been the pièce de résistance, the cornerstone of Jerilyn Brusseau's bakery-café from its very beginning. Ten years ago she bought a vacant Shell gas station in Edmonds, carted away the pumps to make a parking lot, cleaned out the rubble, painted the place, moved in bake ovens and stoves, put up a sign out front, and opened brusseau's (she does not capitalize the *b*).

Brusseau's first offering opening day was her Grandmother's Cinnamon rolls—a delicious pastry rich with brown sugar, nuts, eggs, butter, and two kinds of flour, white and whole-wheat. It has remained the baked good of choice in a tantalizing array of delicious things that has thirty-two people working two and a half shifts a day to keep abreast. The café, too, has become the center of much of the town's social and culinary activities, beginning early in the morning with breakfast, through lunch and an early dinner. By seven o'clock dining has ended but people come by to pick up "take-out" meals.

Edmonds (pop. 27,340) is a sophisticated suburb of Seattle and brusseau's, up the hill from the wharves where Puget Sound ferry boats dock, has been compared to a Parisian café.

There was a strong, cool breeze blowing up from the water and across the patio so we forsook alfresco and sat at a table inside. It was midmorning and customers were chatting, sipping, and sampling. Jerilyn introduced us to four of the town's ministers meeting informally over coffee and cinnamon rolls at the next table. They were discussing the good weather that had blessed the town for the past few days. It was also the children's hour, with young mothers and babies near by. A constant stream of people came to the table to ask Jerilyn how she was, and where has she been? Good question. She had been away for several days—to Russia in fact. The customers had missed her. The buzzes and hums from the bakery and the open kitchen and from the tables were warm and friendly. "Family noises," said Jerilyn.

She is a handsome, vibrant woman in her forties, with a brilliant, rewarding smile. She grew up on a dairy farm in Oklahoma and became a medical laboratory technologist before turning to the restaurant business.

When brusseau's was launched, she said, "I didn't know a thing about the business but I knew a lot about food." Her main entrepreneurial strengths, she explained, are of a great family tradition of hospitality, and a lifelong interest in food and preparations. Smoking is not allowed, something a bit avant-garde when the place opened a decade ago. No additives find their way into the baked goods, and she won't hear of using mixes, despite some early advice that she wouldn't be able to stay in business without them. "I'm adamant on that," she said.

Brusseau's customers are fiercely loyal. Every day of the week since 1979 one elderly couple has come midmorning for coffee and cinnamon rolls, and returns midafternoon for coffee and a "treat" from among the pastries. Jerilyn laughed: "And then on Sunday they 'go out' they explain, by visiting a different restaurant."

Enter the Russians.

It began several years ago when a group of visiting Russian journalists and writers, escorted by U.S. newsmen, including Jerilyn's brother, came to brusseau's for breakfast.

"I was terrified. Here was the enemy coming to my café! What kind of people were they? I grew up thinking the Russians were out to get us. I had lost a twenty-one-year-old brother in Vietnam and that complicated my thinking. When the van pulled up in front of the restaurant the first person out was this Soviet earth mother—flowing long hair and a long sort of drapey peasant skirt. She picked me up with a flourish and whirled me around in a real big bear hug! *That* was my introduction to the Soviets—and I had never even touched one before!

"The earth mother, who was one of Russia's most famous poets, read poetry. I served them cinnamon rolls. It was a ball. We had so much fun, we adjourned to the waterfront park for a picnic."

Things were never to be the same again in Jerilyn's life.

"My stereotype of the Russians as an enemy collapsed completely. They were warm and caring. They worried about heart disease and they wanted to spend more time with their families. We went to a salmon barbecue; we ate cinnamon rolls by the dozens and shared our lives.

"When we said good-bye, one of the Russian journalists turned to me and, with great feeling, said: 'Around the table we are all one family.'

"How can we do more to encourage this friendship? Then it came to me—we can cook together! Kitchens aren't armed. Kitchens are safe places. We can sit around the table and eat together and become friends."

So began Peace Table.

"I knew that if I could have a chance to cook for the Soviets in Russia, we would not need a translator—the food would speak for itself. So I got myself a visa."

During her first trip to the USSR, which she paid for herself, Jerilyn spent five weeks knocking on doors of often incredulous cooks and bureaucrats explaining her dream of an exchange of cooks between the two countries. She made six trips back to the Soviet Union laying the groundwork for her vision of culinary diplomacy.

Later, sixteen chefs from the Pacific Northwest flew with Brusseau to privately owned cooperative restaurants in Moscow, Tbilisi, Leningrad, and Tashkent. They took with them a taste of the United States— smoked salmon, black cod, fresh oysters, cranberries, apples, and the ingredients for cinnamon rolls.

"I knew that we would be friends for life if I could just get them to smell my grandmother's warm cinnamon rolls. And it worked!"

The Americans had heard a lot about boring Russian food, cabbage day after day. But the Peace Table group came home raving about the thick, unpasteurized sour cream; yogurt so delicious that people who think they don't like it relish it; the crusty rounds of Uzbek bread; the butter and the cheese.

On another trip Brusseau visited Georgia, and was astounded. "It's an Eden. A land of unbelievable abundance. The markets are stacked with mountains of grapes, apples, peaches, apricots, walnuts, and plums. Everything. You have to pinch yourself to realize that you are in Russia where in other regions people have nothing. It doesn't compute. Food rots waiting for trucks and rail cars that never come. Sad."

She is pleased that Peace Table has made a contribution to the new understanding between the United States and the former Soviet Union. She has since taken Peace Table to Jordan for a similar food and cultural exchange between Israelis and Palestinians. Vietnam is next.

GRANDMOTHER'S CINNAMON ROLLS

[MAKES 16 LARGE ROLLS]

Two flours are used in making the rolls—all-purpose white and whole-wheat pastry flour. The latter is sometimes difficult to find, so I substitute white pastry flour or whole-wheat flour used in bread baking. There is a slight difference in texture, but the result is nevertheless delicious.

INGREDIENTS

DOUGH
3 cups all-purpose white flour
2 packages dry yeast
½ cup granulated sugar
2 teaspoons salt
2 cups milk
⅓ cup unsalted butter, room temperature
2 eggs
½ cup raisins
2 cups whole-wheat pastry flour or whole-wheat flour for bread

FILLING
2 cups (4 sticks) unsalted butter, melted
3 cups dark brown sugar
3 tablespoons ground cinnamon
2 cups chopped walnuts or pecans or almonds (optional)

EQUIPMENT

Two 9 x 13-inch metal or ceramic baking pans—not glass, which tends to caramelize sugar too quickly—well greased

PREPARATION BY
HAND OR MIXER
8 mins.

For the dough: In a large mixing or mixer bowl measure the white flour, dry yeast, sugar, and salt. Blend.

In a medium saucepan pour the milk and add the butter. Heat over a low flame until most of the butter is melted—but not long enough to scald the milk. Pour the heated milk into the flour-yeast, and stir to make a light batter. Lightly beat the eggs in a small bowl and add these to the dough mixture. Beat with a spoon or the mixer flat beater until the eggs are absorbed.

Add the raisins. Add the whole-wheat flour, ¼ cup at a time, to form a dense mass that can be lifted to the work surface, or left in the bowl under the dough hook. The dough should be smooth, satiny, somewhat resilient, and not sticky.

FIRST RISING
45 mins.

Shape the dough into a ball and place in a large greased bowl, turning the ball over to grease the top. Cover with plastic wrap. Let rise in a warm place until double in bulk, about 45 minutes.

FILLING
5 mins.

While the dough is rising, melt the butter and in a bowl mix it together with the brown sugar and cinnamon.

SHAPING
15 mins.

Turn the dough onto a large floured board. Roll out to a 24 x 20-inch rectangle. Spread the entire rectangle with the butter-sugar mixture and sprinkle with nuts, if desired.

Roll the rectangle tightly from the long side (the filling may be slightly runny and the dough will be soft). Make certain the seam side is on the bottom. Shape with your hands to make a cylinder uniform from end to end.

With a sharp knife, cut the roll into 16 equal portions. Place in the two well-greased baking pans, cut side down.

SECOND RISING
30–40 mins.

Cover the pans with plastic wrap or a warm, damp towel and let the dough rise until almost doubled in size, 30 to 40 minutes.

PREHEAT

Preheat the oven to 350° while the rolls are rising.

BAKING
350°
35 mins.

Bake the rolls until browned and all the filling is bubbly, about 35 minutes.

FINAL STEP

Take the rolls from the oven and immediately invert onto serving platters or a cookie sheet to allow the syrup to drip from the pan onto the rolls. (The dripping is the secret of these successful rolls, Jerilyn explained.)

TURKEY SALAD
WITH TARRAGON AND HAZELNUTS

[SERVES 6]

Now that the turkey comes to market tailored and packaged in a variety of shapes and mixtures, it is possible to be highly selective without committing the budget and menu to the whole bird.

Breast of turkey is an example, and a fine-tasting one at that. Especially in this salad by Jerilyn.

INGREDIENTS

TURKEY
2 pounds turkey breast
2 stalks celery, coarsely chopped
1 medium onion, chopped
1 large carrot, chopped
2 bay leaves, broken
½ teaspoon salt
1 tablespoon salad oil, to brush
1 teaspoon dried thyme

continued

SALAD
½ cup hazelnuts
1 small red onion, coarsely chopped
4 stalks celery, coarsely chopped
¼ cup finely chopped fresh parsley
1 tablespoon dried, or 3 tablespoons chopped fresh tarragon
Salt and pepper, to taste
¾ to 1 cup mayonnaise

EQUIPMENT | One roaster or small oven pan

PREHEAT | Preheat the oven to 350°.

ROASTING
350°
2 hours

For the turkey breast: Place the breast in the pan, add 1 inch of water, the vegetables, bay leaves, and salt. Brush the breast with the salad oil and thyme. Cover the pan with foil and bake for 2 hours, or until the breast meat tests done. Discard the vegetables and herb. Chop the meat into bite-sized pieces.

30 mins. | For the hazelnuts: Place the hazelnuts on a cookie sheet in the 350° oven for 20 minutes, stirring often. Remove immediately from the oven. Wait 5 minutes, then place the nuts in a clean dish towel for 5 minutes. Rub vigorously in the towel to remove the outer skins. Chop coarsely.

FINAL STEP | Combine all of the ingredients in a bowl and serve.

WILD EDIBLE GREEN SALAD WITH FRESH FLOWERS

[SERVES 6 TO 8]

It is not possible to be in the Northwest without the feeling of being as one with the land, the forests, the meadows, the streams, the lakes, and the blue skies. So it is not the least bit out of the ordinary to be offered by Jerilyn a green salad of edible wild things decorated with flower petals and blossoms.

The salad is dressed with a blueberry vinaigrette.

INGREDIENTS | *DRESSING*
¼ cup safflower oil
¼ cup water
1 tablespoon lemon juice
5 tablespoons blueberry vinegar
2 tablespoons fresh or frozen blueberries
1 tablespoon finely chopped shallot

Here is a list of wild and cultivated greens that are to be chosen for the salad. The amount of each depends entirely on availability at the moment.

Shepherd's purse	*Chickweed*
Sheep's sorrel	*Wild chrysanthemum*
Russian kale	*Corn salad*
Wild mustard	*Beet greens*
Nasturtium leaves	*Lemon balm*
Rocket leaves and blossoms	

BLOSSOMS TO GARNISH

Pansies	*Marigolds*
Calendulas	*Violas*
Fava bean	*Lavender*

PREPARATION
1 hour

For the dressing: Mix all the ingredients together well and let stand for at least 1 hour until the flavors develop.

FINAL STEP

Place the greens in a glass bowl, sprinkle with flower petals and blossoms, and drizzle lightly with dressing.

~~~~~*GLACIER, WASHINGTON*

Innisfree—Lynn and Fred Berman

> *I will arise and go now, and go to Innisfree.*
> WILLIAM BUTLER YEATS

Innisfree is a small restaurant tucked in the deep woods in the shadow of Mount Baker (elevation 10,877 feet) in Washington, ten miles below the Canadian border. The food, the drive, and the hospitality make worthwhile the two-hour travel time from Seattle; as *Le Guide Michelin* would put it, "worth a special journey."

Its location in the mountains was picked with care by Lynn and Fred Berman, two ex-Californians now in their mid-forties, who for six years had farmed a quarter-acre plot of ground in Norway, and returned to America in search of a small farm of equal beauty and fertility in a similar

mountain setting. They found it near the village of Glacier, off the
Mount Baker Highway: twenty acres of woods and pasture and an old
frame farmhouse nearly hidden by brambles and old fruit trees. Around
the property at all points of the compass was the forest, and lording over
it all were the mountains and Mount Baker. "It's our little piece of
Norway," said Fred.

In the beginning, a restaurant was not in mind. There was to be a
working farm, a truck garden, a small dairy, and whatever else they could
coax the old place to be after it was rescued from the wilds. The deer
had found the fruit trees and the raccoons were harvesting the fish pond.

"The plan was that here in the shadow of Mount Baker we would
grow things and live off the land and make a living as we had done in
Norway. There, everything we ate we produced ourselves on that tiny
piece of land. We joined our neighbors to fish in the fjord below our
farms and regularly came home with one hundred kilos of fish. It was
not sport fishing. It was sustenance fishing. Food we didn't eat we took
to the town market and sold for spending money; we even put aside some
in savings."

The Mount Baker soil was fertile and crops grew bountifully; two
jersey cows had beautiful calves, and gave cream-rich milk for home-
churned butter; and six ewes had frisky lambs. Bees made pounds of
honey. In the meantime, Berman led a movement to open a farmers'
market in the small city of Bellingham on Puget Sound, thirty miles west,
so that he and other farmers would have an outlet for the flood of cabbages, lettuce, carrots, peppers, beans, corn, beets, Brussels sprouts, and
more that was beginning to flow from their fields. But Bellingham
couldn't or wouldn't support the undertaking, and the market collapsed.

That year Berman plowed under several thousand heads of lettuce, each one of which had been lovingly put into the ground by hand.

They would open a restaurant.

"We had always liked to cook. We were good cooks; at least our friends said we were. We would have it over others who opened restaurants—we know food from the ground up, literally. And we had so much of it!"

Two hundred feet beyond the farmhouse, across the pasture, through a small wood and over a footbridge was an A-frame house for sale alongside the highway. The Bermans bought it, added a kitchen and wine cellar, and a year later opened its doors as the Innisfree.

The name is important to the Bermans. On the ship to Scandinavia in 1972 they told a fellow passenger about their pilgrimage to make a new life for their family in Norway. He read them the lines from William Butler Yeats's "The Lake Isle of Innisfree":

> *I will arise and go now, and go to*
> *Innisfree,*
> *And a small cabin build there, of clay*
> *and wattles made;*
> *Nine bean-rows will I have there, a hive*
> *for the honey-bee,*
> *And live alone in the bee-loud glade.*

In the past half-dozen years the A-frame has been enlarged so that upwards of twenty-five guests can be seated, and the old house, completely rebuilt, looks over the pond now alive with fish and crayfish. Wild ducks and geese call frequently. Kingfishers plunge beneath the surface for minnows.

Innisfree has prospered. In the summer, diners come from mountain resorts across the Canadian border, and in winter, from the ski fields farther up the mountain. Complete dependence on the farm alone has been modified somewhat, but the Bermans stick tenaciously to the credo of "regional self-sufficiency." He says: "For example, we serve only fish from our streams and Puget Sound nearby. No exotics from distant places."

Fred laughed: "We didn't do a market study of any kind to determine how much business we might have, nor where we would get our customers. We went into it totally cold turkey. Blind. We had the farm and we wanted to share this wonderful food. We assumed that if our meals were well prepared and priced right people would find us, even up here on the mountain. They did, but it took a while.

"In the beginning we were so naïve about dining hours, for instance, that we closed the restaurant for the day at six o'clock so I could milk the cows!"

BAY FOREST CREPES

[SERVES 6]

Shrimp from the bay and mushrooms from the forest blend together with kale and shallots in this delicious crepe.

In the Northwest, plan to spend a clear, crisp autumn day after the first rainfall on a hike in the woods. The chanterelles will be exploding at your feet. Their bright red color will blend in with the fall colors of leaves, so be careful where you step. Also, be sure you know your mushrooms or are with someone who does because picking the wrong mushrooms can make you sick. Bring along a pocketknife and a small paintbrush. Cut the mushrooms close to the ground and brush the debris off before placing in a basket.

If chanterelles are not to be found wild in your woodlands, they are often available in the produce sections of supermarkets, fresh as well as dried.

When making crepes, assume the first few are to test the consistency of the batter, which can be thickened or thinned with a bit more flour or a splash of milk. Don't hesitate to get it right.

INGREDIENTS

CREPES
4 eggs
2 cups milk
½ cup (1 stick) unsalted butter, melted
1¼ cups all-purpose flour
Pinch of salt

FILLING
2 tablespoons clarified butter (see page 241)
4 tablespoons sliced shallots
2 cups chanterelles
½ teaspoon Vegit (dehydrated vegetable seasoning—optional)
Pinch of white pepper
1 pound large uncooked prawns, peeled and deveined
1 cup kale, washed, center rib removed, and cut into strips

1 ounce dry sherry
½ to ¾ cup cream

Note: The prawns may be cut lengthwise to stretch the amount.

PREPARATION
5 mins.

For the crepes: In a medium deep bowl, beat the eggs until blended. Add the remaining ingredients. Beat until smooth and no lumps of flour remain.

COOKING
10 mins.

Heat a 9-inch skillet with sloping sides until medium hot. Using a small ladle, pour in just enough batter to leave a thin coating in the pan when tilted in all directions.

The crepe is ready to turn when just slightly brown and beginning to pull away from the pan at the edges. The easiest way to turn the crepe over is with your fingers, a heatproof rubber spatula is another option. No more than 30 to 60 seconds are needed for each side.

Lay the crepes on a rack to cool.

FILLING
15 mins.

In a large skillet over medium heat, melt the butter and sauté the shallots until translucent. Add the chanterelles, Vegit, and pepper.

When the mushrooms just begin to get limp, add the prawns. The prawns are done when they curl and turn opaque, about 4 minutes. *Don't overcook!*

Add the kale strips and *quickly* stir all the ingredients together.

Immediately remove the prawns and vegetables with a slotted spoon, cover, and keep warm. Leave the liquid in the skillet. Add the sherry and cream and reduce the mixture to a thick custardlike consistency. Remove from the heat and return the prawns and vegetables to the skillet to coat with the sauce.

ASSEMBLING
5–10 mins.

Fold the crepes in half and half again to make a wedge shaped cone. Fill the cones and pour a bit of the sauce over the top. Serve immediately.

KUMLE
(Potato Dumpling)

[SERVES 6]

Kumle is a delicious potato dumpling of sorts than can be served in a stew or soup. Or it will stand on its own nicely, sometimes plain, or sometimes with a bit of sausage or meat inside.

Kumle has as many names and ways of being prepared as there are dialects in Norway—*kompe, poteballer, raspeballer,* and *potetklubb* are but a few.

Lynn explained the effect *kumle* has on her: "I've been served *kumle* and made it many times with always the same effect. I always feel very comforted and satisfied and overcome with the need to lie down and take a nap afterward."

INGREDIENTS

8 large potatoes (russet or Idaho), 6 raw and 2 cooked
½ to ¾ cup unbleached white flour
3 to 4 tablespoons barley flour
1 teaspoon salt
Browned clarified butter (see page 241) or homemade gravy

PREPARATION
20 mins.

Peel and either finely grate or rice the raw and cooked potatoes in a food mill. Add the 2 flours and salt. The type and freshness will determine how much flour is needed. The mixture should have the consistency of a thick porridge.

Wet your hands in cold water and form the potato mixture into individual balls that are somewhere between the size of a golf and tennis ball.

BOILING
35 mins.

Boil a pot of water and drop the balls into it. Bring to a boil again, reduce the heat, and cook the balls over medium heat for about 30 minutes.

FINAL STEP

Drain and serve warm with browned clarified butter or your favorite gravy.

Another version is to chill the leftover balls, slice, and fry in butter for a delicious and hearty breakfast or lunch. Somewhat like potato cakes.

CHOCOLATE-HAZELNUT TORTE

[MAKES ONE 9-INCH ROUND TORTE]

Somehow the great Northwest forest setting of the Innisfree Restaurant for this hazelnut torte seems entirely appropriate.

INGREDIENTS

12 ounces dark bittersweet chocolate
¾ cup (1½ sticks) unsalted butter, room temperature
4 eggs, separated
½ cup sugar
1 cup ground hazelnuts
¼ cup all-purpose flour

EQUIPMENT

One 9-inch cake pan, buttered and dusted with flour

PREHEAT

Preheat the oven to 350°.

PREPARATION
25 mins.

Melt the chocolate and butter in the top of a double boiler set above boiling water, but not touching, about 10 minutes. Allow to cool.

In a large mixing bowl beat the egg yolks and sugar until the yolks are thick and yellow. Add the chocolate to the yolks, mixing well. Stir in the hazelnuts and flour.

Beat the egg whites until stiff and fold into the chocolate mixture.

BAKING
350°
25–30 mins.

Pour the batter into the prepared cake pan and bake for 25 to 30 minutes, or until cracks begin to form on the surface of the cake.

COOLING
15 mins.

Cool the torte for 15 minutes in the cake pan, then unmold onto a cooling rack.

FINAL STEP

The torte may be served plain, or glazed with a thin layer of melted bittersweet chocolate.

✕✕✕✕✕PORTLAND, OREGON

A Dinner of Things—Richard Nelson

Richard Nelson is one of the best cooks in the Pacific Northwest, and through his no-nonsense food columns in the Portland *Oregonian*, he has taught hundreds how to poach a salmon, clean a crab, sauté a clam, and make his South Dakota grandmother's Spoon Bread Soufflé.

Nelson, in his sixties and not a tall man, looked up from across a wide maple work table. He has a choice of how he looks at the world. At that moment he was wearing the pair of glasses for distance. His half-lens reading glasses were tied on a ribbon around his neck. He shifts frequently from one to the other.

A pronouncement was forthcoming (Richard speaks with quiet authority): "Tonight we are not having *dinner*—we are just doing *things*!"

Shopping for "things" began when we drove to the farmers' market in the nearby small city of Beaverton. It was a pleasure to watch a knowledgeable shopper work at his craft. With authority quickly recognized by the tradesmen, Richard walked among the market stalls touching this, joking about price, smelling that, pinching a leaf here and pulling off a leaf there, until he had an armload of lettuce, strawberries, and red peppers plus a big bag of homegrown hazelnuts for munching as

we shopped. Next stop: Strohecker's Super Market for crab meat that had come in earlier in the morning from the shore.

Impressive credentials underlie Richard's assuredness and confidence. He has taught a thousand students, written hundreds of columns, authored a highly recognized cookbook, appeared on dozens of television shows, and was a student and associate of the late James Beard. Richard is not imperious. He simply knows who he is. I felt that if a dozen unexpected guests dropped in for dinner at this very moment Richard would not be the least bit flustered. He would stretch one pound of crab into some delicious dish. Dinner would be served on time.

But tonight is to be a relaxed affair for four. Marje and I, Richard and his longtime friend and associate, Charles Kofler. Together they have this gracious and contemporary house high in the hills above Portland with a view across the Willamette River to mountains on the far side of the Columbia River. We were standing on the deck admiring the view framed by a forest of stately pines.

"It is always ten degrees cooler up here than in the city," said Charles, who manages the art shop in the Portland Museum of Art. "Today it was ninety-two degrees down there—and so comfortable here." A raccoon ambled across the lower yard.

Suddenly a lion roared! I couldn't believe it.

"We're a real jungle. Lions roar and elephants trumpet." He smiled and pointed to a forested hill across the valley. "The Portland Zoo. Lots of lions."

Nelson first came to Portland on a vacation trip from a career as a stage designer in New York City. "I liked it so well I never went back." It was here he met and began assisting James Beard in his summertime cooking classes at Seaside on the Oregon coast. A decade later Nelson opened his own cooking school in Portland and began writing two food columns—"Kitchen Basics" and "Richard Nelson Talks Food"—for the Portland daily newspaper, the *Oregonian*.

"I grew up on a ranch in South Dakota, eating wonderful food cooked by my grandmother. She could create amazing things from the little things that were at hand, the memories of her magic with the skillet and a pot and pan are with me all the time."

For ten years Richard wrote his columns about American food, which he defined as good basic ingredients properly cooked without unnecessary seasonings or sauces to mask the true flavor. He no longer writes about food. "The wheel went around too many times."

Nelson was chopping the red peppers he had bought earlier in the day. "The key to my cooking has always been its simplicity—and that's the way we're going tonight!"

CASSEROLE OF DEVILED CRAB

[SERVES 8]

One of Richard's favorite dishes, deviled crab is really a hot salad and can be made from any kind of fresh crab—Dungeness, king, blue, or stone.

INGREDIENTS
2 pounds Dungeness crab meat
2 cups cracker crumbs
1 cup finely diced celery
¾ cup chopped onion
¾ cup (1½ sticks) unsalted butter, melted
¾ cup light cream or whole milk
1½ teaspoons dry mustard
½ teaspoon salt
Dash cayenne pepper
2 tablespoons chopped fresh parsley
1 tablespoon chopped green bell pepper
Dash hot pepper sauce

EQUIPMENT   One shallow casserole, buttered

PREHEAT   Preheat the oven to 350°.

PREPARATION
5–10 mins.   Rinse the crab meat in cold water; drain and combine with the crumbs, celery, and onion. Add the melted butter and cream or milk. Season with the remaining ingredients.

continued

BAKING
350°
30 mins.

Mix thoroughly and bake, covered, in the prepared casserole for 30 minutes. For a crustier top, bake uncovered.

FINAL STEP

While dining on this all-crab dish, think about variations combining scallops, shrimp, and crab; or substitute shrimp or scallops for the crab meat. Be certain the amount totals 2 pounds.

BAKED BEETS

[SERVES 6 TO 8]

Richard found this recipe in the *White House Cook Book*, written and dedicated to the wives of presidents in the late 1800s.

INGREDIENTS

6 to 8 medium to large beets, unpeeled, unwashed
3 to 4 tablespoons (about ½ stick) unsalted butter or margarine, melted
1 teaspoon sugar
Salt and freshly ground black pepper, to taste

EQUIPMENT

One Dutch oven or casserole lined with foil

PREHEAT

Preheat the oven to 400°.

PREPARATION
5 mins.

Do not wash the beets: Remove any soil with a dry paper towel. Moisture will cause the beets to steam, and you do not want this to happen. Leave ½ inch of the stem and the root of the beets. Place them in the foil-lined baking dish.

BAKING
400°
1 hour

Cover and bake for 1 hour.

ASSEMBLING
15 mins.

Remove from the oven and allow to cool for about 5 minutes.

When the beets are cool, remove the stems and skin. Leave the roots on if you are serving the beets whole; remove if you are dicing or slicing them. The skin is easily removed simply by slipping it off with your fingers.

Place the skinned beets, sliced, diced, or whole, in a saucepan or skillet. Add the melted butter and season with the sugar, salt, and pepper. Heat through over a low flame. Serve hot.

SPOON BREAD SOUFFLÉ

[SERVES 6]

Richard's favorite dish is Spoon Bread Soufflé. The garlic cheese can be bought commercially in 5-ounce jars or made by mixing 1 teaspoon of mashed garlic with ½ cup grated mild Cheddar.

INGREDIENTS
2 cups whole milk
½ cup white cornmeal
½ cup (1 stick) unsalted butter
One 5-ounce jar garlic cheese (see above)
4 eggs, separated
1 teaspoon baking powder
1 teaspoon salt
1 teaspoon sugar

EQUIPMENT
One 2-quart casserole, well buttered

PREHEAT
Preheat the oven to 325°.

PREPARATION
20 mins.
Combine the milk and cornmeal in a saucepan. Cook, stirring constantly, to the consistency of a thick cream sauce, 5 minutes. Be careful not to burn.

Remove from the heat and transfer to a large bowl; add the butter, stirring it in as it melts. Add the garlic cheese and stir until smooth. Cool. Add well-beaten egg yolks, the baking powder, salt, and sugar and mix well. Beat the egg whites to a stiff peak and fold into the cornmeal mixture.

BAKING
325°
45–50 mins.
Pour the batter into the casserole and bake for 45 to 50 minutes, or until the top is puffed and golden.

Serve immediately.

On the Road—SEASIDE, OREGON

Razor Clams

I did everything but wade into the surf to dig for the most elusive and delicious of shellfish, the Pacific razor clam. "I will march into the Pacific if that is the only avenue open to me to get the clams," I blustered to my friend John Pincetich, whose house on the Oregon coast is near the ocean.

He glanced at his watch. "You may if you wish, but you will be over your head before you reach the place where the clams are. You clam at low tide or not at all, and on my calendar that comes in the middle of the night. Besides, digging is allowed only on odd days, and today is the twelfth. Sorry."

There was a chill breeze off the water and I was not unhappy to be deterred. Marje and I had clammed many years ago for the Pismo clam at a beach in southern California where we had parked our Airstream trailer overnight, but I was younger then and didn't mind being buffeted by heavy waves and a cold wind.

Because of overharvesting, there is only a small window of opportunity for clamming along the Oregon/Washington coasts, hence the tough restrictions on when clams can be dug. There are razor clams in Alaska and on the East Coast but clams from the Northwest are considered by far the finest tasting. At maturity, they measure about five inches long and from one and a half to two inches wide. They have a thin, lacquerlike shell with sharp edges; diggers must grasp the clams from the hinged side, which always faces toward the ocean. The clams are captured either with a shovel or a "clam gun," a hollow metal cylinder that is forced deep into the sand surrounding the clam and which sucks the mollusk from its burrow when the plunger is raised. The trick is to do it fast. A clam that senses it is about to be dug, or gunned up, can work its way down into wet sand with incredible speed.

With the tide and time running against us, John asked the Bell Buoy if they would put aside a dozen or so razor clams for us, as well as demonstrate how to clean them. I had a feeling my friend, a native of Astoria, up the coast a few miles, who had spent his youth during the Great Depression fishing for salmon at the mouth of the Columbia River, was not excited about such a prosaic catch as a clam.

Lucille Stinnett at the Bell Buoy had put our live clams on reserve in a gallon bucket under the counter. "Start with boiling hot water—but only for a moment," she said as she put the clams in a colander and held them under a tap of steaming hot water until she saw the shells open. She immediately plunged the colander of clams in a bucket of cold water. "Too long in hot water will toughen them."

She picked up a clam, slipped the narrow blade of a long knife between the half-opened shells and cut the meat loose. It dropped into her hand. She cut off the brown tip of the neck. Holding the clam body with the neck (sometimes called its "digger") hanging, she carefully pushed the sharp blade up through the neck and body. With a slight tug on the knife, the blade sliced through the length of meat, laying the clam open and flat, ready for frying.

An impressive performance. I tried one or two clams with a modicum of success. After all, Lucille has been doing it for two decades—I for two minutes.

We left the Bell Buoy richer by a dozen clams.

PORTLAND, OREGON

Razor Clams—Patty Pedersen

Patty Pedersen is a fine cook, though she protests that she is not a great one. "I cook simply—I don't do sauces."

We were standing in her big kitchen in an equally big house in a fashionable suburb of Portland. It seemed to me that the kitchen, if called on to do so, could accommodate a whole battalion of kitchen help without stress or strain. But it is all hers. She and her husband, a Portland orthodontist, hunt, fish, and cook. The several freezers hold venison, elk, duck, geese, salmon, halibut, sturgeon, and a family favorite, razor clams.

"She does the best razor clams on the Pacific coast," said Richard Nelson, food author, columnist, and teacher as well as a first-rate cook himself, as we drove up to her house. I had hoped to bring my Bell Buoy clams with me, but Richard assured me that Patty's would be as good.

Patty said: "These have been frozen, but fast, and they have been wrapped in aluminum foil to prevent freezer burn. These will be just as delicious as ones that are fresh dug. Frozen like this they can be sent any place in the country."

Earlier that morning, Patty had placed the clams to thaw in a colander in the sink so they would not be sitting in water as they thawed. "Drain them or they will be tough," she warned.

RAZOR CLAMS, TO FRY

[SERVES 4 TO 6, DEPENDING ON SIZE]

"There is a crisp tang to their flavor which makes them unique, and these clams should always be cooked as delicately as possible—like wild mushrooms—to preserve this flavor," said Patty. "They should never, never be deep-fried."

INGREDIENTS	*12 saltine crackers*
	2 eggs
	4 tablespoons milk
	Dash Tabasco
	24 medium razor clams
	3 tablespoons each corn oil and butter
	Salt and freshly ground pepper, to taste
	Lemon slices
EQUIPMENT	One cookie sheet or platter
PREPARATION 25 mins.	Crush the crackers with a rolling pin. Do not use a food processor, which will spin them too fine.

In a shallow platter beat the eggs together. Add the milk and Tabasco.

Dry the clams with a paper towel. Dip each clam in the eggs, drain off any excess. Place them in the crumbs to coat.

Place on a cookie sheet or platter to allow the coated clams to rest for 15 minutes.

FRYING
25 mins.

While the clams are resting, heat the oil first and then drop in the butter. Heat but *not* so hot as to smoke.

Fry each clam to a golden brown, 1½ minutes on each side. It is important not to overcook the clams, or they will be tough.

FINAL STEP

Remove the clams from the pan with a slotted spoon, sprinkle with salt and pepper, serve with lemon slices, and eat them right away.

︿︿︿︿*PORTLAND, OREGON*

The Genoa—Fred and Amelia Hard

By pure happenstance we arrived at The Genoa, one of the best *ristorantes* in the Pacific Northwest. It was one of those friend-of-a-friend routines that worked out wonderfully. Rather, deliciously.

It began when Al Cobine, a bandleader, composer, and arranger of note and a friend of mine in Indiana, said one day, "If your cookbook takes you to Portland, look up a friend of mine, Fred Hard. He owns a restaurant, called The Genoa, I think." His friend had a graduate degree in music from the university and had played bass in Al's big band group. He was a fine jazz musician. I filed the information.

When I decided to include Portland in my itinerary, Al's words pinged. I called a friend out there. No, he'd never heard of The Genoa. But he had a friend who knew Portland's restaurant scene quite well. The report came back promptly: a great little place that featured Northern Italian food, a specialty I was looking for. I called Fred, allowing I was a friend of Al's. Bless friends.

It *was* a great little place—the food was outstanding; Fred and Amelia Hard were delightful; the ambiance was Italian.

When Fred left Indiana he joined the faculty at Portland's prestigious Reed College as professor of English. Amelia, ten years his junior, was his student. After her graduation they were married. She worked in the college library until one day both decided they'd had it up to here with the structured life of academe and quit.

Amelia: "When I left the library, a friend—a waiter—asked me if I would like to try working as a waitress. 'You would make a wonderful one,' he said. I was willing to try anything. I loved it. I really enjoyed working with the public. I took delight in explaining to a guest how a dish was prepared and cooked and to what taste buds it might appeal. I was a darned good waitress—and still am."

With Amelia now a waitress, Fred went back to a career he never really left—music. Dance bands and combos. He also found time to move into a third career, bartending. Now both were working at The Genoa.

One day they were offered The Genoa by the owners, who were moving away.

Fred: "We went on a retreat for three days to think about it. We discussed it at great length, soberly and not-so-soberly. Either way we came up with the same conclusion: If we failed to make the move, if we didn't say yes, not only was there the risk that The Genoa, which we had come to love so dearly, might fall into the wrong hands and be destroyed, but we would forever wonder 'What if . . . ?' So we bought it."

Amelia: "We made two changes. We abolished all titles in the kitchen. No longer is there a chef. One of the three cooks (and I am one of them) is Cook number one for two weeks and then he or she drops back to assist until all of the cooks have been rotated. It's wonderful.

There's no burn-out, something that befalls a surprising number of chefs. Now there is time for those not number one to test recipes, experiment, and research. It is a constant recharging of energies.

"The second change: I had been watching the kitchen for four years and now that we owned the place it was my chance to make small but subtle changes. I could hardly wait to get into the kitchen to go to work. I was like a kid about to get her hands on her first pair of skates."

The Genoa's food is at once elegant, traditional, earthy, and solid. No one leaves the restaurant hungry.

Fred: "We are blessed with a mini-climate similar to Northern Italy's, and what they grow we grow. We have fresh porcini mushrooms brought to our door regularly and at a price we can afford—five dollars a pound. We have a wonderful source of quail and pheasant. Veal is raised on its mother's milk and is not confined. Our sausage man makes a fine prosciutto. We have a wide range of regional cheeses. Fish is heaven here! Our butcher is a saint. The wife of the man who supplies our rabbits supplies almost all of our herbs. Yes, blessed."

I wanted to know what his role was in the scheme of things.

"Actually, I am here under false pretenses. I am what I call Genoa's support services. While I have a good palate, I am better at fixing things. Changing light bulbs. Keeping books. That sort of thing."

Amelia: "He is a man who can put his hand on a sick mixer and it will come to life. He feels the spirit of the machine and gives it comfort. Really he does."

"In sum," Fred continued, "I think our relationship is in near-perfect balance. She expresses her creativity with food; mine is with music. And then I have this rudimentary mechanical mind which allows me to deal with refrigerators and all of the things that go wrong. I have a strong supportive role here, but don't ask me to do a particular sauce."

The dinner set before us was a seven-course classical feast. Yes, feast.

It began with *funghi grigliati e brushetta*, thick slices of local porcini mushrooms that had been grilled over charcoal, topped with olive oil, garlic, and parsley. It moved to *Zuppa di Cozze*, a lovely creamy mussel soup. The third course was *risotto con la zucca*, rice cooked with chunks of sweet-meat squash and onions. The fourth course was *Branzino alla Livornese*, a fillet of fresh rock bass sautéed. Delicious.

Marje and I parted company on the entrées. I ordered *gamberi alla Milanese*, large Mexican Gulf shrimp marinated in olive oil, garlic, shallots, thyme, and saffron and sautéed in butter. Marje's choice was *scaloppine di vitello con Marsala a funghi*, thin scallops of range-raised Oregon veal tenderloin sautéed in butter with fresh local chanterelle mushrooms. Then came *dolci*, a choice of seven homemade pastries. To complete the meal, *frutta*.

I refused to weigh in for several days following.

ZUPPA DI COZZE
(Creamy Mussel Soup)

[SERVES 4 TO 6]

Smooth as velvet, and delicious. The stock is prepared much as it is in the recipe for *Branzino alla Livornese* (below). Salmon is plentiful nowadays in most markets so fish for this stock should be easy to come by. There should be 2 cups of stock for this recipe.

INGREDIENTS

STOCK
2 pounds salmon trimmings
1 medium onion, sliced
¼ teaspoon whole black peppercorns
1 sprig of fresh thyme
¼ teaspoon fennel seeds
Handful of parsley stems

2 pounds live mussels
2 tablespoons unsalted butter
2 medium carrots, peeled and thinly sliced
2 medium onions, coarsely chopped
*2 ripe tomatoes, cored, peeled, and seeded, or 3 cans pear
    tomatoes*
1 garlic clove, chopped
1¼ cups dry white wine
1 large bay leaf
1 sprig of fresh thyme
2 shallots, chopped
¼ teaspoon saffron threads, dried for 5 minutes in 300° oven
2 to 3 tablespoons boiling water
1 cup whipping cream
½ to 1 cup Pernod, as desired
1 teaspoon salt, to taste
½ teaspoon freshly ground pepper, ground very fine

EQUIPMENT

One stainless-steel or enameled saucepan large enough to hold the mussels in 2 layers and liquids; length of cheesecloth to strain liquid

STOCK
35 mins.

(*Note:* The fish stock can be prepared 1 or 2 days in advance.) Place all of the stock ingredients in the pot and add cold water to cover. Bring to a simmer, skim off the scum, and simmer for 30 minutes more. Strain through a fine strainer.

PREPARATION
15 mins.

Wash the mussels well, scrubbing them with a stiff brush to remove the sand. Discard any that have partially opened shells. Set aside.

COOKING
35 mins.

Melt the butter in a large saucepan, cover and cook the carrots and onions over medium-low heat until they are very soft but not browned, about 20 minutes. Add the chopped tomatoes and garlic, cover, and cook for an additional 15 minutes. Remove from the heat and set aside.

STEAMING
10 mins.

In the large pan pour ¾ cup of wine, and add the bay leaf, thyme, and shallots. Add the mussels. Cover the pan and steam the mussels over high heat until they have all opened, about 5 minutes. Be aware mussels do not open very wide.

Immediately remove the mussels to a bowl, strain the steaming liquid through the cheesecloth. Set the mussels and liquid aside.

SIMMERING
10 mins.

Combine the salmon stock and mussel liquid. There should be 3 cups—if not, add water. Pour this into the pan with the cooked vegetables, and add the remaining ½ cup of wine. Bring to a simmer for 10 minutes.

ASSEMBLING
20–25 mins.

Strain the soup and puree the solids in a food processor or blender until very smooth, adding the soup liquid, if necessary, to facilitate pureeing. Pour all of the liquid and puree back into the saucepan.

Grind the dried saffron threads in a mortar with a pestle until powdered; add a few tablespoons of boiling water to the mortar to dissolve the saffron. Add this to the soup.

Add the cream and Pernod (start with the lesser amount and add more if you like) and salt and pepper. Set the soup aside while you shell the mussels.

Remove the mussels from their shells, and pull out the beards which protrude. Reheat the soup gently (don't let it boil).

FINAL STEP

Heat the bowls with hot water before serving. Divide the mussels evenly among the bowls. Ladle the soup over the mussels and serve immediately.

BRANZINO ALLA LIVORNESE
(Rock Bass with Fresh Tomatoes and Basil)

[SERVES 4 TO 6]

The fish stock is easy to make, especially if you can get the necessary fixings from a fisherman friend or the friendly fishmonger at the market. Otherwise, I sometimes use a fish food base such as Minor's or a bottled clam juice. (*Note:* Be sure you have 2 cups of fish stock for this recipe.)

The dish itself takes only a few minutes to prepare and must be served immediately. So, have the preliminaries out of the way early.

INGREDIENTS

STOCK
2 pounds fresh lean fish, heads and trimmings (bass, snapper, halibut, flounder)
1 large onion, thinly sliced
1 cup dry white wine
1 teaspoon lemon juice
¼ teaspoon salt

2 ripe tomatoes, cored, peeled, and seeded, or 1 small can pear tomatoes
12 large fresh basil leaves, or 1 tablespoon dried
1½ pounds rock bass or perch fillets
1 cup flour
½ teaspoon salt, or to taste
Pinch of freshly ground black pepper
4 tablespoons (½ stick) clarified unsalted butter (see page 241), to sauté
6 tablespoons unsalted butter, chilled, to sauce

STOCK
35 mins.

For the fish stock: Place all of the ingredients in a large stainless-steel or enameled pot, and add fresh cold water to cover, about 4 cups, cover and bring to a simmer, skim off the scum, and continue simmering for 30 minutes. Strain through a fine strainer, and use or refrigerate immediately.

PREPARATION
10 mins.

Chop the tomatoes and set aside.
Wash the basil leaves and dry with a paper towel.
Cut the bass into 6-ounce servings, and set aside.
In a shallow pan mix the flour with the salt and pepper, and set aside.

COOKING
5 mins.

Heat the clarified butter in a frying pan large enough to hold all the fish pieces without crowding. Dredge the fish pieces in the seasoned flour, shaking off the excess.

When the butter has slightly deepened in color, put in the fish and sauté until nicely browned on both sides, no more than 5 minutes total. Regulate the heat under the pan so that the butter never gets darker than a deep yellow.

When the fish is cooked, remove to warmed serving plates.

SAUCE
6–8 mins.

Pour the fish stock into the frying pan and reduce it over high heat until it has a syrupy consistency, stirring frequently, about 4 minutes. Chop the basil coarsely and add with the tomatoes. Continue stirring 2 more minutes.

Remove the pan from the heat and whisk in the 6 table-spoons of chilled butter, a tablespoon at a time, until it is all incorporated into the sauce. The sauce should look creamy, not oily. Taste the sauce for salt and pepper, remembering that the fish pieces are already seasoned. Pour the sauce over the fish. Serve immediately.

⋙PORTLAND, OREGON

Heathman Bakery and Pub—Greg Higgins

In the heart of downtown Portland is a remarkable wood-fired oven for bread baking. I can imagine my good friend, the great Parisian baker, Pierre Poilane, standing before it in admiration.

By chance I discovered the oven walking past the open door of the B. Moloch/Heathman Bakery and Pub. I smelled the heavenly smell of fresh-baked French bread. I went in.

And there it stood, a ten-ton beautiful behemoth, its iron door open to a field of golden fat loaves bathed in the reflected heat of a bank of glowing red coals at the far end of the long chamber. The baker, Greg Higgins, slipped the long-handled wooden peel under a half dozen of the golden *boules* and pulled them out. The crusts crackled and snapped in the cold air.

The bakery and pub, and microbrewery adjoining, was the creation of Mark Stevenson, who owns the four-star Heathman Hotel. He wanted a home for eight whimsical oil paintings by a nineteenth-century carica-turist B. Moloch, purchased in a Paris antique shop. Greg Higgins, the

baker, was the hotel's executive chef at the time and wanted more than anything else to have an authentic wood-fired oven for hearth-baked breads and pizzas.

They found an old building nearby that was ideal for the project. "High-tech primitive," it came to be called. A chimney had to be pushed up through five stories and, to meet the city's tough pollution regulations, fitted with an afterburner to clean up emissions. The vaulted firebox in which the bread is baked rests on layers of fire brick laid on a thick concrete pad. Packed between the arched dome of fire bricks and the outside walls are nine yards of sand.

"What we did was to create a thermal mass!"

Equally remarkable is his design of the "smoke box" for smoking meats. The air temperature as the smoke leaves is between 700° and 800°, much too hot for proper smoking, so it is cooled as it passes through a series of baffles before entering the smoke box higher up the chimney.

Greg climbed the stairs leading to the smoke box which is about ten feet above the floor.

"Fruit wood—apple, cherry, peach—pruned from Oregon orchards gives everything a rich flavor. We do some custom smoking. This month, all together we will smoke about four hundred ducks, fifteen hundred pounds of salmon, and a ton and a half of sausages, not to mention a few hams and several bacon slabs. It does smoke-dried tomatoes that are out of this world."

But it is the hearth-baked loaf that is his pride.

"I have been astounded at the beautiful loaves it bakes. The coals are banked overnight and then first thing in the morning I open the door, stick in my hand, like my grandmother did with her old range. If it feels just right I load the bread. If it's too hot, I throw in some ice. First we do breads, blister red peppers, and roast beef in the mellow heat. Midmorning we fire up again for four or five dozen *calzoni* for the luncheon trade. And we are doing pizza throughout all of this. More breads in the afternoon.

"The fire was allowed to go out for the first time a year ago when we had to replace some bricks. It wasn't really cool even then and the poor guy who had climbed inside the oven to reset the bricks almost roasted!"

A list of breads that are to go to the oven is posted nearby: San Francisco sourdough, whole-wheat onion, semolina sourdough, Russian rye, Swedish rye, beer bread, pesto bread, orange raisin wheat, pumpernickel, egg raisin, and cardamom oat rolls. His *pain de campagne* and walnut onion are from my *Breads of France*.

An enormous plate-glass window separates the bakery and pub from Widmer Microbrewery. Pub customers watch the brewery workers brew and bottle. The brewery sends over spent grains and fermented wort to leaven and give texture to some of the breads. "It's a happy symbiosis that has existed between the baker and the brewer for centuries," Greg said.

A trim, handsome thirty-two-year-old man, Greg carries himself like the athlete he is, racing bicycles when he can get away from the bakery. But most of his life is spent at the bakery by choice. He is serious about food. His approach to it is no-nonsense.

"I am happiest baking bread," Greg explained. "It's simple. It's hard to screw up. It's rewarding. People love it. We don't advertise, but they come from miles around. It has become the signature item for the whole operation."

I sampled slices of a half-dozen still-warm loaves and lunched on an all-vegetable pizza (marvelous crispy crust made with semolina dough) and a stein of Widmer's best, and walked out of the bakery euphoric—with four big loaves in my arms.

SEMOLINA AND ALE BREAD

[MAKES 4 LOAVES]

This bread nicely combines the talents of Heathman Bakery and the Widmer Brewery next door. The dough can be shaped thin for an excellent pizza base as is done in the Heathman.

Semolina flour is a yellow granular flour made from durum wheat.

It is used primarily in this country for making pastry and only occasionally for bread. It can be found in health food stores and ordered from catalogs.

The Heathman makes two delicious variations to this recipe: The first is to add 1 cup pesto to the dough while mixing, the other is to add ½ cup chopped dried tomatoes and ½ cup grated Romano cheese.

INGREDIENTS	*3 cups semolina flour* *2 packages dry yeast* *2 cups ale* *2 tablespoons olive oil, plus extras for brushing* *2½ cups water* *1 tablespoon sugar* *7 cups bread or unbleached flour, approximately* *2 tablespoons coarse sea or kosher salt* *Freshly ground black pepper, to sprinkle*
EQUIPMENT	Two cookie sheets, oiled and sprinkled with coarse cornmeal, or three medium (8 x 4-inch) loaf pans, greased or Teflon
PREPARATION BY HAND OR MIXER 10 mins.	In a large bowl or mixing bowl combine the semolina flour, yeast, ale, olive oil, water, and sugar and blend well with a wooden spoon or mixer flat beater.
RESTING 30 mins.	Cover and set aside for 30 minutes while the mixture proofs (begins to foam).
KNEADING 8 mins.	Add the bread flour, ½ cup at a time, to make a rough mass that cleans the sides of the mixing bowl. If it is slack and inclined to be sticky, add liberal sprinkles of flour. Lightly flour the work surface and turn the dough into the center of it, or leave it under the mixer's dough hook. Knead until smooth and elastic, about 8 minutes.
FIRST RISING 35 mins.	Brush the dough lightly with olive oil and place in a large bowl. Cover with plastic wrap and set aside until the dough doubles in bulk, about 35 minutes.
SHAPING 10 mins.	For *baguettes* (long, slender) or *boules* (round), divide the dough into 4 pieces and shape. Place on the 2 cookie sheets. For regular loaves, shape the dough to fit.
SECOND RISING 40 mins.	Brush the loaves with olive oil, cover, and set aside for the dough to double in bulk, about 40 minutes.
PREHEAT	While the dough is rising, preheat the oven to 375°.

BAKING 375° 30–45 mins.	Score the loaves with a sharp knife or razor blade. Sprinkle with the coarse salt and black pepper. Bake until evenly brown, about 30 to 45 minutes.
FINAL STEP	Remove the bread from the oven and place the loaves on a wire rack until cooled. This bread freezes well.

PAIN DE CAMPAGNE
(French Country Loaf)

[MAKES 4 MEDIUM LOAVES OR 1 LARGE HEARTH LOAF]

The Heathman is now baking this husky, rough country loaf that initially I brought back from Monsieur André David's *boulangerie* in Honfleur on the Normandy coast of France, when I was researching and writing *The Breads of France*. The decorating technique for making wheat stalks baked on the crust is described below.

INGREDIENTS	*STARTER* *1 tablespoon honey* *1 cup hot water (120°–130°)* *1 package dry yeast* *1 cup bread or all-purpose flour, approximately* *1 cup whole-wheat flour* *DOUGH* *2 cups hot water (120°–130°)* *All of the starter* *1 tablespoon salt* *2 cups whole-wheat flour* *2 to 3 cups all-purpose or bread flour, approximately*
EQUIPMENT	One or two baking sheets, greased and sprinkled with cornmeal, or Teflon. The number of sheets depends on the number of loaves to be made, and on the size of the oven.
BEFOREHAND 4 hours– overnight	To make the starter, in a large bowl dissolve the honey in the hot water and add the yeast. Add ½ cup each white and whole-wheat flours to make a thick batter. Add the balance of the flour to make a shaggy mass that can be worked with the hands. Knead for 3 minutes. Toss in liberal sprinkles of flour if slack or sticky. Cover the bowl with plastic wrap and leave at room temper-

ature for at least 4 hours. Left overnight it will gather even more flavor and strength.

PREPARATION BY HAND OR MIXER
10 mins.

To make the dough, pour the hot water over the starter. Stir with a wooden spoon or rubber scraper, or the mixer flat beater, to break up the dough. Add the salt.

Place 2 cups each of whole-wheat and white flours at the side of the mixing bowl—and add equal parts of each, ½ cup at a time, first stirring with a utensil and then working the dough with your hands, or with the dough hook. It may take more white flour to make a mass that is not sticky. Lift from the bowl if to be kneaded by hand, or leave in the mixer bowl if with the dough hook.

KNEADING
10 mins.

If by hand, place the dough on the floured work surface and begin to knead the dough aggressively with a strong push-turn-fold motion. If the dough is slack and sticky, add sprinkles of flour. Once in a while lift the dough high above the work surface and bring it down with a crash to speed the process. Do this 3 or 4 times, and then resume kneading. Knead by hand or with the hook for 10 minutes.

FIRST RISING
3 hours

Place the ball of dough in a greased bowl, cover tightly with plastic wrap, and leave at room temperature for the dough to double in volume, about 3 hours.

SHAPING
10 mins.

Push down the dough and turn out on a well-floured work surface. Divide the dough into the desired number of pieces and shape with cupped hands into tight balls. Reserve 1 cup of dough to make the wheat stalks later, if desired.

Place on baking sheets and press down to flatten slightly.

SECOND RISING
2½ hours

Leave the loaves under wax paper to *triple* in size, about 2½ hours at room temperature.

DECORATING
10–15 mins.

The wheat stalks need a large round loaf that measures at least 12 inches across to do the stalks justice.

Shortly before the loaf or loaves are completely risen, divide the reserved cup of dough into 3 pieces. Roll each into a long strand (under the palms) 12 to 14 inches long—no thicker than a lead pencil.

Place the strands parallel and, beginning 4 inches from one end, braid to the end. Turn the braid around and separate to make it convenient to cut the wheat design on each strand.

With sharp-pointed scissors, make small cuts down 5 inches of a strand—alternating cuts right, center, and left—to create grains of wheat protruding from the stalk before harvest. Leave the remainder of the stalk uncut and bare. Repeat the pattern for each strand.

Before placing them on the loaf, lightly brush the top with water, and position the wheat stalks. Fan the upper stalks apart.

PREHEAT

Preheat the oven to 425° about 20 minutes before baking and place a broiler pan on the bottom rack. Five minutes before the bread goes in the oven, pour 1 cup of hot water in the pan to create a moist, steamy oven.

BAKING
425°
40–50 mins.

Place the loaves on the middle rack. Midway through the bake period shift the loaves to balance the effect of the oven's heat.

The loaves are done when golden brown, in 40 to 50 minutes. The bottom crust will sound hard and hollow when tapped with the forefinger.

FINAL STEP

Place the loaves on a metal rack to cool. Freezes well.

If for a party or simply out of pride, before slicing present the loaf complete with wheat stalks at the table.

~~~~~SEAVIEW, WASHINGTON

Shelburne / Shoalwater—David Campiche and Laurie Anderson / Tony and Ann Kischner / Chef Cheri Walker

Under the roof of an old Victorian house in the village of Seaview (pop. 638), on a remote stretch of the Washington coast, is a noteworthy establishment for food and shelter. It is run by two couples in tandem—one at the inn, the other at the restaurant.

The food is so good, the beds so firm, and the hospitality so warm that it would be unthinkable for Marje and me to go anywhere else if we are within a day's journey of the The Shelburne Inn and its companion restaurant, The Shoalwater.

David Campiche   Ann Kischner

Despite its out-of-the-way location on the Long Beach Peninsula that extends north from the mouth of the Columbia River, The Shelburne has been discovered. Both inn and restaurant have been acclaimed, praised, photographed, televised, and written about by the national media. It bears its honors well.

The innkeepers are David Campiche and Laurie Anderson, who had the imagination and daring in 1977 to purchase the old inn that had been established a hundred years earlier as a summer retreat for Portland families who came down the Columbia River on the sternwheeler *T. J. Potter* to Astoria, transferred to a ferry for a ride across the river, and there climbed aboard a coach on the narrow-gauge Clamshell Railroad for the twenty-five-mile ride up the narrow peninsula to Seaview, and on to Oysterville.

The Shelburne sits on the edge of S.R. 103, and directly across the street from Sid's Supermarket, but that's all left behind when you push open the frosted-glass front doors and step into another era. Lovely stained-glass windows in floral patterns, salvaged from a nineteenth-century English church, have replaced all of the ordinary clear-pane windows, bathing the restaurant, the lounge, and the pub in warm, muted colors. The open-beam ceiling is strung with brass chandeliers, a red overstuffed davenport faces the brick fireplace, and, in the bedrooms, brass bedsteads are covered with colorful handmade quilts. There are no televisions in any of the inn's sixteen guest rooms. The old building is in the National Register of Historic Places.

This morning there were a dozen of us for breakfast, served family style at a big oak table. Not an ordinary bed-and-breakfast breakfast but a meal that can only be described as scrumptious, or if you will, sumptuous.

Choices: banana-pecan pancakes with fresh-picked blueberries or wild mushroom omelette with homemade pesto sauce; or savory crepes filled with ham, herbs, and scrambled eggs topped with salsa and crème fraîche; or scrambled eggs with Stilton cheese, apples, and caviar made in-house by the innkeeper from fresh silver salmon roe. Accompanying each entrée: just-baked gingerbread muffins; sautéed potatoes with garlic, fennel, and peppers; freshly ground coffee; and a platter of fruit.

All this is from the inn's kitchen.

David: "When Laurie and I bought The Shelburne twelve years ago we had the dream all innkeepers have—work hard during the summer months and then coast the rest of the year. I am a potter, and I saw myself as a three-month innkeeper and a nine-month potter. Ha! That was a dream. I've had to give up pots, at least for the past decade!"

In addition to a fourteen-hour day as innkeeper, David is a volunteer fireman. A radio above the kitchen range was tuned to the firehouse. It suddenly came alive with a loud beep. The voice of a dispatcher was calling for an ambulance. David continued slicing celery stalks. But what the voice said next froze the knife in midair. "Driver," the voice was without emotion, "go immediately to the health room at Ilwaco High School . . . a student has withdrawals!"

David turned the knife in his hand. "So, you see . . . even here . . . we are not so remote after all. . . . Sad . . ."

Back to cutting.

"In the beginning our breakfasts were strictly continental—one of Laurie's muffins, a slice of toast, fruit, and coffee or tea. Then one day we added a coddled egg. I had been smoking my own spicy sausages, so we added a sausage. I was fishing, so we added a slice of salmon pie. The next thing you know we are famous for our breakfasts!"

The Shoalwater restaurant, arguably one of the best places to dine on the Oregon/Washington coast, is less than six paces across the lounge of The Shelburne Inn. It is the domain of Tony and Ann Kischner, restaurateurs, whose kitchen will occasionally borrow a cup of sugar from The Shelburne's but that is as close as the two ever get.

Ann Kischner, the pastry chef: "We like it that way. We four are good friends; unfortunately we no longer have time to get together for a picnic on the beach or to go to a movie as we did in the beginning— before we were discovered." She laughed. "We still try to sit down with a cup of coffee once a week to talk about problems that pop up."

Tony and Ann came to Seaview ten years ago when they learned from the man who supplied snails to the Seattle restaurant Tony managed that The Shelburne was seeking someone to take over its dining room that had been recently run by two women.

Tony: "We knew from the beginning that we would base our cuisine on the abundance of fresh, regional foods. How can you go wrong with salmon, sturgeon, clams, and oysters pulled from nearby Willapa Bay, the Columbia, and the Pacific? Wild mushrooms are in abundance and so are berries and the local escargot."

A fisherman had just delivered a sturgeon as I walked into the kitchen with Tony. Five rows of bony plates extended the length of its body. Its tail was like a shark's. It would not win a prize among fish for beauty. For a long time the sturgeon was considered a trash fish, and caught only for its roe (for caviar) and its air bladder (isinglass). The carcass was thrown away until someone realized just how delicious its meat was. Today it is overfished and must be protected—only sturgeon between four and six feet in length can be kept. Most of the sturgeon that fishermen bring to The Shoalwater are those that have been caught in salmon nets. These are considered "incidental catch" and can be kept.

"Sturgeon is now as pricey as salmon," said Tony. "For fine dining, I take sturgeon over salmon anytime—except during the spring salmon run when we can get those incredibly fat, moist, and rich salmon that have spent the last three years in cold arctic waters.

"The sturgeon is a curious prehistoric creature that has changed little in a number of million years. It is a bottom fish that vacuums up everything it finds. The incredible thing is that whatever it does produces this wonderful meat.

"We treat it differently than other fish when it comes to the kitchen. Unlike other fish that must be immediately killed, cleaned, bled, and iced, we leave the sturgeon to expire on its own anywhere from twelve to fourteen hours after it's pulled from the water. We don't touch it. If we did, the meat would be as tough as shoe leather."

At dinner we had sturgeon. The meat was white, moist, not fat, sweet, and with a taste somewhat like mahimahi, one of my favorite fish. In the kitchen I watched Chef Cheri Walker reverently place it on the grill for just a few minutes. On the plate she surrounded it with gingered apple, leek, and a sweet red pepper sauce. But I began with a sautéed Dungeness crab cake with ginger mayonnaise, and then, in my almost-insatiable hunger for seafood, I shared with Marje a plate of pan-fried oysters from Willapa Bay, just a few miles away. And then I begged a bite of her grilled fillet of Chinook salmon, with blueberry and cranberry mustard sauce. I watched a neighboring diner relish his first taste of pan-fried yellow-eye rockfish. He told me it was served with ginger, lime, and cilantro butter sauce, and a homemade salsa. At that point I was beyond envy.

To my regret I did not have the steamed Willapa Bay littleneck clams. And I put off until another evening the baked marinated Pacific halibut and the roast Northwest free-range veal loin and the sautéed pecan-coated chicken breast with Dijon mustard and sour cream sauce. Not to mention smoked salmon and whitefish sausage and Willapa smoked oysters.

Yes, to my regret.

DAVID'S SPICY SAUSAGE

[MAKES ABOUT 12 POUNDS]

This sausage, made with no preservatives, can be stuffed into casings, smoked, or rendered for bulk patties. At The Shelburne, a favorite is bulk sausage sautéed with pecans, currants, and red onions. Molasses, wine vinegar, soy and oyster sauce are added and then the mixture is flamed in sherry. It is served in an omelette with Parmesan cheese and crème fraîche.

Not your everyday breakfast dish but splendid for a special brunch.

INGREDIENTS	*10 pounds pork steak, cut into 1-inch cubes* *1 each green and red bell pepper, finely chopped* *2 heads garlic, minced* *½ cup finely chopped Italian parsley* *½ cup finely chopped fresh oregano* *¼ cup fresh chives, chopped medium fine* *2 tablespoons freshly ground black pepper* *4 tablespoons cuminseed* *1 tablespoon cayenne pepper* *Salt, to taste* *2 cups red table wine*
EQUIPMENT	Meat or sausage grinder, with ¼-inch horn if to be stuffed; sausage casings, if to be stuffed
MARINATING overnight	Mix all of the ingredients together and allow to marinate overnight in a cool place. Stir occasionally.
STUFFING 1 hour	Push the mixture through the meat grinder. Stuff directly into a casing or reserve for bulk sausage.
FINAL STEP	If cased, smoke lightly for 3 to 4 hours. It is superb.

COUNTRY SALMON PIE

[SERVES 5]

In some parts of the country this might be considered a quiche, but at The Shelburne it is a pie with a delicious Parmesan cheese crust.

INGREDIENTS

CRUST
2 cups flour
¾ cup grated Parmesan cheese
1 cup (2 sticks) unsalted butter, chilled
3 tablespoons ice water

FILLING
7 ounces smoked salmon
½ large onion, diced
1 garlic clove, minced
1½ tablespoons butter
1 cup sour cream
3 eggs
¾ cup grated Gruyère cheese
½ tablespoon chopped fresh dill, or 1 teaspoon
*   dried, plus extra for garnish*
¼ teaspoon salt

EQUIPMENT

One 8-inch springform pan

PREHEAT

Preheat the oven to 375°. (The oven will be used to partially bake the crust before filling and to bake the pie.)

PREPARATION
10 mins.

For the crust: Combine the flour and grated Parmesan cheese. Cut in the butter until the mixture resembles small peas. Sprinkle with the chilled water. Form into dough with your hands. Be careful not to overwork.

Press the dough into the bottom and up the sides of the springform pan.

BAKING
10 mins.

Place the empty shell in the oven to bake for just 10 minutes.

FILLING
10 mins.

Break the salmon into bite-sized pieces, removing any skin or bones, and set aside.

In a small skillet sauté the onion and garlic in the butter until the onions are soft and translucent, about 6 minutes.

Beat the sour cream and eggs until blended. Stir the salmon into the sour cream mixture along with the sautéed onion, ½ cup of Gruyère cheese, the dillweed, and salt.

| BAKING 375° 55–60 mins. | Pour into the partially baked crust and top with the remaining ¼ cup of cheese. Bake for 55 to 60 minutes. |

BAKING
375°
55–60 mins.

Pour into the partially baked crust and top with the remaining ¼ cup of cheese. Bake for 55 to 60 minutes.

COOLING
15 mins.

Cool in the baking pan for 15 minutes. Then remove the pan's sides.

FINAL STEP

Cut the pie into wedges, and serve garnished with fresh dill.

FIDDLEHEAD FERN OMELETTE

[SERVES 3]

Much of the fun of eating at The Shelburne comes from the treasures of the land. The fiddlehead fern, also known as the bracken fern, is one such treasure. Only the very tender tip of the fern is sought, just as it pushes from the ground in a tight roll about the size of a quarter. The fiddlehead is as tasty as asparagus.

The prepared ferns are served in an omelette with Parmesan cheese.

David: "The guests consume this delicacy with a fervor that continues to amaze even us!"

INGREDIENTS

FERNS
2 pounds fiddlehead ferns, blanched and cleaned,
    tender curled portion only
½ Spanish onion, finely chopped
6 tablespoons unsalted butter
3 tablespoons Irish whiskey
½ cup heavy cream
Salt and freshly ground black pepper, to taste
Fresh dill, chopped, to taste

OMELETTE
12 eggs
3 tablespoons cream
Salt, to taste
6 tablespoons unsalted butter, for pan (none needed
    for Teflon pan)
1 cup Parmesan cheese, freshly grated

4 sprigs of dill, to garnish

PREPARATION
10 mins.

For the ferns: In a skillet briefly sauté the ferns and onion in 4 tablespoons of hot butter, about 6 minutes. Add the whiskey and with a match burn off the alcohol. Add the cream and reduce by half or until the cream thickens to a heavier sauce, about 4 minutes. Season to taste with salt, pepper, and dill. Add the remaining 2 tablespoons of butter and cook only until married with the sauce. Remove from the heat.

COOKING
12 mins.

For one omelette: Lightly beat together 4 eggs, 1 tablespoon cream, and salt. Melt 2 tablespoons of butter in an omelette pan, and pour in the eggs. When the eggs have hardened on one side (just barely golden), about 2 minutes, add a quarter each of the fern filling and grated Parmesan cheese over half of the omelette. Gently fold the omelette in half. Cook for a minute. The inside should be moist. Carefully slip the omelette onto a serving plate. Repeat for the other 2 omelettes.

FINAL STEP

Garnish each omelette with a sprig of dill and serve immediately.

STURGEON AND GINGERED APPLESAUCE

[SERVES 8]

There are about 2 dozen species of sturgeon. Some live at sea yet spawn in fresh water, while other are purely freshwater fish. The white sturgeon, a *transmontanus*, is found in Northwest rivers and can reach 15 feet in length.

INGREDIENTS

SAUCE
1 tablespoon butter
1 leek, thinly sliced, white part only
½ Granny Smith or Gravenstein apple, unpeeled, diced
1 green bell pepper, seeded and diced
⅓ cup sliced gingerroot (don't peel)
1 cup apple juice
1 cup heavy cream
2 ounces balsamic vinegar
Salt and pepper, to taste

STURGEON
Eight 8-ounce sturgeon fillets
Unsalted butter, melted, to brush
Leek and bell peppers, julienned, to garnish

PREPARATION
20 mins.

For the sauce: Melt the butter in a saucepan and sauté the leek, apple, pepper, and gingerroot over low heat until the apple is soft and starts to fall apart, 10 minutes. Add the apple juice.

Puree the mixture. (Be careful not to fill the blender too full; hot liquid can explode out of the blender.)

Press the puree through a fine strainer or cheesecloth into a saucepan. Combine the puree with the cream, vinegar, salt, and pepper.

Keep the sauce hot in a double boiler until the sturgeon is grilled and ready to be served.

GRILLING
15 mins.

For the sturgeon: Brush the sturgeon fillets with butter and grill over a hot flame, 3 minutes on each side. They can also be cooked under a broiler, about 3 minutes per side. Don't overcook the fish. It is best when just a touch underdone in the center.

FINAL STEP

Present the fillet set in the center of a puddle of sauce. Garnish with slices of leek and strips of green pepper.

DUCK LIVER PÂTÉ

[SERVES 20]

This is a party-sized pâté, the recipe for which can readily be cut in half or even into one quarter to serve a more intimate group.

When making the forcemeat for this or any pâté, Laurie suggests overseasoning the mixture, because the flavors will leech out a bit while the meat cooks.

Slice into 20 pieces and serve with cranberry chutney, pickled asparagus, and fresh French bread.

INGREDIENTS

10 ounces each chicken and duck livers
½ cup each brandy and heavy cream
1 tablespoon freshly ground black pepper
10 ounces fatback, thinly sliced (to line mold and cover pâté),
    plus 10 ounces fatback, finely diced (to include in pâté)
10 ounces ground pork
½ cup port wine
½ cup brandy
½ cup crème fraîche
4 eggs
½ teaspoon crushed juniper berries
1 tablespoon épices fines (fine mixed spices)
1 teaspoon coarse salt
1 teaspoon white pepper
1 cup each fresh or frozen cranberries and blueberries

continued

EQUIPMENT — One 13 x 4 x 4-inch mold; pie weights; a bain-marie or water bath or a pan somewhat larger than the pâté mold itself

MARINATING
overnight — Marinate the chicken and duck livers in the brandy, cream, and black pepper overnight. Refrigerate.

Line the mold with the sliced fatback, and reserve in the refrigerator.

PREHEAT — Preheat the oven to 350° 20 minutes before baking the pâté.

PREPARATION
15 mins. — Blend the pork and diced fatback in a processor or blender until smooth and creamy. Add the port, brandy, crème fraîche, and eggs. Blend thoroughly. Add the spices, salt, pepper, and livers. Blend but do not overprocess.

In the mold alternate the forcemeat with the berries in layers. Cover with a layer of fatback. Place a piece of foil over the top, and weight with pie weights.

BAKING
350°
1 hour 15 mins. — Set the mold in a water bath two thirds up the sides of the pan. Bake for 1 hour and 15 minutes, or until a knife inserted in the middle of the pâté comes out clean.

RESTING
30 mins. — Turn the oven off. Leave the pâté in the oven with the door ajar for 30 minutes.

FINAL STEP — Cool. Refrigerate before serving.

PUB BUN

[MAKES 6 LARGE TURNOVERS—MEAL-SIZED]

Ann's barbecue sauce is the delicious ingredient that sets this chicken-filled Pub Bun apart from any other meat turnover I've ever had. And I report as a turnover buff. The Pub Bun is not served in The Shoalwater dining room but across the lobby in the Heron and Beaver Pub, and only at lunch. Wonderful to eat on the premises or to take with you on the road, in a boat, or on a hike.

INGREDIENTS — *SAUCE*
1 cup each red wine vinegar and red chili sauce (cocktail sauce)
5 tablespoons Worcestershire sauce
6 tablespoons veal or duck demiglace (optional)
1½ tablespoons butter
⅓ cup brown sugar
1 tablespoon minced garlic

Dash Tabasco
2 teaspoons dry mustard
½ teaspoon each dried thyme and oregano
1 teaspoon salt
1½ teaspoons each paprika and chili powder

CHICKEN
6 whole chicken breasts, skinned and boned
1 teaspoon each chopped garlic and dried basil
2 tablespoons olive oil
1 onion, sliced into thin strips

BUN
3 pounds French Bread dough (see page 182), after first rising
*   cut apart 6 equal ½-pound pieces*
1 egg yolk and 2 tablespoons milk, to glaze

EQUIPMENT

One jelly-roll pan, lightly greased or covered with parchment paper

PREPARATION
10 mins.

For the sauce: Combine all the ingredients in a saucepan and heat to a boil. Reduce the heat and simmer, uncovered, for 10 minutes. Set aside.

MARINATING
1–2 hours

Marinate the chicken breasts in the barbecue sauce for 1 to 2 hours.
   Slice the chicken into thin strips.

COOKING
10 mins.

For the chicken: In a skillet briefly sauté the chicken strips with the garlic and basil in 1 tablespoon of olive oil. Cook until the chicken turns white, about 4 minutes. It should not be completely cooked. Remove from the pan and set aside.
   Add the remaining tablespoon of olive oil to the skillet and over medium heat cook the onion until soft and translucent, but not brown, about 6 minutes.
   Add the barbecue sauce and stir well. Remove from the heat.

PREHEAT

Preheat the oven to 400°.

ASSEMBLING
20 mins.

Roll each piece of dough into a flat 5 x 7-inch rectangle or an 8-inch round.
   Place the equivalent of 1 chicken breast and 1 tablespoon of onion in the center of each dough piece. Spread over it about 1 tablespoon of sauce. Leave a clear margin around the edge of the dough so the seal will hold when pinched together. Pull up the sides to the middle. Pinch together well.

continued

BAKING
400°
15–20 mins.

Place the turnovers seam *down* on the jelly-roll pan. Brush with the egg glaze. Bake for 15 to 20 minutes, or until well browned.

FINAL STEP

Serve with extra barbecue sauce at hand to be spread on or be dipped into!

⋙*On the Road—SALISHAN, OREGON, AND BEYOND*

Whales, Ships, Seals

On the 150-mile drive down the spectacular coast highway (U.S. 101) from The Shelburne there were so many stops to watch whales, ships, seals, pounding waves, otters, and hundreds of small craft bobbing through the Chinook salmon run that it was late afternoon before we drove up to Salishan Lodge.

Everything about Salishan is spectacular. Its 150 rooms are spread in tiers among fir and hemlock trees on a high bluff overlooking Siletz Bay and, beyond, the Pacific. The rooms are connected by covered bridges and walkways that protect from winter's mists, fogs, and rain and lead down the slope to the main lodge.

Dinner was a celebration of sorts, for the next day we left the Pacific coast and, for the first time in two months, the van faced east into the morning sun, headed back to Indiana.

There was regret to leave the magnificent coast, but at the same time an excitement with the promise of what would be around the next ten thousand curves.

In the morning began the journey up and down the Coast Range of mountains, across the wide and fertile Willamette Valley, and up and over the Cascades. The mountains were at once exhilarating and depressing. Just as you felt transported into an undefiled wilderness came the shock of hundreds of acres of the ugly detritus of clear-cut logging.

"Oh, no!" Marje cried. "It's mine! It's a national forest. It belongs to *me!*"

Nevertheless, an army of saws and tractors and trucks had moved across a battlefield to leave nothing but stumps, broken limbs, soil, and rocks that seemed embarrassed to lie naked in the sun after having been sheltered for centuries.

It was like looking at a beautiful woman who shows a dreadful gap where a front tooth should be when she smiles.

A Basque Cook—Eusebia Susaeta

Eusebia Susaeta, who is Basque, is a ranch cook, and a good one. Her husband, Bassilio, is foreman of a ranch running fourteen hundred head of cattle. They came from the Spanish Pyrenees forty years ago; only he speaks English. Housekeeping on a remote Idaho ranch, cooking three meals a day, seven days a week, for a husband and kids and a dozen Basque cowhands left little time to learn a language she didn't need.

I needed help. Basque is considered one of the most difficult languages in the world to learn. Called Eskuara, it falls harsh and loud on the ear. "After all," said my interpreter, smiling, "it is supposed to be the pure language of Eden, the tongue with which Adam wooed Eve."

My interpreter was an old friend and a distinguished Idaho rancher/politician, Peter T. Cenarrusa, who had taken a few days off work in Boise as secretary of state, to be the bridge between me and Eusebia, his cousin. Pete and I first met thirty years ago when I wrote an article on this many-faceted man who was a Basque sheep rancher, Speaker of the Idaho House of Representatives, and an ex-Marine combat pilot who flew his own plane to distant pastures in the mountains to keep in touch with his Basque sheepherders and their flocks.

It was midmorning when the four of us—two Cenarrusas and the two Claytons—drove down the lane to a large two-story brick house, surrounded with flowers, a big garden alongside. There were several young heifers penned near the back door. Four kittens came tumbling down the steps. Eusebia waved. She had just caught a fat hen that she had been chasing across the chicken yard. Its neck wrung, it was about to be plucked and made ready for lunch.

We walked into the kitchen.

Eusebia, who is sixty-two, is a tightly packed bundle of energy. Short, no more than five feet; slender, perhaps a hundred pounds, she danced around the big kitchen which was hers alone.

Eusebia, speaking through Pete, laid out the day. Three of their six cowboys and her husband would be coming in from the range about noon. They would be hungry, so the food must be on the table. We would join them.

"The first thing she has to do," said Pete, "is to start the bread. Usually she bakes for the entire week on Saturday, but today is different. She is keeping it small—just three loaves and two dozen rolls."

She reached under the table for a tin bucket, wide and deep. She stirred in the yeast and water and followed with salt and flour, the latter she dipped from a twenty-four-pound bag. The rim of the bucket on the table was at her eye level. Standing on tiptoes she could just see into it. She put the bucket on a chair and tried to knead. The bucket slipped and turned.

There was a volley of Basque words! She was not happy with the arrangement.

"She says that despite company she is going to do it the way she usually does it—put the bucket on the floor," Pete said. The bucket went to the floor with Eusebia kneeling over it. She began to knead with a strong, forceful rhythm, banging her fists against the dough.

"The dough wouldn't dare to resist," Pete said with a grin.

Eusebia now had two hours before the men would come in from working with the cattle, and in 120 minutes she would:

• Let the dough rise before she shaped and baked three loaves and two dozen cloverleaf rolls.

- Prepare and bake a cinnamon flan.
- Cook a pot of garbanzos and red beans.
- Starting with the fresh chicken, put together and bake a paëlla.
- Chop apart several large pieces of frozen round steaks.
- Country-fry the eight steaks, place them in a big iron pot to bake.
- Simmer a light vegetable pasta soup in a stock made from the chicken's giblets, legs, neck, and wing tips.
- Roast red peppers and sauté with garlic bits to make a sauce for the meat.
- Toss a salad of lettuce, tomatoes, and mushrooms, with an olive oil and vinegar dressing.
- Make a huge pot of coffee the old-fashioned way—toss the coffee into the water, bring to a boil, allow it to settle, pour.
- Arrange a platter of fresh fruit for a centerpiece.

This she did with no help from the company who watched in awe.

It was a few minutes after noon when Bassilio and the three cow-hands, who also live in the house, came to the dining table freshly scrubbed. We were all at the table except Eusebia, who sat on a chair near the kitchen sipping coffee ready to spring into action if somebody wanted something.

The meal was hearty Basque, meant to stick to the ribs of hard-working and hard-riding cowboys. It was not haute cuisine. It wasn't meant to be.

OLLON PETCHU PAËLLA
(Breast of Chicken Paëlla)

[SERVES 6]

With a flock of barnyard hens as near as her back door, Eusebia makes this marvelous chicken dish often.

INGREDIENTS

¼ cup olive oil
3 garlic cloves, bruised and chopped
2 double breasts of chicken (4 pieces)
½ cup each ham and chorizo or other spicy sausage, diced small
⅓ cup pimento or red bell pepper strips
3 tablespoons minced onion
1 tablespoon minced fresh parsley
⅛ teaspoon each saffron and cayenne
Salt and black pepper, to taste
1 cup raw rice
2 cups chicken stock, homemade (see page 562) or store-bought
½ cup dry white wine
1 cup tomato sauce

EQUIPMENT

One 2-quart casserole

PREHEAT

Preheat the oven to 350°.

COOKING
20–25 mins.

In a large skillet heat the olive oil and drop in the garlic. Cook for 4 or 5 minutes over medium heat. With a slotted spoon remove and discard the garlic.

Add the chicken breasts and cook until browned—no longer, about 8 minutes. Set the chicken aside in the casserole and keep warm.

Place the skillet over medium heat and add the ham, chorizo, pimento, onion, parsley, saffron, cayenne, salt, and pepper. Cook the mixture until the onions are soft and translucent, 5 to 8 minutes.

Add the rice, stirring to coat the grains with oil.

Stir in the chicken stock, wine, and tomato sauce. Bring to a boil. Pour the mixture into the casserole with the chicken.

BAKING
350°
25–35 mins.

Cover the casserole and bake until the rice is cooked (al dente), about 25 to 35 minutes.

Serve hot.

KARAMELO BUDINA
(Caramel-Cinnamon Flan)

[SERVES 8]

Flans and custards are Basque favorites.

INGREDIENTS	*1 cup granulated sugar* *½ cup water* *1 (8-ounce) can evaporated milk* *2 cups fresh milk* *½ teaspoon salt* *1 stick cinnamon* *8 eggs* *1 tablespoon vanilla extract*
EQUIPMENT	One 2-quart deep-dish pie or flan pan of choice, or custard cups; 1 pan larger than flan pan for water bath
PREHEAT	Preheat the oven to 325°.
CARAMELIZING 10–12 mins.	To caramelize the pans or cups, cook ½ cup of sugar and the water at high heat in a stainless-steel saucepan. Stir only until the sugar is dissolved, 4 minutes. The mixture will bubble and the water will evaporate. Continue cooking until the sugar begins turning tan in color, about 6 to 8 minutes. The syrup burns easily, so watch it carefully! Just before it gets to the color of a dark rum, pour into the cold pan. Slide the caramel from side to side quickly so that it will be distributed evenly in the bottom of the pan. Set aside.
PREPARATION 10–12 mins.	In a large saucepan heat both milks, the salt, and cinnamon stick over medium heat, stirring occasionally until the milk scalds and tiny bubbles appear around the surface, 10 to 12 minutes. Remove from the heat but cover and keep warm. Remove the cinnamon stick. Beat the eggs in a large mixer bowl for about 1 minute. Add the remaining ½ cup of sugar and the vanilla. Gradually pour into the egg mixture, beating only until well blended. Pour the mixture into the pan coated with caramel.
BAKING 325° 1 hour 10 mins.	Place the flan pan in a water bath of 1-inch-deep water in the large pan. Bake for about 1 hour and 10 minutes, or until a knife comes out clean when inserted in the center.

continued

COOLING
8 hours–
overnight

Cool and refrigerate for at least 8 hours or overnight.

FINAL STEP

Cut around the cold custard in an up-and-down motion with a straight table knife to loosen from the pan. Carefully turn the custard over onto a platter by placing the platter on top of the pan and quickly turning over. Do this over the sink, as the caramel may drip during the turning process.

Slice and serve as you would a cake.

><><><>*On the Road—*

EN ROUTE TO JACKSON HOLE, WYOMING

The Forty-ninth

Today was our forty-ninth anniversary. A lot of miles have been traveled since the day we drove away from Marje's parents' home in Indiana where the ceremony was held. The day was unforgettable. The old grandfather clock in the living room had not struck for years. Exactly at noon, when I said "I do"—it struck twelve times with vigor. So loud in fact that the pastor stopped the service until the bongs ceased.

At that time I was not a sports fan, blissfully unaware when I made reservations at Cincinnati's Netherland Plaza for our wedding night that we had chosen the headquarters for fans swarming into town for the 1940 World Series opening the next day. The town was packed. My best man and friends had filled our hub caps with rocks that clanked and banged in slow traffic right up to the hotel door, much to the amusement of a throng of baseball fans and the broadly grinning doorman. At two o'clock in the morning a construction crew moved under our window to hammer together a line of bleachers for the parade. I have not forgotten the time of year for the World Series or our anniversary ever since.

The big celebration, our fiftieth, will be next year. Tonight, after a long day on the road, we will probably walk Timothy, eat a light meal, have a glass of wine, and shake hands to celebrate the fact we are still such good friends.

Good night, Marje.

JACKSON HOLE, WYOMING

Chocolate— Pat Opler

Jackson Hole loves its food!

It's a refrain we heard again and again as the van cruised in the shadow of the Grand Teton mountains from dude ranch to dude ranch and from restaurant to bistro to café. There was something about the mountain air that sharpened the appetite and challenged the least of cooks to excel.

Pat Opler is a transplanted Chicagoan who has lived in Jackson for a decade. When months earlier she said she would be my Jackson Hole guide, I jumped at the offer. "This is a wonderful place," she said as we walked through one of the arches shaped with elk horns at each corner of the town square.

"We are as close to an egalitarian society as you can hope to get. Walk into Nora's Fish Creek Inn for one of her fabulous breakfasts and you can't tell the Easterners from the cowhands. They're all in jeans and boots and Stetsons.

"And they're all talking about the same thing. If it's summer, it's fly fishing. If it's winter, it's skiing."

Jackson is the town (pop. 4,500). Jackson Hole encompasses the town and the surrounding valley floor. To early fur trappers, a protected valley where they could winter-over was a "hole." And this was a good one.

Pat, the center of most every cultural endeavor in the valley, leaves town occasionally to travel the world with her husband, president of the Chicago candy firm that makes "The World's Finest Chocolate, Inc."—those rich velvety bars that every fund-raiser in the country has at one time or another peddled door to door. "We're in the field of sweet fund-raising." Pat laughed.

But her heart is in Wyoming—in a beautiful big log house on a high aspen-covered bluff overlooking Fish Creek where it flows into the Snake River. The snow-capped mountains, off the front deck, are a magnificent backdrop to the valley scene. Beavers splash in the stream below and the occasional long-legged moose comes up the hill, steps over the fence, and grazes in her garden.

Pat, an outstanding cook, occasionally teaches a cooking class for neighbors. At breakfast on our last morning in Jackson Hole she served a coffee cake made with poppy seeds soaked in buttermilk. One bite and I wanted the recipe.

True to her devotion to chocolate, the last thing she handed Marje as we went out the door was two wrapped wedges of the World's Best Chocolate Cake.

"To assuage the pangs of hunger on the road," she said, smiling.

Assuage it did. Deliciously so. Her recipe follows.

POPPY SEED–BUTTERMILK COFFEE CAKE

[SERVES 12]

The poppy seeds for this recipe are soaked in buttermilk touched with almond extract. A delicious combination.

INGREDIENTS

¼ cup poppy seeds
1 cup buttermilk
1 teaspoon almond extract
1½ cups sugar, plus ⅛ cup, to sprinkle
4 eggs, separated
1 cup (2 sticks) unsalted butter, room temperature
2½ cups all-purpose flour
1 teaspoon baking powder
1 teaspoon baking soda
½ teaspoon salt
2 teaspoons ground cinnamon, to sprinkle

EQUIPMENT	One tube or Bundt pan, greased
BEFOREHAND 30 mins.	In a small bowl soak the poppy seeds in the buttermilk and almond extract for 30 minutes.
PREHEAT	Preheat the oven to 350° 20 minutes before baking.
PREPARATION 15 mins.	In a large bowl cream the 1½ cups sugar, egg yolks, butter, and soaked poppy seeds until smooth. In a separate bowl stir together the flour, baking powder, baking soda, and salt. Set aside for a moment. Beat the egg whites until soft peaks form.
ASSEMBLING 10 mins.	Stir the flour into the buttermilk mixture just until the dry ingredients are moistened. Don't overmix. Stir a quarter of the egg whites into the batter to lighten. Fold the lightened batter into the remaining egg whites. Pour half of the batter into the greased tube pan. Sprinkle half of the cinnamon on top of the batter, taking care not to have the cinnamon touch the outer perimeter. Pour the remaining batter over. Tap the tube pan firmly on the counter to concentrate the batter evenly in the pan. Sprinkle the remaining cinnamon and sugar lightly on top of the batter.
BAKING 350° 50 mins.	Bake for about 50 minutes. Test for doneness with a testing pin, broom straw, or toothpick.
FINAL STEP	Remove the coffee cake from the oven and let cool for a few minutes before turning it over onto a wire rack.

WORLD'S FINEST CHOCOLATE CAKE

[MAKES ONE 9-INCH CAKE]

Chocolate is not only America's favorite flavor, it is also the world's favorite flavor. Between eleven and twelve pounds of chocolate are consumed annually by each American. Seventeen pounds are enjoyed yearly by Western Europeans.

Here is one way to help your consumption top the national average, but be aware: It is addictive!

INGREDIENTS

CAKE
¼ *cup raisins*
¼ *cup rum or bourbon*
7 ounces best-quality sweet dark chocolate
3 tablespoons water
½ *cup (1 stick) unsalted butter*
3 eggs, separated
⅔ *cup granulated sugar*
⅔ *cup ground almonds (not too finely)*
4½ *tablespoons cake flour*

FROSTING
3 tablespoons best-quality dark sweet chocolate, melted
3 tablespoons unsalted butter
3 tablespoons confectioners' sugar

EQUIPMENT

One 9-inch cake pan lined with double layer of wax paper

PREHEAT

Preheat the oven to 375°.

BEFOREHAND
30 mins.

Steep the raisins in the rum or bourbon for 30 minutes.

PREPARATION
12 mins.

In a saucepan melt the chocolate with the water, 8–10 minutes. Stir in the butter until smooth.

Beat the egg yolks with the sugar until the mixture is light yellow. Stir the yolks into the chocolate. Then add the nuts, flour, and raisins, including the liquor.

Whip the egg whites with a whisk until they hold their shape. Pour the whites gently into the chocolate batter and fold together.

BAKING
375°
25 mins.

Pour the batter into the prepared pan and bake for 25 minutes.

COOLING
1 hour

Remove the cake from the oven and after 1 hour of cooling, run a knife around the cake edge and invert onto a serving plate.

FROSTING
5 mins.

In a double boiler melt the chocolate and stir in the butter. Stir in the confectioners' sugar. Pour the frosting over the cake.

FINAL STEP

This cake can easily be frozen first and then wrapped tightly. Unwrap while still frozen in order not to remove the glaze.

⋙JACKSON HOLE, WYOMING

Working Dude Ranch— Darcy Crowder

The season for dude ranches in Jackson Hole was winding down, but some kitchens were still cooking for a few die-hard guests and the hands.

It was black as pitch—hours before sunrise—when we drove north thirty miles to the Triangle X Ranch, a working dude ranch that has been in the John Turner family for more than half a century. It was at the Triangle X that John Wayne, in his first western film, rode horseback for the first time. Every dude about to mount a Triangle X horse for the first time is told the Wayne story.

The ranch house was as black as the night. No lights. I shouted and a lantern appeared.

"Sorry about this," a friendly voice called out, "but it happens every now and then—no electricity." It was the cook, Darcy Crowder. She led the way into her kitchen. Suddenly the lights came on—just in time— for I was about to step into a crate of eggs.

Darcy, who is younger than thirty, has worked as a ranch cook for six years. This morning she was making breakfast for a dozen staff people, who were getting ready to batten down the guest cottages for the winter, as well as for four or five guests determined to catch just one more trout before the season ends or it snows.

Though the ranch urges the catch-and-release of fish, Darcy was baking a beautiful sixteen-inch cutthroat trout that a guest could not bring himself to release. She draped strips of bacon over the fish, but it was obvious that she wished it were back in the water.

Breakfast was hearty. If you wanted four eggs you could have four eggs. The word *diet* never came up. The oatmeal was creamy; the sausage, crisply fried. Pans of thick but light biscuits came from the oven. A big dish of sausage gravy was passed around. Rich coffee.

Through the window I could see the sun peek over the mountain. The black silhouette of the jagged peaks against the pink sky. Stunning!

COWBOY COBBLER

[SERVES 6]

Darcy's reputation as a ranch cook has been enhanced greatly in the valley by her Cowboy Cobbler. Her favorite fruit is peach, but frequently she uses apples, cherries, or berries. For a large bunch of hungry campers, double the recipe and cook in a Dutch oven tucked in the coals.

INGREDIENTS	*½ cup (1 stick) unsalted butter or margarine*
	1 egg
	1 cup milk
	1 teaspoon vanilla extract
	1 cup sugar
	1 cup all-purpose flour
	1 teaspoon baking powder
	2 teaspoons salt, or to taste
	4 cups sliced fresh peaches, or fruit of choice
EQUIPMENT	One 9 x 13-inch baking pan or Dutch oven
PREHEAT	Preheat the oven to 375°.
PREPARATION 10 mins.	Melt the butter or margarine slowly in the baking pan over low heat or in the oven while putting together the other ingredients. Tilt to spread evenly.
	In a bowl stir together the egg, milk, and vanilla. Add the sugar, flour, baking powder, and salt. Mix thoroughly.
	Pour the batter evenly over the melted butter, but *do not mix or try to spread.* Arrange the fruit evenly over the batter. *Do not mix.*
BAKING 375° 45 mins.	Bake the cobbler for 45 minutes or until the crust is a golden brown.
FINAL STEP	Remove from the oven. Serve warm. Darcy serves it with rich cream or ice cream. Go for it!

CRESCENT H RANCH, JACKSON HOLE, WYOMING

Upscale—
Chefs Rebecca VanNess and Susan Schop

Susan Schop, *center*,
Rebecca VanNess, *right*

The sun was up when we drove back to Jackson from a visit to Yellowstone. We passed one small herd of buffalo and a dozen or so elk drifting down to the National Elk Refuge on the outskirts of the town where hundreds come to winter.

The food at the Crescent H Ranch next day was a different matter —considerably more upscale. The ranch is considered one of the three or four best dude ranches in the country, and it is expensive—$2,200 a week for one person. This does not include the optional $200 a day for a fishing guide. While the ranch appeals chiefly to fly fisherman who prowl Fish Creek, above the Opler's place, as well as the Green, Yellowstone, and Snake rivers, guests can ride, hike, bird-watch or just be in the contemplative mode.

And they eat. Very well indeed. Yet trout is seldom on the menu. Like the Triangle X, most times the fish are set free—after a photograph.

The ranch guests have been gone several days and the staff was preparing to shutter the buildings for the winter. Only the kitchen was open.

Chef Rebecca VanNess said, "Our guests are a pretty sophisticated bunch of people. They have traveled widely and they have eaten in the best restaurants, so it's a challenge for the kitchen to come up with something they didn't have last week in Chicago or New Orleans or Paris."

It was noon when we arrived. Rebecca and Susan Schop, the pastry chef, have spent the morning putting together several dishes that would be typical of the fare served their guests. The dishes were elegant in looks and elegant in taste. Lucky dudes!

First, a poached salmon (flown from Seattle) and served with a touch of dill cream. Next, a small square of grilled swordfish with an orange-soy marinade. Then a slice of roast tenderloin of veal stuffed with spinach, pine nuts, and mushrooms, with a dollop of mustard cream sauce. But best of all, I thought, was the strudel—mushrooms, onions, cream cheese, sour cream, and Parmesan cheese folded in phyllo and baked. Her recipe follows.

"Most of our guests protest that they are on diets and trying to lose weight, so we serve small portions. Ample but not overpowering. People are funny. The cholesterol thing, you know. They will eat two or three eggs for breakfast and then deny themselves a cream sauce at dinner, or have the cream sauce and have just one egg the next morning."

MUSHROOM STRUDEL

[MAKES 2 STRUDELS; SERVES 6 OR 8]

This is one of Chef VanNess's favorite dishes and also one of the ranch guests', too.

INGREDIENTS
20 sheets phyllo dough
½ cup onion, cut into ¼-inch dice
3 tablespoons unsalted butter, plus 1 cup (2 sticks), melted, to brush
1 pound mushrooms, thinly sliced
¼ cup sherry
1 teaspoon salt
8 ounces cream cheese, room temperature
1 cup sour cream
⅓ cup chopped fresh parsley
2 garlic cloves, minced
Juice and zest of 1 lemon
1 teaspoon dried dill
1 teaspoon dried thyme
1 teaspoon freshly ground black pepper
½ cup grated Parmesan cheese
1 cup bread crumbs, approximately

EQUIPMENT   One baking sheet, Teflon coated or greased

BEFOREHAND   If frozen, be certain to thaw the phyllo dough according to the
several hours   package instructions.

COOKING   In a skillet, over medium heat, sauté the onion in the 3 table-
20 mins.   spoons of butter until the onion turns soft, about 8 minutes. Add
the mushrooms and cook for an additional 6 minutes. Stir in the
sherry and salt, and cook until absorbed. Remove from the heat
and drain the excess moisture through a sieve, but don't press.
Return the mixture to the skillet. Cut the cream cheese into
small cubes and add to the mushrooms. Stir until melted.
Stir in the remaining ingredients except the bread crumbs.
Now stir in the bread crumbs with care—don't overload and
make too dry. Keep the mixture moist.
Cool slightly before assembling.

PREHEAT   Preheat the oven to 375°.

ASSEMBLING   (*Note*: Two strudels, with 10 phyllo leaves each, will be made.)
20 mins.   Place the first sheet of phyllo on the work surface. Brush
with some melted butter and repeat for a total of 10 layers. Spoon
and spread half of the mushroom mixture on the phyllo, leaving
a 2-inch margin on the edges; roll up and squeeze the ends tight.
Place seam side down on the greased baking sheet. Brush the top
with butter. Repeat for the second roll.

BAKING   Bake for about 25 minutes, or until golden brown.
375°
25 mins.

FINAL STEP   Remove from the oven and cut into serving pieces. If desired, a
dill or thyme cream sauce may be served underneath. The strudel can be frozen.

LIME AND WHITE CHOCOLATE TORTE

[SERVES 8]

Chef Schop makes this a torte of 8-inch circles. The first time I made the
torte I cut the recipe in half and made 6-inch circles. I thought I should
go small before I went large. It worked equally well, and was equally
delicious.

INGREDIENTS

COOKIE LAYERS
1 cup (2 sticks) unsalted butter, room temperature
1 cup sugar
4 eggs
1 teaspoon vanilla extract
1½ cups sifted all-purpose flour

LIME CURD
Juice and zest of 8 limes
6 eggs, plus 5 egg yolks
1½ cups sugar
½ cup (1 stick) unsalted butter, melted

MOUSSE
10 ounces white chocolate
2 eggs, separated
2 teaspoons sugar
¼ ounce raspberry liqueur
1½ cups heavy cream

TOPPING
½ pint heavy cream, to whip
1 tablespoon light rum or liquor of choice
White chocolate, shaved into curls

EQUIPMENT

Parchment paper; two or more baking sheets; a double boiler or water bath

PREHEAT

Preheat the oven to 350°.

PREPARATION
10 mins.

For the cookie layers: Draw a dozen 8-inch circles on the parchment paper; turn the sheets so the drawings will be the under side when filled. In a bowl cream the butter and sugar together until light and fluffy. Beat in the eggs one at a time. Add the vanilla and flour.

Divide the batter among the circles and spread evenly and thinly. Place as many of the filled circles as possible onto the baking sheets. In most ovens the layers will be baked in several batches.

BAKING
350°
18–24 mins.

Bake until the edges are lightly browned—no more. It will take about 6 to 8 minutes per batch, but watch carefully.

COOLING
5 mins.

Remove the cookie pans from the oven. As soon as they have cooled sufficiently to touch, gently peel off each of the papers.

If left on, the paper may stick to the layer. Put aside but don't stack unless separated by wax paper.

Repeat until all the filled circles are done.

WHIPPING
10 mins.

For the lime curd: Combine the lime juice, whole eggs, egg yolks, and sugar in the top of a double boiler. Whip over low heat—with the water barely bubbling—until the mixture resembles hollandaise. Whip the melted butter into the mixture and incorporate well. Fold in the lime zest.

Chill. Reserve until ready to use.

BLENDING
15 mins.

For the white chocolate mousse: Melt the chocolate and set aside for a moment. Whip the egg yolks, sugar, and raspberry liqueur until the mixture is pale. Add the chocolate to the mixture and cool. Whip the egg whites until stiff and fold into the chocolate mixture. Whip the cream and fold into the mixture.

Chill. Reserve until ready to use.

ASSEMBLING

Begin with the first cookie layer and stack—alternating the chilled fillings of lime curd and mousse until the final cookie layer is on the top.

Cover with whipped cream flavored with rum. Decorate the top with white chocolate curls.

⋙JACKSON, WYOMING

Wort Hotel—Chef Alan Myers

When 2,023 bright shiny silver dollars were sealed under polyethylene in the bar top of the old Wort Hotel they named it the Silver Dollar Bar. Almost as an afterthought they added "and Grill" so folks would know that food could also be had.

Recently, the hotel brought Executive Chef Alan Myers down from Washington State to create new dishes to pep up the grill's old steak-and-potato image. While steak and ribs are still on the menu to please the old clientele, Chef Myers has created a whole range of dishes with buffalo, elk, moose, grouse, duck, and venison.

Chef Myers is a tall, imposing man in his late twenties, who sports a

large droopy mustache and carries himself as though he would be as comfortable on a basketball floor as in a kitchen. He came to Jackson from Salish Lodge at Snoqualmie Falls in Washington.

We dined on an array of his new dishes—venison sausage; venison hash with eggs and hollandaise sauce; corn chowder; plus a triple grill that included buffalo medallions with a cracked pepper and walnut sauce, barbecued sirloin beef tip, and duck sausage. Not to mention a spinach salad with warm cubes of breast of chicken accompanied by corn muffins.

CORN CHOWDER

[SERVES 6]

A bowl of this corn-rich chowder is topped with two cheeses—Cheddar and Parmesan—before it is placed in an oven broiler to brown. Fresh corn in season is best, of course, but frozen corn will do almost as well.

INGREDIENTS

4 slices day-old bread
¼ pound bacon, cut into ½-inch pieces
1 cup onions, diced small
¾ cup celery, diced small
¾ cup carrots, diced small
1 teaspoon finely chopped garlic
2 tablespoons flour
4 cups fresh or frozen corn kernels
6 cups chicken stock
1 teaspoon white pepper
2 medium potatoes, unpeeled and diced
2 cups half-and-half
6 slices Cheddar cheese
1½ cups grated Parmesan cheese
½ cup chopped green onions, to garnish

PREPARATION
10 mins.

Cut the croutons with a 2-inch biscuit or cookie cutter and toast in a 350° oven for 8–10 minutes.

COOKING
45 mins.

In a large saucepan sauté the bacon over medium heat till done but not crisp, about 6 minutes. Add the diced onions, celery, carrots, and garlic. Cover the pan and cook briefly, until the vegetables are al dente, not soft, about 8 minutes.

Stir the flour into the mixture until it absorbs the bacon fat and cooks a bit.

Add the corn and chicken stock and bring to a boil. Season with pepper. Add the potatoes. Cook until the potatoes are just done, about 15 minutes. Reduce the heat and simmer for 30 minutes. Remove from the heat.

Heat the cream until bubbles form around the perimeter. Pour into the chowder and blend.

ASSEMBLING
5–10 mins.

In each bowl or cup pour a portion of chowder and float 1 crouton. Cover this with a slice of Cheddar cheese and a heavy pinch of grated Parmesan.

BROILING
6 mins.

Place the bowls in the oven under the broiler until the cheese is a golden brown, about 6 minutes.

Top the chowder with the green onion bits and serve.

MOUNTAIN GAME HASH

[SERVES 6]

This is a hunter's hash that is at home in mountain country and does equally well elsewhere. While Chef Myers's recipe calls for a sausage made with venison and buffalo meat (recipe follows), the hash is equally tasty made with other kinds of sausages.

INGREDIENTS

BROWN SAUCE
1 tablespoon cornstarch or arrowroot
½ cup beef stock, homemade (see page 560) or store-bought

1 pound game sausage in bulk
1 onion, peeled and finely diced
1 green bell pepper, finely diced
1 pound red potatoes, cooked and cut into small cubes
6 eggs poached, to top hash
1 cup hollandaise sauce

PREPARATION
10 mins.

For the brown sauce: In a saucepan blend the cornstarch or arrowroot with 1 tablespoon of the stock. Then beat in the rest of the stock. Simmer for 5 minutes, or until the sauce is lightly thickened. Set aside.

COOKING
28 mins.

In a medium skillet sauté the sausage until brown. Remove the meat from the skillet, drain off all but 1 tablespoon of the fat.

Place the onion and pepper in the skillet, cover, and smother until the onions are soft and shiny, about 8 minutes.

Stir the sausage into the onion-pepper mixture. Add the potatoes and brown sauce. Cover and simmer gently over low heat for 15 minutes. Set aside and keep hot while preparing the eggs and hollandaise.

FINAL STEP

Top a serving of hash with a poached egg and crown with a dollop of hollandaise sauce. A mountain man's dish!

VENISON-BUFFALO SAUSAGE

[MAKES ABOUT 5 POUNDS]

If there is a hunter in the family or among friends, it will be relatively easy to obtain a piece of venison for this sausage. Buffalo may be more difficult to get, but meat from ranch-raised animals can sometimes be found in specialty meat markets that carry game. If no buffalo, use beef.

If you have appropriate barbecue equipment you may wish to smoke the sausage in bulk form or in casings, as does Chef Myers.

INGREDIENTS	*3 pounds venison* *1 pound buffalo meat or stew beef* *1 pound beef suet* *½ teaspoon ground mace or grated nutmeg* *½ teaspoon crushed red chili pepper* *½ teaspoon dried oregano* *1 teaspoon cayenne* *2 tablespoons roughly ground black pepper* *1 teaspoon finely chopped garlic* *2 teaspoons salt* *2 tablespoons chopped fresh parsley* *½ cup water*
EQUIPMENT	Meat grinder (or the friendly butcher). Don't use a food processor; it chews the meat.
PREPARATION 10 mins.	Grind the meats and fat together in the meat grinder twice; coarsely first, then regrind. Perhaps you could ask the butcher or game processing plant to do it, if you have no grinder available.
MIXING 10 mins.	Place the ground meat in a large bowl and add the remaining ingredients mixing with a light motion. Use your hand as a rake. Do not squeeze and squash the meat. It will toughen the meat proteins.
CHILLING overnight	Cover and refrigerate the mixture for several hours or overnight to marry the ingredients.
FINAL STEP	Form into patties or stuff into hog casings and fry or, if desired, smoke.

▰▰▰▰*MOOSE, WYOMING*

Gros Ventre River Ranch— Chef Christian Peschcke-Koedt

The Gros Ventre River Ranch, a working outfit where cowboys tend cattle and dudes, is on the eastern boundary of Grand Teton National Park along the banks of the tumbling Gros Ventre (pronounced "grow vahnt") River, a tributary of the Snake. While it is a working ranch, it is also one of the top-of-the-scale dude ranches in Jackson Hole. The main lodge, guest cabins, and corrals are set amidst meadows, pines, and aspen.

On a sun-splashed patio overlooking mountains and river I had one of the best pasta dishes served on our three-year journey across the country. It carried one of the chef's three names, Peschcke. Full name: Christian Peschcke-Koedt. The middle name, which means chimney sweep, has been carried down through several generations by his Polish forebearers.

Christian, in his twenties, studied food at Columbia State College in California, cooked summers for 250 guests a day at a Yosemite summer camp-resort, and came to Jackson Hole where he was given culinary freedom.

He exercised it well.

PASTA PRIMA PESCHCKE

[SERVES 6]

INGREDIENTS
6 chicken breast fillets
¼ cup white wine
Dash freshly ground white pepper
1 pound bacon, cut into bits
1 pound mushrooms, thinly sliced
1 tablespoon butter or margarine
1 pound fettuccine noodles
¼ cup olive oil, to coat noodles

SAUCE
1 cup sour cream
1 cup (2 sticks) unsalted butter, melted
¾ cup grated Monterey Jack cheese
½ cup dry white wine
½ cup grated Parmesan cheese
¼ cup grated mozzarella cheese
4 garlic cloves, minced
½ cup finely chopped fresh parsley, to garnish

COOKING
25 mins.

Poach the chicken fillets in white wine, uncovered, seasoned with a dash of white pepper, about 10 minutes. Cut into small bite-sized pieces and set aside.

In a medium skillet fry the bacon bits until crisp. Remove from the skillet and drain the bacon on paper towels. Set aside.

Over medium heat sauté the mushrooms in butter for about 5 minutes.

Prepare the noodles al dente (resistant to the bite). Drain and lightly coat with olive oil.

SAUCE
8 mins.

In a saucepan add all of the sauce ingredients except the parsley and stir until it becomes a smooth sauce, about 8 minutes.

ASSEMBLING
5 mins.

Pour the sauce over the noodles and mix together well. Top with the chicken, bacon bits, and mushrooms.

Sprinkle lightly with parsley and serve.

〰〰〰〰〰*On the Road—SALT LAKE CITY, UTAH*

"This Is the Place"
[Brigham Young on locating the church]

Salt Lake City is a comfortable place to be. It has the Great Salt Lake at its front door, and the Wasatch Mountains at its back. It is built to human scale. There's room to breathe. There are no skyscrapers marching along narrow streets to intimidate the spirit. The tall slender spires of the Mormon Temple in Temple Square rise gracefully above a small forest of trees. Sidewalks are wide and shaded. Streets are impressively broad. The church elders who laid out the city in the mid-1800s saw to that when they decreed that streets must be wide enough to allow a wagon train pulled by oxen to make a 180° turn in the middle of a block. The airport is not congested; planes seem to keep to schedules here.

I like the Mormons' city.

It is an old friend, and, as one is with old friends, I am aware of changes. I first came here when Temple Square was protected only by a graceful wrought-iron fence which, visually at least, allowed the church buildings—the Temple and the Tabernacle and others—to blend harmoniously into the rest of the city, much as the White House does in Washington. Today I walked to the square to discover that the old fence has been replaced with a ten-foot-high, thick concrete wall. Security against craziness, I suppose, but I find it discomforting. The Square has suddenly become an enclave. A duchy. A principality. There are gates and they are open and you are welcome to enter. But it is not the same.

Across the street from the Temple is the old and gracious Hotel Utah. Sad to report, it is no longer a hotel but administrative offices of the church. The Angel Moroni standing atop the highest steeple of the Temple looks down on the building. Many nights I have slept under its protective gaze.

▰▰▰▰SALT LAKE CITY, UTAH

A Mormon Cook—Carol Bartholomew

The greatest work you will ever do will be within the walls of your own home.

DAVID O. MCKAY,
President, LDS (1951–1970)

Carol Bartholomew cooks for a husband and six sons—ages five to fifteen —and once a week sees that the family pet, Cornelia, a small corn snake (*Elaphe guttata*) living in a glass box near the refrigerator gets a mouse. She does this in a kitchen of average size and with only the usual appliances.

The family is Mormon, members of the Church of Jesus Christ of Latter-Day Saints (LDS) which Brigham Young settled here with his famous dictum, "This is the place!" Both Carol and her husband, Wynn, a lawyer, were born into the church. She holds two degrees in education from the University of Utah. They were married when they were nearly thirty, late in life by church standards.

"I taught school in California for a while, summered in Hawaii, and had a grand old time until I decided—after a courtship with Wynn—it was time for me to settle down and be what I wanted to be, a Mom."

Carol's reputation as a cook goes far beyond her seven men. She has won a basket of blue ribbons for her pies and salads, and has been flown to Mississippi to make her Paprika Chicken in a national chicken cooking contest. When I asked Salt Lake City food editors to give me the name of one of the best cooks in town, the reply, without hesitation, was Carol Bartholomew. I had also asked that the cook be Mormon because I wanted to know more about the church's reverence for food that goes back to the wilderness years when seagulls descended on a plague of locusts to save the settlement from certain famine.

"We have a joke among us LDS mothers that you can't possibly be active in the church if you don't bake your own bread, can your own fruit, hang your own wallpaper, knit, sew, crochet, and have lots of babies." She laughed. "And in a way it is true.

"But I do the things I like to do. I like cooking. I like canning and food storage, but I hate sewing. I hate to hang wallpaper. I hate to paint, and I am not particularly crazy about gardening. When someone looks at me accusingly and says: 'You mean you don't do your own wallpapering?' Yeah, I don't like wallpapering and I am still a good mother. And I don't breast-feed my kids. I use Similac and, guess what, they still love me."

Carol, Marje, and I were in the kitchen baking—three large loaves of white bread, four dozen large cinnamon rolls.

"You can bet on it. Two dozen of these rolls will be gone one hour after the boys get home from school," she said. "They eat constantly. I don't encourage it. It just happens. And I hear it gets worse! I used to bake all the bread, but I just couldn't keep up with their appetites. So now we supplement it with store-bought."

There are four basic foods that the church believes essential to survival in the event of personal or community misfortune—wheat, sugar or honey, powdered milk, and salt—and all the Mormon families are urged to keep a two-year supply on hand. In addition to packaged foods, she stores three hundred pounds of wheat, which is rotated regularly to keep ahead of the bugs, and borrows a small grinder from the LDS church down the street to mill flour.

There is a big garden back of the house. It used to be even bigger until Carol decided she didn't like gardening. That space went for fruit trees. Now she bottles and dehydrates fruit. ("Bottling" is the peculiar use of a word for what the rest of the country calls "canning.")

Last summer she drove out to a farm and bought all the van would hold of sweet corn. For one day she did nothing but blanch, cut corn from the cob, and package the forty quarts that went into the freezer, enough to last the family for a year. But not without cost. The stove was burned out after eight hours of constant high heat. It was only then she learned that Whirlpool makes a special heavy-duty unit for Mormon cooks to withstand the rigors of so much canning and blanching. She now has one, and this year had no problem with corn. She also made quarts of strawberry, raspberry, and peach jams, as well as dozens of cans of peaches and applesauce.

"I will buy a hundred dollars worth of chickens at a time on sale and freeze them. Several of us will go together to buy hundred-pound bags of nuts. The boys love pizza so when mozzarella cheese goes on sale at a dollar sixty-nine a pound, I buy a huge quantity, shred it in the food processor, put it in small plastic bags, and freeze it. I buy fifty-pound bags of rice, twenty-five-pound bags each of sugar and flour, and syrup in gallon jugs.

"The Safeway supermarket in Salt Lake City could never understand this kind of buying, and finally gave up and went out of business."

There is a sophistication about Salt Lake City, especially with food, that comes as a surprise to a visitor. It is not *despite* the church but because of it. Each year hundreds of young people go out as missionaries to carry their faith throughout the world. For two years they live among native peoples whether in Germany or Japan or Tahiti. In turn, "convert immigrants" come from foreign places to live a while in Salt Lake City or just for a brief visit.

"Wynn was on mission two years in Japan. He spoke the language and ate the food. I came back from Hawaii fascinated with Polynesian dishes. As a result, Oriental food is our choice, kids included."

Yet equally high among family favorites are Carol's ranch stew, doughnuts from a recipe that has been passed down through several generations of Mormons, as well as a dinner wrapped in foil and dropped on glowing campfire coals.

RANCH STEW

[SERVES 6 TO 8]

Mormons have a unique situation with family meals on Sundays, Carol explained. First of all, active churchgoers attend meetings for three hours. (In order to accommodate members who must travel great distances to church meetings, three basic weekly meetings are consolidated into one time block.) This means that after church, family members arrive home ravenous and restless, and it is wise to serve after-church meals which can be cooked during church or which are easy and quick to prepare.

Ranch Stew, which cooks for 5 hours, is an ideal Sunday meal. And delicious any other time as well.

INGREDIENTS

2 pounds beef stew meat, cubed
2 cups peeled, sliced carrots
1 cup sliced celery
One 10½-ounce can condensed tomato soup
1 can (from above) water
2 tablespoons tapioca
2 medium onions, chopped
2 medium potatoes, peeled or unpeeled, cut into bite-sized
  pieces
2 teaspoons salt
¼ teaspoon freshly ground black pepper
1 tablespoon Worcestershire sauce

EQUIPMENT

One Dutch oven or ovenproof sauce pot with tight-fitting lid—this is an ideal crockpot stew

PREPARATION
5 mins.

Combine all of the ingredients in the Dutch oven or pot.

BAKING
250°
5 hours

Bake for 5 hours. Do not remove the lid during baking time.

BRIGHAM YOUNG'S BUTTERMILK DOUGHNUTS

[MAKES ABOUT 18 DOUGHNUTS]

Brigham Young ate only 2 meals a day, but they were substantial. At breakfast, he often ate cornmeal mush, hot doughnuts with syrup, codfish gravy, and a roasted squab from his pigeon house. As a cereal, he ate a bowl of popcorn covered with rich milk.

INGREDIENTS

¾ cup buttermilk
½ cup granulated sugar
¼ teaspoon baking powder
½ teaspoon baking soda
½ teaspoon salt
¼ teaspoon grated nutmeg
1 egg
1½ tablespoons butter, melted
2 cups all-purpose flour
Vegetable oil or shortening, to fry
Confectioners' or granulated sugar, to dust

EQUIPMENT

One large heavy frying pan; frying or candy thermometer

PREPARATION 30–50 mins.	Mix the milk, sugar, baking powder, baking soda, salt, nutmeg, egg, and butter in a large bowl. Add the flour gradually, using just enough so that the dough is firm enough to handle yet as soft as possible. Allow it to stand for 15 minutes. If the dough should seem thin, chill it for 30 minutes before rolling.
SHAPING	Turn the dough out onto a lightly floured board and knead it for a few minutes. Roll out to about ¾ inch thick. Cut it with a floured doughnut cutter or sharp knife into 3-inch rounds, cutting out and saving the centers. They are delicious when fried.
REST 5 mins.	Place the doughnuts on a lightly floured piece of wax paper and let them rest for about 5 minutes.
FRYING 360° 6 mins. each batch	Using a large, heavy pan and a thermometer, heat about 3 inches of oil or shortening to 360°. Fry 3 doughnuts at a time, about 3 minutes, turning them with a fork or tongs when one side is browned, and continue to fry until brown all over, about 6 minutes. Reheat the fat to 360° before frying the next batch. Fry the holes separately.
FINAL STEP	Drain on paper towels and dust with sugar.

FOIL DINNER DELUXE

[SERVES 1]

This is Carol's complete out-of-doors meal for her boys or anyone with a big appetite! Drop it on the hot coals and in 20 minutes there's a large dinner for a hungry hiker, cyclist, swimmer, or whomever is just lounging around camp.

INGREDIENTS	*1 potato, peeled and sliced* *2 carrots, peeled and sliced* *½ pound lean ground beef* *One 4 x ¼ x 1-inch strip of Cheddar cheese* *½ teaspoon seasoned salt (Lawry's)* *⅓ onion, thinly sliced* *½ cup pineapple chunks* *3 slices crisp-fried bacon, chopped* *Barbecue sauce, to taste*
EQUIPMENT	Lay out and cut an 18 x 12-inch piece of extra-heavy-duty aluminum foil

continued

PREPARATION
4 mins.

Parboil both the potato and carrot slices for 3 to 4 minutes. Drain and set aside.

ASSEMBLING
10 mins.

Fashion the ground meat into an oblong piece 5 x 2 x 2 inches. Split the meat in half and tuck in the slice of cheese. Seal the meat around the edges and place in the center of the foil. Sprinkle with the seasoned salt.

Place over the meat, in this order: potato, carrots, onion, pineapple, and bacon.

Pour the barbecue sauce over all.

Fold and seal the foil securely. The packet is ready to be cooked now or refrigerate for later.

GRILLING
20 mins.

When the time and place are right, place the foil dinner over hot coals and cook for 20 minutes, with sealed side of foil up.

The package will be steamy hot to open so take care.

⋙⋙⋙ SIOUX CITY, IOWA

A Game Dinner—Penny Fee

Game is a healthy, warming and savory food,
fit for the most delicate palate and easy to digest.
In the hands of an experienced cook, game can
provide dishes of the highest quality which raise the
culinary art to the level of a science.
                                    BRILLAT-SAVARIN *(1755–1826)*

Game cookery has always puzzled me. So much of it is a matter of judgment based on long experience. There is no butcher to vouch for the tenderness of a chop or loin, no butcher to bone a leg or tie a roast. In the wild you take what's offered, as is. No money-back guarantee.

My father was the editor of a small country newspaper in Indiana and was often gifted with game by local hunters who appreciated a mention in the *Zionsville Times* of their prowess in the field. Over the years

this mixed bag included squirrels, rabbits, ducks, coots, geese, frogs, turtles, and, on one occasion, a muskrat proffered as something it wasn't, much to my mother's distress. To make certain the meat of whatever it was was tender, my mother cooked it for a long time. Tenderness, not taste, was her goal. The wild flavor was lost. Squirrel tasted like rabbit that tasted like coot. But delicious.

Our dinner with Penny Fee and her husband was different. She was making not one but two game dinners, one immediately following the other. We were in Sioux City for a short stay, so she and her hunter husband, Paul, wanted us to enjoy a range of game tastes and textures.

The first dinner was ruffed grouse, the finest of all the game birds, Paul believes. Larger than a quail, each bird weighs about one pound. The meat is all white (the bird walks more than it flies so no dark meat in its muscle structure). To accompany the grouse were wild rice and corn niblets cut fresh from the cob.

The second dinner, was Hasenpfeffer, the traditional German dish of rabbit marinated in vinegar. This time we feasted on two wild rabbits which had been taken in early winter when rabbits are plump. (I suffered a pang each time Penny referred to them as "bunnies.") A tiny pumpkin, no more than three inches across, its seeds scooped out, had been filled with maple syrup and butter before the top was replaced and baked. Delicious. Also with the Hasenpfeffer were its traditional companions— potato pancakes, rye bread, and beer. The dessert for this most satisfying two-entrée game dinner was a pear, perfectly poached, with an almond custard sauce.

It was the kind of dinner after which I would have loved to lounge before a fire with a fine cognac in one hand and a long, fragrant Havana cigar in the other. Trouble is, I no longer smoke.

We talked about game cookery.

Penny: "Quail and grouse are very similar. Grouse is considerably larger but it is prepared the same way. We do as little to them as possible. On occasion, if it's not fat, we may wrap the bird in bacon. These birds were fat so all I did was sauté them in a little butter and olive oil in a medium-hot skillet to give them a rich brown color—and then into the oven with a light marinade of cranberry sauce, chicken broth, onion, and a touch of crème de cassis."

Paul: "We try not to make game something it is not. These are wild birds. They are supposed to taste like wild birds. I tell my friends, 'If you don't like the taste of wild birds, don't eat wild birds. If you do, expect the wild flavor.' "

Penny, the cook and a high school French teacher, met Paul, the hunter and a Sioux City physician, after she returned from France where she had escorted several high school students including the eldest of Paul's four sons. Paul was a widower. Their first date was a one-hundred-mile drive to Omaha to dine in a fine French restaurant.

"I was impressed," said Penny.

The second date was something else again. She was taken ice fishing by father and sons. The boys ranged in age from seven to fourteen. "We caught a string of beautiful bluegills and then I was invited to the house to fry them. You wouldn't believe their kitchen! Five bachelors! Pots and pans and dishes piled everywhere. I did the fillets and made corn fritters. They loved it; said I was the best cook ever. Would I come back and cook again?

"The third date was to admire the ducks feeding in the flooded cornfields on his farm along the Missouri River. I knew then I was destined to be a game cook. We were married two years later."

Paul is now the sole hunter in the house. The four boys have grown and left home. One is a doctor, one a lawyer, and two are in college.

Penny does not hunt. "Before we got the hunting dogs, I was the dog—walking and flushing the birds. Now, with the dogs, I go along to be outdoors and to be the hunter's companion. But not with a gun."

The Fees have a game dinner at least twice a week during the hunting seasons and once or twice a month other times.

Over coffee Penny and Paul spelled out their list of do's and don'ts for wild game.

• "If you shoot it, you eat it! That's been the rule in raising our four boys as hunters.
• "Game birds are rare and precious. Know what you are doing. Don't be greedy, and don't waste anything." (Penny earlier that evening had served a delicious pâté made with grouse livers and truffles.)

- "We shoot rabbits for meat, not sport!
- "If the rabbit has fat around its kidneys it is probably healthy, no trichinosis. [Author's note: I once brought home a rabbit that I had chased down on foot in an open field. My father would not let my mother cook it. "Any rabbit my son can catch has to be sick."]
- "Birds. Let them hang for the weekend or, if it is warm, just a day.
- "Clean game well. Try not to cut the intestines. If shot through, cut out the exit wound and area around it.
- "Look game over well. Try to remove all shot. Warn guests that despite the cook's best efforts they may bite into a shot.
- "Don't overcook or it will be gray and stringy.
- "Don't oversoak in salt water.
- "Wines and liquors in cooking help to tenderize game and enhance its flavor.
- "To freeze game, place pieces in a milk carton, fill with water and freeze.
- "Finally, don't expect game to taste like something it isn't. Enhance its flavor, but don't try to mask it."

QUAIL LIVER PÂTÉ

[MAKES ½ POUND]

A creamy smooth pâté dotted with bits of truffle. If short of quail livers, try grouse or pheasant.

INGREDIENTS
1 cup quail, grouse, or pheasant livers
½ medium onion, coarsely chopped
½ garlic clove, bruised and chopped
2 tablespoons flour
½ teaspoon salt
¼ teaspoon each allspice and white pepper
2 tablespoons unsalted butter, room temperature
½ cup whipping cream
1 tablespoon cognac
¼ teaspoon grated nutmeg
Truffles, minced

EQUIPMENT
One 1-quart mold—small casserole, pâté or galantine mold—greased; a sieve; 1 large baking pan to hold mold

PREHEAT
Preheat the oven to 325°.

continued

PREPARATION
15 mins.

Place all of the ingredients *except* the truffle bits (to be added later) in a blender. Blend until smooth. Through a sieve pour into the prepared mold. Stir in the truffles.

BAKING
325°
1 hour 15 mins.

Cover the dish or mold with a tightly fitting lid or piece of foil and set in a larger pan. Fill the pan halfway up with boiling water. Bake for 1 hour and 15 minutes.
    Cool, then refrigerate.

FINAL STEP

Set out 30 minutes before serving. Serve with toast points.

WILD DUCK WITH SAUSAGE, APPLE, KRAUT, AND BEER

[SERVES 4 TO 5]

Penny uses older, darker, and less plump ducks in this recipe. No matter, they are tender and flavorful. Precise ingredient amounts are difficult to give, because they depend on the size, condition, and number of ducks.

PREPARATION
10 mins.

Fill duck cavities with pieces of uncooked pork sausage links, raw onion pieces, raw unpeeled apple pieces. Put in a greased roaster.
    Top ducks with 1 large can sauerkraut and 1 bottle of beer. Caraway seeds are optional.

BAKING
350°
55 mins.

Preheat oven to 350°. Cover and cook for 40 minutes. Uncover so ducks can brown, about 15 minutes.

FINAL STEP

Ladle juices over duck pieces and serve.

HASENPFEFFER

[SERVES 6]

If wild rabbits are not at hand, try domestic ones. Either way, delicious, especially when served with potato pancakes, rye bread, and beer.

INGREDIENTS

6 to 8 slices bacon, finely chopped
2 wild rabbits
½ teaspoon each salt and freshly ground black pepper
½ cup flour
½ cup onions, finely chopped
¾ cup red wine vinegar

1 cup chicken stock, homemade (see page 562) or store-bought
1 bay leaf

EQUIPMENT

One 5-quart roaster or flameproof casserole with tight-fitting lid

PREPARATION
20 mins.

In the roaster or casserole cook the bacon over moderate heat, stirring and turning it frequently, until it is crisp, 10 minutes. Drain on paper towels. Set the pan and bacon fat aside for a few moments.

Cut the rabbit into serving pieces. Cut away and discard the belly meat. Into a brown paper bag put the salt, pepper, and flour. Shake the bag with a few rabbit pieces at a time to coat with the flour mixture.

PREHEAT

Preheat the oven to 325°.

BROWNING
30 mins.

Heat the bacon fat over high heat until it sputters.

Add the rabbits, a few pieces at a time, and brown them on all sides, regulating the heat so they color evenly and quickly without burning, about 10 minutes. As they are done, transfer to a serving plate.

Pour off all but 2 tablespoons of fat and cook the onions in it until they are soft and translucent. Pour in the vinegar and chicken stock and add the bay leaf. Bring to a boil over high heat, scraping in any brown bits clinging to the bottom and sides of the pan.

BAKING
325°
1½ hours

Return the rabbit and juices to the roaster or casserole. Add the drained bacon. Cover the vessel tightly, and simmer for 1½ hours, or until the rabbits are tender but not falling apart.

FINAL STEP

Serve the rabbit directly from the roaster or casserole, or arrange the pieces attractively on a heated platter.

VENISON MEDALLIONS IN BING CHERRY SAUCE

[SERVES 6]

When I asked Penny to write down the recipe for this venison recipe, she added this footnote: "This is wonderful!"

When working out your timetable, plan to marinate the venison for at least 2 hours. Overnight is better. Serve with wild rice, topped with toasted pine nuts and watercress. If no cress, use endive or, as a last resort, parsley.

INGREDIENTS

6 to 8 venison tenderloins, 1 inch thick

MARINADE
2 tablespoons olive oil
2 onions, chopped
1 garlic clove, bruised and chopped
1 carrot, coarsely chopped
1 cup beef stock (see page 560) or bouillon
1 teaspoon beef extract
1 cup dry white wine
¾ cup red wine vinegar
8 juniper berries
1 teaspoon dried thyme
½ teaspoon dried coriander
1 teaspoon freshly ground black pepper
1 bay leaf

SAUCE
2 cups fresh or frozen pitted Bing cherries
1 cup ruby port
3 tablespoons Bing cherry jam

¼ cup (½ stick) unsalted butter
Fresh sage leaves, to garnish

EQUIPMENT

One large heavy frying pan

PREPARATION
10 mins.

Trim off all the fat and membranes from the meat. Cut the meat 1 inch thick. Place in a glass pan.

COOKING
1 hour 10 mins.

For the marinade: In a large saucepan heat the olive oil and add the onions, garlic, and carrot. Cook until the onions are soft and translucent, about 8 minutes. When well browned, add the remaining ingredients, and bring to a boil. Reduce heat, and simmer for 1 hour. Strain.

MARINATING
2 hours–
overnight

Pour the marinade over the venison to marinate for at least 2 hours, but overnight is best.

SAUCE
12 mins.

For the sauce: Drain the medallions, and reserve the marinade. Blot the meat well with paper towels and put it aside to await cooking.

In a saucepan boil the marinade to half its original volume. Check for seasoning—it may need more salt. Add the cherries and port to the sauce. Add the cherry jam. Simmer until the jam is melted, 12 minutes. Again taste for seasoning. Put aside until the meat is cooked.

FRYING
2–4 mins.
per batch

Heat the heavy frying pan and melt the butter until it sizzles. Cook the medallions (don't crowd in the pan) quickly for 1 to 2 minutes on each side.

FINAL STEP

Put a spoonful of sauce under each medallion as you place it on a heated serving plate. Serve the balance of the sauce separately. Garnish with fresh sage leaves.

〰〰〰 *On the Road—PEORIA, ILLINOIS*

Going Home

We had been on the road for ten weeks—seventy days and seventy nights —and we were now within one overnight of home.

Road weary after 9,350 miles? Not really. It always surprises me that we are not. We could keep on driving to new places if there were not bills at home to pay and leaves to rake.

Timothy, our constant companion except for a few days in kennels in big cities where hotels prefer he not be a guest, never tires of scrambling aboard the red van in the mornings. He immediately jumps on the backseat where he has a blanket and a pillow. Later in the morning he will move to the front of the van where the transmission warms a place on the rug. If it's a hot day, he retreats a few feet to catch the breeze from the air conditioner. When the van is moving slowly through traffic Timothy likes an open window, but when it picks up speed it hurts his ears when the wind begins to whistle.

While Timothy has a box in the van for sleeping, he doesn't use it much anymore; nevertheless, he is particular about its position. It must be next to the big carton of books. I had moved his box one morning, but I failed to push it back in place as I should have. Marje and I came back from a breakfast stop to find that he had torn the box apart trying to tug it back to where it belonged. The box also goes into the motel room at night to give him a feel of home.

Normally he is not destructive, but the smell of fresh-baked Norwegian *Sandbakkels* stored in the back of the van in a large plastic box completely undid him. The cookies had been left to mellow for several days before eating. Timothy was not aware of this caveat, so when we left him alone in the van he pawed his way through a small opening to pull out and eat half the *Sandbakkels*.

We never leave Timothy alone in a motel or hotel room. He's happy to stay in the van when we are at dinner or visiting a museum or busy in someone's kitchen. Unchaperoned pets can act crazy at times in strange places, even trustworthy creatures like Timothy. A deposit of $5 to $25 against pet damage is perfunctory in many motels and hotels across the country, and I think it fair. One exception. In a phone conversation with the manager of a hotel on San Francisco's Nob Hill about reservations, I asked if small pets were allowed. "Oh, yes," he said in a gracious voice, "We like pets. All we ask is a thousand-dollar deposit."

Timothy slept elsewhere that night.

VII NEW ENGLAND via CHESAPEAKE BAY

Pennsylvania Maryland Massachusetts

Maine Vermont New York

The New Old Order

The land in Lancaster County is legendary Amish and Mennonite country. Or it was. It is now a developer's dream. The small Old Order Amish farms are being gobbled up for tract houses and light industry. The young people, seduced by high wages in factories and shops, are leaving the farms. As a consequence, with land prices skyrocketing, the old folks are selling the homeplaces—some have been in families for more than 250 years—and moving to town and to church retirement villages in Southern states. While some folks have grown too old to farm, others have no heirs. And some can't resist $10,000 an acre for land that cost them little or nothing.

The land is a rare blend of silt loam on limestone which needs no irrigation and is the most productive farm land east of the Mississippi. Each year hundreds of acres of this precious soil are torn up and covered by golf courses, amusement parks, shopping malls, and parking lots as well as houses and factories. In fact, Lancaster has taken on the ambiance of a gigantic theme park with 5 million visitors annually coming to buy antiques and gawk at the Plain Sect farmers and their families coming into town in their horse-drawn buggies.

We had visited Lancaster forty years before and had found it a charming, believable community that was authentically Old Order Amish. Horse and buggies far outnumbered cars. Amish meals could be got in homes and small restaurants, not like today, with meals taken in cavernous barnlike structures that seat hundreds of guests at a time.

Tonight we ate in one such place—Good 'n Plenty Family Style

Eating. There were a dozen tour buses parked in a lot the size of a football field. Inside, a battalion of young women in Amish costume—modest print dress, apron, and lace cap—were rushing food from the kitchen. It was set before us family style, in deep bowls and wide platters —mustard pickles (chowchow); applesauce; chicken potpie; ham with pineapple; fried fish; fried chicken; mashed potatoes; gravy; corn; squash; pepper slaw; stewed tomatoes; cottage cheese; bread and butter; apple butter; shoofly, rhubarb, and raspberry pies; ice cream; caramel custard; iced tea; milk; lemonade; and soft drinks. Price: $12.50.

No question about it, it was the place for a hungry man and one who likes to dine with the multitude.

There was one magic moment tonight. I had walked a distance along the edge of a freshly plowed field behind the motel to look at the night sky away from the dazzle of highway lights. It was quiet. Then I heard it. The fast clop-clop-clop of a horse's iron-shod hooves striking against the hard pavement. I could see only the dim lights of a buggy coming fast down the backcountry road. Occasionally a spark flew as a metal shoe caught a stone just so.

It was a magic moment for the driver, too. He was calling softly to the horse, telling it what a good steed it was and that they would soon be home. I could sense more than see horse, man, and carriage as they came abreast of me, perhaps fifty feet away. Then they were gone—their place in the night marked only by a tiny taillight receding in the distance.

For a moment I had stood in another century.

LUSBY, MARYLAND

A Chesapeake Bay Compound—Frances Fischer, Peggy Simpich, E. Gertrude Bernadine Bean, and Lillian Wells

Lusby is a settlement of a few thousand souls on the western side of Chesapeake Bay, just north of where the Patuxent River flows into the bigger body of water. It is about a sixty-mile drive southeast of Washington, D.C.

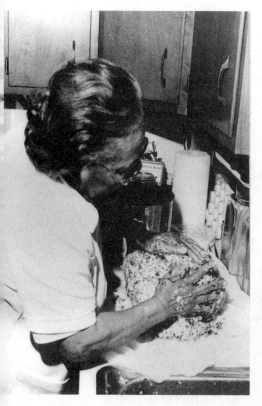

E. Gertrude Bernadine Bean

Frances Fischer

A newcomer to the community is my friend Bill Simpich. Many years ago we were fellow executives of a New York public relations firm; I was its man in San Francisco while Bill was based in the home office. The invitation from Bill to visit was irresistible. Family and friends would do specialties of the area, Bill wrote. Peggy Simpich would prepare Crab Cakes. Her sister, Frances Fischer, would do her Crab Imperial; while a neighbor, Lenore Shaw, would arrange for two acclaimed black cooks who lived nearby to come to her house and stuff a ham, Maryland style.

Yes, I replied in haste, we would be there.

There are three houses in the Simpich "compound" at the end of a narrow gravel road behind the small rural church, the Olivet United Methodist. Grassy lawns slope gently down to Mill Creek which, in turn, leads into the Patuxent River. On the water there is a steady procession of pleasure boats as well as watermen making their way to and from the fishing grounds outside. Bill, an Annapolis graduate, traded a sailboat for a traditional waterman's vessel that has ample room on the open deck behind the wheelhouse for a load of fish, oysters, or crab. But the boat is used chiefly by children and grandchildren who come to summer on the water. Sunk in the water at the end of the dock are his crab pots that provide the families with an occasional crab feast.

The preparation of the ham began one dreary morning in Lusby. The two women were shredding the second head of cabbage when I came dripping wet out of a rainstorm and into Lee Shaw's kitchen where work on the ham was just beginning.

"Miss B" (Mrs. E. Gertrude Bernadine Bean) was seated on a stool offering a suggestion now and then to Lillian Wells, who was doing her first stuffed ham. Miss B, who is accepted throughout the community as one of its finest cooks, cooks not only for her husband, a waterman on Chesapeake Bay, and family and friends but caters for social affairs for miles around. Lillian, director of the local Senior Companion Program, and also a fine cook, had taken the day off to help her friend, Miss B. It was a joint project for the visitors' benefit.

The salt-cured or "corned" ham was parboiling in a big pot of simmering water. While the ham cooked, Lillian was hand-cranking a small mountain of vegetables through a food grinder to make the stuffing.

After the ham is parboiled, said Miss B, it will be lifted from the water and allowed to cool.

"The cuts are the most important thing," she said, picking up a razor-sharp knife she has brought with her from home. "This is a medium-size ham, so I'll make my cuts over the top and sides, not on the bottom as I would do with a larger ham. Some folks make their cuts all the way through so they can stuff from top and bottom, but I don't do it that way. I just go deep—about as deep as my fingers."

Miss B made a total of fourteen cuts, about three inches long, between the strings holding the ham together. The cuts were lengthwise, along the grain.

She vigorously attacked each cut with a handful of vegetables, tamping in the mixture with her fingertips. For half an hour she returned again and again to each cut to wedge in the most she could.

When it seemed the ham must be full enough to burst, Miss B pronounced it done. It was tightly wrapped in cheesecloth, tied, and placed back in the kettle. It simmered for about four hours.

It was sliced and served warm at dinner. It would be equally delicious cold, Miss B said.

Miss B has only cooked with a salt-cured ham, but she said other country hams should have the same good flavor.

CRAB IMPERIAL

[SERVES 6]

Fran Fischer calls herself the compound's "mother." She and her husband and kids were the first to come here in the late 1940s. In the summers that followed there came a stream of houseguests from New York and Washington. Finally it was decided that the guests who came most frequently should build their own houses, thus creating the three-house compound.

"Look, I cook but I don't consider myself a cook," she protested when Bill Simpich introduced her as one of the best cooks on Chesapeake Bay. "I knew nothing about cooking when I got married, but I married a man who loved to eat so I thought I'd better have at least a grasp of the fundamentals over and above boiling water."

She was standing at the counter picking over a mound of white crab meat for shell fragments.

"This is not lump meat, the very best, but backfin, which is all I could get today. It's picked from in between the back fins, and there are usually shell fragments that must be picked out.

"These I didn't catch. While I have crab pots off my dock, I bait them only when the children are coming down. Then I serve them the easy way. I steam the crabs, stack them on a picnic table, and let everybody pick his own."

Butter is an important ingredient to her Crab Imperial.

"And I melt it and set it aside as the very first thing even though it is added last. The full 1½ tablespoons of lemon is important. So is mustard, but it doesn't have to be the fancy kind. French's ordinary hot dog mustard is fine."

The recipe is for 6, to be baked in individual ramekins such as scallop shells or a shallow baking dish.

INGREDIENTS	_1 tablespoon unsalted butter, melted_
	1 pound crab meat
	¼ teaspoon salt
	1 cup mayonnaise
	½ tablespoon prepared mustard
	½ teaspoon Worcestershire sauce
	1½ tablespoons lemon juice
	Paprika, to dust tops
EQUIPMENT	Six ramekins or seashells for individual servings, or one 6-cup flat baking dish
PREHEAT	Preheat the oven to 400° 10 minutes before mixing the ingredients.

continued

PREPARATION
10 mins.

Melt the butter first. Set aside.

In a large bowl mix all of the ingredients together in the order listed above, except for the butter, which is added last.

When thoroughly mixed, divide the crab among the ramekins (or put in the baking dish), sprinkle a pinch of paprika over each, and place in the oven.

BAKING
400°
15 mins.

Bake for 15 minutes, or until it is bubbling.

Serve immediately.

CRAB CAKES

[SERVES 6]

I realized I had never eaten a crab cake—a real-for-sure crab cake worthy of its name and pedigree, a Maryland crab cake that is mostly crab and little cake—until Peggy Simpich set hers before us at dinner. The first bite told me that until that moment I had been doing business with counterfeiters who loaded their crab cakes with crumbs and fillings and not much crab.

Peggy uses only 9 crushed crackers in the 1 pound of crab meat to help the 2 eggs and a bit of mayonnaise hold the soft and wet mixture together until she can get it into the pan.

Crab cakes make a fine entrée, a sandwich, or, in a smaller size, a delicious hors d'oeuvre.

INGREDIENTS

9 saltine crackers
¼ cup chopped onion
1 teaspoon cooking oil
1 pound crab meat
2 eggs, room temperature
3 tablespoons mayonnaise
Dash Worcestershire sauce
½ teaspoon salt, or to taste
1 tablespoon peanut oil, preferably

PREPARATION
13 mins.

Crush the crackers into small crumbs under a rolling pin or bottle and set aside.

Sauté the chopped onion in the oil until soft, about 8 minutes. Set aside.

ASSEMBLING
5 mins.

In a large bowl gently mix together all of the ingredients except the oil. The mixture will be wet. Allow about ⅓ cup of the crab mixture for each cake. On the work surface pat and flatten the meat into cakes.

COOKING
10 mins. per
batch

Heat the peanut oil in a skillet over medium flame. Gently slide the cakes off a spatula into the oil. It is best to do no more than 4 or 5 at a time. Sauté each side for about 5 minutes so the egg is cooked and the cakes are lightly browned.

FINAL STEP

Serve hot.

If by chance all the crab cakes have not been cooked, wrap each separately and freeze. A delicious surprise to spring on the family later.

SOUTHERN MARYLAND STUFFED HAM

[SERVES 12, WITH AMPLE LEFTOVERS]

> *The making of a ham dinner, like the making of a gentleman, starts a long, long time before the event.*
>
> W. B. COURTNEY,
> "Congress Eate It Up"

A Southern Maryland Stuffed Ham is stuffed in the most peculiar way.

The large cavity left in the center of the ham when the butcher removes the bone *disappears* when the meat is tied into a compact bundle with a strong cord. The ham is parboiled. Several long, deep slits are cut and stuffed with a mixture of chopped vegetables—cabbage, kale, onions, and celery—and spices. The ham is wrapped in cheesecloth, boiled for several hours, cooled, the cords cut away, and the meat sliced to reveal deep pockets of green vegetables. Delicious. A ham lover's delight.

INGREDIENTS

One 12-pound country ham, salt-cured preferred
2 large heads of cabbage
1 pound kale
2 pounds fresh or frozen onions
1 bunch celery
2 tablespoons salt
2 tablespoons freshly ground black pepper
2 tablespoons celery seed
3 tablespoons dry mustard
3 tablespoons cayenne (crushed red pepper)
6 to 8 cups hot pot liquor from ham kettle, approximately

EQUIPMENT

One kettle, with cover and bottom rack, large enough to hold ham and water to cover, usually 30 to 40 quarts; 1 smaller kettle in which to mix chopped vegetables and seasonings; food grinder (I use a KitchenAid with shredder attachment through which I can push a steady flow of vegetables. A Cuisinart will do the job but the bowl must be emptied several times); one 4 x 4-foot piece of cheesecloth, double thickness

PREPARATION

Ask the butcher to debone the ham and to tie it with 1 cord lengthwise, 3 cords around its girth. This leaves ample space for the cuts that will be filled with the stuffing.

PARBOILING
1½ hours

In the kettle cover the ham with water, bring to a boil, reduce the heat, and parboil for 1½ hours.

VEGETABLES
25 mins.

Choose a blade for the food grinder to cut the vegetables finely as for slaw.

While the ham is cooking, core the cabbage and discard the coarse outer leaves. Strip the kale from its heavy stems, rinse clean and dry. Peel the onions. Shred all of the vegetables.

Place all of the shredded vegetables in the smaller kettle, add the salt and spices. When the ham is cooked and removed from the kettle, pour 6 to 8 cups of the hot ham liquor over the vegetables to soften and moisten. (Don't make them too soupy.) Mix thoroughly and set aside until the meat is cool enough to cut and stuff.

COOLING
30 mins.

Allow the ham to cool, about 30 minutes, until it is comfortable to handle. Reserve the balance of the liquor in the big kettle for the ham later.

STUFFING
50 mins.

With a sharp knife cut 12 to 14 deep pockets in the ham (see page 486).

Stuffing is not a tidy operation and the only way to do it is with your hands. So, jump in! Use a large pan to hold the ham and to allow you to retrieve stuffing when it drops out as you work it into the cuts (see page 486).

Squeeze each handful of stuffing to take out some of the moisture. Pack each cut as tightly as you can—and then go back and do it again and again. Push it in hard with your fingers. Now do it again.

In determined hands, the cuts will accept an unbelievable amount of stuffing.

Place the ham on the cheesecloth. Spread the remainder of the stuffing over the ham, lifting up the cloth to hold the stuffing against the sides. (This excess stuffing will be served as a side dish later.)

Tie the cheesecloth tightly and securely and place the ham back in the large kettle. Add water necessary to cover.

COOKING
3–4 hours

Bring the water to a boil, reduce heat, and simmer partially covered for 3 to 4 hours—about 15 minutes per pound.

FINAL STEP

Remove the ham from the kettle and allow it to cool. It can be sliced and served warm, although some Maryland cooks let the ham cool 2 hours in the pot likker. They then refrigerate it overnight, in the cloth, before slicing and serving cold.

Serve the extra stuffing that was spread over the top of the ham as a side dish.

ᐳᐳᐳᐳᐳOn the Road—GETTYSBURG, PENNSYLVANIA

Outflanked

I am a Civil War buff and I have visited the Gettysburg battlefield a number of times but not with Marje, who usually does not share my enthusiasm for this piece of the American experience. Today she did, and for two hours we were in the hands of Phil Cole, a professional guide we booked at the Visitors' Center. He drove our van, which made it easier for me to concentrate on battle formations. However, I discovered he did not like me to interrupt his smooth-flowing military commentary with such questions as "Who harvests the corn growing in this field?," "Is there vandalism in the park?," and "What's that big bird? (Answers: a local farmer who leases the field. Yes, considerable, especially broken stone guns and swords on monuments. Turkey buzzard.)

After one thousand monuments and cannons along forty miles of scenic avenue, we returned to the motel. Tour buses had surrounded the place in our absence. We were outnumbered and outflanked.

I asked the motel manager about the noise factor with so many visitors. "Not bad," he said. "It's spring and high school kids by the thousands are coming on class tours. Now that the weather is nice we are getting a lot of elderly folks on tour, too.

"The good part of it is they don't seem to get in each other's way. The adults are in bed early while the kids yell and scream and chase each other around the pool all evening. They're noisy but early the next morning while the kids are in bed, and wish to stay there, the adults get revenge. They are up early and outside the rooms laughing and scratching and calling to friends across the patio. They outdo the youngsters."

We planned to leave midmorning, in the window of opportunity between generations.

⋙ MARSHFIELD, MASSACHUSETTS

Miss Bradford

When Elizabeth Bradford was born, her brother, who later would become governor of Massachusetts, looked down in the crib and then up at his mother: "Why, she is just a wee bit, isn't she!" From that moment and for the eighty-four years to the present, she has been known to the family as We-bits and Wibs.

This will help explain why so many recipes in the Bradford family's notebooks and files begin with—"This came from Aunt Wibs. . . ."

Bradford history both in and out of the kitchen goes back 350 years. From one of Massachusetts's most distinguished families, Miss Bradford is a ninth-generation direct descendant of Plimoth Plantation's longtime Pilgrim governor William Bradford, who, among other achievements, appropriately, established Thanksgiving Day.

Miss Bradford and her brother, Charles, live on the outskirts of

Marshfield (pop. 3,300) in a charming Colonial house, part of a show-place farm once owned by a nephew of P. T. Barnum. Some walls erected in the late 1600s are part of the old house. A graduate of the Windsor School and Radcliffe College, for many years she taught children with learning disabilities in schools in Boston and Marshfield. She retired a dozen years ago.

"Mother was an old-fashioned cook and she loved it," said Miss Bradford. "She didn't care how much trouble it was to prepare a dish. I can't say that I have the same dedication. While I am *the* cook in this small household, I don't consider myself *a* cook. I am not a gourmet. I don't live to eat."

She was not convincing. It became clear as we talked about her mother's and grandmother's recipes—some are two hundred years old and written in ink on well-thumbed pages held in an old leather binder —that she has had a long and loving acquaintanceship with all of them, from potted pigeons to Irish moss blancmange, a pudding, and many of her own, one of which is Perfect Mince for Pies.

"Mother called her recipes 'receipts and rules.' For example, her rule for the tops of the traditional Thanksgiving pies reads: 'Be sure to cover the mince pies with a lattice crust, as mince always has 'slats'; the 'civered' is apple, and the 'open' is squash."

LUMBERJACKS—GINGER COOKIES

[MAKES 4 DOZEN COOKIES]

This recipe was brought to the Bradford house a century ago by a cook who had baked them by the thousands for hungry lumberjacks in a Maine logging camp. "No matter how often she made them," Miss Bradford said, "the men thought they were wonderful."

While Miss Bradford pressed her cookies flat with the bottom of a glass, I press them into shape with my thumb. The neighborhood kids now ask for "thumbies."

The camp cook used whatever shortening she had—bacon or ham fat, chicken fat, beef drippings, lard, or "whatever." The choice is yours. I use vegetable shortening.

INGREDIENTS
1 cup molasses
1 cup brown or white sugar
1 cup shortening, of choice

continued

1 egg, beaten
2 teaspoons ground ginger, or more if desired
1½ teaspoons baking soda
1 teaspoon salt
2 cups all-purpose flour, approximately

EQUIPMENT

One or 2 baking sheets, greased or lined with parchment paper. (A second sheet speeds the operation. While one sheet of cookies cools, the second sheet can be filled and go into the oven.)

PREHEAT

Preheat the oven to 350°.

PREPARATION
BY HAND OR
MIXER
15 mins.

In a mixing or mixer bowl stir together the molasses, sugar, and shortening until creamy. Add the beaten egg and blend. Stir in the ginger, baking soda, and salt.

Add the flour, ¼ cup at time, until the dough is a mass that will not stick to the fingers when pinched.

SHAPING
10 mins.
per sheet

Place the dough on the work surface alongside the baking sheet. Pinch off a piece of dough and roll it between your palms into a round ball the size of a marble or large grape. Place the dough ball on the baking sheet and flatten thin with the bottom of a glass dipped in flour. (Dipping the glass in water also works, while I flatten mine with a thumb.)

Repeat until the sheet is filled with paper-thin cookies.

BAKING
350°
12–15 mins.

Bake for about 12 to 15 minutes. Don't scorch. They should be lightly browned. Allow the cookies to cool on the baking sheet, since they are quite fragile when hot.

FINAL STEP

When the cookies have cooled, store in an airtight container.

These cookies will keep for weeks in a tin box. If the cookies in time should lose their crispness, give them new life in a 250° oven for 10 minutes. The dough can keep almost indefinitely in the refrigerator.

PERFECT MINCE FOR PIES

[MAKES ABOUT 3 QUARTS FOR 3 PIES]

Ask for Civil War Pie at the Bradford table and you will be served a slice of mincemeat pie with this filling.

"When my niece, Rebecca Chase, was a little girl, Mother baked this pie and during the course of dinner Mother remarked that 'this is a mince pie Grandmother baked during the Civil War.' The next day at second-grade show-and-tell Rebecca stood beside her desk to announce: 'Yesterday I had a pie made in the Civil War.' "

INGREDIENTS

2 pounds ground beef, as for hamburger
1 pound suet
3 apples
2 lemons
2½ cups apple cider
1½ pounds seedless raisins
1 pound currants
2 cups sugar
1 cup molasses
1 tablespoon grated nutmeg
1 tablespoon salt, or to taste
¾ tablespoon each ground cloves and ground cinnamon
2½ cups sherry and brandy mixed

EQUIPMENT

Food mill; sterilized jars or a crock

PREPARATION
40 mins.

In a skillet fry the ground beef over low heat, just until the pink is gone, about 5 minutes. Discard the grease.

Cut the suet into pieces and feed though a food chopper using the finest blade. Mix the hamburger and suet together in a large bowl.

Finely chop the apples and add to the meat. Seed the lemons, finely chop, and add to the mixture.

Bring the cider to a boil and pour into the mixture.

Add all of the other ingredients, except the sherry-brandy mixture, which will be added *after* cooking.

COOKING
10 mins.

In a large saucepan bring the mincemeat to a boil, reduce the heat, and simmer for 5 minutes.

COOLING
10 mins.

Allow the mince to cool, add half of the sherry-brandy, reserving the balance for bake day.

AGING
3 weeks

Pour the mincemeat into the sterilized jars, cover tightly, and keep in a cool place. Shake or stir the mincemeat daily for 3 weeks. The mincemeat may also be kept in a crock and covered with plastic wrap stretched over the top.

FINAL STEP

As the filling is used for pies, add some of the remaining sherry-brandy mixture to each.

Lay a dozen plump raisins and 6 paper-thin slices of citron on top of the filling in each shell. Top with a lattice crust and bake at 400° for about 40 to 50 minutes.

THREE-X SPONGE CAKE

[MAKES 1 CAKE]

While it may sound like a recipe put together by a mathematician out of whimsy, the instructions for making this deliciously moist sponge cake have been handed down for generations by Bradford women. And always verbally.

Bradford cooks have been challenged to memorize the instructions as did their mothers, grandmothers, sisters, and aunts. It is a matter of Bradford pride that they have not been written down, that is, until now.

"Think of it always in multiples of three," Miss Bradford said. "The weight of three eggs in sugar plus half that weight in sifted flour and the zest of two lemon halves and the juice of a third. These ingredients—except the yolks—are divided into thirds. The egg whites are dropped into three small bowls."

The recipe that follows is in a somewhat simplified form.

Why did Miss Bradford suggest that it be in this book? She and her brother were concerned that this longtime family favorite would be lost to posterity if it were not recorded.

"Despite family tradition, the cake is simply too good for that to happen, I believe," said Miss Bradford.

The basic 3-X recipe of the weight of 3 eggs makes a small cake, indeed. In the following recipe I have tripled the ingredients to make a bountiful 9-inch cake—again multiples of 3.

INGREDIENTS	*9 large eggs (weight: 20 ounces)* *3 cups sugar (weight: 20 ounces)* *3 cups sifted all-purpose flour (weight: 10 ounces)* *Juice and zest of 1 lemon*
EQUIPMENT	One large and 3 small bowls; one 10-inch tube or bundt pan, buttered and dusted with flour
PREPARATION 20 mins.	(*Note:* Miss Bradford insisted that the yolks in a large bowl be beaten by hand. The whites may be whipped by an electric mixer. The dry ingredients are placed in small piles on wax paper on the work surface until needed.) Separate the eggs—yolks in a large bowl, whites equally in the 3 small bowls. Keep the whites chilled in the refrigerator until needed. Divide the sugar into thirds. Sift and divide flour into thirds. Divide the lemon zest. The juice, however, can be added at one time during the first mixture.
PREHEAT	Preheat the oven to 300°.

<table>
<tr><td>BEATING
20 mins.</td><td>Beat the eggs yolks to a light yellow. (Miss Bradford does it on a large platter with a flat whisk.) Add one third of the sugar, one third of the flour, one third of the lemon zest, and all of the lemon juice to the yolks. Beat.

In the small bowl or mixer bowl beat 3 egg whites until dry and peaked. Fold the whites into the big bowl.

Add the next third of the dry ingredients, plus 3 more beaten egg whites.

Add the final third of the dry ingredients plus the last 3 beaten egg whites.</td></tr>
</table>

BAKING 300° 30 mins. 350° 30 mins.	Pour the batter into the prepared pan and place in the moderate oven. Bake for 30 minutes, increase the heat to 350°, and bake for another 30 minutes. Test for doneness with a cake testing pin. The top will be lightly browned and somewhat rough, like a macaroon.
FINAL STEP	Place the cake on a rack. When the cake has cooled, turn it out (and over) onto a plate—and then over again to present the macaroon top. Delicious served with fresh berries or peaches.

〜〜〜〜NORTH ANDOVER, MASSACHUSETTS

A New England Cook—Beverly Jones

My correspondence with Beverly Jones had progressed to the point where we were sharing deep culinary secrets. When she wrote, "I would rather have something authentic *occasionally*, like real whipped cream on a slice of apple pie, than something not authentic *routinely*, like Cool Whip," I knew she was my kind of cook. When she followed with "moderation not abstention makes better sense," I placed her in my kitchen pantheon.

A handsome blond woman, Bev Jones is fortyish, a mother of four (one a West Point cadet), and wife of a tall, rangy G.E. engineer. She's ebullient about life. She radiates exuberance about everything she does. And she is an exceptionally fine cook.

Beverly, Massachusetts-born and a University of Massachusetts graduate with a home economics degree, taught in the inner-city schools of Pittsburgh for several years when she and Lewis were first married. "I was lucky. The kids were first-generation Czechoslovakian. They were the sweetest children. Well-behaved. Smart kids. Anxious to learn. They were a generation behind the big-city kids. Thank goodness! They even brought presents to the teacher. Imagine!"

The Jones house is authentically early American situated in an estate setting of broad lawns and magnificent oak and maple trees. It had been out in the country before the city of North Andover grew around it. Out back there is a grassy hill up which horses pulled wagons into the upper reaches of a barn that is no longer there. Only a few stones of the old foundation peek through the grass. Several outbuildings, silver-gray with age, still stand. One is filled with garden equipment and lawn mowers. On the south side of another outbuilding is a patch of rhubarb, planted there to catch the warm rays of a springtime sun to coax the plants out of dormancy for the first rhubarb pie of the new spring.

The three of us—Beverly, Marje, and I—spent the day cooking traditional New England dishes in the big kitchen of the old house. We began with fresh cranberry muffins as a midmorning snack and then moved on to fish chowder for lunch. Both delicious.

The tempo picked up with Indian pudding, to be topped with ice cream, that welcomed the two Jones kids when they got home from school in the afternoon. At intervals the Jones station wagon raced down the driveway to shop for fiddlehead ferns (the season was just beginning), and, finally, a selection of lobster, scallops, shrimp, and several scrod fillets.

Next stop was the rhubarb patch in front of the old work shed. Dessert for dinner—deep-dish rhubarb pie made with a cream cheese pastry.

Next chore was to clean the fiddleheads, a crisp, crunchy springtime delicacy in the Northeast as well as in the Northwest (see Fiddlehead Fern Omelette, page 437). They are ostrich ferns before the fronds unfurl. When these little ferns come up along riverbanks and streams during May, the heads are covered with a thin brown membrane. As the heads grow, the membrane breaks into flakes.

Beverly brushed off the brown flakes of the half pound she bought for dinner. "They're easy to prepare. Place them in a saucepan, salt, add a half inch of water, and bring to steaming point over high heat. Lower the heat and cook, probably five to ten minutes, and then test them with a fork. Don't overcook or they get slimy. Yes, slimy. There is just no other way to express the state they will be in. Tonight I will serve them with salt, pepper, and butter.

"I also microwave fiddleheads. It's even easier. Dot with butter, sprinkle with lemon juice, cover with Saran Wrap (to steam), and punch in the level and time."

Daughter Christina was home from school and she was peeling and chunking butternut squash for dinner. Son Josh had been mowing the big yard. He called a momentary halt and came into the kitchen for a bowl of frozen cranberry shrub his mother had made the night before.

I mentioned to Beverly that I was nearly overwhelmed by the work she was cramming into a dozen hours.

"Moderation?" I asked.

"Well," Beverly said, laughing, "this day is special. I want you and Marje to experience all of the good things we love in Massachusetts, so I am compressing three days into one. Enjoy."

NEW ENGLAND FISH CHOWDER

[SERVES 8 TO 10]

If possible, buy a whole fish to start this chowder for it will provide the stock as well as the meat. There are two other options: Beg a fish frame for stock from the fishmonger at the time you buy the fillets, or make a stock with a commercial food base (Gourmet Edge is a good one) of fish or chicken bouillon. At times I have used bottled clam juice with good results.

The following recipe assumes you are starting with the whole fish.

INGREDIENTS

STOCK
4 pounds haddock, cod, or scrod, cleaned
4 cups cold water
4 sprigs parsley, stems and all
2 bay leaves
2 stalks celery, chopped
½ onion, roughly cut
8 peppercorns

¼ pound salt pork, cut into ¼-inch dice
2 large onions, finely chopped
⅓ cup flour
1 pound potatoes, cut into ¼-inch dice
1 cup cream or evaporated milk
2 quarts whole milk
½ cup (1 stick) unsalted butter, room temperature
Salt and freshly ground black pepper, to taste
Dash monosodium glutamate (optional)

EQUIPMENT

One large stockpot

PREPARATION
25 mins.

Place the whole fish in the stockpot and cover with 4 cups of water. Stir in the remaining stock ingredients. Simmer the fish for 15 minutes over medium-low heat, or until the fish flakes when picked by a fork.

Remove the fish and set aside on a platter to cool. Pick the meat off the bones and reserve.

SIMMERING
30–40 mins.

Put the bones back in the stock and simmer for an additional 30 to 40 minutes. Strain and reserve the stock. Discard the bones.

While the stock is simmering, fry down the salt pork in a large skillet until the cubes are golden, about 8 to 10 minutes. Remove with a slotted spoon and drain on paper toweling. Set aside to garnish the chowder when served.

ASSEMBLING
20 mins.

For the chowder: Sauté the onions in the pork fat until the onions are golden and soft. Add the flour, stirring to make a roux. Cook for 3 to 4 minutes.

Cook the diced potatoes in the fish stock until barely tender, about 10 to 15 minutes.

Carefully, to avoid splattering, add 2 cups of hot stock to the roux, stirring until thickened, and add to the potatoes and fish stock in the large pot.

Heat the cream and milk together in a saucepan and when hot—but not scalding—pour into the fish stock. Bit by bit stir in the soft butter. Add the salt and freshly ground black pepper. A dash of monosodium glutamate is optional.

Add the fish and bring the pot back to hot before serving.

FINAL STEP

Serve hot with a sprinkling of the reserved crisp pork cubes on top.

The chowder base, before the addition of potatoes, cream, milk, and butter, may be frozen. Those should be cooked and added at serving time.

CRANBERRY MUFFINS

[MAKES 1 DOZEN LARGE MUFFINS OR 24 SMALL]

These muffins are delightfully tart and nutty. The cranberries are chopped frozen so they won't squash, nor will the red juice spread through the batter when mixed.

INGREDIENTS

STREUSEL
¼ cup chopped walnuts
¼ cup brown sugar
2 tablespoons flour
2 tablespoons rolled oats or bread crumbs
¼ teaspoon ground cinnamon
1 teaspoon orange zest

BATTER
2 eggs
1 cup granulated sugar
½ cup (1 stick) unsalted butter, melted
1 cup (8 ounces) lemon yogurt
2 cups flour
1 teaspoon baking powder
1 teaspoon orange zest
1 cup frozen cranberries
¼ cup chopped walnuts

EQUIPMENT

Tins for a dozen large or 24 small muffins, greased or Teflon

PREHEAT

Preheat the oven to 375° before mixing the batter.

PREPARATION
15 mins.

For the streusel: Mix all of the ingredients together in a bowl and set aside.

For the batter: In a large bowl beat together the eggs, sugar, and melted butter. Stir in the yogurt, flour, baking powder, and orange zest.

Roughly chop the frozen cranberries, and stir into the batter. Add the walnuts.

ASSEMBLING
5 mins.

Spoon the batter into the muffin tins to three-quarters full. Sprinkle the streusel mix on top of the batter.

BAKING
375°
25 mins.

Bake for 25 minutes, until browned and muffins test done.

FINAL STEP

Remove the muffins from the oven and cool on a wire rack.

⋙⋙⋗PORT CLYDE, MAINE

Lobster Dinner—Anne Johnson

When you are invited to the Johnsons' for a Maine lobster dinner you make every effort to be there. The sea cannot provide a more delicious food. Hollywood cannot script a more fitting locale. The Johnsons' cooking is superb.

The Johnson house sits within two hundred feet of the Atlantic Ocean; only a strip of lawn and a narrow shoreline of massive granite slabs and boulders lay between it and the water. After having been landlocked in Indiana for long periods, it is always an exciting moment for me to walk to the edge of the open ocean and fantasize what strange and wonderful landfall lies beyond the horizon. In this instance, I lost some of that wonder when Treby Johnson said he thought it would be Bordeaux, on the French coast, which is all right but not quite the exotic place I could wish for.

Anne Johnson is an accomplished cook. To the delight and encouragement of her mother, Anne, at age eight, stood on a kitchen chair to stir her first endeavor, a chocolate pudding. "Mother didn't mind how much of a mess I made in the kitchen just so I cleaned it up."

The culinary accomplishments of Treby are limited to just one—a caramel corn concoction that must bake for an hour in the oven. Treby's talents lie in other directions, ranging from lobster steaming (more about that later) to neighborly advice on real estate and financial matters. He retired a few years back as head of a heating oil company in Augusta, the state capital, about forty miles away, where they spend the winter months away from the coast's raw weather. There will be a surprise in store if you look to your right as you walk across the lawn to the house.

There, resting on the grass, is the "African Queen." It says so in bold black letters painted on the prow of the twenty-foot green dory. Like the big hunk of steam engine Humphrey Bogart nursed down the Ruki River, this vessel has what looks like an engine in the middle, standing six feet tall, with all the necessary pipes and valves and fittings, a steam whistle, and a ten-foot-tall stack.

Fired up and puffing smoke and steam, with an occasional whistle blast, this African Queen does *lobsters!*

Treby explains. "This is an oil-fired steam boiler that once supplied heat to an old mansion in Augusta. I stripped off the insulation so all of the machinery and pipes would show, painted it black, and set it in the dory.

"You see this pipe? This is a steam line running fifty feet underground to the garage, where I do the lobsters."

The pipe connects to a stainless-steel box, about the size of a bushel basket, fastened to the outside wall of the garage.

"I fire up the Queen, get a good head of steam going, and then walk over here, drop in the lobsters, and close the cover. I turn a valve and in shoots the steam. Twenty minutes later my lobsters are done."

Treby was doing only six lobsters for tonight's dinner, not worth the bother of using the Queen.

There was one night in particular, which he delights to recall, when he and the African Queen did a special batch of lobsters.

"A business associate from New York City who had never been to Maine came for a visit. He had heard all about our lobsters, of course, so I promised him a fine lobster feast. I told him I'd show him how we harvested them. He could help. He was pretty much a city fella and didn't know much about lobstering."

Treby and I walked to the water's edge past a wooden fence on which hung dozens of brightly colored buoys broken loose from lobster traps and cast up on the rocks.

"When the tide goes out," he explained, "it leaves all these nooks and crannies in the rocks filled with water.

"So before my guest arrived I had a dozen big lobsters sent over here to the house. I put on my heavy gloves, because they're mean rascals, and I dropped a lobster in the pool here, another lobster over there, until I had them scattered in pools all along the front of the house.

"When he got here I said, 'Why don't we go down to the rocks and see if we can find enough lobsters for dinner?' He thought that was a great idea.

" 'Here's one,' he shouted. 'And, look, here's another one—and over there is another one.' He could hardly contain himself.

"I found a couple. He found more. 'I've never had so much fun,' my friend cried. Finally when we had collected the dozen I said, 'I think this is enough for today, don't you? We don't need any more.' "

Treby swore that to this day his friend believes that all you do in Maine to get a lobster for dinner is to step out your front door.

In the kitchen Anne was at work. We were to have lobster; scallops baked in cream; scalloped tomato casserole; lightly boiled fiddlehead ferns; New England baked beans; spinach and rice salad, and Indian Pudding.

One lobster was left when dinner was over. Anne urged us to take it to our house. "Promise me you'll make Lobster Scramble with it for breakfast," she said.

Marje said she had never heard of lobster scramble, but, yes, she would try it in the morning.

I thanked Anne for her introduction to scramble, which I now think is the most delicious way to have a lobster. We were so taken with it that I bought lobsters for scramble on three successive mornings.

LOBSTER SCRAMBLE

[SERVES 2]

Here is Lobster Scramble in Anne's own words.

"It is one of the most delicious ways ever to serve lobster—and so simple. Remove all of the meat from a 1½-pound lobster and cut it into bite-sized pieces. Have the meat at room temperature, of course. In a bowl stir 4 eggs with a tablespoon of cream or rich milk. Add salt and pepper to taste. Heat butter in a skillet over medium heat. Stir in the lobster pieces and the eggs. Take the skillet off the heat while the eggs are still moist. Lobster and eggs are truly meant for each other."

BAKED SCALLOPS

[SERVES 6]

This was my first taste of Baked Scallops. I liked them.

INGREDIENTS	*1½ pounds scallops, washed and wiped dry* *¼ teaspoon each garlic powder and seasoned salt* *Pinch of freshly ground black pepper* *Cream or half-and-half to cover scallops* *1 cup bread crumbs* *½ cup crumbled cornflakes* *¼ cup (½ stick) unsalted butter, melted*
EQUIPMENT	One casserole or baking dish large enough for scallops to fit in single layer, sprayed with Pam
PREHEAT	Preheat the oven to 425°.
PREPARATION 10 mins.	Place the scallops in the baking dish in a single layer. Season with the garlic powder, seasoned salt, and pepper. Pour the cream to the top of the scallops—not over them. Spread the bread and cornflake crumbs over the top of the scallops. Drizzle the butter over the surface.
BAKING 425° 12 mins.	Bake uncovered for 12 minutes.
FINAL STEP	Take from the oven and serve from the casserole.

MAINE BAKED BEANS

[SERVES 8]

The wonderful aroma all day long of beans baking in a Maine kitchen is almost as good as when they are eaten. Maine people feel that baking beans is one of the best of all regional cooking customs.

Some cooks in New England like all maple syrup and no molasses in which to bake their beans, while others prefer all molasses, usually unsulfured, which gives the beans a richer and stronger flavor.

INGREDIENTS	*2 cups white pea beans (see page 248)* *¼ cup each maple syrup and unsulfured molasses* *4 teaspoons dry mustard* *1 teaspoon salt* *1 medium onion* *6 to 8 whole cloves* *½ pound salt pork*
EQUIPMENT	One 3- to 4-quart bean pot
BEFOREHAND overnight	Pick over the dry beans. Wash them. Place in a large bowl, cover with water, and soak overnight. If you forget to soak the beans, boil them until the skins of a spoonful of beans will pop open when you blow on them, about 5 minutes. Drain the beans.
PREHEAT	Preheat the oven to 250°.
PREPARATION 15 mins.	In a deep bowl mix the maple syrup, molasses, dry mustard, and salt. Stir in the drained beans and mix together until all of the beans are coated. Stud the onion with whole cloves and place on the bottom of the bean pot. Ladle the beans and seasoning into the pot and over the onion. Score the salt pork with cuts down to the rind. Rinse in hot water and place on top of the beans. Add boiling water, about 3 cups or enough to cover the beans. Cover the bean pot with its lid or a piece of heavy foil.
BAKING 250° 8 hours	Bake the beans for 8 hours. They should not be stirred, but they do need attention occasionally, for they need to be kept covered with liquid at all times. The bean pot itself needs to be kept covered until the last hour of baking then removed so the beans will brown on top and the pork will become crisp.

FINAL STEP

Serve the beans directly from the pot.

Leftover beans may be refrigerated in the same pot; tightly covered with foil and plastic wrap, they can be kept safely for a week to 10 days. The beans will absorb the cooking liquid as they stand; add a little water before reheating them in the oven.

INDIAN PUDDING

[SERVES 4]

One of the most traditional of Colonial America's desserts, Indian Pudding is even more traditional than apple pie, which actually has a European heritage.

INGREDIENTS

3 cups milk
¼ cup cornmeal
1 teaspoon salt
½ cup molasses
1 teaspoon ground cinnamon
½ teaspoon ground ginger
2 eggs, beaten

EQUIPMENT

One 2-quart crock or casserole, generously buttered

PREHEAT

Preheat the oven to 325°.

PREPARATION
10 mins.

In a large saucepan, heat 2 cups of milk to just below boiling. In a medium bowl, combine the cornmeal, salt, molasses, cinnamon, and ginger. Gradually whisk in the scalded milk.

COOKING
15 mins.

Pour the pudding mixture into the saucepan, and cook over moderate heat, stirring, until the mixture boils, thickens, and becomes creamy, about 15 minutes. Stir in the eggs.

BAKING
325°
3 hours

Pour the pudding into the buttered crock or casserole and bake in the middle of the oven for 1 hour. Do not cover. Pour the remaining cup of cold milk into the pudding as it bakes, stirring it well, baking about 2 hours longer. The longer the pudding bakes, the darker and thicker it gets. It is done when a tablespoon of pudding lifted from the crock holds its shape.

FINAL STEP

Serve the pudding at once, directly from the baking dish, or let cool and serve at room temperature.

Indian Pudding may be accompanied by unsweetened cream or vanilla ice cream, if you like.

>>>>>_On the Road—PORT CLYDE, MAINE_

Taciturn?

New Englanders have a reputation, deserved or not, of being spare with words. They are spoken of as closemouthed and taciturn. Where others need dozens of words to express a sentiment, these people do it with "yup" and "nope." Or so cartoonists, writers, and playwrights would have you believe.

I have news for them.

I stopped at a roadside lobster/restaurant/souvenir shop to buy yet another lobster for a Lobster Scramble. I pointed out my choice of lobster to the young man standing by the glass tank. He had been feeding a fire under a black kettle of boiling water when I drove up. He said it would take about fifteen minutes to boil the creature. I went inside the store where two ladies were arranging a new supply of souvenirs on the shelves and a third was fussing with the cash register.

Fifteen minutes to wait, keep in mind.

In those few minutes I learned:

• The lady behind the cash register was born in Maine sixty-one years ago and owns the place.

• The competing lobster stand directly across the road is run by her husband: "We get along better three hundred feet apart."

• She wants to sell the business and move someplace where it is warm in winter. Probably Florida, where the family goes for three months.

• These are her sisters helping. One runs the gift shop, the other the restaurant. Her mother comes in occasionally to help dust.

• That's her grandson doing my lobster. He's not married. He recently graduated from a Florida flight school and wants to fly for Delta or United.

She was still talking when I picked up my lobster and left.

~~~~~~MONTPELIER, VERMONT

New England Culinary Institute— Chefs Lyndon Vikler and David Miles

David Miles

There are four seasons in Vermont—Foliage, Winter, Mud, and Summer.

Foliage is October, when the leaves peak in a riot of colors to dazzle the thousands of out-of-state visitors touring the back roads. Every guest bed in the state has been booked for months in advance.

Winter is skiing.

Mud is spring, when water from melting ice and snow saturates the gardens and fields but cannot drain because the granite underneath won't allow it.

Summer is a short span of a few weeks, yet the harvests in the orchards and gardens demand superlatives.

David Miles, Manhattan-born but now a deeply committed Vermonter, was telling me about life and times and food in the Green Mountain State. We were seated in the Elm Street Cafe, one of the best places to eat in Montpelier, and one that affords a rich learning experience for the students in the New England Culinary Institute located here. For eight years he has been on its faculty. In addition to teaching food theory and meat fabrication, he is responsible for the smooth running of the school's restaurant, which is only a block or so from the State House. The restaurant enjoys a brisk trade with legislators when they are in town and all the time with lawyers of which, per capita, there are more than in any other capital city.

David is coauthor of a cookbook, *Fresh from Vermont*, published by the state's quarterly travel magazine, *Vermont Life*.

"We have an incredibly short growing season in Vermont," he said, "but the results are fabulous despite the weather. Two years ago we had frost every month—I mean *every* month! It doesn't happen every year but often enough to give you pause about starting a garden. A true Vermonter takes it in his stride and plants a large one anyway.

"The results are unbelievable. People who have cooked with California and Florida produce are blown away with the quality and flavor of Vermont fruits and vegetables."

The culinary institute, highly regarded by chefs and hoteliers across the country, has its main campus on a hilltop overlooking Montpelier. A satellite campus is at Essex, near Burlington, the state's largest city. There the chefs and students do all the food service for a luxury hotel, The Inn at Essex.

Later I talked with Pam Wilkins, a native Vermonter, who shares David's enthusiasm about produce grown in the state.

"It should come as no great surprise, really," she said. "After all, here you are dealing with an agricultural society. Its people are thrifty. They make do out of necessity. And they do it exceptionally well. A true Vermonter, for example, always has a big black soup kettle sitting on the back burner for every kitchen scrap, trimming, and bone. Nothing is wasted. It smells great. It tastes great.

"Out behind the house, even in town, you'll find a few chickens for eggs and meat, and perhaps a couple of rabbits. On the edge of town they'll have a milk cow and a young porker or two. Maybe a sheep."

I said that I had not seen a single hog as we drove across the state. "The reason," she said, "is that they keep the pigs penned in close because of the foul weather, and put them down [butcher] young."

A first-year student (it takes two years to graduate), Pam is thirty-eight years old. She is now fulfilling a longtime ambition to have a country inn in rural Vermont. "You are not going to make any money unless you know how to use everything you get and present it in the right way. The school is good for that. We learn not to waste, which appeals to my Vermont frugality." With a degree in accounting, she had been an auditor for the U.S. Postal Service for fifteen years. But she longed to get into food. It has not been easy. She is at school for a long day that begins at 5:30 A.M. and does not end until about 4:00 P.M.

"It helps remembering back when I pulled all-nighters before exams in college—and survived.

"My husband and kids urged me to do this—and then helped make it possible. My seventeen-year-old son takes care of his three-year-old brother. Imagine, he has given me a year of free baby-sitting. And then my husband fills in where and when he is needed."

With our discussions focused chiefly on Vermont's superb garden produce, I chose two of Elm Street Cafe's excellent salads for the book.

GRILLED CHICKEN, SNOW PEAS, AND CASHEW SALAD

[SERVES 6]

This salad with a soy-sesame vinaigrette dressing is the creation of faculty chef Lyndon Vikler.

INGREDIENTS

MARINADE
1 cup soy sauce
¼ cup sesame oil
½ cup finely chopped green onions
3 tablespoons red wine vinegar
3 tablespoons minced fresh ginger
2 tablespoons sugar
1½ teaspoons minced garlic
Dash cayenne pepper

3 to 4 (1½ pounds) whole chicken breasts, boneless and skinless

continued

DRESSING
1 tablespoon sugar
2 tablespoons soy sauce
3 tablespoons vinegar of choice
2 tablespoons sesame seeds
1 teaspoon salt

SALAD
2 heads of salad greens (Boston red leaf or romaine and finely sliced iceberg head lettuce)
1 cup grated carrots
50 snow peas, stemmed, blanched, and shocked (rinsed in cold water)
6 water chestnuts, thinly sliced, or 3 peeled broccoli stems, thinly sliced
1 cup alfalfa sprouts

⅔ cup chopped roasted cashews or slivered almonds

MARINATING
1–2 hours

Combine in a bowl all of the marinade ingredients, and marinate the chicken for 1 to 2 hours in the refrigerator before grilling.

GRILLING
6 mins.

Grill the chicken over medium-hot coals for 3 minutes on each side. Baste with the marinade. Don't overcook. Remove the meat from the grill and when cool shred into bite-sized pieces.

ASSEMBLING
15 mins.

Combine the dressing ingredients in a small bowl.

Toss the salad greens in dressing, but use it sparingly. Mound the lettuce in the center of each of 6 salad plates. Top with grated carrot, moistened with the dressing. Arrange the snow peas in a pyramid over the greens. Arrange strips of chicken in the same pyramid fashion, alternating with water chestnuts or broccoli stem slices.

Surround the salad with a thin ring of alfalfa sprouts.

FINAL STEP

Garnish with a sprinkling of cashews or almonds.

It is a handsome presentation. Serve with pride.

CRACKED WHEAT SALAD WITH CHICKEN AND VEGETABLES

[SERVES 4]

This salad by Chef Miles received an A+ in my kitchen notebook. It contains a generous amount of bulgur (cracked wheat), which I especially like for its nutty flavor and crunchy texture.

INGREDIENTS

MARINADE
1 garlic clove, peeled, smashed
¼ cup chopped fresh parsley
Juice of 1 lemon
½ teaspoon freshly ground black pepper
⅓ cup olive oil

1 pound boneless, skinless chicken breasts

CRACKED WHEAT
1 cup bulgur (cracked wheat)
1 teaspoon salt
Boiling water, to cover while soaking

DRESSING
2 tablespoons white wine vinegar
1 tablespoon lemon juice
Dash Tabasco sauce
¼ cup olive oil

SALAD
4 green onions, sliced
12 sugar snaps, trimmed, blanched, chilled, cut into ½-inch
*   pieces*
1 small zucchini, washed and diced small
1 tomato, seeded and diced
1 red bell pepper, seeded and diced
½ cup chopped fresh parsley
½ cup chopped romaine lettuce

BASE AND GARNISHES
Romaine lettuce, large leaves for salad base
½ cup crumbled feta cheese
2 small tomatoes, cut into 8 wedges
8 whole black olives, pitted
8 wedges pita bread, toasted

continued

MARINATING
1 hour

Mix the marinade ingredients in a bowl. Marinate the chicken breasts for 1 hour or more in the refrigerator.

GRILLING
6 to 8 mins.

The marinated chicken can be grilled beforehand in a broiler or over a grill until just done, about 6 to 8 minutes. Don't overcook. Set aside for at least 10 minutes before shredding into bite-sized pieces.

SOAKING
20 mins.

Place the bulgur and salt in a bowl and pour boiling hot water over them. Let soak for no more than 20 minutes. The bulgur grains should be al dente, not mealy. Pour into a sieve and with a rubber spatula press out any excess water. Set aside.

DRESSING
5 mins.

To make the salad dressing, combine in a small bowl the vinegar, lemon juice, and Tabasco sauce. Whisk in the olive oil to blend.

ASSEMBLING
10 mins.

In a large bowl toss together the bulgur and all of the salad ingredients including the chopped romaine lettuce. Toss lightly with the dressing.

Cover 4 dinner plates with the large lettuce leaves. Mound the salad on the leaves and top with shredded chicken. Garish with a sprinkle of feta cheese, the tomato wedges, and olives.

FINAL STEP

Serve with 2 toasted pita wedges per plate.

▰▰▰WEST TOWNSHEND, VERMONT

Windham Hill Inn—Ken and Linda Busteed

When Ken and Linda Busteed left Indiana eight years ago to buy a country inn in Vermont's Green Mountains, they little dreamed that Windham Hill Inn would become celebrated not only among travelers but among aspiring innkeepers who regularly come to see how the Busteeds do it.

Up the mountain from the village of West Townshend, through a birch and pine forest, I turned the van into the drive, past the barn (five guest rooms), and parked in front of the rambling 160-year-old white clapboard house (ten guest rooms).

When I stepped out of the van I realized the air was filled with the excited high-pitched twitter of barn swallows crisscrossing the sky as they swooped down to the banks of a nearby pond, standing momentarily on wobbly legs unaccustomed to walking, to scoop up dabs of mud. With a whir of wings, they lifted off and flew to nests taking form under the eaves of the barn.

"Hospitality here," Marje said as she watched the nest builders.

Others have thought so too, for the inn has collected kudos galore as one of the best inns in America. The governor of Vermont, Madeleine Kumin, a frequent guest: "Windham Hill lives up to the expectations of any New Yorker or Bostonian who conjures up a romantic vision of a Vermont country inn." Then she added almost as an afterthought: "It also lives up to what a Vermonter expects a Vermont country inn to be!"

It becomes quickly apparent to a Windham Hill guest that the cuisine here is special. Good food far above the ordinary.

In five-course dinners over two days the dishes ranged from asparagus *en croûte*, sherried peach bisque, shrimp vichyssoise, bitter lemon sorbet, pork tenderloin with maple-mustard sauce (see below) to beef with braised onions, mushroom nut strudel, green beans in a bundle tied with lemon rind, walnut mousse, and strawberries Pompidou, a shortcake with fruit spooned on top of a small meringue case and topped with crème fraîche.

Linda Busteed is self-taught, a natural cook. She had cooked at home for a family of five, but never for dozens daily. When she realized that it was she who was to become the baker/cook/chef of the inn, she signed up for cooking classes in Indianapolis, read a number of cookbooks, and clipped recipes from every food magazine on which she could lay her hand.

Linda: "Actually, taking over in this kitchen was *not* a challenge. The previous cook/owner did what she called home-style cooking, principally meat and potatoes. One night while she was still here she braised a cut of beef smothered in Franco-American gravy. After dinner I overheard one guest say: 'I thought the lamb tonight was wonderful!' "

Ken, with degrees in math and chemistry from Wagner College, left an executive position with the Indiana Health Services Corporation to come to Vermont. Linda, a graduate of the New York School of Interior Design, had foregone a career in home decorating in Indianapolis for this life as an innkeeper.

It was winter when the two of them first saw Windham Hill. A deep blanket of snow lay over the mountain and the inn.

Ken: "It looked beautiful! It really did. Right out of Currier and Ives. Any moment I expected a horse-drawn sleigh to come out of the barn with bells jingling. I didn't realize what problems lay hidden under the snow. While it was beautiful on the outside, we were hit with its dreariness when we stepped inside. God! I mean dreary!"

Linda: "We finally said, yes, we would buy it. We rushed back to Indiana to sell our house and arrange financing for this place. Looking back, I can see that the greatest joy we had was fantasizing about the things we would do—furnish it with antiques, tear out this wall, partition that room, rebuild the kitchen, serve this dish, and on and on through the night. It was fun."

Ken: "We had three small boys and a dog in the back of the station wagon when we drove up the hill that spring day to become innkeepers. It was as if someone had dropped a two-ton block on our heads. The snow had melted. It was the mud season. Everything lay exposed, warts and all. The place looked terrible. We were overwhelmed. Devastated is what we were."

Linda: "And our first guests were coming in two days. Somehow we got by. Gradually things changed for the better."

The Busteeds, both in their mid-fifties, are proud of what they have achieved. He has written numerous magazine articles on inn management and regularly holds seminars for budding innkeepers in the New England states.

Ken: "When you ask a longtime innkeeper about going into the business, the first thing he'll do is warn you about the long hours and the low return. But you really don't listen. You are in love with the idea. You refuse to believe there is a down side.

"The hours are unbelievably long. I mean long as in l-o-n-g. The commitment it total. I thought I had been working long hours in the corporation, but it was nothing compared to innkeeping. Here it is literally twenty-four hours a day, seven days a week. For eight years Linda has been doing all of the baking and cooking and, in her spare time, the decorating. We have fifteen rooms, usually about thirty guests, which means we are not big enough to hire more staff and too big to do it all ourselves."

Yet in the late evening when the dinner guests have left and the kitchen is closed, the Busteeds get away from it all with a dinner prepared by Linda in the small kitchen in their apartment. "Sometimes by candle-light and always with a glass of wine," she said.

"It keeps us sane."

PORK TENDERLOIN
WITH MAPLE-MUSTARD SAUCE

[SERVES 4]

Pork tenderloin is marinated in a mixture that includes 9 herbs plus salt, then after it is baked a sauce of pure Vermont maple syrup and Dijon mustard completes it nicely. A great combination.

INGREDIENTS	*MARINADE* *5 bay leaves* *1 teaspoon each ground cloves, grated nutmeg, dried thyme* *½ teaspoon each cayenne pepper, ground allspice, ground cinnamon, dried basil, freshly ground black pepper, and salt* *2 pork tenderloins, about 3 pounds total* *Olive oil, to rub meat* *SAUCE* *¾ cup pure Vermont maple syrup* *½ cup Dijon mustard*
EQUIPMENT	One medium roaster
MARINATING 2–3 hours	Mix the marinade spices in a small bowl and rub into the meat. Cover the meat and refrigerate for 2 or 3 hours.
PREHEAT	Preheat the oven to 375°. Bring the meat to room temperature.
ROASTING 375° 30 mins.	Rub the meat generously with olive oil. Place in the roaster and roast until the meat's internal temperature reaches 150°, about 30 minutes.

continued

While the meat is cooking, whisk together the maple syrup and mustard.

FINAL STEP   Slice the meat and serve with the maple syrup–mustard sauce.

CLAIM-TO-FAME GRIDDLE CAKES

[MAKES 18 6-INCH AND 24 4-INCH CAKES]

Making and serving these good griddle cakes will allow anyone to stake a claim to fame. These are tender and darker than most griddle cakes, thanks to the whole-wheat flour. Linda drops the batter on the griddle with a plunger-type doughnut maker. The result is an interesting ring-shaped griddle cake with a center that's just perfect for an extra dollop of syrup.

INGREDIENTS   *½ cup stone-ground whole-wheat flour*
2 tablespoons cornmeal
½ teaspoon baking powder
½ teaspoon salt
¼ teaspoon baking soda
1 egg
2 tablespoons cottage cheese
½ cup buttermilk
2 tablespoons corn oil
1 tablespoon pure maple syrup

EQUIPMENT   Griddle, oiled

PREPARATION
5 mins.   In a large bowl stir together all of the dry ingredients. Place the moist ingredients in an electric blender or food processor. Blend at medium speed or a few bursts in the food processor.

Pour the liquid mix into the flour, stirring until the batter is well blended.

COOKING
time depends
on griddle size   Ladle some batter onto the oiled grill, turn the griddle cake when slightly puffed and bubbles appear, in 2 or 3 minutes. Cook for another 2 to 3 minutes or until golden brown. Repeat until the batter is used up.

FINAL STEP   Great served with butter and warm Vermont maple syrup.

STEAMED CRANBERRY PUDDING

[SERVES 10 TO 12]

Simmered in water like Boston brown bread, this delicious steamed pudding is served with a white vanilla sauce topped with a candied cherry.

INGREDIENTS
1½ cups all-purpose flour
2 teaspoons baking soda
⅓ cup hot water (120°–130°)
½ cup dark molasses
2 cups fresh or frozen cranberries

SAUCE
½ cup granulated sugar
1 cup half-and-half
½ cup (1 stick) unsalted butter
1 teaspoon vanilla extract

12 candied cherries, to garnish

EQUIPMENT
Two 1-pound coffee cans, each greased and fitted with a disc of buttered wax paper cut to fit the bottom of the container; 1 large kettle

PREPARATION
12 mins.
In a large bowl stir together the flour and baking soda.
In a small bowl stir the hot water into the molasses and add the cranberries. When thoroughly blended, pour the mixture slowly into the dry ingredients. Stir just enough to mix. Don't overstir. The batter will be very thick.

SHAPING
10 mins.
Divide the batter between the 2 cans. Tie a foil cover tightly over the top of each. Don't puncture.

STEAMING
2 hours
In the bottom of a large kettle with a cover place a rack on which the cans can rest. Pour hot water up to half the height of the cans, and bring the water to a slow boil.
It may be necessary to add more water during the 2-hour period. Steam until the pudding is springy to the touch and no longer sticky. Probe one with a toothpick or metal skewer—if it comes out clean and dry, the puddings are done.

COOLING
1½ hours
Remove the puddings from the kettle and allow the tins to cool before turning them on their sides and slipping the puddings out, about 30 minutes. Work with care because the puddings are fragile. Place them on a cooling rack before wrapping them in foil to put in the refrigerator to chill before serving.

continued

SAUCE

5 mins.

For the sauce: Stir together in a saucepan the sugar, half-and-half, and butter. Gently simmer over low heat for about 5 minutes. Stir in the vanilla.

FINAL STEP

Cover each slice of pudding with a generous serving of sauce. Garnish with a candied cherry.

MAPLE–POPPY SEED DRESSING

[MAKES 1 PINT]

This salad dressing put together by Linda, with Vermont's famous maple syrup as its chief ingredient, is delicious on fruit or spinach salad. Simple to make, it keeps for several weeks in a jar stored at room temperature.

INGREDIENTS

¾ cup maple syrup
1¼ teaspoons salt
½ cup apple cider vinegar
1⅓ cups cooking oil
1½ teaspoons dry mustard
3 teaspoons poppy seeds

PREPARATION

5 mins.

Mix all the ingredients together and store at room temperature.

✕✕✕✕✕SPRAGUETOWN ROAD, GREENWICH, UPSTATE NEW YORK

Rock Hill Bakehouse— Michael and Wendy London

Emma, a Jersey cow with soft, luminous eyes, polished horns, and slender hocks, set the tone of this visit to Rock Hill Bakehouse. She was being milked when we walked up the hill, past the springhouse, to the small barn where she mothers Lily, her calf.

This could only happen at Michael London's, where a registered milk cow is on a daily diet of eight loaves of whole-wheat and rye breads, supplemented by a ration of cornmeal and bran. If the supply of her loaves should run short, Michael will fire up the ovens to do a special bake just for her. In gratitude, Emma gives two gallons of rich creamy milk each day, so much, in fact, that the surplus is churned into butter and stockpiled in the freezer. (Emma's unusual but rewarding diet was discovered by Michael in an old French farm journal and approved by Emma's veterinarian.)

Michael and Wendy London, two of the best bread and pastry bakers anywhere, France included, came into our lives more than a decade ago with a call inviting us to drop by sometime to visit their bake shop in Saratoga Springs in upstate New York. Drop by we did. Not once but many times. Whenever I need to be inspired to be creative in baking I go to watch these two wholly dedicated people at work.

Several years ago I urged Craig Claiborne, *The New York Times* food columnist and a friend, to visit the Londons. Greatly impressed, he compared the Londons' breads and pastries with those of such famous European shops as Demel's in Vienna, Wittamer in Brussels, Peltier in Paris, and Zauner in Bad Ischl, Austria.

Michael, a handsome man in his early fifties, was teaching contemporary poetry at Skidmore College in Saratoga Springs when he decided baking was what he really wanted to do, and left to apprentice in bakeries in this country and in Italy and France. He was baking in Greenwich Village when he met and married Wendy Wadham, a beautiful young woman who also lived in the Village, baking and selling bread, which she delivered by bicycle.

The bake shop they opened several years later in Saratoga Springs was a huge success but, lamentably, only in the summer months when the town overflowed with visitors to the city's famed racetracks and spas. It wasn't enough.

In 1985 they moved to the country to raise their two young children in a bucolic environment—and bake bread.

Michael speaks of bread with respect bordering on reverence. When he talks of baking he drops such aphorisms as:

- "My aim all along has been to bring together a loaf of bread that is, in and of itself, a complete food."
- "There is a fascinating alchemy in bread baking."
- "The optimal life forces are in a loaf of bread."
- "The elements in a loaf of bread are so elemental that I want to begin with the earth to grow my grain."
- "It is exciting to be the steward of all of these forces."
- "Bread made with a natural starter, rather than a commercial yeast, has more structural integrity."
- "We moved to the country. We moved to the fields. We moved to the bread of the vine." (Translation: His starter is made with fermented grapes.)

The Rock Hill Bakehouse is actually the kitchen/porch in a two-hundred-year-old red-brick farmhouse on eighty-five acres of hilly, rock-strewn pasture and woods near the small town of Greenwich, close to the Vermont state line. Five times a week a truckload of several thousand big crusty loaves—sourdough white and rye, *baguettes*, *pain au levain*, *boules*, and *miches*—go to specialty food shops and upscale grocers from Albany and Schenectady to New York City, where Bloomingdale's is a major outlet. Customers also include neighboring farm families with whom the Londons barter for eggs, honey, fruit, vegetables, and the occasional ham and roast. Mail order, too, has boomed.

The London loaves—chewy and with an old-world flavor and open texture—are in such demand that a large part of the operation will be moved to nearby Schuylerville, a small town of one thousand.

"Wendy and I will continue to bake here in the country at least once a week to take care of our neighbors—and Emma." The labor force in the Schuylerville bakery is three young men in their mid-twenties, who studied under Michael. One is his son Josh.

With the ovens out of the kitchen, the Londons plan to turn the house back as it was in the Federalist period when it was built. A wood-fired brick oven and open hearth at which to cook will be built into the kitchen. It will be the place where customers calling at the house for bread will be welcomed. There will be little or no plumbing. Water will be brought from the well house. Already some of the rooms are lit only by candle; the electrical wiring has been pulled out.

MAX'S LOAF

[MAKES 1 LOAF]

The Max of Max's Loaf is the Londons' son, whose birth his father celebrated by creating this supremely healthful bread of whole-wheat flour, pure honey, and sunflower seeds. There have been thousands of loaves of this bread baked in the London ovens since Max was born a dozen years ago.

INGREDIENTS

¼ cup honey, clover preferred
½ cup buttermilk
1¼ cups hot water (120°–130°)
2 teaspoons salt, if desired
2 packages dry yeast
4 cups whole-wheat flour, approximately
½ cup toasted sunflower seeds, plus 1 cup untoasted, for crust
1 egg yolk and 1 tablespoon milk, to brush

EQUIPMENT

One large (9 x 5-inch) baking pan, greased or Teflon

PREPARATION
BY HAND OR
MIXER
10 mins.

In a mixing or mixer bowl combine the honey, buttermilk, water, and salt. Stir to melt the honey. Add the yeast, 2 cups of flour, and the toasted sunflower seeds. Beat to blend with a wooden spoon or a mixer flat beater. Add the balance of the flour, ½ cup at a time, working it into the dough with the mixer or by hand. (*Caution:* Don't overload the dough with flour too quickly. Give the flour time to be absorbed into the dough, otherwise it may turn into a hard ball.)

When the dough is a rough mass, lift to the floured work surface—or leave in the mixer bowl if using a dough hook.

KNEADING
8 mins.

The dough will become less sticky and more elastic as the kneading continues, but it will never have the elasticity of a white flour dough. If by hand, use a dough blade to help turn and work the dough.

Knead by hand or in the mixer for 8 minutes.

PREPARATION
BY PROCESSOR
5 mins.

This is a dense dough that some food processors cannot prepare successfully. Try it with the plastic dough blade, but if the machine labors under the load, finish the mixing by hand.

Place 2 cups of whole-wheat flour in the bowl and add the honey, buttermilk, water, salt, and yeast. Pulse to blend and dissolve the yeast. Add the toasted sunflower seeds, and the balance of the whole-wheat flour—¼ cup at a time—until the dough forms a ball that is carried around the bowl by the blade.

KNEADING
40 secs.

Process to knead for 40 seconds.

FIRST RISING
20 mins.

Drop the dough into a greased bowl, cover tightly with plastic wrap, and leave at room temperature to rise for 20 minutes.

SECOND RISING
40 mins.

Remove the plastic wrap, punch down the dough with your fingers, turn the dough over—and replace the plastic cover. Leave to rise a second time for 40 minutes.

SHAPING
10 mins.

Turn the dough onto the work surface and press it into an oval roughly the length of the baking pan. Fold the oval in half and pinch the seam together. Let rest for a moment. Spread the untoasted sunflower seeds on the work surface.

Brush the top and sides of the loaf with the egg-milk mixture. Carefully hold the loaf in both hands—invert it over the seeds, and roll it gently back and forth to pick up the seeds.

Place the shaped loaf in the prepared pan. Tuck in the ends and press down with the flat of your hand.

THIRD RISING
45 mins.

Cover the pan with wax paper or a clean towel and leave until the dough has risen about 1 inch above the top of the pan, about 45 minutes.

PREHEAT

Preheat the oven to 375° about 20 minutes before baking.

BAKING
375°
40 mins.

Place the loaf in the oven and bake in the moderate oven for about 40 minutes, or until the loaf tests done.

FINAL STEP

Unmold the loaf and let it stand seed side up on a rack until cool.

JEWISH RYE

[MAKES 2 LARGE ROUND LOAVES]

One of the most celebrated—and delicious—rye breads is one known by several names—Jewish, New York, and Seeded. Its great flavor also rests with the leavening, a sour made with rye flour and onion slices (to give it acidity).

Michael has traveled widely searching for recipes, and this one he found in a Jewish bakery in New York City.

INGREDIENTS

1½ cups soaked rye bread pieces (see Beforehand below)
3 cups rye sour (recipe follows)
1 package dry yeast
1 tablespoon salt
3 teaspoons caraway seeds (more if you like the flavor), plus
    1 tablespoon, to sprinkle
4 cups bread or unbleached flour, approximately
1 egg, beaten, and 1 tablespoon water, to brush

EQUIPMENT

One baking sheet dusted with cornmeal or greased

BEFOREHAND
5 mins.

Soak in water a half-dozen crusty slices of a previously baked loaf of rye. Squeeze dry. Set aside 1½ cups for this recipe; the balance can be refrigerated or frozen for later use.

PREPARATION
BY HAND OR
MIXER
18 mins.

In a large bowl (or mixer bowl) drop in the squeezed-dry pieces of rye bread. Add the rye sour. With a wooden spoon or a mixer flat beater stir until the bread is thoroughly incorporated into the sour. Stir in the dry yeast, salt, and 3 teaspoons of caraway seeds.

Add 2 cups of the white flour and mix vigorously into the sour. Add more flour, ¼ cup at a time, stirring first with a wooden spoon and then with your hands, or with the mixer. The dough may be sticky at first, but it will become elastic and smooth as it is worked. Lift the dough from the bowl and place it on the floured work surface.

KNEADING
8 mins.

Knead the dough under a dough hook or with your hands for 8 minutes. Use a strong push-turn-fold motion, adding sprinkles of flour if the dough is sticky. But don't overload the dough with flour. It is better to keep it on the slack side.

PREPARATION
BY PROCESSOR
5 mins.

Soak the bread, as above.
    Use a plastic dough blade.
    Place the bread pieces and the sour in the processor work bowl. Pulse several times to make certain the two are thoroughly

blended. Add the yeast, salt, and caraway seeds. Pulse, and leave for a minute or two for the yeast particles to dissolve.

Add the white flour, ½ cup at a time, until the batter becomes a solid and is carried around the bowl by the force of the blade.

KNEADING
45 secs.
Keep the machine running and knead for 45 seconds. The dough may be too dense for some machines to operate, so turn the dough onto the work surface and proceed by hand.

FIRST RISING
30 mins.
Place the dough in a bowl, cover with plastic wrap, and leave at room temperature for 30 minutes.

SHAPING
5 mins.
Punch down the dough and turn out onto a floured work surface. Divide into 2 pieces. The dough may be fashioned into round loaves or long plump ones. Place the loaves on a baking sheet.

SECOND RISING
30 mins.
Cover the loaves with wax paper and put aside to rise for 30 minutes to proof only three quarters—not the usual full proof of double in volume. This is not critical, but it is nice to be able to come close.

PREHEAT
Preheat the oven to 450°, and prepare a cup of hot water to pour into a pan on the bottom shelf 3 minutes before putting in the loaves. This will create the steam used in commercial ovens.

BAKING
450°
40 mins.
Cut the top of the loaves into a pattern with a razor blade or sharp knife. Try a tick-tac-toe design or diagonal cuts across the top. Brush with the egg yolk and water mixture. Sprinkle with the tablespoon of caraway seeds.

Place in the hot oven. Midway through the bake period turn the loaves around so they brown evenly. The loaves will bake a deep brown in about 40 minutes. Turn one loaf over and tap the bottom crust to determine if it is done. If it is not hard and crusty, return to the oven for 5 or 10 minutes.

FINAL STEP
Place the loaves on a wire rack to cool.

This is a delicious loaf that will be hard to keep in supply.

Rye Sour

[MAKES 8 CUPS]

This sour may be kept alive and well in the refrigerator for several weeks (stirred and fed occasionally with a tablespoon of flour), but the onion chunks should be removed and discarded after the first day.

INGREDIENTS

2 medium onions, coarsely chopped
2 cups rye flour, stone-ground preferred
3½ cups hot water (120°–130°)
2 packages dry yeast
1 tablespoon caraway seeds

EQUIPMENT

A length of cheesecloth in which to tie the onion pieces

PREPARATION
Overnight

Tie the onion pieces into a bag made of cheesecloth. Put aside for the moment.

In a large bowl measure the rye flour and water. Stir to mix. Sprinkle on the yeast and work into the rye mixture. Add the caraway seeds.

When the mixture is thoroughly blended, push the onion down into the center of the sour. Cover tightly with plastic wrap and put aside overnight but no more than 24 hours.

FINAL STEP

Lift out the onions, scrape the sour off the cloth, and discard the onions. The sour can now be used.

VIII   LOUISIANA

The Closing Chapter

The journey south to Louisiana wasn't a question of saving the best for last, it just happened that way. It would be the closing chapter, the final 3,238 miles. The food would be Creole and Cajun, a new experience, and it would be in the springtime, before heat and humidity and mosquitoes. The first travels in the book were to Mississippi and Alabama, so it seemed fitting to schedule Louisiana for the last, with the rest of America in between.

Two things would be missing, however. One, the van. It had served well across the plains, up and down the mountains, wetting its tires in both oceans as well as in the Gulf of Mexico. It carried three of us and a lot of luggage and gear in comfort. Marje and Timothy shared the back divan a great deal of the time. There were none of the usual long-distance, passenger-car complaints about cramped seats, thanks to seats that swiveled and turned and reclined.

With the van, too, came a feeling of being an equal with the big guys on the highway, the trucks. The van rode tall and we looked out over the top of traffic to scenery far ahead just as the truckers do. We could look the truckers square in the eyes when we passed, rather than straining to look up to see who or what was driving, a curiosity-driven quirk of mine. Then, too, the van was painted a cardinal red trimmed in silver which made it stand out in a parking lot or when ordering it from the parking valet.

Our garage was not large enough for the van, so rather than let it stand out in another harsh Indiana winter we gave it up when the lease

529

expired. Timothy was brokenhearted. He sat for hours by the driveway waiting for the van to appear, which would have meant "Hurrah, we're off again!"

But the van did not appear for the last trip, nor did Timothy go. There wasn't room for him plus equipage. We drove the family four-door Buick sedan, trustworthy, conservative, and a dull gray. No panache.

Three things stood out about the trip to Louisiana.

Had I been collecting states, this would have been a good day. We drove through six states—Indiana, Illinois, Missouri, Arkansas, Tennessee, and Mississippi—and crossed the Mississippi River twice, all before nightfall. A record of some sort.

Second, I was struck with the high cost of cornflakes in Mississippi! On the second morning, we stopped for breakfast at the Family Restaurant off I-55, just a few miles into the state. The place looked passable on the outside, but it certainly wasn't on the inside. Grubby and greasy. But we had made the commitment, besides the next possible stopping place was a distance beyond. The coffee, Marje said, was hot, and my cornflakes, which seemed a safe item to order, were satisfactorily crisp.

Then I saw the bill: $1.19 for the cornflakes. I looked at the weight on the box: 11/16th of an ounce. I quickly calculated that one pound would cost $7.68! "That can't be correct," I protested to the cashier. "You are right," she said, "it should have been $1.14," and gave me back a nickel. I took my 5¢ and stomped out. Later I bought an assortment of breakfast cereals, including cornflakes, just to find what that little box would have cost the Family restaurant, had the cashier gone across the street to buy it retail: 32¢, a markup of 200 percent! (I thought this was outrageous until several months later I saw the price of the same box of cereal in the Hilton Airport Café in San Francisco: $2.95! And two days after that at the Kona Hilton Hotel in Hawaii, the same *less-than-an-ounce* box: $4.50!)

At the very least it gave me something to think about the rest of the day, because nothing else happened on the long drive from the northern end of Mississippi to the southern, and on into New Orleans.

That was the third thing that I noted in my journal. Nothing!

With the exception of a few miles on either side of Jackson and through the city, I-55 seemed to lie in a forested corridor that stretched without a hill or village or barn or cows or horses or cultivated fields for more than three hundred miles. Hour after hour we zipped down an avenue through piney woods. The sameness became remarkable.

"I get the same lonesome feeling I sometimes had driving across the western plains with nothing but highway stretching ahead," Marje said.

It began to change on the outskirts of New Orleans and the lonesome feeling vanished.

▰▰▰▰▰ *NEW ORLEANS, LOUISIANA*

The Josephine—Mary Ann Weilbaecher,
Patrick Fahey

JUDI BOTTONI

The dinner was Creole, a meal that embraced a dozen cultures. It was French but not quite. It was Spanish but not quite. Indian? African? German? It was all of these—and more. It was Creole—a wonderful amalgam, a blend come together over several centuries in New Orleans.

We were twelve at dinner. Our host was Patrick Fahey on whose steamboat Marje and I had traveled down the Mississippi River from St. Paul to St. Louis six months before. In addition to being president of the company that operates both the *Mississippi Queen* and the *Delta Queen*, Patrick is an exceptional home cook. When he learned I was searching for authentic Creole dishes for my book, he said he probably could put something together that would help and at the same time be fun to do. Because he has been on the New Orleans scene for only a few years he turned to a friend, a true New Orleanian, Mary Ann Weilbaecher, mistress of The Josephine, a guesthouse, and one of the city's notable cooks.

"Would you do the dinner?" asked Patrick.

"Yes, but only if you do the shopping," replied Mary Ann.

So the steamboat executive dropped anchor and, with basket in hand, began one of several trips to the market for dinner. It was not an easy chore. "You can take these shrimp right back to the man," Mary Ann ordered when he appeared at the kitchen door after one of a half-dozen sorties into town with a bundle of shrimp in hand. "I don't care what the man told you—these have been frozen! You take my meaning?" Patrick, a handsome, curly-headed bachelor in his forties, who can hold his own with steamboat captains, river pilots, and board chairmen, took her meaning, nodded, turned, and left to exchange the crustaceans for ones that *positively* had never been frozen.

It was the kind of dinner party that good food and fine wine make memorable. The guests were a London architect, the bureau chief for the Associated Press, a movie agent/director, a financier, several steamboat company people, the Claytons, and the hostess and her husband. Very few of us were acquainted when we came to the house, but two hours later, following dessert, a motion was made and carried unanimously that this affair be held annually. It was that kind of evening.

Earlier Mary Ann and I talked in the kitchen.

"Dinner will begin with a 'classic' Creole dish—boiled shrimp and fresh crab meat with New Orleans remoulade sauce. Then we will have *Gumbo Z'Herbes*—we also call it Green Gumbo because of all the vegetable tops in it—which breaks all the rules for gumbo. It uses neither okra or filé (powdered sassafras). It is the only gumbo in which the roux is not prepared first. Originally it was a Lenten dish, so it contained no meat, seafood, or game. Tonight, however, I have added a few bits of ham.

"The crawfish season has just began, which means that we are having *étouffée*. The crawfish are small right now but especially sweet and tender. The *étouffée* will be served on "popcorn" rice. It is an old strain of rice that smells like popcorn when it is cooked. I would have used a different rice, but Patrick insisted you have this one.

"It was his way of aggravating me!" She laughed.

"Dessert will be bread pudding. You can't have a Creole dinner without it. It's traditional New Orleans, but I make it in a different way from all the others. It's a secret. After dinner it will be café brûlot New Orleans, coffee flamed with brandy and Grand Marnier."

It all transpired as planned. Beautifully so. The shrimp were fresh. While the traditional sauce for the traditional Bread Pudding is a whiskey or rum sauce, she garnished each serving with strawberries and blackberries.

Mary Ann was born in the city of New Orleans, not across the river, which in her view disqualifies anyone from claiming full New Orleans citizenship. A graduate of Louisiana State University and a home economics teacher for several years, Mary Ann and her husband, Dan Fuselier, toured France one year searching for a new direction in their lives. They discovered innkeeping and returned to New Orleans to begin lives as innkeepers. In a mansion built in the Italianate style in 1870, they created the lovely Josephine, so named for the tree-lined street that runs past the house.

"We restored the main parlors and the six guest rooms to reflect the graceful life-style of an old New Orleans home. We furnished the place with French antiques, gilt mirrors, and silverboards. I have always given big dinner parties and had lots of guests and have done some catering and some special dinners, like tonight, and it all has come together beautifully in The Josephine."

SHRIMP AND CRAB REMOULADE

[SERVES 4]

New Orleans remoulade sauce is highly seasoned and reddish in color. The sauce can be prepared in advance and refrigerated, but don't sauce the shrimp and crab until a few minutes before serving or they will get soggy. The sauce is adapted from Mary Ann's "very favorite cookbook of all times"—*The New Orleans Cookbook* written by Richard H. Collin (Alfred A. Knopf, 1977).

INGREDIENTS

1 bunch green onions, roughly chopped, plus 1 minced
2 stalks celery, roughly chopped, plus 1 tablespoon minced
3 sprigs of parsley, chopped, plus 2 teaspoons minced
3 tablespoons Creole mustard or of choice
5 teaspoons paprika
1 teaspoon salt
½ teaspoon freshly ground black pepper
¼ teaspoon cayenne
½ teaspoon basil
6 tablespoons white vinegar
5 teaspoons fresh lemon juice
¾ cup extra-virgin olive oil
Lettuce leaves to arrange under seafood
½ pound cooked shrimp, peeled, deveined, and chilled
½ pound cooked crab meat, chilled, lump preferred

EQUIPMENT

Food mill

PREPARATION
10 mins.

For the remoulade, puree the pieces of chopped green onions, celery, and parsley and pour into a china or stainless-steel bowl. Add the seasonings, vinegar, and lemon juice and blend well with a wooden spoon.

Gradually add the olive oil, stirring constantly.

When well blended, add the minced green onions, celery, and parsley. Stir to blend.

REFRIGERATING
3 hours

Cover the bowl with plastic wrap and refrigerate for at least 3 hours.

continued

FINAL STEP   At serving time, place lettuce leaves on each salad plate. Arrange the shrimp and crab pieces on the leaves. Stir the sauce to blend and then pour about ¼ cup over each portion. The sauce should completely cover the meats. Serve well chilled. Additional sauce may be passed.

GUMBO Z'HERBES
(Green Gumbo)

[SERVES 8 OR MORE]

Gumbo Z'Herbes is a celebration of garden greens. Go into the garden and pick almost anything and it will be right for this unusual Lenten dish that was traditionally served on Good Friday. Legend has it that you will make as many friends as the number of different greens you put in the gumbo.

The flavor that comes from combining many different greens is what makes this gumbo so delicious. In addition to the greens Mary Ann used in her gumbo, she had the choice of others: green onions, watercress, beet tops, radish tops, chicory, and a small head of green cabbage.

No longer a Lenten dish, *Gumbo Z'Herbes* is most often prepared with meat as it is here. The meat is cubed small when the gumbo is the soup course, cut larger when it is the entrée. It is served over rice.

Her recipe is adopted from the well-thumbed, tattered, and torn pages of Richard H. Collin's *New Orleans Cookbook*.

INGREDIENTS   *GREENS*
(a minimum of 5 is adequate, 7 perfect. A bunch is described as a handful.)
1 bunch collard greens
1 bunch mustard greens
1 bunch turnip greens
1 bunch parsley
1 bunch spinach
1 bunch carrot tops
1 bunch lettuce
⅓ cup cold water

ROUX
½ cup vegetable oil
⅔ cup flour

BASE
1 cup chopped onions
½ pound each *lean ham, smoked sausage, and veal, cut into
    ½-inch cubes*

SEASONINGS
1 teaspoon salt
¼ teaspoon freshly ground black pepper
⅛ teaspoon cayenne
2 bay leaves, crushed
½ teaspoon each *dried thyme and marjoram*
2 whole cloves
6 whole allspice

8 cups cold water

EQUIPMENT

One heavy 3- to 4-quart saucepan; one large 7- to 8-quart heavy pot or kettle

**PREPARATION
20 mins.**

Rinse the greens under cold running water. Let the excess water run off, shake the greens lightly. Place the greens in the heavy saucepan, add the cold water, and turn the heat to high. When the liquid in the bottom of the pan begins to boil, cover the pan tightly, reduce heat to medium, and cook the greens for 12 to 15 minutes, or until just tender.

Remove the pan from the heat and drain the greens by dumping them into a colander placed in a large bowl to catch the liquid formed during the cooking. Reserve the liquid. When the greens cool, chop them fine and set aside.

**COOKING
1½ hours**

In the large pot or kettle, heat the oil over high heat. Reduce the heat to low and gradually add the flour, stirring constantly. Cook over the low heat, *always stirring*, until a golden brown roux is formed—the color of peanut butter.

Quickly add the chopped onions, stir thoroughly, and continue browning for 5 minutes longer, still stirring. Add the ham, sausage, and veal cubes and the liquid reserved from cooking the greens.

Mix well, then gradually stir in the chopped cooked greens. Add the seasonings. Keep the heat low, gradually add the cold water, stirring to mix thoroughly. Raise the heat to bring the gumbo to a boil, lower the heat, partially cover, and simmer for about 1¼ hours.

FINAL STEP

Best served over boiled rice. The gumbo can be refrigerated for several days and frozen for several weeks.

BREAD PUDDING

[SERVES 6]

Crepes Suzette and Bananas Foster flamed at the table may be a more spectacular presentation, but in New Orleans they rank behind Bread Pudding in popularity. Originally devised as a way to use stale French bread, Bread Pudding has become a local art form. Every good New Orleans cook has his or her own version, prepared from a jealously guarded secret recipe.

The bread should be dry and slightly hard, to give the pudding the proper chewing texture after it is baked.

Mary Ann's secret: While other recipes call for the bread to be cut or torn into pieces and soaked in milk before it goes into the casserole to be baked, she will have none of that.

She fits whole slices of French bread including crusts into the baking dish; the milk is then poured slowly over the slices, allowing it to be absorbed. There is no presoak. At one point she took my pen and printed on my notepad: DO NOT SOAK!

She works with a basic formula that can be easily expanded for a larger yield: 2 eggs and ½ cup sugar for each cup of milk.

INGREDIENTS

French bread, cut into 1-inch slices, enough to fill casserole or baking dish in 3 layers (about 12 baguette slices)
½ cup (1 stick) unsalted clarified butter (see page 241), for slices
½ cup raisins, if desired
4 cups milk
8 eggs, beaten
2 cups sugar
2 teaspoons vanilla extract
1 teaspoon ground cinnamon
½ teaspoon salt
Choice of berries or cherries, to garnish

EQUIPMENT

One 5-cup casserole or baking dish (6 x 3-inch), buttered; one pan of water (1 inch deep) in which to set the baking dish during baking

PREHEAT

Preheat the oven to 400°.

PREPARATION
20 mins.

First, to assure a snug fit, arrange the bread slices in layers in the baking dish. Turn out the slices, dip both sides in clarified butter, and return to the dish. Tuck in small pieces to fill out the layers. Sprinkle in raisins between the layers, if desired.

In a small bowl beat together the remaining ingredients.

With a wire whip beat until the mixture is smooth and thick. Pour over the bread slices. Press down so they are submerged.

Depending on the porosity of the bread, the slices may rise above the surface to give you a rich brown crust.

BAKING
400°
45 mins.

Place the baking dish in the pan of water and put in the oven for 45 minutes. Check doneness with a knife.

FINAL STEP

Serve the pudding warm. While many New Orleans cooks serve the pudding with a whiskey or a rum sauce, Mary Ann simply places a spoonful of macerated strawberries and blackberries or cherries with a bit of juice on top.

Bread pudding is delicious served cold, but my choice is warm.

〰〰〰〰LAKE CHARLES, LOUISIANA

Cajun—Jude Theriot

My friend Jude Theriot is Cajun. He traces an ancestry back through seven generations to a Thomas Theriot, who as a child fled with his mother from the British in Canada to the bayou wilderness of southwest Louisiana.

Today the term "Cajun," a derivative of "Acadian," is applied to anyone of French heritage living or born in the bayou country of Louisiana. Bayou is the Choctaw Indian word for the streams that weave a vast network through the swamps and marshes on which the early Cajuns moved about in small pirogues.

Jude is a big man. He stands tall, more than six feet, with an impressive girth. He fills out every inch of a chef's jacket when he stands before a class. It is quite evident that he loves food, especially Cajun.

Jude stands tall, too, among educators in that part of the state, where he is assistant superintendent of schools in Calcasieu Parish (Lake Charles). Jude, who holds advanced degrees from three universities, fit in a career as a French chef before he became a school administrator.

It is Cajun cooking in which he takes particular pride. He has written four cookbooks, mostly about Cajun food, which he promotes in a killing

schedule of autograph parties, demonstrations, and cooking-school classes. I met him the first time when he found his way to my small Indiana city to give Cajun cooking classes and sell books. He has returned on demand several times. Thanks to Jude, there is an active cell of Cajun cooks in town.

My favorite cookbook is his *La Cuisine Cajun*, an excellent guide for a beginner.

"Cajun cooking," Jude explained, "is the cooking of a simple country people, unlike Creole, which has been influenced by a half-dozen cultures. Our way of life here has been nurtured by the lavish bayou system, which yields a wealth of fresh seafood, while the land provides an abundance of game. When my family came here from Canada they found the growing season especially long and it allowed them—as it has us—to have a variety of vegetables, spices, and seasonings available all year long."

The Cajuns' French heritage had taught them the French style of cooking with all the sauces and seasonings, but here in the bayou country many of the traditional ingredients were unavailable.

"Cajuns started with what they knew and incorporated that with whatever they could get. Sauces became gravies and meats and seafoods were cooked in sauces for a richer flavor. Variety became the mark of our cooking. A true Cajun cook prides himself on the ability to do what everybody does, but in such a unique way that only he can re-create the exact taste experience."

Some Cajun cooks, said Jude, are subtle in their spicing and seasoning. Others are heavy-handed. Many are in between or sometimes one way, sometimes the other, depending on the mood. Ease of preparation, he explained, is an essential characteristic of Cajun cooking.

"Remember, Cajun cooking was originally done in backwoods kitchens without fancy equipment or supplies. It involved cooking with heavy black pots for even heat distribution, simple utensils, plenty of fresh ingredients, and plenty of different spices, seasonings, seafood, and meats."

Jude agreed that Cajun cooking can be somewhat time-consuming.

"But not difficult." It often calls for a large list of ingredients, but that should be no problem. It only enhances the dish and helps to make it special. "It is the blending of flavors that creates a treat," he said.

CRAWFISH SKILLET

[SERVES 8]

A beloved staple in the South and one that is growing in favor among Northern cooks is the crawfish. As a kid I knew them as crawdads and ignored them when I went swimming in the creek. No longer! I have grown fond of them, especially prepared this way by Jude.

Jude tells us that the little creature is a descendant of the Maine lobster. After the Cajuns were exiled from Nova Scotia, the lobsters yearned for the Cajuns so much that they set off across the country to find them. The journey over mountains was so long and treacherous that the creatures began to shrink in size. By the time they found the Cajuns in Louisiana, all that was left of the crustaceans' former greatness was their tremendous flavor, which they managed to store in their succulent tails. Upon their arrival, a great festival was held, and all the great Cajun crawfish dishes—*étouffée* (stew), jambalaya, gumbo, bisque, *boulettes* (meatballs), pies, and fried and boiled crawfish—were created.

"Cajuns don't doubt the veracity of this story, even though some non-Cajuns have difficulty with it," Jude said.

More and more crawfish are being commercially grown and shipped to large Northern cities. Medium shrimp, fresh, peeled, and deveined may be substituted, but sauté for 4½ minutes instead of 3 minutes when using shrimp.

There is no need to make this dish in advance, because it takes less than 10 minutes to cook after chopping all the ingredients and arranging them in order.

This is a great one-dish meal. Serve it with French bread. The toasted almonds add a delightful crunch.

INGREDIENTS
¼ cup peanut oil
½ cup (1 stick) unsalted butter
1 pound fresh crawfish tails, or 1¼ pounds uncooked shrimp,
    peeled and deveined
1 tablespoon minced celery
1 tablespoon minced carrot
1 bunch green onions, tops and bottoms, chopped
2 medium bell peppers, sliced into strips
8 large mushrooms, sliced
2 firm red tomatoes, sliced into wedges
2½ cups cooked white rice
1¼ teaspoons salt
½ teaspoon each Tabasco sauce and black pepper
¼ teaspoon each dried sweet basil and filé powder
1 tablespoon white wine
¼ cup sliced toasted almonds
½ cup minced fresh parsley

EQUIPMENT
One very heavy 10- to 12-inch skillet with high sides—since it must hold the entire dish at various stages

COOKING
5 mins.
Heat the peanut oil in the skillet over medium-high heat, until it begins to smoke. Add the butter and move it around so that it melts quickly. Add the crawfish tails or shrimp, celery, and carrot, and sauté for 3 minutes.

Add the green onions and mix well. Add the bell peppers, mix well, and sauté for 30 seconds. Add the mushrooms and tomatoes. Stir briefly just to coat the mushrooms. Remove the skillet from the heat.

ASSEMBLING
5 mins.
Add the cooked rice, salt, Tabasco, black pepper, sweet basil, filé powder, and wine and mix until all of the rice is coated with the pan liquid. Add the almonds and parsley and mix very well.

Serve at once!

SHRIMP ÉTOUFFÉE
(Shrimp Stew)

[SERVES 8]

People in the bayou country still gather their own shrimp for one of their most popular Cajun dishes, étouffée. Gulf shrimp are especially flavorful, more so than their ocean cousins.

This dish lends itself to being made ahead of time. You can either refrigerate or freeze the dish after it has been completely cooked. To reheat, just thaw in the refrigerator and place over medium-low heat until the shrimp are hot, then serve over rice.

This is low in calories (210 calories in one serving) but great in taste.

INGREDIENTS

½ cup (1 stick) unsalted butter
3 medium onions, chopped
½ cup thinly sliced celery
2 garlic cloves, minced
3 tablespoons diced bell pepper
1 tablespoon tomato paste
2 pounds uncooked shrimp, peeled and deveined
2 tablespoons flour
1 teaspoon salt
1½ teaspoons Jude's Seafood Seasoning Mix (see recipe below)
½ teaspoon Tabasco
½ cup seafood stock or bottled clam juice or water
1 cup chopped green onions, tops and bottoms
¼ cup minced fresh parsley
Cooked white rice, to accompany

EQUIPMENT

One large heavy skillet or pot

COOKING
30–35 mins.

Melt the butter in the skillet or pot over medium heat. Sauté the onions, celery, garlic, and bell pepper until the onions are lightly browned around the edges, about 8 minutes.

Add the tomato paste and blend well. Add the shrimp and cook over medium heat until they are nicely pink, about 5 minutes. Add the flour and blend well. Add the salt, seafood seasoning mix, and Tabasco. Stir well and cook for 1 minute.

Slowly add the seafood stock or clam juice and lower the heat. Cover the skillet and let the dish simmer for 12 to 15 minutes, stirring often to prevent sticking. Remove the cover, add the green onion and parsley, and cook for an additional 3 minutes.

Serve at once over cooked white rice.

Jude's Seafood Seasoning Mix

Excellent for seasoning all seafood. Use as you would any seasoning mix. Don't add extra salt to the dish.

Filé powder, one of the ingredients in the mix, is pounded dried sassafras leaves and is used to thicken the gumbo.

INGREDIENTS

¼ cup salt
2 tablespoons cayenne pepper
1 tablespoon each freshly ground black pepper, white pepper,
    and garlic powder
2 tablespoons paprika
1½ tablespoons onion powder
1 teaspoon dried sweet basil
½ teaspoon each dry hot mustard and ground bay leaves
¼ teaspoon each filé powder, dried thyme, and dried tarragon
⅛ teaspoon each dried oregano and dried rosemary

PREPARATION
5 mins.

Mix all the ingredients together well and store in a tightly covered glass jar to use as needed.

FINAL STEP

Season and enjoy. Only 4 calories per teaspoon.

CATFISH COURTBOUILLON

[SERVES 6]

In Cajun country the great boiled fish dish is Catfish Courtbouillon (one word, pronounced coo-bee-yon). It is a happy adaptation of a French cook's court bouillon (two words), a light tasty stock made without meat, used in delicate soups and sauces.

"No one does it better than Dee Dee Guidry," Jude said as we walked down the street from his office to Mama's Fried Chicken and Seafood. A big American flag on a short staff waved across the words "Lunches Daily —Open 7 A.M. to 3 P.M." painted on the front window. A small blue neon sign blinked LITE.

Mrs. Guidry and T.J., her husband, started the restaurant a dozen years ago because they were bored with doing nothing in retirement.

"They have built up quite a business cooking for those of us who like good down-home Cajun cooking," said Jude, "and they have done it in a modest place with a half-dozen tables and four counter stools—and a selection of good Cajun dishes."

This is an adaptation of Mrs. Guidry's recipe for the courtbouillon she served us for lunch. Delicious. I have changed it slightly.

As you do with so many Cajun and Creole recipes—"First, you make a roux"—the flour and fat (usually vegetable oil) mixture that is cooked slowly until the mixture is brown and has a nutlike aroma and taste. It serves as a base and thickening agent for a wide variety of dishes.

INGREDIENTS

½ cup vegetable oil
½ cup all-purpose flour
1¾ cups finely chopped onion
1 cup thinly sliced green onions, tops and bottoms
¾ cup finely chopped green bell pepper
1 tablespoon finely minced garlic
⅓ cup finely chopped celery
3 cups coarsely chopped, drained canned tomatoes
1 tablespoon finely minced fresh parsley
3 whole bay leaves, broken into quarters
½ teaspoon dried thyme
¼ teaspoon dried marjoram
6 whole allspice
2 teaspoons salt
½ teaspoon freshly ground black pepper
⅛ teaspoon cayenne
½ teaspoon dried basil
2½ tablespoons fresh lemon juice
1 cup dry red wine
3 cups water
1½ pounds catfish fillets

EQUIPMENT

One heavy 4- to 5-quart pot

PREPARATION
25 mins.

(*Note:* Prepare the chopped and minced vegetables before start-ing the roux and set aside in one bowl. Chop the tomatoes sepa-rately and reserve. Collect all of the herbs and spices beforehand. This makes it easier to put together the courtbouil-lon in an orderly fashion without a frantic last-minute search for a forgotten ingredient.)

(*Caution:* The basis for the roux is *hot* oil. Don't grow care-less in the 25 minutes of constant stirring and allow the mixing spoon to slosh about. It can burn. Even one drop can raise a blister.)

Heat the oil in the pot. Add the flour, lower the heat, and cook over low heat, *stirring constantly*, until a roux the color of peanut butter is formed, about 25 minutes. Do not allow it to blacken or it will taste scorched and must be done over.

COOKING
50–55 mins.

Add the onion, green onions, pepper, garlic, and celery and brown for 8 to 10 minutes, stirring constantly. Add the chopped tomatoes, seasonings, lemon juice, and red wine. Stir to mix thoroughly, then slowly add the water, mixing well.

Bring to a boil, then lower the heat, and simmer uncovered

for 35 minutes. Stir frequently to prevent scorching and to allow the sauce to thicken.

Add the catfish pieces. Cook for 8 to 10 minutes, then remove the pot from the heat.

FINAL STEP   In a soup bowl, over rice, serve fish with plenty of liquid and supply soup spoons. French bread goes well with it.

IX   A FAMILY ALBUM
of RECIPES

Linda Clayton
and Susan Bernato

For good food I need never go outside my family circle, which for a century and a half, and surely even before that, has been producing good cooks. In my lifetime it began with my grandmother Condon, who, at the age of fourteen, married my grandfather, Clark Condon, the depot agent in the Indiana town where I was born. Her parents came from Germany, so her cooking was a blend of her family's favorites and those of her groom, my English-Scotch grandfather. In later years, when Grandpa came to our house, my mother served leg of lamb, his favorite, something that did not fit into my grandmother's scheme of cooking.

Very early in girlhood, Lenora, my mother, the eldest of six children, was in the kitchen helping to cook for a ménage that at times numbered more than a dozen as relatives came for lengthy visits because, as one uncle said to my mother, "the food is so damned good."

My mother was not an imaginative cook. She did not create new dishes. When she won a cluster of state fair blue ribbons for her cooking, it was for cakes and pies and cookies she had been baking for us at home for several decades. Her repertoire was unchanging, but when it featured pot roast, you knew it would be the best-tasting pot roast ever set upon the table. My school chums knew this, and because my mother loved to cook for hungry boys there were always extra kids at the table. A half century later I received a letter from a grade-school friend who said one of his fondest recollections as a youth was eating my mother's golden, butter-rich breaded tenderloin.

No matter what special dish she placed before members of the Bridge Club, the most discerning group in town, it was her rolls that drew the most flattering remarks from the men—and requests for the recipe from wives. Her recipe follows.

Martha, my kid sister, had the rich background of my mother's cooking. She was fourteen when she won first prize at the state fair for her chocolate cake, which later that afternoon was presented to the governor. She went on to spend a dozen years in Belgium, Monaco, and France, which sharpened her already considerable culinary skills. My brother-in-law, a gourmet's gourmet, demanded perfection in everything and found it in my sister's kitchen. A favorite dish is *moules à la marinière*, mussels in a rich broth of wine, onions, celery, garlic, and spices.

I was so smitten in my pursuit of Miss Marjorie Roach, the campus beauty, that it never occurred to me to ask if she knew her way around the kitchen. She didn't. When we were married she stood in awe of my mother's cooking. Thanks to my mother's encouragement, however, that feeling didn't last. Marje was as quick as she was pretty, and before long our table was a joy. Her cooking now reflects the years we lived in San Francisco and Honolulu and travels in this country and abroad. Her salads are outstanding. Her dish in the family album: broiler salad.

One of the early photographs I have of Susan, our daughter, was taken when she was two years old, standing on a stool beside her grandmother Clayton while the two of them rolled a piecrust. From that early brush with food, Susan went on to become an excellent cook. She was baking delicious breads, cakes, and pies long before I became a food professional by writing cookbooks. Her forte was and is baked goods. Her recipe for Mexican-inspired *pan dulce* follows.

The first time Marje and I met Linda Clayton, our daughter-in-law to be, she was preparing a luncheon among the big stones on the bank of a wilderness river in Idaho. Within fifteen minutes she had put together a table of driftwood, moved stones to be sat upon, put down a bright tablecloth (with linen napkins), opened a bottle of wine, laid out hors d'oeuvres, and turned to grilling the trout. She continues to impress me with her style, knowledge of food, and her vitality. Her recipe for roasted beef brisket is here.

LENORA'S YEAST ROLLS

[MAKES 2 TO 3 DOZEN ROLLS]

My mother called these, simply, her "yeast rolls."

INGREDIENTS

1 egg, room temperature
¼ cup sugar
½ cup mashed cooked potato or prepared "instant" mashed potato
¾ cup milk, room temperature
⅓ cup unsalted butter, softened, plus ¼ cup (½ stick), melted, to brush
½ teaspoon salt
3 to 3½ cups all-purpose flour, approximately
1 package dry yeast

continued

EQUIPMENT

One baking sheet or sheets for Parker House rolls, *or* two 8- or 9-inch cake pans, buttered, for Pan Rolls

PREPARATION
BY HAND OR
MIXER
15 mins.

In a large bowl or mixer bowl, blend the egg and sugar. Add the potato, milk, softened butter, and salt. Mix together either with a wooden spoon or mixer flat beater. Add 2 cups of flour and the yeast. Beat for 100 strokes, or 1 minute in the mixer. Gradually add flour, ½ cup at a time, first with the wooden spoon and then by hand as the dough becomes firm. If in the mixer, attach the dough hook.

Work the flour into a moist ball until it cleans the sides of the bowl and has lost much of its stickiness. Under the dough hook, the dough will clean the sides of the bowl and form a ball about the revolving hook.

It is an easy dough to work because of its high butterfat content.

KNEADING
8 mins.

If by hand, turn the soft dough onto a floured work surface and knead with a strong push-turn-fold motion until the dough becomes smooth and velvety under your hands. If the ball of dough sticks to the sides of the bowl during kneading, add sprinkles of flour. Knead for 8 minutes.

PREPARATION
BY PROCESSOR
3 mins.

Attach the steel blade. The sequence of adding ingredients varies from above. Measure 1½ cups of flour into the work bowl and add the yeast, sugar, and salt. Pulse to blend. With the processor running, pour the milk through the feed tube, and add the egg and the softened butter. Add flour, ¼ cup at a time, either by taking off the cover or using the feed tube, until the batter becomes a rough mass of dough.

If the ball of dough does not clean the sides of the bowl, add small portions of flour.

KNEADING
1 min.

When the dough has formed a ball, process for 1 minute to knead. Stop the machine and test the dough with your fingers. If it is too dry, add water by the teaspoon with the machine running; if it is too wet, add flour by the tablespoon. The dough should be very elastic when stretched between your hands. If not, return to the work bowl and process for a few more seconds.

FIRST RISING
1¼ hours

Return the dough to the bowl, stretch a length of plastic wrap across the top, and leave at room temperature until the dough has risen to double in volume, about 1¼ hours.

SHAPING
20 mins.

For Parker House rolls: Dust the work surface with flour. Divide the dough in half. Roll the first piece into a circle, ⅜ inch thick.

Cut rounds with a 2½- or 3-inch biscuit cutter. Make a crease across the center of the small rounds of dough with a rolling pin or the handle of a knife. Carefully roll toward each end to create a valley through the center of the round. The center will be about ⅛ inch thick while the ends will be thicker. Or you may press the rounded handle of a knife into the dough to achieve the same results. Keep the rolling pin or knife handle dusted with flour as you work.

Carefully brush each round to within ¼ inch of the edges with a little of the melted butter. This will allow the baked roll to open as a pocket.

Fold over the round of dough so the cut edges just meet. Pinch with your fingers to seal, and press the folded edge (the hinge) securely. Place each about ½ inch apart on a baking sheet as completed. Repeat with the remainder of the dough, as desired. You should get 28 to 32 rolls in all.

15 mins.

For pan rolls: Dust the work surface with flour. Divide the dough into 2 pieces and, with your hands, roll one piece of dough into a 12-inch rope. Cut into 12 pieces. Shape each piece into a tight ball under a cupped palm. Arrange in the pans. You should have 24 balls in all.

SECOND RISING
30 mins.

Brush tops with some melted butter, cover the dough with wax paper, and leave at room temperature until rolls have doubled in size, about 30 minutes.

PREHEAT

Preheat the oven to 400° 20 minutes before the bake period.

BAKING
400°
12–15 mins.

Place the rolls in the oven and bake until a golden brown, about 12 to 15 minutes.

FINAL STEP

Remove from the oven and immediately brush with the remaining melted butter. Place on a metal rack to cool.

Delicious served warm from the oven.

MOULES À LA MARINIÈRE
(Mussels in Broth)

[SERVES 4]

One of the memorable meals of my life was *moules à la marinière* served alfresco under a canopy of grapevines at my sister's house high in the hills looking across at Prince Ranier's *palais* in Monaco. The view was spectacular. The mussels never better. Here is Martha's recipe.

INGREDIENTS	*4 pounds mussels (approximately 60)* *½ cup (1 stick) butter* *½ cup olive oil* *2 medium onions, finely chopped* *2 stalks celery, finely chopped* *1 teaspoon fresh red chili pepper, finely chopped,* or *½ teaspoon dry flakes* *2 garlic cloves, mashed and chopped* *6 sprigs of parsley, chopped* *1 tablespoon chopped fresh basil* *1 tablespoon dried oregano* *2 cups dry Sauterne or white wine of choice*
PREPARATION 20 mins.	Scrub the mussels clean in cold water and remove their "beards." Set aside for the moment.

COOKING
25–30 mins.
	In a large pot melt the butter and add the olive oil. Add the onions, celery, chili pepper, and garlic and cook, covered, until the onions and celery are translucent and soft, about 10 to 15 minutes.
	    Add the parsley, basil, and oregano and cook for an additional 10 minutes. Add the wine; heat but don't boil!
	    Add the mussels. Increase the heat to a light boil. Cook for 6 to 7 minutes, or until the mussels begin to open. Cook for an additional 3 minutes. Remove the pot from the heat.

FINAL STEP	Serve the mussels and the broth in large bowls. Have plenty of rough peasant bread to dunk.

BROILER SALAD

[SERVES 4 TO 6]

Broiler Salad at our table is always an occasion for it brings back memories of our life in Honolulu in the late 1940s when the celebrated Canlis' Broiler restaurant was in a metal shed across Kalakaua Avenue from the Moana Hotel. We fell in love with its steaks and the salad. The salad has been with us for almost 50 years. Marje has made some minor adjustments, but I know Pete Canlis, who was a friend and neighbor, would approve.

The cardinal rule among all great salad makers is to tear the lettuce by hand into bite-sized pieces. Never cut.

INGREDIENTS

2 heads of romaine lettuce
⅓ pound bacon, sliced
1 egg
1 tablespoon extra-virgin olive oil
½ teaspoon salt
1 large garlic clove, skin removed
2 tomatoes, peeled, seeded, and cubed into bite size
¼ cup chopped green onions
1 tablespoon chopped fresh mint
½ teaspoon dried oregano
½ cup grated Romano cheese

DRESSING
Juice of 1 lemon
2 teaspoons red wine vinegar
1 teaspoon freshly ground black pepper, or more to taste
¼ cup extra-virgin olive oil

¼ cup croutons

PREPARATION
20 mins.

Wash and dry the lettuce leaves, separating each leaf. Chill.
Fry the bacon and crumble.
Coddle the egg for 1 minute in boiling water.

ASSEMBLING
15 mins.

Pour the olive oil into a large salad bowl. Add the salt. Rub the bowl firmly with the clove of garlic and at the same time mix well the oil and salt. Discard the garlic clove.

Tear the lettuce into bite-sized pieces, add to the bowl with oil and toss.

Add the tomato cubes, green onions, mint, oregano, cheese, and bacon.

For the dressing: Whisk together the dressing ingredients and add the coddled egg, whisking until smooth. Pour the dressing over the salad, toss well, coating all the lettuce and tossing together all of the ingredients. Sprinkle the croutons on and serve.

PAN DULCE
(Sweet Bread)

[MAKES 2 SMALL (8-INCH) LOAVES OR 1 LARGE LOAF]

Susan is a baker, and this loaf is one of her best.

It is as much a joy to watch her shape a piece of dough as it is to see her work a piece of glass into a leaded glass window or stitch together a quilt. I believe her talented fingers came from my mother, but then I may be somewhat prejudiced.

After the rich dough is spread with filling, rolled like a jelly roll, and allowed to rise, diagonal cuts are made across the top with a razor blade just to the depth of the filling. The result is a sweet bread that looks to be bursting with dark chocolate goodness. Which it is.

INGREDIENTS	*3 cups all-purpose flour, approximately* *½ cup milk, room temperature* *1 package dry yeast* *1 teaspoon salt* *¼ cup sugar* *1 egg, room temperature* *3 tablespoons butter or margarine, room temperature* *FILLING* *¼ cup sugar* *⅓ cup flour* *2 tablespoons butter or margarine, room temperature* *1 egg* *1 tablespoon cocoa or ground semisweet chocolate* *1 egg yolk and 1 tablespoon milk, to brush*
EQUIPMENT	One 11 x 17-inch baking sheet, greased or Teflon; a razor blade
PREPARATION BY HAND OR MIXER 12 mins.	In a mixing bowl measure 1 cup of flour and add the milk, yeast, salt, and sugar. Stir to blend well. Add the egg and butter or margarine. Blend with a wooden spoon for 100 strokes, or for 1 minute with the mixer flat beater. Add additional flour, ¼ cup at a time, until the dough has formed a soft ball.
KNEADING 10 mins.	If by hand, turn onto a floured work surface to knead. If using the mixer, attach a dough hook. Knead with a strong push-turn-fold rhythmic motion, adding sprinkles of flour if the dough sticks to the hand or the work surface. In the mixer, add sprinkles, as needed, until the ball of dough cleans the sides of the

bowl and rotates with the dough hook. Knead by hand or with the mixer for 10 minutes, until the dough is soft and elastic.

FIRST RISING
1 hour

Turn the dough into a bowl, cover tightly with plastic wrap, and put aside at room temperature to double in volume, about 1 hour or more.

FILLING

While the dough is rising, prepare the filling. In a bowl combine the sugar, flour, butter or margarine, and egg and beat together until creamy. Add the cocoa or chocolate. While this may be made without the chocolate, it is more dramatic and flavorful with.

SHAPING
10 mins.

Punch down the dough, divide into 2 pieces if for 2 loaves. Put one piece aside for the moment. Roll the dough into an 8-inch square about ¼ inch thick. Leaving a ½-inch margin around the edges clear of filling, spread half the filling.

Roll like a jelly roll. Tightly pinch the edge of the dough into the body of the dough so the filling does not bubble out when the dough begins to expand.

Place the roll on the baking sheet with the seam under.

Repeat with the second loaf.

SECOND RISING
45 mins.

Cover the loaves lightly with plastic wrap and put aside to double in size, about 45 minutes.

PREHEAT

Preheat the oven to 325° about 20 minutes before baking.

BAKING
325°
50 mins.

With a razor blade make diagonal cuts about 2 inches apart across the top of each loaf—through the dough to expose the filling. Brush the dough with the egg and milk mixture.

Place the loaves on the middle shelf of the moderate oven. If the tops seem to brown too rapidly in the latter part of the baking, cover with a piece of brown paper or foil. Bake for about 50 minutes, or until the loaves are a deep brown.

COOLING
1 hour

Remove the bread from the oven and allow it to cool for about 10 minutes. Carefully turn it onto a metal cooling rack because it is somewhat fragile when hot.

FINAL STEP

Slice and serve. It may be served warm or toasted *after* it has initially cooled. Bread hot from the oven is not completely baked!

BEEF BRISKET

[SERVES 6]

The secret of this recipe for Linda's roasted beef brisket is the very, very slow cooking of an inexpensive cut of meat. The recipe came from her grandmother, Bessie Paperny, who immigrated from a small village in Latvia at the turn of the century.

One of the pleasures of doing this dish is its easy preparation. Allow about 1 hour roasting for each pound of meat.

INGREDIENTS	*2 garlic cloves, mashed and chopped* *2 teaspoons salt* *2 teaspoons freshly ground black pepper* *2 teaspoons paprika* *One 3-pound beef brisket* *¼ cup red wine or sherry* *2 tablespoons Worcestershire sauce* *2 cups beef stock, homemade (see page 560) or store-bought* *1 lemon, thinly sliced* *1 large onion, thinly sliced* *2 cups potatoes with skins, cut into small chunks* *2 cups carrots, cut into 1-inch chunks*
EQUIPMENT	One medium roasting pan with cover
MARINATING 1 hour or overnight	In a small bowl mix together the garlic, salt, pepper, and paprika and rub it into the brisket. Place the meat in a plastic bag and allow it to marinate for an hour or more. It may be left overnight in the refrigerator.
PREHEAT	Preheat the oven to 325°.
BRAISING 12 mins.	Place the roasting pan over a high heat and braise the brisket on all sides until browned.
ASSEMBLING 5 mins.	In a bowl stir together the wine, Worcestershire sauce, and beef stock and pour over the brisket. Place the lemon and onion slices over the top of the meat. The potatoes and carrots will come later.
BAKING 325° 3–3½ hours	Place the roasting pan in the oven, cover, and bake for 2 hours. After 1 hour, look to be certain the surrounding liquid has not cooked away. If so, add more stock, wine, or water. After 2 hours, uncover and add the potatoes and carrots. Leave the cover *off* and roast for an additional hour. For extra tenderness and flavor, Linda's mother slices the

meat into serving portions and returns the brisket to the oven for another 30 minutes.

FINAL STEP

After 3 hours the meat should be fork tender. Slice and serve with the vegetables.

1977–1992

APPENDIX: BASIC RECIPES

Rather than repeat the full recipe for a basic stock or a piecrust each time one is called for in the preparation of a dish, I have selected the following recipes from my book *The Complete Book of Soups and Stews* (Simon & Schuster, 1984) and *The Complete Book of Pastry, Sweet and Savory* (Simon & Schuster, 1981).

Stock is the liquid in which meat or meat bones, fowl or fowl bones, fish or fish bones, and vegetables are cooked to extract their flavors.

The choice is yours, of course, whether to use homemade or store-bought stocks. The resulting soups will differ, of course, but that's the fun of tasting and testing until you strike the right combination that brings the greatest pleasure to the palate.

The chinois mentioned in the stock recipe is a metal strainer, conical in shape and size and reminiscent of the Asian head covering of another era. An ordinary sieve is good for straining, but most have limited capacity when stock is poured through to separate the solids from the liquids. With care, however, a sieve can be used.

Mirepoix is a mixture of vegetables, usually onion, celery, and carrots, cooked with the stock to impart flavor. They are then discarded.

The *sachet d'épice* is a bundle of herbs and spices placed in a metal tea ball or tied in a cloth or cheesecloth bag to flavor the stock. It is also known as a *bouquet garni* or herb bouquet.

WHITE STOCK
(Fonds Blanc)

[MAKES APPROXIMATELY 6 QUARTS]

Originally white stock was made primarily with veal bones, but today it is made with nearly any combination of beef, veal, or poultry bones. This recipe calls for beef bones, but feel free to make substitutions.

INGREDIENTS

5 pounds meaty beef bones, cut into short lengths
2 teaspoons salt

MIREPOIX
1½ pounds onions, chopped
½ pound carrots, scrubbed, chopped
½ pound celery, including leaves, chopped

SACHET D'ÉPICE
2 cloves
3 garlic cloves, bruised
3 bay leaves
1 tablespoon black peppercorns
½ teaspoon dried thyme

6 to 8 parsley stems, tied together

EQUIPMENT

One large (12- or 16-quart) stockpot or kettle; chinois or sieve; cheesecloth (optional)

PREPARATION
15 mins.

Rinse the bones under running water and place in the stockpot. Cover the bones with water and bring to a boil. Immediately pour off the water, which will carry with it scum and bits and pieces of flesh and bone.

COOKING
6–8 hours

Cover again with water to a depth of 4 inches above bones and add cold water as necessary to maintain liquid at this level during long simmering. Bring the water to a boil, reduce heat, and simmer partially covered with the lid at an angle for at least 6 to 8 hours. Kitchens in fine restaurants allow it to simmer for up to 12 hours.

Skim the surface repeatedly as foam collects. Stir the pot once or twice during the first hour so the bones don't stick to the bottom.

Add salt as the stock begins to simmer, and stir to blend.

Add the vegetables to the stock for the final 2 hours.

Thirty minutes before the stock is finished add the *sachet d'épice* and the parsley.

continued

COOLING
1½ hours, at
least

Place the chinois or sieve over a large bowl or pot to receive the stock and pour the stock through. If possible arrange a cold-water bath in the sink in which to set the bowl or pot, to cool it rapidly and prevent the strained stock from souring. Stir frequently. If this can't be done, place the pot in the refrigerator. (I have placed stockpots in snowbanks outside the kitchen door.)

FINAL STEP

Stock will keep refrigerated 2 to 3 days in covered containers but should be reheated and cooled again if to be kept for several more days. Stock freezes well for long periods. Pour the stock into convenient 4- to 6-cup plastic freezer containers. Label with the contents, date, and volume. Cover and freeze.

BEEF OR BROWN STOCK
(Fonds Brun)

[MAKES APPROXIMATELY 6 TO 8 QUARTS]

While beef stock is easy to make, it does take a watchful eye over a long period of time. The result will be several quarts of rich stock to use now or freeze for use in weeks and months to come.

Beef bones and vegetables are browned and caramelized in the oven before they are simmered with water in the stockpot to give the stock its rich color and pronounced good taste.

When the bones and vegetables are placed in the stockpot, they are cooked at a simmer or gentle boil. Anything more vigorous would make the stock cloudy and limit its use.

INGREDIENTS

3 pounds meaty beef and/or veal bones, fresh or frozen

MIREPOIX
1 pound onions, roughly cut
½ pound each celery and carrots, cut into 2-inch pieces
3 cups fresh or canned whole tomatoes, or 1½ cups tomato
    paste or tomato puree
1 tablespoon salt, kosher preferred

8 quarts cold water

SACHET D'ÉPICE
1 clove
1 garlic clove

2 bay leaves, crumbled
½ teaspoon peppercorns
½ teaspoon dried thyme

5 to 6 stems parsley, tied in bundle

EQUIPMENT	One large roasting pan; large (12- to 16-quart) stockpot or kettle; chinois or sieve; cheesecloth (optional)
PREHEAT	Preheat the oven to 400°.
PREPARATION 30 mins.	If the bones are fresh, boil them one time in water to cover, and drain. Bones that have been frozen—and today most of them are—need not be boiled.
	Trim fat from any meat there is, as fat is the biggest enemy of stock and will have to be taken off later if not now.
BAKING 400° 2 hours	Scatter the meat and *mirepoix* vegetables over the baking pan. Sprinkle with kosher salt. Place the pan on the middle or lower rack in the hot oven.
	Check the pan frequently and stir the meat and vegetables with a wooden spoon each time. Lower the heat if the vegetables are getting too brown and likely to burn—especially those around the edges of the pan.
	Remove the pan from the oven after about 2 hours.
COOKING 4–6 hours	Scrape everything in the baking pan into the stockpot, including the *fonds* or crusty residue from the bottom of the pan. To loosen the *fonds*, deglaze with a cup of water poured into the pan. Much of the flavor is in the *fonds* so be certain to scrape off all you can.
	Pour in the 8 quarts cold water and bring to a boil, skimming off sediments as they rise to the surface. Simmer partially covered with the lid at an angle for 4 to 6 hours—the longer the better—to extract all of the flavor of the ingredients.
	Stir gently once or twice to free any sediment to allow it to rise to the surface.
	A half hour before the stock is to be finished, add the *sachet d'épice* and parsley.
RESTING 1 hour	When the stock is cooked, turn off the heat and let it rest for 1 hour. Discard the *sachet d'épice* and parsley.
STRAINING 15 mins.	Ladle the stock through a chinois or sieve into a bowl or pot. For sediment-free stock, ladle through a double or triple thickness of moistened cheesecloth.
COOLING 1–2 hours	Cool the stock before storing. Placing the stockpot or kettle in the sink and running cold water around it is perhaps the best

way to achieve this. Stir frequently. Putting the stock outside in cold weather (in a sheltered spot away from little creatures) is a good way to cool it.

FINAL STEP When the stock is cooled, refrigerate the amount that is to be used the next day or so, and freeze the rest.
Discard the cooked bones and vegetables.

CHICKEN STOCK
(Fonds Blanc de Volaille)

[MAKES 6 QUARTS]

Homemade chicken stock has a texture and richness on the tongue that few, if any, commercial products can equal. The stock is so easy and economical to make that store-bought stock should be used only because of time constraints. The bigger and older the chicken, the richer the stock. Young chickens just don't have what it takes!

INGREDIENTS *6 pounds chicken, whole or in parts*
2 teaspoons salt
8 quarts water

MIREPOIX
1½ pounds onions, roughly chopped
¾ pound each carrots and celery, coarsely chopped

SACHET D'ÉPICE
2 cloves
3 garlic cloves, mashed
3 bay leaves, crumbled
½ teaspoon each black peppercorns and dried thyme

5 to 6 stems parsley, tied in bundle

EQUIPMENT One large (6- to 8-quart) stockpot; chinois or sieve; cheesecloth (optional)

PREPARATION
10 mins. Wash the chicken or chicken pieces under cold running water. Place in the stockpot, add the salt and cover with the water.

COOKING
3 hours Bring the stock to a gentle boil, reduce the heat to a simmer, and cook for 1 hour. Skim frequently as the sediment comes to the surface. Do not cover. For a concentrated stock, don't replenish water as it evaporates. Otherwise, add water.

Add the *mirepoix* and return to a simmer. Continue to cook for 2 more hours.

Thirty minutes before the stock is cooked, drop in the *sachet d'épice* and parsley.

RESTING
30 mins.

When the stock has finished cooking, remove from the heat and put aside to rest and cool. Chicken stock is the most susceptible of all the primary stocks to spoiling or souring and its temperature should be lowered as quickly as possible.

COOLING
1–2 hours

Cold water flowing around the stockpot will dissipate heat quickly. If the stockpot is too large for the sink, divide the stock among smaller containers to cool. Stir occasionally to move the warm stock at the center out to the cool sides.

STRAINING
20 mins.

Strain the stock by ladling through the chinois or sieve. Straining a second time through moistened cheesecloth will remove almost all of the sediment. Discard the *sachet d'épice*, parsley, and vegetables. The meat from the chicken can be used in other dishes, but don't expect it to have much flavor.

FINAL STEP

The stock may be refrigerated for 2 or 3 days, but it should be brought to a boil if it is to be held longer. Frozen stock can be kept for at least a year at 0° F.

FISH STOCK OR FUMET
(Fumet Blanc de Poisson)

[MAKES ABOUT 6 QUARTS]

Fish bones, stripped of meat, but with tails and heads attached, seem unlikely ingredients for a fine, light stock that is the foundation for great seafood soup, stews, and chowders. Not all fish bones make good stock, but the bones and big heads of round fish do—cod, red snapper, grouper, striped bass, haddock, and others. Flatfish—sole, flounder, and halibut—do not.

A fish frame is one of the cheapest ingredients used in stock preparation. Usually the fish vendor is delighted to get rid of it, and so is the fisherman next door. The frame should be used the same day it's available. Cut the gills from the fish head or they will make the stock bitter.

564   APPENDIX

INGREDIENTS
4 pounds fish bones, coarsely chopped, heads and trimmings
2 tablespoons butter, margarine, or oil

MIREPOIX
1 pound onions, coarsely chopped
½ pound celery, with tops, chopped
½ pound leeks, with green tops, chopped
6 sprigs of parsley, including stems

1 teaspoon salt
1 teaspoon lemon juice
5 quarts water

SACHET D'ÉPICE
1 clove
1 garlic clove, mashed
1 bay leaf, crumbled
¼ teaspoon dried thyme
½ teaspoon black peppercorns

EQUIPMENT
One large (8- to 10-quart) stockpot or kettle; chinois or sieve; cheesecloth (optional)

PREPARATION
20 mins.
Rinse the fish bones and heads in cold running water and chop the bones coarsely into 3- or 4-inch lengths.

COOKING
1 hour
In the stockpot or kettle heat the butter, margarine, or oil until bubbling. Add the fish pieces, stir into the butter, cover tightly with a lid, and cook over medium heat for 5 minutes.

Mix the *mirepoix* and add to stockpot along with the salt and lemon juice. Cover again and continue cooking for an additional 10 minutes, or a total of 15 minutes.

Cover with the 5 quarts water and bring to a boil. Lower heat, add the *sachet d'épice*, and simmer, uncovered for 45 minutes. Skim if necessary.

RESTING
30 mins.
Take the pot off the heat and let the stock rest for 30 minutes before straining through the chinois or sieve. Put the fish stock through cheesecloth to catch any tiny fish eggs, which become hard as buckshot when cooked.

COOLING
1 hour
Cool the strained stock in a water bath and then refrigerate or freeze.

FINAL STEP
The stock will keep 3 days refrigerated or 3 months frozen.

BASIC PIECRUST

[FOR 1 8- OR 9-INCH SHELL OR APPROXIMATELY 4 TARTLET SHELLS. DOUBLE THE
INGREDIENTS FOR A TWO-CRUST PIE]

One of the finest piecrust doughs—and one of the most widely used in
kitchens across the country—is this easy-to-prepare dough using lard or
vegetable shortening or a combination of the two. This dough produces
a "medium-flaky" crust.

INGREDIENTS

1 cup all-purpose flour
¼ teaspoon salt
6 tablespoons lard or vegetable shortening, chilled
1 teaspoon sugar (optional)
1 teaspoon vinegar (optional)
2 tablespoons egg (half of 1 slightly beaten egg; optional)
2 to 3 tablespoons cold water (If the optional vinegar and egg
    are used, reduce water by half.)

EQUIPMENT

One 8- or 9-inch pan or 4 tartlet pans

PREPARATION BY
HAND
5 mins.

Into a medium bowl measure the flour and salt. With a knife,
cut the lard or shortening into several small pieces and drop into
the flour. Toss and work the fat and flour together with a pastry
blender, two knives or your fingers working quickly, until the
mixture resembles coarse meal, with irregular particles ranging
in size from tiny grains of rice to small peas.

Add the sugar, vinegar, and egg, if desired. Pour each ingredient into the flour mixture and stir to blend before adding the
next.

Add cold water, a tablespoon at a time, and stir with a fork,
gently tossing the loose particles around the bowl to absorb moisture. Add water as needed to bring the particles together in a
moist (but not wet) mass that holds together with no dry or
crumbly places apparent.

PREPARATION BY
ELECTRIC MIXER
4 mins.

Measure the flour and salt into the mixer bowl. Cut the fat into
several small pieces and drop into the flour. Start mixer at slow
speed and stir until the mixture resembles coarse meal, about 1
minute.

Add the sugar, vinegar, and egg, if desired, and mix briefly.
Add the water, a tablespoon at a time, and mix until the mass is
moist and forms a rough ball. Don't overmix.

PREPARATION
BY FOOD
PROCESSOR
3 mins.

With the metal blade attached, add the flour, salt, and fat to the
work bowl. Process with two or three short bursts, or until the
mixture is the consistency of coarse meal. Stop the machine.

continued

Add the sugar, vinegar, and egg, if desired. (Operate the machine in short bursts so as not to overmix.) Pour the cold water through the feed tube. Stop as soon as the dough begins to form a rough, moist mass.

COOLING
4 hours or
longer

Wrap the ball of dough in plastic wrap or foil and place in the refrigerator to mature and chill. Remove the dough from the refrigerator about ½ hour before rolling or it will be difficult to work.

ROLLING/
SHAPING
10 mins.

If making a double crust, divide the dough into two pieces, one slightly larger for the bottom crust. Dust the work surface lightly with flour. Roll the piece into a circle ½-inch larger than the diameter of the inverted pie pan you're using. Keep a light dusting of flour under and on the dough so that it does not stick as it is rolled.

Fold the dough in half, then into quarters and lift into the pan. Carefully unfold and push gently against the sides of the pan to shape. Trim the dough around the rim leaving a ½-inch margin to be folded over the top crust or tucked under the rim to make a thicker and higher crust around the pie, especially if the filling is juicy.

Dampen the edge of the lower crust with moisture from the pie or with water. Roll out the dough for the top crust, fill the bottom crust with the filling, then lift the dough onto the filling following the directions above. With a razor or sharp knife cut a decorative design in the top to allow steam to escape. Flute a decorative edge using your fingers or with a fork press the top edge of the dough into the lower.

For a lattice top, roll the remaining dough into a circle large enough to provide strips of various lengths to cross the pie. Cut 12 or 14 strips, ½-inch wide, with a pastry cutter or a sharp knife.

If making a lattice top with a store-bought crust—usually two crusts are packaged together—invert the second crust and let the dough thaw 20 minutes before rolling into a slightly larger circle and cutting the dough into ½-inch wide strips as above.

Arrange the strips in a lattice work pattern, weaving over and under, if desired. The strips may also be twisted when laid down. Moisten the edge of the bottom crust, then pinch the ends of the strips to the edge to seal. The strips may also be pressed around the edge of the pan and over the ends of the crossed lattice pieces. Sprinkle with sugar or brush with a mixture of one egg and a tablespoon of cream or milk.

INDEX

Permissions

About the Author

BERNARD CLAYTON, JR., began his career as a reporter and foreign correspondent. Baking was his hobby. As a result, he has experimented with various modern techniques, developing his craft. He has been writing cookbooks for twenty years, beginning with the *The Complete Book of Breads*. When he travels, Mr. Clayton investigates historical and regional recipes, conversing with bakers and cooks around the world. He is also the author of *The Breads of France*, *The Complete Book of Pastry*, *The Complete Book of Soups and Stews*, and *Bernard Clayton's New Complete Book of Breads*. He lives with his wife in Bloomington, Indiana.